My Life of Ministry, Writing, Teaching, and Traveling

My Life of Ministry, Writing, Teaching, and Traveling

The Autobiography of an Old Mines Missionary

Mark G. Boyer

WIPF & STOCK · Eugene, Oregon

MY LIFE OF MINISTRY, WRITING, TEACHING, AND TRAVELING
The Autobiography of an Old Mines Missionary

Copyright © 2021 Mark G. Boyer. All rights reserved. Except for brief quotations in critical publications or reviews, no part of this book may be reproduced in any manner without prior written permission from the publisher. Write: Permissions, Wipf and Stock Publishers, 199 W. 8th Ave., Suite 3, Eugene, OR 97401.

Wipf & Stock
An Imprint of Wipf and Stock Publishers
199 W. 8th Ave., Suite 3
Eugene, OR 97401

www.wipfandstock.com

PAPERBACK ISBN: 978-1-7252-8799-0
HARDCOVER ISBN: 978-1-7252-8800-3
EBOOK ISBN: 978-1-7252-8801-0

02/02/21

Dedicated to all
whose life threads
narrated in this book
are woven into my lifetime tapestry.

> "The days of our life are seventy years,
> or perhaps eighty, if we are strong;
> even then their span is only toil and trouble;
> they are soon gone, and we fly away."
>
> —PSALM 90:10

> "If all goes well with us, the evening of life is a time of homecoming,
> a time when all the elements of our life come together in harmony,
> a time of healing, unity, and peace."
>
> —MICHAEL CASEY

> "We forget that each of us is actually a tragic-comic amalgamation
> of countless reproductions and survivals, randomness, sheer dumb luck,
> fumbles, misdirection, and unnoticed generosities."
>
> —ART DEWEY

> "God can speak a single truth into a single life, at a single moment of time:
> and this truth cannot be known until it is heard."
>
> —MILES HOLLINGWORTH

Contents

Introduction | ix

1. From Birth to First Grade | 1
2. From Second Grade through Fifth Grade | 10
3. From Sixth Grade through Eighth Grade | 24
4. High School | 32
5. College | 48
6. St. Meinrad and Ordinations | 59
7. Assignments in the Diocese of Springfield-Cape Girardeau | 73
8. Teaching at Missouri State University | 174
9. Mountain Climbing and Colorado | 181
10. Ocean Cruises 1979–1990 | 278
11. Other Travels | 316
12. Writing | 351
13. Genuine Human Encounters | 424
14. Three Major Incidents and Memorable Retreats | 492
15. Conclusion | 506

Indices | 511
Recent Books by Mark G. Boyer | 537

Introduction

Title

I HAVE NAMED THIS book *My Life of Ministry, Writing, Teaching, and Traveling: The Autobiography of an Old Mines Missionary* because that is what this work is all about. I present my life as a child growing up in a French village about sixty miles south of St. Louis in the middle of the twentieth century. In my writing I have often referred to my first eighteen years as my French ghetto phase! After eighteen years of life in Old Mines, the oldest settlement in the state of Missouri, I moved to St. Louis for four years and then to St. Meinrad, Indiana, for four years where education opened my eyes to a world very much larger than my village of origin. Life continued for me after ordination as a priest in the Roman Catholic Church in Springfield, Missouri, the third largest city in the state, and Joplin, Missouri. Through new environments, experiences, and travel, my village life was transformed into an international one. Because life is the thread stitching together this book, I cannot easily separate parts of it into neatly woven chapters. As Art Dewey states in one of the epigrams, "We forget that each of us is actually a tragic-comic amalgamation of countless reproductions and survivals, randomness, sheer dumb luck, fumbles, misdirection, and unnoticed generosities."

Thus, to make this book manageable, I have divided my life into four categories. The first deals with ministry. I spent twenty years of my life—almost 30 percent—preparing for ministry, which lasted officially for forty years—57 percent—as a priest. Ministry is not doing something but being someone to others. In an epigram Miles Hollingworth states, "God can speak a single truth into a single life, at a single moment of time: and this truth cannot be known until it is heard." I heard God speaking to me and calling me early in my pre-teenage life, and I answered that call age-appropriately throughout high school, college, and graduate school as I followed the twists and turns in understanding the truth I heard. The chapter on ministry also contains the stories of those people whose life threads over forty years are woven into my lifetime tapestry, because they cannot be separated easily.

The second category deals with writing. My writing career began with poetry; some poems are found in this book. After finding an audience for poems, I heard a call from a publisher to write a book. That volume has become sixty-four books with a few more yet to come. The chapter on writing also contains the stories of those editors whose life threads of almost fifty years are woven into my lifetime tapestry, because they cannot be separated easily.

Teaching is the third category of my life. After playing school with my sister when we were children, I began substituting in elementary school when I was in high school. In college I taught elementary school religion classes. In post-graduate school I was a teaching assistant. And two years after ordination I was teaching high school religion classes and Latin. I answered a call to teach the Literature and World of the New Testament in the Religious Studies Department of Missouri State University—what had been Southwest Missouri State University when I began. The chapter on teaching also contains the stories of those students whose life threads of over thirty-seven years are woven into my lifetime tapestry, because they cannot be separated easily.

The fourth category of my life is travel. At a very early age, I found myself loving to travel. At first it was an over-night play date with a cousin or a day trip to a state park or other attraction. My parents made frequent trips to the St. Louis Zoo. Teachers in junior high school and high school took me on trips, and in college and during my post-graduate years, I will never forget exploring various parts of the United States. Later, I discovered the beauty of the Caribbean islands while serving as chaplain on ocean cruises. I longed to go to Europe, and my first trip there whetted my appetite for more. The chapters on mountain climbing, ocean cruises, and other travels also contain the stories of those companions whose life threads of over sixty years are woven into my lifetime tapestry, because they cannot be separated easily.

The subtitle of this book, *The Autobiography of an Old Mines Missionary*, further situates me in my middle-of-the-twentieth-century context. First, this is my autobiography, written during my seventieth year of life on earth. In biblical numerology, seven represents completion; it is the sum of three, the divine order, and four, the created order. Multiplying by ten intensifies it. This is why the Psalm 90:10 epigram states: "The days of our life are seventy years, or perhaps eighty, if we are strong; even then their span is only toil and trouble; they are soon gone, and we fly away." I decided that this was a good year to write this account of my life. Both of my parents died when they were in their seventieth year of life. I'm hoping for eighty, as the psalm states, because I am strong, and modern medicine should be able to keep me alive for at least another ten years. I count any years over eighty as bonus ones. Michael Casey, in an epigram, expresses my feelings not only about turning seventy, but also writing my autobiography: "If all goes well with us, the evening of life is a time of homecoming, a time when all the elements of our life come together in harmony, a time of healing, unity, and peace."

Second, I hail from Old Mines, Missouri, the oldest settlement in the state of Missouri, beginning in 1723. The village was founded by the French from Illinois, who crossed the Mississippi River; by the French who followed the Mississippi River once they were kicked out of Canada by the British; by the French who followed the

Introduction

Mississippi River from Louisiana. At various times in history all of them met in the village of Old Mines to dig for silver, lead, and barite (tiff) and to build log homes, raise families, and engage in commerce. While they spoke different dialects of French, they also created their own patois, which only my grandparents spoke when I was growing up. While my mother's and father's generation might understand some of their French, my generation never learned it. I remember hearing my grandparents and others of their generation tell tales about their struggles to learn English in elementary school. While the village was never incorporated, its boundaries remain marked today with reduced speed zone signs along Missouri Highway 21.

Third, I began considering myself a missionary in the summer of 1969, while hearing a talk about the need for priests in the western parts of the U.S. That was another one of those God-speaking-truth moments, which I knew when I heard it. While I tinkered with being a missionary to a western state, I was first drawn to stop studying for the Archdiocese of St. Louis, in which I lived, and transfer to the relatively new, as of 1956, diocese of Jefferson City. How that story came to naught is narrated later. My desire to be a missionary got tweaked, when, in 1972, I joined the Diocese of Springfield-Cape Girardeau, also created in 1956, whose northern boundary was only 20 miles south of Old Mines! The Diocese of Springfield-Cape Girardeau is still described as being a missionary diocese; it comprises the thirty-nine counties of southern Missouri from east to west or about one-third of the state. I began working in this mission territory in 1975 and continue to do so to this day.

Thus, *My Life of Ministry, Writing, Teaching, and Traveling: The Autobiography of an Old Mines Missionary*, is about the threads of the lives of those to whom I have ministered, the lives of those who have read my books, the lives of those I have taught, and the lives of those with whom I have travelled and how all the lives of many other people are woven into my lifetime tapestry. Some of their threads are short, while some of their threads are long. No matter, they form a scene that is my autobiography of this Old Mines missionary.

Three Notes

First, all the names of people mentioned in this book are real. After thinking and rethinking about this for a very long time, I decided not to change the names of people whose stories are woven into my narrative. Most are people I've been privileged to know, and they have had both positive and negative effects on me. I want readers to know about their threads woven into my tapestry; some are light threads and some are dark threads! I have found out who I am by recognizing that I know myself with and through others. Furthermore, if any one of those named herein were asked, I'm sure the story he or she would tell might be different from the narrative I have presented. These are my versions of the stories, and my perspectives may be different from the way others would tell the stories. Thus, there can be two versions of the same story;

Introduction

it all depends on who is telling it! When those mentioned in this book write their autobiography, they can present their version of the story. I apologize if any story offends anyone.

Second, in general, a story about a person woven into my tapestry appears in this autobiography in the narrative where he or she emerges in my life, such as growing up, college, post-graduate work, ministry, mountain climbing, writing, traveling, etc. In a few instances, some people's names are found in more than one area because, for example, I both mountain-climbed and traveled with him, or I knew her from two different venues.

Third, while I have not provided footnotes for quotations from e-mails, letters, and cards, all references to such documents are mentioned in the text. The documents are stored in my private library files. When relying upon my memories and not paper documents, I indicate that by stating that I remember such an event or encounter.

1

From Birth to First Grade

I WAS THE FIRSTBORN son of Jesse Lee and Verna Marie Boyer. My parents were married in St. Joachim Church, Old Mines, Missouri, on November 27, 1948. I was born in the Bonne Terre Hospital on a Saturday two-thirds of the way through January 1950. At the time of my birth, my father was 32 years old, and my mother was 25 years old. My birth certificate has my name spelled incorrectly; it states I am Mark *Gerad* Boyer. The fact of the matter is I am Mark *Gerard* Boyer.

I was named after no one in my family. No one in my hometown village of Old Mines had the name *Mark*. Furthermore, since I was a firstborn, my second name came from St. Gerard, patron of pregnant women, to whom my mother had devotion. Both of my parents were cradle Catholics; however, my father was more religious—in terms of going to church—than my mother.

My fraternal grandparents were Charles and Meade Boyer, who lived in Old Mines. I have very few memories of them, as they died when I was very young. I do remember seeing each of them in his or her coffin waked in their home in Old Mines, as was the custom in the 1950s. My father had a twin sister, Lena, along with brothers named William (Bill) and Thomas and another sister named Juliette. My maternal grandparents were named Ernest and Margaret Boyer, and they lived two- to three-tenths of a mile down the hill from where I lived. I have more memories of them than I have of my fraternal grandparents because they lived into my early adulthood. My mother had two sisters: Thelma and Alberta. Before my parents married, my father's brother, Thomas, had married my mother's sister, Thelma. That made their two children—and the other five to whom my father and mother gave birth—my double first cousins.

My maternal grandfather's brother, Francis, married my father's twin sister, Lena. Thus, my mother's uncle was also her brother-in-law. The three children born from the union of Francis and Lena Boyer were my first cousins through my father and my second cousins through my mother. And what is interesting in all this family history is that no one ever changed her name!

My Life of Ministry, Writing, Teaching, and Traveling

After I was born, my parents gave birth to my five brothers and sisters: Jane Marie, Michael Jerome (deceased), Diane Marie, Joseph Lee (deceased), and Jeffrey Allen, who lived to be only six years old, dying in 1969. Michael, who was mentally handicapped, lived well into his 60s despite the fact that when he was born, he was not expected to live past twenty-one years of age. Joseph lived into his early 60s; his death was the result of too much alcohol consumption, too much tobacco inhalation, and work with asbestos. My father was a welder in the railroad shops for Missouri Pacific in DeSoto, Missouri, a town about 12 miles north of Old Mines. He and other men who worked in the shops car pooled to work five days a week.

Harry S. Truman was president of the United States when I was born. A three-bedroom home cost $8,450. The average U.S. citizen's annual income was $3,319. A new car could be purchased for about $1,300 and filled with gasoline for $.27 a gallon. A loaf of bread cost $.14, and a gallon of milk cost $.82. The price was high for milk because it was pasteurized; I was the first child in my neighborhood not to be given raw milk in addition to the milk my mother supplied.

I was born under the sign of Aquarius and in the year of the Tiger, which indicates aggressiveness, courageousness, candidness, and sensitivity. Of course I didn't know it then, but I would discover later in my life how well all that described me. I would spend many hours searching to know who I was, and I had already been told at my birth!

I was baptized in St. Joachim Church within two weeks after I was born. I was clothed in a white gown, wrapped in a blanket with a white cap tied onto my head, and taken to the church by my father; my mother was still recuperating from my birth and did not attend. At church my father was met by my designated godparents: Thomas, my father's brother, and Thelma, my mother's sister.

The only story told to me about my baptism was the one about me almost dying. As the ceremony was about to get started, the priest, associate pastor Father Bernard Suellentrop, opened the blanket and noticed that I was turning blue. The ribbon holding the cap on my head had slipped down under my chin to my throat and was suffocating me. They untied the ribbon and took off the cap in order to save my life. If it hadn't been for that priest, I wouldn't be writing these memoirs today. I didn't know it then, of course, but Suellentrop, who was moved from my home parish to another after a few years as associate pastor of St. Joachim Parish, would return as pastor and have a great effect on me and my own journey to the priesthood.

I remember little of my first six years. As a little boy, I remember playing cowboys and Indians outside our home with my cousins. We strapped on holsters with pistols that fired caps and carried poles to which had been attached pieces of old white sheets—we called them flags—and spent hours hiding behind trees and galloping on our stick horses through the yard around our houses. When I wasn't playing cowboys and Indians, I was busy making mud cookies; while other children just dug some dirt, mixed it with water, spooned it onto a hard surface, and let it dry, I perfected mud cookies. After digging dirt, I would move it over a piece of screen to sift it. The rocks would be eliminated, and I would have fine dust to mix with water. Once it was all stirred, I would spoon the mixture onto newspapers that had been spread over an old wooden crate; the newspapers kept the mud from sticking to the wood. The mud cookies were placed in the sun; once they were dried, they were easily removed from the newspaper and placed in a box. I had the best mud cookies in the neighborhood!

Sometime before I went into first grade, I had to be taken to the doctor to have my head sewed together. I do not remember the year. I had been playing outside by myself in a small metal car that my parents had bought for me. It was one of the toys that was big enough to get in and sit down and peddle around. However, after falling over in it, one of the front fenders was bent and rubbing against the front wheel; that made it hard to peddle. So, unknown to my mother, I went into the smokehouse—what we called a shed—and found my father's hatchet; one end of it was shaped like a hammer, and the other end of it had a sharpened blade on it. As I went to raise the hatched over my head to hit the fender with the hammer part of it, I actually hit my head with the blade part. Of course, blood began to pour out as I poured out screams and tears.

My mother came outside, saw what I had done, got a towel and put it on my head, called my grandmother to come and watch my brothers and sisters, put me in the car, and took me to our family doctor about six miles away in a town named Potosi. We had to wait for our turn to see him. He looked at my wound, washed it with some kind of antiseptic, poured some kind of powder in it, anesthetized my scalp, and sewed together the wound. He used a material we referred to as catgut, which disappeared as the wound healed. My wound was the talk of the neighborhood for days, and I was forbidden ever to go into the shed again and get the hatchet for any reason. All that remains is the scar that is still visible on my head.

Preschool and kindergarten didn't exist when I was growing up. My parents did not provide any education; both had only graduated from eighth grade. So, my first experience of any education occurred in first grade. On September 4, 1956, at the age of six years old, the day after Labor Day, I entered first grade in St. Joachim Elementary School, Old Mines. I remember leaving home that day. My mother had requested that two of my second cousins from the neighborhood, Ronald and Janet Politte, come to our house to walk me down the half-mile gravel road to the highway, where we would catch the school bus. Before we left, my mother took my picture in front of our old black car. I was dressed in blue jeans and a soft-collared shirt. I carried a book satchel in which my mother had placed school supplies, consisting of a Big Chief tablet, a big pencil, and a small notebook. In the outside small pocket of the satchel, she had placed a peanut butter and Karo syrup sandwich for me for a snack.

After catching the school bus, getting to school, and getting off of the bus, my cousins led me to my first grade classroom in the school. As I walked into the room, I remember seeing the old fashioned desk with a short rail around the top and a small figure sitting behind it dressed in black from head to toe—except for the lower part of her wimple, which was white—and only her face showing. I knew what to say when I saw her, since I had been primed by my parents: "Praised be the Incarnate Word. Good morning, sister." She responded, "Forever. Amen. Good morning." Then, she asked me my name and showed me where to sit.

My seat was in the second row from the window, about three desks from the front. Sister Laura Magowan, a very young woman who had come from Ireland and been trained in San Antonio, Texas, at the Sisters of Charity of the Incarnate Word Motherhouse, had fifty first-graders in her classroom. Our desks were the very old style made of wood and painted brown. A short rail ran across the top of the desk; below the rail on the right side was a hole for an ink bottle (which we didn't need and never used except to look through the hole to see what was below). The left of the ink bottle was an indentation that had been cut into the wood to look like a trough; it was a place to put a pencil to keep it from rolling off the top of the desk, which was slanted slightly toward the seat. Below the ink well and trough were hinges which attached the top of the desk to the rest of the desk; the top of the desk could be raised and things could be placed inside the compartment that raising the top of the desk revealed. Below the desk was another compartment, open only on one side; it was like a shelf where books and paper could be placed.

Iron fancywork held together the desk and the seat, which itself could be raised. Both the desk and the seat were bolted to rough, unfinished boards which ran like railroad tracks in each row in the classroom. Sometimes two, three, or four desks and seats were bolted to the same boards, and at others times only one or two were bolted to the same boards.

After sitting in my seat behind my desk, Magowan instructed me to empty my book satchel into the desk, placing whatever I had on the shelf under the desk. This I did. Then, she instructed that the book satchel should be placed on the floor next to my seat, and I should wait for further instructions.

This gave me time to look around the room. I did not know any other first-grader. I remember seeing a bulletin board along the top of the long green blackboards that covered the front wall and the side wall opposite the window. There were storage cupboards in the back of the room. The bulletin board over the side blackboard contained black cats with red bow ties over which were printed white letters. These I would later learn were my A, B, Cs. On the blackboard in the front of the room to the right side someone had painted numbers from one to a hundred in neat rows of ten. These, too, I would learn in future days.

It wasn't long until Magowan instructed all her fifty students to stand near their desks, pick up their empty book satchels, and march in single file out the door into the hall and place the satchels on hooks provided under shelves on both sides of the hall. The boys had the right side of the hall, and the girls had the left side of the hall. I had problems immediately; the handle on my satchel would not go in between the double hook; I had been instructed to place it on the lower hook. The top hook would be saved for the coats we would wear to school once it got cold.

Magowan saw me struggling to get the satchel's handle over the hook. She came to me—I was scared to death, of course—took the satchel handle and turned it sideways, and it went right onto the hook. The handle was slimmer sideways, and it would slide right on the bottom hook.

After returning from the hall to our desks, we were instructed to get out our tablets. I got out my rainbow one—it was the small one—and Magowan immediately told me to put it away. She wanted the Big Chief tablet on my desk, because it had lines drawn on each page in light blue ink. On the lines we were supposed to draw circles, filling up a whole page with them. I remember the girl next to me, Mary Lou Bourisaw, who drew beautiful circles, according to Magowan, except they were small and only on one line tall. Sister had instructed us to draw them two lines tall.

The other thing I remember about my first day in school was going to the bathroom. At some point in the morning, Magowan asked if any boy knew where the boys' bathroom was. She asked me, and I didn't know. Finally, she found a boy who knew where it was—down the steps to the basement. The girls' bathroom was just down the hall from our classroom. To the right of each bathroom door was a porcelain drinking fountain with three faucets; each sent an arched stream of water when the handle below was turned to the left. After going to the bathroom, each student got in line to get a drink of water.

The boys' bathroom was huge to me. I had never seen a porcelain urinal, so I wasn't sure what they were for until I saw another boy stand in front of it, unzip his pants, and pee into it. I remember thinking that was a much better idea than the toilet bowl. There were several toilet bowls against the opposite wall, each having its own enclosed space and door. I thought of them as mini-outhouses. After all, this is what we had at my house, until my father had a well dug, built a bathroom, installed fixtures, and connected plumbing to the bathroom and plumbing from the bathroom to the septic tank outside. I remember watching the well drillers, and I can still remember the pounding sound of the instrument used to get through rock and dirt to water well below the surface of the earth. I also remember the iron well casing being lowered and pounded into the well once it was finished, as well as the black plastic pipes and steel jet which were lowered down the casing into the water. The pump and storage tank were placed under the house. Because the pipes from the top of the well casing to the house had to buried to be kept from freezing in the winter, they also had to be dug in order to pull them out of the well to repair a leak or remove a gravel lodged in the intake valve of the jet. Many times those pipes were pulled with the help of family and friends. Thus, while indoor plumbing was not new to me, to see so many urinals and toilets was! There were also three porcelain sinks in the boys' bathroom for washing hands, and a cloth towel dispenser than needed to be pulled in order to get a clean spot on the yards of towel that simultaneously unrolled from the top and re-rolled at the bottom when tugged.

Another thing that I remember about my first day in school was distinguishing my name from Martha Boyer's name. When a first-grader is working at his desk—drawing circles on a Big Chief tablet sheet—he is not focused on discerned listening! I didn't want to respond to Magowan's calling Martha's name, but I also did not want to miss responding to my name being called. I remember that Martha had the same problem of not responding when my name was called.

As we learned our A, B, Cs in first grade, I remember Gale Paul, the daughter of the man who owned the fleet of buses that the school rented, going up and down the side bulletin board pointing out the letters as she said them with a yard stick. She often led the class in the recitation of our A, B, Cs. I remember how proud I felt when I could say them to myself, while she pointed them out.

We learned our numbers in the same way. Sister stood at the front board with a pointer, and we would recite the numbers. At first we only recited numbers from one to ten; then we went from ten to twenty. Every week we added another decade until we made it to a hundred. I liked all this learning. I liked school!

Once we had our letters memorized, we began reading. We had a particular book for each small group into which we had been divided. When we had mastered that book, we were given a test and, if we did well, we went on to the next book. Sometimes in our groups we would read the same book over and over; David and Ann were the characters who populated our books. And they had a dog named Spot. Those three dominated all our readers. When reading, we sat on small brown and red chairs in the front of the room in a circle while the other groups in their desks completed phonic workbook exercises.

We also had morning and afternoon recesses which amounted to sliding on the playground metal slide, done, of course, in an order with Magowan's supervision. We also played other games, like the farmer in the dell or ring around the rosy. Some of the games that I wanted to play, like jacks, seemed to be labeled as girl activities; boys were not supposed to play jacks; they were supposed to play marbles instead. I played jacks at home, and sometimes I got girls to let me play jacks with them at school. I was an odd young boy!

In early December of 1956, Magowan began preparing us for the Christmas program which would be presented to our parents. Every grade would be featured with a carol or two or a skit or tableau of some kind. The first grade carol—I don't remember what it was—concluded with all the boys turning around toward the back of the stage and bending down, revealing a letter pinned to the back of their jeans. All the letters spelled Merry Christmas. Being the shy kid that I was, I tried everything possible to get out of doing this. I begged my mother to take me out of the program, but nothing happened. Even on the day of the performance, I begged her not to make me wear that letter on my butt and proceed to show it to the audience. All of this was fruitless, and

I ended up with the letter on my jeans and turned around and bent over on cue—even though I was embarrassed and turned bright red. I couldn't wait until that school program was over.

See, I was the type of shy kid who was even afraid of Santa Claus. Santa Claus would set up a small building on an empty lot in downtown DeSoto, Missouri, where we often went grocery shopping. I remember my mother asking me if I wanted to see Santa Claus, and I remember telling her I did not. She forced me out of the car and pulled me by the hand to Santa's room, where I was lifted up onto his lap while crying and screaming. I do not remember telling him anything; all I did was cry and beg to be put down and taken back to the car. Seeing Santa Claus was a very traumatic experience for me! I remember several such trips, and I remember hating being forced to do this!

After Christmas Magowan began preparing us for our First Confession, which had to precede our First Communion. We memorized the ritual: enter the confessional booth; say, "Bless me father, for I have sinned; this is my first confession"; present our sins by number of times committed (such as, "I disobeyed my parents" six times or "I hit my sister" two times); listen attentively to the penance (prayers) the priest told us to say; recite the act of contrition; listen to the prayer in Latin the priest prayed; and listen as the priest dismissed us. After memorizing what we needed to know, we went from school to church and made our first confession. The confessional booths had room for kneeling penitents on either side of the priest sitting in the middle. When it was my turn, the priest slid open a screen, and I whispered my memorized words and my list of sins to the priest I could not see. I listened as he told me to say the Lord's Prayer one time. Then, I said my Act of Contrition. After being dismissed and while I was leaving, he closed the screen through which we whispered on my side and opened the one on the other side so he could hear the confession of the person kneeling and waiting on the other side. Then, the process was repeated until all the confessions were heard. After our first confession, we would make many more confessions, especially as a class during Advent and Lent, and we were encouraged to join our parents when they went to confession on Saturday afternoon. Of course, as I got older, I discovered I would have more sins to whisper to the priest behind the screen!

In the spring of our first-grade year, Magowan was responsible for preparing us for our First Communion. We had to memorize answers to questions in the *Baltimore Catechism* and certain prayers. Sister would take us to church and practice receiving communion. We were taught how to kneel, where to put our hands, how soon we should swallow the host the priest put on our tongue. Finally, the big day arrived on May 5, 1957, and all of us processed into church together and filed into the pews reserved for us in the front. The boys, dressed in slacks with a white shirt and dark tie, sat on the right (known as St. Joseph side), and the girls, dressed in white prom dresses with veils, sat on the left (known as the Blessed Virgin Mary side); our parents sat behind us.

After going to the communion rail, receiving communion for the first time, we returned to our pews and knelt in prayer. Then, immediately after Magowan clicked her clapper, we began reciting in unison the prayers we had memorized. When the Mass was finished, we processed out of the church together to the outside where our parents found us. I remember my mother taking a picture of me with Magowan; I still have the picture. We went home and had a big celebration with a meal, a cake, and gifts given to me. Most first-graders received a first communion kit, consisting of a prayer book with its case, a rosary with its case, and a small statute of St. Joseph for boys and of the Blessed Virgin Mary for girls. For first-graders this was a big deal; it was like graduating from college. We now had the right to get in the communion line at any Mass and proceed to the communion rail to receive on our tongue the host from the priest's hand. Until we made our first communion, we were not permitted to be in the communion line; we had to wait in the pew while our parents joined the procession to the front, received communion, and returned to the pew where we sat or kneeled waiting. We were not permitted to touch the host; if by chance the priest missed our stuck-out tongue or the host fell off, an altar boy would catch it with the paten he held under our chin. And if that didn't happen, then we may be able to keep it off of the floor by catching it in the communion cloth under which we placed our hands while kneeling at the communion rail.

One of the gifts I received for First Communion was a large Sunday Missal, a book that contained the prayers of the Mass in Latin on one side of the page and in English on the other side. A missal was a status symbol for a Catholic first-grader. I would carry that book with me to Sunday Mass, and people would look at me and say that I was on the ball—or so my young mind imagined! I usually got up early and went to the 6 a.m. Mass with my mother. As my sisters and brothers got old enough to attend Sunday Mass, they would usually go with my father to the 10:30 a.m. Mass.

The final event of the school year in May was the school carnival sponsored by the high school students, who occupied the second floor of our two-story school. I remember how anxious all us were to get out of school to attend the carnival and spend whatever dollar or two we may have had. After school during the morning, we were dismissed for the afternoon to enjoy the cotton candy, soda, ice cream, and games until we ran out of money or the buses showed up to take us home. I remember never winning anything at any of the carnival games.

The last day of my first-grade year was over. I remember that joy of knowing that I had passed first grade, I had made my First Confession and First Communion, and a whole summer was ahead of me for play. My report card for four of six reporting periods—no report was given to first graders for the first two reporting periods—contained all VGs (Very Good), Gs (Good), or Ss (Satisfactory). Only one area, Art, had Xs (Improvement Needed). I could not illustrate simple ideas with crayons or water colors! My parents were not concerned about my inability to draw and neither was I. Next year, I would be a pro at school as I entered second grade.

Summer consisted of June, July, and August; we did not begin school until the Tuesday after Labor Day in September. The three months of summer gave me time to play with my cousins in Brown Hollow, the name of the area in which we lived. My mother also enrolled me in a reading program sponsored by the Washington County Library. After reading a certain number of books, I got a certificate, which my mother posted on a dining room wall. Many Sunday evenings were spent with cousins in Old Mines. This gave my father the opportunity to visit his sisters while we played games, primarily softball.

2

From Second Grade through Fifth Grade

IN FIRST GRADE I had learned my A, B, Cs and could print both upper case and lower case letters. In second grade I learned cursive, a method of writing letters that connected them together. By the end of second grade, I was able to write a sentence with the letters of each word connected. Furthermore, I was able to sign my name.

My second-grade teacher was Loreda Boyer, an unmarried woman who gave meaning to the phrases *old maid* and *mean*. She was a strict disciplinarian and put up with nothing that second-grade students could offer. When she said to be quiet, we were quiet. When she taught us cursive writing, every letter had to match the model posted on the bulletin board above the green blackboard in the second-grade classroom and the one she wrote repeatedly on the board for us to imitate. Boyer was one of the few lay teachers in my school who had a Missouri Teaching Certificate.

Besides learning cursive, I also prepared for Confirmation. Our religion class period consisted of learning the answers to the questions about Confirmation in the *Baltimore Catechism*. Most of my first-grade classmates had returned for second grade; a few had moved away or decided to go elsewhere. Once we had covered the Confirmation material, we went to church to practice for what would happen when the bishop came to confirm us. Boyer was assisted by Sister Francis Clare, a Sister of Charity of the Incarnate Word. I think Sister came into our classroom to teach religion. In 1957, lay teachers could not be trusted to teach religion accurately in a Catholic school!

Since we lived in the Archdiocese of St. Louis, Archbishop Joseph E. Ritter—who was later named a Cardinal—came to confirm us. In those days, we processed into church with several other grades of Confirmation candidates (known as confirmandi) with our sponsor behind us. The boys sat on the right side of the church and the girls sat on the left side of the church. Sponsors took pews immediately behind the candidates, so that there was a row of confirmandi followed by a row of sponsors, confirmandi, sponsors, etc.

While my parents left it up to me to choose a sponsor, they presented only two possibilities. I could ask my uncle—my father's brother, Thomas—who was my godfather, or I could ask a family friend who lived down the highway, Oliver Osia. I chose Oliver Osia, even though I didn't know him that well; I didn't choose my uncle because he annoyed me almost every time I saw him. Today we would call him a bully.

I was a very shy boy, scared of anything new. I was easily embarrassed and indicated it by my face turning bright red. I also had lots of freckles from one cheek across my nose to the other. I had inherited my father's red-head complexion with my mother's black hair. My uncle Thomas often told me that he would take axle grease and rub it on my face to remove the freckles. He was also a big baseball fan whose idea of manhood was sports and cars. He spent any time not at work or listening to baseball on the radio tinkering on a car in his garage. Sometimes he listened to baseball on the radio while working on his car in his garage. His idea of fun, from my perspective, was getting his hands greasy with black stains under his fingernails. I did not like sports; I was not good at any sport; I detested getting my hands dirty with grease and using gasoline to remove it. I hated listening to baseball on the radio. Thus, because I did not fit in, he bullied me!

My mother made me play little league baseball, and I hated every minute of it. She had told me that if I didn't play baseball, I would not be permitted to visit my great-grandmother, who lived on a hill about a quarter of a mile up the road from where we lived. I loved to walk the path that wound its way through the woods to her log-cabin home. So, I played baseball. I was scared of the baseball. When it was my turn at bat, I just stood in front of home plate, hoping that the pitcher would walk me. When my team took the field, I was always sent to the outfield, where I hoped that no one would hit a ball, because I couldn't catch it!

I hated the summer evening when we had to go to the baseball field and play little league baseball. In subsequent years I begged my mother not to make me go, but I was always threatened with a privilege being taken away. So, to avoid losing the privilege, I put on my glove and protective helmet and went out on the field, promising myself that one day I would no longer have to endure this. I don't know why, but after a few years my parents, finally, gave up and stopped forcing me to play little league baseball. Maybe they came to their senses and realized that I was not good at sports!

I preferred the arts. I was interested in sewing and cooking and painting and flower gardening. My Aunt Ann (Mary Ann Ackerson), who lived with my great-grandmother, taught me to sew on her self-propelled Singer sewing machine. While holding fabric with both hands on top of the machine, my feet moved the lever that had a huge wheel attached around which was a belt connected to a smaller wheel on the machine that made the needle go up and down through the fabric to the bobbin. Ackerson also taught me how to cook; I learned how to bake pies in the oven of a wood-burning kitchen stove, as well as how to prepare other food on that stove. She taught me all about flowers, because her yard was full of them; I often helped plant seeds, cut back dead growth, transplant, and bring blossoms into the house for all to enjoy. On Sunday afternoon, I often spent time chopping dried kitchen wood and then carrying it into the kitchen and placing it in the wood box for burning during the week.

Ackerson was an orphan. Both of her parents died one day apart of typhoid fever when she was a small child. So, my great-grandmother, Sarah Osia, had taken her and raised her. She had two brothers and one sister; each of them had been taken by others and raised. In those days, there were no adoption procedures to follow.

My uncle Thomas often told me that sewing and cooking were things women did, and I needed to learn how to do manly things. If he had heard that I was sewing or planting flowers or cooking, he would embarrass me, telling me that I was acting like a girl. Again, today, we would call this bullying; in those days we didn't have a name for such behavior. So, that is why I decided not to choose him to be my Confirmation sponsor.

Our practice for the Confirmation ceremony paid off. The archbishop processed into the sanctuary of St. Joachim Church with several priests, who assisted him. We approached the communion rail and knelt down, while our sponsor put his or her right hand on our right shoulder. The bishop dipped his thumb in Sacred Chrism Oil and traced the sign of the cross with it on our foreheads, saying something in Latin. Then, he gently tapped our cheek, saying something else in Latin. A priest followed him with a cotton ball, which he used to wipe off the oil the archbishop had just smeared on our forehead. Once that was done, we returned to our pew to await the end of the ceremony.

To say that I was scared of the archbishop would be an understatement. I was terrified to be in his presence, but I knew that I had to go through with it. I remember forcing myself to walk out of the pew and go to the communion rail and kneel down while Oliver Osia was standing behind me. Once I got back to my pew, all I could feel was relief that another ordeal was finished. That was October 7, 1957, exactly six months after my First Communion.

My report card for second grade contains lots of Gs (Good) and Ss (Satisfactory). Only in Religion did I get a VG (Very Good). However, several Ps (Poor) had appeared; one was in the category of obeying rules and regulations promptly; the other was in physical education. I couldn't have identified it then, but at seven and eight years old I was becoming a critical thinker, questioning the reasons for rules and regulations. I also got one X (Improvement Needed) on that second-grade report card under the category "listens attentively." I was listening, but I was questioning, and that was not acceptable either at school or at home!

I got in trouble at home all the time for daring to ask questions, for talking back to my parents, for seeing the world differently than they did. When I was punished corporally—switched, fly-swatted, belted, or made to kneel by my bed—I remember thinking not only about the injustice that I was enduring, but also about how my way of seeing was not only not understood, but not even considered as possible truth. Today, we would label such discipline child abuse—and in some ways it was. I was becoming a child whose parents did not know what to do with me; they reverted to what their parents had done with them: beat them. They maintained the positions their parents had taught them and tried in vain to get me to conform. Of course, I refused!

I find very little in my memories of third grade. My teacher was Marjorie Bourisaw, about whom I remember nothing. My report card for 1958 to 1959 contains lots of Es (Exceptionally high achievement) and Hs (High average achievement). The only X (Improvement needed) was under the "speaks distinctly" subhead of the English category.

Joan Politte was my fourth-grade teacher from 1959 to 1960. She declared that I had completed grade four on May 27, 1960, and signed her name on my report card. I remember nothing outstanding about Politte, but she sprinkled Es, Hs, and Gs after Religion, Reading, English, Spelling, Handwriting, Arithmetic, Geography, and Art on my report card.

Even though Angela Portell declared that I had completed grade five on May 26, 1961, fifth grade was a low point in my elementary education. It is important to note that in those days the classroom teacher taught all the subjects for a designed period of time every day, five days a week. Most classes began with Religion. Then there followed several subjects, a bathroom break, more subjects, lunch, recess, more subjects, a bathroom break, and the final subjects for the day.

One of the subjects I came to hate in fifth grade was spelling. I didn't hate the spelling of words; I hated the memorization of the definitions of the words in the back of the spelling book. Once a week Portell would make the boys form a line on one side of the classroom and the girls on the other side of the classroom. Then, she would say one of the spelling words for that week. The next person in line would have to spell the word and recite the memorized definition of it from the speller. If you missed either spelling the word correctly or the definition, you had to sit down and write the word and its definition a hundred times. That kept everyone in their desks occupied while the remainder of students continued the spelling bee. Whoever was left standing won some kind of prize trinket. On Friday, we always had a written spelling test.

I could not see the sense in memorizing the definitions of words; to me it was a waste of time. So, while I could spell a word correctly most of the time, I did not memorize the definition. Thus, I would always be seated immediately after my turn in the spelling bee. At the first parent-teacher conference, Portell told my mother what I was not doing, and, of course, my parents talked to me about why I did not do all of my homework and memorize the definitions of the spelling words. I explained to them that I thought it was a waste of time with no purpose; they told me that I was going to memorize the definitions. And so for a few weeks I did, only to regress when no one was paying any attention.

My fifth-grade report card is full of only Gs. My love for school was waning. The only thing that kept me from crashing was altar boy training. A boy could not become an altar boy until he was in fifth grade, and every boy wanted to become an altar boy.

The associate pastor of the parish, who was Father Joseph Capazzi, was responsible for teaching fifth-grade boys to be altar servers.

Once a week the boys went to church and awaited Capazzi's presence. He began by teaching us the Latin responses. We had a little book titled *How to Serve Low Mass*, which contained the Latin we had to learn with the English sound of each Latin word printed above it. Week-by-week Capizzi would go over the Latin, have us recite it, take home the book and memorize it, and return the next week to recite it for Capizzi, who would teach us the next part.

After getting all the Latin memorized—and there were pages of it—he began to teach us the choreography of the Mass. We learned when and where to kneel, when and where to sit, when and where to stand, when and to where to move the huge *Roman Missal* on its wooden book stand, etc. As we added each part each week, we connected the choreography to the Latin that we needed to recite. Once all this was done, we were ready to serve our first Mass at 6:30 a.m. However, we did not serve our first Mass alone. For a whole week we vested in cassock and surplice and knelt, stood, and bowed next to the older altar servers who were present. Thus, for that week there were four altar servers, whereas there would have been only two regularly. On the last day of the week, the older altar servers let us serve, while they took our places and coached us through the Mass.

Finally, once Capizzi thought that we both knew the Latin and had the choreography down were we assigned to serve Mass without older altar servers being present. For some fifth-grade boys, this meant a repeat of the week-long process. Once we had serving Low Mass mastered, then we were trained to serve High Mass, Tuesday Night Devotions with Benediction, and Funerals.

Altar boys in fifth grade seldom got to serve a funeral; high school men usually did that. But when we did get to serve a funeral, it meant that we would be out of class for several hours. We would be sent to church by our teacher to prepare for the funeral. Then, once the funeral Mass was finished, we would go with the priest to the cemetery. So, by the time we got back to our classroom, most of the morning would have elapsed. Furthermore, after serving a funeral, the funeral director would often hand the altar servers a dollar each—which was a lot of money in the late 1950s and early 1960s. On a rare day, an altar server might be given a five-dollar bill; in that case, we thought we were rich!

Altar servers also functioned at school Masses. Depending on the grade one was in, a class may go to church for Mass once, twice, or three times a week. A school Mass was said at 8:30 a.m. or 9 a.m. every day to accommodate students. Once attendance was taken and the lunch count sent to the kitchen, we would form a line and process to church; boys would sit on the right and girls would sit on the left. If an altar boy made a mistake during the school Mass, he was sure to hear about it that day during lunch and recess. His fellow altar boys would point it out to him; sometimes the nuns would point it out to him. Everything connected to religion had to be done accurately.

From Second Grade through Fifth Grade

Even though I loved to serve Mass, serving Mass was fearsome. If an altar boy made a mistake—no matter how small—he would be severely reprimanded after Mass by the priest. Mass was supposed to be served perfectly. Some priests would severely criticize the boy who made a mistake; some would slap him across the face; some would make him kneel in the sacristy for fifteen or thirty minutes. Making a mistake meant punishment of some kind, and, of course, that instilled fear in altar servers. It became the reason many boys quit serving after getting disciplined. I don't remember ever being disciplined by the priest, and that may explain why I never quit serving. But the fear never left, either.

Because I was not good at sports, I was always chosen last for a team, like softball. Most of the boys played softball after lunch, and because I was no good, I usually pitched. The other boys thought it was the safest place for me because they didn't have to worry about me not catching a ball at a base or in the outfield. Once outdoor cement basketball courts were installed on the playground, I never attempted to play basketball; I didn't understand the game, and I didn't like all the pushing and shoving that went along with it. If I didn't play softball—baseball was prohibited by the school—I walked around the playground with one or two other boys who either didn't like sports or weren't good at them either. Somehow we found comfort in each other's company.

Another event I remember from fifth grade was the visit of the principal, Mother Ambrosia Hartigan, an over six-foot tall Incarnate Word nun. She was called Mother because she was the superior of the other sisters who taught in our school. Hartigan was built like a football player. Thus, her size, not to mention her disciplinary techniques, scared me. I'm sure that Portell had asked her to come and visit our fifth-grade classroom. When she came in, all of us stood and declared, "Praised be the Incarnate Word. Good afternoon, Mother." She responded with, "Forever. Amen. Good afternoon, students. You may be seated." And we sat down. In her hand she carried a yard stick!

It was Geography class. So, after asking Portell what our homework assignment had been, Hartigan told us to put our homework on our desk, and she would walk around the classroom to see that it was done. She walked down one isle and up another, looking at finished and not-done homework. If the homework was not done or if it was done and messy, she took the yard stick and whacked the student with it several times; it made no difference if you were a boy or a girl. I did not have my homework done, but she missed my aisle and didn't see that I didn't have it done. That day I escaped getting beaten with a yard stick, but it was clear that a reign of terror best characterized the educational system in my school. I guess that teachers thought that their students would learn if they were intimidated and beaten by the principal!

Sometime during these early elementary school years, I got the idea of building a shrine to the Blessed Virgin Mary under a sandstone bluff that protruded on the path through the woods between my house and my great-grandmother's cabin. I remember spending time with a hammer and screwdriver chipping away small pieces of sandstone under a rock ledge until two large pieces came out, forming a perfect spot six- to eight-inches tall for a statue of Mary.

Students were always selling religious items to make money for the school. Sometimes we sold all-occasion cards or Christmas cards. Sometimes we sold rosaries. This time we were selling plastic statues of Mary that had a base with a rosary inside. My parents had bought me one, and so I took the statue and placed it in the shrine I had made. A little later I got some cement and poured a flat surface upon which to place the statue. Someone came along the path and shot the statue with a pellet gun, breaking it into many plastic pieces.

Since Ackerson, who lived with my great-grandmother, liked the shrine, she found me a mental statue of the Blessed Virgin Mary; that statue was placed in the shrine and stayed there until I moved away many years later. Throughout my elementary school years and into my high school years, the shrine continued to expand. I added an altar above it out of wood and covered the wood with tin foil. I collected used glass candle holders from church and put small candles in them. I built a small wooden storage cabinet under the altar.

Over time the altar was enclosed on three sides with a roof put on it. A side altar was constructed over another shrine to the Blessed Virgin Mary a few feet away from the original. This shrine featured a large—at least two feet tall—white, plastic statue of Mary. Whatever money I earned from mowing grass or splitting wood was saved to buy wood for construction, candles, cloth, or other things for the shrine. Ultimately, a free-standing altar in front of the shrine was built out of cement that I mixed and poured at the site. Finally, all the wood of the old shrine was removed and replaced with concrete in order to withstand the elements.

Building the shrine in the woods was one way I enhanced my spirituality. The shrine was my place to pray, to be alone, to work on this project, and to renovate it as new ideas came to me and funding was available to pay for them. The focus was always on the Blessed Virgin Mary, whose statue occupied the original crevice hammered out of the sandstone. I spent hours of my life there in prayer and worship and work.

During these early elementary school years, my mother took me to the Washington County Library in Potosi to increase my reading skills. We had no books at home, because my parents didn't read. And because my parents didn't read, neither I nor my siblings were read to by our parents. But, as already indicated above, the Washington Country Library had a reading program every summer. I had to read a certain number of books in order to get a certificate. I got my first certificate, titled "By Rocket to Adventure Club" in the summer of 1958, duly signed by Mrs. Larry J. Casey, Librarian, and featuring a space rocket and gold foil medallion stapled on top of two pieces of purple ribbon. I remember proudly displaying it on the wall in our dining room at home.

I have another such document, called a diploma, for having read fifteen books of literary merit—and in so doing traveled to Alaska the forty-ninth state—also signed by Casey. Since it has no date on it, I presume that this reading occurred in the summer of 1959, since that was the year Alaska was admitted to the union. A third certificate of award was presented to me on August 13, 1960, for completing a reading project, which is not indicated. This certificate is signed by Mrs. Mark H. Moore, acting librarian. So, from the end of grade two through the end of grade four I was involved in reading by checking out books from the local library.

I remember the thrill of getting our own set of encyclopedias at home. The grocery store in DeSoto, where my mother shopped, offered a new volume every week, and she purchased it. The encyclopedia volumes were displayed on a bookshelf in our living room. To me and my siblings these were sacred books—the family Bible sat next to them—used for school homework with the greatest of care and replaced when finished with appropriate thanksgiving. I think those encyclopedia volumes inspired me to form my own library in time. My love of learning was growing, but for a few years it would be curtailed by fear.

Because I grew up in an all-Catholic area, not only did we abide by the regulations of Catholicism—like eating no meat on Fridays, attending Mass on Sundays, performing our Easter Duty (confession and communion during the Easter Season)—but we practiced folk religion. Folk religion flowed from the Church, but was not officially a part of the Catholic Church.

For example, on Holy Saturday, the day before Easter Sunday, my siblings and I would gather around the kitchen table to dye hard-boiled eggs prepared by our mother. After listening to our elders narrate how they made dyes from coffee and plants, we considered ourselves lucky to have a kit of Easter egg dyes. I remember opening the packets of powder into a tea cup or mug and watching as mother poured boiling water into the container. Then, taking a teaspoon we would stir the powder and water until we had cups of pastel blue, red, and yellow, the primary colors from which other colors could be made. We would place a white, hard-boiled egg on the spoon and lower it carefully into the cup being sure that it was submerged completely into the dye. Then we would wait for a while before lifting it up to see how well the color had taken to the egg. Sometimes we would lift out the egg and roll it onto a dish towel to dry; other times we would lower it back into the dye to get a deeper color; and once in a while we would take it out of one cup and put it into another in order to achieve still yet another color, like green from blue and yellow, or like orange from red and yellow.

Once all the hard-boiled eggs were dyed and dried, they were placed around a lamb cake, which my mother had baked the day before and placed on a tray. She had an aluminum lamb cake mold which featured a reclining lamb. After mixing the ingredients for a cake, she would pour the batter into the bottom half of the mold, attach the top half of the mold, tie the halves together with wire in three places, and bake the cake. After it came out of the oven, the top half of the mold was removed so the cake, which had risen to the top half of the mold, could cool. After that it was removed carefully from the bottom half of the mold and stood on a tray. Then, it was coated with white icing and coconut. Two raisins served as the lamb's eyes; three or four raisins formed its upturned mouth; and a half of a Maraschino cherry served as its nose. All around the recumbent lamb was planted green paper grass, and upon the grass were placed the dyed Easter eggs. Once the project was completed, my mother would take the tray with the lamb and eggs and place it on a bureau in the dining room of our home.

On Easter Sunday morning we would awaken to find Easter baskets with our names on them in the living room. Some were on the sofa, and some were on the chairs. Because there were six children, both sofa and chairs were used as receptacles for the baskets filled with candy peeps, chocolate eggs, and other sugary delights. The eggs from around the lamb cake would be missing. If it were a sunny Easter morning, they would be hidden outside in the yard; if it were a rainy Easter morning, they would be hidden in the living room and dining room of the house. My siblings and I were given empty containers and told to find them. So, we would search the yard or the rooms locating the eggs and, after finding one, carefully place it in our container. My mother usually had a total of how many eggs had been hidden, but often what we had in containers did not add to that total. So, we would have to search until we found the missing egg or two. I remember some years when we found Easter eggs months later; thinking we had found a prize, mother would take the egg and place it in the trash immediately!

A unique custom in the French village in which I grew up was known as fighting with Easter eggs. Adults and children would choose an egg and hold it in a fist with just the top of it exposed. Another person would hold an egg and smash it against the one being held. Whichever egg didn't break was considered the winner of the fight; he or she would then repeat the process with another person and be declared either the winner or the looser depending on what happened to his or her Easter egg. Adults often brought Easter eggs to Church with them on Easter Sunday and stood outside the building engaging in fighting. At home the fighting took place after sitting at the table but before eating Easter lunch. Once everyone's egg was broken, he or she finished removing the shell and ate it with the meal. Once the meal was finished, the lamb cake was carried to the table, where it was sliced and served as desert. For the next few days of the Easter Season we continued to eat hard-boiled eggs and lamb cake with our lunch and/or dinner.

Another custom was getting chicks and/or ducks for Easter. After they were hatched, they were dyed pastel blue, green, red, yellow, and pink and sold in a variety of stores. Chicks and ducklings needed to be kept warm and given food and water; often they were placed in a cardboard box near a stove and covered with a towel at night. Once they were big enough to be put outside in a coop, they went there. Over the course of several weeks they grew feathers and the pastel dyes disappeared. In a few months, they were taken out of the coop and placed in the chicken yard attached to the shed, where they roosted at night and, if hens, left eggs in the nests during the day.

When attending Mass on Easter Sunday, it was customary to bring an empty bottle. Once Mass was finished, people brought their empty bottles and jars to the huge tub of water in the sanctuary of the church. Known as Easter water, that water had been blessed during the Easter Vigil the night before. Once the bottle was filled with Easter water, it was taken home, and sometime on Easter Sunday it was sprinkled by one member of the family on all others, and all over the house, inside and outside, as a protector. It was also sprinkled on chicks, ducklings, dogs, cats, and livestock. The folk belief is that it would protect them from death and make them fruitful.

The Sunday before Easter, Palm Sunday, featured another aspect of folk religion. Palms were blessed only at the earliest Mass and then left on tables for people attending later Masses to pick up and take home. Palm branches were brought home and placed behind a cross or a picture of a saint. If one knew how to do so, he or she might weave the various strands of the branch into a cross or something else. During lightning and thunder storms, palm branches were burned in an ash tray or bowl to drive away the lightning and thunder. While the dried palm branches were being burned, blessed candles obtained on February 2, the Feast of the Presentation of the Lord, could be lit to protect the home from the storm. Because my father was especially afraid of storms, he would gather everyone together in one room and make everyone kneel around the beds therein while we prayed the rosary and my mother lit a blessed candle and burned pieces of palm branches. Today, I stand back in utter wonder at how we survived over the years without catching the house on fire with the multiple open flames we displayed during a storm!

Folk religion was also manifested at Christmastime. A week or so before Christmas, my mother would put together a cardboard fireplace which featured a red electric bulb with an attached fan propelled by the heat once the bulb grew hot. Behind red tissue paper flames on brown cardboard logs, it looked like a fire was burning in the fireplace. On the mantel my mother placed her nativity scene made of painted plaster figurines. Those replaced the wax figures which had melted in one summer's heat! However, if the plaster figures fell off the fireplace or got knocked off because of the instability of the cardboard, they broke in multiple pieces which had to be glued back together. Of course, once plastic was invented, the mostly broken-and-glued-together plaster figurines gave way to plastic ones. My sister, Jane, and I would sit in a large red rocking chair and practice Christmas carols after supper with the light creating fire in the fireplace.

Along with the erection of the cardboard fireplace was the decorating of the Christmas tree. I remember my father taking his ax into the woods and chopping down a cedar tree, which he brought home and lodged in a bucket of rocks filled with water. When I got older, this became my responsibility. The tree was brought into the house through the living room door—called the front door, which was hardly every opened or used—and placed in a corner of the living room. The box of decorations was hauled out of the dining room or living room closet and electric lights were put on the tree, followed by ornaments and tinsel. Those electric lights were the kind that when one bulb burned out, none of the bulbs lighted. One had to take a fresh bulb and go through the string of lights, unscrewing a bulb, putting in the fresh one, and repeating the process until the whole string lighted. The bucket which held the tree was filled with water and wrapped in a piece of cloth, and gifts large and small were placed under it, until Christmas eve, when, with my great-grandmother—Osia—and my Aunt—Ackerson—my siblings and I would distribute the gifts to the person named on the tag on the outside of the package and all would sit around the living room with the lights on the tree burning and open the gifts. Once all that was done and the paper mess was cleaned up, some gifts were put away immediately, and others were placed under the tree to be put away later.

Later in the evening, once everyone was asleep, Santa came. My siblings and I would put our names on the sofa or on a chair in the living room before going to bed. Also, we would usually put a few cookies on a plate and put it on the fireplace mantel. During the night, Santa Clause would place our gift under our name. Because we did not have a real fireplace, we never thought about him coming down the chimney; in our house, Santa came through the front door which was left unlocked on Christmas Eve! Thus, on Christmas morning, after awakening, we ran to the living room to see what Santa had left us. The cookies would be gone, of course. The rest of Christmas Day was spent playing with our new toy.

Because I was very much into folk religion, I began to erect an outdoor nativity scene that changed over the years. It began with a stand placed into the ground outside a living room window. A creche, made by my father, was placed on the stand, and small plastic figures depicting the nativity of Jesus—Jesus, Mary, Joseph, shepherds, sheep, wise men, and a camel—were placed in it. Three cedar trees, which I had cut in the woods, were planted in the ground around the stand, and electric lights were strung on the trees. They were plugged into the socket of the front porch light and turned on and off from inside the house. All of us liked to look through the front window and see the lights glowing in the dark outside. In time, the small plastic figurines gave way to large plastic ones lit by a small light bulb within. My father and I made a large creche to accommodate the larger statues. That was placed outside on the ground before the front window and several cedar trees were cut and placed around it. Over the course of the years, strings of large colored lights were added to the annual display.

My sister, Jane, and I often played Mass. I was the priest, and she was the congregation. The altar was the shelf on the kitchen sideboard, where we would take a glass with water and a plate with bread—a large round host created by smashing white bread down and cutting out a piece with the rim of a glass—and cover them with a dish towel. I would tie a bath towel around my neck and drape it over my shoulders. When we weren't playing church, we would play school, teaching each other what we had learned recently.

From Second Grade through Fifth Grade

I also remember watching my father push his lawnmower in the front yard. I asked him if I could push it through the grass, and he told me that it was harder than it looked. He pushed the two wheels which turned three or four blades which cut the grass. I tried pushing it, but I could not make it move. Later, when he bought a gasoline-powered lawn mower, he began to cut grass all around the yard that surrounded our house. A few summers he paid me fifty cents a day to keep the grass cut both inside the yard and outside the yard. I no more finished cutting it all and it was time to begin again.

At some point in my early years we got Bantam chickens. My father had built a chicken house and surrounded it with a pen about five or six feet high. Bantam chickens are smaller than regular chickens, and I don't know from where my parents got them. But I do remember them bringing the chickens home and putting them in the pen and how they immediately flew out of it! They had to be caught and put in the chicken house while dad added another five or six feet to the fence. Then he had to cut the tree branch that hung in the pen because they were flying to the branch and escaping. Finally, with everything high enough and tree branches trimmed, the Bantams came to our house to stay. They were excellent egg-layers, even though the eggs were smaller than usual chicken eggs. The hens always laid a clutch of eggs in the spring, sat on them for three weeks, and hatched anywhere from eight to ten chicks. Over the years the number of chickens increased, and some found ways to escape the pen and at night roost in the trees. I remember tracking one hen to a nest of ten chicks under an old Model A Ford that was parked at the edge of the woods near our house. I never knew the origins of the Model A Ford, I just presume that it belonged to my parents until it stopped running one day and got parked in the space where it sat for years and years. Like other men of his time, my father worked on the family car, which replaced the Ford. Also, he was always attempting to make something useful for the house.

One of the more joyous things I remember about these years was my mother baking themed cakes. She had found a book that demonstrated how to cut a sheet cake into pieces and create something—like a face or animal—by assembling the pieces in a specific way and icing them accordingly. She also had purchased three round cake pans of descending size in order to make wedding cakes. With her metal tube decorator and its several tips through which icing was squeezed, she decorated the three-layer cake for weddings in our area. In addition to making the Easter lamb cake mentioned above, my mother also had a metal rabbit mold, but she never made a rabbit cake because the ears seemed to break off when it was taken out of the mold. I remember borrowing that mold, taking it to Ackerson's cabin, and making the rabbit cake successfully. I stabilized the rabbit's ears by putting toothpicks in them!

Another interest I had during these years was preparing flower gardens, which we called flower beds. My first ones were around the fence behind the area of the yard in which existed the clothes lines, where wet wash was hung to dry. I planted a variety of flower seeds or got transplants from Ackerson to put there. Then, I moved on to a small triangular-shaped parcel of ground surrounded by roads which crossed to our house. I planted all kinds of roses, daffodils, gladiolas, moss, etc. There was even an old washing machine tub that I sank partially into the ground, filled with water, into which I placed gold fish. I built a wooden fence along one side of the garden for the sweet peas to climb on and tended the plants for years until I moved away from home. I remember going into the woods and digging small maple trees, which I brought to the garden and planted in order to give shade to the plants. The flower garden was the place that nourished my spirituality in silence as I watched things grow and bloom.

We were financially poor, but we didn't know it. My father worked as a welder on box cars for the Missouri Pacific Railroad in the shop in DeSoto, Missouri, and he made just enough money to pay the household bills for electricity, propane, fuel oil, and food. I remember seeing my mother standing at the kitchen sink after coming home from grocery shopping and mixing a gallon of regular milk with a gallon of powdered milk to have enough milk for six children. My brothers and sisters and I would not drink reconstituted powdered milk because we did not like the taste, but when it was mixed with regular milk, we could not taste it.

Being poor meant that we only saw a doctor when absolutely necessary and no home remedies, like a hot toddy—warm whisky mixed with lemon juice—was working. There were two doctors in Potosi, the seat of Washington County, Missouri. My parents preferred one of them over the other one. They made house calls in those days driving off the main highway and over gravel roads into the woods. Usually, but not always, all my brothers and sisters and I were sick at the same time with chicken pox, measles, mumps, colds, etc. We would be in bed when the doctor arrived in winter. I remember his very cold stethoscope being placed on my chest to listen to my heart and lungs and his thermometer being stuck in my mouth to take my temperature. After that, he usually pulled a vial of serum out of his black bag, which he placed on the bed, along with a needle. After filling the needle with serum, he would instruct me to roll over, pull down my pajamas, and put the shot in my hip. Then, he would pull out a small envelope from his black bag and a large bottle of pills. He would pour tablets into the envelope, being careful to count them as they fell into the small envelope. Then, he would take out his ink pen and write directions for administering the medicine on the front of the envelope. He would hand the medicine to my mother, who would pay him with cash, and tell her that would take care of me. Then, he would repeat the same procedures for my brothers and sisters. The only time we went to the doctor's office was in an emergency, such as the need for stitches on one's head or hand, or after stepping on a nail in a piece of wood, or severely burning a finger. There was no hospital, emergency room, or clinic in the wide area where we lived.

As a child growing up in Brown Hollow with my maternal great-grandmother, my maternal grandfather and grandmother, my double uncle and aunt and my double first cousins, a great uncle and aunt and their many children, a widow great aunt, and an unmarried great aunt, I had plenty of people to visit and other children with whom to

From Second Grade through Fifth Grade

play. Our favorite game was cowboys and Indians outside. All the children had holsters and guns that fired caps. By the time we reached junior high, most boys owned a bee-bee gun. Inside we played checkers, Chinese checkers, cards—rummy, pinochle, and solitaire—Battleship, and Monopoly. I owned a farm barn complete with all kinds of toy animals. One Christmas I got an electric train made out of metal. The engine pulled several cars around a metal track and puffed smoke out of its stack; my nephew now owns it. I also remember getting an erector set with bolts and nuts and metal pieces from which I could build things. I loved to play jacks or pick-up sticks. On TV we watched Jeopardy. In the winter, when the snow was packed, we had plenty of hills to ride down on our sleds. I remember several times when the huge propane truck came to our house to refill our tank and crushed the snow, making it perfect for a half-mile sled trip. In the afternoon I would come into the house, after removing my goulashes on the back porch, and take off my wet gloves to dry near the fuel-oil stove, and hang my sock cap and coat on the rack in the kitchen. Then, because jeans were usually wet from the knees down, I would take those off, hang them up to dry on the clothesline above the stove, and put on dry pants. While I was doing that, the same actions were being repeated by my brothers and sisters and cousins all around Brown Hollow.

3

From Sixth Grade through Eighth Grade

THE REIGN OF TERROR begun in fifth grade continued into sixth grade. Every student in St. Joachim School feared Sister Cronin Smullen, another Incarnate Word nun, who ruled sixth grade. Smullen's classroom was a war zone, and everyone knew it. She taught with a small flag pole—minus the flag—in one hand and her teacher's copy of the textbook in the other.

I remember a classmate, James Pashia, a smart boy who had skipped a grade because he was intelligent, standing at the side blackboard with a piece of chalk in his hand performing a mathematical function of some kind. He didn't know what to do, but every time he wrote the wrong number on the board, Smullen, who was standing behind him, whacked him across the back and buttocks with her small flag pole. The underlying presupposition was that beating him would somehow help him to figure out the solution to the mathematical problem! After a long while and many strokes later, she ordered him to sit down, and she proceeded to call another student to the board who was able to solve the problem.

Smullen was a short woman, whose desk sat on a raised platform so she could look over her students to be sure they were always doing what she told them to do. Our religion class consisted of Bible History. What that meant was that we memorized biblical stories and recited them in unison as a class. There were other exercises in the textbook, like true and false statements, fill in the blank statements, and vocabulary words to learn. However, Smullen excelled at making us memorize Bible stories. If she noticed that a student's lips were not moving during unison recitation, indicating that he or she had not memorized the story, the flag pole was applied to the student's body. Frequently, she would tell us to form a line, lead us down the hall, knock on another classroom door, announce to the teacher that we were going to recite a story, tell us to walk into the classroom and stand on both sides of it, and begin the recitation of the story into which all of us would chime. Once we were finished, she would march us back to our classroom.

Every afternoon we had a short snack break. Smullen would go to the back of the classroom with her set of keys, open the cabinet with the padlock on it, take out candy, popcorn, and cookies, and proceed to sell them to the students who had money with which to buy them. The candy was what some students had given her for a special occasion, like Christmas. The popcorn and cookies were assigned to students to bring to her. Yes, she sold back to her students the very things they had given her! One piece of candy cost a penny. Popcorn cost five cents. And cookies cost ten cents. She kept the money to spend on her next trip home to Ireland.

The popcorn had to be placed in a smaller container, so she had a method of making a cone-like container out of newspaper and filling it with popcorn. One of the girls in the class was always assigned to help her sell things every afternoon. I remember Smullen telling her to make a cone for another student who wanted to buy popcorn. The girl couldn't figure out how to make it correctly, so Smullen slapped her across the face with the back of her hand and told her how stupid she was.

I came from a poor family, as did other students. So, we did not have money to spend on afternoon treats. We remained in our desks in fear, because sometimes when no one had any money to buy anything, all of us might be in trouble and liable to be beat with the flag pole. We always hoped that someone would buy something once the store was open.

Another incident from sixth grade further identifies the fear and terror we endured. For some reason one day I was buying my lunch from the cafeteria; I usually took my lunch, prepared by my mother, in a brown paper bag. Most often it was a bologna sandwich with something else to go with it. One item on my lunch tray was peas, and I did not like peas. So, while Smullen, who had lunch duty that week, wasn't watching, I and another boy spooned the peas into our empty milk cartons and proceeded to the trash cans and tray-deposit cart. Smullen was standing there and saw that our trays were empty. We tossed the milk cartons into the trash can, placed the silverware in the proper container, and stacked the trays on the cart. We had beaten the system and disposed of the peas—or so we thought!

The Incarnate Word nuns made us eat every bite of food that the cafeteria ladies spooned onto our trays, even if we told them that we didn't want what they were about to put on the tray. Furthermore, we were not permitted to leave the cafeteria and go outside for recess until we had eaten everything on our tray. No food was to be thrown away—ever! That's why the other boy and I had put our peas in our empty milk cartons.

Unknown to us, Smullen had watched us put the peas into the milk carton. She said nothing to us about it when we threw the cartons away and put our trays on the cart. However, once recess was over and we filed back into the sixth-grade classroom, Smullen called our names and commanded us to come forward and stand in front of her desk. She asked us if we had eaten all our lunch; and, of course, we said we had. Then, she told us that she had watched us put the peas into our milk cartons. She asked me why I did that. I explained that we did not eat peas at home, and I did not like them. Both of us knew that we were going to get a beating with the flag pole. However, for some reason, she told us to sit down; she was going to call our parents that evening. And so she did.

My mother had to make a trip to the school that evening to see her. I do not know what happened because I stayed home after confessing to the dastardly deed. When my mother got home, she told me that I didn't have to eat peas, and that, if Smullen ever hit me with the flag pole, I should inform her about it. She had told Smullen that she was never to touch me or to stop me from scraping food off my tray if I didn't want it. I counted that as one small victory, but I lived in fear that Smullen would find a way to get even.

With all the terror and fear of sixth grade, there was one bright shining time that I remember fondly. Another Incarnate Word nun, Sister Yvonne Degonia, originally from my hometown, was teaching third grade from 1961 to 1962, when I was in sixth grade, in the convent, which had several classrooms on the first floor; the nuns lived on the second floor. Degonia had taken an interest in me, and she offered to teach me the names of everything used in church. I was enthusiastic, to say the least. So, once or twice a week after school I went to her classroom, and there she taught me the names for chalice, paten, corporal, purificator, etc. She had a book with pictures of the items, and I memorized the names for them.

Degonia's classroom was a place of refuge. Instead of fearing her, I respected her. When I forgot the name of something, she went back over it with me. Often, she would present me with a holy card or medal or some other religious object. I didn't know it then, but Degonia was awakening deeper spirituality within me, while all else around me was killing it. She was a refuge from the terror that comprised most of the school day.

Smullen got her revenge on my sixth-grade report card. It is peppered with Ls (low average achievement) and Gs (good or average achievement). There isn't a single E (exceptionally high achievement) or H (high average achievement) anywhere on the scholastic record part of the card! Nevertheless, she declared that I had completed grade six on May 27, 1962.

For grade seven, I was taught by Agnes Courtway for a few months. Because she was pregnant, she was replaced by another lay teacher by the middle of the first quarter when she left to have her baby. All I remember about Courtway was her discipline—my fellow students and I called her mean—and the fact that her idea of teaching history was to write every question from her teacher's manual on the board, make us write the questions on a sheet of paper, and then give them as homework. We had to write the question on another sheet of paper and answer it by including the question in our answer. It was a colossal waste of time because all I ever did was search the chapter of the textbook to find the answer and write it. Needless to say, I learned little history using that method.

From Sixth Grade through Eighth Grade

An interesting fact that students today have never heard of—but we practiced with devotion—was textbook covering. Every book we used, no matter if it had a hard cover or a soft cover on it, had to be covered with either a white paper cover with advertising provided by the school or book publisher, or with a brown paper bag which had been cut to form a large sheet of paper. Whichever was used, it had to be folded correctly and put on the book correctly. An uncovered textbook would result in a warning, a slap across the face, a flag pole swat on the knuckles or another part of one's anatomy, or having the book confiscated by the teacher. Teachers were adamant that books had paper covers on them.

After Courtway left to have her baby, Rose Ann Coleman took over the seventh grade. While she was less violent that her predecessors, she worked her students hard. Her basic philosophy was that the more classroom work done and homework assigned, the more knowledge gained. Even in seventh grade I disagreed with that philosophy, but did what I was told. While Courtway had given me Gs on the personality record of my report card, Coleman gave me Es (almost always acts in the manner indicated for respecting authority, showing courtesy, keeping desk and work neat, and completing work on time). She did give me a G (acts in manner indicated most of the time) for using extra time well.

I missed eleven days of school in the third quarter of seventh grade because I caught either the measles or the mumps and had to stay home to recuperate. Vaccines had not yet been developed for such childhood diseases, including chicken pox. Once a student got chicken pox, measles, or mumps, he or she usually passed it around to other students and to his or her brothers and sisters at home. That meant that a whole family may have these childhood diseases at one time.

I remember trying to do my school work at home when afflicted with one of those childhood diseases, but could not understand a particular algebra problem. When I returned to school, Hartigan, who was teaching seventh grade mathematics, came to my desk—of course I was scared—and showed me what I was doing wrong and helped me to correct my homework. I remember being shocked by her kindness and gentleness that day. She did not yell at me or hit me or insult my ignorance in any way; she showed me how to solve correctly the equations I did not understand. That image caused friction with the yard-stick wielding principal I had experienced in fifth grade.

The other event that I remember from seventh grade was the death of my great-grandmother. I had known her for years and, when she had become too sick to go to Sunday Mass, I had stayed with her while Ackerson went to Mass. While Ackerson was attending church, I baked pies and did other cooking, keeping an eye on Sarah Osia.

Osia was a woman who remembered crossing the Mississippi River in a canoe. I was near her bed when she took her last breath and those gathered around her declared her to be dead. Her death was the first death of a family member in which I actually participated. I remember the deaths of my paternal grandparents, Charles and Meade Boyer, but I was just a little boy who was scared of dead people. I remember nothing of their funerals, but I do remember seeing them waked in their coffins in the living room of their home. I vividly remember my great-grandmother being waked in her log cabin. A sofa bed had to be removed from the room so there was a place for her coffin. For several days family and friends stopped by with food, to view the body, and to pray.

My seventh-grade classroom was situated in such a way as I could see the old cemetery where my great-grandmother was to be buried. I remember gazing out the window watching the workers dig her grave on the hillside next to my great-grandfather's grave, Zeno Osia, who had died before I was born, and next to her son's grave who had died when he was seventeen. I also remember serving her funeral as an altar boy. Funerals in the early 1960s were dreary celebrations. The priest wore black vestments; the choir sang morbid music. Osia's coffin was surrounded by unbleached candles, while we prayed for the salvation of her soul.

After the funeral, my parents asked me if I would stay the night with Ackerson. She was not my blood aunt, but probably more of an aunt than any blood aunt ever was. She had been adopted by my great-grandmother after her parents died of typhoid fever on consecutive days. There were no formal adoption procedures in those days; whoever could take an orphan child, simply took him or her and raised him or her. Ackerson had a sister and two brothers, and each of them was taken by a different couple to raise.

My great-grandmother had left her log cabin and its contents to Ackerson, who had a job at the shoe factory in Potosi, Missouri. Before Osia's death, Ackerson hired someone to stay with Osia while she went to work on the weekdays. On Sunday while Ackerson went to Mass, I stayed with her, and sometimes my sister, Jane, stayed with both of us. Since I was the oldest of my siblings at fourteen years old, my parents asked me to spend a few nights with her until some of her grieving was over.

What began as a few nights, turned into a few months, and then into five years. I never went back home permanently. Yes, I went home every day, but for all practical purposes I had moved a quarter mile up the road. Ackerson became my second mother. For some unknown reason, she understood me and fostered spiritual growth within me. She taught me how to cook, how to sew, how to embroider, how to keep house, how to split wood, how to white-wash, and more. We prayed together. She checked my homework and listened to me recite anything I needed to memorize for school. We got up in the middle of the night together to go to church and pray during the hour of adoration assigned to her when the parish was having its Forty Hours of Devotions. We went on short trips together. We shopped together. She referred to me as her partner, because I was.

My daily routine usually consisted of waking up and getting out of the featherbed in which my great-grandmother had died when Ackerson had to get up and go to work. She would drop me off at my house, where my mother would be fixing breakfast for my siblings. Shortly thereafter, all of us would walk down the hill on the gravel road to the paved highway to catch the bus to school. After a day at school, I would come home, do my chores, eat supper with my family, and head up the hill on the path through the woods to Ackerson's cabin. I'd sit in the kitchen of the two-room home and do my homework. When finished, I'd join Ackerson, who was either watching TV or praying in the other room. I'd pray, and we would go to bed. And the routine would repeat itself the next day. The only variance in this routine was Sunday, when, after getting to Ackerson's by mid-afternoon, I would chop kitchen wood for the week and join her for dinner. We would watch TV together and go to bed in preparation for the work and school week ahead. Of course, I didn't know how long this was going to last when I was in seventh grade.

While Courtway gave me only Gs (good or average achievement) and Ls (low average achievement), Coleman gave Gs, Hs (high average achievement) and one E on my scholastic record for religion; I had scored 100 percent on my semester examination. On May 31, 1963, Coleman declared that I had completed seventh grade.

The reign of terror ended with eighth grade. Our home room teacher was Sister Evangelista Politte, another Incarnate Word nun; she was from the Old Mines area and she understood her students. She treated us with respect and, thus, got us involved in all types of things that brought about learning. One of our accomplishments was the eight-grade newspaper we produced, titled "Highlights of SJS" (St. Joachim School). I don't know who typed it on the stencils that had to be cut with typewriter letters, but I had a poem printed on the first of eleven pages, titled "Using Them Correctly." The title referred to the eight parts of speech: noun, verb, pronoun, adverb, adjective, preposition, conjunction, and interjection.

I had a fourth of a column story on page 2 about my father building a wooden shrine for a St. Joseph the Worker statue. The wooden box for the statue was attached to a tree in a grove on the playground on February 5, 1964, and blessed by the pastor of the parish, Suellentrop.

Politte got the class involved in putting on a play, titled "The Quest." It premiered for the student body on December 19, 1963, and was repeated for parents and others on December 22. I remember being in charge of the lightning; I had to learn which breakers turned on which stage lights. We didn't have a huge stage in the school basement, but we did have three banks of colored lights. Once I had the lighting worked out, I had to stay standing by the breaker box to turn on and turn off lights for each scene of the play. That also meant that I was in charge of opening and closing the curtain, since the ropes for doing so were located near the breaker box. I remember loving those responsibilities.

Politte took the class on trips, one such to the bank in Potosi, a town located about six miles south of the school. After the tour of the bank, we toured the office of the *Independent-Journal*, the local newspaper. We also traveled to Jefferson City to tour the capitol building, the Missouri Supreme Court building, and other places on an eighth-grade trip. I remember taking a minute to slip into St. Peter Church near the capitol building to see it. When I came out, I could not find my group. However, Politte found me in a just a few minutes.

Before Christmas in 1963, Politte's art project for her class was to make a Christmas centerpiece. Not only was it an art project, but it was also a contest. While I don't remember exactly what mine looked like, it won first place. The seventh-grade students judged the contest. This was a validation of my creative side and my interest in the arts. For Christmas Day the eighth and seventh grade students led the music for the 7:30 a.m. Mass. We sang carols before Mass started and during the Mass at specific times.

Another thing Politte started was a volunteer patrol. Volunteer eighth-grade students donned an orange belt that had a strap that went over the right shoulder. Then, we patrolled the corridors, rest rooms, and cafeteria during the noon recess and the parking lot, when the buses arrived to transport students from school to their homes. We also organized games for the lower grades. I remember being an active member of this patrol. It was instituted to develop leadership skills in us and to add more order to the school. Basically, we made sure that all students in the elementary school were where they were supposed to be at all times and that no one got run over on the playground/parking area by a bus.

My eighth-grade report card contains mostly Gs for academics and Es and Gs for personality development. I completed eighth grade and prepared for high school. There was no eighth-grade graduation ceremony, as that had been eliminated in the hope that we would go on to high school. Both of my parents were very proud of their eighth-grade education; neither of them had the opportunity to go to high school. Both got jobs right after eighth grade to support themselves. I was destined to attend high school; my parents would not even let me think of not doing so. Besides, I wanted to become a priest, and I had to have a high school education in order to get into the seminary college.

When the associate pastor had asked the altar boys during a routine meeting if anyone was interested in the high school seminary, I raised my hand. When I asked my mother about it, she told me that I needed to attend the Catholic High School and decide after that if I still wanted to be a priest. I was ready to move to St. Louis and attend one of the high school seminaries—St. Louis had two: Prep North and Prep South. I'm sure my parents could not afford to send me to a prep school, and that is why my mother told me to attend our Catholic High School. I remember wanting to be a priest from early in my life. At some time during my middle school years, a Divine Word priest had given a vocation presentation in my school; I wanted to be a priest. So, I completed the card he gave me and indicated my interest. He stayed in contact with me throughout my high school and college career.

Because Politte had done such a good job with the eighth grade, primarily ending the reign of terror, many of our parents urged her to continue on with us into high school and be our homeroom sponsor. And she did. Sadly, many of my eighth-grade classmates did not come back to our Catholic High School. Some of them wanted to play sports, and we had no sports program. Some of them wanted to be in a band, and we had no band program. Some wanted to take classes in subjects my school did not offer. Some could not afford the tuition to attend a private high school. And still others wanted to get out of the Catholic environment in which they had been for eight years. Our numbers were very diminished when members enrolled for classes in St. Joachim High School in the spring of 1964 and got ready to become freshmen that fall.

At some point during these years, I got a bicycle. My grandparents favored their youngest daughter's children, and, even though they lived about fifteen miles away, my grandfather bought them bicycles, which they rode in Brown Hollow when they came to visit him. I begged my father for one, but, because we were poor, he could not afford it. However, one Saturday after my cousins came bicycle riding by our house, my father took me to Western Auto, which was located at a gas station a few miles from our house, and he bought a bicycle for me. I don't know where he got the money or how he paid for it, but I had a red bicycle.

We brought it home, and I took it up the hill to show it to Ackerson. Then, I began the trip down the hill on the gravel road. The road from her house to ours had one ninety-degree turn in it. I turned the handlebars of my bicycle, but the wheel would not turn. I went straight into a large tree on the corner of the ninety-degree turn. I didn't hurt the bicycle, but I did skin my knees and elbows a lot. I walked the bicycle home, and my father realized that the screw bolting the handlebars to the wheel was loose. He tightened it, and that solved the problem for future rides.

4

High School

Freshman

I ENTERED ST. JOACHIM High School in September 1964; I was fourteen years old. The reign of terror of fifth, sixth, and seventh grade still haunted me and my classmates. Our eighth-grade sponsor, Politte, moved on with us to be our homeroom sponsor for our freshman year of high school. Lots of change was taking place in our Catholicism as a result of the Second Vatican Council that had concluded just a few years before. One change was that the nuns could return to their baptismal name if they wanted to instead of keeping the name they received when making religious profession. Politte chose to return to her baptismal name; even though she was the same person, we now called her Sister Rose Mary Politte. The nuns had also changed their multi-layered black habits and huge veils for a simple black dress and shorter veil. Ultimately, they would do away with the habit completely.

Politte had kept in contact with some of her eighth-grade students during the summer between the end of eighth grade and the beginning of high school. She spent the summer in St. Louis at the Incarnate Word Motherhouse that was then located in the suburb of Normandy. I have a short note she wrote to me, thanking me for a gift I had given her at the end of the school year and asking me about the dance we were permitted to attend in June of 1964. The incoming Sophomore, Junior, and Senior high school students held a dance in the school cafeteria and invited the incoming Freshmen to come and become a part of the youth group. Most of my classmates were there.

Another change that occurred for my class was in our religion textbook. In eighth grade the *Baltimore Catechism* was replaced with a new textbook; a new religious studies curriculum was being born and my class was getting just the end of it. The Mass was also changing to the Celebration of the Eucharist. We were being taught how to pray the Mass in English. We were singing hymns. And an altar was being used for Mass that faced the congregation occasionally. By the end of my senior year, a permanent altar would be placed in the church at which the priest could stand facing the congregation.

At some point early in our freshmen year, we were initiated into high school by the senior class. All I remember about the week of initiation was how much I hated it. We had to put on clothes that made us look stupid. We had to memorize a paragraph that extolled seniors and recite it every time we came across a senior in the hall, on the playground, or in the cafeteria. We had to do whatever a senior told us to do. It was humiliating to me, and I hated every day of it. I found it embarrassing and demeaning.

Hartigan, the principal, taught algebra, and the associate pastor, Father Anthony Jansen, who had been recently ordained, taught our religion class, using the first volume of a four-volume series, called *Lord and King Series*. The first-year religion course book was *Jesus Christ, Lord of History* by Vincent M. Novak. Published earlier in 1964 by Holt, Rinehart, and Winston, Inc. of New York, it was a hardbound narrative of biblical and religious history with questions to be answered at the end of every chapter. Jansen gave us essay tests, something we had never had before, to see how well we understood what we read out loud in class after which he commented.

Jansen was also responsible for boys' physical education classes, another period I hated. We had to buy white gym shorts, white T-shirts, and tennis shoes. We had five minutes to go to the changing rooms located in a separate building behind the school, take off our school clothes, put on our physical education clothes, and be wherever Jansen had told us to be. It is important to note here that none of us wore shorts in those days; shorts were worn only by professional sports players. All of us wore blue jeans or dress slacks with a soft collar shirt all year long. So, while some freshmen boys didn't mind putting on shorts, I detested it. I was embarrassed to wear shorts. Those days were nothing like today in which shorts are standard dress for boys and men from spring through summer and into fall.

Sometimes we went to the huge baseball field behind the cemetery and, after some calisthenics, played rag football. I was always embarrassed to stick a red rag in the back waistline of my shorts. We couldn't play tackle football because we had no equipment. Not only did I not understand the game of football, I couldn't play it. I was no good at sports!

Because we did not have a gym, Jansen had us play basketball on the concrete court behind the school, dodge ball in the parking lot, softball in the lower field, or some other sport. When it was too cold to go outside, we did calisthenics on the concrete floor of the cafeteria as that was the only indoor space available to us. Jansen was into running—lots of running. After being brought to the big field, we often had to run laps around it. If someone talked back to him or joked about something, that person was given laps to run. I prayed every day that PE would be cancelled, and once in a while my prayers were answered—and we got to enjoy a study hall.

Politte and Sister (Mary of the Assumption) Frances Vetter divided citizenship, English, general science, and glee club among themselves to teach us. My freshmen report card does not indicate who taught what subjects.

We changed rooms for every subject on the second floor of the school. A student would ring a bell in the hall to indicate that a period was finished and it was time for us to pick up our books and things and move to the next classroom. Of course, all this was brand new to us at first and a little intimidating. We had no desk to call our own; we had lockers in the hall in which to put our belongings, and we could buy a combination lock from the principal to use on our locker. In the few minutes that we had between classes we had to open our locker, put away what we had, get out what we needed for the next class, and get to the next classroom before the bell rang again or we would be tardy—and that carried fearful consequences.

Throughout our elementary school education, we never changed from one classroom to another; the teachers may change, but we stayed in our desks. Now, we had no desk to call our own; the teachers stayed in place, and we moved from classroom to classroom all day long.

Backpacks had not come into existence yet, so our book bags usually consisted of a large, tough plastic bag into which we placed our books in order to take them home and bring them back to school. If we couldn't find a heavy plastic bag at home, we could purchase one from the school supplies closet sponsored by the school. The school supplies closet was open before school to sell paper, pencils, ink pens, erasers, and book bags. While teaches weren't as insistent on students using real ink (in cartridges or otherwise) as they had been from grade two through grade eight, most of the time we had to prepare written assignments using real ink; ball point pens were never permitted.

My freshman year of high school report card indicates that I was an average student, earning 4 3/4 credits for the 1964–1965 school year. I earned full credits in algebra, citizenship, English, and general science. I earned 1/4 credits in glee club, physical education, and religion. Except for algebra in which I made As, my grades for the rest of the subjects were Bs and Cs. By the end of my freshman year, I was well on my way to earning the 17 units I needed to graduate from high school.

Sophomore

In my sophomore year of high school, the report card changed to report slips. Every teacher gave us a slip of paper with our grade for that class on it. Our home room teacher was Sister (Ita Patrice) Patricia Kennedy, a short lady who had great difficulty controlling us. A great change had occurred during the summer of 1965 in the staffing of the high school. A new principal had been appointed, Sister Stephen Marie Glennon, a member of the Incarnate Word nuns. She brought with her some new sisters to teach in St. Joachim High School. The first layman was also hired. Those teachers who had initiated the reign of terror were gone.

Sister Rosita Hyland, a very quiet but poised woman, taught general business, at which I excelled, and English II. Sister (Albina) Mary Sheila Foley taught biology. Jansen taught religion. Glennon taught glee club, choral singing, and music appreciation—all rolled into one. The layman, Thomas Davis, taught world history and boys PE. He had little or no control over his classes, because most of the time he was not sure of what he was speaking. That is why he lasted only one year as a high school teacher.

With the reign of terror a few years behind me, I began to learn for the sake of learning. I earned As in general business, biology, and religion. I earned Bs in English and physical education. And I earned Cs in world history and glee club. At the end of my sophomore year of high school, I had earned 4 3/4 credits; that gave me 9½ units toward graduation. I was halfway there.

Junior

I was becoming a real student. By my junior year, 1966–1967, I was well on my way to academic success and my report slips prove it. I had As in English, social studies, physics, geometry, typewriting, religion, and choral. I had a B in physical education and a B on the federal constitution test. I earned 5 3/4 units my junior year, giving me 15 3/4 toward the 17 I needed for graduation.

When the nuns returned after summer break to begin a new school year, Hyland had been named principal of the school and superior of the convent. With her were seven more nuns, most of whom taught in the high school. The convent in which they lived on the second floor was too small, not to mention the fact that the old clapboard-covered, two-story building needed renovation. Instead of renovating it, the plans were drawn for a new convent to be built during the summer of 1967. A capital campaign was underway in the parish to fund this building project, and students raised money to contribute to it as well.

Our home room teacher was Sister (Margaret) Alice Marie Holden, who also taught English. I remember falling in love with Shakespeare that year. Holden acted out all the parts of the plays we read in class; she played records of the lines of the plays being recited by famous Shakespearean actors. Because I checked out every Shakespeare play we had in the cabinet in the back of the room and read it, I do not remember which plays we read together in class except *Julius Caesar*. After reading a play we would write papers about the characters.

This was also the year I fell in love with the *Canterbury Tales*. Holden followed the same process, reading the tales out loud to us, explaining what they were about, and letting us listen to recordings of them. Again, we wrote papers about the characters.

Holden awakened in me a love of literature. After I had learned to type in Hyland's typewriting class, I bought a portable typewriter from the local Western Auto store for $50 and paid it off over a number of months. Not only did I write stories of all kinds, but I typed them and presented them to Holden to read and offer me feedback. And she did.

She taught a section on poetry, which got me writing poetry. In the fall issue of *The Torch*, St. Joachim High School newspaper, I had my first poem published: "One Tree, One God, One Man." Here it is:

> Strong and mighty tree you are,
> Standing there, there, afar,
> Planted there by one command,
> Cared for by the Lord's own hand.
>
> Nourished by the one who cares,
> He made you without a snare,
> You are strong, yet weak you be,
> Stand up straight and firm and see.
>
> Looking up behold and see,
> Holy Godhead, one in three,
> One we stand, divided we fall,
> God, Himself stands with us all.
>
> On your mighty branches strong,
> He can rest and see the wrong,
> That is caused by me today,
> Hoping that I'll change some way.
>
> Now he waits for me and you,
> Knowing just what we can do,
> Offering mercy when we pray,
> Even though we've turned away.
>
> Back to trees—they seem to speak,
> For the strong ones and the weak,
> Fighting strong yet standing still,
> Far, far off upon the hill.
>
> Of God's Kingdom you belong,
> Glorious tree forever strong,
> Bearing food for me to eat,
> Feeding worlds about your feet.

One last thought for creatures here,
Mighty tree who knows no fear,
You were made somewhat like I,
You were made by God to die.

Once again I stand and see,
Oh how straight you speak to me,
After death you bud anew,
Heaven is the life I view.

Holden was the moderator of the school paper. Either she or Hyland had convinced me to join the staff of the paper as a typist; I was very good at typewriting, and so I joined the staff of *The Torch* as a typist. I received a 43-word per minute typewriting speed award in April 1967 to demonstrate what a good typist I was.

In one of the spring issues of *The Torch*, I had two articles published. They were titled, "Deadly as Cancer: Chronic Respiratory Disease and Cigarette Smoking" and "The Kingdom of Heaven Is Liken to a Hunter." For this fifteen-page issue, I was the sole typist. In typewriting class, we had learned how to prepare columns of text, and so I experimented with single, double, and triple columns on a page. Furthermore, because word processors had not yet been invented, I justified the text by putting in extra spaces between words. Holden was very pleased with my creativity.

She got me to read J.R.R. Tolkien's *The Hobbit*, and to write a book review of it in the last issue of *The Torch* in 1967. That issue also reported that I had received second prize in our school science fair. Kennedy had gotten her students more involved in science beyond a school science fair. She took fifteen students, me included, to the South Central Missouri Science Fair held at the University of Missouri at Rolla on April 14–15, 1967. My exhibit was titled "Demonstration with Temperature-Sensitive Paint." Even though I did not earn an award, three of Kennedy's students did receive second and third places. And a fourth student received the Bausch and Lomb Honorary Science award. Also, in the last issue of *The Torch* for the 1966–1967 school year was my short story, titled "Jerry Finds a Friend."

In addition to English taught by Holden, and typewriting by Hyland, Kennedy taught physics and geometry; Sister James Joseph McBeath taught social studies; and Suellentrop taught religion and gave tough essay tests over the material covered in class. Sister Juliette De'Clue taught choral music, and Jansen taught physical education, which I continued to hate.

One highlight of my junior year of high school was a Junior-Senior field trip. After attending the 6 a.m. Mass on Sunday, April 30, members of the two classes boarded a bus that took them to Union Station in St. Louis, where they caught a train to Springfield, Illinois. There, the classes toured the chambers of the House and Senate in the State Capitol Building. Then, a bus took them to Abraham Lincoln's home for a tour. After that, the bus took them to the grave site of all the Lincolns and New Salem

State Park, where Lincoln had spent six years of his life. The St. Nicholas Hotel was the site for dinner, which was followed by the film "How to Succeed in Business" and a train ride back to St. Louis and a bus ride back to Old Mines.

Another highlight of my junior year of high school was the Junior-Senior Prom. I had been elected president of my class, and Mary Ann Politte had been elected vice-president at the beginning of the school year. The members of the class knew that if they wanted prom to be a success, they needed to elect real leaders, and Politte and I were those leaders.

In early November of 1966, during a class meeting, we led the class in selecting the theme "Hawaii and the Islands." We appointed committees to oversee all the various aspects of the banquet, held the evening before the prom, and the prom itself. We conducted fund raisers to buy supplies. When all was ready, we decorated the cafeteria, arranged the tables, held the banquet, and then held the prom. Politte was my date for the prom. Basically, the two of us organized both events and directed the rest of our classmates in what needed to be done.

We had a tradition that during the banquet the Junior class president would present prophecies or predictions about members of the Senior class. With the help of Politte, I crafted the humorous predictions, typed them on sheets of paper that I glued together to form a scroll, and read them during the banquet. Also, during the banquet, I gave the farewell address to the senior class of 1967. Once the banquet and prom were finished, all that remained was the end of the school year. On May 24, 1967, I received a perfect attendance award for the 1966–1967 school year which demonstrated my commitment to my education. I was also given a recognition of excellence in scholarship award and an achievement in science award from Future Scientists of America.

From June 17 to 24, 1967, I attend the annual Boys State on the campus of Central Missouri State College, Warrensburg, Missouri. Boys State was a mythical fifty-first state organized and administered for citizenship training purposes under the auspices of the Department of Missouri and the American Legion. The session was seven days long; its purpose was to educate youth in the duties, privileges, rights, and responsibilities of American citizenship.

The instructional program had three phases: schools, functional activities, and general assemblies. I attended law school and became a lawyer on June 22, after passing my bar examination, and then I was appointed city attorney for Shelby City of which I was a member with sixty other young men. Frank Strong was our city counselor, and he was assisted by Jack McDonald. I was sponsored by American Legion Post 285 in Potosi, Missouri. As city attorney, I prepared cases against violators of city ordinances, and I provided legal advice to the mayor.

The functional activity that went along with attending law school included learning about the operation of the courts, legislative assemblies, administration of law enforcement, etc. General assemblies were scheduled throughout the week to deal with issues that affected all the boys in attendance. General assemblies were also for the purpose of lectures on topics of interest to all in attendance.

While there were ample opportunities to play sports, like football and basketball, I did not participate in them, as I was not good at sports. I did play volleyball and ping-pong.

After I returned home, I gave a four-page speech to the gentlemen of the American Legion, explaining what Boys State was, how I participated in it, and thanking them for having made this experience available to me. Boys State helped me prepare for my senior year of high school.

While I didn't have a formal job in high school, I did work for my father, mowing the huge lawn we had; it took two or three days. I also worked for my grandfather doing whatever odd jobs with which he needed help. Primarily, I earned spending money from Ackerson, with whom I lived, with yard work and by splitting wood.

While most of my classmates had gotten their driver's license as soon as they turned sixteen years old, I was in no hurry to get mine. Once I had it, I had nothing to drive but the family car. I had taken the written test one time before and failed it, because I did not study the material! One August 2, 1967, before beginning my senior year of high school, I took the written test and passed it with a score of 95. Then, I took the driving test and passed it with a score of 76. My first driver's license for the State of Missouri cost me $2.

Senior

I excelled during my senior year of high school. I knew that my parents could not afford to pay the tuition (I later found out that they had not paid any tuition since my freshman year of high school), so I volunteered after school for a few hours every day to help the principal, Hyland, in any way she needed. She had Politte as a paid student secretary, so I did whatever Politte or Hyland told me to do. When we were finished with work, one of Politte's parents, one of my parents, or Ackerson would come and get us and take us home. It was convenient because to get to my home we had to pass Politte's home.

I was inspired to donate more time to the school by one of the previous year's seniors: Wayne Pratt. I admired him from a distance because he assumed leadership roles that other students could not have even attempted. He dressed in a collared shirt with tie and dress slacks most days. Pratt was Hyland's right-hand man throughout his senior year in high school. He stayed after school to help in any way needed. He ran the projectors that showed the films we watched every other week or so. He was responsible for ringing the bell to end and begin classes. During my junior year of high school, Pratt became the model leader of who I wanted to be and what I wanted to do. I often thought about Pratt when I was in high school. While I never spoke to him about the subjects that deeply mattered to me, after he graduated from high school, I followed his lead. I wore a light blue shirt and tie with dress slacks to school every day during my senior year of high school, because I was sure that I would be called on to represent the school in some way. I also inherited his responsibilities to ring the bell to begin and to end class and run the projector when we watched a film.

Hyland always had plenty for Politte and me to do. Sometimes we took letters she dictated to us; then, we typed them and presented them to her for her signature. At other times we filed papers, placed stickers from standardized tests on permanent records, recorded grades on permanent records. I often ran errands around the school or cleaned closets and reorganized the materials stored in them.

Besides spending a couple of hours every afternoon after school, I also served as the projectionist for films shown to the student body, as already noted above. Every other week a 16mm film would arrive at the school in three, four, or five film canisters. I was responsible for getting the film out of Hyland's office, taking it to the cafeteria, and getting the two projectors ready, each with a reel of film threaded through its intricate mechanism. I had learned how to do this from Pratt, the previous projectionist. After showing a reel of film, I knew the cue to switch to the other projector. Then, I would rewind the film, tape it, and put it back in its canister while getting ready to switch back to that projector when needed. I even learned how to splice film when it broke or for some unknown reason got jammed in the projector's system.

Our teachers considered the viewing of films as part of our education. Most of the films we saw were classics, which we would never have seen if they were not shown in school. Besides the films shown in school, we often took bus trips to St. Louis to see superior films, like *Camelot* or *Doctor Zhivago*.

Hyland gave me a master key to the school in my senior year. I had gotten into the habit of coming to the 6:15 a.m. Mass every day. I would ride with Ackerson, who was on her way to work in Potosi, and merely had to drop me off in front of the church. After Mass I would go to the cafeteria where I would eat the breakfast sandwich I brought with me. Before I got the key, Hyland saw me standing outside the school one morning waiting for someone to let me in. She gave me the key because she didn't want me standing outside in the weather. It became my responsibility to open the school after Mass if the janitor had not yet shown up. If he was delayed for any reason, I also opened the doors to the classrooms so students could get in.

The key that Hyland entrusted to me meant that I was responsible and worthy of trust. I respected her greatly because she was not scared to trust me. How many students would be given a master key to their school today? Something as simple as that key helped me to grow by leaps and bounds. Furthermore, it gave me prestige, because no other senior had a key to the school!

As noted above, I was also the bell ringer for classes. I had a large bell that I moved around on the second floor. When it was time to begin class, I rang the bell. When it was time to end class, I rang the bell. Throughout the school day, I rang the bell for high school students. The school did not have an electric bell of any kind, so a hand-held bell needed to be rung. I had to be a wrist-watch watcher, keeping my eye on the time. Once in a while, some student would think it funny to hide the bell; I would merely stand in the hall and shout, "Ring, ring, ring." Students would laugh, but the change of classes went on nevertheless.

Sometime during junior or senior year, I was put in charge of altar boys. It was my responsibility to meet with them and train them appropriately. While most of the boys in my class had stopped being altar boys when they entered high school, I had continued. In preparation for special ceremonies, I left class, gathered the boys I needed from the elementary and high school, and went to church to practice. I had mastered most of the ceremonies, and both priests respected me for that. I remember one Easter Vigil a few years after Vatican II ended when the Roman Catholic Church was in the midst of making a transition from services in Latin to English along with a change in basic ceremonies. I choreographed the whole thing, serving as Master of Ceremonies and directing priest and altar boys alike.

I got more approval at school and church that I did at home. My father was a good man, but he was never in the best of health. He tried to teach me what we would today call "man stuff," like fixing things, especially cars—which I hated because I didn't like getting my hands dirty—and hunting. I preferred cooking and baking for which I was criticized unmercifully by my uncles, cousins, and even my father because they thought of those as "women's stuff." From those experiences I've learned not to impose who I want someone to be on any person. I learned to listen to a person tell me who he or she is.

The first major event of our senior year in high school was ring day. October 6, 1967, was the day the seniors got their rings. After participating in the Mass of the Sacred Heart, Suellentrop blessed the rings and Jansen placed them on the finger of each senior. Parents who were free, attended the ceremony; those who were working got to see the ring that evening. A ring dance was held in the school cafeteria from 8 to 11 p.m.

The ring was crafted in gold with the words St. Joachim 1955—the year when the high school was started—surrounding a blue stone upon which was a gold J. On the left side of the center were the numerals 19 and on the right the numerals 68. On the left side of the band was the Incarnate Word emblem, and on the right side the cross and crown emblem. Seen only from inside the ring, embedded in the blue stone was an image of the Sacred Heart of Jesus. And engraved to the right of the blue stone were my initials. The rings were manufactured by Herff Jones, Indianapolis, Indiana. I think my parents paid thirty dollars for the ring, which I wore on my left hand for several years.

The faculty moderator of *The Torch* was Sister (Rose) Carol Bird, and I became the editor. My first issue, consisting of nineteen pages, was dated October 27, 1967. I had five typists who prepared the stencils, and two people who took care of circulation—passing out copies of the paper to the rest of the one hundred-member-plus student body. I ran off the copies on this now-primitive duplicating machine by placing the type-cut stencils on an ink drum and feeding paper over it by cranking the drum with its attached handle. The ink seeped through the stencil and stuck to the paper. While it was very messy, this printer, which existed only in the rectory basement, was the best we had in 1968.

In my second issue as editor, January 31, 1968, I ran a story about the dedication of the new convent that had occurred on December 10, 1967. The number of Incarnate Word nuns coming to St. Joachim School, Old Mines, had increased, but there was no room for them in the two-story white clapboard building they had occupied. After a capital campaign for the adults and many fundraisers by the students, the new convent was ready for occupation. The actual construction had begun in the spring of 1967 just as our junior year of high school was coming to an end. When we left school for the summer, the foundation had been dug and a cement basement had been poured. Finally, by late fall, the building was ready to be occupied.

After prayers of thanksgiving in St. Joachim Church, the congregation gathered outside in front of the new building while the pastor, Suellentrop, the principal, Hyland, and the speaker, Msgr. Vincent Naes, a former pastor of the parish, gathered on the second-floor balcony outside for the blessing of the new convent.

The new convent included an office, a parlor, a community room, a chapel, a dining room, a kitchen, and a utility room on the first floor with ten bedrooms—each with a sink—and toilets and showers on the second floor. As the article stated, it was a dream come true for the nuns.

In preparation for moving into the new convent, I remember helping Hyland clean the chapel in the old convent before it was demolished and decide what was to be brought to the new. I had functioned as an altar boy in the old chapel many times when Mass was said there. As Hyland prepared to throw away old candelabra and vestments, I set them aside to take home and use in my shrine in the woods. Only things that could be used in the new chapel were transported to the new one.

That issue of *The Torch* also reported that fifty-three high school students had taken the bus to St. Louis on January 21, 1968, to participate in the televised Mass from a local TV station studio. Suellentrop was the celebrant of the Mass, and St. Joachim High School students formed the congregation, answering the prayers and singing the songs. Following the Mass and lunch, the buses took the students to a theater to see the film *Camelot*.

One thing the pastor, Suellentrop, and the principle, Hyland, did for the high school students was expose them to the greater world around them. Other than other trips already mentioned, several times during my high school years we went to St. Louis to appear on the televised Mass. On the Sunday morning when the live Mass was being shown on a local TV station, we took a bus from St. Joachim High School to the TV station in St. Louis. We had spent hours and hours preparing for this day. Once we unloaded the bus, we went into the church-like studio where we received instructions from the director of the live televised Mass. At the appointed time, we celebrated the Eucharist just as if we were at home in our parish church. After all was completed, we went to eat at a White Castle or McDonalds, and then there was usually a movie to see before heading home on the bus for the sixty-mile trip back to our parents waiting in their cars in the school parking lot. "I saw you on TV," could be heard repeatedly from parents, who were proud of their teenage sons and daughters on TV.

There were many trips to Bush Stadium to see a Cardinal's baseball game. I remember boarding the school bus in the afternoon, getting to the stadium, buying a score card, finding my seat, and eating salted-in-the-shell peanuts! I often purchased several extra bags of the difficult-to-find nuts and brought them home with me for enjoyment later.

Also, in the January 31, 1968, issue of *The Torch* was an article on me attending the Eleventh Annual Junior Journalist Press Conference held on Saturday, December 9, 1967, on the Washington University Campus, St. Louis. There was an article on the Student Council, whose moderator was the associate pastor, Jansen. There was another article on the Parish School of Religion teachers—the new name for CCD (Confraternity of Christian Doctrine)—and how the pastor and associate pastor had taken seven of us to St. Louis for dinner on January 7, an evening I remember very well. My mother had prompted me how to dine correctly in a fancy restaurant that set each place with a cloth napkin, several forks, several spoons, and several plates.

For me the most important announcement in the January 31 issue of *The Torch* was my reception of the Outstanding Teenager of America Award, which was presented to me by Hyland during a January Student Council Assembly. This award recognized my outstanding ability, accomplishments, and service. My accomplishments were printed in an annual publication which was placed in libraries throughout the country. The OTAA program was sponsored by the nonprofit Outstanding American Foundation.

Our homeroom teacher for our senior year was Hyland, who also taught bookkeeping and algebra. Sister (Catherine) Evelyn Lambert taught chemistry, while Suellentrop taught religion, and Bird taught English. McBeath taught American History. De'Clue taught choral, and Jansen continued to teach physical education.

I remember having one specific conflict with Jansen. On a day when *The Torch* needed to be finished and printed—something else I did by taking the stencils to the rectory copy machine—I skipped Jansen's physical education class, telling another student to tell him I was working on the newspaper. The next day he came and got me out of class and took me to the counseling room where he proceeded to become angry, telling me how upset he was that I had skipped his class. I explained that I was working on *The Torch* along with a lot of other things. I had to decide what I was going to do, and I did. I knew someone would be upset. When tears began to roll down my face as I recounted all the things for which I was responsible, he let me return to class. He never brought it up again.

Some of the nuns offered adult education classes one night a week in an attempt to bring more educational opportunities to the people of the Old Mines area. Because I was good at typing, I helped Hyland teach typewriting. I also taught in the Confraternity of Christian Doctrine program, which, as indicated above, had become PSR, working with other teachers. PSR classes were the religion courses students who were not in Catholic school attended once during the week.

On February 20, 1968, I was one of the first six students to be inducted into the St. Louis IX Chapter of the National Honor Society, which had a charter (number 13806) dated October 20, 1967. A very formal ceremony was held with me serving as Master of Ceremonies. After the singing of the National Anthem, Suellentrop gave an invocation, various students explained the four NHS requirements of character, scholarship, leadership, and service, and then Hyland inducted us into the NHS. We finished the evening by singing our St. Joachim School song:

> Our hearts are filled up to the brim with love for you, St. Joachim.
> We pledge with great sincerity, affection, prayer, and loyalty.
> Oh, alma mater dear;
> Your students gather here, sing laud:
> Your praised never dim,
> We praise you, St. Joachim!

I was such a good Master of Ceremonies that I was invited to come back at the end of my first year of college for the second NHS induction ceremony on May 19, 1969, during which ten more students were added to the St. Louis IX Chapter of the National Honor Society.

My third issue of *The Torch* (April 8, 1968) featured a story on the Junior-Senior boys retreat on February 13 at St. Pius X Monastery in Pevely, Missouri, located on the banks of the Mississippi River. After classes that day, I joined the other Junior and Senior boys for the over-night retreat. I remember sharing a room with Paul Ricar, with whom no one else wanted to room. This was my first experience of taking a shower; I had seen people taking showers on TV, but I had never had one before. All we had at home was a bath tub, which was a step up from my mother's huge wash tub! After getting settled, we were served dinner. Then, we listened as two Benedictine monks gave us conferences on various topics that young Catholic men needed to hear that evening and throughout the next day. The retreat day ended with a celebration of Eucharist. As the boys were being picked up by four drivers, the girls were delivered to the retreat center for their over-night stay.

Also named in the April 8 edition of *The Torch* were the co-editors for the 1968–1969 school year; instead of their being a single editor, two junior girls had agreed to serve as co-editors of the school paper. That ten-page issue contained the usual essay contest winners, each high school class' past and upcoming events, poems, and short stories.

High School

The last issue of *The Torch* for which I served as editor was dated May 22, 1968. Its ten pages carried stories on career day for the seniors, a story on what each senior was planning to do after graduation, short stories, and poetry. In the senior interview story, the writer recorded the following about me: "Mark Boyer's plans for the future are college and priesthood. When asked, 'What is the most exciting thing to happen to you?' he replied, 'Graduation. I've completed the twelve years of school!' He would go to St. Joachim High School, if he had to do it over. His advice to the students is to study hard."

The last issue of *The Torch* also previewed the upcoming graduation program for seniors. And it reflected upon the Junior-Senior "Rendezvous of the Stars" banquet and prom. The banquet, held May 9, featured speeches by Suellentrop, Jansen, and Hyland. I presented a thank you speech. The mothers of the junior class prepared and served the meal. And I presented the valedictorian address, since I was declared valedictorian of my senior class. I spoke on an old Arabian quotation that addressed the four kinds of men: the one who knows not and knows not he knows not; the one who knows not and knows he knows not; the one who knows and knows not he knows; and the one who knows and knows he knows.

The prom, held May 10, featured the formal presentation of the seniors with their dates before the first dance. I took Freda Pratt to the prom. I had intended on taking Politte with whom I worked after school, but she was dating Pratt's brother. So, I invited Pratt's sister, who readily accepted my invitation

Graduation was held on Sunday, May 26. It began with a baccalaureate Mass at 7:30 that morning. All fourteen members of St. Joachim High School Senior class walked in procession, dressed in cap and gown. After participating in the Mass, we went to the school cafeteria for sweet rolls with juice and coffee served by the sophomore class. The actual graduation ceremony took place at 4 p.m. in St. Joachim Church. Following the procession of the seniors into the church, a hymn, and act of consecration to the Blessed Virgin Mary, Monsignor Joseph Kennedy, pastor of St. Philip Neri Parish, St. Louis, under whom Suellentrop had served as associate pastor before coming to St. Joachim, Old Mines, as pastor, delivered a sermon. After this Suellentrop handed the diplomas to Kennedy, who was seated and who presented them to each graduate as he or she knelt before him while Jansen called each name.

My classmates included: JoAnn Bone, Marilyn Bone, John Boyer, Michael Coleman, Jerry Declue, Robert Finch, Wayne Koch, James Pashia, Mary Ann Politte, Geraldine Sampson, Kenny Sansoucie, Catherine Singer, and George Wall. Out of the fifty who had started first grade together, only fourteen remained. Some had moved away; some had gone to Potosi High School; some had quit high school to get a job. I have a group senior class picture, taken in the recreation room of the new convent, with all present except Finch.

After receiving our diplomas, the senior awards were given by Hyland. Most of the awards were presented to me. I received a certificate designating me as valedictorian of the class of 1968; a perfect attendance award for the 1967–1968 school year; an excellence in scholarship award; an award of appreciation for faithful service, loyalty, and devotion to St. Joachim School; the good citizenship medal presented by the Francois Valle Chapter of the Daughters of the American Revolution; a certificate of proficiency in twentieth-century bookkeeping; and a regents' scholarship to Southeast Missouri State College, Cape Girardeau.

Another hymn followed the awards ceremony along with benediction conducted by Father Clement J. Burghoff, pastor of St. James Parish, Potosi, and the recessional. Also present was Father Joseph Ryan, who had been an associate pastor of St. Joachim Parish in 1951–1952. I remember my mother taking photographs of me with Kennedy, the pastor, and the associate pastor. I also have a photograph of me and my first-grade teacher, Magowan, who was present. I have a photograph of me and Hyland. Following the picture-taking, I went home with my parents to enjoy dinner and a special graduation cake. I remember feeling very empty during that evening because high school was over. It was like I wanted to do something, but I didn't know what I wanted to do. After twelve years in St. Joachim School, a chapter of my life had closed, and I had to wait for three months for the next one to begin.

I finished my senior year with a report card full of As and Bs. I earned 5 3/4 units, giving me 21 units for the 17 required for graduation in the State of Missouri. And out of fourteen students I was ranked first!

A few days after graduation, I traveled to St. Louis with my uncle and his son to where they worked. Their place of work was in an industrial area. I spent the day going from one business to the next putting in my application for a job. I found one in a billboard printing factory. I was hired on a Friday to keep the place clean; by the time I got back the next Monday I was already promoted to the position of an assistant printer! I learned how to take paper stencils, grease them, and stick them to silk screens. I learned how to move the squeegee across the silk screen, print the image on a huge sheet of billboard paper, and then move the sheet to the drying rack without smudging it. I also learned how to clean the silk screen press in order to prepare it for the next stencil.

I hated this work because it was so hot and noisy in the factory. I hated this summer job because it involved getting grease all over me, not to mention the harmful and stinky chemicals we used to clean silk screens and squeegees. I could never seem to please the boss with my printing efforts. So, I preferred to be on the assembly line, putting together packets of advertising brochures and information that would be distributed by other companies. I got off work an hour before my uncle and cousin with whom I rode to work, so I would get into their car, roll down the windows, sit in the back seat, and read *Reader's Digest*, which I had received as a high school graduation gift. I couldn't wait for summer to end, so I could leave that place and begin my first year in the college seminary.

High School

When not working in St. Louis, I dated Patricia Boyer from Tiff, Missouri, all during the summer of 1968. We went to the drive-in to see movies, to dances, and did several other things together. Near the end of the summer she told me she was not interested in the relationship that we were developing. While I remember being saddened by the break-up, I also remember seeing it as a confirmation that the next chapter of my life would begin with the college seminary.

5

College

Throughout the summer of 1968, I prepared for entrance into Cardinal Glennon, the college seminary for the Archdiocese of St. Louis. I had been interviewed by the rector at some time in the spring, and I had scored high enough on the entry exams to be admitted. My mother helped by gathering the items on the list that had been sent to me. I needed a cassock, which she got from a young man who had spent some time in a seminary: Thomas Paul. I needed two surplices, which she made. All my clothes had to have name tags sewed into them with the laundry number assigned to me; the laundry tags were purchased from Sears. I needed cloth napkins for the dining room which my mother made. Piece by piece things were gathered and prepared for the sixty-mile trip to St. Louis.

The hardest part for me was leaving the home I had with Ackerson. I had lived with her for over five years in the two-room cabin she inherited from my great-grandmother. I knew I would miss feeding the wood stove in the main room. I knew I would miss the winter chill of the kitchen, at whose table I spent many hours doing high school homework while the fire in the cook stove was permitted to go out so a new fire could be laid to be lit first thing the next morning.

I had gotten use to the uneven floor in the main room; the floor boards had been nailed to logs lying on the ground which shifted over the years. I enjoyed sleeping in my feather bed, which was hot in the summer, but warm in the winter; it was the same bed in which my great-grandmother had died. During the summer, we would sleep with the screened door and screened window open, and so we could hear the night chirps of insects and birds. We would not turn on the electric lights in the summer in order not to draw the bugs to the screens; rather, we would light the coal oil lamp and sit in its dim glow.

Ackerson had taught me how to repair the dabbed walls inside. In a bucket, dirt and straw were mixed with water to a firm consistency. Then, the mud mixture was spread onto the logs of the walls and permitted to dry. Once dry, the mud was whitewashed; a mixture of lime with water was brushed on the mud and let dry. Gradually as more of the white-wash was brushed on, the walls became white, and the clean smell of lime permeated the room. All four walls of the main room in which we slept and watched TV were white-washed, as well as the walls of the porches. The kitchen had cardboard tacked to the logs over which wall paper had been pasted.

During college and post-graduate school, when I would come home, I would stay there. Ackerson gave me the extra room that was on the north side of the main room. In those days there was no door connecting that room to the main room; to get to it I had to walk out of the main room and down the porch a few steps to the door that admitted me to the extra room. Later, an uncle with a chain saw would cut the logs in the main room and create a door from it to the extra room. That room, along with an upstairs room, had been added to the two-room cabin for my grandmother and grandfather after they were married and before they could afford to build a home. In the upstairs room over their room they raised three daughters, one of whom was my mother.

The extra room contained a double bed and a matching chest of drawers along with other pieces of furniture and a wood stove for heat. It had one window to let in a little light. In that room I stored many of my things while I was in college and in post-graduate school. In fact, many of my personal belongings remained there until I went to Springfield, Missouri, in 1976.

We had no bathroom, but we did have an outhouse. Bathing was done with a wash pan of warm water, a wash cloth, soap, and a towel. In the wintertime, we stood near the stove to stay warm while we washed our face, then our arms and chest, then our butt and legs. Most of the time, we took baths only a few times a week. One of us would wash while the other did something outside or in the kitchen.

Ackerson and I had become mother and son. We ate together. We traveled to church together. We worked outside together. We washed clothes together. We fixed the roof, repaired the chicken house, cut the grass, and more together. While I often had dinner with my parents and siblings, I spent most of my time during those over-five years with Ackerson.

Just when I thought that the reign of terror from elementary school was in my past, I entered Cardinal Glennon College to discover that it was alive and well there. In those post-Vatican II days, the Vincentian priests who ran the seminary college had no idea what to do with college seminarians. Most of the Vincentians who taught in the seminary also lived there in a section of the huge building that was off limits to students. Many of the Vincentians who taught there were there because there was nowhere else to put them; some of them had alcohol issues while others had multiple psychological disorders. They were not models for young men to imitate, but I was willing to endure it because I wanted to be a priest, and I had to go through the college seminary to reach that goal. The four years I spent in Cardinal Glennon College were the worst of my academic life!

After arriving at Cardinal Glennon College, I was assigned to live in one of the two dormitories. Each second-floor dormitory for freshmen consisted of a huge open L-shaped room filled with single beds that had two drawers under them with walking space a few feet away from each other. Near each bed was a chair, and all along the wall were small lockers to which I was assigned two. On the other side of the room were rows of sinks, and behind the sinks were rows of private shower stalls and private toilets. There was no personal privacy except in the library, where I studied. After the first semester, the half of the freshmen class in one dormitory exchanged with the other half in the other dormitory for the second semester. I hated the arrangement. The only thing that kept me there during my freshman year was the promise of getting a private room for my sophomore, junior, and senior years.

In between the completion of my first year of college and the beginning of my second year, I got a job working in the summer program at Cruise School, the public elementary school located a couple of miles from my home. I worked as a teacher's aide, being responsible to help with students doing academic work, serving the mid-morning snack, and supervising recess activities.

Once this summer employment was over, I began to prepare to furnish my room in Cardinal Glennon College. The room, chosen in a lottery, was about twelve feet by twelve feet. It came with a bed, a book shelf, a desk, two lockers built into the wall, and a sink. I furnished mine with a rocking chair, a table with a lamp my grandmother gave me, a swag lamp my mother earned from collecting stamps issued by the grocery store, an aquarium on a stand I had built, and a bed spread and curtains that my mother made out of another bed spread that matched.

Ackerson went with me when I made a trip to St. Louis about a week before school began. She helped me bring in my things, arrange the furniture, hang the curtains, and make the bed. I wanted to be ready when school began; all that remained was to bring my clothes. On one wall I hung the forty-one inch by forty-nine inch crocheted Nativity that my mother had made for me over the summer. I had made a wooden frame for it over which had been tacked heavy plastic in the front—glass would have been too heavy—the crocheted piece, orange cloth, and brown paper taped and sealed it on the back. My mother had told me that she would make me something for my room, and I asked her to crochet the Nativity. She had made a smaller one after she married my father, and it hung in the living room of our home.

Except for eight or ten of us, most of the freshmen class had attended one of the two preparatory high school seminaries and knew each other. They had their social groups; those of us who had attended a regular high school found it difficult to fit in. I was befriended by Denny Schaab, who like me, was not athletic and didn't fit in with most of the men with whom he had spent four years of high school. Schaab got me interested in playing tennis, which I continued to do for many years. He also got to know a man from the Diocese of Jefferson City, Ronald Jewell, whom he befriended. For a long time the three of us would make it a point to spend time together, especially on Sunday for lunch. The cafeteria did not provide lunch on Sunday, so seminarians were left to their own devices. I had a hot plate and a pot and used to fix soup in my room. Someone else brought cheese and crackers, and someone brought cookies.

In some ways the college seminary was like being in a prison. We had a strict schedule to follow which began with morning prayer, followed by breakfast, classes, late morning Mass, lunch, and afternoon classes or what was called work order; every student in the school had to spend time during the week working around the school. After work order, there may be time for homework or sports before meditation time, evening prayer, and supper. Most evenings were free to do homework.

While not many seminarians had cars, those who did were not permitted to keep them on seminary property. There were two cars that could be signed out; the cost for using the cars was so much per mile. Several upper class students were responsible for the upkeep of the cars. A sign-out clipboard was kept on a table outside one of the dorms. A student had to plan way in advance and get his name on the list in order to checkout a car, especially if it was going to be for more than an hour or two.

There were no student telephones in the building except a pay phone on each side of the building. Seminarians were to use the telephones only for emergency purposes. Incoming calls from family or friends were not encouraged. When someone answered the phone, he had to find the person requested by the caller—and that was not always easy to do.

Lunch and dinner were formal dining affairs. Some faculty sat at a head table in the dining room at which students served. Students had assigned tables where personal cloth napkins were kept on the chair seats. Someone from each table went to the kitchen to get food after a faculty member rang a bell indicating silence and then led prayer. Once the meal was finished, the faculty member rang the bell again and led prayer again. At this point any announcements that needed to be made were spoken. Then, all were dismissed to whatever the next activity of the day may be.

During classes and for meals clerical attire was required. For the 1968–1969 school year—for the first time—students could wear clergy shirts instead of cassocks, although cassocks were perfectly acceptable. For Mass, cassock and surplice were required.

Work order kept the cost of education down and assured the school of plenty of hours of manual labor. One could volunteer to work outside mowing the grounds, cutting brush, fixing things. Inside, one could volunteer to clean toilets, showers, and the halls. I worked in the library. I began working in the accession area, taking a hot electric pen and, with a white tape that left itself on book bindings when traced with the hot pen, put the Dewey Decimal numbers on the spine of new books.

In the accession area there was a table with a rack attached in which the book could be placed to hold it secure. Inside the book were the Library of Congress cards, which had been ordered by the assistant librarian and upon which she had written the Dewey Decimal number. Once I traced the number on the spine of the book, another seminarian put a cover on the book while a third seminarian took the cards and alphabetized them for filing in the card catalogue. Usually, there were three cards, one each for title, author, and subject; sometimes there were more cards to file if a book had multiple authors or fit into several different subjects.

When all the accessioning had been done, the assistant librarian would give the three or four of us other jobs to do. We might be assigned to pull the cards from the card catalogue for books that were being taken out of circulation. We might be sent to the stacks (the rows of shelves with the books on them) to find a book that someone wanted or to search for a book that may have been put in the wrong place. Or if there was a backlog of reshelving to do, we might take books and put them back on the shelves.

I worked in the library at Cardinal Glennon College for four years. My senior year I was named the student head librarian. That meant that I had a key both to the library itself and to the librarians' office. In that office was the only modern copy machine in the building. If someone needed a copy of something, I accepted the fee and made the copy for him. Besides making copies, I had other responsibilities. I oversaw the student staff, making sure that all jobs were done correctly. If a student did not appear for work order, it was my responsibility to find out where he was. After looking through book catalogues, I could recommend books to the head librarian to be added to the collection. In the office, I had a desk at which I could work.

At the last work order before we went home for Christmas, the librarians and the seminarian staff always had a Christmas party which began with Mass celebrated in the library. The head librarian would invite a priest she knew to come for the Mass; sometimes we also had a deacon from Kenrick Seminary located a few blocks away from the college seminary. After Mass, we enjoyed cake, cookies, punch, and other types of Christmas treats.

During all four years I spent at Cardinal Glennon, Clementine Linzee served as the head librarian, and Marybeth Gladiaux was the assistant librarian. Besides their usual duties, they were available to help students find materials for research papers.

As seminarians, we had no choice of majors; we had to major in philosophy, although we could minor in lots of other subjects. For the first and second semesters of my freshman year in the college seminary I took twenty credit hours, although I got credit for only a few of them. Some courses were mandatory, but no credit was awarded, such as a two-hour theology course that wasn't even graded or an orientation course which consisted of the Dean of Studies, Father James Graham, a Vincentian priest, reading the school catalogue to us. I did get credit for courses in rhetoric, Latin, French, math, and music. In the second semesters of freshman year we began to work on our major by taking a course in logic—the only course for which I received an A. When I first got there, we had classes on Monday, Wednesday, and Friday, and on Tuesday, Thursday, and Saturday. I think it was after my Sophomore year that Saturday classes were cancelled and those on Tuesday and Thursday were lengthened to make up for no longer having Saturday classes.

College

Two college instructors stand out during that first year. The first was Father Raymond Ross, who taught Latin and served as Vice-Rector. Everyone was afraid of Ross. However, he recognized that several of us in his class had not studied Latin before; those who had gone to the preparatory high school seminaries had studied the language, which was required in college. So, he decided to take the three or four of us out of the regular Latin class and teach us separately in the evening; we were graded on how well we did in the evening class. He didn't have to do that, of course, but he must have seen something in us. Instead of letting us fail the class, he helped us pass it.

But just as he was a help, he could also scare seminarians. I remember being in his second semester Latin class when he spotted a seminarian with his class ring on his finger. High school seminarians did not get class rings like those of us who had gone to a regular high school did. Ross asked the seminarian why he had the ring on and proceeded to berate him for continuing to wear it. I was sitting a few desks over, and I had my high school class ring on. Very slowly I slipped it off my finger with one hand, placing it within my fist so that it could not be seen. I did not want to be singled out for reproof by Ross should he notice that I, too, had a class ring on my finger.

Another person who stands out during that first year was Robert Gardner, who taught the essentials of music. The first semester he played classical music records and taught us how to appreciate such music. The second semester he wanted us to learn to play the scales on the piano. I had no training of any kind on a musical instrument, but I tried to master the keys of the piano. Of course, I failed meeting his expectations. So, for one of two times in my entire educational career, I received a F on my report card. I didn't like Gardner, and he didn't like me. He also taught rhetoric, and didn't think that I pronounced some words correctly. So, he would embarrass me in front of my classmates making me say words over and over again until they sounded the way he wanted me to say them.

The seminary rector for both my freshman and sophomore year was Father Francis A. Gaydos, a Vincentian priest who had interviewed me in the spring of my senior year in high school. I had no dealings with him during my freshman year, except for an interview near its end. Because the seminarians always put on a talent show in the spring, Gaydos asked me why I was not involved in it. I explained that I was not the talent show type. While we talked, he kept insisting that he knew that I wanted to be a part of it, and I kept telling him that I had no such desire. He got angry with me for speaking my truth, and I knew then that I was in some kind of trouble.

That trouble presented itself during the spring of my sophomore year. Some of the members of my class had discovered that I knew how to sew, so they asked me to help with the costumes for the talent show. Those presenting a skit based on a part of a Shakespearean play wanted a loin cloth sewed over their pants to give the effect of a mediaeval costume and for humorous effects. I hand sewed about a half a dozen of these. The Monday after the weekend musical was over I was summoned to the rector's office, and I had no idea why I was told to go there. After I sat down Gaydos asked me if I had been involved with the costumes, and I acknowledged that I had—I was credited on the program for participating in the costuming along with several others.

Gaydos began to tell me how inappropriate he thought the costumes were that I had worked on. He berated me for over thirty minutes, putting me down, telling me that I had made a big mistake. I told him that I only sewed what I had been asked to sew; it made no difference to him. I was wrong, and he was right. He ended by telling me that I would be lucky not to be kicked out of the seminary. But I wasn't.

Following the reign of terror of Gaydos, Father Ignatius Melito, CM, was named rector of the college seminary in 1970. I do not know what happened to Gaydos; Melito was a bit better. In my junior year of college, I had decided to minor in English, and Melito was the English professor. Since there were only five or six of us taking his courses, we went to his office for our classes. I took courses in the Canterbury Tales, poetry, Romantic Poets, Shakespeare, and Twentieth Century American Fiction, earning Cs and Bs in them. Melito did not like my style of writing.

I also earned a minor in Greek. Two semesters of elementary Greek were taught by Sister Isaac Jogues, a School Sister of Notre Dame. She was a wonderful teacher, who cared about her students. Her method was to present, explain, practice, and drill. Learning Greek from her was fun. In my senior year, I took two more semesters of Greek from Father Francis Agnew, CM, who came from Kenrick Seminary to teach the small class of which I was a member. We read parts of the New Testament in Greek, and he commented on the style and grammar of the Greek as we translated it.

During the summer following our Sophomore year of college, we were required to spend six weeks in what was called a Priestly Formation Program (PFP). We moved across the creek to Kenrick Seminary, where the program was held. Each week was devoted to a different topic, which was presented by an expert in the topic. I remember three topics that really grabbed my attention.

One of them was liturgy. I do not remember who presented the week on liturgy, but he led us through several mediaeval rituals which fascinated me. I served as sacristan for the six weeks, which meant that I was responsible for preparing the chapel for Mass every day and for any other liturgies we were going to celebrate.

The second topic I remember is the week on psychology. Rumors from previous classes involved in PFP had circulated about this week of introspection and sharing. Because I was a basic introvert, I didn't even want to think about this week. We were engaged in all kinds of sharing exercises in small groups. I hated every minute of sharing what I considered personal information. However, if I had refused to do so, I would have found myself dismissed from the program and from the seminary. So, I scripted what I was going to say, and, following my notes when it was my turn, told of my hopes and dreams in being a diocesan priest.

The third topic that caused me to change my mind about becoming a priest for the Archdiocese of St. Louis was missions. A presenter talked about the lack of priests in the western U.S., as well as in many countries. I had never thought about anything missionary before. So, I began to investigate other dioceses in Missouri. One of my forty-one classmates—Jewell—had become a good friend through our four years of college seminary together. He was from Mexico, Missouri, a small town within the geographical boundaries of the Diocese of Jefferson City, which had been created in 1956. He invited me to apply to the Diocese of Jefferson City. Jewell put me in contact with his vocation director, Father Anthony O'Connell.

However, in order to be accepted into the Diocese of Jefferson City, I had to be dismissed from the Archdiocese of St. Louis. At that time, Cardinal Archbishop John J. Carberry's secretary, Msgr. Fenton Runge, was in charge of seminarians, even though he knew very few—if any—of us. In 1971, I wrote a letter to him requesting that he release me so that I could be a seminarian for the Diocese of Jefferson City. He never answered my first letter. So, after months and months of waiting, I wrote another very angry letter requesting that he release me. Again, I got no response. However, Runge wrote a letter to Melito, informing him about my letter and instructing him to chastise me. After being called to his office one day, he told me that I needed to stop writing letters or I would be kicked out of the seminary.

Because I wanted the transfer to the Diocese of Jefferson City to be finished before I graduated from Cardinal Glennon College, I had been in contact with O'Connell, the Director of Seminarians and the Rector of St. Thomas High School Seminary in Hannibal, Missouri. O'Connell had written me several times indicating that the diocese was interested in accepting me as a seminarian. However, according to him, his hands were tied until I was released from the Archdiocese of St. Louis.

Unknown to me before graduation, Runge also had written to O'Connell, who, during the summer of 1972, wrote me a letter informing me that the Diocese of Jefferson City was no longer interested in me as a seminarian because of my disrespect for authority. Of course, at that time, I had no idea that O'Connell was sleeping with high school seminarians. That fact became known about twenty-five years later—after he had been ordained a bishop and sent to a diocese in Florida to succeed a bishop who had been accused of child molestation. All this later helped me to understand why he dropped me as a seminarian. Anyone who spoke back to authority was not the person he would be able to get into his bed! In my naiveté, I did not realize that I did not need any permission to change from one diocese to another.

While all this was taking place, I continued studying at Cardinal Glennon College. Most of the courses were taught by faculty who should not have been teaching in a college seminary. The Vincentians smoked and drank heavily; one philosophy teacher was found passed out on the floor of his room when students went to get him for class. Their only methodology in teaching was lecture; if we memorized the material, we could pass the test.

Faculty from outside the seminary were much better. They taught elsewhere in St. Louis, so they had methodologies that better suited the students who sat in front of them. However, few of them had any tolerance for creativity. The college seminary was four years of educational endurance instead of learning. Within me were stirrings of critical thinking; I wanted to test my ideas and see how they held up to scrutiny, but most faculty members were only interested in what they considered to be the correct question and answer.

For example, Father Melvin Reitzer, a Franciscan Capuchin, who taught some philosophy courses, encouraged critical thinking. I remember getting very good grades from him for my creative work in his course. John Wickersham, another philosophy instructor, taught a course in aesthetics that I will never forget. He invited large group discussion. Likewise, the art teacher, Sister Maria Liebeck, a Daughter of Charity, was interested in developing the creative side of her students.

Then there was Marian Koevenig, who taught English composition. If I didn't write the paper exactly the way she wanted it, I got a very low grade. Father John Byrne taught education; he sat a desk for every class and read his notes to us. His hero, Gabriel Moran, was the only educator who knew anything about education. Even Melito had a set paradigm of what he wanted; there was no room for creativity in the English courses I took from him.

Besides working in the seminary to offset the cost of education, some of us were also involved in ministry outside of the seminary, called apostolic work. I do not remember how I got involved in the Confraternity of Christian Doctrine program at St. Sebastian School in St. Louis, but I participated in that program on Saturday mornings for several years after Saturday classes were cancelled in CGC. I taught sixth grade religion. Sometime I was assisted by Ted Agniel, a seminarian from Jefferson City, who was more of a kid than the sixth graders! I taught under the supervision of Sister Ann Catherine Shaw, a Sister of Charity of the Incarnate Word, the same religious community of nuns that had taught me in elementary and high school.

If you were to look at "The Eleventh Commencement Exercises of Cardinal Glennon College" booklet from May 13, 1972, you would find my black and white photograph with my name—Mark G. Boyer—printed below it. I am dressed in a black cassock with a white Roman collar. Underneath of my name is the name of my home parish: "St. Joachim, Old Mines." What is even more interesting is the line below that: "Diocese of Jefferson City."

So, after St. Louis Auxiliary Bishop Joseph A. McNicholas handed me my A.B. in Philosophy college degree, I walked over to Bishop Michael F. McAuliffe, the Ordinary of the Diocese of Jefferson City, to shake his hand. Little did I know at that time that I had been duped by O'Connell. That fact would be revealed about a month later.

After I received O'Connell's letter rejecting my application to join the Diocese of Jefferson City, I wrote to Bishop William Baum of the Diocese of Springfield-Cape Girardeau—comprising the southern third of the state of Missouri—informing him that I was interested in becoming a seminarian for his diocese. Within a few days a response arrived in the mail. He was interested. He invited me to go to Springfield and meet him. I did. Being very truthful, I told him what had been happening to me over the past two years. He told me that he didn't need a letter from St. Louis to accept me into his diocese. He also told me that I was free to pick a school of theology to attend. "Tell the authorities to send the bill to me," he said. In my senior year of college, I had visited St. Meinrad School of Theology, run by the Benedictine monks in southern Indiana, and I fell in love with the place. Baum was happy with my decision, and I left his office being a theology seminarian for the Diocese of Springfield-Cape Girardeau. It was so simple!

However, within a few months after I arrived at St. Meinrad, Baum was appointed Archbishop of Washington, DC, and the Diocese of Springfield-Cape Girardeau would be without a bishop for about a year. That would lead to the next set of problems I needed to conquer.

On May 13, 1972, I was awarded a Bachelor of Arts degree by Cardinal Glennon College. I had finished a major in philosophy, earned 140 college credit hours, had a GPA of 2.58, and ranked 26.5 out of forty-two students. The worst four years of my academic life were over. The reign of terror was coming to an end. At that point in time, while I thought I was going to study for the Diocese of Jefferson City, I had hope that a better future awaited me.

During the summer of 1972, I served as secretary in my home parish of St. Joachim. The pastor, Father Richard Suren, had offered me the job after the regular secretary—Mary Ann Politte—had indicated that she wanted the summer free. I was responsible for picking up the collection deposit at the bank on Monday morning, recording the contributions of parishioners in a ledger, answering the telephone and door, preparing the weekly bulletin, and lots of other things. Suren invited me to join him and the associate pastor, Father Edward Schramm, for lunch and dinner every day. He asked me to live in the convent once the sisters left for the summer. I had a huge house with ten bedrooms on the top floor and a kitchen, dining room, and community room with chapel and two offices on the first floor. Furthermore, the house was air conditioned.

When I wasn't being the parish secretary, I played tennis, read, and watched TV. One project I worked on that summer of 1972 was passed on to me by Schramm. He had been chosen by the local ministerial alliance to decorate a space in Washington County Memorial Hospital as a Chapel Quiet Room. He didn't have a clue as to what needed to be done. I gathered some drift wood and formed an ecumenical cross from it. I got someone to make a small table-altar upon which I placed a single large candle stand, candle, and Bible. The three items together were perfect for a chapel to be used by Christians both Catholic and Protestant. A photo of the finished place appeared in the October 5, 1972, issue of *The Independent-Journal*, a newspaper published in Potosi, Missouri.

My focus the summer of 1972 was looking forward to the fall; I would be in a major seminary—St. Meinrad School of Theology—which, I hoped, would foster both my academic and spiritual growth. I needed a car to drive from Old Mines to

St. Meinrad, Indiana. One Saturday during the summer, Ackerson took me to Potosi and bought my first and only used car for $500. It was in bad shape. There was always something wrong with it—even the trunk leaked—but it got me to and from Indiana for four years, needing lots of work along the way!

6

St. Meinrad and Ordinations

St. Meinrad

I ARRIVED IN SOUTHERN Indiana at St. Meinrad School of Theology in St. Meinrad on September 5, 1972. There were forty-nine first-year theologians in my class. We were the first class to participate in a revised curriculum following the Second Vatican Council. Our first semester consisted of two classes: Ancient Church History (three credit hours) and the Religious Dimension of Human Existence (nine credit hours). The later was a type of interdisciplinary approach to the introduction of theology. We also chose from a variety of in-service ministry options, which were recorded as pass or fail.

There were a lot of in-service options in the area. I taught in St. Meinrad Parish School of Religion program my first year there. In subsequent years, I assisted in the continuing education program for priests. I traveled to Evansville to help in a parish on the weekends—sometimes preaching. I did a variety of things in various places in southern Indiana in order to prepare for ordination to the priesthood.

I had fallen in love with St. Meinrad when I had visited early in the spring of 1972. The School of Theology was overflowing in 1972; because of the large first-year class, some of us had to be housed in the college area, which was also full of students. I was one of those theologians who was assigned to live in the college area, a part of a floor that had been renovated so that it featured a common area surrounded by bedrooms on two sides, a study area on one side, and windows on the other side. I had a roommate, who had been in St. Meinrad College and returned to study theology. Because he was from Evansville, he was not around much, and he decided to leave the seminary at Thanksgiving time. That meant that I had the room to myself for the rest of the first semester and for all of the second semester. That suited me just fine!

While some parts of the college dormitories had been renovated, the sinks, toilets, and urinals were all located in a different section of the building, known as Newman Hall, what had one time been a high school seminary. A huge room featured sink after sink in the middle of the floor with toilets alongside one wall and urinals around the other side. Showers—believe it or not—were located in the basement of Newman Hall. Since I was a theologian, I was able to shower in the next section, known as Sherwood Hall, where I would live in a private room with a sink for my second, third, and fourth year of theology. In Sherwood Hall, the toilets and urinals were located in one room, and the showers were located in another room. It still meant that we had to wear a bath robe—at the minimum a towel—from our rooms to the showers, and carry soap, shampoo, and a towel with us.

The School of Theology began the day with breakfast, although few of us were ever present for the first meal of the day. A few first-year theologians, me included, met with Father Jerome (Jerry) Neufelder, the Spiritual Director for the School of Theology, for breakfast as soon as the meal was ready to be served. We became a small community throughout the four years we were there.

After breakfast we had our first class. Then, it was off to the Archabbey Church for morning prayer. That was followed by more classes, lunch, classes, free time for study or work or play, Mass, dinner, and study, work, or play. We were not required to wear clerical attire, as I had to do in the college seminary in St. Louis, and we did not wear cassocks and surplices for Mass in the St. Thomas Aquinas Chapel located on the fourth floor of Sherwood Hall. The only time I did not attend Mass in Sherwood Hall was on Sunday, when I joined the Benedictine monks for Mass in the Archabbey Church.

Once the semester got started and I figured out what was there "on the hill," as everyone referred to St. Meinrad Archabbey, monastery, school of theology, college, guest house, press, and more, I began to join the monks for Saturday Evening Prayer and Sunday Evening Prayer, and fell in love with sung Vespers. I also joined the monks for special celebrations during the liturgical year. A few times during the year, the students in the college and the school of theology joined the monks for Mass, such as on the Solemnity of St. Meinrad, January 21.

One of the first things first-year theologians needed to do was to choose a spiritual director. Robert Higginbotham, a third-year theologian, became my mentor in this regard. I met him at dinner one night, and he seemed like someone I could trust. After dinner we went outside and walked around the hill, talking about spiritual direction. I remember stopping and sitting on a bench with him; he recommended Father Sebastian Leonard, a priest-monk, who lived in a hall down the hill and served as its moderator. I made a point to see Leonard, and he accepted me as one of his directees. Leonard got me reading the Bible every day and deepened my appreciation of the liturgy. He listened to me one evening intently as I told him about my desire to write about my life; he named it homesickness, and he was correct. In many ways over two years, Leonard got me grounded in spirituality.

In some ways, being at St. Meinrad was a lot like having entered Cardinal Glennon College. Many of the members of my class had graduated from St. Meinrad College, just like many of my college classmates had graduated from St. Louis Preparatory

High School Seminary. While there were more theologians from around the U.S. in my first-year theology class, there were many who had attended St. Meinrad College. Thus, they knew each other, had formed their own social groups, and made it hard for the new students to get to know them. Thus, I, like many other men from around the U.S., formed my own group. I got to be friends with four or five others, and we formed a subgroup among ourselves, often going to Archabbey Church together for prayer, going out to eat together, doing laundry together, and other things.

When my roommate left at Thanksgiving, I decided to pursue the work-study program in which he had been involved. I had gotten most of the details from him in our conversations. So, I found the appropriate office, completed the necessary paperwork, and got a job working in the Development Office. Several days a week in the afternoon I did whatever Janet Werne, my boss, told me to do. I filed papers, sorted materials, and lots of other things. When she learned that I could type, I began to be placed in charge of the then-modern word processor. I would feed it stationery and watch as it typed letter after letter to alumni, personalizing each one with the appropriate name and address.

I got to know the other people who worked in the development office, too. I continued to work there until my third-year of theology, when I apprenticed myself to Father Ephrem Carr as a teaching assistant, working with first-year students. Another teaching assisting, Thomas Morrison, and I were responsible for teaching the first two weeks of his classes until he returned from Europe. This we did. For the rest of the two semesters I read research papers and met with students to help them refine their writing abilities.

I ended the first semester of my first year as a theologian with all Bs, earning another B in the inter-term of January 1973. The month of January offered students the opportunity to participate in a class at one of several schools of theology in and around southern Indiana. First-year theologians had to choose from courses offered on campus. I took the History and Theology of Western Liturgy course.

In November 1972, I should have made my Declaration of Candidacy for Diaconate and Priesthood ordinations and been Instituted in the Ministry of Lector. However, because the Diocese of Springfield-Cape Girardeau did not have a bishop (Baum had been transferred to Washington, DC) and because my class was the first to receive the newly instituted ministries (the minor orders having been abrogated), I was not permitted to share in either of those. The seminary rector, Father Daniel Buechlein, OSB, could not get assurance from the administrator of the Diocese of Springfield-Cape Girardeau, Msgr. John J. Rynish, that I was a seminarian for the diocese.

Finally, a year later on November 30, 1973, I made my declaration of candidacy and was instituted as a lector by Archbishop George J. Biskup of Indianapolis. My certificates are signed by Rynish, the administrator of the Diocese of Springfield-Cape Girardeau. On October 26, 1974, I was instituted into the ministry of Acolyte by Bishop Charles G. Maloney, Auxiliary Bishop of Louisville. This certificate is signed by Bishop

Bernard F. Law, who had been named the bishop of Springfield-Cape Girardeau in the meantime. I did not declare candidacy nor was I instituted in the ministries of lector and acolyte with my class; all these were done with the class behind me.

The second semester of my first year of theology (1973) found me taking fifteen hours of credit along with in-service ministry. My courses included Fundamental Theology, Introduction to Preaching, Ancient Church History II, History of Religious Life, and the History of Israel (Old Testament). By the end of the second semester, I was well on my academic way with a 3.4 grade point average and ranked eleventh in my class of 45. Four classmates had left either before or after Christmas.

During the summer between the end of my first year of theology and the beginning of my second year of theology, I worked as the secretary of my home parish, St. Joachim, in Old Mines, Missouri. The pastor, Suren, again had asked me to take over for the summer while the usual secretary, Politte (who was now Pratt) took off the summer months. I was responsible for recording contributions, recording baptisms, marriages, deaths, going to the bank to pick up the deposit receipt, producing the weekly bulletin, and lots more.

Suren invited me to join the associate pastor and him for lunch. After the Incarnate Word nuns, who taught in the school, left for the summer, he asked me to move into the convent and live there until they returned in the fall; I lived in the convent in order to keep anyone from breaking into the building. When the nuns did return, Suren invited me to take the guest room in the rectory. From that point on, the guest room became my room when I was home until I was ordained to the priesthood.

During that summer of 1973 the parish was preparing to celebrate its 150th anniversary, having been founded in 1822. The area known as Old Mines was marking its 250th anniversary, having been founded in 1723 by Philippe Francois Renault. One of the many events marking the dual anniversary was an outdoor pageant, fair, picnic, craft demonstrations, and other activities over the first weekend of September. So, throughout the summer I worked with others in organizing and getting ready for this momentous occasion.

Besides doing a lot of the office work necessary, I also designed the outdoor stage, which was built by some men in the parish and painted by some youth of the parish, upon which was enacted the pageant. While still a senior in Cardinal Glennon College in the fall of 1971, I finished editing, writing, and laying out what became known as my first book: *History of St. Joachim Church 1822–1972, 1723–1973* (Kansas City, MO: Yearbook House), a 200-page, coffee-table size tome. The cover featured a shield imposed over an outline of the church's facade; there were three fleur-de-lis, representing the French in Old Mines as members of the Archdiocese of St. Louis and in honor of the one God in three persons; there were a crossed pick and shovel, representing the mining that had taken place in the area, first for silver, then lead, then barite (tiff); there was a blank lower section, representing the future to be completed; and there was a banner with "St. Joachim" printed on it. One of my college classmates, Mark A. Dolan, designed it.

St. Meinrad and Ordinations

During the summer of 1971, when I had served as secretary for the parish while the usual one took vacation time, Suren said something about putting together a parish history book, and I volunteered to do it. I spent a lot of that summer gathering information from the parish records and files, researching in various places—such as the local newspaper office, the court house, and the archives of the Archdiocese of St. Louis, making notes, preparing text, gathering photos, finding a publisher, and learning how to prepare the pages to be submitted to the publisher. After telling Suren that I needed a typewriter to take with me to Cardinal Glennon College so that I could finish the work during the fall semester of my senior year of college (1971–1972), he gave me one from the school. It was a manual Olympic office model, and it not only served the purpose for preparing text, but it accompanied me through my four years of theology and well into my first few years of priesthood. I typed many papers on that machine before it became obsolete with the advent of electric typewriters, then word processors, and then computers.

During the fall of 1971, while finishing up the book, I got several other of my college classmates involved in the necessary photography. Richard H. Risse and Schaab agreed to take pictures of everything from famous tomb stones in the parish cemetery to pages out of the very old parish registers. They had the cameras, the lenses, and the skills to do all this. A college friend, Vernon J. Meyer, Jr., did the proofreading. The seventh and eighth grade students in the school sold the ads to pay for the project under the direction of Sister Mary Ellen O'Connor, who had become the principal of St. Joachim School.

Once all the pages had been submitted to the publisher, the wait for the final product began. In the spring of 1972, the boxes of spiral-bound books arrived, and they were an immediate hit with parishioners and others alike. I laid claim to three copies, since that is the only salary I ever received for writing the book, except for the typewriter and the typing stand it sat on. Because I wrote and edited the history book, I was involved in planning the anniversary celebration during the summer of 1973.

Near the end of the second semester of my first year in St. Meinrad School of Theology, I was asked by Neufelder to be the prayer coordinator for the school. He told me that he had noticed that I always attended morning and evening prayer and that he and others thought I should be given this position. I accepted the position. However, this meant that I had to be at St. Meinrad a week ahead of when the fall 1973 semester began to introduce first-year theologians to the prayer program for theology students. In order to fulfill my responsibilities of prayer coordinator, I drove to St. Meinrad for a week and then headed back to Old Mines for the big celebration, which began with a flag raising (I designed and sewed the Old Mines flag) and was followed by all kinds of carnival games, demonstrations of ancient crafts with demonstrators dressed in appropriate period attire, a meal, and the pageant in the evening. On Sunday morning I had to head back to Indiana, because classes began on Monday morning.

My Life of Ministry, Writing, Teaching, and Traveling

My second-year theology class had dropped to forty-three members. Serving as prayer coordinator meant that I had to be sure that leaders had volunteered to prepare morning and evening prayer. I took fifteen hours of courses and continued to work in the development office on campus. I also prepared to go to Indiana University, Bloomington, for the second semester to work on a Master of Arts in Religious Studies degree as part of a joint program worked out by St. Meinrad and IU.

Three others members from my class—Noah Casey, Chrysostom (Daniel) Conway, and James Dvorscak—were going to participate in this program. So, we took a three-hour course called Readings in Religious Studies during the fall of 1973 to prepare for the spring of 1974 on the IU campus. This meant that my ministry as prayer coordinator for St. Meinrad School of Theology was short lived; it lasted for only one semester. It also meant that the four of us would not be able to participate in the interterm at St. Meinrad because we had to report to IU for classes in mid-January.

So, mid-January 1974 found me living in Eigemann Hall on the IU campus and taking courses in Modern Christian Thought, Topics in the History of Christianity, the Religious Element in Culture, and North American Indian Folklore. These were days of signing up for courses by going to a gym and visiting departmental tables upon which were sheets of paper where students put their names for courses they intended to take. After that was done, one went to a payment table, where he paid for the courses he intended to take.

Even though the vocation director—Msgr. Stephen Schneider—for the Diocese of Springfield-Cape Girardeau had approved my going to IU, I had not yet received the check to cover the cost. In those days, dioceses paid for all of a seminarian's education. Because I did not have the funds, I was put on a list that indicated that I would pay for my courses within a couple of days. As soon as this was done, I called Schneider, and explained to him that I needed a check to complete my registration at IU. I asked him to do all he could to get it to me so that I could pay my bill. Needless to say, I did not want to have all my registration work cancelled and have to start over a few days later. I agonized all weekend over the arrival of the check. However, on Monday the check arrived, and I headed directly to the treasurer's office to complete payment and registration for my courses.

By the time the snow finally melted—it snowed a lot that winter!—and spring arrived in Bloomington, I had finished all the course work for my MA degree in Religious Studies; it was mid-May 1974. IU accepted eight hours of credit for courses I had taken in St. Meinrad. All that remained was the writing of the thesis, which was worth six credit hours; the thesis would not be accomplished for a few years.

The one semester spent on the IU campus of thirty thousand students made me hungry for St. Meinrad, to which I headed for the summer session of 1974. Those students who attended IU were required to participate in the summer session following the semester at IU in order to pick up the required courses they missed while being at IU. So, during the summer session, I took Theological Anthropology, Moral

Theology, Prophecy, and Religion in Drama and Literature. It was a heavy load of twelve hours for summer!

However, the last course listed above would affect me for the rest of my life and lead to my developing a film program at Missouri State University in the Department of Religious Studies. The other effect of summer school was my friendship with two very different people. One was Sister Mary Caroline Marchal, with whom I would be friends for six or seven years; she broke off the friendship after objecting to me serving as a chaplain on cruise ships. The other was Dick (Richard) Wildeman, a theologian one year behind me from whom I learned what non-possessive love is.

Besides attending class—of which I did a lot because of taking twelve hours—the small summer school session became a small Christian community, composed of a few priests, some nuns, a few lay people, and a few seminarians. Marchal was in charge of summer activities, and so she drew me in on helping in many different ways. It was very hot and humid that summer in southern Indiana near the Ohio River. It was so hot some nights that some of us took our bedding to the conference room, which was air conditioned, and slept on the floor. At the closing Mass of the summer session, presided over by Carr, I preached the homily on what we learned from each other by relating to each other.

Because there were only a couple of weeks between the end of the summer session and the beginning of the fall semester, I did not get to work that summer. For the fall semester of my third year of theology, I took courses in Theology of the Church, Christian Marriage, Jesus and the Synoptic Gospels, Catholic Epistles, and the Church in the Age of Reformation. By the end of 1974, I was ranked first out of thirty-seven classmates in academics.

When not studying, I was working as Carr's teaching assistant, as indicated above. I read first-year theologians' papers and met with them to discuss how they could improve. When Carr was busy with other things or when he thought Morrison and I could handle his class, I taught Ancient Church History. I had also gotten involved in monastic liturgical services, volunteering to serve on special occasions. I loved the monastic liturgies and was willing to participate at any time.

For the January 1975 inter-term, I took an introductory course on Oriental Churches, taught by Carr. Besides the background given and the study of the various rites, Carr chose to celebrate several of the rites with the class. In the evenings we made our way to the Byzantine Chapel located under the Archabbey Church and celebrated Masses that were foreign to all of us who knew only the Roman (Western) Rite.

Ordinations

Besides taking courses for the spring 1975 semester in Sacraments, Pauline Christianity, Liturgy, Canon Law, and Preaching, I prepared to be ordained a Transitional Deacon. A lot of planning went into this event. This was to be the first ordination ever to take place in historic St. Joachim Church, in which still hung the banners from the 1973 double anniversary celebration. The Vocation Director for the Diocese of Springfield-Cape Girardeau, Schneider, had arranged with Bernard F. Law, Bishop of Springfield-Cape Girardeau, to ordain me in my home parish, even though it was located within the boundary of the Archdiocese of St. Louis. The Archbishop of St. Louis, Carberry, had to give permission for the ordination to take place; he did, but he would not permit Law to carry his crosier, a sign of jurisdiction.

I had garnered the help of fellow St. Meinrad seminarians and a St. Meinrad Archabbey monk-deacon. Concelebrating priests included the current pastor and former pastors—Suren and Suellentrop—and current and former associate pastors—Jansen, Father Edward J. Schramm, and Father James M. Moll. Deacon Brother Jeremy King, OSB, was from St. Meinrad Archabbey, St. Meinrad, Indiana, and Deacon Dennis Schaefer was from the Diocese of Belleville, Illinois. My good friend, Wildeman (Diocese of Evansville, Indiana), served as the primary Master of Ceremonies and was assisted by my other good friends, Meyer (Archdiocese of Santa Fe, New Mexico), and Jerome Martinez (Archdiocese of Santa Fe, New Mexico).

Incense was handled by David Tscherne (Diocese of Toledo, Ohio); the cross was carried by Brother Michael Buttner, OSB, from Belmont Abbey, NC; and the ritual book was carried by Peter Libasci (Diocese of Rockville Centre, New York). Four altar servers from the parish served as acolytes and miter bearers: Kevin Thebeau, Tim Coleman, Tim Bone, and Donnie Battreal.

I had asked Steven LeBlanc (Diocese of Lafayette, Louisiana) to serve as music director, Morrison (Diocese of Charleston, South Carolina) to play the organ, and David Martin (Diocese of Evansville, Indiana) to play the guitar. The choir was formed by R. Mark Duchaine (Diocese of Sioux City, Iowa), John Giel (Diocese of Orlando, Florida), Glenn Macip (Diocese of Lafayette, Louisiana), and Henry Tully (Archdiocese of Indianapolis, Indiana). Timothy Berg (Archdiocese of Sant Fe, New Mexico) was in charge of taking black and white pictures. My cousins, Dennis Boyer and P. Gregory Boyer, were the readers for the ordination Mass.

Good friends Joey and Barb Bone had agreed to be in charge of housing for all the seminarians, since there was no motel in the area. So, they arranged to have each seminarian stay with a local family. When seminarians arrived by the car full at St. Joachim Church from southern Indiana, the host families were called to come and pick them up, take them home, and get them settled. The host family had a schedule for rehearsal and other things in which the seminarians needed to participate.

On March 8, 1975, the Vigil (Saturday) of the Fourth Sunday of Lent, I was ordained to the Diaconate by Law. I was the second deacon he ordained after he was ordained to the episcopacy. Suren, the pastor of the parish, welcomed all to the historic celebration; the church was almost full. Schneider presented me to Law for ordination, after which Jansen clothed me in stole and dalmatic. My mother, Verna, was present, along with my second mother, Ackerson, my grandmother, Margaret, and lots of other relatives, friends, and a few priests from the Diocese of Springfield-Cape Girardeau and the Archdiocese of St. Louis.

Following the ordination Mass, the St. Anne's Sodality of the parish sponsored a reception in the school cafeteria. A meal was served to the seminarians, overseen by Sister Achille Bugnitz, CCVI, and the food was provided by the Knights of Columbus. Seminarians spent another night with their host families and headed back to St. Meinrad on Sunday morning, as did I, after serving as deacon at one of the parish Masses.

At the ordination Mass, Law had announced that for the summer I would be serving in the Diocese of Springfield-Cape Girardeau in St. Eustachius Parish, Portageville, Missouri, located in the bootheel, with the pastor, Father Amel Shibley, who was at my ordination Mass. So, when the spring semester was finished, I headed to Portageville to spend the summer in parish ministry.

Shibley was willing to have a deacon present because it meant less work for him! I preached at every Mass—Sunday and weekday. Anyone wanting to get married was referred to me. What was interesting was that Shibley had no objections to what I did as long as it removed work for him. However, he would not let me do anything creative, and always warned me not to upset anyone in the parish.

I had a bedroom on the second floor of the rectory with a bathroom and shower. Shibley had a bedroom with a half-bath, and so we had to share the shower as well as the living room. He warned me that he often sat in his favorite chair in the living room in nothing other than his underwear, and he did. He often spoke about sex, and by today's standards would be found guilty of not only verbal abuse, but physical abuse. One of his common practices was to grab me from behind when I was walking up the steps ahead of him. While I didn't like it then, I didn't know what to do about it. I didn't want to cause problems with my first assignment in the diocese. It was a form of bullying and abuse, but I didn't know that then!

On the first floor of the rectory there was a kitchen, dining room, and Shibley's office. He would not allow me to have an office on the first floor; instead he sent me to the basement, where there was a desk. Before I could use the basement, I had to clean it. It was full of dried floral arrangements, lots of junk, and other stuff. I created a clean place at the bottom of the steps, spread a large carpet I had found over the concrete floor, placed the desk and a couple of chairs and lamps upon it, arranged my typewriter and stand, and spent a lot of time there working. One of Shibley's favorite things to do was to open the basement door and ask, "What are you doing?" When I would inform him, he would make some comment like, "That's not work," or "You're not doing anything important."

It was not until April 4, 2019—after Bishop Edward Rice published a list of priests of the diocese with allegations of abuse—that I was compelled to report Shibley's verbal abuse about not wanting me in his house, only being given the basement as a place to work, his language about sex, and the grabbing of my butt, him sitting in his underwear in common spaces, and other talk that made me very uncomfortable.

That letter was never answered by Rice; he gave it to William Holtmeyer, the Diocesan Director of the Office of Child and Youth Protection.

Holtmeyer wrote to me on April 10, 2019, stating. "The details of your experience are truly disturbing; that should not have happened to you, and I am sorry for the wound it may have caused you." Shibley died in 2002; his name had been placed on the list of those clergy who were alleged to have sexually abused minors. "But your experience shines additional light on the mistreatment of adults, as well," wrote Holtmeyer. He asked me to review the materials he enclosed with the letter and to return a form indicating that I had been informed about the Rights of the Victim/Survivor. I did that on April 12, 2019. I included a note indicating that I had processed this a long time ago, and that I did not want to revisit it. I merely wanted to report what Shibley did. I wanted to make clear that I am not what happened to me.

In early September 1975 I headed back to St. Meinrad for the fall semester of 1975. I took courses in Penance and Moral Problems, Liturgy, Applied Theology, and Preaching. Because I was a deacon and there wasn't one in St. Meinrad Archabbey, I often served as deacon at monastic celebrations. I loved participating in monastic prayer. On some occasions, after Mass, I was invited to join the monks in their dining room for dinner. For some reason I never really considered joining the monastery; I was too focused on diocesan priesthood.

After Christmas I was back in St. Eustachius Parish, rearranging my office in the basement and preaching at every Mass. Shibley was gone on a cruise for a week and Father James Seyer, a retired priest, came and spent the week. He was a very strange man, telling jokes that were not all that funny all the time, and hurrying through the Mass, like there was a fire in the church. He and I engaged in several conversations in which I remember explaining the purpose of the three orations—Collect, Prayer Over the Gifts, Prayer after Communion—of the Mass. Shibley had told me not to make him angry in any way because he would not come back when Shibley needed him again. I prepared two couples for marriage to take place later in the spring. I often played softball with the children in the school during recess. I taught a religion class in the school. Basically, I did all the work which Shibley did not want to do!

Knowing what I was getting into from the past summer, I spent more time in the basement making stoles and putting together the booklet for my ordination to the priesthood in April 1976. My classmates and I made a trip to St. Meinrad during the spring to process our experiences in parishes. We wrote case studies and presented them to each other for consideration. Our supervisors, in my case Shibley, were supposed to be with us, but Shibley refused to go to St. Meinrad. Thus, I was alone.

After Easter 1976 I made a private retreat with the monks at the now-closed St. Pius X Monastery in Pevely, Missouri. Then, I headed to Old Mines to finish preparation for my ordination to the priesthood on Saturday, April 24, 1976. Law had agreed to ordain me on the day before my feast day, St. Mark, April 25, so I could say my first Mass on my patron's feast day. Before I had left St. Meinrad for Christmas, I had organized ministers to assist in the ordination ceremony.

The pastor in my home parish of St. Joachim had changed from Suren to Father Theodore R. Brug. I asked Deacon Kevin J. Bryan from the Archdiocese of Louisville, Kentucky, and Deacon Brother Noah Casey, OSB, from St. Meinrad Archabbey, St. Meinrad, Indiana, to serve as assisting deacons. Wildeman was the primary Master of Ceremonies, assisted by Meyer and Deacon Joseph N. Dant and Paul M. Shikany, both from the Archdiocese of Indianapolis, Indiana.

Tscherne was now a deacon, but chose to be thurifer nevertheless. Buttner carried the paschal candle instead of the cross, and Libasci served again as book bearer. My cousins were readers. LeBlanc, also a deacon now, was music director, assisted by Deacon Morrison on the organ, Anthony J. Trosley (Diocese of Peoria, Illinois) on the guitar, and Girard M. Sherba (Diocese of Raleigh, North Carolina) on the flute. The choir consisted of Giel, Tully, who had been ordained a deacon, Michael E. Nelsen (Diocese of Rockford, Illinois), and Roger L. Leveillee (Diocese of Springfield-Cape Girardeau, Missouri). Berg was again in charge of photography. Altar servers were Timothy Bone and John Wilson.

Among the priest concelebrants were Moll, Suren, Shibley, Schneider, Father Thomas E. Reidy, Chancellor of the Diocese of Springfield-Cape Girardeau, and Carr. There were other priests present from the Archdiocese of St. Louis and from the Diocese of Springfield-Cape Girardeau.

Brug welcomed all to the celebration on this Saturday in the Octave of Easter. Schneider presented me to Law for ordination. And after I was ordained, Suren clothed me in stole and chasuble; the privilege of doing this was my going-away gift to him when he left the parish during the summer of 1975. An Old Mine's native, Sister Lorraine Bourisaw, CCVI, had sewn a set of twenty-five stoles—reversible with white on one side and green on the other—for all priest concelebrants as her ordination gift to me. Both of my parents, Jesse and Verna, were present, along with my second mother, Ackerson, and many other relatives and friends. Near the end of the Mass, Law announced that my first priestly assignment would be as associate pastor of St. Agnes Cathedral, Springfield, to which I would report on May 31. Following the Mass, I gave a first blessing to all who waited in the church; then, a meal was served for all in the school cafeteria.

All of the ministers coming from St. Meinrad were paired with host families as had been done for my diaconate ordination. They arrived at the church on Friday, were picked up by their host family, got settled, and were brought back for a rehearsal. After the meal on Saturday they were entertained by their host families and brought back for some entertainment sponsored by the students in St. Joachim School. After the entertainment, host families took the seminarians home in preparation for my first Mass the following day.

On Sunday afternoon, April 25, I presided over the Eucharist for the first time and sang Eucharistic Prayer III. Concelebrating priests included Brug, Moll, Shibley, Carr, Suellentrop, who had baptized me 26 years earlier and who delivered the homily, and Father James E. Hanson, the only other priest from St. Joachim Parish, Old Mines, in active ministry. My assisting deacons were Paul D. Koetter (Archdiocese of Indianapolis, Indiana) and Tscherne.

Wildeman was Master of Ceremonies, assisted by Meyer and Shikany. Dant was responsible for incense, Buttner carried the Paschal Candle, and Libasci was book bearer. My cousins were readers, and Thomas Wilson and Glen Osia were altar servers. The music director, organist, guitarist, flutist, and choir were the same as the day before. Berg took photographs.

Both of my parents were present, along with Ackerson, and my uncle and aunt, who were also my godparents, Thomas and Thelma Boyer, and who bought the stole and chasuble I wore for my first Mass. We used unleavened bread that had been backed by a friend. Both the Nambe silver chalice given to me by my parents and the wooden chalice made by the monks at St. Meinrad and given to me by Ackerson were used. Other chalices were crystal, another ordination gift from another friend, Marchal. Following the Mass, there was a reception in the school cafeteria.

Most of the seminarians headed back to St. Meinrad that Sunday afternoon and evening, because they had class the next day. I, too, had to be there on Monday for our final class seminar and graduation. Before graduation we had a Mass; since I was one of three members of my class who had already been ordained to priesthood, I was chosen to preside over the graduation Mass. On Thursday, April 29, 1976, Archabbot Gabriel Verkamp, OSB, awarded me my Master of Divinity diploma. I didn't know it at the time, but academically I ranked first in my class of thirty-six.

After saying good-bye to classmates, I headed home for a month of celebrations in St. Joachim Parish and several weddings in St. Eustachius Parish. I made it a point to have Mass in the homes of all my uncles and aunts as a thanksgiving to them for their support over the years. They invited their friends to participate and to share cake and coffee afterward.

I would be remiss if I did not mention the Rural Parish Workers of Christ the King, a secular institute of women who lived and worked in St. Joachim Parish. They created banners for the church and offered their St. Michael House for the evening entertainment after my ordination. I went to their headquarters, celebrated Mass with them, and shared dinner one evening before May 31.

With the help of a few cousins who had a van, I gathered my belongings and a few pieces of furniture and headed to Springfield on May 30. There I met my first pastor, Msgr. John H. Westhues, who had been the founding chancellor of the diocese and was pastor of St. Agnes Cathedral. The associate pastor I was replacing was still living there because his new assignment was not effective for a few months. So, I was given the guest room, where I put a few of my things, stored others in the rectory basement, and began my parish ministry.

My professors in St. Meinrad School of Theology taught me how to think critically and how to be creative. They nourished my inquisitiveness and challenged my growth. They enabled me to develop a solid theological foundation and a deeper appreciation for a love of the liturgy. While these were the best years of my academic life, I was abused both verbally and physically by Shibley during the summer of 1975 and the spring of 1976 I spent in Portageville. Because of my naiveté, I didn't realize I was being abused at the time; I merely accepted it as part of the clerical culture. Furthermore, because Shibley was so well liked by the priests of the diocese and Law—since he sent me there—I doubt they would have understood what I was talking about should I have reported him for what he did to me. Eight years later, Law was transferred to Boston, where he covered up his priests' abuse of children; once this fact became public, he was forced to resign in 2002. So, I doubt that Law would have believed me even if I had told him about the six months I endured in Portageville.

As to the other thirty-five members of my 1976 ordination class, some are still in active ministry or retired, some are dead, and some have left active ministry. As to those who assisted at my own ordinations, Law ended up in Rome, where he retired and died, unable to return to the U.S. for fear of prosecution for what he did in Boston. Suellentrop, Suren, Schramm, Brug, Leveillee, and Shibley are dead. Jansen and Moll left active ministry. Hanson is retired in Old Mines.

Schneider admitted to child abuse and was defrocked. King is a priest-monk of St. Meinrad Archabbey. Schaefer is a priest of the Diocese of Belleville. Wildeman was ordained to the priesthood and then left active ministry to marry. Meyer was ordained a priest for the Diocese of Phoenix, and left active ministry after he and his bishop disagreed on a number of issues; he now serves as pastor of a United Church of Christ parish in Phoenix.

Martinez was named a monsignor and continues in priestly ministry in the Archdiocese of Santa Fe; Tscherne serves as a priest in the Diocese of Toledo. Buttner, who was a priest-monk of Belmont Abbey, served as registrar for Belmont College for a number of years, then left the monastery to become a priest of the Diocese of Charlotte. Libasci was ordained a priest and later ordained an auxiliary bishop of the Diocese of Rockville Centre; then he was named the bishop of the Diocese of Manchester, New Hampshire. LeBlanc serves as a priest in the Diocese of Lafayette; Morrison served as a priest in the Diocese of Charleston, but is now retired; Martin serves as a priest in the Diocese of Evansville; Tully serves as a priest of the Archdiocese of Indianapolis; Trosley serves as a priest in the Diocese of Peoria; Bryan serves as a priest in the Archdiocese of Louisville; Casey, a priest-monk who worked in St. Meinrad College for a number of years, left St. Meinrad Archabbey and became a priest of the Archdiocese of Indianapolis, where he died; Dant serves as a priest in the Archdiocese of Indianapolis; Giel serves as a priest in the Diocese of Orlando;

Duchaine was named a monsignor and serves in the Diocese of Sioux City; Koetter was named a monsignor and serves in the Archdiocese of Indianapolis.

Reidy retired as the chancellor of the Diocese of Springfield-Cape Girardeau in 2019; Carr, after teaching in Rome for a long time, returned to St. Meinrad Archabbey; Sherba was named a monsignor and serves as chancellor of the Diocese of Raleigh; others who were involved in my ordinations and first Mass and named above, I do not know what happened to them.

7

Assignments in the Diocese of Springfield-Cape Girardeau

Associate Pastor of St. Agnes Cathedral Parish

My first priestly assignment in the Diocese of Springfield-Cape Girardeau was associate pastor of St. Agnes Cathedral Parish, Springfield. I reported for duty there on May 30, 1976, arriving around mid-day with a van containing my few possessions driven by my cousins. The pastor, Westhues, was not ready to receive me, neither were any members of his staff. The associate pastor I was replacing was still in his rooms and would remain there for three months. I was assigned to the guest room, which did have a private bathroom. Basically, I had a bed, a desk, and a chair. Most of my personal belongings had to be taken to the basement, where they were stored until I could move into the rooms I would eventually inhabit.

I walked into a team that had been functioning for a few years. The members of the team—pastor, associate, religious education director, finance manager, and secretary—were not excited about adding a new member. I felt like a pin ball with the staff as flippers, sending me rolling from one side of the parish to the other. From working in my home parish, I had some idea of what a parish was and how it functioned, but I did not know who I was. I had been so focused on academics and completing my studies that I had spent little time asking myself who I was and what I wanted to do in terms of priestly ministry.

Because I really wasn't needed yet as an associate pastor, I was sent on weekends to substitute for priests who were absent for some reason. I didn't know the diocese, because I had only visited Springfield a few times; I had never lived in the diocese. While I went to many parishes for weekend Masses, one place I remember well was Our Lady of the Ozarks, Forsyth, Missouri. I went there for a weekend during the summer of 1976 and said several Masses for the people. While eating Sunday lunch at one of the restaurants, a lady, Ruth Hamilton, who had been at one of the Masses and recognized me, invited me to come and see a cabin on her property.

My Life of Ministry, Writing, Teaching, and Traveling

When I finished lunch, I followed her home to a huge house that sat on a cliff overlooking Powersite Dam. Below the house there was a log cabin. She showed me around her house and took me to the cabin, even showing me where the key was kept. It was an old slave cabin that her husband, Alexander Hamilton, had rescued—from what was now Bull Shoals Lake—while the dam was being built. He dismantled it log by log and stone by stone, numbered all the pieces, and reassembled it on their property below their home. It consisted of one room with a stone fireplace at one end. At the other end Hamilton had added on a room in which he installed a toilet, a shower, a sink, a hot water heater, and a refrigerator. There were two single beds in the one room, several chairs and tables, and rugs scattered on the wooden floor.

Ruth explained that before Alexander died, they had used the cabin as a guest house and, primarily, as a place to serve drinks and hors d'oeuvres before moving to the main house for dinner. She was not using it in 1976, and she offered it to me anytime I wanted a place to get away to for a few days. After looking around it, I thanked her for the offer, promised that I would call if I decided to use it, and headed back to Springfield. A few weeks later, I called her and made my way to the cabin for a day or two.

During the two years of my assignment as associate pastor of St. Agnes Cathedral, I used the cabin often, spending the night in it, and spending my day off reading and sitting in the sun. It was a very quiet place, and Hamilton never bothered me except to welcome me. I used the cabin for years and years, taking high school male students there for weekends, once I began as a high school teacher, and making private retreats there. When I brought a group of high school students to the cabin, they brought sleeping bags to spread on the floor for the night. Hamilton always welcomed them and me to the cabin and prepared a breakfast for all of us on the morning of our choosing. She always called the students "your boys," and loved entertaining them. Finally, near the end of one visit, Hamilton informed me that she was selling the property and moving closer to her daughter. She offered to introduce me to the new owners, but we could not work out a time to meet them. So, after many years of use, my time in the cabin came to an end.

Once Father Fergus Monaghan, the associate pastor of St. Agnes Cathedral, left for his new assignment, I was able to move into the two rooms which he had occupied. I had new curtains made for the windows, had the double bed placed in the guest room and the single bed in there put in my bedroom in order to have more space. There was a desk in my sitting room and bookshelves upon which I placed my unpacked boxes of books which were the beginning of my library. Since I had little in terms of furniture, I went to several flea markets and found a corner desk, which I put in my bedroom, and a small rocking chair which I placed in my bedroom. The corner desk was my workspace for completing the writing of my MA thesis.

During my third and fourth year of theology at St. Meinrad School of Theology, I had worked on my thesis for the Master's Degree in Religious Studies at IU. I had chosen the topic of the Lamarques in Old Mines; this came as a result of working on the History of St. Joachim Parish that I had written in 1972–1973. I had made a trip to Ste. Genevieve to research the Bolduc family from which Mrs. Lamarque had come. Her father had been a rich merchant in Ste. Genevieve. After marrying Lamarque, they moved to Old Mines, where she used her fortune to enlarge the church, build the first school, and repurchase the parish property after a pastor had sold it! All the old Ste. Genevieve records were in French, but I had a friend in the seminary who willingly translated for me the copies I had made.

I also made a trip to Jefferson City, Missouri, to research the Missouri Supreme Court case concerning Mrs. Lamarque in the Missouri Supreme Court Archives. The papers I read were all hand written; I had copies made of both times the Lamarque case had made it to the Missouri Supreme Court: the first time the case came in error; the second time it came it brought a decision that hurt the Catholic Church. Gradually, I worked on writing my thesis on my day off or when I had a few hours to spend on it. The handwritten pages were typed by Marilyn Vydra, a part-time secretary who worked a few days a week to manage priests' correspondence or whatever else was asked of her.

The cathedral parish was a bee hive of activity. The phone rang constantly; the doorbell rang many times every day. There were meetings both day and night. A live-in cook prepared three meals a day for Westhues, me, and Father Phillip Bucher and Schneider, who lived there the first year I was there. After they moved out and Msgr. Sylvester Baur replaced Westhues as pastor, Bucher's rooms were taken over by Father Val Reker, and Schneider's room was taken over by Father James L. Reynolds, who was to become my best priest friend.

Westhues was a very good friend with Sister Rachel Dietz, OSB, religious education director, so I was like a third wheel when we met as a staff. I was responsible for visiting classes in the school and training altar servers. When I got there, the practice was that we preached only every other weekend at all the Masses. So, on one weekend Westhues preached at the Masses he celebrated and at the Masses I celebrated; the next weekend I preached at the Masses he celebrated and at the ones I celebrated. It didn't take long for me to dislike that arrangement, because I preferred to preach at the Masses I celebrated. I liked developing a theme and using it throughout the liturgy, and I was a much better homilist than Westhues; Westhues loved it because it meant that he didn't have to prepare a homily every week. When, after a few months, I told him that I preferred to preach at the Masses I celebrated and only them, he reluctantly changed the practice.

When Law came to celebrate Mass at the cathedral, I usually served as his Master of Ceremonies for the Chrism Mass, ordinations, Palm Sunday, Holy Thursday, Good Friday, and the Easter Vigil. The cathedral organist, Helen Howard, and I would sit down together and plan the services; then, I would present them to Law for his approval. I remember one Easter Vigil that we had planned that he did not like and changed what we wanted to do.

On January 25, 1977, I wrote to Law, after previously speaking to him, about the possibility of me making an application to become bi-ritual, being able to celebrate the Byzantine Liturgy according to the Melkite Rite. I had been involved in the bi-ritual celebration of the Byzantine Liturgy at St. Meinrad Seminary, and I wanted to continue my interest in it. In my letter to Law, I stated that I wanted to be bi-ritual to teach others about the rite. I also told him that it would continue to enrich my spirituality. There was also a pastoral reason to getting permission to be bi-ritual: I could help the Melkite Rite Parish in Kansas City, Missouri. I also had the endorsement of Father Pat H. Hoffman, who ministered to the parish in Kansas City. Law wrote to me that he had decided this was not a good idea. Later, I discovered that he had granted another priest, Shibley, the privilege of being bi-ritual, but he would not grant it to me.

It was very hard to make changes with Westhues and Dietz, who did a lot of whatever she wanted. I tried using my skills at decorating the cathedral, only to be criticized by Dietz most of the time. I remember one celebration of the Solemnity of St. Agnes, the cathedral's patroness. I had placed the statue of St. Agnes behind the altar and surrounded it with living palm plants (since Agnes was a martyr). When Dietz walked into the cathedral, she immediately voiced her shock that I would place that arrangement in front of the tabernacle. For Lent one year I had a large wooden cross made and two smaller crosses and placed those behind the altar; since Westhues insisted that more than one cross be used for Good Friday, I used all three for the veneration of the cross; this brought comments about using the crosses for the two co-crucified thieves instead of the one for Jesus for adoration.

As the tension continued to mount, a meeting was called to discuss what was going on with staff. After requesting examples of why I felt that I was not accepted there from Dietz, I proceeded to give example after example of the negativity I had experienced. Both of them listened and understood.

After one year as associate with Westhues, Law moved Westhues to Joplin and brought in Bauer as pastor. The cook went with Westhues to Joplin; before Bauer got there, I hired a different cook for the house. Bauer was known for his frugality. He took all the small light bulbs out of their sockets up and down the indoor steps to the second floor. He removed the outside light from the back door that many of us used to enter the rectory. He turned off the air conditioners in the cathedral when it was not being used. When the air conditioning in the rectory broke in the heat of the summer and Bauer was in the hospital for a few days, I got it fixed, even though he didn't want to spend the money to fix it. I once told him that if I got hit on the head when I was trying to enter the rectory at night because there was no light outside the back door, I was going to sue him. Within a day the light was back!

Bauer imposed his frugality on everyone. Dietz left. Reynolds moved out. The cook quit. And I had had enough of a hot rectory, a hot church, and imposed frugality. I firmly believed in not wasting things, but there was a point when turning off the hot water, which Bauer had done, went too far. Imagine my wondering why there was no hot water, going to the basement, and discovering that the hot water heater had been turned off! When I met with Law after two years as associate pastor, he wanted me to go to Cape Girardeau as associate of St. Mary Cathedral there. I did not want to go to Cape Girardeau, and I told him so. He continued to insist, reminding me that I had promised him obedience when he ordained me. I began to cry, and that moved him to ask me what I suggested. I told him that I would like to go to Joplin to be with Westhues. He told me that I would have to learn how to work with other priests, but made a deal with me: If I would go to Joplin to be part-time associate in the parish and teach part-time in McAuley Regional Catholic High School, he would send me there. I agreed.

It was during these two years that two important things took place. The first was that I began to study psychology on my own through reading in order to discover who I was. I did not like parish ministry, but I did not know why I didn't like it. I did not like visiting the sick in their homes or in the hospital. I did not like the daily events of the parish, even daily Mass. I had begun to hate everything about parish life to the point that I dreaded facing it for another day.

The second thing that took place was a telephone call from Gerrit tenZythoff, who was in the process of establishing the Religious Studies Department at Southwest Missouri State University (now Missouri State University). He offered me a position there, which, because I was moving to Joplin, I could not accept. Little did I know that in 1987 I would be offered the same position again by a different department head, and this time I would accept it.

So, in August 1978, I, with the assistance of a St. Agnes Cathedral eighth-grade student, packed my books and other belongings. Someone from the parish offered to loan and drive a truck with my things to Joplin. Off I went to St. Mary Parish rectory, where I would face the next obstacles in my life.

Associate of St. Mary Parish and Chaplain of McAuley High School

I arrived with my belongings and greeted Westhues and his cook. I was shown to my rooms, and noticed that there was not a single bookshelf in any room. I spoke with Westhues about this; we decided that I would go to the hardware store, buy lumber and bricks, and build temporary bookshelves in my room. I enlisted the help of a student Westhues recommended, who stained the lumber while I built the shelves. Once I got moved in, I went to meet the principal of McAuley High School, Sister Norbert Flesch, RSM. Besides being chaplain of the school, I would be teaching one class of religion to Sophomores. I met other faculty members, got a copy of my textbook, and prepared for the school year.

In the parish, my skills were needed in decorating the church, working with the musicians and choir, and planning liturgies. I spent a year working with Westhues and the two religious education directors, Sister Pat Lewter and Sister Faye Huelsmann,

St. Joseph nuns from Concordia, Kansas. The nuns and I attempted to get some parish policies together so that we had boundaries within which to work. Westhues would agree, but then do whatever he wanted anyway. In other words, it was the same song, second verse for me.

On November 7, 1978, I was very frustrated with Westhues and St. Mary Parish. As I wrote in a memorandum, in an attempt to straighten out my life and remove some of the frustrations and anxieties, I was no longer celebrating the 8 a.m. daily Mass, the 5:30 p.m. Sunday Mass, and the 5:30 p.m. First Friday Mass. Those were very sparsely attended Masses with little or no participation. They did not foster or nourish faith, and they were hurting my own faith. Sunday, the Lord's Day, should have the afternoon and evening free, especially in light of the fact that I was putting in ten-hour days, six days a week. Because of the few participants in the Sunday evening Mass and the fact that there was also one at the other parish in Joplin, St. Peter the Apostle, I advised that it be cancelled at St. Mary. Westhues did not know how to react except to say that he would take the Masses I was not going to celebrate. I was beginning to realize that I did not want to spend the rest of my life being a parish priest.

However, I excelled in high school work. I loved being back in school. I got to know my students, and they got to know and like me. They told me that I was a hard teacher, and they ranked me along Ted Monseur, who taught current events and history; Susan Monseur, who taught math; and Sister Jean Adam, RSM, who taught religion and French. When Law came to visit the school and dedicate an altar and ambo I had had made for the school Masses, they told him that I should be permitted to go into teaching full time. When he asked me about it, I told him that I wanted to go into teaching full time.

In June 1979, my frustration level and unhappiness level had reached an all-time high. I wrote in my journal that I needed to do something for me before I could minister to anyone. I wanted to be happy, but I was not happy in parish work. I knew there was a place for me in the world, and I hoped there was one for me in the Diocese of Springfield-Cape Girardeau. I admitted to myself that I was a teacher, a scholar, and a liturgist. I also admitted to myself that I had needs to be met. I had experienced some depression. I created a chart of the differences in views of ministry between me and the bishop. I listed my personal needs, parish needs, and how my ministry at St. Mary Parish did not fulfill me, but my work in school did. I realized that I could no longer say yes to parish work; I had been an educator since I was in high school, and I found joy and fulfillment in that. So, in August 1979, I left St. Mary Parish and moved to St. Peter Parish, where I was to be in residence, and became a full-time faculty member of McAuley High School, where I would teach for the next six years.

Assignments in the Diocese of Springfield-Cape Girardeau

Fulltime Faculty Member of McAuley High School

My place of residence, St. Peter the Apostle Parish Rectory, was pastored by Rev. William Rochford, a priest no one could live with! I moved in there in August 1979, and I was scared to death. I had meant him earlier when Westhues and I had joined him for lunch. As he was walking out of the house to our car, his secretary, Eleanor Goodson, came to the door and screamed, "When does the slave get to eat lunch?" He never answered her, but just kept walking toward our car.

He didn't want me living in the house with him, a fact he made clear the day I was moving in. I explained that I had been assigned by the bishop to live there and help him. He showed me where my two rooms were upstairs and where the kitchen and dining room were downstairs. Basically, the rest of the house was his. Of course, the first thing I needed to do was to clean the two rooms I was going to live in. Rochford, a rather large man, had boxes of stuff piled in every room and in the hall. I moved the boxes stored in my rooms to the sun porch, which served as a storage room. I moved my furniture in, but left most of my books in the boxes in which I had packed them and stored them in the basement. I didn't think I would be living there for long.

However, he gradually began to warm up to me. He always had the coffee on when I got up, so I began to bring a cup full to him. After a while, he began to offer me the Christmas Midnight Mass, the Palm Sunday Mass, or one of the Paschal Triduum Services.

We had only one major disagreement during the four years that I lived there. Because I taught and got to know high school students, they often came to the rectory to see me. I lived on the second floor, and Rochford spent most of his time on the first floor, which meant that he usually answered the door bell. Furthermore, while he loved small children, he was terrified of high school students. One evening a couple of my high school students/friends rang the doorbell, which Rochford answered. He opened the door, saw who it was, yelled at them, closed the door—leaving them outside—and yelled at me upstairs. I came down, opened the door, and invited them in. After they left, I went to where he was watching TV, and I told him that he would never speak to my friends like that again. And he never did.

I was only a block away from McAuley, so I walked to school every day. My classroom was located in what was called the old convent building, which was torn down years ago. I also had an office in that building where the liturgical furniture for Mass was stored. For the next six years I would teach in one of the classrooms in that building. When my classes got too large to fit in one room, I moved across the hall to a larger room. I taught required religion classes to sophomores and juniors, and I taught a Latin elective. I had lunch duty, like any other faculty member, along with playground duty. Adam and I planned and executed Masses and other liturgical services throughout the school year.

My Life of Ministry, Writing, Teaching, and Traveling

While I was teaching at McAuley, I spent some time one year attending Missouri Southern College (later University) to earn a lifetime Missouri Teaching Certificate for Junior High and High School English. I needed only a couple psychology courses, a few education courses, and a couple English classes to earn the certificate. The English classes were independent study on poetry. I earned the certificate on July 28, 1983, after doing my student teaching in the Joplin High School summer program. My master teacher knew that I had been teaching at McAuley since 1978, so she set up the summer English class to be co-taught.

After that was accomplished, I was notified by the registrar of Missouri Southern that I had earned a Bachelor of Science Degree in Education while taking the courses I needed for my lifetime Missouri Teaching Certificate. All I needed to do to get my diploma was to pass the Missouri Constitution Test, which I did. So, in May 1984 I was awarded that diploma.

The first thing I had done the first summer I had free—1980—was get back to working on my MA thesis for my Master's Degree in Religious Studies from IU, Bloomington. I spent the summer correcting and retyping the thesis. I had to get an extension from IU to finish it, but that was not difficult to do. Before this I had submitted the draft that Vydra had typed when I was associate pastor at St. Agnes Cathedral. It had been returned with some corrections and other things that my director thought needed to be done. I had not had the time to work on it with all the moving I had been doing.

So, after correcting the thesis, I submitted it to my director at IU, and it was accepted. It was returned to me with the acceptance page to be copied and bound. I think IU needed two copies; I wanted a copy; and a copy was to be placed in the Old Mines Area Historical Society Library; the society had been founded after the celebration in 1973. With the thesis finished and bound and sent to IU, I was awarded my Master's Degree in Religious Studies on August 31, 1981.

Law was transferred to Boston early in January 1984, and Msgr. John J. Leibrecht from St. Louis was appointed bishop of Springfield-Cape Girardeau in December 1984. Having served the Archdiocese of St. Louis as superintendent of Catholic schools, I expected to have an educator as a bishop. However, Leibrecht was merely an administrator, who, while having a PhD in education, had never been a classroom teacher of any kind.

In the spring of 1985, at a faculty meeting, I had requested that a creative writing course be added to the McAuley High School curriculum. Since I had a teaching certificate in English, I wanted to teach at least one class in English in addition to the religion classes—I had inherited the freshmen class when Adam left—and the Latin classes I taught. The principal, Sister Constance Fifelski, a Dominican nun, who had replaced Flesch a few years before this, thought it was a good idea, too. However, shortly after this decision had been made, I got a telephone call from Leibrecht, asking me to come back to Springfield and run an adult religious education program. I was given some time to think about it.

Assignments in the Diocese of Springfield-Cape Girardeau

I talked to several people about this opportunity, and all agreed that I should accept it. So, I returned Leibrecht's call and told him I would be willing to develop the program. When I asked him where I would live, he told me that I would be in residence at St. Elizabeth Ann Seton Parish. I told him that I preferred to live alone. He told me that was not possible. I told him that I preferred to live alone. He got very angry with me on the telephone, and I gave in.

I had been living alone for almost two years. After living for a year at St. Mary Rectory and for four years in St. Peter Rectory, I had moved to Sacred Heart Rectory in Webb City in August 1983, about ten miles north of Joplin. Rochford had left St. Peter Parish that year and moved to Springfield, and the new pastor did not want me in the house. What I didn't know is that Sacred Heart Parish's pastor's brother was coming back from a leave of absence and was going to be living in Sacred Heart Rectory, too. The pastor was Monaghan, the man I had replaced as associate pastor at St. Agnes. His brother, Justin Monaghan, had left the priesthood and gotten married. Now, he had decided that those decisions were wrong and, after having spent some time praying in a monastery and getting updated theologically, he was getting ready to go back into active pastoral ministry.

Granted, they were brothers, and they were often out late at night. My room was right off of the kitchen. So, when they came in to get a snack, they made a lot of noise and awakened me. Furthermore, I think one of them had been messing with my new word processor in my office/library there, because I found it on one afternoon after arriving home from school.

I had worked in the St. Meinrad Development Office while in the School of Theology in southern Indiana. One new piece of equipment I had used was a pre-computer typewriter that merged addresses to print personalized letters and envelopes. So, some years later, I investigated other pre-computer developments in terms of office equipment. I found a system consisting of an interfaced typewriter and a pre-computer that used large floppy disks upon which information could be stored. The system I bought had one slot for a disk, but the typewriter could be used with or without it. It was perfect for preparing tests and other materials for high school.

I did not like the living arrangements in Webb City; I was living in someone's home. It was like I was non-existent. So, after having moved there in August, erected bookshelves for my library and unpacked all my books, I began to look for another place to live in early November. I found a little white house on Indiana Street in Joplin; the old part of the house was built out of concrete blocks! That part consisted of a small kitchen, a living room, and a bathroom. The additional room, constructed from wood and sheetrock, served as a bedroom and office. I contacted the owner, looked it over, and agreed to rent it.

Of course, it needed to be thoroughly cleaned before I could move in. I spent days with buckets of water and soap scrubbing everything. On Thanksgiving Day 1983 with the help of a few friends, we loaded my packed boxes in a truck and brought them to the white house on Indiana Street, where we unloaded them. Afterward, everyone, including me, scattered to wherever we were having Thanksgiving Dinner. After I returned home that day, I began to erect bookshelves in one part of the living room and put my books on them. I made my bed, and crawled into it for a good night's sleep. While the day had been stressful, I was not stressed. I had a home, and no one else lived in it. The rest of that weekend was spent unpacking and putting things away.

One part of the living room was used as a library. The other part had my few pieces of furniture: a rocking chair, a table, a lamp, and a china closet; later, I bought a TV, which was also placed in the living room. The large bedroom was divided between a sleeping area and an office area, in which I placed a metal desk I had found at an office supply store, an office chair, and my word processing equipment. A good friend, Arthur Hobbs, lent me his old dining room table, which I put in the kitchen. Other friends had cleaned out their kitchen cabinets and given me pots and pans, dishes and silverware, and other things necessary for keeping house.

The only problem was the bathroom shower. It was an old metal shower that was rusted at the bottom and leaked water all over the bathroom floor when it was used. The first time I showered in it, I had a flood. I called the owner, and he promised me he would fix it immediately. He was a very difficult man to get going on anything. I called him repeatedly, asking him when he was going to fix it. He kept promising me that he would get to it, but he never did. His last promise was to fix it between Christmas 1983 and New Year's Day 1984. I returned from a trip a few days after New Year's Day with the expectation that I would have a new shower, but the shower was not done. I was furious, called him, and told him that he had promised me he would have it done. I was ready to move out; that motivated him, but the shower wasn't fixed until mid-January 1984. In the meantime, I went to the local YMCA, which I had joined while living at St. Peter Rectory, and showered there every day. I still stand in amazement at how much I was able to bear when I had the solitude and living conditions I craved.

I had gotten into the attic of the white house in order to store some things there. I noticed that the hot water heater exhaust pipe did not connect to the outside, but vented into the attic. I called the owner and told him that had to be fixed; all it needed was a piece of pipe that connected the hot water heater exhaust to the vent in the roof. Within a few days he was there to fix it.

Only one other issue had to be addressed, and that was the gas stove in the bedroom/office. I tried turning on the stove, but it would not work. So, I summoned the owner, who came in a few days and fixed it. After that I was able to turn down the wall heater in the living room and use only the stove in the bedroom at night in order to save money on utility bills.

After I was all moved in and settled, I wrote Law a letter explaining what I had done and why I had done it! I never received an answer to that letter. All I ever got was a short note from the chancellor, Reidy, asking me if I needed anything. I told him that a little help with finances would we welcome, and he saw to it that a check arrived every month to help me with my rent.

When I left my home in the morning, I would turn down the wall heater to low; likewise, the bedroom heater would be turned to low. In the wintertime when I got home, the house was cold and took a while to warm up. In the summertime, it was very hot. I bought a small window air conditioner and had it installed in my bedroom/office, but I only turned it on for sleep during the night because I couldn't afford the electricity to run it during the day. The rest of the day I had the windows open. I lived in the white house until the summer of 1985, when I left Joplin and McAuley Regional High School and returned to Springfield to run the diocesan adult education program and live in St. Elizabeth Ann Seton Rectory.

Resource Person for Adult Religious Education Programs

I had met with the pastor of St. Elizabeth Ann Seton Parish, Father Michael McDevitt, before I moved into the rectory. He showed me an upstairs room that would be my bedroom, and the large basement, where I could put my library and some of my furniture. Before leaving Joplin, I had boxed my household items for storage, since the rectory was a fully functioning house. Those boxes were put in the attic of the SEAS Rectory.

Again, I organized a space into an office area, a library area, and a TV watching area. A small unused room upstairs with a window was arranged for my house plants. Once I got settled, I met with Leibrecht, who did not have a clue as to what he wanted me to do in terms of adult education. I began by offering mini-courses, which were advertised in the diocesan newsletter; these led to talks and retreats. I also worked with two Daughters of Charity, who ran the diocesan religious education office, writing articles for their monthly newsletter. Until I showed up, they had no idea that I would be working in adult education; Leibrecht had never explained to them what he wanted me to do, because he did not know.

I gave presentations on adult approaches to faith, the Bible, and spirituality; the book of Revelation; Christology; death; eucharist; Holy Week; images; gospel Infancy Narratives; John's Gospel; liturgical spirituality; Luke-Acts; Mariology; Matthew's Gospel; morality; Paul; the Profession of Faith; Reformation church history; resurrection; sacraments; values; world religions; synoptic gospels; mission; and more. I also gave retreats on Advent, confirmation, covenant, discipleship, dry bones, eucharist, evangelization, exodus, feet, gifts, Holy Spirit, journey of faith, liturgical spirituality, parables, peace, salt, and more.

Besides providing various educational programs for adults and youth in the parishes, I was also assigned to help at the Ecumenical Center at Southwest Missouri State University (now Missouri State University). I did very little there except teach a mini-course or two because I did not have time. I was busy in St. Elizabeth Ann Seton Parish, with adult education offerings, and with retreats. I was quickly learning that the bishop had no idea how much time it took to prepare materials for courses and retreats, serve in Seton Parish, and have any time leftover for other things.

For all that work I was using my own equipment. I had purchased a Systel System, what today would be known as a primitive word processor. I could store my work on very large floppy disks and print it on the typewriter whose keyboard enabled me to enter it on the screen. After getting started I asked Reidy if there were funds available to support my equipment needs, and he told me no. Thus, I used my own personal equipment for diocesan work. I asked for help to offset the cost of pre-computer equipment, and the diocese refused me!

After the first year of talks and retreats all across southern Missouri, Leibrecht asked me to assist Robert Lee, the editor of *The Mirror*, the diocesan newspaper. After speaking to both of us, I was asked to begin in September 1986. One day a week I would go to *The Mirror* office and read through news copy that had come over the Catholic News Service wire. I would pull articles that had some type of educational bent to them for publication by Lee, whom I disliked because of his arrogance and his inability to refrain from hugging and kissing me!

I didn't realize it at the time, but Leibrecht was trying to find a way to get Lee out of the newspaper office. Lee's last issue of *The Mirror* looked just like his first, and he was editor for about 30 years. There had been no changes, no redesign, no growth in the paper. The pastors were up in arms because there was nothing worth reading in the paper that they had to provide to every parishioner in the parish. Leibrecht wanted me to enhance the appearance of the paper, which I was not able to do as long as Lee was editor.

I hated living in St. Elizabeth Ann Seton Rectory with McDevitt. He would not put dirty dishes in the dishwasher; he set them in the sink, where they often remained for days until the housekeeper showed up and put them in the dishwasher. I was often sick the year I lived in Seton Rectory because of the germs multiplying in the kitchen sink. I once asked him if he could put the dirty dishes in the dish washer, and he told me that he would not do it.

He believed in an open-door policy. I do not know how many people had keys to the rectory, but I never knew who might be roaming through the residence. One evening I came home, parked my car in the garage, and entered the living room to find a small group of people sitting around the coffee table having a meeting. This was not the type of home I wanted; it did not nourish my solitude. In fact, it stressed me.

At one point, the rectory was broken into. Little was taken except my typewriter and word processing equipment, even though every room had been searched. Insurance covered the replacement cost of new equipment. Whoever the thief was, he had failed to take the operating disk with him, so what he stole would do him no good. The replacement equipment was improved; the new system could operate on two, huge floppy disks and switch back and forth between the two drives.

McDevitt was often gone from the parish, and I was responsible for filling in for him for Masses. He was not present for Palm Sunday; I had all the Masses. He was often gone for several weekdays in a row, and I was responsible for the weekday Masses. I didn't think that I was in parish ministry, but every time I turned around, I was working in Seton Parish.

One day McDevitt, who was Diocesan Vocation Director, asked me if I would mind if a seminarian came to live with us for the summer. I told him that I did not want anyone else in the house; it was too small and too crowded already. What I didn't know at the time was that he had already made arrangements for the seminarian to move into the guest room. This meant that the seminarian would have to share my bathroom. I was very upset when I came home one day to discover a seminarian in the house. I was furious with McDevitt.

The housekeeper also drove me crazy. She was always attempting to take care of me. While I appreciated her generosity, I was a very self-sufficient man. When I was working in my space in the basement, she would often come down—even if I had the door closed—to talk or investigate what I was doing. She insisted on fixing lunch for me on days when I was in the house working.

Every time I met with Leibrecht to report what I had been doing, I told him that I wanted to live alone. He didn't like hearing it, and put me off by telling me that he would consider it at priestly assignment time (July). Several more times I talked to him about it. He never got back to me about the issue; after a year, the chancellor, Reidy, called me and told me that I was free to find a house or apartment to rent. I found a house, and couldn't wait to move in.

Near the end of my second year serving as Resource Person for Adult Education Programs and assisting Lee in *The Mirror* office, Leibrecht announced to the chancery staff that Lee was retiring as of July 1, 1987, and that a search was going to take place for a new editor. This is exactly for what Leibrecht had hoped; he had put enough pressure on Lee to improve *The Mirror*—something Lee could not do—that he decided to retire. Several staff members told me that I should apply for the job, but I told them that I knew nothing about running a newspaper. One person in particular, Vydra, Director of Diocesan Communications and former thesis typist for me at St. Agnes Cathedral eight years before, urged me over and over again to apply for the job. So, I did, and I was named editor of *The Mirror* on July 6, 1987.

Editor of *The Mirror*

The first thing I did was hire Lee for the month of July as editor, because I had made a promise to a then-priest-friend to substitute in his parish in Colorado for the month of July. Lee gladly accepted; in fact, he was supposed to work for me part-time; however, he did little work. Once I got home in late July and took over as editor, I remember asking myself, "What have I gotten myself into?"

The appointment letter I got from Leibrecht stated, "I want to work with you and improve the paper in whatever ways we can see together." Over the next fourteen and a half years, I learned that that sentence meant that Leibrecht wanted to improve the paper as long as he could take credit for it. He wanted to be the editor, yet he knew nothing about it. I got to work to get my first issue ready to be printed. I had learned the basics from Lee, and I set out to use those skills.

I learned quickly that the equipment that came with *The Mirror* was outdated to say the least. It was old typesetting equipment that left impressions on photographic paper that had to be developed. Once the typesetting was done, printed, developed, and dried, it was cut into strips, waxed, and pasted on layout boards. Catholic News Service sent eight to twelve articles every day over a wire feed, and they were automatically printed by a dot matrix printer. Like any other copy, the typesetter had to (re)type everything into typesetting equipment. It took hours to have enough set copy to put together a weekly newspaper.

Mike Banasik

Besides outdated equipment, I inherited a typesetter and a secretary. The typesetter resigned her position after I had given her specific instructions about required attendance at an event which she failed to attend. I advertised the opening of the position and conducted interviews of potential employees. One in particular caught my attention: Mike Banasik. He was a young man who was recuperating from an almost-fatal car accident. Because I was new at the position in which I found myself, I failed to ask enough questions and to ask about typing proficiency. The typesetter's job was to enter copy into the Compugraphic equipment according to margins established by me. Once the copy was entered, it had to be printed on rolled photo paper and then fed into another piece of equipment with several chemicals in which it was developed. Then it was allowed to dry before I cut and pasted it on layout boards. Accurate typing was essential in preparing copy for layout. Quickly, I learned that Banasik was a very slow and inaccurate typist. It took him a long time to enter an article. Furthermore, his entry work was not accurate; there were lots of misspellings of words. So, after noticing those things, I instructed him to work on accuracy by proofreading the copy before he developed it. I thought that the speed would come as he remained at the job. With his proofreading accuracy improved, and with his daily work entry speed also improved. In order to eliminate almost all typographic errors, we began having my secretary proofread the entire paper and give it to Banasik to issue corrections.

He made up for his lack of skill by becoming a friend and then using me through the friendship. He took advantage of breaks—extending them much longer than they were to be; asking me to take him home when he did not have a ride because he could not drive; and giving me gifts. Because he was impotent as a result of the accident and unable to father a child with his wife, he used me and other chancery staff to write letters of recommendation for him and his wife to adopt a baby.

In the beginning, Banasik came to work with a cane. The automobile accident broke a number of his bones and left him in the hospital for a long time. I don't remember what job he had before the accident, but he saw the typesetting job as a way to enter the work force again. Gradually, his navigational ability improved, even though he walked with a limp.

Because we worked together closely, I got to know Banasik very well. We began to discuss a variety of things, and what began to surface was his anger with God for the accident he was in and the suffering he had endured as a result of it. He had been affected physically, sexually, and spiritually by the accident; the result was anger with which he failed to deal. On March 11, 1988, I had come to recognize that his anger resulted in drunkenness. Before that, I discovered, it had been drugs. He lived with the illusion that he had power over his anger, but he didn't. When he purchased a six pack of beer, he couldn't stop until he had consumed all the cans of beer. If he purchased a bottle of bourbon, he couldn't stop until the bottle was empty. The alcohol freed him to release his anger under the guise that he would be forgiven by me for not coming to work or being late or by his wife by saying, "I'm sorry."

I agreed to help him process his anger by staying after work and discussing various aspects of it. While I thought he was improving, Banasik was just telling me what he thought I wanted to hear. I figured that out quickly, also realizing that I was being used. Because he could not drive, I would have to take him home after our sessions together. I have notes dated November 13, 1988, about four days when he never showed up for work or came in late. One time he called me from a bar to pick him up and take him home; he was drunk. Taking him home after work became commonplace; I thought I was helping him. I forgave him for being late because he always seemed to have a good excuse.

Finally, on November 13, 1988, I explained that he needed to be at work at 8 a.m., that he needed to observe break times without ten- or fifteen-minute extensions, that he needed to stop wondering around and spending long conversations on the telephone, and that he needed to take his lunch break during the usual time. Because he had missed work, I explained that he needed to put in two hours of overtime for the next two weeks until he was caught up on typesetting. I had a weekly newspaper to produce, and I needed typeset copy to do so.

On April 18, 1989, I realized that being Banasik's boss, counselor, and friend had gotten all mixed together. So, I sat down with him and explained that I, his boss, had hired him to do work, which was not getting done. I told him that I had hired him to make my work easier. I explained that if there were more tardiness, leaving early, not getting projects accomplished, I was going to fire him. I explained that the friendship was over and that it was going to be an employer-employee relationship from then forward. I kept records of his tardiness returning from break, and deducted the extra time from his time sheet before I signed it. I threatened to have the telephone removed from his office because he spent a lot of time talking to people instead of working. I also set daily goals as to what had to be accomplished.

As his counselor, I told him that he needed help that I was not able to give. He played games with me by only telling me what he thought I wanted to hear. Mutual truthfulness had not been forthcoming. So, I was not serving as his counselor any longer. I made it clear that as his friend, he would not be using me anymore. He had disrupted my whole life, causing me worry about getting the newspaper done on time because he missed work. That disruption affected my personal writing, my peace of mind, my sleep, and drained me of psychic energy. He had been to my home for dinner a time or two and seen the pottery I had. For the previous Christmas he had given me a pottery pitcher and drinking cups. At that session I returned the pottery to him, explaining that I could not keep it because it represented the mixing of roles that I was now straightening out.

It wasn't long after that Banasik left employment by *The Mirror*. A secretarial position opened in the Marriage Tribunal in the same office complex, and he applied for and got that job. I would still see him around the office, but that was the end of my involvement with him. I hired his replacement, and the daily tasks of getting a weekly newspaper into print continued with much less drama and much more creativity.

Communications Advisory Board

In the meantime, I had been hiring a young woman, Leslie Mayes, to do some copy entry for the paper. She applied for his job, and I hired her. She set to work to exploit the old equipment we had to its limits. In the meantime, Vydra, who ran the Diocesan Communication Department, and I formed the Communications Advisory Board (CAB), and this group of professional communications specialists gave us the clout we needed to propose desktop publishing. With their guidance I began to renovate the way we produced the newspaper, sell all the old equipment, and buy computers.

One of the first things I had done after being named editor was to find a printer in the Springfield area. Lee's method was to put the waxed layout boards in a box with the sized photos and put the box on a bus across southern Missouri to Cape Girardeau, where the paper was printed and mailed. Once the paper left Springfield, I had no way to control whatever happened to it. The printer in Cape Girardeau was not interested in producing quality copy; what often resulted was a mess. So, the CAB suggested that I let out a bid to several printers in the Springfield area and interview them. After doing so, I chose a printer in Bolivar, who had a representative who not only personally picked up the copy every week, but helped *The Mirror* staff to adapt to the growing technological advances occurring in newspaper work.

It wasn't long before Catholic News Service copy was able to be captured on a computer, downloaded, and transferred on a floppy disk to the Macintosh computer where it was edited and stored for future use. Ultimately, all copy was required to be submitted on disk. This was followed by digital photography. *The Mirror* staff had been responsible for running a dark room, in which we developed film and printed pictures. With digital cameras and the ability to download photos directly onto the Macintosh, the dark room became a dinosaur. I remember closing it and selling the equipment.

I began to attend Catholic Press Association meetings, where I learned what other Catholic editors were doing. I also started attending the Associated Church Press, where I learned what other Christian editors were doing. The Society for Newspaper Design convention is where I learned what the general newspaper world was doing. *The Mirror* began to enter newspaper competitions; we didn't win anything at first. But as I got to see what others were doing and implement it in *The Mirror*, we began to win journalism awards in a variety of categories. By the time I left as editor, *The Mirror* had won twenty-seven journalism awards.

Of course, with winning awards came more stress from Leibrecht, who was jealous of my success. After all, I did not have a degree in journalism; I had learned from others and then tweaked what I learned to fit my own needs. The first time the paper won a couple of awards I wrote a short story about it for the paper. Leibrecht called me to his office and told me that some priests did not think I should be publicizing the awards. When asked, he couldn't tell me why. It didn't take me long to figure out it was because of his jealously.

Among the clergy, no one is supposed to be more successful than anyone else, especially if it is a priest who is more successful than his bishop! All are supposed to remain at some common denominator level. I, of course, didn't agree with that. I had already been a very successful student—I held two undergraduate degrees and two graduate degrees; I was also a very successful high school teacher. Now, I had become a very successful newspaper editor, and this latter success brought with it clerical jealously.

The "From the bishop's desk" positive notes on the newspaper's improvements quickly turned negative. No changes were to be made without first getting the bishop's permission. Getting Leibrecht to change was very difficult in anything. Another note told me that I was to change nothing in the bishop's column; I had been fixing the grammar and editing it to fit the space on the page that was allotted for it. One time he didn't like a headline, another time it was a misspelled word that escaped the proofreaders. Any little thing was an opportunity for him to write a note to criticize me.

What Leibrecht couldn't tolerate was someone who was better at something than he was. I was making him look good with an award-winning newspaper, but almost everyone knew that I was behind the changes. And that irritated Leibrecht, and it manifested itself as jealously.

I remember attending an afternoon of reflection before the celebration of the annual Chrism Mass, which I was covering for *The Mirror*. On the way out of the cathedral to a happy hour, Leibrecht approached me among a group of priests to remind me of something I have now long forgotten. One of the priests turned to me and asked, "Why would he think you would forget about that?" I remember thinking to myself because that was his way of reminding me that he was in charge. That was a way to embarrass me in front of other clergy in order to curb my success.

DDF Campaign 1988

After being named editor of *The Mirror*, I discovered that I was responsible for some things that had absolutely no connection whatsoever to editing a newspaper. The first was the annual Diocesan Development Fund campaign. I was responsible for developing the campaign: choosing a theme, creating a poster, publicizing information. On August 20, 1987, just after being appointed as editor on July 6, I attended a DDF meeting to plan for the campaign in May of 1988. In those days, Father Ralph J. (Jake) Duffner led the campaign for the diocese. With Duffner; Vydra; Jan Smith, Diocesan Finance Director; and me, Leibrecht asked us to stay behind after the laity responsible for DDF left and reamed us out because we proposed a stewardship approach to DDF. He wanted a fund-raiser. We sat around a table and listened to his tirade for about fifteen minutes.

On February 19, 1988, in preparation for DDF Sunday—the first Sunday of May—during a DDF meeting I presented the materials I had and explained that it took four days, two weekends, to develop fund-raising posters and brochures—because I was not a trained fund-raiser. Duffner made fun of it. At the same meeting Leibrecht began to circulate the sample of the materials I brought and toss them at me even before he read them. He didn't like them. No one at that meeting voiced, "Thank You," for the work I had done. A year or two after this and after lots of urging, a professional fund-raiser was hired to take over the DDF campaign.

I had made it a point to prepare a staff photo every year, similar to a class photo, so it was easy to see who was working in The Catholic Center on any given year. On August 12, 1988, as I was preparing the first, he made it clear that he didn't like the arrangement before I even had a chance to say that there were other possibilities. And on August 18, 1988, I heard what I would discover was a usual process of saying before a gathered group of people—staff, DDF, etc.—"I want to see you." The put-downs continued after that at a Liturgy Workshop in which I worked with Extraordinary Ministers of the Eucharist in Cape Girardeau on November 6, 1994. He attended my presentation, which began with the theology of the assembly as church and its role to participate. After getting the participants to reflect on how architecture affects participation, I pointed out how everything we participate in is a stadium, round- or oval-shaped. The best arrangement for a church to foster participation, I concluded, was circular. He butted in while I was speaking and made it clear that no circular churches would be built in the diocese as long as he was bishop! Even at a staff day—a day devoted to the continuing education of The Catholic Center staff members—he took fifteen minutes to put down a method of theological reflection that I presented. In all of the fourteen and a half years that I served as editor, never once at a staff meeting did he ever refer to or address me as Father Boyer; I was always Mark. Other priests on staff—and there were three or four others—were always referred to or addressed as Father. After one particular staff meeting, the Director of Family Life, Troy Casteel, followed me into my office and asked me, "Why does he never refer to you as Father Mark?" And I told him, "He does not respect me."

Editor Leibrecht 1988

On February 11, 1988, I received a memorandum from Leibrecht stating that he would like to meet with me "monthly to discuss briefly what is happening with *The Mirror*." He wrote: "You could go over future plans with me, keep me informed about projects and topics you will be covering, etc. At the same time, I will have an on-going opportunity of sharing some of my own ideas with you." So, I began to present my ideas on February 17 about finding a printer in the Springfield area, going to the Catholic Press Association meeting in May, finding a part-time person to help with photography, dark room, advertising, and reporting. I, with Vydra's help, was forming the Communications Advisory Board (CAB) and developing a parish reporter's workshop to be held in various places in the diocese. I explained that I was not running a creative resources department, and that the next DDF campaign needed to be led by a professional fund-raiser. He wanted sixteen pages for an issue, an increase from twelve. I was interested in more advertising to cover the costs, but he insisted that there be no more than one full page of advertising. Over the years, he raised this issue over and over again when he noticed that a few ads may be on a page other than that devoted to advertising. While advertising brought in only a few dollars in terms of offsetting costs, I could never understand why he didn't want more of it since the DDF was supporting the cost of producing *The Mirror*.

On May 19, 1988, I got a hand written letter about changing the practice of continuing stories from later—meaning the back page—to previous pages. "I want this to take place, and yet have you take advantage of color to make an attractive page." At the subsequent meeting I explained that I had learned that the last page is like the front page; it ought to have something that leads the reader back into the paper. In a similar vein he wanted "the paper to have less 'continued'" articles. His suggestion was to remove the photo on the page. I explained that "jumping" the article was to get the reader to see another part of the paper. If a photo was removed, then page-appeal would be lost. The reader's eyes are drawn to the picture first. "What are the guidelines for twelve, sixteen, or twenty pages in the paper?" was the third point of the letter. He also wanted to know printing cost differentials and postal differentials. I explained there were no guidelines yet, as I was still operating with the budget left by the former editor. I was working on my first budget, and a lot depended on what was going on news wise. He stated that he wanted to have all that information before the June 4 CAB meeting. See, the CAB, composed of media professionals, was giving me direction that he didn't like! It was at his insistence that Vydra and I form the CAB, but he didn't like the direction it was steering me.

The CAB directed that I find a printer in Springfield—not in Cape Girardeau—that I go to desk-top publishing, and that I do some re-arranging of some of the sections of the paper. The members suggested that all the columns be grouped together and put at the back of the paper. Leibrecht refused to have his column moved from page three because Lee, the former editor, had told him that was the first thing readers would see when they opened the paper! Over the years, as I attended Catholic Press, Associated Church Press, and Society for Newspaper Design meetings—at the suggestion of CAB members—I made more changes to improve the quality of the paper. I was called to meetings with Leibrecht repeatedly because someone didn't like something in the paper. On January 27, 1998, I received a hand-written note: "I'd like to suggest that no additional changes be made in *The Mirror* until we have had a chance to talk. I'd like to know what the master plan is and the philosophy guiding it."

Earlier in March of 1994, I got a hand-written note expressing dislike for the headline I had prepared for his column, which was about the Blessed Sacrament and Blessed Sacrament Chapels. In his words, "The headline engenders feelings, in my opinion, which keeps the reader from entering into the real topic which is the Blessed Sacrament." I replied with my own hand-written letter on March 23, 1994, explained that one of the points he was making was about the place for eucharistic reservation. "So that is how I wrote the headline." I continued: "I didn't write the headline to 'engender feelings' but to do what headlines are supposed to do: get the reader to read. I didn't see the headline as a problem, since it states what the liturgical norm of the Church is concerning Blessed Sacrament chapels." I continued: "I try to do the best job I can, especially in light of the fact that for the past eight weeks your column was two to three hours late. Also, my staff and I would like a note now and then about something that you liked about an issue. It would help bolster morale." At the subsequent meeting about this, I told him that he was free to write his own headline for his column, but that would set me free from his criticism, and he declined to do so.

Over the years I threw away a lot of what I began calling "nasty notes." Those I kept had no dates written on them. "The logo for the Stand Firm in Faith column, I prefer, have only the symbol of the flame and ewer." He didn't like the boot in it! "I'd like to offer *The Mirror* an award for 'Most Insensitive Headline' for its lead story in the January 30 issue. Not good!" I do not remember what that story was. "I hope we don't have any more 'you can have it all' in 'the holy will prosper' article in *The Mirror*. Mary Kay Cosmetics philosophy, it seems to me, we do not need." I have no idea to what that once referred. On October 18, 2000, Leibrecht's secretary brought a letter addressed to a person living in Ozark, Missouri, with her note, stating: "The bishop wants this in this week's *The Mirror* in a prominent place. He knows you'll need to re-do some things but wants it in this week." This was one of only many last-minute decisions that caused me and my staff stress, once we had the paper laid out and proofread before the printer came to get it!

Clerical Dress Issue 1989

After being asked to supply a rationale for why I did not wear clerical attire in the Chancery Office, on January 20, 1989, I submitted an essay to Leibrecht explaining that when covering stories, taking pictures, or functioning as a supply priest, I always wore a Roman collar. But my work in *The Mirror* offices involved corrosive chemicals in the dark room, stain-causing fluids in the old Compugraphic equipment, and wax in the lay-out room. Those substances ruined clothes and could not be removed. The former editor wore jeans, I reminded him, for the same reason. The memorandum I received on January 30, 1989, stated that I "wear clerical attire at the Chancery as much as possible." Leibrecht continued, "There can be some practical steps you can take: for instance, it certainly is not necessary that you wear expensive clerical attire. I hope you understand my expressed wish that you wear clerical attire at the Chancery as much as possible." So, for staff meetings I wore clerical attire; the rest of the time I went to my offices and worked there so as not to be seen!

Carmel Issue 1991

One thing I learned quickly after being ordained is that if I ever said Yes to something one time, I would end up with it for a very long time. Such was the issue of ministry to the eight nuns at the Carmel of St. Anne. I was no more than named editor, and I was asked to volunteer to help with Mass at the Carmel. I did. However, I was never officially appointed to serve the Carmelites. In a February of 1991 meeting, I explained to Leibrecht that the stress of producing a weekly newspaper, which he had told me was a full-time job when he appointed me, along with all my other responsibilities, dictated that I remove Carmel from my list. Furthermore, I did not agree with what the Carmelites fostered: people attending Mass there with no parish contact and little participation. Having daily Mass for eight cloistered sisters was a luxury we could not afford as far as I was concerned.

On February 26, 1991, Leibrecht sent me a memorandum. It stated, "I would like to postpone a decision regarding Carmel and deal with it when I am going over all new assignments for August 1991." He explained that his rationale was to have a better grasp of the whole picture—whatever that was—at that time. I was told to wait to discuss the issue until the larger picture was clearer. He did not listen to me about Carmel. So, On February 27, 1991, I wrote to him:

> I cannot wait until August concerning Carmel. I am frustrated and I hate going out there. By the very fact that no priest likes going out there, that should tell you something. I volunteered to help out with Carmel five years ago, after I was told that *The Mirror* was a full-time ministry. I volunteered to function as chaplain after the previous chaplain was moved. I have been chaplain for two years, but for the past few months I have not been able to manage it, and I need to be released from this responsibility for personal reasons. I will finish out the month of March as the schedule is done. This is one thing that I cannot put off anymore. I have thought this through carefully many times and the answer keeps coming back the same. I regret having to do this, but I have to do this for myself. I hope you understand.

I also gave him a copy of a letter that the Carmelite sisters had sent to a number of people who came there on a regular basis for Mass, when they should have been going to their parishes. They were trying to keep them coming, whereas I was trying to send them to the parishes to which they belonged. I was given a copy of the letter by one of the people who was concerned about what was going on at Carmel. "I think the letter reflects the severity of the situation at Carmel." I had presented to him a list of ten options for ministering to the eight sisters at Carmel; among them were getting area priests to sign up for a Mass, to get all the parishes in Springfield to take a day at Carmel, to let the sisters invite area clergy, and to run an ad for a chaplain in Catholic papers. I never heard another word about Carmel after that. He had no concern for me and my needs; all he saw was a warm body that knew how to say Mass, and he had a place to send it!

Subscription Issue 1988 and 1994

On February 27, 1988, the CAB adopted a proposal that changed the diocesan policy of updating all parish lists of subscribers in February to staggering them throughout the year. I presented the proposal to Leibrecht on March 9, 1988, and he advised that it be taken to the Presbyteral Council for consideration. It was approved by the council on April 11, 1988, with two amendments: no parish would be scheduled to update lists during June, July, and August and each parish would be given two months to make changes. A memorandum arrived from Leibrecht on April 13, 1988, with the amendments suggested by the members of the council. There was also the following: "Is there some way to making sure that billings for *The Mirror* do not arrive at the same time as billings for insurance, for instance, from the diocese?" How could I control that? And, "Is it possible to remember that some parishes have secretaries who do the work while many of our parishes must have the work done by the pastor himself?" So noted! The new policy about staggering the updating of parish lists throughout the year went into effect July 1, 1988.

A very disturbing paragraph also appeared in that April 13, 1988, memorandum from Leibrecht. He noted that there was some negative feeling about the diocesan policy that every household should receive a copy of *The Mirror* among the members of the Presbyteral Council. "I told the Presbyteral Council that I remain committed to the policy but that if, even in the light of the commitment I have, they want to discuss it, I would be open to listening. The policy will probably be on some future agenda, and I would want you with me at that particular meeting." That discussion never came up, and I was more than happy that I didn't have to engage in this laborious policy-changing process again.

Thus, the diocesan policy concerning *The Mirror* remained: Every household in every parish was to receive a copy of *The Mirror*, which was to be paid by the household, and, if not, by the parish in which the household belonged. Bucher, the pastor of Our Lady of the Lake Parish in Branson, Missouri, invited people to have their names removed from the parish's *The Mirror* list in his March 13, 1994, parish bulletin. He had done this before when he was pastor of Immaculate Conception Parish in Springfield, and his successor returned all those to the parish list when he became pastor. On March 17, 1994, I sent the bulletin, which had been brought to me by one of our volunteer proofreaders, to Leibrecht with a memorandum, asking him to write to Bucher and ask him to present the diocesan newspaper in a positive light. "If a pastor cannot directly remove the names of subscribers from the parish list, then, it would seem, that he cannot do it indirectly by inviting them to request that their names be removed," I wrote.

Furthermore, because Bucher was a Vicar General, the Promoter of Justice and Defender of the Bond in the Marriage Tribunal, and a Diocesan Consultor, I raised the question of what kind of good example this presented to the rest of the clergy. What I didn't know was that Bucher and Leibrecht were friends and golf buddies. The only response I got to my memo was this: "Let me know of the change in Branson's *The Mirror* list. Then I'll decide what step to take." I sent a long list of households being removed, but no letter telling Bucher to stop was ever written.

The Historical Jesus 1996

In the March 1, 1996, issue of *The Mirror*, I pulled four articles from Religion News Service to which we subscribed, another recommendation from CAB; all four dealt with biblical issues including the historical Jesus. One tackled the question about the mention of Jesus' brothers in the New Testament. It clearly stated the difference between historical investigation and doctrine, presenting Catholic doctrine and what the *Catechism of the Catholic Church* teaches. Another asked if the apostle James wrote the letter attributed to him. The third examined biases in biblical translations, and the last looked at Jesus as both human (historical investigation) and divine (doctrine). I considered the articles to be adult religious education materials. They both presented the

Catholic point of view concerning doctrine, and they presented modern biblical scholarship. Some readers didn't like the articles and wrote letters to Leibrecht about them. I got a few letters and phone calls, too, and explained what the articles stated, namely, that there was a difference between historical investigation and doctrinal belief.

On February 29, 1996, a memorandum arrived from Leibrecht. He wanted to know what the guidelines were that I used to decide what material to use from RNS? According to his interpretation: "Two RNS articles are built around questioning the virgin birth. Another article relates to the divinity of Jesus." He also wanted information about the Jesus Seminar, whose meetings and writings were the bases for the articles. Thinking all this was sincere, I went to a March 21 meeting with my guidelines and Jesus Seminar information in hand. As I wrote in a memo on March 25, "The topic for the meeting was his anger with me and condemnation of me for reporting what some Catholic scholars are saying and to inform me that he was going to tell the priests at the upcoming Chrism Masses that I was wrong to report the opinions of some scholars, hinting at, but never specifically stating, a lack of faith on my part in the doctrines of the Church." I explained that I reached that conclusion because he informed me that there was only one guideline: "articles must build up faith." I continued: "When I asked for clarification as to the meaning of that, you told me that I was not to challenge the faith of the readers of *The Mirror*. Later, you said, I was to challenge only to the point of bringing them along in understanding." The reader will note the ambiguousness of the answers.

In my memo I noted that he had not asked for the guidelines I use, nor had he asked for the information on the Jesus Seminar that I prepared. He merely told me that he "had consulted some bishops who 'stay up with these things,'" which meant that he wasn't interested in the topic. I concluded my memo, writing:

> Summoning me to your office like a child and then proceeding to question my credibility and my faith under pretext of what I perceived that the memo requested violates justice and my adult, human dignity. I will not be treated like a child again. Any disagreement that we may have can be worked out once both sides understand each other clearly. If you cannot or will not understand and will not treat me with human respect, then it is time for you to get rid of me and to find an editor whom you will understand and respect. The credibility of the paper to report news about religion as unbiased as possible is more important than who the editor is. If I need to step down to keep *The Mirror's* credibility from slipping, then that is more important. I don't want to see torn down what I have worked so hard to build up.

On the same day, March 25, 1996, I sent Leibrecht a three-page memo appealing to his sense of justice and understanding. I tried to educate a man with a doctorate in education! I urged him to re-read the questionable articles, understand the methodology. I wrote:

> My mandate from you is to provide adult religious education resources for people. When people get upset about learning something new or hearing of the opinion of someone, it provides the opportunity to teach them not to condemn until they understand; that scholarly investigation does not attack doctrine; that the doctrines of the Church can be found in the *Catechism of the Catholic Church*; that Scripture gives rise to some, but not all, doctrines; etc. In other words, understanding leads to and provides the opportunity for faith.

I also gave examples of other things that could be read as an attack on doctrine, such as reviewing a R-rated film, an article on Buddhism, or a history of pretzels during Lent. I also explained that the content of the articles could be found in all major news magazines and newspapers. I ended the memo by seeking understanding without agreement that brings forth justice. I asked him not to condemn me at the dinner before the Chrism Mass.

The next day, March 26, 1996, I received another memo from Leibrecht. It rehashed the purpose of *The Mirror*: "to support and build up the faith-life of Catholic people." It questioned the appropriateness of the articles I chose for *The Mirror*, using the word "pastoral" over and over with no definition. I was instructed "to take into consideration the pastoral implications of my editorial judgments." Thus, no matter what materials I chose from whatever source, I could also be wrong! My perspective was that the articles were valuable from a religious education perspective of an educator, but from his point of view "RNS material should not have been in *The Mirror*" because it sparked people to write letters. "I continue to support *The Mirror* and yourself," he wrote. What he didn't write is that he supported me unless he disagreed with an article I chose for the paper. He added, "I feel confident that my remarks after the Chrism Mass dinners will be fair to all parties concerned." Still yet another memorandum arrived, dated April 4, 1996, with this self-congratulatory paragraph: "My remarks to the priests at the Chrism Mass dinners went very well and contained compliments from the men themselves about *The Mirror* and your work with it. I would like to think that those compliments were occasioned by the manner in which I was able to speak about the March 1 issue of the paper."

The man just could not distinguish between the Jesus of history and the Christ of faith. This issue resurfaced on August 17, 1998. In my August 7, 1998, column, I examined how most biblical scholars did not think that Jesus set out to found a church. In a lengthy paragraph, Leibrecht presented what Richard McBrien said about the question: no, if is meant a new religious organization; yes, if is meant lay-found foundations in indirect ways. He wanted me to write that the church had its origin in Jesus, yet he remarked, "Jesus had no institutional master plan." Then, he quoted what the *Catechism of the Catholic Church* said.

In another lengthy paragraph I was instructed to give context to what theologians and scholars say and critique it and provide Catholic context, which is exactly what was presented in my column. I was told I should have explained the difference between my use of *found* and the use of *established* or *instituted*. I had chosen my word carefully in order to avoid what seemed to be unavoidable. He also wanted the theologian's or scholar's specific form of Christianity identified; see, this would enable readers to question their veracity. Like many memoranda before this one, it ended with Leibrecht being happy to discuss the issue further; that meant that there would be no discussion. I would be put down and told I was wrong, even though he could not find a basis for that in my carefully-worded column.

Readership Survey 1996

During Lent in 1996, *The Mirror* conducted a readership survey at the suggestion of the CAB. Every seventh name on *The Mirror* subscription mailing list was sent a copy of the survey questions and a bubble-form to use to complete the survey along with directions to choose an answer and color the dot on the form that corresponded with the person's choice. After the deadline for returning the survey in the postage-paid envelope which accompanied it, I took the forms to the computer center at Southwest Missouri State University (now Missouri State University) to have the results tabulated. I gave a copy of the results to Leibrecht. On April 4, 1996, he indicated that he had not examined them carefully. "I would very much appreciate some of your initial thoughts about the survey results, and I will offer a few thoughts myself," he wrote. He wanted to meet to do this in mid-April. So, on April 19, I brought what I concluded from the 458 responses received. Seventy-one percent of respondents, ages thirty-one to sixty-one, read *The Mirror* for five to sixty minutes every week. They did not use the free movie review line provided by the Catholic Conference of Bishops. People were willing to pay $12 to $16 for a yearly subscription. Over half of the readers have other sources of Catholic news and made over $31,000 yearly. The *MCC Messenger*, a quarterly insert in the paper, was rarely or never read. And some people were angry about getting *The Mirror*.

Once again, the sincerity of the request was not the purpose of the meeting. My interpretations of the data were all wrong. Furthermore, he nailed me with some people who had complained that it was hard to get things into *The Mirror*. When I asked who those people were, I got no response. The emphasis was on that people perceive this. I explained that I cannot change what people may perceive; I need empirical data of when they have tried to get something in the paper and it didn't happen. My guess was that it was too late to meet the deadline. The bottom line of the meeting was that my interpretations of the survey results were all wrong, and his were all correct. And that was the end of that meeting!

Assignments in the Diocese of Springfield-Cape Girardeau

MCC Messenger 1996, 2000

The *Missouri Catholic Conference Messenger* was a thorn in my editorial life. As the 1996 survey indicated, people didn't read it. It arrived as a four page insert, poorly laid out and looking nothing like *The Mirror*. In fact, it made *The Mirror* look bad. Anything in the issue in which it was inserted that I wanted to enter into a newspaper contest was immediately disqualified because of it; that is how bad it was! I had been explaining this poor quality to Leibrecht, but, of course, he was not going to bring it up at a province meeting of the bishops of Missouri. On March 14, 1996, I received the worst material I had ever seen. On March 18, I sent a copy of all the articles to Leibrecht with a memo attached. I asked him to read all the pages "and note the grammatical errors, the typos, the separations of words, etc." I also received color mug shots for a black and white newspaper! "From a journalism point of view, most of this is garbage," I wrote. "Members of my staff and proofreaders told me how bad they thought it was. Furthermore, one half of the cost of printing it was being borne by *The Mirror*. I asked Leibrecht to compare what I got with what I attempted to do with it in the March 22 issue of *The Mirror*. I'm sure that the copy was not read and the comparison was not done. Nothing happened on the conference level except the reception of more of the same on a quarterly basis.

I even submitted a proposal from the CAB, whose members had repeatedly complained about the poor quality of the *MCC Messenger*, to the MCC. We, the members of CAB, suggested that the MCC hire a part-time reporter, who would file stories with the four editors of diocesan newspapers in the province of Missouri. That reporter would write interviews and feature articles and explore issues that faced Catholics in Missouri. The two-and-a-half-page proposal offered a variety of suggestions for other stories, such as about legislative issues, analysis of legislative positions, responses from ordinary people, etc. The proposal also advocated that input concerning needs from the four dioceses in Missouri would be the guide for the reporter, who would be responsible for meeting those needs. The reporter's salary would be paid by the funds saved from producing the *MCC Messenger*. Needless to say, that proposal went nowhere!

Four years later in 2000 the poor quality continued. In order to conform the material to the style of *The Mirror*, I had requested that the material not be laid out, but that we lay it out so it looked like our newspaper. On October 9, 2000, I got part of the material for the next issue of the *MCC Messenger*. I sent an e-mail to Candy Smith, who worked in the MCC office. As an editor, I called attention to the difference between questions and statements; the article presented statements, not questions with answers as the article stated. I called attention to the shift from one person to the other and the use of *we* with no plural antecedent noun. I said that wordiness is not a virtue; the material needed to be edited. I called attention to the lack of the use of needed commas and run-on sentences.

Well, Smith didn't like my e-mail. So, she turned it over to Deacon Lawrence A. Weber, the Executive Director of the MCC, who sent me a FAX on October 10, 2000, which defended the use of question and answer for clearly stated statements, the use of poor grammar, and the late arrival of the material. Of course, he also sent a copy of his correspondence to Leibrecht, who wasted no time writing a memo on October 12, 2000, wanting to see me. On the same day he wrote a FAX to Weber, apologizing for the harshness of my e-mail to Smith and assuring Weber that the tone of my e-mail did not represent the spirit of the diocese. What is to be noted in his missive to Weber is that he did not address any of the concerns about the quality of the *MCC Messenger* materials that I raised. We met, and I got put down for attempting to raise awareness of the downright poor quality of MCC materials. Nothing was ever done about it. The poor quality continues to this day!

Deadlines 1997, 1998

As already mentioned above, Leibrecht's column often was late. His deadline was 10 a.m. on Wednesday before the paper was proofread on Thursday and went to press on Friday. My staff and I were supposed to do the impossible when it was late. He wanted quality, but that couldn't be achieved unless we had all the pieces to fit them together. I asked over and over again to keep his column to two double-spaced typed pages because that was the room allotted to the column. If it went over that, it had to be severely edited; there was no page to which to jump it because all the other pages were finished. No matter how hard I tried to urge him to adhere to his deadline—which was the very last one for every issue of the paper—he ignored it. Sometimes it was on time; other times the column came right before lunch or after lunch. Then, the staff and I had to rush to finish the page.

The issue of deadlines came very much forward in 1997. Publishing the new assignments for diocesan clergy was not only kept secret for some reason, but became Leibrecht's fixation. Before I left for vacation in July 1997, I finished two issues of the paper. The one dated July 25 was finished except for his column. I had sent a memorandum to him three weeks before I left, I explained in a July 23 memo, that both issues of July would be done before I went on vacation. In my memo, I stated, "Before I went on vacation, I spoke to Reidy—in your absence—about assignments. He told me that there were only a few and that publishing them in the August 8 issue would be fine." See, the Copy Coordinator, Leslie Mayes, who by now had been married twice (Hunter Eidson), called me while I was in Colorado and told me that he had asked that the assignments appear in the July 25 issue. As I explained to him, "I told her that I couldn't write a story from Colorado and have it ready to go on the day I returned to the office." Hunter Eidson tried, but she couldn't write. When I saw what she had written, I went with my original plan because the day I returned to the office

Leibrecht's column needed to be edited and laid onto the page where it belonged, the paper needed to be proofread, and it had to be ready for the printer.

The next day, July 24, 1997, I received this memorandum from Leibrecht: "As you know, the practice has been to make the appointments in mid-July with *The Mirror* announcing them in the first subsequent issue. I truly believe that with that consistent practice, you should have made provision for that to happen whether you were on vacation or not." I concluded that among my editorial responsibilities was predicting the future, after I had already sent a memo indicating the deadline for the issue in question. His memo continued: "In this particular instance I gave a specific instruction on what was to be done, namely, that the appointments were to be carried in the July 25 issue. Countermanding that instruction or failing to follow it is not acceptable, whatever the problems may be." Now, I concluded, *The Mirror* staff was charged with doing the impossible. We were supposed to get into print material we didn't have! The irony of all this is that no one cared about priestly appointments in *The Mirror*. The priests moving from one parish to the next had already told their parishioners; announcing them in *The Mirror* was not new news to them, because they already knew.

Based on the information given to me and presented above, namely, that the priestly assignments would be announced in mid-July and be printed in the last issue of July, in 1988, I finished the first issue of July and went on vacation. Leibrecht then changed his mind. He wanted them in the first issue of July. When I got home, a July 1, 1998, memorandum sat on my desk. Of course, it began with the need to see me. "As editor, you should have approached me to see which issue, July 10 or July 24, would be *The Mirror* in which the assignments were announced," he wrote. "You know July is the month and yet you made no inquiry of which July issue should be prepared for the announcements." It was my fault that he had changed his mind!

There was also a letter from Hunter Eidson on my desk, dated July 1, narrating how Leibrecht's secretary had been sent to inquire about the publication of assignments in the July 10 issue and being told that the issue was finished. Then Leibrecht summoned Eidson to his office, and she told him the same thing, namely, that she was not authorized to redesign the paper. She wrote that he indicated that there was no question, the announcements were going in July 10. He authorized her to tear up the July 10 issue and put the announcements in it. She gave him the telephone numbers where I could be reached, but he did not want to talk to me. In her letter to me, Hunter Eidson wrote: "I was to pursue gathering the information, photos, etc. and that he would deal with Mark upon his return, but there was to be no other arrangements made other than publishing the information he gave me to go into the July 10 issue. The appointments were to go to press the morning of July 6, no other story."

Hunter Eidson wrote another letter on July 6, 1998, informing me that the appointments of twelve priests were in the July 10 issue. Repeatedly she expressed her dislike of being caught between the bishop and me. According to her letter, he made contact with her six times. She had called me in Colorado, and I had told her not to do it; I was not authorizing the tearing up of an issue of the paper that was finished, and there was nothing I could do from Colorado. Leibrecht was being unreasonable and contradicting his own previous directive. Furthermore, I could not control what she chose to do or not do when faced with his directive. When I returned to the office, I sorted out this with Hunter Eidson, then I wrote a July 16, 1998, memo to Leibrecht.

"This time I'm not accepting the blame nor the responsibility for what you failed to do," I began. I quoted the July 24, 1997, memorandum that priestly assignments would be made in mid-July and announced in the last issue of July. I also quoted from that memo that they would "always appear in the second issue of July." I explained that I had arranged my vacation to be back in time to write the story for the second issue of July. "I don't know when you changed your mind after the memorandum and verbal order of last year, but you never informed me about it. So, I am not accepting responsibility for this. I did what I had been told to do." I had also issued a sheet of deadlines in May, and on that sheet was the following notice: "The July 10 issues of *The Mirror* will be delivered by noon on Friday, June 19. Note the change in the deadline day."

In his July 1 memo, he wrote: "I feel sorry for Leslie in this matter because she has been caught in the middle. Because she is doing exactly what I instructed her to do, I want absolutely no negative repercussions toward her because it would clearly be unfair to her." In my July 16 memo, I wrote: "She was doing what I told her to do, based on the memorandum you sent to me last year. You put her in the bind by insisting that she first write the article about the priests' assignments and then proceed to tear up the pages of *The Mirror* which were completed. Leslie is not a staff writer nor is she the newspaper page designer. Any unfairness to Leslie has been done by you. It's not only unfairness, it's plainly a case of the lack of justice and the failure to check your own memorandum." I told him that he had belittled me in front of my staff and behind my back. He owed an apology both to Hunter Eidson and to me. The only response I got was dated July 20, 1998, with an appointment to meet with him to plan the following year's assignments for priests. I gave him the dates for the summer, every-other-week publication schedule for 1999. "Please indicate the issue in which you want the assignments to appear, and they will be published in it."

Redesign 1999

After attending many Society of Newspaper Design conventions, I was convinced that *The Mirror* needed to be redesigned. The newspaper redesign guru was Tony Sutton. After getting the redesign project as a line item costing ten thousand dollars in the budget, I proceeded to make arrangement with Sutton to work on the redesign process. After a few months of work and dialogue with me, Sutton presented *The Mirror* redesigned. My staff and I agreed to launch the redesign with the first issue of January 2000. Once the redesign was completed, it was presented to Leibrecht, who decided that he would redesign the redesign.

So, on September 24, 1999, I got a two-page memorandum with "a few questions and suggestions." The first suggestion was about putting in news briefs. That was a good idea, and so I proceeded to place them on the last inside page to fill the space over advertising. On December 9, 1999, I got this memorandum: "Let's replace the RNS column on the right side of the front page each week with News Briefs." He didn't like anything from Religion News Service, and this was his way of getting rid of the commentary column that began on the right-hand column. In a December 10, 1999, memo to Leibrecht, I explained that "news briefs on the front page will not improve the paper." I continued: "The purpose of the front page of a tabloid is not to give bits of news but to present a story (or two) that gets the reader inside the paper and a commentary or opinion piece that also draws the reader inside the paper." After spending ten thousand dollars I suggested that it was best to leave the redesign as Sutton had suggested. The news briefs continued to be placed on the inside last page.

In his September 24 memorandum, he wanted the page head on page 16 changed from adult education, but didn't know what he wanted it to be! He suggested adult faith, and that was fine with me.

The third suggestion was to find a way "to do things at the last minute." He wanted "to address those problems and have a procedure which allows late-breaking news or information in an issue a week earlier than it might otherwise appear." With a staff of three full-time people, of course, this was impossible. The copy had to be written or taken off one of the news feeds we used. Then, it had to be laid out, proofread by my secretary, proofread by a volunteer, corrected, and sent to the printer. In the process of attempting to be "more current on some matters," we would have to tear up several pages, basically starting over. Because news feed copy was often corrected or changed, I didn't want to risk getting an incorrect story in the paper at the last minute. I told Leibrecht we would see what it was, and then evaluate the possibility of getting a story in the paper at the last minute with the other last-minute columns (his included) that often arrived late.

Then, he informed me in his memorandum that he had taken the redesign to the Presbyteral Council meeting, without informing me. The priests at the meeting had their own observations, according to him. They noted the quality of photographs which I had brought about and wanted to know if that would continue. They also wanted to see more diocesan news. I explained that I welcomed more diocesan news if we had staff to write it. They also wanted *The Mirror* to be more pastorally sensitive, which meant they wanted nothing in it that might disturb anyone. I remember saying to myself, "How am I supposed to know that?"

Father Tom Ehrich Column 2000

My question to myself was not answered, but on September 14, 2000, Jill Sisney, MD, wrote to Leibrecht, telling him that Father Tom Ehrich's column was "biased, misinformed, and hostile." She was referencing Ehrich's reflections in the front-page commentary about his recent doctor's appointment and how long he had to wait past the appointment time to see his doctor. Sisney, a Catholic doctor, didn't like the comments Ehrich, an Episcopal priest, made in his Religion News Service column. And, of course, Leibrecht didn't either. He answered Sisney's letter, sending a copy of both her letter and is response to me, writing, "Ehrich painted with too broad a brush by generalizing individual real problems into a description of the medical profession as a whole." He added, "Little understanding of a doctor's side of the story was present in his highly judgmental remarks."

I had received several other letters about the same column. Since I had been directed to print every letter received by *The Mirror*, and later I had been instructed to write a short editor's response to the letter, I received an October 5, 2000, memorandum from Leibrecht calling my response "overly defensive." In my response, I had explained that Ehrich did not write an article in terms of news, but he wrote an opinion column or commentary. Leibrecht wrote, "As an editor, you probably interpret the meaning of the word more narrowly but that does not mean the word cannot be appropriately used in its broader definition as did both writers of letters to the editor."

My editor's response said that nowhere in the commentary did Ehrich state that all doctors were like the one he encountered. Leibrecht referred to Sisney's statement in her letter about Ehrich's claim that some doctors may have had a neurotic need to validate themselves by forcing patients to wait. According to Leibrecht: "Sisney was criticizing Father Ehrich's willingness to ascribe neuroticism to doctors who have people waiting. Father Ehrich was no longer talking about one doctor he encountered." Leibrecht didn't like my suggestion that Sisney's patients be surveyed to see what they think. He told me that I was going after her. I had also stated that Ehrich's words and letters offering other perspectives were valued because they were based on individual personal experience. Leibrecht asked, "Are the two opinions of equal validity? They are subjective but what about objectivity?"

The next day, October 6, 2000, I responded to Leibrecht's memorandum. I stated that I didn't think I was too defensive, in light of the fact that Ehrich's words had a colored banner over the title stating: Commentary. "When a reader writes about someone's article, it means he or she is reading it as news—not as the commentary it is labeled as." I explained that when specific journalism words are used interchangeably, no one knows that they mean. I also pointed out that Ehrich didn't say the sentence about doctors' neuroticism; patients, who shared his experience, had said them. I also stated that I was not going after Sisney. I posed an honest question. What would the results be if she poled her patients? Ehrich had done that much. I continued:

> Both opinions are valid based on human experience, but the not-waiting one loses hands down to the experience of people waiting for a doctor, when you ask around. Ask around this building and elsewhere and you'll discover how many people think Ehrich is right because he interprets their experiences.

> Have you ever had to wait for thirty minutes or more in a doctor's office? If
> you haven't, then you have no idea of what the rest of us deal with on a day-
> to-day basis. I have waited and waited and waited just in the past year for up
> to an hour to see a doctor.

I concluded by suggesting that Leibrecht read the rest of the letters that continued to arrive about this issue and were printed in *The Mirror*. "So far, they all support Ehrich (and me)," I wrote.

Reflection 2000

Near the end of 2000, I reflected on my life. I looked over the various dimensions of it, and I discovered that the only place where I found negativity was with *The Mirror*. I was receiving great evaluations as a teacher from my students at Southwest Missouri State University (now Missouri State University). The nineteen books I had written were selling well. I was getting positive evaluations from the adult education sessions I had been giving. I had excellent evaluations from the workshops I had given on church building renovation in Arkansas and other church building consultations. The only negativity I found was with Leibrecht in *The Mirror*. So, I decided that it was time for a change. However, before that, there was more negativity with which to deal.

Jim Keusenkothen 2001

On February 4, 2001, I received a letter from Jim Keusenkothen taking issue with Leibrecht's "Walking Together" column in the January 19, 2001, issue of *The Mirror*. Leibrecht had reviewed *The Complete Idiots Guide to Understanding Catholicism*. Keusenkothen wrote, "I must preface my remarks by mentioning my reservations about writing this letter because I do not make it a common practice to publicly disagree with Catholic bishops." Keusenkothen had read the book and stated that for several reasons he would not recommend it to anyone seriously looking for a better understanding of Catholicism. Then, in his two-page letter he went on to list seven examples of how he thought the book did not represent true Catholicism. "I sincerely hope that Leibrecht will perhaps take a closer look at this book and reconsider his endorsement of it before it causes serious harm to the faith of some innocent reader." In a PS he asked me to give a copy of his letter to Leibrecht in the hope that he would respond to it either personally or in his weekly column. I did as I had been asked; I prepared the letter for print in *The Mirror*, as I had been told by Leibrecht to print every letter received.

After giving Leibrecht a copy of the letter, I got a note from Leibrecht, who wrote, "I'll write him and also make reference to his concerns in a future column of mine. No need to print his lengthy letter." I couldn't believe what I was reading! This violated the policy of the man who had made it, namely, that every letter to the editor was to be printed. So, on February 12, 2001, I wrote a letter to Keusenkothen to inform him that I had done as he asked and given a copy of his letter to Leibrecht. "A couple of days later, the bishop sent me a memo telling me not to print it," I wrote. "That is why I am writing to you. Since I have been told not to print it, I want you to know why you will not see your letter appear in *The Mirror*." I continued:

> Because I think you make some excellent points about *The Complete Idiots Guide to Understanding Catholicism*, I think your letter deserves to be printed. Other readers of that book need to know the distortions you point out. So, if you would like to see it in print, you will need to submit it again or write another letter without the PS requesting that it be given to the bishop/publisher first. At this point, I can do nothing more.

On February 14, 2001, I received a letter sent via FAX from Keusenkothen, stating that he had received my letter in which I mentioned that Leibrecht told me not to print it. "Did the bishop state that he would respond to it, either to me directly or in his column?" he asked. "I would be happy to resubmit my letter but only if Bishop Leibrecht does not intend to respond to it." He included an e-mail address where I could answer him, and I did answer him the same day. I sent an e-mail, stating, "To answer your question about what the bishop is going to do concerning your letter, I do not know." I also asked him not to mention that I had sent a letter to him. Then, I wrote, "See, to be quite frank, I've caught the bishop in a two-faced position. I was told to be sure to print all the letters to the editor, but this one, because it was about his column, I was told not to print. I wrote to you to protect my own integrity and let you know why your letter would not be printed." Then, I repeated what I had written in my letter to him, namely, if he resubmitted the letter, I would print it. Later the same day, Keusenkothen sent me another FAX, informing that he had e-mailed Leibrecht asking him to respond. If he did not respond, he would resubmit the letter to me for publication.

On February 14, 2001, Leibrecht answered Keusenkothen's concerns with his own two-page letter in which he acknowledged not having read the book in question in its entirety. Then, he went on to address each of Keusenkothen's issues raised in his original letter. He introduced his defense by stating, "I probably would not agree with everything in the book nor with the way it is presented. That is true of most books I read." Attached to a copy of Leibrecht's letter to Keusenkothen and a copy of Keusenkothen's letter was a red note: "After finally taking the time to look more closely at Jim Keusenkothen's letter, I've decided not to do anything in my column. It doesn't warrant it."

I replied to the note with my own: "Following your previous directive that I publish all letters to the editor, Jim Keusenkothen's letter to the editor is scheduled for March 2, 2001. There is room for the whole letter in that issue of *The Mirror*." However, because Keusenkothen had gotten what he wanted—an answer to his letter—his letter never appeared in *The Mirror*.

Assignments in the Diocese of Springfield-Cape Girardeau

Call to Action 2001

On February 23, 2001, *The Mirror* carried an article titled "What is Call to Action?" As the editor's note at the very beginning of the story stated, "Several readers have requested the following article." I asked Melissa Gray, one of my stringers, to do the necessary research and write it. Also, in the editor's note was the following: "The information below is given as information only. *The Mirror* neither fosters nor discourages participation in Call to Action." On February 21, 2001, I received a letter from Leibrecht attacking the editor's note: "Such a stated policy by a diocesan agency is not yours to make, but mine as bishop." Then, there followed the following paragraph:

> From this time forward, if there is any article for *The Mirror* whose appropriateness you or the average reader finds questionable, its publication will require my prior approval. Experience with the new understanding during the months ahead will assist in clarifying what is and is not acceptable.

I tried explaining that no one was setting any kind of policy; in fact, the word *policy* was not used. The editor's note was a standard disclaimer designed to keep letters from readers being sent accusing *The Mirror* of propagating Call to Action. It set no policy; it was neutral, neither advocating nor endorsing. No one of eight previous readers interpreted the disclaimer as policy, and no reasonable person would conclude a policy being set. Of course, the episcopal mind was set, and no reasonable word could be heard! More and more the publisher wanted to be the editor. The reader will immediately notice that Leibrecht's policy leaves me in a double bind: It is up to me to determine appropriateness, and it leaves him plenty of room to tell me that I was wrong!

What is interesting is on February 23, 2001, I received an e-mail from William Bishop, who served as movie-review editor. Along with the reviews, he wrote: "By the way, there was a story about Call to Action. Why did you print the disclaimer before the article? I didn't find the story any more provocative than some of the others that run in *The Mirror*. Just curious?" On the same day, I replied:

> I printed the disclaimer because I didn't want letters saying that *The Mirror* was supporting Call to Action. I printed that disclaimer in order to eliminate any potential angry letters which are usually sent to the bishop. Then I get called on the carpet for it. But this time I was nailed anyway, since the bishop accused me of setting diocesan policy. If you can see anything about a policy in that editor's note, I'd like to hear about it. The word *policy* isn't even used.

Later in the day, I got this e-mail from Bishop:

> You mean policy vis-à-vis Call to Action? Meaning that the diocese supports Call to Action and that is the diocesan policy? No, I did not read it that way at all. In fact, I believed that I knew exactly why you did it, and your response confirmed it. I was just somewhat surprised because you don't generally shy

away from any controversy that a story may generate. For that matter, I bet you will get some letters, the disclaimer notwithstanding. But that's OK. Keep up the good work. I think a little controversy is a good thing (as long as you can keep your job).

On March 2, 2001, I sent an e-mail to my good friend Father James Reynolds recounting the saga of the Call to Action article. In that e-mail, I told Reynolds that Leibrecht had told me "that because there was a 'for more information' paragraph at the end, that *The Mirror* was supporting Call to Action and he, as bishop, did not want to support it." I continued to tell Reynolds: "I kept repeating to him what he was telling me and how I understood how he was reaching the conclusion he was reaching, but that it was in error. Never once did he repeat to me the position I was explaining to him, which means he never heard me." I concluded, "His position was correct and that was the truth."

American Catholic Church 2001

In the May 18, 2001, issue of *The Mirror*, there appeared an article about the American Catholic Church growing in Springfield; it was written by Christine Ballew-Gonzales, a part-time staff writer, reporter, and substitute print and online editor whom I had hired on June 30, 2000. On May 21, 2001, both Ballew-Gonzales and I got a memorandum from Leibrecht: "One of the key roles of *The Mirror* is to educate," began the memorandum. "In my opinion, the article on the American Catholic Church was seriously deficient in addressing that role." After posing multiple questions, he wrote about procedures that "could be put in place so that an article which falls short of what it could be educationally can be edited into something more instructive for the average reader." The reader will notice that only Leibrecht considered the article educationally to be lacking; neither of the editors did so.

Because I had been out of town attending press meetings, Ballew-Gonzales had been acting editor in my stead. She left me an e-mail about the "lovely letter from the bishop"—"a poison pen letter," she called it—requesting that we see him, of course. I responded to her email by telling her to forget it and sit back and see what happens. I did not follow up, and I think he forget all about it.

New Editor 2001

In the spring of 2001, a search committee had been formed to find a new editor for *The Mirror*. I had asked to be released from that job as soon as possible. However, the committee had not surfaced the person Leibrecht wanted; thus, the official word was that no competent candidate could be found even though several had applied. So, I continued for another six months as editor until another committee could be formed and begin the process again. A sabbatical awaited me once a new editor was in place. The deadline for applicants was October 17, 2001. Finally, the committee released its recommendation: Leslie Eidson (who had dropped the Hunter from her last name).

I had hired Leslie A. Mayes on June 21, 1989 as part-time help with entry work. At that time, wire copy arrived printed by a dot-matrix, self-feed printer on continuous-feed paper. Her job, named Copy Coordinator, was to sit in front of a computer, enter copy from the news wire and other sources, proofread it, and save it on a small floppy disk, which could be given to the typesetter to prepare for layout. Once the typesetter resigned his position, she applied for the job, and I gave it to her because she knew the basic process for producing a weekly newspaper. Over the course of the years, Mayes married a man with the last name of Hunter with Leibrecht as the witness; she divorced Hunter a few years after the marriage and had it annulled in the Catholic Church. Then, she married a man named Eidson.

Over the course of the years until cell phones became the norm, I repeatedly had to call her attention to the time she spent on the office telephone taking care of personal matters, walking around the building and stopping to talk at other desks, and then charging over-time in order to get all her work done. In 1993, she applied for an executive secretary job in the same building without saying anything to me; I found out about it after the position was filled. She had graduated from high school and taken some courses at SMSU (now MSU) over two years. However, she had no college degree. So, imagine my surprise—after reading the add advertising the search for an editor that stated the diocese was searching for a qualified applicant with experience as an editor and a degree in a related field with excellent written and verbal communication skills—when I heard that Eidson had applied for the job without telling me and then been named editor. The only conclusion I could reach is that is what Leibrecht wanted; he thought he could control her. After all, he already had several times. He told her what to do, and she did it.

Leibrecht appointed her editor on December 7, 2001, effective January 10, 2002. The announcement appeared in the December 14 issue of *The Mirror* with a news release issued by Vydra, Diocesan Communications Director, on December 13. My last issue was January 11, 2002. In a December 6, 2001, letter to the leadership of the diocese, Leibrecht wrote, "I met with the search committee following its interviews with six candidates and accepted its recommendation that I interview two of the six as finalists." He continued, "My decision was made after those two interviews." Of course, we do not know who the other finalist was. Certainly, the search committee would not have recommended a candidate to the bishop who did not have a college degree!

Another candidate for the job of editor was Ballew-Gonzales, who had a degree in journalism, served as my substitute editor, and served as editor as the web edition of the paper. On December 14, 2001, Ballew-Gonzales narrated what Leibrecht told her:

> He told me to go to his office after liturgy. Behind closed doors, he told me how sorry he was and how disappointed I must be (even pointed out that I had been refused the job twice) and how much he wants to help. When I explained how shocking his decision of who to name editor seemed to me and other people, he went into this protracted explanation of the selection process. Here's what it came down to: Eidson had no experience or degree, the other candidate had post-graduate degrees in theology and media but no experience, and me, extensive experience and education. Basically, the whole stupid conversation was his feeble attempt to convince me that one plus one equals three.

I responded by warning her not to be deceived. "He thinks that he can manipulate you into thinking he is right so that you won't stir up anything," I wrote to her. I explained how he did that with me; I called it a suppression technique. In my case it was always a put down of some kind. I warned her not to fall into his pit. On December 17, 2001, Ballew-Gonzales e-mailed me again. She wrote: "It was very transparent and a weak try at getting me to think all was kosher, when it is clearly not." She continued: "I doubt he knows or even cares how fake it all sounds. He must think you and I are both idiots!"

Meanwhile, on December 5, 2001, I sent a confidential e-mail to people who worked for me in various capacities. I told them that they needed to know the story behind the story, namely, that while Eidson had twelve years of experience as copy coordinator for *The Mirror*, she had no college degree or journalism training, she had never written an article, and she had poor grammar skills. Those facts, I told my faithful employees, would affect the material they submitted. I advised them to consider this free information to use as they saw fit.

E-mails poured in. Mary Hart, a columnist, wrote: "I am stunned. You are a gifted editor and writer, as well as an academic, and for your replacement to have no skills in those areas is mind-boggling. I can't imagine what will happen to the paper." Karla Essner, a reporter, wrote: "Thank you so much for your advance notice of the change of command. I want you to know that it has been an honor, a privilege, and a horizon-broadening learning experience to work for you and with you." Another person wrote: "One can't be replaced with a secretary. It just looks that way. All will see that as the planning that you've done runs out soon. She's in over her head without a bit of theology. So, the theological adult education aspect of *The Mirror* is now finished, because, as you and I both know, you can't educate if you yourself are not educated." Melissa Gray, a stringer, e-mailed me: "I appreciate the information you sent to me. You have pushed me in so many different directions and shown me that I am capable of doing more than I ever imagined. You have taught me more in the six years we have been working together than any professor, editor, or colleague that I have come in contact with." There were a number of other e-mails, but these give the reader a glimpse of what many of them said.

Assignments in the Diocese of Springfield-Cape Girardeau

Reynolds's concern was me leaving The Catholic Center. "If you leave, The Catholic Center will have no professional theological person on its staff—a sad prospect indeed." I replied to his remark in our March 2, 2001, exchange, writing about being tired of listening to Leibrecht tell me that I was wrong all the time. I wrote to Reynolds that I could not continue to walk around coals never knowing what he would decide is not appropriate or inaccurate or wrong after it is in print. "See, it's one of the cases where it's OK until Leibrecht declares it wrong," I wrote in my e-mail. "So, how do I ever know? And sometimes it's not wrong until someone writes him a letter, then, it's wrong." After the new editor was appointed, I sent Reynolds an e-mail, and he responded with disbelief.

On January 15, 2002, I received an e-mail from Ballew-Gonzales informing me that Eidson had removed her from her position as web editor. "I was told to remove my name from everything that said I was web-edition editor. According to her and Leibrecht, the web edition is an experiment that failed." She continued: "I was berated for everything that she feels is wrong with the web edition. I was told that everything is going to change and that she didn't want me to work from home anymore." Humorously, she continued, "There's lots more; I could go on and on and on—this exercise in humiliation lasted a full two hours, which I spent looking around the office for something sharp to stab myself with." Then, she added: "Eidson is just smart enough to know that she's not qualified and I am; that's why she's running over me in this way. People who are competent in leadership let other competent people do their jobs."

I responded on the say day with an e-mail, writing, "Eidson is threatened, of course, by your expertise, just like Leibrecht was threatened by mine. Some people in power cannot stand to work with others who know more than they do, and they are too stupid to realize their loss." I explained to Ballew-Gonzales:

> Eidson is too stupid to realize that after Leibrecht uses her to get what he wants that she will be forced out too because of her own inability to be an editor. She has the illusion of power that he has let her have in order to get rid of those who threaten him. He has done it before. So, she will use her power to do his dirty work, then he will use his power to force her out because of her inability. The way that will work is he will ask the board she is supposed to form to evaluate her, and he will get the priests to do the same. Then, he will blame the board and the priests for having to force her out. It is how he plays church politics.

I urged Ballew-Gonzales to get out of the sick system in which she found herself. "I spent the past ten years fighting it," I wrote. "I have some idea of not only how it works, but how sick it truly is. I could tell you story after story of what Leibrecht has done to me over the past ten years in order to force me out. I refused to go (to play his game) until I decided that it was taking too much of a toll on me spiritually, physically, and psychologically." I urged her not to stay in that toxic environment, but to get out. And she did.

On January 18, 2002, I received a letter from Leibrecht commenting on my words to Reidy. The tradition at The Catholic Center was that a staff party was held when someone left or moved on to another job. I had told Reidy that I didn't want a staff party because it was always a fake occasion. After all the abuse I had received from Leibrecht, I didn't want him standing up and telling the party-goers how great I was and what a great job I did. I told Reidy that I would be happy to accept a check for the amount of money that would be spent on a staff party, or he could have one, but I was not going to be there. Leibrecht wrote, "I told Reidy that we would certainly respect your pleasure on the matter." Enclosed was a check for use during my sabbatical. Leibrecht's letter was full of kind words, falling all over himself to be nice and wishing me all the best and being fraternal! It wasn't sincere, and I knew it.

On April 5, 2002, I inquired about a news release I had sent to Eidson about my new book, *Using Film to Teach New Testament*. I got a two-word reply on April 5, stating, "It isn't." I asked, "Why not? I think I'm owed an answer." I got a reply from her on April 7, telling me that her plans were to do a story on my then-upcoming work in religious education. "I thought your activities during your writing sabbatical would naturally be a part of that piece." Then, there was another paragraph which startled me:

> Oh, and as a personal side note: In light of all the caustic e-mails with me as the subject matter that transpired between you and Ballew-Gonzales and Father Jim Reynolds (among others) at the occasion of my appointment, not to mention all the unsolicited outside verbal commentary to *The Mirror* freelancers and columnists . . . In the future, let's not talk about what you're genuinely owed, shall we?

What I discovered is that The Catholic Center had changed computer servers, and when that was done, all the old deleted e-mails reappeared. Eidson had read all of them; it made no difference to her if they were private or not! I told Reidy about what was done. He told me that he asked her if she read them, and she told him she had not. He believed her rather than the words I had in print. She lied; otherwise, she could not have written the words above in her April 7, 2002, e-mail. No action was ever taken on this issue.

I have often wondered why I continued as editor for fourteen and half years. I continued because I was ministering to people who wanted to learn and grow, no matter what. It was like having a classroom of seventeen thousand students, and I was their teacher. The man who should have been their teacher, Leibrecht, wasn't even a good student—and he had a degree in education! At one point during those years, he asked me to show him how to use a computer. So, one day I went to his office and sat with him in front of his computer. I told him to type in something, and I discovered that he didn't know the keyboard! How could a man make it through high school, college, and post-graduate work without knowing the keyboard? How did he type papers? That was the first and last computer lesson I gave him. I just continued on despite all the negativity until my health could not deal with it anymore. Even my staff would ask about getting something positive from Leibrecht once in a while. Yes, I have a few notes thanking me or there is a paragraph at the end of a nasty memorandum telling me that I was doing a good job, but these are not sincere. The very way they are written or typed on paper betray their honesty. They are like sitting in Leibrecht's office; he always welcomed me to sit on the couch which engulfed a single person while he sat in a large straight-back chair. That was his way of diminishing people by the use of physical environment. A different dynamic arose once I began to pull up the other large straight-back chair and sit opposite him.

Readers will notice basically only negative comments in Leibrecht's letters, memorandums, notes, etc. Even when I brought back journalism awards, no congratulations were ever issued. I outshined Leibrecht, and he couldn't stand it. All insincere recognitions were always attached to nasty notes at the end as though they were after thoughts or an attempt at a complimentary close! Besides the narratives I reveal above, I have a four-inch thick folder of other Leibrecht letters, memorandums, red notes, white notes, etc. A whole book could be written from these to illustrate further the negativity that was generated by him towards me!

Joan Ward

Out of all the people I hired and fired as editor of *The Mirror*, the one who outshines all of them was Joan Ward. When I became editor in 1987, I inherited an outdated system of sharing a secretary with the Religious Education Office. At first the arrangement was half-time for each or two and one-half days a week for each. By 1995, the needs had shifted to four days a week for *The Mirror* and one day a week for religious education. There were other tangled webs—such as joint ownership of a computer, printer, and the percent of rent paid by the office space occupied by the secretary for two different offices. In September 1995 I set out to untangle that web. I wanted a full-time employee who would serve as the Office Manager for *The Mirror*. I knew that this would be a task, but it needed to be done. The opportunity was ripe because the newspaper-religious education secretary was retiring. And I knew who I wanted to replace her.

Ward worked part-time in the financial development office. Over the years both of us had been in The Catholic Center, I had watched her take responsibility for projects and accomplish them. She knew her way around computers, and she knew how to get help if she didn't. I arranged a meeting with her one day and set my proposal before her. She was excited, and so was I. Gradually, a new data system had been brought into the building, the process of printing labels had been changed, bookkeeping for advertising accounts had moved from accounting to *The Mirror*, and a pool of proofreaders needed to be managed. So, after speaking to Ward about all this, on

September 29, 1995, I submitted a detailed proposal of how to accomplish this to the office of administration. And to my surprise it was accepted.

From November 15, 1995, Ward became the office manager for *The Mirror*. It was the best decision that I ever made as editor. She went to work immediately organizing the office. She worked on keeping the database up to date; she collected past-due parish payments and advertising revenues; she organized files; she set goals and objectives for herself and achieved them. "I think the quality of your work is outstanding. More has been done in the past year than I could have ever hoped for," I wrote in her first performance review. She had streamlined the day-to-day work, and that made her available to assume additional responsibilities. Ward could handle people and me. In my dealings with Leibrecht, she often counselled me about how to deal with him. "Pick your battles carefully," I remember her saying. Over the years I shifted more and more of my responsibilities to her. "Ward is doing exactly what I wanted her to do; she's managing the office and helping organize others, especially *The Mirror* staff," I wrote on her performance review. She learned the skills she needed to get her work done. To my knowledge, she did not play office politics; she supported me and kept me on target until I left as editor. A few years after Eidson was named editor, Ward retired.

The Mirror Awards

During my fourteen and one-half years as editor of *The Mirror*, I oversaw the winning of twenty-seven journalism awards. They are: 1990, Associated Church Press Award of Merit for newspaper graphics; 1991, Associated Church Press Award of Honorable Mention for professional resource; 1991, Catholic Press Association third place Journalism Award for best news reporting on a local or state issue; 1992, Associated Church Press Award of Merit for front page; 1994, Associated Church Press Award of Merit for feature article, newspaper or news service; 1994, Catholic Press Association second place Journalism Award for general excellence; 1994, Catholic Press Association second place Journalism Award for best feature story; 1995, Associated Church Press First Place for Best In Class: Regional Newspaper; 1995, Associated Church Press Honorable Mention for department: newspaper/news service; 1995, Associated Church Press Award of Excellence for in-depth coverage, newspaper; 1996, Catholic Press Association Honorable Mention for best seasonal issue: "Christmas"; 1996, Catholic Press Association Third Place for best reporting on a special age group, special issue: "Youth and Youth Ministry"; 1996, Catholic Press Association Third Place for best photo story: "The Holy Land: Ancient and Promised"; 1996, Associated Church Press Award of Merit for professional resource; 1996, Associated Church Press Award of Merit for personal experience, first person account; 1996, Certificate of Commendation, American Psychiatric Association for feature article; 1997, Associated Church Press, Award of Merit for theme issue, section, or series: newspaper/news service; 1997, Associate Church Press, Honorable Mention for newspaper front page;

1997, Associated Church Press, Honorable Mention for photography with article or cutline: newspaper, newsletter or news service; 1998, Catholic Press Association, First Place, best one shot special section—specific situation, event or issue: "Prayer"; 1998, Catholic Press Association, Third Place for best regular column (spiritual life) "Passages" by Robert Hodgson, Jr.; 1999, Catholic Press Association, Honorable Mention for "Family Graces" by Mary Hood-Hart; 2000, Catholic Press Association, Second Place for feature writing, "Take a Hike, See God's Canvas" by Dan Rice; 2001, Associated Church Press, Award of Merit for Letters to the Editor; 2001, Associated Church Press, Award of Excellence for Theological Reflection; 2002, Catholic Press Association, Honorable Mention for best personality profile, "Changing Perspective: Jackson Native Peace Corps Volunteer in Morocco" by Karla S. Essner; 2002, Catholic Press Association, Honorable Mention for Best Front Page Tabloid.

Know Myself

In 1986, after having taught in McAuley Regional High School from 1978 to 1985, and after having run an adult education program for a year, I decided to jump into the know-myself-better programs. I began with the Myers-Briggs Type Indicator. I began by answering the 126 questions which would yield a type once their answers were scored. I discovered that I was an INTJ. The I indicated that I was an introvert, relating more easily to the inner world of ideas than to the outer world of people and things. The N indicated that I used my intuition more than my senses; I would rather look for possibilities and relationships than work with known facts. My ability to think was represented by the T; I based my judgments more on impersonal analysis and logic than on personal values. The J indicated that I had a judging attitude; I liked a planned, decided, orderly way of life better than a flexible, spontaneous way.

The explanation on the back of the Myers-Briggs report form informed me that INTJs usually have original minds and great drive for their own ideas and purposes. I did not yet have a clue as to how true that was. In fields that appeal to them, INTJs have a fine power to organize a job and carry it through with or without help. How true that was about my seven years of teaching in McAuley High School. How true that would be during my tenure as editor of *The Mirror*. And my organizations skills would shine during my thirty years of teaching in Missouri State University (formerly Southwest Missouri State University) even while I was founding a new parish in Nixa, Missouri, and cleaning up messes left by former pastors in Mountain Grove, Cabool, and Shell Knob. The Myers-Briggs report form identified me as skeptical, critical, independent, determined, and often stubborn. Those characteristics gave me the ability to minister, teach, and write books. I'm not sure that I ever learned to yield less important points in order to win the most important points as the report indicated.

My quest for self-knowledge continued in 1987 in learning about Neuro-Linguistic Programming (NLP) and attending a workshop on it in Des Moines, Iowa.

NLP is considered to be a pseudoscientific approach to communication, personal development, and psychotherapy. It was developed in the 1970s. Its creators—Richard Bandler and John Grinder—claim there is a connection between neurological processes (neuro-), language (linguistic) and behavioral patterns learned through experience (programming), and that these can be changed to achieve specific goals in life. NLP methodology suggests that a person can model the skills of exceptional people, allowing anyone to acquire those skills. I was interested in NLP because the two nuns I worked with in St. Mary Parish, Joplin (1978–1980), were trained in it.

The workshop raised my awareness concerning the language I used about sight, hearing, feeling, smelling, and tasting. I was taught about eye-accessing cues, which indicate if another accesses information by seeing, by hearing, or by feeling. I learned about anchoring, the experience of remembering something because of a certain place. Throughout my teaching career I used this to remember my students' names by asking them to sit in the same seat while I created a seating chart. I also taught students that they would use their seat in my class to access the information I taught. I learned about body language, not only my own, but how to read that of others and mirror it back to them in moments of agreement. The power of words, what we would refer to as their connotations, was also covered in the workshop.

I have never stopped using what I learned in that two-day workshop. We receive and process experiences through our five senses (neuro-). We assign meaning to those experiences in both verbal and non-verbal communication systems (linguistic), which are coded and ordered in our brains. We have the ability to organize our communication and neurological systems to achieve specific, desired outcomes (programming). This workshop taught me awareness about myself and how to be aware of others' response to me.

In 1990, I began to explore the Enneagram. I attended several workshops and completed the Enneagram Inventory to discover that I was a type eight personality. The explanation of a type eight was labeled challenger. The interpretation states that type eight people prided themselves on being strong and powerful. They are quite confident, fearless, and assertive in grappling with problems and mobilizing others for good causes. According to the interpretation, type eight folks may lack strength to confront their own weakness and insecurity. In work or ministry, they are natural leaders who welcome difficult tasks, especially those that pertain to justice. Their emphasis on strength and confrontation reflects the power of God and Jesus' confrontation of injustice. According to the interpretation, I needed to learn to be vulnerable, like Jesus, who, through the power of God, assumed the weakness of the human condition.

In 2012, I explored the Boundary Questionnaire, a tool designed to show a person where he or she possibly falls on a continuum between a thick boundary and a thin boundary. The 146 questions cover twelve categories, such as sleep, thoughts and feelings, sensitivity, neatness, and opinions about a lot of different things. The end result of the scoring is a number that places one on the above-mentioned continuum. It did not surprise me that I fell in between the thick boundary and the middle of the continuum.

When not participating in such standard tools for self-knowledge, I learned a lot more about myself, my likes and dislikes, by reading the works of M. Scott Peck and Wayne Dyer. I also read extensively about personality types, the Enneagram, NLP, and much more. I reached the conclusion through my reading and study that it was OK for me to be me!

Then I discovered James Fowler's stages of faith psychology which described me as a universalizer. Not only did I understand myself better, but I began to understand why others couldn't understand me. There are very few universalizers; most people do not get to this stage of faith. Universalizers seek inclusive justice and the realization of love, according to Fowler. We spend ourselves transforming the present reality in the direction of transcendent actuality. We are not normal as viewed by others. We possess an enlarged vision of universal community and possess ultimate respect for being. Without meaning to, we are experienced as subversive of religious—and other—structures, often dying at the hands of those we hope to change and being more honored after death that during life. We love life, yet hold it loosely. We see truth where others cannot, and we can live with the paradox of multiple truths. Because we see the largest picture possible, we often possess blind spots. Fowler argues that we do not seek this stage of adult faith; rather, we are drawn to it by the providence of God. We see what life is meant to be and live toward it. So, we oppose unjust structures, feel a sense of homelessness here, and yearn for the absolute value of the kingdom of God. As I studied Fowler, I discovered myself set free to be me and to pursue justice.

Chaplain of St. Anne Carmelite Monastery: Accident

I had no more than been named editor of *The Mirror*, and I was asked to serve as chaplain at the St. Anne Carmelite Monastery, consisting of eight nuns behind a grill (screen). At first in 1987 I was to assist the pastor of Immaculate Conception Parish, Springfield, who was responsible for providing the nuns with a chaplain. A year later, I was appointed chaplain of the Carmelite Monastery with the help of Rev. Gregory Zatina, who was supposed to organize who went there for Mass; Zatina left active priestly ministry. In 1989, McDevitt was supposed to provide some help for me at the Carmel. I continued as chaplain for one more year, and then I resigned because I could not take it anymore.

I said Mass at an altar facing eight nuns behind a screen with a few other people in attendance behind me. Those others were not supposed to be there; they should have been in their parishes. The liturgies were lifeless. It was like having two different congregations—because they were!—and neither participated to any degree. For my own spiritual life, I gave a letter to Leibrecht explaining why I was resigning instead of waiting for several months, as he wanted me to do. The albatross around my neck had been released. I had one principal responsibility, and that was *The Mirror*, and that is all I wanted. That had been to what Leibrecht and I had agreed in 1987, but he had added on the chaplaincy. One door was left open, however; he had never written a letter of appointment. Thus, he could not be upset with me.

On a rainy morning in January 1987 I went to the Carmel for Mass. I didn't know that the rain had frozen on the steps when I walked out of the sacristy after Mass. I walked on the sidewalk towards my Isuzu and I slipped off of the two steps coated with ice. I rolled down the small embankment, and came to stop. There was no one around, and I knew that no sister would ever see me lying on the ground. So, I forced myself to get up, got the scraper out of the Isuzu, remove the ice from the windshield, and drove home. Immediately, I called my friend Chris Haik, who was also my landlord and a nurse. She rushed over, informed me that I was going into shock, and took me to the emergency room of St. John's Hospital (now Mercy Hospital).

A nurse was appointed to start an IV drip. First, she tried finding a vein in my left elbow, then, when she couldn't get one, in my right elbow, and she couldn't get one. Another nurse tried the top of my left hand with failure for the third time. Finally, Haik intervened and told them to get a nurse who knew how to find veins that moved. A nurse got one on my right hand. I needed to get x-rays to be sure that I had not broken anything. Finally, a dye was injected into my IV while a series of x-rays were taken. The doctor announced that other than being bruised, I had a contusion in my right hip. I was given muscle relaxers and dismissed. Haik took me home with her and put me to bed in her guest room for a few days. When I called the Carmelites in the afternoon to tell them what had happened, they were not concerned about me; all they wanted to know was who was going to come the next day to say Mass for them. I told them that I did not know; I had called the chancellor, and it was up to him to find someone.

In either 1987 or 1988, my sister, her husband, and their three children came to Springfield to join me for Thanksgiving. I told the Carmelites that they were coming and that I wanted them to meet each other. At first the Carmelites did not want to meet my sister's family; the superior told me that they preferred not to do so. I insisted. So, after Mass on Thanksgiving morning, my sister, her family, and I went to the parlor and with a screen between the Carmelites and us met each other. The Sisters asked a few questions of my nieces and nephew, and that was it. The meeting was over.

While still a chaplain at Carmel, on March 31, 1988, Father William Rochford, the pastor of Holy Trinity Parish, Marshfield, Missouri, died. I lived with Rochford in Joplin at St. Peter Rectory from 1979 to 1983. After the funeral, Leibrecht asked me to go to the parish for weekend Masses. The first weekend I went there I discovered that that there was a Saturday evening Mass and two Sunday morning Masses, and that was one more Mass that the parishioners needed. When Leibrecht asked me to go there, he also asked if I wanted to be appointed as the pastoral administrator, and I told him to appoint the nun who worked in the parish as the parish life coordinator, which he did. After the first weekend, I told the nun to meet with the parish council and decide which two Masses they wanted for a weekend; I was not going to continue with three. At first she objected, saying that was a decision the future pastor should make; I told her that I would say two Masses per weekend. The next weekend, she informed me that we would have a Saturday evening Mass and one on Sunday morning. I continued as the supply priest after Rochford died for three months until Father Thomas Kiefer was appointed pastor. Over thirty years later, Kiefer continues to thank me for having cancelled one Sunday Mass instead of leaving it for him to do.

In August of 1998, while still editor of *The Mirror*, I went back to Marshfield one weekend between the resignation of one pastor and the arrival of another one only for the weekends; my job was to smooth out issues left by the former leader. The first Saturday evening I got there after the former pastor's resignation, I was met by the parish council president, who filled me in on what was going on. She and I, assisted by others, put the church back in the renovated state it had four years before. In a letter to the new weekend pastor on August 17, 1998, I wrote, "There has been a lot of division in the parish over the past two years and about half of the people left." After discussing other matters that I thought the new weekend pastor should know, I wished him well, telling him, "The people are looking forward to you being with them. They were asking me about you after both Masses."

Likewise, in between my two stints in Marshfield I spent six weekends going to St. Francis de Sales Parish in Lebanon, Missouri. One pastor left before the next one was scheduled to arrive. The first Saturday evening I was there, fully aware that the previous pastor was noted for hurrying the Mass to make it as short as possible, I began my homily and a man seated in the back of the church got up and proceeded to walk down the aisle toward the altar. I remember his shoes clicking on the floor. When he got to the altar, he genuflected, walked over to a candle stand, dropped in several coins—the clinking of the metal coins in the metal collection box could be heard throughout the church—lit a candle, knelt, prayed, got up, returned to the center aisle, genuflected, and turned around to return to his place. I had stopped talking when he dropped the coins into the metal collection box. After he genuflected and turned around, I asked him, "Do you do this during Mass every Saturday?" And he replied, "I do!" I said, "This is the last Saturday you will do it as long as I am here." He walked back to his place in the church. I don't know what happened to him or even if he came to Mass as long as I was there, but no one got up to light a candle during my homily for the next five weeks. After Mass several parishioners congratulated me, saying that needed to be done a long time ago.

House Living 1986–2002

In 1986, while involved in adult religious education, I left the Seton Rectory and moved to a rental house on Lois Street in Springfield. It was a two-bedroom, one-bathroom home. One bedroom became my office. I had a living room that opened up into a dining room, a small kitchen, and a one-car garage. My library, which had continued to grow, was spread through every room, lining the walls with books. Anything that would not fit in the house was stored in the garage. I lived in that house until the end of 1994.

In 1994 the finance officer, Janet Smith, approached me one day in The Catholic Center—the name given to the renovated high school to which the chancery offices and *The Mirror* moved in 1989—and asked me if I was interested in living in property owned by the diocese on National Avenue in Springfield. It had once been the home for three Jesuit priests followed by the home of a nun. I said that I wanted to see it before I agreed to live in it.

The diocesan property manager and the finance officer and I agreed on a day and a time to view the property. It was in terrible shape; a different color of carpet in every room sewn together under archways from room to room; doors only on bedrooms and bathrooms; a huge window air conditioner in every room; dark drapes permitting no light to enter the space; cracked plaster everywhere, especially around the fireplaces; a tub with no shower; and on and on. After touring the facility, I said that I would move into it if it were fixed up, but that I was not moving into a dump. So, the diocese got a contractor and pumped about thirty-thousand dollars into it.

The old boiler and radiators were removed and central heat and air conditioning were installed. All the windows were replaced and mini-blinds installed instead of curtains. The green kitchen cabinets were painted white. I picked out the carpet that was installed in every room of the house along with the paint for the walls. When the house was finished in the fall of 1994, I agreed to move in after Christmas, or early 1995.

I thought I was moving into a mansion. The home had a den, three bedrooms, a bathroom and a half bathroom, a very long living room, a dining room, a large kitchen, a utility room, and closets in every bedroom. I was able to have a large office/library, a bedroom, and a guest room. A large group of people could gather in the living room, and one or two could meet in the den. Friends, who had raised seven children, gave me their huge dining room table, which fit perfectly in the dining room. What had been my dining room table in the previous house fit in the kitchen in a breakfast area!

I liked living in that house, and would have stayed there longer than the eight years I lived there if I could have gotten the diocese to do a few things that I wanted done. I wanted the unused front porch turned into a sun room. I wanted the back door and the garage connected with a breezeway. As appliances, like the hot water heater, went out, instead of the property manager overseeing the installation of the new one, it became my responsibility. When plaster began to fall from around the fireplace and I reported it, nothing was done about it. The southwest corner of the house's foundation was sinking, but no one cared. After I moved in, I had cleaned up the huge front and back yards, removing brush that had grown over the years when the house sat empty. While I was learning new home repair skills—like plastering—all my work was not for my benefit. And I knew who would be blamed for not having things repaired when the day came for me to move out.

My Home

So, after my neighbor—who had become a good friend—to the west of me died in the fall of 2001, I marshaled my financial resources and made an offer to her relatives to purchase her house. I had thought about buying a house for a while, as I wanted a place to retire to one day. I knew everything about the house next door on Stanford, as I had often changed light bulbs or helped in other ways.

In the year before she died, the lady who lived in it, Allegra Mahler, had a new roof put on it and a new sewer hook-up installed. Three years before she died, she had the back porch turned into an enclosed sun porch and had the whole house electrically rewired. The house was small, except for the sun porch, but it did have a basement with a full bathroom. Upstairs there was a living room, a dining room, two bedrooms, a bathroom, and a kitchen with a breakfast nook. It was perfect for me.

Mahler's family—nephew and niece-in-law—accepted my offer, and I bought it in May 2002. I was able to pay for it by selling my Wal-Mart stock, cashing in a few certificates of deposit I had, and using my savings. I immediately applied for a home equity loan so that I could renovate it. Before anything was moved into it, I got a contractor who agreed to begin my renovation plans while I worked on getting the home equity loan; I now refer to this as phase one renovation plans. A double set of doors was walled shut from the living room to one of the bedrooms, which I turned into an office. French doors were hung from the entrance to the dining room from the living room, and a single French door was hung in the entrance from the dining room to my office. The breakfast nook was removed in the small kitchen, and cabinets with a counter top were installed. Since the former owner had the whole house wallpapered a few years before, I kept most of the walls as they were, except for the dining room and kitchen, which I had pained an off white. Also, all the woodwork throughout the house was painted white.

In the basement, only one half was finished; that is where I put my library and a home chapel. On the other side, I had a fourth of the basement finished near the bathroom, and that room became the guest room. The other fourth served as the utility room with washer and dryer, the filing cabinet room, and extra library room. Because the renovations had not cost as much as I had anticipated, I had shelves built in the two-car garage/shop and a potting shed built behind the garage.

Friends helped me move in July 20, 2002, from one house to the one next door! I knew where every item was going to be put. Furthermore, I had spent part of the summer preparing the bookshelves for the basement and getting the library in order; the books were on the shelves. After spending the morning moving, a friend served lunch in the backyard to all the workers. Most of them then left, but a few stayed around to help with specific small projects.

Finally, late in the afternoon, everyone left, and I realized that I was not just home, but I was in my home. I had never felt so secure in my life. I had years of work ahead of me to make flower gardens and vegetable gardens. I had a home equity loan in the amount of about fifty thousand dollars that needed to be paid. But I was in my home, and I loved it.

After getting settled on July 30, 2002, I wrote a letter to Leibrecht explaining that I had moved. I listed the condition of the house on South National Avenue, and I explained that I could not get the man in charge of diocesan properties to take care of it. According to Leibrecht's August 2, 2002, letter, "The underlying issue is whether a diocesan priest can independently of the bishop simply move wherever he himself decides." That was not the issue. I had never been assigned to live in the house on National Avenue; so, there was little he could do about it. In an August 13, 2002, letter I explained: "I possess no official letter of assignment to live at that diocesan property. If my memory serves me correctly, I was asked if I would live there, about eight years ago, if the property was improved. I agreed to do so." I continued: "If I would have had an official letter of assignment, I would have asked your permission to move." I explained: "When I agreed to live at the South National Avenue property, there was enough per diem to maintain that house. When the per diem was cut, I was placed in financial double jeopardy. It takes more than $350 a month to supply and maintain that large house." In my August 13, 2002, letter, I also listed in an eight-line paragraph the obligations that the diocese did not meet on my signed renter's agreement.

On August 19, 2002, Leibrecht had to admit that "there is no document of assignment, but that makes the assignment no less valid." The logic of that statement leaves the reader wondering. According to him, now the issue "is about contact, whether verbal or written, about the permission you need from the bishop to change residences." Also, he asked me who the landlord was of the house in which I was now living. On August 21, 2002, I wrote, "I am the landlord." His response was to write me a letter, assigning me to live in my own house! When I told my best friend, Reynolds, about this, he just laughed!

After the first phase of renovations to my home built in 1918, I had a home equity loan of about fifty thousand dollars to pay off. Every extra nickel went to decreasing that loan. By 2007, I was ready for phase two, which consisted of both outdoor and indoor work.

The exposed roof joists needed to be either painted or covered; I chose metal covering. The open front porch was enclosed, and the outside was covered in vinyl siding. The front porch was, basically, useless until I enclosed it. When it rained, the water blew in. When it snowed, the snow piled up on it. By enclosing it, putting in windows and a glass door, and creating a place for the postal carrier and package delivery persons to put parcels, I made it a useful room. About a year later, I had an electric heater installed on it so I could keep house plants there during the winter.

After removing the green indoor-outdoor carpet from the front porch and the front steps, the steps were discovered to be cracked in many places. My contractor for this second phase of renovation, Wade Flaming from Executive Remodeling Concepts, employed the services of a man who specialized in old houses. He showed up one evening with a sledge hammer. He swung the hammer one time hitting the steps. They immediately crumbled into a heap of cement, bricks, rocks, and other leftover building materials. Then he told me that is how people used to make steps; they would pile together rocks, bricks, and lots of other things and pour cement over the pile, creating the steps. In time, moisture would get into the pile and cause the cement to crack and break apart. That was exactly what had happened here. So, once the pile of rubble was hauled away, the forms for a new set of steps—complete with rebar—were prepared and concrete was poured.

All windows in the house were replaced with double-pane, double-hung, vinyl windows. The putty was falling out of the old windows, which were protected by old storm windows whose plastic pieces were deteriorated; the storm windows would not stay in their tracks and were easily moved by the wind. Flaming told me that no one repaired old windows anymore. Furthermore, the old windows' ropes that led to a weighted counterbalance were all rotted. So, the spaces were measured and new windows were ordered and installed.

The concrete foundation of the house had been plastered over and painted. Flaming's man, who specialized in the renovation of old houses, informed me about the plaster and the paint that would never stay stuck because plaster absorbs moisture. So, I agreed that the plaster had to be removed and the outdoor basement walls covered with a cement finish. I told the man to match the mortar between the bricks with the finish to be applied to the foundation. In this way, the white foundation was removed, the cement was sealed, and the mortar matched everywhere.

The four basement windows—each a different size and each constructed differently—were replaced with insulated blocks of glass. A new faucet was installed on the kitchen sick, and latches were installed on several kitchen cabinets in order to keep the doors shut.

Maybe the largest renovation of all was the removal of all the carpet in the house, the linoleum in the kitchen, and the covering on the stairs from the basement to the kitchen; all was replaced with ceramic tile. Beginning with the living room, furniture was moved to another room in the house or to the garage. The carpet and its pad were removed and hauled away. Concrete board was cut and nailed to the wood subfloor. Then, the ceramic tile was glued down and grouted. Once a room was finished, the furniture was brought back into it, and the process of removing furniture from another room, removing carpet, putting down concrete board, and setting tile continued. It took the tiler a month to finish every room in the house.

While the gutters were removed for work to be done on the exposed roof joists, it rained, and water began to come into the basement, where there had been no water for all the years that I had lived there. Cracks were discovered in the foundation; those needed to be repaired. The year 2007 was very rainy and lots of water came into the basement. So, in order to keep this from happening again, two large sump pumps were installed. This did not solve the entire problem; so, in 2008, two small sump pumps were installed in the lowest points of the basement floor and hoses were run from them to the two large sump pumps. Later, in 2017 two more small pumps which sit on the floor with hoses to the sump pumps were purchased for use in other low areas of the basement. That fixed the problem of water in the basement.

Other minor renovations of phase two included the installation of a door bell for the front door, a new dusk-to-dawn light near the garage, new house numbers both on the front of the house and over the garage, painting exposed basement walls inside where cracks had been repaired, installation of a control joint along a wall of the house to stop the cracking in the mortar, and the installation of a new metal rail along the new front steps. I sanded and painted the gutters so they could be reused, and I sanded and painted the two wooden awnings over the windows on either side of the fireplace since they were custom made.

By the middle of July when all the renovation work had been completed, I had spent over forty-four thousand dollars, and I was back in debt to U.S. Bank with my home equity loan. I did not know that a year later my best friend, Reynolds, would die and leave me stock, which when liquidated resulted in sixty thousand dollars. In 2008, I used part of that money to pay off my home equity loan and dedicated a room to Reynold's memory.

This meant that phase three of renovation could be done. So, in July 2008, Flaming began work on several projects. Because rain was blowing through some of the sun porch windows, the roof needed to be extended by several feet in order to create a little veranda. This was accomplished with white corrugated PCV panels; they let in light but kept out rain. Any exposed wood, such as the sun porch and garage were covered with vinyl siding. Two new white metal garage doors were installed, and two double-hung, vinyl windows were installed in the garage to replace the old metal and glass windows. A gate was built and installed on the east side of the garage. The two smaller sump pumps, already mentioned, were installed in the basement. A wooden privacy fence was installed between me and my neighbor to the west; she failed to trim a line of bushes that fell into my yard and made it very hard to mow; the fence was designed to keep the bushes out of my yard. Furthermore, I installed flower gardens all along the fence; I accomplished that feat by the end of the summer.

The cost of the second phase of renovation was almost sixteen thousand dollars; part of it was paid with Reynolds's gift, and a part of it was paid over the next year. In November of 2008, I had the sun porch roof—made of tar paper—replaced and sealed for an additional eight hundred dollars.

In 2009, I bought a two-thousand-dollar outbuilding and had the interior finished as a hot tub room for $4,400. The hot tub had been purchased a year or two before and sat in the garage until I had it moved into its new home. In the meantime, I developed a skin disease that did not like the chemicals that needed to be added to the hot tub water. So, I sold the hot tub a few years later and turned the room into a library annex, using the money from the sale to buy book shelves.

By 2010 I was debt free again, but I was interested in an addition to the sun porch with a fountain in it. After meeting with Flaming, we designed an additional space to be added on to the sun porch in which would be placed a cascading water feature constructed of native rocks. The 8' X 14' room needed to have two drains that ran under its concrete floor in order not to form a dam in the back yard. The area was excavated, the drains were installed, and the concrete foundation poured. Windows were installed all around, while the outside was covered in vinyl siding to match the rest of the house. A few other minor repairs to things in the house—such as replacing a three-way light switch and faucet replacements in the upstairs bathroom—are included in the twenty-four-thousand-dollar total. No more work could be done until that home equity loan was paid.

My home equity loan was paid off by the end of 2012. I had been using the sauna at the fitness center with no reaction from my skin disease. So, I decided to have a custom outdoor sauna installed. I began by purchasing an outbuilding. Then, Flaming and his crew took over. They turned it into an outdoor sauna, complete with a dressing area, cedar walls and benches, a glass door, and other necessary things. The total cost was over twenty-thousand dollars.

The only room in the house that had never been touched, except for painting in 2002, was the upstairs bathroom. I could not decide what I wanted to do in there. Finally, a plan emerged. Flaming was in charge of the renovation. The tub was removed and a custom walk-in shower was built out of cultured marble. In order to accomplish this, a wall had to be built partially in front of the bathroom window, which hung partially over the tub; the tub was removed. Between the new and old wall, a very small linen closet was created. White wooden cabinets were built and installed on either side of the medicine chest to match those found in the kitchen; they have an open shelf area on the bottom and doors on the top all the way to the ceiling. A new sink was made of cultured marble to match the new shower. Other things included a new electrical outlet, and using the old white tile from the tub area to finish off any other area in the room. The pink floor tile was not disturbed, nor was the toilet. Everything was painted white.

In order to accomplish this project, I had chosen a cultured marble titled salt and pepper. It was almost black, but bordered more on gray. The color scheme for the bathroom was to be black and white. New plumbing had to be done. A new wall had to be built and a subfloor for the shower had to be installed. The new counter top had to be made. Flaming had two weeks to get the renovation done, but it took two additional months to get the renovations finished. I had to wait and wait to get the splash guard for the sink installed and for minor repairs to be done to the cabinets. This fourteen-thousand-dollar renovation almost cost Flaming his job as my home contractor. I had worked with the man since 2007, and I had never experienced such inability to finish a project.

Once the bathroom renovation was paid, a new roof was put on the sun porch in 2016. The old corrugated veranda roof could not be replaced, so a roof extension was built with soffit to match the rest of the house before the new white roof was installed. Also, new rain gutters were installed to replace the paint-peeling old ones. Finally, brown edging was installed on the stairway tiles both to protect their edges and to give me a clear view of where the step was located. In 2018, new dusk-to-dawn lights were installed over the sun porch entrance and front porch entrance, along with other miscellaneous repairs that needed to be made, such as replacement of an outdoor water faucet and two rubber thresholds on doors. For all practical purposes my home was ready for my retirement!

Death of Parents

While recuperating from my fall at the Carmelite Monastery in 1987, my father died. Because of the contusion I suffered from that fall, I was not able to drive. In order to get out of a chair, I had to place my right leg on top of the left one and raise myself out of a chair with my arms. I asked the chancellor to find someone to drive me to my hometown so I could celebrate my father's wake and funeral Mass; he did. Moving very slowly I led the wake service and prepared for the funeral Mass the next day. I asked Father Paul McLoughlin to serve as Master of Ceremonies for the Mass because I knew there would be other priests present; Leibrecht also informed me that he would be present.

During my father's funeral Mass, I used the account of the death of Jesus in Mark's Gospel. The theme there is abandonment; Jesus is abandoned by all his disciples before he is crucified. My homily was about the feeling of abandonment my father had experienced in his life with his many health issues, the primary one being Parkinson's Disease. However, abandonment leads to new life, and that was what we were celebrating with my father's funeral Mass. After Communion, Leibrecht said the prayers for the final commendation. But before he said those prayers, he had to say something. He proceeded to bring in John's Gospel, which contains the unique scene of Jesus entrusting his mother to the beloved disciple and the disciple he loved to his mother. In other words, Leibrecht completely dismantled my homily by placing Mary at the foot of the cross to negate the theme of abandonment that I had presented. I couldn't believe what I was hearing, as Leibrecht supposedly corrected my homily.

In 1995, after suffering heart and kidney failure my mother died. Again, I asked McLoughlin to serve as Master of Ceremonies for the funeral Mass. A number of priests from both the Archdiocese of St. Louis and the Diocese of Springfield-Cape Girardeau were present for the funeral Mass. Leibrecht had informed me that he would be there, too. He was going to be in Cape Girardeau for the weekend before the funeral Mass. I gave him the time. The priests were vested and in place. The hearse with the coffin and my brothers and sisters and others were outside and ready for the procession into the church, but there was no bishop. So, after waiting a few minutes, we began without him. He showed up during the Liturgy of the Word. McLoughlin slipped into the sacristy and helped him get ready, then at an opportune time led him to his place in the sanctuary. After the Mass was finished and we formed a procession to the cemetery, he apologized for being late. I knew that he was late because of me; he always had to downplay me in order to elevate himself and make himself important!

LIMEX

After having been involved in various ways in adult religious education for years, I decided to pursue LIMEX in 1996. LIMEX—Loyola's Institute for Ministry Extension Program—consisted of ten master's level courses with each course containing ten sessions. It was a local cohort program; this meant that a small group of people would be committed to each other for all ten sessions—each lasting three hours—of each course. If a session had to be missed because of an emergency, the person missing it had to gather two other members of the cohort and make up the session before the next scheduled meeting. At the end of the course, a researched reflective essay was produced and sent to a reader at Loyola University, New Orleans, Louisiana. The reader assigned a letter grade to the paper which became the grade given for the course. A number of cohorts had been formed in the Diocese of Springfield-Cape Girardeau. Since I was involved in adult religious education, I decided that I wanted to find out what this adult education training program was all about.

I had asked Leibrecht if the diocese would pay the tuition for this program, since I was doing this to become a better religious educator. He refused to pay the five hundred dollar per course expense, but agreed that the diocese would pay half of it. His reasons were that I would benefit personally; therefore, my personal benefit was worth one-half the cost of the tuition that I would pay! I was not pleased with his decision, but I wanted to experience the program; thus, I paid one half of the cost of each course.

The Springfield LIMEX cohort began in February 1997; there was an organization meeting in January. The eight or ten of us—I don't' remember how many—gathered with one of us who served as the facilitator for our first session. Each three-hour session began with sharing the answers to questions that we had written after reading the assigned material. Usually there was a video to watch and questions for discussion about it. After a short break with refreshments supplied by members of the cohort on a rotation basis, there may have been a total group activity or smaller groups that fed into a total group activity based on what was read, discussed, and learned in the session. At the end of each session the facilitator gave us our assigned readings and questions to prepare for the next session.

I belonged to a very aggressive group; the members decided that they could get through three courses a year. Thus, after finishing course ten in the spring of 2000, we graduated from the program. I did not go to the graduation ceremony in New Orleans because I already had a master's degree in religious studies. At a point near the end of the general program, we had to decide exactly in what each of us wanted to major. I chose adult education; that meant that I had to pursue materials alone and file a report about what I had read with the final paper for the course, integrating something from my private learning into the required paper. I earned a Master's Degree in Adult Religious Education as a result.

I remember spending many weekends reading the assigned material for the next session of a course and preparing answers for the questions which accompanied the reading for the weeknight upon which we had agreed to meet from 6 p.m. to 9 p.m. Some of the reading reconnected me to my days in classes at St. Meinrad School of Theology; I became aware of how well I had learned and was now relearning the material. Some material was new, and it had to be read carefully and methodically in order to spark an idea to research for the next paper due at the end of a course.

Needless to say, the members of the cohort to which I belonged became good friends through their commitment to each other. I remember a number of times inviting them to come to my home in order to discuss our final paper topic for each course. We would sit in my living room and present the topic we were preparing to write about. Since I was a writer, I would help each person develop a thesis statement and outline in order to ensure success for the paper. Through dialogue, discussion, and clarification, we helped each other through the program. Along the way of the three years together, a few people dropped out of the program, decided that it was not meeting their needs any longer, or moved because of work. The six of us who finished the program served as teachers, and all of us served as students. This was very different from the classes I continued to teach at SMSU (now MSU) while also serving as editor of *The Mirror*. Most of the members of the cohort moved away once the course was finished. There is one with whom I remain in contact: Cyndi Berry.

Silver Jubilee

Near the end of the twentieth century I began to plan for my twenty-fifth anniversary of ordination to the priesthood. I was editor of *The Mirror* and not associated with any parish, and, thus, there was no place for me to hold a celebration. Most clergy mark twenty-five years with a Mass in their parish and a dinner that follows. As I thought about all this, I decided that I would host an adult education event. I could use facilities at The Catholic Center, called the Pallotti Center—since I worked there—for the adult education conference and St. Agnes Cathedral Chapel for the Mass that would follow it. I submitted a twenty-fifth anniversary category in my budget for *The Mirror* in the spring of 2000 to cover the cost of my celebration in 2001. The Diocesan Director of Finance told me that Leibrecht had not approved that category. His philosophy was that no priest working at The Catholic Center would have his anniversary celebration covered by his budget.

Needless to write, I was upset by this. I had been the editor of an award-winning newspaper since 1987, and I couldn't believe that my silver jubilee would not be supported by the very institution I served. If I had been in a parish, the celebration would have been paid for by the parishioners. So, I decided to take my celebration to a hotel in Springfield. After meeting with several hotel management staff members in various places, I settled on the Quality Inn (which became a Days Inn) and signed a contract on May 20, 2000, for the use of meeting rooms and the serving of lunch to those who attended the all-day conference.

The meeting and banquet reservation agreement listed the order for the day. Continental Breakfast would be served at 8:30 a.m. in one of the four sections of the meeting room. The other three sections would be arranged using all four sides. The musicians and choir were located behind the ambo at one short end. At the opposite end was the altar with chairs for attendees behind it. On one long end were chairs with the presider's chair located among three or four rows of other chairs but highlighted with the rug upon which it sat. Across from the priest's chair were three or four rows of chairs for attendees. The space was used both for the conference presentations and for Mass that brought the day to an end.

Melissa Bosso served as my second in command for the day. She supervised the continental breakfast and dealt with issues that arose behind the scenes. Ken Pesek served as Master of Ceremonies for the conference; he introduced speakers and kept everything on time. Hospitality was provided by Jan Smith, who was assisted by Joan Ward, Nancy Derryberry, and Jim and Dorothy Askren.

I had chosen the theme for the day as early as 1999—Understanding Mark and His Gospel—when I wrote to five friends and asked them to give presentations on aspects of Mark's Gospel. In the conference space, three adult education presentations were given in the morning: Robert Hodgson, who worked for the American Bible Society, gave an overview of the structure of Mark's Gospel. Bernard Brandon Scott, who was the Darbeth Distinguished Professor of New Testament at the Phillips Theological Seminary on the campus of the University of Tulsa and my professor of New Testament in St. Meinrad School of Theology, spoke about parables. The good news that God's kingdom has come near was addressed by Mark Given, a colleague in the Religious Studies Department at Southwest Missouri State University (now Missouri State University).

Following the three morning conferences, lunch was served on the Terrace in Days Inn to 130 or more people. Before leaving the conference hall, my first-grade teacher,

Sister Laura Magowan, CCVI, said the lunchtime prayer. Margaret Bishop served as the luncheon supervisor; she was assisted by the luncheon seaters: Jerry and June Beck, Sheri Kinler, and Raamah Crim. After the hour break for lunch, Charles W. Hedrick, another colleague from the Religious Studies Department at SMSU (now MSU), gave a presentation on healings and miracles in Mark's Gospel. Discipleship in Mark's Gospel was addressed by Pauline Nugent, CCVI, professor of modern and classical languages at SMSU (now MSU). After a thirty-minute break during which everyone exited the hall, all regathered for the Celebration of Evening Prayer and Eucharist.

As they re-entered the hall, they were greeted by teams of foot washers under the leadership of Robin Zeka and Cyndi Love (now Berry). As each person stopped, sat down, and removed his or her shoes and socks, his or her feet were washed and dried with a towel while Mary Beth Wittry, director of music from Immaculate Conception Parish, Springfield, conducted the choir from the same parish, along with all present, in singing two songs from Taize: "Let Us Sing to the Lord" and "Veni Sancte Spiritus (Come, Holy Spirit)." In the "Ministers for the Conference, Evening Prayer, and Eucharist" pamphlet I had prepared for the day, I wrote that foot-washing "serves as a reminder that our common Christian vocation of service springs from another bath—baptism. All of us are simultaneous foot-washers and foot-washees. When it comes to Christian ministry, each of us is a channel through which God's power flows."

Once the foot washing was completed, I went and sat in my chair vested in a new chasuble made by Dorothy Askren and June Beck, while all others found a seat. After a few minutes of silence, we rose and sang the gathering hymn: "Go Up to the Altar of God." After the usual greeting and introduction, we sat and sang Evening Prayer together. "Our prayer is God's work for us, not our work for God," I wrote in the pamphlet. "Through the psalms and the canticle, we praise God for God's wonderful saving acts among us." I urged everyone to let the words wash over them like water. Incense was placed on charcoal in a large clay pot by Laura Vinyard, as we sang: "Like burning incense, Lord, let my prayer rise up to you." In the pamphlet, I wrote, "Let the incense carry the prayer from your center to God. Let God pray in you." After a psalm prayer, a part of Psalm 103 was sung, followed by a psalm prayer, and then we sang Revelation 19:1–7, which was followed with a psalm prayer.

Once the psalms and canticle of Evening Prayer were finished, the Glory to God was begun by the choir and all present joined in the refrain. Following the Opening Prayer, Jeremiah 1:4–10 was proclaimed by Matthew S. Miller. All joined in the Responsorial Psalm 90, then John Kossler read 1 Corinthians 2:1–16. During the singing of the Alleluia, the Master of Ceremonies, Nathan Laurin, the two altar servers, Matthew Laurin and Hunter Owensby, and I carrying the Book of Gospels formed a procession from the altar to the ambo, where I proclaimed Mark 1:1–20. My homily was about the call to discipleship that everyone present had experienced in his or her life. I referred to the call as a response we make to God with our total selves to be in partnership with God. It is only the degree of our cooperation with God that differs from one person to another. After giving a few examples, I invited all present to join me in celebrating our response to God's call to partnership.

After the homily we professed our faith together, and Thomas Crim led all in the general intercessions. A collection, under the direction of Pap and Jane Pashia, David and Laura Ingram, Bill and Audrey McElyea, and Matthew Pashia was held for Food for the Poor. Matthew Pashia presented the collection to me, while Brenda Jackson, who had baked the bread, presented the bread, and Zach Kinler presented the wine.

Following the Eucharistic Prayer, I was assisted in the distribution of communion followed by the purification of the vessels by Jim and Brenda Jackson, Keith and Robin Zeka, Ed and Julie Rice, Natalie Villmer, Sister Mary Ellen O'Connor, Sharon Wiedelman, Bosso, and Love (Berry). After a little quiet time, all stood to sing the Canticle of Mary to conclude Evening Prayer. The Prayer after Communion, the blessing, dismissal, and postlude followed. A few people stayed around to talk about the day and the environment Chris Haik and Pam Detten had created for the conference/Mass space. Others admired the liturgical furniture—altar, ambo, presider's chair, processional cross, Paschal Candle stand, and candle holders made by Patrick J. Murphy. I had asked Murphy to make the pieces for my silver jubilee celebration knowing that one day I would retire and install them in a chapel in my home. Murphy charged me $5,370 for materials and labor. All those wooden pieces are in my home chapel and used every day.

Christine Ballew-Gonzales supervised a table of my books for sale. And once everything was finished for the day, Patrick H. Murphy loaded all the liturgical furniture into his truck and took it to my house, where he unloaded it.

After all expenses were paid—invitations, postage, speakers, luncheon, audio equipment, dry erase board, screen, liturgical furniture, printing, etc.—I figured that I had spent $10,000 on the educational conference marking my twenty-five years as a priest. The Church contributed nothing toward the expenses incurred in "Understanding Mark and His Gospel"!

Sabbatical 2002

After years of negativity and notes from Leibrecht that indicated to me that it was time for me to resign my position as editor of *The Mirror*, I attempted to resign in 2000, but no suitable candidate could be surfaced to replace me. I had plans for a sabbatical for the last four months of 2001, but those plans had to be cancelled. Leibrecht asked me to continue as editor through the end of 2001. Finally, after a new search, the bishop named Leslie Hunter Eidson, who served as my copy coordinator, to replace me. She had no college degree, and the only training is what she got from me. Many people, such as Reynolds, could not believe that she was named the editor. I'm sure she was named editor because Leibrecht thought that he could control her in ways that he could not control me. While I didn't want to see the paper deteriorate to the level it was when I inherited it, I wanted out. However, the paper did return to its former, non-professional look rather quickly.

My sabbatical began in January 2002 and was to last until May 2002. I stayed home, and continued to teach classes at Southwest Missouri State University (now Missouri State University). The sabbatical had four components: writing, reading, prayer, and study in preparation for my new assignment as assistant to Sister Rosalie Digenan, a Daughter of Charity, who ran the religious education office for the diocese. Working with her I was to develop adult education programs. Another component of the sabbatical was buying the house on Stanford Street, which occurred in May 2002, as described above.

Canonical Pastor of Sacred Heart Parish, Mountain Grove, and St. Michael Parish, Cabool, and Adult Education

Near the end of my sabbatical time in 2002, I was asked to make an appointment with Leibrecht to talk about my future assignments. There was already an agreement that I would work in the religious education office in the area of adult education. I met with him on May 14, 2002; at that meeting he informed me that he intended to cut in half the per diem (meaning *per day* and referring to the cost of daily needs not included in one's salary) I had been getting since July 1, 2000. That per diem, seven hundred dollars a month, was supposed to cover costs that would have ordinarily been covered by a parish, such as food, cleaning, laundry, telephone, etc. In response to that meeting and at the bishop's request, I prepared a report of the per diem I had been receiving from July 1, 1987, when I had become editor of *The Mirror*. What had been $485 a month (sixteen dollars a day) had increased gradually over fifteen years to seven hundred dollars a month (twenty-three dollars a day). In a letter I explained to Leibrecht, "The per diem was increased gradually through the past fifteen years to correspond to the increase in the cost of living, the increase in per-mile allotment, and the increase in food prices and other things associated with running a household."

As I was preparing the per diem report, I consulted with my accountant who told me that in 2002 the Internal Revenue Service considered a per diem to be thirty-two dollars a day, and that included only food and incidentals. He also told me that the IRS considered the Springfield per diem to be between thirty-six dollars per day and thirty-eight dollars per day. I wrote to Leibrecht, stating: "With that in mind and considering that my per diem (of twenty-three dollars per day) covers not only food, but house cleaning, dry cleaning, laundry, telephone, and other things associated with running a household—such as dishwasher soap, laundry detergent, bath soap, shampoo, small appliance repair/replacement, cooking utensils and replacement, foil, plastic wrap, bathroom cleaning agents, toilet tissue, toilet bowl cleaner, tissues, light bulbs, garbage bags, napkins, furnace filters, paper towels, etc.—I don't see how it can be reduced to less than the twenty-three dollars per day (seven hundred dollars per month) that it is now."

Because I was about to begin work with Digenan in the area of adult education, I had submitted a budget to her for the next year. I told the bishop that I was willing to eliminate items from that proposed budget, such as books and subscriptions, conferences, travel, hotels, etc. in order to save over a thousand dollars. I also offered to resume mowing the yard, paying the cost of garbage service, and absorbing the cost for other incidental things.

On May 29, 2002, I received the bishop's reply to my letter. He wrote: "I want to follow the criterion of having your per diem somewhat similar to those of the other two priests being paid a per diem by The Catholic Center. An allotment of $4,200 is more than either of the two other men receive. I understand fully that your criterion on this matter differs from this, but I believe this is a fairer way of approaching the issue." In other words, he was cutting my per diem in half; this meant that I would be getting less than I had received fifteen years before! And that, in Leibrecht's estimation was fair! Once Leibrecht made up his mind about anything there was no reason that could be presented that would cause him to change it no matter how unjust the decision was. As I thought about this, I concluded that I was being punished for two things: I had left *The Mirror*, and I had bought a house and moved into it. Leibrecht didn't like either of those.

After thinking about this for a few days, on June 3, 2002, I wrote to Reidy, inquiring "about the proper procedure to follow concerning the due process of an appeal." I stated that the bishop's decision was unjust; "it violates the basic tenants of justice." I asked him, "Who would begin work in a new ministry and receive less than he received fifteen years ago?" I concluded: "If my per diem is cut to $11.25 per day, which meal should I buy? Because I consider this an unjust decision, I am appealing it. However, because I do not know the proper procedure for due process in such a matter, I need information outlining what I need to do."

It was not until June 25, 2002, that Reidy answered my letter. He did provide the name of the Vatican Office, the name of the person to contact in it, and the address. In his letter to me, he presented factors that went into making the decision to reduce the per diem—all budgetary. He wrote, "The adjusted figure in your case is not inconsistent with amounts spent for food, etc., by priests living alone in rectories. And, it is somewhat more than what is provided for other diocesan priests living outside of rectories." Since neither Reidy nor Leibrecht had been in a grocery store for years—if ever—neither had a clue as to what it actually cost to live. Both of them had housekeepers who did their grocery shopping for them. In a rectory, if the price of milk, eggs, and cheese goes up, that is absorbed by the rectory budget; it never affects the budget of the priests who live there. The increased costs of house cleaning, dry cleaning, laundry, telephone, and other things associated with running a household never affect the priests who live in the rectory and receive all such services. In most cases, they wouldn't even be aware that the cost of something had risen!

On July 2, 2002, I sent a letter to Dario Cardinal Castrillon-Hoyos, Prefect of the Congregation for the Clergy, in Rome, Italy. In two pages I explained what was happening. I presented copies of everything that I had given to Leibrecht and Reidy. I wrote: "Reducing my current per diem to $350 per month means that I will be getting $135 less per month than I did in 1987—fifteen years ago. Thus, I appeal Bishop John Leibrecht's decision to you on the basis of the justice that should be rendered to me, and I humbly ask that you seriously consider my appeal and find in my favor that the per diem not be reduced from its current seven hundred dollars per month." I explained that I was not asking for a raise. "I am merely requesting that my per diem not be cut in half."

I did not receive a reply to my letter until June 25, 2003—almost a year later. After quoting a section of Canon 281, which states that clerics deserve remuneration that befits their conditions, he made an application to my appeal. He wrote that the application "can result in priests of the same diocese receiving differing amounts of compensation, depending upon their condition and the nature of their office." He continued:

> Bishop Leibrecht has made a determination that priests living within the Diocese of Springfield-Cape Girardeau who receive a per diem in addition to their ordinary remuneration should receive a similar amount. According to this determination, Bishop Leibrecht has lowered your per diem to be consistent with that received by other priests in the same condition. By itself, this action constitutes no injustice. However, the remuneration that you receive must be sufficient to provide for the necessities of your life and the just remuneration of those whose services you need. You have made no assertions in your petition to this congregation that your current compensation is inadequate. In the absence of an assertion that the present reduction in your per diem has resulted in an injustice or caused you to lack the necessities of life, this congregation declines to overturn the decision of your ordinary.

I remember sitting in wonder after reading that paragraph. I thought to myself: What more could I have provided. The remuneration I was receiving was not sufficient to provide for the services that I needed. I was supplying the difference from my salary. My whole letter was a petition that the current compensation was inadequate; the reduction of the per diem to an amount less than fifteen years before was an injustice. I was not in the same condition as the other priests receiving a per diem; they lived in an apartment; I lived in a house. What they required for living in an apartment was less than what was required for living in a house.

On August 18, 2003, I appealed Castrillon-Hoyos's decision by supplying what seemed to be lacking, according to him, in my July 2, 2002, letter of petition to him. I recounted every step of this petition, specifically stating that "cutting the per diem in half would not enable me to provide for the necessities of life." I hoped that this would indicate that the compensation was inadequate. I explained that $11.50 per day does not provide for the necessities of life. "Dinner alone cannot be covered by $11.50 per day. Add to that telephone charges (twenty dollars per month), housecleaning charges (sixty dollars per month), laundry (twenty dollars per month), and other things associated with running a household is not covered by $11.50 per day." I explained that I was getting $135 less per month than I did in 1987. I asked that the seven hundred dollars per diem per month be restored.

A very short reply arrived on October 1, 2003, from Castrillon-Hoyos. "There is nothing contained in your amended petition which would cause a change in the disposition contained in our letter to you dated 25 June 2003." There was no doubt in my mind that this was an injustice and that I was being punished for having left *The Mirror* and bought a house in which to live and one day retire.

Furthermore, my assignment to work in adult religious education hadn't yet begun when I was also asked to serve as canonical pastor of Sacred Heart Parish, Mountain Grove, and St. Michael Parish, Cabool, Missouri. After a meeting with Leibrecht, who asked me whether I wanted to be named pastor or canonical pastor, I suggested canonical pastor with permanent deacon Joseph Kurtenbach named as Parish Life Coordinator of both places. I'm sure that is what Leibrecht wanted, and I didn't want any more friction between the two of us. On July 2, 2002, he named Kurtenbach Parish Life Coordinator of both parishes. So, in August 2002, I began driving 150 miles round trip every weekend to Mountain Grove and Cabool for a Sunday Mass in each place.

However, Father Justin Huelsing, OMI, left Mountain Grove on Monday, August 5, twelve days before my assignment was to take place. That meant that I had to cancel my vacation plans and go to Cabool and Mountain Grove the weekends of August 10–11 and August 14–15 for Masses. In the process of leaving, Huelsing took all the food in the rectory with him; he left not a single can, box, or frozen item. He also took any Mass Offerings with him. He left a mess of things scattered around the house that he didn't take. The stink of dog urine on the carpets was so strong that no one could stand it. A section of kitchen cabinets had been taken out to make room for a new refrigerator that wouldn't fit in the old space, but the repair work was never done. Junk was piled everywhere. Mouse traps in every room indicated that the house was full of vermin. Add to this the malfunctioning air conditioning, and any other human being would have understood readily why I bought my own house and moved into it!

In order to facilitate the adult religious education aspect of my work, I had to change the schedule at the two parishes. The Saturday evening Mass at Cabool had to be cancelled, since most adult education would be done on Saturday across southern Missouri and I couldn't get to Cabool in time for a 5 p.m. Saturday Mass. It was moved to early Sunday morning and was followed by a later Sunday morning Mass in Mountain Grove.

I had no more than gotten to Mountain Grove and Cabool when an e-mail arrived on September 16, 2002, from Jody Hubner, a former member of Sacred Heart

Parish. In the beginning of her e-mail she stated that she was interested in knowing more about my goals and intentions for the parish. That, of course, was a cover for what followed. "I did not feel very welcome at Mass on Sunday," was the heart of the e-mail, also expressed as having a heavy heart! Everything that followed was a list of her feelings: I had attacked the previous pastor, her directive about taking communion to an elder lady in the front pew, music practice before Mass, singing four hymns, hosting a parish picnic, and staying after Mass to visit with parishioners. "I want to help you," she wrote, "if you will let me, make your transition into the canonical pastor role at Sacred Heart smoother."

I set aside her e-mail until September 23, 2002, when I answered it. I stated that it was important "not to reach conclusions before she established the facts." I continued, "Because you did not establish the facts, your conclusions are erroneous, and, I might add, based on feelings, which are often deceptive and lead people astray from the facts." I tried to help her understand that her feelings were due "to the fact that she was not a member of the parish, which had been moving on and changing when she was not there, but came only to visit." I explained that the members of the parish had moved on without her. Then, I addressed the issues she raised in her e-mail.

What she felt about my having insulted the previous pastor was a catechetical moment. I explained to her, "I continue to discover that many people don't know what I'm talking about, so I try to explain it to them." I narrated how the parish had been learning new music, which I had been teaching a few minutes before Mass was to begin. I also explained that we were not singing four hymns at every Mass since that was not necessary. I wrote: "We will sing more music during the more important church seasons, like Christmas and Easter. During other seasons, we will vary the music to reflect the solemnity of the season. No one is taking anything away. We're just not going to do it all every Sunday. And I might add, this has nothing to do with how long Mass takes—another of your erroneous conclusions."

I took time to catechize Hubner about canon law's prohibition about the use of artificial music or pre-recorded music during Mass. The same is true about candle tubes instead of real candles and artificial flowers. "Nothing that is not real should be used in worship; God deserves our best and what is real—not what is fake."

I corrected her erroneous presupposition about me not visiting with people. "When coffee and doughnuts are served in the parish hall, I am there." I explained that since she had not been present when I had, she didn't know that information and didn't bother to ask me about it. I concluded my e-mail by suggesting that she get all necessary information before reaching conclusions based on feelings instead of facts. "The parish has moved and is moving forward," I stated.

Later the same day, I got a response, once again based on feelings. It was like my e-mail had not been read. "I have never felt unwelcome in a Catholic Church," she began. I responded by stating that I would not accept responsibility for how she felt. She did admit that she had not been a member of the parish for eight years. I couldn't understand how she would think that nothing would happen in the parish while she was away! I asked her to consider that fact. What was now taking place in the parish did not concern her; she was not a member. She accused me of not respecting the people of the parish. I wrote: "I didn't say a thing about the people of Sacred Heart. Most of them are cooperating with me and giving me positive feedback." She ended her response by stating that she would be back soon and would not be so appalled the next time. I informed her: "You don't have to attend, and you don't have to listen. If you do, it's a choice. You can choose to go elsewhere." I never heard from her again; my e-mail had stopped the manipulation that she was attempting to employ.

Because one never knew what might pop up next, every weekend was an adventure. On January 18, 2004, a very conservative Catholic member of the parish, Jack Keene, sent me an e-mail about saying Mass facing the altar instead of the people. He had found an exception to the church's preference that the priest face the people in a question posed by someone in a church where that was not possible. The Congregation for Divine Worship and the Discipline of the Sacraments had addressed the question and answered it on September 25, 2000. The answer explained that the priest facing the apse was not to be excluded because in some churches facing the people was not possible. In my January 19, 2004, response, I explained, quoting from the answer itself, that the exception had to do with "the topography of the place, the availability of space, the artistic value of the existing alar, the sensibility of the people participating in the celebrations in a particular church, etc." I explained that there are some churches where there is no room for an altar enabling the priest to face the people. It is not the priest's personal choice of which way to face; in some cases, it is dictated by the architecture. In new and renovated churches, altars are now freestanding, and, therefore, the priest faces the people. I explained that facing the people could not be mandated but, according to the General Instruction of the Roman Missal, "desirable whenever possible." The answer itself stated, "The position towards the assembly seems more convenient inasmuch as it makes communication easier, without excluding the other possibility." The other possibility, namely facing the apse, could not be excluded because the topography of some churches prohibited the desired position of facing the people. I was not about to begin celebrating the Eucharist with my back to the people in a church that had been renovated with a freestanding altar!

As I began to initiate changes in both parishes—like getting rid of artificial flowers, decreasing the use of electronic music, and cleaning up clutter—some people began to complain to Kurtenbach, who gave me an ultimatum to stop. One change consisted of eliminating the closing hymn during Ordinary Time. Because a few people didn't like that, Kurtenbach got someone from outside the parish to come forward at the end of a Sunday Mass and announce a closing hymn and proceed to lead the singing of it. I said nothing.

However, the next Sunday I was in the vestibule before Mass looking for this woman. And, sure enough, she appeared. In the midst of others, I asked her to talk to me, but she continued to walk past me. I touched her arm to get her attention, and she stopped. I told her that if she did at the end of this Mass that day what she had done the week before I was going to the rectory, call the police, and have her arrested for disturbing the peace. I asked her if she understood what I had told her. She indicated that she did, and I proceeded to celebrate Sunday Mass. I had foiled Kurtenbach's plan.

The next Sunday she was not present, but Kurtenbach told me that he had called a parish meeting with the Regional Moderator for the following Thursday evening, and he expected me to be there. I told him that he had no authority to call a meeting, and, since I had not called it or approved it, I would not be present. He told me that the woman was accusing me of grabbing her; I told him that was not the case, and there were plenty of witnesses who would say the same.

I did not attend the meeting, and I heard nothing about it during the week. However, on Sunday after saying Mass in Cabool and joining the parishioners for coffee and doughnuts after Mass, they gave me several Thank You cards signed by almost everyone in the parish. Notes of appreciation were written in the cards. I still did not know what had happened at the meeting.

I went to Mountain Grove for Mass, and everyone was extremely nice to me. After Mass more Thank You cards were given to me. I still did not know what had occurred at the meeting. A parishioner who took communion to those in the local nursing home had asked me to go with her that Sunday to anoint those there. When she got in my car so we could go together, I asked her what went on at the meeting. And she began to tell me about the accusation by the woman and how parishioners stood up and defended me. I will never forget her words, "Father, you would have loved it." In other words, Kurtenbach's plan blew up in his face.

At a later time, I got a copy of the minutes of that November 7, 2002, Listening Session. According to the minutes, forty-two people were in attendance, along with Kurtenbach and the regional moderator, Father Daniel Hirtz. According to the minutes, "A letter was read from a woman who one Sunday got up and sang a closing hymn. The letter said that the next Sunday [I], after saying, 'Excuse me,' to her two times, walked over and grabbed her arm hard. [I] then told her that if she did that again, [I] would have her arrested." Next, the minutes narrate: "Two people who were in the back of the church at the time of this incident said that was not the way it happened. They said he did not grab her hard, that he simply touched her arm to get her attention."

Kurtenbach filed a report about the meeting with Leibrecht, although a copy of what he sent was never given to me. Leibrecht sent him a letter acknowledging receipt of his report about "the meeting" that "went extremely well." Leibrecht also commented on "this event which certainly seems to have advanced a certain sense of healing." For the rest of the two years that I was there, I did not have too much more trouble with Kurtenbach. I even cut down on his preaching time and explained carefully what I expected of him. From time to time I had to correct him or remind him that he was not in charge of the liturgy.

Assignments in the Diocese of Springfield-Cape Girardeau

I spent a lot of time cleaning drawers and cabinets in both churches in April 2003. The result was seven bags of trash that needed to be hauled away. I made it clear in a hand-written letter to Kurtenbach that I wanted no more clutter anywhere. I took down a rack he had erected in the gathering space of Sacred Heart Church because he did not clear it with me. "I am really fed up with this," I wrote in my April 20, 2003, letter. "I thought I had made it very clear that you are to do nothing without first talking about it to me. That means nothing." Again, I stated that I wanted no more pamphlets, books, posters, etc. stuck on walls or windows. I told him to stop leaving the ritual book and corporal on the altar. "Show the altar the respect it deserves by not leaving things on it," I wrote. There were several things in the rectory that he was supposed to be working on; I made it clear that those projects needed to be addressed while clutter was eliminated.

Also, in April 2003, I endured what I have come to name the "Funeral from Hell." A member of the St. Michael Parish in Cabool, Jean Pinkston, had moved to a nursing home away from the parish when she was no longer able to take care of herself. When she died, her family wanted her funeral in the parish church in Cabool. I agreed to celebrate her funeral Mass on a Saturday with her wake on a Friday evening.

I arrived at the funeral home in Cabool in plenty of time to meet with the funeral director and the family of the deceased woman. From the funeral director, I learned that the deceased was a veteran, and so her coffin was draped with the American flag. After speaking briefly to him, one of Pinkston's adult children came to talk to me. She identified herself and told me that she was representing her other four or five siblings. Immediately, she told me what she was going to do at the wake and what part I would play in it. I explained to her that I was going to use the *Order of Christian Funerals* wake service, and that she was free to do whatever she wished before or after. She insisted that I was going to begin by leading the rosary because her mother prayed it. I informed her that I was not going to do that because that was not what the church proscribed for funerals. This upset her. I told her she or one of her siblings could lead the rosary, but she didn't want to do that. I looked around and saw members of the parish, and I told her that she could get one of them to lead a rosary if that is what she insisted on doing. She didn't need me for that devotion. I told her that if she had something else she wanted to do, I would be happy to leave and let her do it.

As she continued to try to get her way, I became aware that she and her siblings did not practice their Catholicism. This became apparent as she agreed to have a parishioner lead the rosary followed by me leading the wake service. Then we moved on to the next day's funeral Mass. I explained that the American flag would be taken off her mother's coffin before the casket entered the church, and that a white pall would be placed on the coffin. She objected sternly to this, indicating that her mother would not want the pall. So, I told her that we could omit the pall, but the flag would need to be removed. I showed her in the *Order of Christian Funerals* where it stated that flags on caskets were not permitted during funeral Masses. She was furious, and again told

My Life of Ministry, Writing, Teaching, and Traveling

me she did not want a pall on her mother's coffin; she wanted the flag. I told her that could not happen. She seemed to agree.

Then, she informed me that she had chosen hymns for the funeral Mass. I asked how that could have been possible since she did not have a copy of the hymn book we used in the parish. She told me that she was going to play Celtic music. I countered by informing her that recorded music was forbidden in the church and that the people of the parish would sing hymns appropriate for funerals. Then, she stated that she wanted to say a few words at the homily time; I told her that was impossible. I would preach the homily. On and on this discussion went. I realized that she did not want me there; all she wanted was the use of the church to do whatever she had planned. Then the wake began. While a parishioner led the rosary, I waited in the hall. Then, I prayed the wake service inviting those present to join in the responses to the prayers. Parishioners responded; family members sat quietly.

Once I finished the wake, I walked toward the door of the funeral home to leave. Several parishioners, who had overhead all the dialogue, told me they were sorry about all this. I thanked them for their support and headed to the rectory in Mountain Grove. On the next morning I got to St. Michael Church early to open it, greet the parishioners who came to the funeral, post the numbers of the hymns we were going to sing, and discuss the use of the pall with the parishioner who had donated it to the church. I told her about the previous night's conversation, and that she was free to see if she could convince the deceased's daughter to use it.

When the procession with the hearse carrying the casket and the members of the family arrived, all their car windows were rolled down and they were blaring Celtic music from the CD players in their cars! As the hearse backed into the church sidewalk to unload the casket, the family let the music blare for a while before turning off their radios in their cars. The American flag was removed at the front door, and the person with the pall indicated that she had gotten permission to use it. About twenty parishioners came into the church and sat on one side. The family followed the casket into the church and sat half-way back on the other side. The parishioners sang the hymns and recited the prayers of the funeral Mass. The family didn't know the hymns nor the prayers! Not a one of them came to communion. They had not been in a Catholic Church for years!

After the Mass the altar servers and I led the casket out of the church with the family behind. The pall was removed and the flag was placed on the coffin before it was loaded into the hearse for the trip to the cemetery. The altar servers and I got into the hearse with the funeral director. At the cemetery, we led the casket, family, and others to the grave site. I said the prayers from the *Order of Christian Funerals*, and then the servers and I went back to the hearse to wait for the funeral director. And that is what we did: wait! We waited and waited while talking among ourselves. Finally, the funeral director appeared and told us that the daughter was leading her own graveside rites, reading from a book, and talking. He said he should be back soon, while he handed each of the altar servers a ten-dollar bill. About fifteen minutes later, he returned to tell us that what the daughter was doing was still going on. He said that he had never seen anything like this before. He handed each of the altar servers a five-dollar bill. Finally, thirty minutes later, he returned and said it was over, finally! He drove us back to the church. Never before or after did I celebrate a funeral that was so full of friction like that one was. The family thought I would do as I was told, but I quickly made it clear that I would do as the church told me. No one was going to hijack the parish church in order to lead her own version of a Catholic funeral.

I do not know what Kurtenbach was writing or telling Leibrecht. On July 2, 2003, Leibrecht called a meeting after having met with both Kurtenbach and me individually. That meeting occurred on August 19, 2003. According to Leibrecht's memorandum, the focus was a review of the Parish Life Coordinator policy. We were to meet with each other every other Sunday, to work together to help the parish council of each parish look to the future and do some visioning. I was responsible for creating that process. The memorandum also made clear that my responsibility was the sacramental life of the parish, while I supervised the Parish Life Coordinator. Leibrecht also wanted copies of any written communication between the two of us. I don't' know what Kurtenbach sent to him, but I never sent him anything.

There is no doubt that Kurtenbach needed direction. On January 18, 2004, I went to St. Michael Church for Mass to discover that the new speakers that had been ordered had been installed by him. He had left the wires connecting them on the floor. I had to explain that violated every fire code and hazard plan known to anyone, and if the diocesan insurer made a spot inspection, the parish would be liable to lose its coverage due to the blatant disregard for safety. I gave him to February 1 to hide the wires under the carpet or employ some other approach. I added this to my January 18 e-mail: "And in the future before you make any repairs or any changes, I will need a detailed plan of how it is to be done." How many times had I said and written that before?

On February 25, 2004, I made a list of things that I had already addressed several times before. The ritual book and corporal were still being left on the altar; a poster was taped to the wall, the speakers in St. Michael Church had wires on the floor; he scheduled an adult education session without waiting for the results of the survey the parish was conducting; the guest bathroom in the rectory was not fixed; he had removed the corpus from both processional crosses; there was a skunk smell in the rectory; he was training people to be extraordinary ministers of the eucharist without talking to me first.

On March 7, 2004, in writing I requested dates when the guest bathroom in the rectory would be repaired, when the heat in the kitchen would be fixed, when bare light bulbs would be covered, when a professional sound person would be hired to installs the speakers in St. Michael Church, when a RCIA team would be formed. I also made it clear again that any action that he was going to do needed to be put in writing, brought to the parish council, and approved by the parish council and me before it could be done. I also made it clear that no more literature about abortion would appear in the bulletin without my approval. I also listed four liturgical matters that needed his attention. Realizing that my March 7, 2004, list could be misinterpreted, on March 14, 2004, I rewrote my list, turning it into specific questions about each item on the list. On March 25, 2004, I got a handwritten page of some answers. The guest bathroom repairs had been made. He would take no further action on the sound system. He had two other people on an RCIA team. "I refuse to go along with your micromanaging," he wrote in response to the procedures to be followed. Out of my eleven notes, four were not addressed.

I replied to Kurtenbach's handwritten letter on April 3, 2004. I reminded him that it was my responsibility to supervise him. "The bishop stressed that at the meeting we had with him," I wrote. Then, I listed six items that needed attention. First, the guest bathroom in the rectory was not yet fixed, as there was a hole in the tiles, and tiles needed to be replaced. "I want it completely fixed, as it should be," I wrote. I requested a plan that explained when and by whom that would be done by April 15. Second, the sound system in St. Michael Church still needed to have the speakers installed correctly. I appointed Kurtenbach to get a professional person to explain what needed to be done and to give an estimate of the cost. That was to be brought to the parish council for approval. I wanted a report by April 15. Third, a man needed to be added to the RCIA team.

Number four:

> You can refuse all you want to do the following. However, in my role as supervisor of what you do, you will do what I tell you or you will answer to the bishop. It is standard diocesan operating procedures that before any action (plans, repairs, fixing, budget, etc.) is begun, it is to be put in writing, be brought to the parish council and approved by the council, and then brought to me and approved by me. The parish council is an advisory body to me. You lead and administer it in cooperation with me. Canon Law holds me responsible for whatever is done; it does not hold you responsible.

Fifth, there would be no more information about abortion in the bulletin without my permission. And sixth, no posters were to be affixed to walls, windows, or doors in the churches or in the rectory without my prior approval. The DDF posters were to be given to me to be put in their proper places. See, I was already in plans for founding a new parish, and I needed to push Kurtenbach to get projects done before I left Sacred Heart and St. Michael parishes.

I fulfilled my responsibility in leading a visioning process. First, I got Digenan to give a presentation to a combined meeting of parish councils on the role of the parish council. Second, I began to meet with both parish councils together to lead the process of developing a long-range vision for each parish. Step by step the members of the parish councils identified values, the ways the values were manifest, what needed to be done to preserve the value, the future of the value, the resources needed for the future, and the actions needing to be taken. Before I left both parishes, eleven values had been surfaced and processed. I do not know what follow through occurred after I left both parishes.

My major work in adult religious education with Digenan was conducting a six-phase workshop in several places across southern Missouri. We gathered LIMEX graduates and empowered them to be adult educators. In these all-day sessions, we covered the content of national adult education directives and offered many suggestions as to how to implement them in their parishes. The biggest obstacle to adult education was not having adult educators; the biggest obstacle were pastors of parishes who didn't want adult education to take place. It raised questions which they didn't want to have to answer. The empowerment of adult educators came to an end right before I began to start a new parish!

Founder and Pastor of St. Francis of Assisi Parish, Nixa

Leibrecht had begun a custom of seeking input from priests concerning their assignments every year. Near the end of January, a letter would arrive in the mail with a form to be completed. There were various options to check on the form, such as stating that one preferred to stay in his current assignment, one preferred to be offered another assignment, etc. For a few years the option about being interested in founding a new parish in Nixa, Missouri, had been on the form.

At first I had dismissed the idea of founding a new parish. Then, I began to consider it a little. Finally, in 2004 I decided to check the line that indicated that I was interested in beginning a new parish in Nixa, a bedroom community of Springfield, located about ten miles south of the Queen City, and see what happened. I returned the form by the end of January.

In March I got a call from Leibrecht asking me how interested I was in founding the new parish, and I told him that I was very interested. He immediately told me that it was going to happen. I was invited to join him and pastors of parishes that surrounded Nixa to establish boundaries for the new parish. I attended the meeting and listened as the boundaries were settled upon. In April the bishop announced to The Catholic Center staff that I would be the pastor of the new parish and found it. I received a letter to be read in the parishes of Mountain Grove and Cabool stating the same. I needed to get busy with founding a parish, an activity about which I knew nothing! On July 6, 2004, the formal decree establishing St. Francis of Assisi Parish in Nixa was issued and signed by Leibrecht and Reidy.

Knowing that I needed a team, I invited a then-friend, Sister Frances Wessel, a School Sister of Notre Dame, to help me. I also invited Bosso, whom I knew from my participation in LIMEX, to serve as Director of Religious Education. The position of Office Manager was given to Sue Geeser. From April through June we looked for a place to meet in Nixa. We drove around the city, looking at business "for rent" signs. We also employed the help of a realtor, who showed us several properties until she landed on the one that would become our home for over six years. The property was not yet finished, but the owner told us that it would be by August 2004 and that we could have input as to the way we wanted it to be finished for our use. So, with those provisions, we outlined what we wanted for a store front church.

The space consisted of three bays of a strip mall. Two bays would be used for worship, and one bay would be used for bathrooms and education. In another year or so, when the fitness center located next to us went out of business, we would take over renting that space, too, turning it into a chapel and two meeting spaces. However, our landlord for all four bays would turn out to be a really difficult person by the time we moved out.

Once I formed a team, we established three meetings in parishes from which potential parishioners would come to form the new parish. We met in Immaculate Conception, Springfield, where I encountered a man who wanted to build a church over the summer! We met in St. Joseph the Worker Parish, Ozark, and we met in St. Elizabeth Ann Seton Parish, Springfield. Potential parishioners came to the meetings and listened as the team members narrated what was going on and described what our dreams and plans were for the new parish. We talked about the committees that would need to be formed and the parish ministers we would need.

After those three meetings were held, we arranged a meeting in Nixa in a Baptist Church. The purpose of that meeting was to organize parish committees and get them meeting and planning and to pick three possible names for the parish. Leibrecht had asked me to submit three names to him, and he would choose one from them. At an evening meeting of potential parishioners, three names were surfaced: Holy Spirit, St. Francis of Assisi, and Mother Teresa. The bishop chose St. Francis of Assisi.

In the meantime, the pastor of Our Lady of the Lake Parish, Branson, was finishing the building of a new church. He had an old church full of liturgical furniture that he wanted to move in order to turn the old church into a hall. He offered the furniture to St. Francis of Assisi for free, and we accepted. The "we" here consisted of the Foundation Committee, whose purpose was to found the parish and its meeting place; its purpose was also to oversee the planning for a permanent facility on the land the new parish owned. This land had been purchased by the diocese ten to fifteen years before I began the process of founding a parish upon it.

Other committees formed included a finance council, a stewardship council, a religious education committee, and a social committee. The finance council was responsible for all parish funds. The stewardship council was responsible for fostering and teaching the concept of stewardship. Anything to do with religious education was handled by that committee under the direction of Bosso; this included religious education teachers. And the social committee was responsible for planning activities that brought people together.

Assignments in the Diocese of Springfield-Cape Girardeau

On the hottest day of summer in July 2004, a Mass was held on the land owned by the new parish in Nixa. Some people borrowed a huge tent and put it up. Musicians prepared liturgical music. A group prepared food. Everyone brought outdoor chairs. Potential parishioners got to meet each other. After the Mass under the tent, a pot luck dinner was enjoyed.

On August 22, 2004, I, after lots of work getting things moved into the temporary facilities and getting them organized, celebrated the first Mass of St. Francis of Assisi Parish. Not only had we accepted the furniture from the Branson parish, but other parishes gave us things they no longer needed or wanted. After sorting through everything, we moved what we knew we could use, and put everything else into storage, where it would stay until we could dispose of it.

At that first Mass, Westhues, my first pastor as a newly-ordained priest, who had retired and was living in St. Agnes Cathedral Rectory, Springfield, installed me as pastor. I invited those present to renew their baptismal promises after which I sprinkled everyone with holy water. The worship space was packed for that first Mass. Little did I know that Wessel was registering everyone who came to that Mass; that would become a real issue in subsequent years.

The following Sunday Leibrecht came and celebrated Mass with everyone. And then the real work began. By the middle of September, we knew how many founding members of the parish we had, and that was nowhere near the number who had been present for the first Mass. However, I was too busy to go over all the registrations that Wessel had completed during the first Mass. I didn't get to that list for two years. In the meantime, the names of over 250 families had been sent to the diocese as part of our annual report. When I finally got the list and narrowed it down to 130 families, which was reported the following year, I was called into Leibrecht's office and asked what had happened. I explained that Wessel had registered everyone, and I had just gotten to the list to correct it. He would not accept that answer. He accused me of running off potential parishioners!

This was only one of the problems that Wessel created for me. As we were getting organized, she had a heart attack and was hospitalized for a few days. After recovery, she came back to work in the parish, but something was wrong. She could not remember anything. The staff and I would agree at a meeting on something, and she would leave the meeting and do exactly the opposite. After this went on for a few months, the other staff members told me that I had to talk to her, and I did. I told her that she had to stop being a lone wolf. She didn't, and, after consultation with her superior in St. Louis, I fired her with the stipulation that she needed help and after recovery I would hire her back. She came back after a few months, did exactly the same thing, and I had to fire her again. After a few more months of recuperation, I hired her for the third time. It was not long before I had to fire her again for the last time. Her superior was present for all this, but her superior could not keep her in St. Louis. The last time, I made it clear that the firing was permanent. Throughout this process, Leibrecht sat on pins and needles, even though Wessel's superior assured him that this was the right thing to do.

After a few years of running the religious education program, Bosso decided that she had done all that she thought she could do. She named her successors, a husband and wife team—Michael and Emily Crites—trained them, and stepped aside. With the assistance of the staff, a team operating proposal was proposed on December 29, 2005, and signed by Sheri Duncan, Finance Committee Chairperson, on January 20, 2006, and by me on January 22, 2006. The proposal outlined the responsibilities which the Criteses were embracing. The husband and wife team were in office for less than two months when they came to a finance council meeting and gave a presentation on how they had reworked the budget to afford things they wanted for youth ministry. Also, they did not like the fact that the Finance Council had defined how funds could be spent at youth conferences in order to counteract the prevailing idea that attending a youth conference was spending time with friends and nothing more. In their February 13, 2006, e-mail, they listed other issues they wanted to discuss. Since I had already accepted the proposed budget from the Finance Council, I told them that they would have to abide by what had already been decided until the new round of budgeting for the next fiscal year began.

After the extended meeting I met with them privately and told them that they would never do that again. They were supposed to present what they needed to the Finance Council whose members would determine what we could afford. On February 18, 2006, they sent me their resignation attack letter based on inadequate information and trumped up reasons about several incidents outside of the parish along with their fundamental disagreements with how parish processes worked. In a February 18, 2006, e-mail, I explained, again, how the processes between three parish consultative councils and parish staff worked. I invited them to take a few days and reconsider their decision and learn from their mistakes. When they didn't respond, I accepted their resignation on February 24, 2006, less than two months after they had been hired. I asked Bosso to come back until I could find a new director of religious education.

Youth ministry, which was technically under the director of religious education, had been handled by a parishioner named Cece Treml. She understood youth ministry to be taking youth to places with the expenses paid by the parish. In June 2007, the Finance Council gave her the youth ministry portion of the budget for 2007–2008. The attached memo stated that there were six activities that it considered to be "'fun' events rather than ministry related," and those would be at the expense of the youth or their family for those who wanted to attend. It also made very clear, due to previous misunderstandings, "If parish funds or grants written in the name of the parish are used for a conference, all attendees must be approved by the parish staff to attend" and those desiring to go must have attended 80 percent of their Whole Community Catechesis (WCC) sessions and be active in a parish ministry.

Assignments in the Diocese of Springfield-Cape Girardeau

The guidelines were put in place because, as recorded in the Parish Council minutes of March 21, 2007, Treml had expressed concern about the fee for a conference being paid for nine of ten youth going. The tenth youth was not a member of the parish. Deb Hinkebein, a staff member, asked Treml if she had followed proper procedure when submitting student names for the conference and if they had been submitted in a timely manner. "She admitted she overlooked the deadline," records the minutes of the meeting. "Hinkebein also asked if she followed proper procedures set by the Finance Council. Treml admitted she failed to do that, that she did not see the importance," records the minutes.

The typical way Treml ran youth ministry was to use money allocated for one item in the budget and use it for something else. The Finance Council commissioned me to meet with her and explain the procedures they expected her to follow. Thus, on April 25, 2007, I met with her and gave her a "Memorandum of Understanding," a two-page document which addressed the nine issues that Treml's behavior had raised. Among those was the Finance Council's ability, with the pastor's approval, to enact policies concerning parish funds, fundraisers, the procedure to get dates for events on the parish calendar, the procedure for requesting parish funds before an event, not writing a personal check and requesting reimbursement after an event, not using funds budgeted for one item to pay for another, the pre-approval of youth by the parish staff to attend an event sponsored by the parish, the events youth would pay for themselves, the procedure to handle last-minute opportunities, and the consultation of parish staff that was required before a decision concerning youth ministry was made. The concern that parish council and finance council had concerning youth was that many of them were not involved in the parish. Also, finance council was stopping Treml's practice of spending her money on non-authorized youth activities and requesting that the parish reimburse her for an event which both council and staff disagreed; once she requested reimbursement for her personal expenditure on youth activities, council members were forced to reimburse her. On April 29, 2007, Treml gave me a letter—with copies sent to Leibrecht, Reidy, the diocesan youth director, the parish religious education director, and the parish council president—which stated that she was resigning as of June 1.

But, of course, that is not all she did! In her letter, she wrote, "I believe I have been maligned in the conversations you said you had with Leibrecht and Reidy. I will be responding to the accusations of mishandling of the parish funds." What is important to note is that she had created this accusation. No one at any time ever accused her of mishandling parish funds. What they accused her of was not following parish procedures. She wanted to tell the youth herself about her resignation. Of course, she didn't like the "Memorandum of Understanding" either. The two-page resignation letter concluded with a ten-line paragraph praising her own accomplishments.

On the same day as I received the letter of resignation, I notified the staff. I asked them about the wisdom of letting her tell the youth that she was resigning and the need to find a replacement for youth ministry leadership. On April 30, 2007, I sent Treml an e-mail accepting her resignation, informing her that she needed to tell the youth on Sunday, May 6, 2007, at the beginning of WCC and let the WCC teachers take it from there, and informing her that I would tell the adults at the end of their WCC session. I also informed her that a notice would appear in the May 13 bulletin.

On May 5, 2007, I sent Treml the letter that I had promised to send in my April 30 e-mail. I accepted her resignation as volunteer youth minister. I restated what I had told her when we met, namely, that she was not a good role model because she was not at Sunday Mass on a regular basis, that her own children had attended less than 50 percent of the WCC sessions, that she procrastinated with plans involving youth and missed deadlines. I explained that paying for youth activities with a personal check and then requesting reimbursement from the parish was not the proper procedure. It was her way of avoiding the procedures put in place by the Finance Council. I named two times when she had bypassed the policy and her approved budget. "You were not authorized to spend parish funds until you had approved by the parish staff those youth you intended to take to the youth conference," I wrote. "You were not authorized to spend parish funds for pizza and soda until you had the Finance Council's approval to reallocate funds. That is why the Finance Council does not trust you. You consistently try to find ways to get around policies instead of observing them." After thanking her for the contribution she made to youth ministry, I urged her to get involved in other parish ministries.

In the meantime, Bosso had gotten herself mixed up with Treml. I had begged Bosso not to socialize with parishioners who were running programs because it caused problems. After Treml quit youth ministry, she left the parish and took Bosso with her.

I thought the Treml issue was over. However, on January 17, 2008, I got an e-mail from her. "It was brought to my attention that at the Parish Council meeting last night you all were reviewing why parishioners had left. You were asked specifically about us, and your reply was to the effect 'we have no idea how much money was misappropriated,'" began the e-mail. She continued by telling me that someone else had told her that I had told her the same. "That is twice, with the latest in a public forum, that you have misrepresented the situation and slandered us." She expected an apology at the next Parish Council meeting, and, if that was not forthcoming, she would have her attorney file a defamation of character lawsuit against me.

Who on the Parish Council was giving her such information? I had said nothing about Treml being guilty of "misappropriating or embezzling thousands of dollars of parish funds." I had merely restated the public information found in the March 21, 2007, Parish Council Meeting Minutes that she "had failed to follow parish staff and Finance Council established procedures to which she had admitted during the March 21, 2007, Parish Council Meeting," and that I had a copy of a Memorandum of Understanding with her signature concerning the same. Five people present at the January 16, 2008, Parish Council meeting signed their names to a statement attesting the same. In the meantime, Treml was gathering those who were telling lies and starting rumors to meet with Reidy. Thus, on March 12, 2008, I received a letter from Leibrecht about the conversation he had with Reidy after he met with Treml and two anonymous informants. Leibrecht immediately accepted Treml's truth told to Reidy. "My own experience tells me that anyone of us can say things at a particular time, beyond the facts, which we would not have said given a second opportunity," wrote Leibrecht. On March 20, 2008, I wrote to Leibrecht, informing him that the two anonymous witnesses were lying. I told him that I had documentation from Parish Council attendees and the Finance Council chairperson stating that I said nothing about "misappropriating or embezzling thousands of dollars of parish funds." I explained the policy that Treml had violated twice. "Treml and her two witnesses are lying," I wrote, "and if I had been asked about this, I would have supplied the needed information and as many witnesses as needed to tell the truth." I added: "I am very disappointed that due process was not followed here. I am assumed guilty of something I did not say." Needless to say, the liars were never called to accountability nor were they held responsible for the tarnishing of my name.

The rest of my four-page letter addressed Leibrecht's two paragraphs of remarks in his March 12, 2008, letter about continuing "to hear about the lack of growth at the parish which is now in its fourth year." He added: "The main question I have is: Why aren't the good things going on at St. Francis of Assisi attracting significant numbers of additional parishioners rather than having registered parishioners leave? The parish was founded to serve all Catholics, or almost all Catholics, within its established boundaries." I answered by writing: "I and the parish staff are attempting to serve all the Catholics within our boundaries to the best of our ability. That is very hard to do when they are told that they do not need to abide by those boundaries or, that if they want, they can return to the parish from which they came." Those are words Leibrecht used over and over in both oral and written communication about the Nixa parish.

I listed the difficulties we encountered when we required some pre-baptismal catechesis for parents before baptizing their children when they can go to a neighboring parish and get baptism without required attendance at such a class; when we required catechesis before confirmation, but they could walk in the door of a neighboring parish and be confirmed without it; when we required annulments according to Canon Law when neighboring pastors didn't; when we required enrollment in WCC, but no such requirement existed in neighboring parishes. I presented four or five more issues the staff and I had experienced. The point was that we were adhering to our parish goals. Some adults who came didn't want to have to do anything; so, they left. I continued: "Your focus seems to be on becoming a large parish. The people of St. Francis of Assisi, as they told you at the meeting in June 2007, are not focused on that (see below). They often express their regret at even thinking about becoming as big as other parishes in the area. They like knowing each other and growing together as a community." I could not understand why Leibrecht had to keep harping about growth.

Leibrecht couldn't resist writing one more letter. On March 27, 2008, he sent me two observations. The first chose one sentence out of my four-page letter to him and attacked it. I had expressed disappointment about due process not being followed. He argued it was because he was only seeking information about Treml in his previous letter. His second observation was about addressing the need for additional growth in the parish, and he concluded that we were doing that. There was no mention at all about all the lack of holding people accountable for pre-baptismal catechesis, confirmation catechesis, required annulments, etc. In other words, neighboring pastors would not be held accountable for not requiring parishioners to fulfill the minimum of requirements.

The Parish Council, which was formed after the parish was created and staff members had written a temporary constitution for it, suggested that we add a staff member whose responsibility was to contact Catholics in the Nixa area who were not attending the parish and invite them to come. The bishop had told people that if they didn't want to join the new parish they didn't have to, and many chose not to build the new parish; they continued to attend the parish to which they belonged. The bishop's remarks made it very difficult to enforce any kind of parish boundaries.

After some interviews of people interested in the job, as already mentioned above, Deb Hinkebein was hired for a day or two a week to look into this. The bishop, as indicated above, was concerned about growth in terms of the number of people in the parish. However, it was he who told people that they did not have to attend the new parish, but it was me he held responsible for the lack of growth! While Hinkebein set up welcoming procedures and initiation steps and met with people, the bishop decided to have a parish meeting about growth.

So, on June 13, 2007, a parish meeting, already mentioned above, along with the members of the three consultative councils was held. Present were Leibrecht and Reidy. Leibrecht forced me to sit up front with him—exactly where I didn't want to be because I had told him that a meeting was not a good idea at this point. He addressed the assembly about growth. One by one people stood up and told him what they thought. One told him they did not want to grow into a huge parish. One asked him for the diocesan list of Catholics living in Nixa, but the bishop told him he would not give it to him; that man called the bishop "Satan." On and on this went; all the bishop kept saying was that the parish needed to grow; the people kept telling him that they did not want to become a mega church. Furthermore, Leibrecht had told potential parishioners that if they did not want to join the new parish, they could stay where they were! The drawing of parish boundaries, a process which took several hours with pastors of neighboring parishes in Leibrecht's office, was a null and void activity. I said nothing, as I had already explained this to Leibrecht several times. The only outcome of the meeting was anger on the part of a lot of people; this anger I had to deal with for the next months. I do not know what was in Leibrecht's head; he was hooked on growth that was not going to occur immediately.

Reichers

On May 7, 2008, there arose Barry and Diana Reicher, who should have been awarded a prize for the greatest disturbers of the new parish. According to Diane's five-page e-mail on May 12, 2008, she and her husband started attending on January 21, 2007, after having moved to Nixa from Minnesota. Based on the contents of the e-mail, it was not difficult to conclude that here were people who had been overly-involved in church matters and expected that their sudden emergence on the scene would make room for them in every aspect of parish life. In other words, they thought of themselves as being superior to everyone else and knowing more than anyone else who had founded the new parish.

According to Diana's e-mail, she was writing in order "to be a mirror" to me. Her e-mail was a "confession to the things that were weighing on [her] spiritually and affecting [her] marriage, family, work performance, and membership in the parish." In other words, this was an e-mail designed to manipulate me into doing what she wanted. As the contents of the e-mail attested, she had managed to do this in all the parishes in which she had held membership.

The first item on the list was not having received "a warm welcome" the first time she came to Mass. According to her, she came early to meet me, which she did, and I handed her off to Julie Clarke, after failing to introduce myself to her. Clarke was one of the people we had trained to welcome new people to the parish—whether as members or visitors—give them an etiquette brochure the staff had prepared, and show them around. At this point in time, the parish had hired Hinkebein as a parishioner liaison—outreach coordinator—to facilitate the incorporation of new parishioners and visitors. She had trained a number of people in this process. The operative philosophy was that the priest was not the parish; the people were the parish. What Reicher wanted was for the priest to be the parish; what she got was the people were the parish. This is best illustrated in her example of the then new bishop, James Vann Johnston, who had come to the parish for confirmation. Johnston must have shaken Barry's hand two times. "In less than five minutes, the bishop cared about Barry and showed it by asking his name and shaking his hand," she wrote. "We have not received that in fifteen months."

In my May 9, 2008, reply I explained how she had come into the education space, where the sacristy was located, and the staff and I had just had a conversation about keeping people out of there before Mass on Sunday so that I and the altar servers, other ministers, and catechists could prepare ourselves for our responsibilities. It was the responsibility of the Mass coordinator to do so; Clarke just so happened to be Mass coordinator that Sunday and did what she had been asked to do. Because I needed some quiet time and time for last-minute instruction to ministers, I explained I did not stand at the door welcoming people to church. That was the responsibility of greeters. I apologized for not having introduced myself to her and explained that my presupposition that everyone knew me may have needed to be altered.

I explained the parish committee origin of the etiquette brochure, how staff and parishioners had decided that such an instrument was necessary to educate and inform about some things Catholic that committee members deemed important to know. I also explained that as the founding priest of St. Francis of Assisi Parish, I had made it clear that "this was to be a self-sufficient parish (as is reflected in the pastoral plan) and that I was not going to be the center of attention (meaning that I had to be present for every meeting, event, etc. taking place, that I had to lead every prayer, that I had to do everything); I am not the parish; you (plural) are!" I knew that the flip side of this fostered inequality among parishioners. Those who knew the priest had power that others did not have; it was and is a manipulation game.

She wanted to know why I didn't stand at the door after Mass and greet people as they left. Well, because of Whole Community Catechesis, there should not be people leaving. "I do not think it appropriate that I say good-bye to people who have been encouraged, asked, begged to stay for WCC," I wrote. We asked everyone to stay for adult education while children attended their respective classes. During the summer months, when there were no catechetical sessions, I stood at the door and talked to people as they left. From September through May, I explained, that I had ten minutes between the end of Mass and the beginning of WCC, and I needed those to unvest, refocus, and reorganize since I was the primary adult catechist.

She also accused me of not calling her and her family by name and concluded that I must not care who they were. I apologized. I did know their names, and I couldn't imagine that I had not at least once said their names, but how could I remember all that?

The next five paragraphs of the e-mail laud the Reichers, who were "not fly-by-night Catholics, willing to leave [their] local church because [they] may disagree with the behavior, actions, or opinions of [their] parish priest." She filled me in on their tithing, how her husband and his brothers were altar servers for weddings and funerals when they were young, all the "wonderful priests" they knew, how they had served on a Building Committee and Campaign somewhere, Barry's musical expertise and her financial and parish council expertise, and on and on. It was like a resume for a job application.

Then began the litany of negativity. Item one: Her daughters did not want to be altar servers because they had heard that I yelled at altar servers and "witnessed [my] sharp admonitions through looks and gestures during the Mass." In my reply e-mail, I explained that we had lots of altar servers. "If I am that scary of a person, we'd have no altar servers," I wrote. "Many of my looks and gestures during Mass are agreed upon cues for altar servers," I explained. I asked her to speak to Tyler Durham, the parish Master of Ceremonies, "who is an expert in the cues given to altar servers," and

Michael Clarke, who trains altar servers. If she did so, she would discover that the cues are signals that something needed to be done and not admonishments.

Item two: She didn't like the process of WCC because it made her feel like she was in college; after a ten-minute break at the end of Mass for refreshments, a staff member would ring a bell to indicate that everyone—adults and children—take their seats for their respective catechesis session. She didn't think that we were living up to our mission statement. She was distressed about an incident she didn't witness but heard about through rumor. She didn't like the fact that I fostered attendance at WCC and total parish stewardship. She blamed me for people who had left the parish for a variety of reasons that she knew nothing about. She even provided a critique of my homilies, which focused on issues arising in the parish and usually concerned attendance at WCC and participation in total parish stewardship. Those were the goals of the mission statement and of the three advisory councils of the parish: parish, finance, stewardship.

In my e-mail, I attempted to address her concerns. I began by telling her that I did not suggest that the precepts of the Catholic Church be observed but that they be kept. I explained: "'Suggesting' that a Catholic needs to follow the precepts of the Church is understood in our culture as an option, when, in fact, keeping the precepts of the Catholic Church is required." My reference was to attendance at Mass on Sundays. We had a few youths who skipped Mass in order to attend sports practices. If they were in the confirmation process, they had to attend 80 percent of their WCC class. So, we had high school students who skipped Mass but showed up for WCC in order to be confirmed. Reicher thought that required attendance at Mass and WCC was too stringent; I explained that it was in line with other confirmation processes in other parishes around us.

She didn't like that I had challenged parishioners to give up one trip during the summer of our building fund campaign and contribute what they would have spent to the building fund. I told her that it was not a requirement; it was a challenge. I had challenged parishioners before, and they had responded as the building fund grew. One of the problems in Nixa among parishioners was Catholic identity, which as I explained, we were attempting to restore, as stated in the parish's pastoral plan.

Reicher didn't like the fact that we didn't have fundraisers. I explained: "Because we are a total stewardship parish, we do not have fundraisers. We have been in the process of phasing out all fundraisers from the very beginning; it was a goal set by the stewardship and finance councils that I approved and support. Fundraising contradicts stewardship."

Of course, Reicher sent her e-mail both to the bishop's secretary and the chancellor's secretary. She also sent a copy to Hinkebein, who referred to her e-mail as crap. She also wrote: "I must say your response was more tactful than mine would have been." She added, she "can stop the negativity if she stopped listening and adding to the rumor mill and realize she is not hearing the entire story."

On June 10, 2008, she was at it again. "I believe the fate of having a viable Catholic church in Nixa is at stake," she wrote. Then she began to analyze finances as they had been presented in the bulletin for the past nine months. There were all kinds of alarming calculations with no data to support them. There was an analysis of the parish directories, calculating how many people came and went. There was a bulleted list of six reasons why people left the parish. That two-page e-mail ends with these words: "I have prayed and prayed and prayed for a solution to the decline in finances, membership, and joy at St. Francis of Assisi Church." Of course, she sent this e-mail to a variety of people.

The same day, I answered her concerns, explaining: "The Finance Council is in charge of overseeing the finances of the parish. Since you are not on the Finance Council, you are missing important data that must be taken into consideration. Therefore, your analysis is not accurate in many ways." I also explained that we were in an economic recession. "We have cut our budget to the barest of essentials to demonstrate that we are good stewards." I also addressed her analysis of the parish directories. "The number of photos in the directory does not indicate the number of people registered in the parish," I explained. We had added two families the week before, even though the growth rate in Nixa had slowed; I suggested that she look over the number of families who had moved out of the area instead of grouping them all together as families who had left the parish.

I concluded my short e-mail, writing:

> If you would stop stirring up some of the negativity in the parish, there would be fewer problems. Please consider stopping the part you play and focus on what we have accomplished and build upon it instead of tearing it down. If you would focus your prayer on building up, you would begin to notice the difference. Please use your leadership skills positively to help the parish move confidently into the future instead of spreading doubt and confusion among others.

I do not know if her e-mails were read by Leibrecht and Reidy; I do not know if either one of them ever addressed her concerns, which she continued to voice with another e-mail on June 10, 2008. She insisted on the accuracy of her analysis of everything. But she disclosed, for the first time, her intention: "I am trying to bring the negativity that you exude every week to the parish to your attention." I was not exuding negativity; I was presenting the goals and values of the parish as they had been articulated by the staff and three consultative councils. Reicher didn't like being told what she needed to do by me. So, she projected that negativity upon me, wanting me to be the clay in her hands that I gathered other priests were in other parishes in which she had been a member. It was manipulative control that I was avoiding.

In the meantime, she was also sending notes to staff members. The parish office manager, Sheri Duncan, sent an e-mail to the rest of the staff, recording: "On her offering envelope, she has written a zero in the amount and added these comments: 'I'm silently protesting the way Father treated the seniors. Graduation is not part of the Mass but celebrating the accomplishments of our youth as a parish family is what we parishioners want to do.'" At the Sunday Mass the high school seniors attended, I announced that there would be cake for all in between the end of Mass and the beginning of WCC. While making other announcements, Reicher asked if they would stand; they were in the back getting ready for their reception. I reluctantly—because it was not in the plan made with them and their parents—asked them to stand. According to Reicher, in a letter to Hinkebein, "The encouragement for our youth would not have occurred otherwise." Then, she added, "I am also very disappointed that we did not list each seniors' name in the bulletin." The fact of the matter is that each name was printed in the bulletin. Once again, she was inciting negativity. The high school seniors and their parents had met in late March and decided that an area in the worship space would be reserved for them, there would be cake during the break between Mass and WCC, and the parish would provide a small gift to them. Basically, what we had done in past years would be repeated. In her e-mail to the staff, Duncan stated, "This is what was done. Why all of a sudden is she 'silently' [ha, ha] protesting." She added, "Does this woman ever do anything other than bash the parish?"

Hinkebein proposed a number of reasons to explain her behavior. "Her extreme negative attitude has me extremely concerned especially now that she is distributing a very biased survey to members of the parish," wrote Hinkebein, who had obtained a copy of the document Reicher was circulating among select parishioners. "I think we should take a very proactive approach and arrange to meet with the bishop prior to Reicher's next move. We all know that she will not keep the information from the survey confidential, but will use it against us. It would be in our best interest to stay steps ahead of her rather than always following her lead." Hinkebein asked, "How can one be so concerned about the spirituality of the parish and act so nonspiritual? She is simply vinegar!"

My response on June 11, 2008, was very short. I wrote to Reicher:

> There is a lot that you don't know; you haven't been in the parish from the beginning. Your analyses have to be evaluated against other data and facts that are unknown to you. If you would get focused on the pastoral plan that is in place and support those who are trying to move forward—instead of getting in the way—you would discover lots of growth and development taking place. All I can do is ask you to embrace the plan that guides the parish into the future and facilitate its growth.

But she was not finished. On June 16, 2008, she wrote to Hinkebein; it was an eighteen-page e-mail, rehashing all her complaints about me and the parish. Hinkebein had set up a meeting with her and the finance council chairperson to explain that what she was doing with her analysis was incorrect. However, she wrote to Hinkebein,

"A person from the Finance Council probably does not need to be at the meeting." The rest of her comments about this reveal her high-and-mighty attitude and her inability to listen: "I have the finance reports and can read and analyze the report. I am a Certified Public Accountant, I have a BS degree in Accounting, and I have worked as an accountant for over twenty years." Other than those words, every paragraph was a bash on my behavior, words, letters, attitude. Hinkebein had set a five-point goal for an hour meeting with Reicher: answer finance questions, review her suggestions as to how visitors and potential new members be welcomed, explain the parish mentor program, review her suggestions about how to grow the parish, and establish a future date to discuss confirmation, RCIA, and other concerns.

On June 19, 2008, Hinkebein, Duncan, and Greg Eck, president of the Finance Council, met with Reicher for three hours to address her concerns. Hinkebein filed a complete five-page report about the meeting for the whole staff. The three-person committee restated what I had put in my e-mails in an attempt to help her understand that there were other perspectives. "I think Reicher is misinformed on many subjects," wrote Hinkebein, "and is allowing other parishioners and past parishioners to fuel her uncertainties." She added, "She and the entire family would be a valuable asset to our faith community if she would channel her passions into positive actions."

On June 22, 2008, the Reichers were not in attendance at Mass in St. Francis of Assisi Parish. On June 23, I informed Hinkebein of this. I also informed her that because Barry was a musician playing guitar with the other musicians, I asked the music director what she knew. She informed me that the family was going to St. Joseph the Worker Parish in Ozark. In my e-mail, I wrote, "She told me that they had attempted to recruit her and her family, and she refused to be caught up in the negativity. She said that she has been telling people that her family is staying and building a church." I sent this question to Hinkebein: "How can we get the negative folks to see that they back themselves into a corner and the only way to save face is to leave—after they have stirred up all the crap?" I added, "The majority of the parish is moving forward and onward and is positive. Your notes from the Reicher meeting basically say that they are incapable of conversion, change, ongoing growth, and formation. And the only way to stop it is to create negativity and, when that doesn't stop it, leave the parish. How can we break the pattern?"

On June 25, 2008, Reicher attended the Stewardship Council meeting. After it was finished, she handed Hinkebein a sheet of paper indicating that she was resigning from everything in which she was involved in the parish. However, she was not yet finished. She informed Hinkebein that she had contacted thirty families, but as Hinkebein challenged her about why she was doing that, she recanted and said that it was only twelve of the families of high school graduates. On June 28, 2008, I posed two questions to Hinkebein. The first was about Reicher's involvement in the high school graduates' issue. All that was decided was done so at a meeting with the graduates, the parents, and the staff. We did what they asked. She did not have a graduate in the group. "The only boundaries I set was that we were not going to be graduation for high school with Sunday Mass," I wrote. "Why is this her campaign issue? She wasn't even at the seniors-parents meeting."

My second question was a lot more serious: "What is she going to do to restore all that she has torn down and all the chaos she has created? Doesn't she have some responsibility to the community to fix the mess she created? Or does she just leave it for someone else to mop up? I'm really getting sick of this; it makes me ill and drains me of energy that could be used positively." Hinkebein replied, "I totally agree with everything your shared. It is very draining and frustrating."

Well, Reichers did leave the parish, and they managed to take Craig and Mary Steensland and Jerry and Sallie Knetzke and family with them. Craig had just been elected to parish council and failed to be present for the installation ceremony for new parish council members. Jerry Knetzke, a member of parish council, had been belligerent at some meetings because things were not going his way but the majority parish council way. As far as the Reichers were concerned, the parish was not being run the way they wanted. So, they incited others to join their cause to drive me out, but I refused to go. After all this, the staff and I agreed that we needed to heal all the damage done in the parish because of those few people.

My Aunt-Godmother's Funeral

I kept in contact with my godparents, whom I would see about once a year. My uncle Thomas, who had been a bully to me as a child, developed an appreciation for me once I was ordained a deacon and a priest. When he died in 1994, my aunt Thelma asked me to celebrate his wake and funeral Mass, and so I did. After that I remember her inviting me to come to her home and spend the night when I was in town, and I did. She came to my silver jubilee celebration. She also came and spent a few days with me in Springfield in my home one time. On all occasions she reminded me that she wanted me to have her wake and funeral after she died.

So, on a Sunday evening in September 2009, her son and my double first cousin, P. Gregory (Greg) Boyer, called me to tell me that she had died that evening. He asked me about celebrating her funeral. I told him that because of my commitment to teaching in the university and St. Francis of Assisi Parish, Nixa, I would be able to travel to Old Mines, Missouri, for her wake on the following Friday evening and her funeral Mass the next morning. He agreed to those plans. I spent all day Monday preparing her wake service and funeral Mass along with homilies for both.

At some time in the afternoon, my sister, Jane Pashia, called me to tell me that one of our other uncles, Martin Pinson—married to my mother's sister, Theresa—had committed suicide. He was a heavy smoker and suffered for a long time from lung cancer. Because of some previous conflicts with that aunt and her adult children, I told my sister that the pastor of their parish would be able to handle it. I was pretty sure that they did not want me there. Just in passing, she mentioned that she was getting ready to leave her home to attend a wake. I asked her, "To whose wake are you going?" And she replied, "They didn't call you, did they?" I asked, "Who didn't call me?" She told me that she was going to our aunt Thelma's wake. She added that our double first cousin Jennifer (Jenny), sister of Greg, had taken charge of her mother's wake and funeral. The wake was Monday evening, and the funeral was Tuesday morning. I told Jane that no one had called me, and that I had spent the day preparing for the wake and funeral. I was very upset! I said to my sister, "Were they going to let me drive 200 miles on Friday for me to discover that aunt Thelma was already buried?" No one ever called me. And to this day I am still awaiting an apology from Greg and Jenny!

Building St. Francis of Assisi Church

While all this was going on, I was meeting regularly with the Foundation Committee of St. Francis of Assisi. Once the parish was established, we began reading my book, *The Liturgical Environment: What the Documents Say*, in order to plan for the building of our own facilities. After that, we met to brainstorm about what we wanted. Gradually, a picture began to emerge. An architect was hired to draw plans. A professional fundraiser was hired to get the money we needed. And, finally, ground was broken on September 20, 2009. We moved in on October 9–10, 2010. The bishop who in 2009 had replaced Leibrecht—who had retired—James Vann Johnston, Jr., blessed the building November 1, 2010.

It consisted of a worship area, a chapel, a meeting room, a committee room/education space room, and offices. The worship space, chapel, meeting room, and offices were finished; the community room was not. It took two days to get everything moved from one location to the other, but we had teams who organized it well. One person at the old site helped get things loaded; I, at the new site, directed where things were to be unloaded and placed. Except for some small things, almost everything was in its place by the end of the second day.

On Wednesday, October 13, 2010, the first Mass was held in St. Clare of Assisi Chapel, and on Sunday, October 17, 2010, the first Mass was held in St. Francis of Assisi Worship Space. The building cost over a million dollars.

After founding St. Francis of Assisi Parish, Nixa, in 2004, I set about training and organizing liturgical ministers and assigning trainers for each group: ushers, lectors, eucharistic ministers, etc. Since altar servers directly affected me, I took direct responsibility for them. Until he left the parish, Laurin had assisted me on special occasions for a year; he was very good at learning what needed to be done during ceremonies and directing other altar servers in their ministries. A young man named Tyler Durham caught my attention after Laurin left the parish. I prepared copies of materials for him to use, and he became my Master of Ceremonies for Holy Week and Christmas and other special celebrations. He had an assistant, who was as alert as he was and whom I hoped to train to take Durham's place once he finished high school and went to college: Mitchell Dotson. Michael Clarke and Julia Kovacs, both high schoolers, took care of training altar servers for regular Masses; Durham trained all of them for special celebrations.

Because we worked closely together, Durham and I became good friends. One time we went to the fitness center pool and swam for a while before getting to my house and eating dinner together. Several times I remember taking him to lunch after going over a specific service, such as the Easter Vigil. We sang the Easter Proclamation together one Easter Vigil, each of us taking some of the lines individually and some of them together. When I sang the Eucharistic Prayer, Durham would stand at the altar with me and turn the pages of the sheet music for me. I also remember us going on several hikes together. After I left the parish in 2011, I lost track of Durham, who went to college and then to graduate school to study music with the hope of writing scores for films one day. I remember contacting him one Christmastime when I heard he was home and inviting him to come to lunch. He did, and we had a good time telling our stories of where we had been and what we had seen and experienced over the past years. That was the last time I saw Durham. In 2009, while still the pastor of St. Francis of Assisi, I dedicated *These Thy Gifts* to Durham, Dotson, Clarke, and Kovacs.

Katy Robling

One time I got an e-mail from Katy Robling, who, with her family, came to the parish but was never registered, never had a photo taken for any parish directory, did not have a name on any parish list, and never contributed to the support of the parish. However, she did have an opinion about everything. In a July 30, 2005, e-mail, after overhearing a conversation I was having with someone else, she wrote, "In light of your remark to me last night that you had more important things to do than set aside more than a half hour of guaranteed, uninterrupted time for me to give you feedback, I am e-mailing my observations instead of meeting with you. You said it as I was walking away." As I explained to her, my remarks had nothing to do with her; my remarks to another person was about coming early for possible confessions and no one showing up. I explained that I was more than willing to set aside time for her because she asked for it; all I wanted to do was to schedule an appointment for thirty minutes, but she wanted me to stop what I was doing and talk to her immediately then. I had tried to establish a day and time to meet, but she would not commit to it.

Her feedback was numbered. On more than one occasion, I had expressed to a number of people my "disappointment with the high school youth." The youth director was very good at raising money for trips and taking youth to meetings and conferences, but never got them involved in parish functions. So, a lot was given to the youth, but there was little return on the investment. Robling wanted me to give more positive feedback, which I explained to her, I didn't give compliments if I didn't think they were deserved. In her e-mail, she pointed out a variety of things in which youth were involved, but none of them were visible to the parish. I affirmed that some youth practiced music with the choir, some babysat, some collected money for a local food pantry, etc., but most of that was invisible, behind the scenes. I wanted to see the youth visibly active in the parish.

The second item on her list was her perception that pointed out mistakes that she and others had made, "sometimes in front of others, which is humiliating." Since I had no idea when I had done that, I wrote, "Please let me know the best way to point out something that needs to be changed." My philosophy was to correct something as quickly as possible so that it did not become the usual way of doing things or start a rumor that I would have to deal with later.

Item number three on her list was about being immediately available again. She wrote, "You seem visibly uncomfortable with my attempts to strike up a conversation with you. Why? Are you just too busy? Do you not like me? Do I make you feel uncomfortable? Am I not smart enough?" I reminded her that I had held more conversations with her than with anyone else. "I am willing to give you whatever time you want by scheduling it; that's the way most people do it." I explained, "I don't' like getting sidelined by 'Can I ask you a question?' which then takes an hour or more to answer. I have a life, too, and other responsibilities and other people to whom I have promised time. I'm not uncomfortable, unless I'm supposed to be somewhere else and I'm getting held up." I tried to make it clear that I was not always immediately available.

Number four consisted of a back-handed compliment. "I so look forward to your sermons because they are quite brilliant. But, also, in almost every sermon you are pointing out the error of our ways. That we are not giving enough of our time, treasure, and talent. After a year now, it is becoming too negative." I responding by informing her that the Stewardship Council wanted me to get the concept of stewardship communicated to the parishioners, since most of them did not understand what being a total stewardship parish meant. I told her that she may not need to hear it, but there were people who did need to hear it. I told her that at that moment we did not have enough funds in the bank to pay the rent on the space we leased. "We have a lot of people who belong to the parish who haven't yet contributed a single dime," I wrote. She suggested writing letters, giving detailed budget reports, setting clear goals. I informed her that all those things had been done! That still did not provoke monetary donations.

The fifth item on her list was about giving her compliments, which she claimed were colored with soft insults. I reminded her that I had paid her compliments many times, thanking her for her service to the parish. She wrote, "I guess I want to hear more than just thanks." She stated that she wanted feedback, but I had tried giving it, only to get such an e-mail as I was responding to at that very time! She wanted feedback as long as it was praise and nothing else!

Item number six: "Sometimes you talk to me and others in a demeaning and condescending manner." I reminded her, "You asked me to teach you, and I told you that it would disturb you, but you insisted." I don't remember the class I was teaching, but it was probably on the historical Jesus. She wrote, "I confessed that I hadn't done my reading for last class. You then opened up the class with that and then told everyone how you don't understand why people pay for classes and then don't do the work." I reminded her that she was the one who organized the class. As a college professor, I experienced that all the time. "I was thinking out loud. I didn't know you were so sensitive. I'll keep my reflections to myself from now on." She mentioned another occasion when another person and she and I were talking, and because I couldn't seem to make myself understood to her, I turned to the other person and asked for help. She didn't like that. I explained that I had made my point about ten times, and I could see that she didn't understand. So, I asked the other person to help me. She mentioned that there was a previous occurrence when she interrupted a confession I was hearing. This time it was my tone of voice that was harsh. I reminded her that I had spoken to her after that had happened. I reminded her that I had to tell her two or three times that I was hearing a confession and that I could not speak with her then and there before she left.

The rest of the multi-page e-mail consisted of a paragraph of praise for who I was. It was a sneaky way to repeat her six previously enumerated points. Her basic premise is that I should not chastise people. I explained that my philosophy about adults is they should be dedicated to the cause. If I kept running after them, they would never grow up and respond. She wanted me to ask people to participate and tell them how much they were needed. I told her that I was pretty sure that didn't work. Her philosophy: "People get their energy from love." While I thought that was true, I knew that was not enough. In the parish, everyone needed to accept responsibility for getting things done. I didn't consider chastising the correct word; I preferred teaching the correct way to do things.

Robling also presented a very psychologized picture of Jesus. She thought that Jesus changed people by loving them. "And that it was his love for them that transformed them, that energized them, that made them want to try harder, that made them want to give more." I reminded her the gospels present Jesus up front and straight on. "He tells people to give away their money and follow him with no mention of how it will make them feel! He tells people to take up their crosses and follow him with no mention that their lives will be better." I told her that she was being challenged to change her view of who Jesus was and what he evoked from people." I asked her, "Do you really think that they would have crucified someone who made them feel good about themselves?"

Robling was a very needy person, who wanted me to meet all her needs. No matter when or what I may be doing, I was supposed to stop when she came into the room. I told her, "The encouragement, support, and fellowship you need must come from within yourself and, hopefully, the community. I cannot give all that to over three hundred people." I don't remember what happened after those three days of e-mailing, July 30—August 1. Most likely, like others who didn't get what they wanted and couldn't seem to grow into adulthood, she probably stopped coming. I cannot say that she left the parish, because she was never a member of it!

Armstrong Granddaughter Funeral

Donald and Therese Armstrong were registered members of St. Francis of Assisi Parish. Their pictures appear in the parish directories that were issued while I was pastor. At some point in time Donald died, but Therese did not make his death known nor request a funeral for him. While I knew who they were, I never interacted with them because they did not stay after Mass for coffee and doughnuts nor participate in adult religious education sessions. I only surmised Donald's death because Therese began coming to Mass without him.

They had a twenty-seven-year-old granddaughter named Gena M. Sobaski, who was killed when a truck ran over her as she walked along a highway in February 2010. After Therese called me and asked me to have a funeral without a Mass, I asked her and Sobaski's parents to meet me after Mass on Sunday in the St. Francis of Assisi meeting room. I asked them to tell me about Sobaski. One by one they began to tell me about her use of illegal drugs and prescription drugs. She had a heart condition that was aggravated by her drug use. She had a friend whose death she had not grieved. She had been in therapy and spent time in rehabilitation centers only to get out and return to drug use. After listening to all this negativity for about twenty minutes, I asked them to say something positive about her. All they could tell me was that she was in the process of turning her life around and that she loved cats!

Because there would be only a few people present for Sobaski's funeral, I suggested that we have it in the small chapel instead of the large church to facilitate participation. Therese was vehement that it be in the church. I explained that the fifteen to twenty people they had indicated who might come would be lost in a space that sat two hundred. The chapel would be the best option, I told her. Again, she insisted that it be in the church; so, I agreed. The family informed me that they had Sobaski's body cremated, so only the cremains would be present for the funeral. They would bring the cremains; I would provide a stand for them. No funeral director would be involved.

After contacting the parish musicians to choose and prepare a few hymns, I set to work on choosing Scripture texts and a homily. I had nothing positive to go on, except for the parents and grandmother telling me that Sobaski was turning her life around, and she loved cats! I didn't perceive from the family at that time that they did not want me to conduct a funeral; they merely wanted to use the church and conduct their own funeral and not have to pay to use a room at a funeral parlor. Because they did not say anything, I proceeded to make plans for a funeral on March 2, 2010. I decided to look at Sobaski's life from two perspectives: tragedy and gift. I explained that it was easy to see her life of drugs and addictions and her death as tragedy. She had not yet discovered her purpose in life. It was harder to see her death as a gift from God to us. I spoke about a personal belief in God that is expressed in and supported by a community of fellow believers, who helps us not to self-destruct and holds us accountable.

I told the few people present, whom I was pretty sure didn't attend any church, that God loves what he creates, and he never stops loving us, no matter what we choose to do. I told them that God calls us over and over again to do his will. "Gina's ashes are a gift from God to us today," I said. "God is teaching us a lesson, a lesson that needs to be learned not just here in St. Francis of Assis Church, not just here in Nixa, but a lesson that needs to be learned throughout the land." I urged them to consider Sobaski's death as a grain of wheat dying and producing much fruit if the lesson her life and death taught was learned. "We can view it as a tragedy. Or we can see it as a gift of a loving God, who will do anything to get us to relate to him in a community of believers." I concluded, "I hope Gena did not die in vain." I knew there was something wrong when no one said anything about taking her ashes to a cemetery. So, after they left the church, I went home.

On March 3, 2010, Megan Sobaski, Gena's sister-in-law, sent an e-mail to Johnston, the parish office, and someone else. The only way I knew about the e-mail is that the parish office manager forwarded it to me. According to Sobaski, the family was very insulted. She stated, "We had met with Father Boyer Sunday afternoon to discuss the services for Gena, and it was understood that he was to bless the ashes and read two Scriptures." Sobaski did not meet with me; thus, she knew nothing about what took place. She accused me of ranting about Gena and how she died. "Gena was addicted to prescription drugs and that's what killed her," she wrote; that was the second non-truth, as she was killed by a truck. Then, she accused me of blaming the family for her death which I had not done. "He never knew the good times with Gena," she wrote. "We all know she was a beautiful person and a great human, but she struggled with a problem she just couldn't fix." Finally, someone came forward with something positive to say about the deceased. More blame was lobbed at me for preaching at the funeral and supposedly lying about what was to take place. I was accused of not mentioning anything else about Gena, but I couldn't mention what I had not been told.

On March 4, 2010, I replied to Sobaski, reminding her that she did not meet with me on Sunday afternoon to plan the funeral in a Catholic Church. "Since the funeral took place in a Catholic Church, I provided from the book we use," I wrote. "From what I gather from your e-mail, your family expected what is usually called a Memorial Service, something that is held in a funeral home and at which various family members speak about the deceased. No one ever said anything about a Memorial Service, because if those at the Sunday meeting had done so, I would have suggested that it be done in the funeral home. Since it was being held in a Catholic Church, I did what we do in the Catholic Church. A homily is always a part of a Catholic funeral." I explained that after listening to Gena's parents and grandmother, I concluded that this was a tragedy. "When I went home, I tried to figure out a way to redeem this young woman's tragic life. So, my homily was an attempt to turn this tragedy into a lesson for all of us to learn about the importance of community, especially a church community that holds us accountable and calls us to growth and development."

Again, I reminded Sobaski that she was not at the planning session; therefore, she did not know what was said there. My guess is that Armstrong told her what she wanted to hear in order to avoid the question about having a non-Catholic funeral in the Catholic church. I explained that I had now learned that the family wanted a Memorial Service, but no one ever told me that. My presumption was that a funeral in a Catholic Church would be Catholic. "I can see that my presumption was incorrect," I wrote; "I hope that you will see that your presumption was incorrect, too."

The same day I got an e-mail from Sobaski's husband, Eric. He acknowledged that they were not at the planning meeting and didn't know what was asked of me except what Armstrong told them. "If that is not what was agreed on, then I am sorry for assuming anything," he wrote. But he still accused me of taking it upon myself to write something that was to be said about Gina's death; he hadn't read my e-mail to his wife very carefully, especially the part about a homily being a part of a Catholic funeral. "I also realize that my parents might not have told you about all the good things that Gena did in her life," he wrote. But I was still responsible for saying something positive when no one had ever told me anything positive. And still, there was nothing positive coming out of his e-mail. However, he did hit on the one note no one liked: "Everybody has their own way that they connect to God; it just doesn't have to be by going to church." He was preaching the part of my homily about the need for community to himself. He concluded his e-mail by stating that I should not have said anything at all. Now I was accused of sticking out my tongue!

Besides those two e-mails being sent, someone else—anonymously, of course—was sending e-mails to parishioners they knew and to the bishop. Someone at the funeral accused me of giving a sermon, not a funeral memorial. That person accused me of talking about buying and selling drugs, the computer as a tool of the devil, pornography, not going to church, and Gena not going to heaven. Of course, I had not spoken about any of that; it was a lie. But it was great fodder for the rumor mill! As I received copies of that e-mail, I learned how quickly one person forwarded it to another or told a version of it to another until what had actually occurred and been said was totally obscured. I got to the point that I began to write in reply: "Since I have learned that these e-mails are being shared with others, I will not be responding to them in the future. If you wish to speak to me about something in person, I will be happy to listen to you."

Later, on March 4, I got a call from Johnston. He told me the family didn't like what I had to say, and, of course, they called him to tell him so. He told me that all they wanted was to use the church; I informed him that they never said a word to me about that. I also told him about the meeting on Sunday afternoon and how they had very little positive reflections to give about Sobaski, that all I had was she was turning her life around and liked cats. He told me that he was happy that he was not in my shoes, because he would not have known what to do either! Then, we said good-by, and that was the end of the Sobaski affair.

Parochial Administrator of Holy Family Parish, Shell Knob, and Diocesan Director of the Society for the Propagation of the Faith

On May 31, 2011, I was assigned by Johnston to be parochial administrator of Holy Family Parish, Shell Knob, located on Table Rock Lake about 60 miles southwest of Springfield. I was also appointed to be the Diocesan Director of the Society for the Propagation of the Faith; this assignment meant that I was responsible for three activities. The first consisted of organizing the Missionary Cooperation Plan, contacting missionary associations and assigning priests to every parish in the diocese for a weekend during the summer where an appeal would be made to help in their work. Following in the footsteps of my predecessor, I needed nine missionary groups—one for each region—to substitute for pastors in the region for one weekend during the summer and make an appeal to the people in the parishes of the region. The collected funds were sent to my office; I wrote an exchange check in November for the total amount collected in each region. So, the first work of the Society for the Propagation of the Faith consisted of organizing summer mission appeals.

The second work of the Society for the Propagation of the Faith involved the annual, second-to-last-Sunday-of-October World Mission Sunday collection. The proceeds from this collection were sent by individual parishes to my office from where I forwarded them to the national office, after deducting any expenses involved for promotional materials and office supplies.

The third work of the Society for the Propagation of the Faith was the distribution of Mass Offerings. My office was a clearing house for Mass Offerings, which were often presented to me by the hundreds. I distributed these to retired priests and parishes that requested them. So, I might receive one-thousand dollars of Mass Offerings from a national society, the diocese, or a parish and send them in batches of thirty to those who had requested them.

Because I continued to teach at Missouri State University, I spent only the weekend in Shell Knob. Usually, I would arrive there on Saturday afternoon and return home on Monday around noon. The first year I was there, I often came home on Sunday afternoon. However, once I started a Monday morning Mass, my return plans changed. I went to Shell Knob thinking that everything was in order; however, exactly the opposite was the case. I soon realized that I had been sent there to clean up the mess from the previous pastor.

My first Saturday afternoon in the parish rectory told me this was the situation. I went to take a shower before Saturday evening Mass, and there was no hot water. The electric hot water heater had gone out, and the previous pastor, Father David Miller, had not had it replaced. Not only had it not been replaced, but the basement (really a tornado shelter) where it was located contained its two previous ancestors including the cardboard boxes in which they had arrived. No one had bothered to clean up the mess or haul away the old hot water heaters.

Next, I went to the relatively new church (built in 2005), to discover that every cabinet and every drawer was stuffed full of old and outdated papers. Even the counters were full of papers and things. The ushers had taken over the priest's sacristy to such a degree that there was no room for me and my briefcase that contained my things. As I opened cabinet after cabinet and drawer after drawer, I began to be depressed upon seeing all the clutter. Upon entering the church, I noticed that the table for the gifts was a stool!

The church was also full of clutter. A huge palm took up a third of the sanctuary. Artificial flowers were everywhere. Nothing was ever put away; it was just left to sit wherever it had been used. The censor hung on its stand in the sanctuary. Papers of all kind filled the ambo. Even the altar had papers and things on it.

The baptismal font, designed to be filled with water, had a big sponge in its bowl; there was no water in the baptism font, but on either side of the doors were two small fonts mounted on the wall with water in them! In other words, the purpose of the font was ignored.

The Saturday night musicians played music that no one knew. My first Saturday evening I asked their leader what we were going to sing, and he told me something one of them had written. I informed him that we would be learning new music because the third edition of *The Roman Missal* was to be implemented that fall. That was the only Mass I saw that group of musicians; they got upset because I told them all of us would have to learn the new music that went with the new English translations of *The Roman Missal* and never returned. They sent me a letter on July 5, 2011, about me not respecting their method, which I didn't know. "It does not appear that we can meet your expectations or requirements for leading the music at Mass," Lou and Kay Hermann wrote. "Therefore, we will not be leading music at the Saturday evening Mass or any other Mass." On July 12, 2011, I wrote a letter to them in which I explained again that the new translation of the Mass and, consequently, new musical arrangements would affect all of us by November 27, when the third edition of *The Roman Missal* went into effect. My plan was to begin the catechesis and introduce changes gradually beginning in September. I wrote: "Thank you for considering helping in this process. Change is difficult for all of us. Musicians have to learn new music for all the parts of the Mass. The assembly has to learn all new responses for the Mass. And the priest has a whole new book that he has to learn. We have to be patient with each other as we move through this process." They never returned while I was administrator of Holy Family Parish; they blamed me for the changes that they were going to have to make!

The Sunday morning Mass featured a woman on the piano. Everyone knew that she was almost drunk or drunk on Sunday morning. This meant that she could not keep time or play the correct notes. When I talked to several people about this, they told me that this had been going on for years and nothing was done about it. On August 26, 2011, I received a copy of letter that Johnston had sent to Mary Lambert in response to a card she had sent to him about me. "I am happy you appreciate Father Mark Boyer," Johnston wrote. On August 27, 2011, I met privately with Lambert. I told her she was to play no more Protestant hymns and no more patriotic songs on holiday weekends and no more Marian hymns except on feasts of the Blessed Virgin Mary. I asked her to observe the seasons of the liturgical year with the amount of music, giving her a copy of *Sing to the Lord,* the U.S. bishops' document on music in Catholic worship. She had been singing Responsorial Psalms she set to folk tunes! I wanted the settings from Oregon Catholic Press used. I gave her a planning sheet for the Mass which was to be submitted to me before the Mass began. I also informed her that beginning on the first Sunday of September we would start to implement pieces of the third edition of *The Roman Missal,* including music.

On September 12, 2011, I sent Lambert an e-mail indicating the hymns that I had chosen for September 18, since she was not adhering to the guidelines I had given to her from Johnston's pastoral letter on the liturgy. Because I was not getting any cooperation from her, I emphasized again that we would not be singing Protestant hymns or patriotic songs. I also needed to know when she planned on implementing the music with the new translations of the Mass. Nothing happened. So, during the catechetical sessions I was conducting after Mass on the third edition of *The Roman Missal,* I began to teach parishioners the new music out of the missal.

On January 1, 2012, after several more attempts to get her to work with me, I suspended Lambert; she was very drunk and hung over from New Year's Eve and couldn't find the music she needed nor keep time. I did not fire her, but later she resigned her position. For six months we sang hymns and learned new music without any musician. Then, a parish council member recommended another pianist, whom I interviewed and hired. She was present occasionally.

Once Saturday evening Masses came to an end with the tourist season, I continued to go to Shell Knob on Saturday afternoon so that I could begin cleaning. I began with the gathering space in which no one could gather because it was filled with stuff. In one corner sat an eternal Christmas tree, which was decorated according to national holidays. Since my first weekend was near July 4, the tree was dressed in red, white, and blue lights and ribbons! Display cases contained religious objects for sale. Tables were full of all kinds of pamphlets; when a table got full, another was set up; when it got full, another was put in place. All of this stuff was removed, moved to the parish hall right next door, or thrown away. In the gathering space I located a desk for ushers and readers in order to get them out of the priest's sacristy.

My next cleaning project was the sacristy. I went through one cabinet every weekend, filling up one to two trash cans with old boxes of contribution envelopes and sheets of paper listing meetings and things from years past. By the time I finished, we actually had room to put the things we needed and get them off of the counters. After this I tackled the work sacristy, and I cleaned it of years of stuff that had been crammed into its cabinets.

While all this was taking place, I began to gather information from parishioners about what else needed to be done. There was no finance council, so I got a few recommendations, appointed five members, and gave them the task of writing a constitution for the finance council based upon the diocesan guidelines. By July 1, 2012, the first members had a working constitution and were making recommendations to me about parish finances and what financial issues needed to be addressed by the parish.

I discovered that all parish council members had been appointed, including the president, who resigned upon my arrival because I made it clear to him that I would deal with complaints and that he did not have to do it in my place. So, after reviewing diocesan guidelines about parish councils, the existing members began to write a constitution for the parish council modeled on those guidelines and hold elections to replace some of the appointed members.

From the parish council I learned about major projects that needed to be tackled. First, the huge clear glass windows in the church needed to be tinted because the sun's rays coming through them were cooking the fabric-covered pews. Once that problem was solved, the pews needed to be recovered. The roof, which had been put on incorrectly, needed to be replaced in order to stop the water damage to the ceiling inside. The parking lot needed to be sealed. And after the diocesan insurance adjuster toured the facilities, he made it clear that the attic needed to be cleaned. Other minor items included the painting of the well house, repair of church gutters, electrical work in the hall, repair of a storm door in the rectory, replacement of an air conditioner unit for the offices, the purchase of a computer for the pastor's office, repair of the rectory sewer and replacement of metal pipes, repair of the rectory deck, carpet cleaning in both the church and the rectory, and more.

I organized a team to tackle the church attic. It was worse than the sacristies. Anything that had ever been used since the parish's founding was stored there. Trucks hauled away tons of junk. One man agreed to take all the wood and burn it in his large fire pit at home. Several people took garbage bags of stuffed animals and other things to nursing homes. The team and I cleaned and cleaned for about six hours until the attic had in it only things we would use.

The parish council appointed one of its members to get estimates on window tinting. Once it accepted one of the estimates, the same person was responsible to oversee the tinting of the church's windows. Right behind that project was the person appointed to oversee the covering of the pews. Cloth was chosen that resembled what was used before. It took over three weeks to recover the seats and backs of all the pews.

Then came the new roof. The contractor for the church and roof subcontractor had both gone out of business. So, the parish had no choice but to put a new roof on the church. Again, a parish council representative was appointed to oversee this project.

While all this work was being done, the parish council also authorized the formation of a social committee, whose responsibilities were to schedule fund raisers to pay for all the repairs and to bring parishioners together. Several annual dinners were scheduled along with other events.

Because I dislodged many people from positions they had held or thought they held in the parish in order to accomplish what needed to be done, some people left the parish and went elsewhere. I tried contacting them by letter, but got few responses. They didn't want to have to pay for the repairs that needed to be made, and they didn't like not having the final say in how something was going to be done. These were the folks who left because I changed the lawn mowing company and had only part of the property mowed; a man volunteered to cut the rest of the grass and bail it into hay two or three times a year. Some people thought that all the property should be mowed, and because they didn't get their way, they left the parish.

Other reasons besides lawn mowing consisted of the formation of the finance council, the formation of a parish council, the changes in the liturgy, the changes in liturgical procedures, the limiting of Saturday night Mass from Memorial Day to Labor Day instead of May through October, and on and on. What caused the most people to leave was the fact that I was not afraid to make the changes that needed to be made. The only project that I did not accomplish during my two years as parochial administrator was the sealing of the parking lot.

Besides cleaning, I faced the implementation of the third edition of *The Roman Missal*. The people had not been prepared for this in any way. I began to hold sessions on the new English translations and practice the new music after Sunday morning Mass; the sessions lasted about an hour. Most people stayed in order to learn about all that was changing. After finishing the sessions on the implementation of *The Roman Missal*, I taught classes on the Bible and planning one's funeral. In other words, I began an adult education program. Anywhere from thirty to sixty people participated in these adult education sessions.

Many people wrote letters to Johnston, sometimes sending a copy to me. In every letter that Johnston answered, he supported me. Sometimes he told the author of the letter to meet with me and discuss whatever issue the writer had. He asked letter-writers not to walk away because they were not happy. He did not respond to their threats to go elsewhere for Mass. Some refused to contribute to the annual Diocesan Development Fund after getting a letter from Johnston inviting them to do so. In all of the letters from very educated people, the most interesting thing mentioned was change and how they didn't like it. I remember asking one lady who came to church early on Sunday morning to make coffee not to go through all the facilities and turn on all the lights everywhere. I asked her only to turn on the kitchen lights. That got a huge negative response.

Miller prepared people for nothing. I learned that funerals were not conducted according to the Church, nor were marriages. Chasubles had no stoles! There was no leadership, no adult education; in fact, when previous changes had been made in the Mass, he told people that they didn't need to change. He often said Mass sitting on a stool, often giving a one-sentence homily. Names of dead people and visitors were on the parish list. Major infrastructure issues were never addressed. All was left for me to deal with and solve, and I did.

Western Master of Ceremonies

While continuing as Diocesan Director of the Society for the Propagation of the Faith, in May 2013, I was appointed to serve as a substitute priest when needed on the western side of the diocese. I was also appointed to be Master of Ceremonies for diocesan celebrations on the west side of the diocese when the diocesan director of liturgy could not be present.

As a substitute priest, I went to parishes for Saturday and Sunday Mass when the pastor, after scheduling with me or through the diocesan chancellor, had to be away for some reason. As Master of Ceremonies, I trained ministers and organized celebrations over which the bishop presided, assisting him with the missal, miter, crosier, and anything else needed. Before he left the diocese in 2015, Johnston sent me a note thanking me for helping him and stating that he knew that I loved the liturgy.

Beginning with my first assignment in St. Agnes Cathedral Parish, I served as a Master of Ceremonies for Law at Christmas, Holy Week, Easter, and other occasions requiring one. I functioned as MC (Master of Ceremonies) for Law when he dedicated Holy Family Church in Shell Knob, Missouri. I served Baum, who dedicated the then-new Immaculate Conception Church in Springfield. And I was MC to Leibrecht when he dedicated Immaculate Heart of Mary Church in Mansfield, Missouri. I can add to this list serving as MC for many confirmations and several ordinations to the diaconate, to the priesthood, and to the episcopacy. So, when Johnston asked me to serve as his MC, I asked him what he wanted me to do. He said, "I want someone to tell me what to do." I replied: "I can do that!"

As I look over my ministry assignments of forty years, I notice that I have spent most of my life cleaning messes left by others. Both my living quarters and the liturgy needed to be cleaned at St. Agnes Cathedral, Springfield. My seven years at McAuley Regional High School in Joplin featured cleaning the religious education department and, at the bishop's urging, cleaning the graduation ceremony. As an adult educator, I cleaned a lot of misconceptions about Catholicism. As editor of *The Mirror* for fourteen and a half years, I cleaned the diocesan newspaper and made it an award-winning enterprise. I cleaned, literally and figuratively, the parishes in Mountain Grove and Cabool. Founding a new parish was nothing other than cleaning. Maybe I did the most cleaning in Shell Knob, along with a lot of cleaning for the Society for the Propagation of the Faith. Teaching is nothing other than cleaning. And in 2013 I was still cleaning in preparation for the bishop. I had spent my life of ministry cleaning, and I was tired.

Retirement

I began thinking about retiring from active ministry in my early 60s in 2014. My reflections on retirement were sparked by the retiring of my friend, Arthur Hobbs, in Joplin. The diocesan retirement policy states that a priest can ask for retirement at age 65, but the bishop does not have to grant it to him. He can ask for it at 70, and the bishop must grant it to him. At age 75, the bishop can ask him to retire. Because I could not draw my full social security benefits until age 66, my preliminary decision was to wait until at least I turned 66. During 2014, I reached a decision to request retirement from active ministry when the bishop sent out his annual survey getting information from priests about their future assignments. In January 2015, I attached a letter to my information sheet requesting retirement on February 1, 2016, after turning 66. This would give the bishop plenty of time to find a replacement for my position as Diocesan Director of the Society for the Propagation of the Faith and plenty of time for him to be trained to take over the position. I chose February 1, 2016, because the fiscal year for the SPOF ends January 31 and I would have turned sixty-six the previous January.

The primary factor motivating me to request retirement was the fact that I spent a lot of time in administration. Put simply, it was not the bookkeeping that was grating on me; it was having to run after both missionaries to get their completed forms into my office and priests to get the funds to my office. In both scenarios, getting back forms and getting in checks often took e-mails and letters—and often multiples of each—to achieve the desired end. Simply put, I was tired of running after people. The other factors influencing my request for retirement were poor eyesight at night and acid reflux.

After writing the letter to the bishop requesting retirement in January 2015, I waited until May to be told by the chancellor that it would be granted. Either he or the bishop had not read carefully what I had written. According to the chancellor, the bishop was ready to grant me retirement in July! I didn't want to retire in July because I could not draw my full social security benefits. I explained to him that I didn't want retirement until February 1, 2016. In the meantime, a successor to me needed to found so that the transition from me to him could be done with ease. Reidy told me to let him know when I thought we were ready to announce my retirement. I accomplished this in October 2015.

This set in motion the wheels to make retirement happen. When I had turned sixty-five in January 2015, I applied for Medicare Part A and found a drug plan cheaper than the co-pay for the Christian Brothers Health Insurance program adopted by the diocese. In October, I applied for Social Security to begin on February 1, 2016, and my diocesan pension to begin at the same time. I also needed to secure Medicare Part

B. I met with my successor, Father Glenn Eftink, in late October to go over everything about the SPOF. Then, I began a budget based on Social Security benefits and my diocesan pension benefits.

As I had thought about retirement, I decided that I would continue to teach at Missouri State University and write. I did not want to stop everything all at once. I wanted to ease gently into retirement. While I did not give a lot of thought as to where I wanted to retire, I presumed that I would stay in Springfield in my home. I had always dreamed of retiring in Colorado and waking up every morning to gaze upon the Rocky Mountains, but the reality of the cost of living there as compared to southern Missouri informed me otherwise. Even if I could sell my home in Springfield, the money I would get from the sale would barely make a down payment on a home in Colorado. And I did not want to go back into debt at age 66. So, the best decision was to continue to live in Springfield in the home I had bought, renovated, and paid in full. I reasoned that I would be easier to maintain the home I had than it would be to start all over again.

Thus, on February 1, 2016, after over forty years of ministry, I retired from active ministry. The days of cleaning messes left by others were over.

Other Ministerial Work

After writing *The Liturgical Environment: What the Documents Say*, I began to give a few workshops to parishes and committees preparing to renovate their churches. I made a trip to Our Lady of the Holy Souls Parish in Little Rock, Arkansas, to view the church and give feedback to the committee. One weekend I preached at all the Masses. Then, I went back to meet with the committee several times as they made their way through the renovation process. The director of the Newman Student Center in Fayetteville, Arkansas, had me come to evaluate the chapel there because it was becoming too small to accommodate the number of Catholics. The pastor of the parish in Bentonville, Arkansas, invited me to preach at all the Masses one weekend and conduct a parish workshop afterward. Because the worship area had been built as a temporary space, they were ready to build a church, but they needed guidance and input. Once the input and response were done, they had a general idea of what they were hiring an architect to do. I served as a consultant to the building of St. Elizabeth Ann Seton Church in Springfield. I met with the committee and asked questions about furnishings, as the building was well on its way. I was the resource person for the building of St. Francis of Assisi complex. I worked with the Trappist monks in Ava, Missouri, and in Conyers, Georgia, touring their facilities and making suggestions as to how they might change their worship environments in order to foster participation. And, of course, because the book is in its third edition, I have no idea of how many people have used it as a guide for building or renovating churches and chapels.

Assignments in the Diocese of Springfield-Cape Girardeau

After retiring I continued to be involved in retreat work. I gave a retreat day on the Easter Vigil to the parishioners in Sacred Heart Parish, Paonia, Colorado, and St. Margaret Mary Parish, Hotchkiss. I also gave a retreat day on Holy Thursday and Good Friday to the same two parishes. Mark's Gospel was the topic of a retreat both for the two parishes in Colorado and a group of women from Our Lady of the Cove Parish, Kimberling City, Missouri, and elsewhere. Thus, being retired from active ministry does not mean that I am retired from all ministry. The 2020 pandemic put an end to most of this kind of ministry, however.

8

Teaching at Missouri State University

IN THE SUMMER OF 1978, I received a telephone call from Gerrit tenZythoff, head of the Department of Religious Studies at Southwest Missouri State University (SMSU). He invited me to apply for a teaching position in the Department of Religious Studies in the College of Humanities. The call came while I was packing to move to St. Mary Parish, Joplin, to assist the pastor there and to teach part-time and serve as chaplain in McAuley Regional Catholic High School. I had to tell tenZythoff that I could not apply for the position he wanted to offer me.

Fast forward to 1989. The then-head of the Department of Religious Studies—James Moyer—called me and invited me to apply for a teaching position. Now, I was living in Springfield and editor of *The Mirror*. In the spring of 1989, I met Moyer in his office in Cheek Hall for an interview after which he hired me to teach a Literature and World of the New Testament course—REL 102—in the fall semester of 1989. In my first college class I had twenty-four students. This was the beginning of a thirty-year career in teaching college students part time.

From the fall semester of 1989 to the spring semester of 1992, I taught a three-credit-hour New Testament course every fall and spring. I did not teach in the fall semester of 1992 because I was on sabbatical from *The Mirror*, a sabbatical SMSU honored. In the spring semester of 1993, I resumed teaching a single Literature and World of the New Testament course, but I was not pleased with myself. I was restless, searching, and unsure if I wanted to continue college teaching. So, I approached Moyer and asked him not to schedule me to teach in the fall semester of 1993 or the spring semester of 1994. He told me that he thought that I would be back, because he knew I liked teaching and got good results from my students. I used the two semesters to reflect and to acknowledge that I did miss teaching. So, I contacted Moyer and told him that I would be ready to begin again as soon as he had a class for me. He told me that he had saved a section of New Testament for me for the fall semester of 1994.

At sometime during that semester I approached Moyer and told him that I thought we needed to develop a film course for the department. Thinking it was a great idea, he told me to develop it. So, I began to think about how I would teach such a course and what its contents would be. By the fall semester of 1995 I was ready for my first Bible and Film class with twenty-two students. My approach at first was to show biblically based films and critique them in light of the biblical text they supposedly portrayed. The three-credit-hour course was listed as a 397-level class under various topics in Religious Studies. I repeated it in the fall semester of 1996, in the spring semester of 1999, the spring semester of 2001, the spring semester of 2002, the spring semester of 2003, the fall semester of 2003, and the spring semester of 2004. By the spring semester of 2005, the course had a permanent listing in the Religious Studies catalogue. It was titled Bible and Film and given the number 319. I had spent multiple hours attending meetings and writing explanatory papers in order to get the course to this point. I taught REL 319 in the summer session of 2005, the fall semester of 2005, the fall semester of 2006, the summer session of 2007, the fall intersession of 2008, the fall intersession of 2009, the fall intersession of 2010, the fall intersession of 2011, the summer intercession of 2012, the fall semester of 2014, and the fall semester of 2015. The department head, John (Jack) Llewellyn, who followed Moyer, didn't like the course and was reluctant to put it on the offered-courses schedule; that is why I taught it in intersessions. Llewellyn was followed by Stephen Berkwitz, who reinstated the course for the fall semester of 2014 and the fall semester of 2015, the last time I taught it.

While I was hired by Moyer to teach the Literature and World of the New Testament, I had developed a Bible and Film course. After teaching those through the spring semester of 2001, I finally convinced Moyer to let me teach a section of the Literature and World of the Old Testament. My first time teaching the Hebrew Bible was in the fall semester of 2001. I taught it again during the summer session of 2006 and the fall semester of 2008.

By 2006 enrollment in Religious Studies courses had begun to drop. My spring semester 2006 New Testament course was cancelled and given to a full-time faculty member who needed to teach the three-credit-hour course to satisfy his full-time status as a professor. My spring semester 2010 New Testament class was cancelled due to poor enrollment. And in the spring semester 2011 no New Testament class was offered to me by the department head. By 2008, seeing what was happening, I applied to teach a one-credit-hour freshman required course titled IDS 110, otherwise known as Introduction to University Life. After meeting with the director of the program, he gave me two separate sections to teach in the fall semester of 2009. By the fall semester of 2010, the course was renamed GEP 101 and was worth two credit hours. I was given one section devoted to service learning; my students worked with a hospice organization in Springfield and reflected and processed their experiences of hospice in the classroom through the topics we were covering. The other section I was given consisted of a learning community, a small group of students who lived together in the dorm and worked on their class assignments together while also sharing in other community activities. The goal of service learning was to apply what was being learned in the classroom in service to others. The goal of a learning community was to develop relationships among students in order to discover each student's strengths and weaknesses; what was one student's strength was another's weakness. By working together students complimented each other.

After working with all three types of freshman introductory courses, in the fall semester of 2011 I taught a regular GEP 101 section, a service learning section, and a learning community section; each section was a two-credit-hour course. The service learning section continued to work with a local hospice, and the learning community members continued to live together in the dorm, study together, and share recreational activities. After receiving further training in service learning, my three fall semester 2012 GEP sections were all service learning. Portland Elementary School in Springfield was the site for all three sections, ranging from eleven to eighteen students. The service learning consisted in offering recess and after-school programs for elementary school students. Thus, elementary students were offered experiences in playing games, photography, dance, etc. There were also after-school sessions for those who needed tutoring in math, reading, or some other skill with which they needed help. Needless to say, the program was a huge success; it made both the principal of the school and me very proud of what college students accomplished during the semester. At the end of the semester the principal held an award-type service in appreciation to my college students for what they had accomplished.

I didn't know it then, but that was the last time I would teach GEP. In the university setting, there had been some discussion on how teachers were assigned to the various one hundred sections of the required freshman class. Full-time faculty wanted to have first dibs on the course because they wanted the extra salary that GEP offered. After lots of discussion, that became the policy by which the director of the program had to abide. Being a per-course faculty member, that is, being hired to teach a specific course or specific courses, I had no clout. So, when the director offered me only one section, I told him that one section could not pull off the recess and after school program at the elementary school. I had already contacted the principal, who was excited to have the program repeated in the fall semester of 2013. After thinking about all this, I decided not to accept the offer of the single section and to resign from the GEP faculty. I enjoyed working with freshmen college students in service-learning sections, and I regretted that I was not able to repeat the success of the previous fall semester. University politics among full-time faculty had figured out a way to make even more money while pushing out the per-course faculty who wanted to teach the classes and were trained to do so.

While teaching the Literature and World of the New Testament, Bible and Film, and Introduction to University Life, I began to get involved in intersession programs. There were three intersessions in the course of the year: one between the end of the spring semester and the beginning of the summer session; one between the end of the summer session and the beginning of the fall semester; and one between the end of the fall semester and the beginning of the spring semester. They lasted from one to three weeks depending on the calendar for a given year.

The first intersession course I taught was in May 2002. Seven students took my course on Generation X, earning one hour of academic credit. Together for five days of one week we explored Generation X for three and a half hours each day. With the success of my first intersession class, in May 2003, I taught a one-credit hour course on Death and the Afterlife. The eight students who took the course and I spent three and a half hours a day in class together for five consecutive days of one week. We also took a field trip to a local funeral home for a guided tour of the facilities and a presentation on the process from death to burial or cremation. In May 2004, I presented a two-credit-hour course on Virtue in Film to five students. We spent two five-day weeks watching and analyzing films in light of the virtues being portrayed by the characters in them. In May 2005, I offered an intersession course on the Matrix trilogy and the Bible; this was repeated in the summer intersession in May 2007. In 2006, during the second block in the spring semester, I taught a course on M. Night Shyamalan and World Religions; this was repeated during the second block of the spring semester in 2007 and the January winter intersession of 2009. For a week in January 2008, the winter intercession, I taught a course on Star Wars and biblical themes. Jesus in Film was the title of my May summer intersession course in 2009. During the winter intersession in January of 2010, I taught a one-credit-hour course on Christmas in the Bible and Film to twelve students; this class was repeated one year later in the winter (January) intersession of 2011 for nine students. My January intersession course for 2012 was on the Holocaust in Film; twenty-three students took that course, which was repeated in the August fall intersession of 2013 for six students. For the fall intersession of 2012 I taught a whimsical course on Lions in the Bible and Film to six students.

After setting up a program with the School of Nursing, the Religious Studies Department Head, Berkwitz, asked me to create a course on Spirituality in the Bible and Film. I taught the two-hour-credit course to twenty-three people during the fall semester of 2013, and repeated it for seven students in the spring semester of 2015. I had eight students enrolled in my August fall intersession 2014 course on Superheroes in Bible and Film; this course was repeated for six students in the August fall intersession 2015 for six students. In the August intersession in the fall of 2016, I taught Sacred Journey in the Bible and Film to five students; each earned one credit hour. The last intersession course I taught was in the August fall intersession of 2017; five students took my Magic Merlin two-hour credit course.

In January of 2005, I began a series of intersessions based on films that would continue to grow over the next years. Eighteen students took my Lord of the Rings and Bible class, which was repeated in May 2005 for eleven more students and repeated again in January 2006 for twenty-three students. In each of those classes students earned one academic credit for the three and a half hours we sat in class for five consecutive days. We watched all three parts of Peter Jackson's *The Lord of the Rings*, and while watching, I presented parallel stories from the Bible. I repeated the course in January 2007 for ten students, in May 2008 for nine students, in May 2010 for eight students, in January 2013 for twenty-four students, in the second block for spring semester 2013 for twenty-four students, and in January 2014 for twelve students. The final time I taught the course was during the spring semester 2016 to twenty-five students, who this time earned two hours of academic credit. After Jackson's success with *The Lord of the Rings* trilogy, he directed a trilogy on *The Hobbit*. So, in the spring semester of 2014, I offered a two-credit-hour course on *The Hobbit, The Lord of the Rings*, and the Bible to nineteen students. In the fall semester of 2015, I taught a two-hour-credit course on the Hobbit and the Bible to twenty-five students.

From the fall semester of 1989 to the fall semester of 2018—thirty years—I taught 2,309 students in one-, two-, and three-hour-academic-credit courses for a total of 285 credit hours taught. A few of my students were acquaintances, a few were friends, a few were good friends, and two became my best friends. I had very few problems. In one New Testament class, in which I was using contemporary films to teach biblical themes, I had one student who brought her father to class with her one day. He didn't like the film she had to watch for the class. So, after class I directed him to the department head, who told him that college students should be able to watch such films and critique them. His daughter withdrew from my class. In another New Testament course, I had a raving fundamentalist present. He thought that everything in the Bible was true, and he used one book to interpret another. He was constantly interrupting me in order to fill in holes found in a gospel with material from another gospel. I had a meeting with him, telling him that he either stopped what he was doing or I would expel him from the course. He calmed down after that.

Another student in a New Testament course failed my class once. Then, he reappeared the next semester to take it over in order to remove the F from his transcript. He failed it again because he did not come to class. After two failures I figured that I would not see him again. However, he reappeared a third time to take the class. He told me that it was his fault that he had failed it two times, but he had reformed his life and was ready to study the material and come to class. I told him that he needed to transfer to another section of New Testament. I considered his failures my own, and I did not want to fail him a third time. He transferred to another professor's New Testament class.

And there was the student who came to my office not having eaten or slept in several days. He was a freshman, and college was overwhelming for him. His parents had not taught him how to get up on his own in the morning, how to cook a few basic meals, and how to go to bed at a certain time at night, let alone how to do his laundry! I helped that young man make a schedule and get his life organized. I remember filling in all the slots of a 24-hour day including eight hours of sleep, time to eat, time to exercise, times of his classes, and time for study. I watched him grow with that schedule throughout the semester and, thus, take control of his life. With a little direction from me, he learned how to do his laundry.

There was the student who was severely manipulated by his parents. He was home schooled and controlled by their verbal abuse that told him he shouldn't go to college and he shouldn't leave home because he was a failure. I employed one of his peers to help me help him make plans to leave home, find a place to live near campus, get a job, and buy a car. I talked with him several times, but the manipulation was too strong for him to break away from it. After four weeks of a fall semester, he withdrew from all his courses. I have never seen him again.

There was the student who appealed her grade to the department head. He told her that she had to appeal it to me first. I recalculated what I had and came up with the same grade as I had written on her grade card. She wanted more, so she appealed to the department head. He talked to me, and I showed him the evidence. Then, he did some research and found that she appealed almost all of her grades; instead of debating the issue, other professors merely raised her grade to be done with it. I refused, and my department head backed me. He told her she could go to the dean, but she dropped it after that.

There was also the high school graduate, who was not accepted by the university because of poor grades but was given a chance to take nine credit hours during the summer session. If she did well, she would be admitted to the fall semester. She was not a good student; in fact, her boyfriend was in the same class. If they were on speaking terms, they sat next to each other. If they were fighting, they sat at the opposite sides of the room. She earned a F in my class; when she appealed the grade to the department head, he raised it to a D without consulting me. That was the only time a grade that I gave got changed by a department head.

Besides teaching college students, in 2015 I began a four-year stint of teaching high school students in a program called Upward Bound. The students came from three high schools in the Springfield area; thus, it was known as TRIO. For six weeks in June and July TRIO sponsored the Upward Bound Academy. Students could take courses in various subjects in order to gain academic credit. For four years—2015, 2016, 2017, and 2018—I taught English in this program. Classes were usually small with only five or six students in a section of Freshmen, Sophomores, and Juniors. I taught grammar, sentence construction, paper-writing of all kinds, and researching with a research paper as the result. While teaching in the program, I watched the enrollment drop because of lack of interest on the part of the students and the time the program was held during the summer break. Over the four years I was involved in the Summer Academy, I taught forty-plus students.

All total, I spent thirty-seven years in a classroom teaching high school students and college students. I learned from my students as they were learning from me. I practiced experimental forms of teaching, often polishing those I liked and dismissing those that did not achieve the goals for which I had hoped. Every few years I rearranged what I was teaching in Bible classes. I went from a lecture format to a film format, to a small group format, to a mixed format, to a discussion format. Teaching was a career I greatly enjoyed. I never retired from teaching. The interest in college religious studies waned, and that resulted in no sections available for part-time faculty to teach.

While spending thirty years teaching at Southwest Missouri State University and Missouri State University, I worked under three different Religious Studies Department heads. Moyer advertised religious studies all the time by attending all kinds of university events. I found him very supportive of me. Two times while he was the department head, he sponsored faculty—full-time and part-time—award banquets. In 1993 and 2004, I received Outstanding Teaching awards, given at the end of the banquet. His successor, Jack Llewellyn, didn't like part-time instructors and cancelled my 319 Bible and Film class. At the end of one summer session, he changed the grade I gave to a student. Llewellyn was succeeded by Stephen Berkwitz, a very quiet leader. Under his leadership, enrollment in Religious Studies steadily dropped until what had been twenty or more part-time instructors under Moyer was reduced to two or three. What I discovered as the years rolled along was that full-time faculty got very comfortable in their positions. They talked a lot about the need to recruit, but they did very little of it. There was security without responsibility in tenure. Without focused recruitment, giving the current secular climate of the U.S., diminished enrollment will continue. In the fall semester of 2019, a former student told me that he was enrolled in a required Religious Studies course with three other students on the first day of class. On the second day of class, there were only two students. And by the time they got to the cut-off time to drop a class, only he remained. Thus, a full-time faculty member was teaching a required course for only one student!

9

Mountain Climbing and Colorado

1975: Vernon Meyer

I GOT MY FIRST glimpse of a mountain in 1975. I was 25 years old, in my third year of post-graduate school, and an ordained transitional deacon of the Roman Catholic Church. Vernon Myer, a friend from Cardinal Glennon College, St. Louis, who had followed me to St. Meinrad School of Theology, St. Meinrad, Indiana, and I decided to take a vacation together in August 1975 before the new school year began.

Meyer was an only child. He was two years behind me in college and post-graduate work, but we cultivated a friendship. After leaving the Archdiocese of St. Louis and coming to St. Meinrad School of Theology, he began to seek a diocese. He was accepted into the Archdiocese of Santa Fe, New Mexico, and he was ordained a transitional deacon in his home parish in St. Louis. I remember serving as Master of Ceremonies for that event. Sometime after that, he transferred to the Diocese of Phoenix and was ordained to the priesthood. His work consisted primarily of education. Thus, it was no surprise when he completed a doctorate. Lots of friction developed between him and his bishop which led to him leaving active ministry in the Roman Catholic Church and becoming the pastor of a United Church of Christ parish. In his later years, he led tours to Europe and to the Holy Land.

In 1975, we headed west to New Mexico, where we visited and stayed with two friends whom we had gotten to know from St. Meinrad: Jerome Martinez and Timothy Berg. Driving into Albuquerque and Santa Fe, New Mexico, I saw the Sandia Mountains, the first time I had ever seen mountains. The Sandia Mountains are just about ten thousand feet in elevation, but they were the most beautiful things I had ever seen. As part of the Sangre de Christo Mountain Chain, they stretch all the way from Colorado through New Mexico and continue into Mexico.

As we toured churches in both cities and even took a tram to the top of Sandia Peak, where we ate dinner at a restaurant overlooking Albuquerque, I was quietly promising myself that I would return and climb those mountains. As I penned in a poem, I felt "at one with the mountain;" I wanted "to be the mountain." In September of 1975, I captured my thoughts in a poem, titled "Colorado Reflections":

> A voice within me seeks to answer
> > the voice I heard.
> I heard it in the trees
> > in the midst of silence
> > it touched my heart.
> I heard it in the stream
> > in the midst of the roar
> > it spoke gently, direct, and firm.
> I heard it in another
> > in the midst of friendship
> > it called me forth.
> I heard it many times before
> > and I didn't know it
> > and I failed to hear it at all.
> But in the mountain air
> > clean, fresh, and thin
> > that unbreathed breath of Spirit
> > filled me and I heard.
> Now I hear it all the time
> > still in the aspen, fir, spruce, and pine
> > still in the foaming stream
> > still in the friendship of another.
> But now I know
> > it is God who indeed dwells on the mountain.

After more days in New Mexico, Meyer and I headed north to Colorado, where I first saw a real mountain! Our drive to the top of Pikes Peak and Mount Evans, two over fourteen thousand feet summits with paved roads to the top, only solidified both my love for the mountains and my desire to return to Colorado to climb them. To commemorate both the trip and my desire to return to climb in the Colorado Rocky Mountains, I framed one of the photos I took of the Maroon Bells, a famous massive located near Aspen, Colorado. That photo still sits on my bookshelf. The three Maroon Bells form a perfect reflection in Maroon Lake. As we left Colorado and headed home to Missouri, I knew that I would be back. I wanted to experience the mountains with more than eyesight.

1976: Dick Wildeman and Paul Koetter

I got my chance to return to the Colorado Rocky Mountains in August 1976. I had been ordained a priest on April 24, 1976, and reported to my first assignment, St. Agnes

Cathedral, Springfield, in late May. Before my ordination, I had made plans with two friends—one from Evansville, Dick Wildeman, and one from Indianapolis, Paul Koetter—to be met by them and picked up at the old Stapleton Airport in Denver. They met me there, picked me up, and whisked me off to Telluride, Colorado, which in 1976 wasn't anything but a small mining town. We stayed with a friend of Wildeman's.

We drove to the East Dallas Divide road and made our way to the Blue Lakes trailhead. None of us had a tent, but we did have a big sheet of plastic and some twine, which, after finding a camping spot, erected a lean-to out of the plastic, inflated our air mattresses, and laid our sleeping bags on top of the cheap air mattresses. The next day we hiked the Blue Lakes Trail, given its name by the three blue lakes that can be seen as one climbs higher and higher on one of the flanks of Mount Sneffels. Once we got to the pass, we had to drop down into Yankee Boy Basin in order to get to the couloir that is the trail to the summit of Sneffels at 14,150 feet.

All of my senses were heightened as we slowly made our way to the saddle and the summit. I couldn't see the summit, but I could feel the rock along the way with both my booted feet and my gloved hands. I could taste the thin air which caused my breathing to quicken and my heart to pound in my chest. I could hear silence. And as we emerged from the last few feet of the couloir, I saw a U.S. flag planted near the rock cairn marking the summit of Mount Sneffels, which was not only my first mountain climbed, but my first fourteener as well. The Colorado Mountain Club had fixed U.S. flags to the summits of all fifty-four fourteeners in Colorado to mark the 1976 Bicentennial celebration of the country.

Along the way to the summit, I found an orange and green crocheted sock cap. At first I was going to leave it where I found it. But my friends urged me to take it and put it on my head, since I did not have this basic piece of clothing. Without another thought, I picked it up and put it on and wore it all the way to the summit. I kept that sock cap for years, wearing it on climbing expeditions. I sold it in a garage sale, after replacing it with a new red one!

After spending about thirty minutes on the summit, we began our descent into Yankee Boy Basin, then up to the pass, and finally down the Blue Lakes Trail to our campsite. We were extremely tired, and we had blistered feet. However, we were experiencing what the song writer John Denver called "a Rocky Mountain high." By the time we got back to our camp near the river, we had decided to strip down, grab a bar of soap, and take a bath in the icy waters.

To commemorate the fulfillment of my 1975 dream, I wrote a poem, titled, "to be Coloradoed," in the style of E.E. Cummings in order to attempt to capture my experiences of climbing Mount Sneffels:

> to place my hand
> up against my unshaven face
> and filled with a wholeness

My Life of Ministry, Writing, Teaching, and Traveling

to be called to dip
into an icy cold stream
by two friends
standing naked in their presence
and not be ashamed
like a pre-fall Adam
a new creature freedomed

to feel the wind against my face
and warm sun on my cheeks and shoulders
sunburned and not hurt

to sing and to pray together
against the background
of an accompanying melodious stream

to watch the morning sun
slip lazily over the mountain top
and in prayed silence Our Father

to climb trudging along a mountainside
being tired
sharing a camp fire
a piece of plastic and some string
a few baked potatoes
sausage, Tang
selves

to light a candle
warding off the darkness
without and within

to be brothers
not in blood but in spirit
feeling your brothers' warm blood
surge through your own body in words
knowing he sustains you
and gives you life
he gives you your freedom
servants of each other

to make up your own games
laughing and crying
not caring who won or lost
for all are winners
silenced and yet so very present
one to another

to gaze at stars
shooting across the open sky
bedding down in sleeping bags
knowing your brothers' presence
at your side

to learn from the silent teaching mountain
a positive simplistic message
forever needed to be learned again
continuous for each generation
and over again

to be hope, faith, love
in these moments of quiet presence
making God present
and presenting him one to another

to remember the good things
of the mountain
so that returning again
to learn over becomes anticipation

to celebrate our freedom
to be our selves
and to sing an endless song
of that celebration is
to be Coloradoed

After a few days in New Mexico, visiting mutual friends, we drove home to Missouri and Indiana. My appetite for the mountains had not been satiated; my climb to the summit of Mount Sneffels served as a taste of the banquet food for which I hungered.

My years in St. Meinrad School of Theology, 1972–1976, brought about my relationship with Richard (Dick) Wildeman, who was one year behind me in school. He had attended St. Meinrad College and graduated from it in 1973. During the summer of 1974, when I was required to attend summer school in order to pick up the courses

I missed while attending Indiana University, Bloomington, Wildeman was also attending courses in preparation to attend IU the next year. I remember noticing him in the summer school program and beginning to establish a relationship with him through conversations during meals in the dining hall. He was a quiet, but insightful person, whom I decided that I would like to know better.

In the autumn semester of 1974, we spent time together. I had made the first move to get to know him, and he had responded. Our relationship grew through working together on summer school parties, walks to Conley Hall, where he was living for the summer school session, and helping him pack at the end of summer school. I felt especially close to him during a trip to Louisville to see John Denver. He took me to Evansville one weekend and introduced me to his home parish, St. Philip, and the pastor, Father Eugene Dewig. In December 1974, before the end of the semester, I told Wildeman how he had helped me grow through our love for each other. I had learned that he had had past experiences of possessive love, and so any relationship seemed to evoke that. Wildeman taught me how to love non-possessively. He also taught me how to pray with others at ease, to trust people, simplicity of life, balanced lifestyle, and more. I narrated how I hoped that I had, in turn, helped him to grow through our relationship by being more himself, open to all his potential, and sharing my friends, interests, and expertise. I had been sensing that our relationship was slowing down or reaching a plateau, and I wanted to keep it growing.

I explained some of my beliefs about relationship. I told Wildeman that the love we shared for and with each other was a mirror of the love God has for all, that love completes us in God, that we give grace to each other when we love, that we bring each other to salvation in the love of Christ, that we never change each other but only challenge each other to grow, that in non-sexual, intimate loving we experience intimacy with God, that in loving Wildeman I experienced a longing for completeness, and that both of us had a lot more to offer each other. I offered him the opportunity to end the relationship. I asked him if he was ready to plunge with me into the mystery of ourselves, the mystery of love, and the mystery of God. Little about our relationship was resolved because Wildeman was spending the spring semester at Indiana University, Bloomington, as I had done the previous year.

Because Wildeman was able to organize himself, I asked him to be the Master of Ceremonies for my diaconate ordination on March 8, 1975. In January 1975, I wrote an unpublished essay on the mystery of love and freedom inspired by the conversations with Wildeman. In the essay I wrote about how Wildeman had taught me to be myself and to permit him to be himself. He taught how to love non-possessively. He gave me love, and he gave me Christ through that love. Wildeman's love for me enabled a freedom in me that I had never encountered before.

In the essay I dedicated to Wildeman, I traced the process of relationship: offer and response. Along the way, love is nourished by thoughtful cards, birthday gifts, deep conversation, dinner together, phone calls, letters, and being together in creative silence. Love is nourished by sharing whatever each person has to offer, no matter if it be laughter, smiles, joys, sorrows, etc. The essay also reflects on the danger of love: exclusivity. Love cannot ever become possessive, because that means the death of the relationship.

The essay expresses the fact that the constant desire for love is a desire for fullness and completeness which can never be totally satisfied. It also develops the idea that each person becomes who he or she is in relationship, in community, with another. The desire for wholeness reveals the love that God has for every person. God's love is synonymous with grace. By loving another, I wrote, we discover that the love we share with the other is the same love that we share with God; it is God's life or grace. We give each other God's life; we give each other grace. In that thirteen-page, handwritten essay, I was not only narrating the experience of my human encounter with Wildeman, but I, unknown at the time, was preparing to write a book on *Human Wholeness* with another human encounter, Matthew S. Ver Miller, at a later time in my life.

On May 15, 1975, at the end of the spring semester at St. Meinrad School of Theology, I wrote a letter to Wildeman which was never delivered. In the five-page handwritten letter, I reflected on the lack of response that I had received from Wildeman after my conversation with him before Christmas. Peter Libasci, a classmate of Wildeman's, and I had visited him at IU at the end of January 1975, and we got hardly any response from him. No response was given to a gift I gave him, except he told me that I was not going to Colorado with him during the summer of 1975. There were no responses to a birthday card, a gift, a letter, etc. In some of our conversations, Wildeman had narrated how others he loved seemed to attempt to possess him. I reflected for myself that I didn't think that was the issue; the issue was that he did not respond to them. They wanted a response, which he read as attempts to possess him. My desire for a response from him was being read as an attempt to possess him. "I don't know why I fell in love with you and why I continue to love you," I wrote in my letter. To myself I resolved to find out where I stood in my relationship with Wildeman. I couldn't maintain a relationship with him without a response on his part. "I may lose you as a friend, but the memories will remain," I wrote.

In the autumn of 1975, I asked Wildeman to serve as Master of Ceremonies for my ordination to priesthood and my first Mass in April 1976; he readily accepted, even noting that he had hoped that I would ask him. I attended his ordination to priesthood in 1977; I remember the joy of attending and sharing with him. After that event we lost contact with each other, even though we did meet accidently a few times in Colorado and, in many years, continued to exchange Christmas cards and letters. At some point in time, Wildeman left active ministry and married. We continue to exchange Christmas cards almost every year.

My Life of Ministry, Writing, Teaching, and Traveling

1977: Greg McEvoy

After climbing my first mountain—Sneffels—I was hooked on mountaineering. I wanted to learn everything about the sport, backpack, hike, climb, and sit around campfires and kitchen tables and tell of my adventures in the high country. While working on a high school retreat in January 1977, I met Greg McEvoy, a high school Junior.

The group of high school students and their teachers and I had gone somewhere—I cannot remember where—for a day of retreating. McEvoy and another student had managed not to join the rest of us by wandering off for an hour or so after we had arrived at our destination. When they showed up, finally, I was assigned to give them a disciplinary talk and get them caught up on what they missed. Of course, neither of them wanted to be at an all-day retreat on a Saturday! I understood that, and they understood that I understood that. So, my disciplinary discourse centered on making the best of the day by getting involved in the activities and not wandering away any more.

I liked McEvoy immediately. I don't know what it was that attracted me to him, but later in the day we caught up with each other and did some talking about all kinds of things. I found out that he was on his high school swim team. He learned that I was infatuated with all things mountain. Over the next few months, we began to get together for movies and other types of activities, including meeting McEvoy's parents. Our relationship blossomed over the next few months.

In the Spring of 1977, I mentioned that I was looking for a companion to go to Colorado in late August before school began again. He was interested; so, we began to make plans for a trip to New Mexico and Colorado. We visited places I had been to before: Albuquerque, Sandia Mountains Tramway, and Santa Fe. Then, we headed to Colorado.

McEvoy reminded me of the beautiful things about youth. Our friendship deepened as we shared our lives and experiences. We continued to get together sometimes with his family and sometimes just the two of us for films, food, and fun. We took a road trip to California in 1978 that took us north along the California coast, into Canada, and back into the United States. In 1979, when McEvoy was a freshman in college, we traveled to New Mexico, Arizona, and Colorado together. I remember McEvoy coming to Joplin to visit me at least once while I was living in St. Peter the Apostle Rectory. However, because of his new relationships in college, dating, and, after graduating, getting a job in the south, we lost contact with each other. I saw him at his grandmother's funeral for the last time. As far as I know, I think he married, but it was a long time after he moved south.

Taking the East Dallas Divide Road in the summer of 1977, we entered the Uncompahgre National Forest and pitched camp near the beginning of the Blue Lakes Trail that I had hiked the year before. Our tent was an orange pup tent that did not have a rain fly. Of course, it rained most of the night! The next morning, after drying out our things, we broke camp and backpacked six miles into the wilderness area. To say that our equipment was primitive is an understatement! I had an outside-frame green backpack, and McEvoy had a day pack. I had never been backpacking in my life! McEvoy carried the food, and I carried almost everything else. We pitched camp just a little below tree line not too far away from the first of the three blue lakes.

The next day we hiked about sixteen miles round trip to Mount Sneffels, the same mountain I had first climbed the year before. Arriving on the summit around 1 p.m., we could not see too much because of the heavy cloud cover. While the U.S. flag that had been there the year before was gone, the pole upon which it had been mounted remained and served to mark the place in the rock cairn where the sign-in register was located.

The Colorado Mountain Club used to keep registers on the summits of most of the fourteeners. The register, which was stored in a piece of two-and-a-half-inch to three-inch pipe with screwed on endcaps, was rolled up; it contained several sheets of paper with columns to write one's name, city, state, and comments about the ascent. When finished, the climber rolled up the register, placed it into the pipe-tube, and screwed on the endcap to protect it from the elements. Periodically, members of the Colorado Mountain Club would collect the full registers, taking them to their headquarters in Denver, and leave a blank one in its place.

After completing the register and eating a snack, McEvoy and I hiked back to our high-country campsite, where we rested, fixed dinner, and prepared to leave the wilderness the next morning. Along the trail we saw deer, marmots (the mountain version of a groundhog), picas (the mountain version of a rat), and ptarmigan (the mountain version of a prairie chicken). Keep in mind that this climb of Mount Sneffels was identical to the one that I had done the year before: Blue Lakes Trail, Yankee Boy Basin, Sneffels, Yankee Boy Basin, Blue Lakes Trail.

Once we backpacked out of the wilderness and got to our car at the trailhead, we headed to Telluride, then a small mining town with only one road in and the same road out. Nestled high in the San Juan Mountains on three sides, we visited Father Sylvester Schoening, to whom I had been introduced the previous year by Wildeman. I had written to Schoening, asking him if it was OK for McEvoy and me to come for a few days and stay in the parish hall, like Wildeman, Koetter, and I had done the previous summer.

Schoening, whom I considered a good friend for years before we had a falling out, was the pastor of St. Patrick Parish in Telluride with a mission parish in Nucla. During the summer, he would set up cots in the parish hall to be used by visitors with sleeping bags. If there weren't enough cots for all the visitors, then the rectory attic had a few mattresses on the floor upon which sleeping bags could be placed. Lots of Schoening's friends took advantage of his hospitality while traveling to Colorado.

High above Telluride and pouring over the edge of the mountain is Bridal Veil Falls, a waterfall that can be seen from almost every place in what was once the small town. Now, of course, Telluride has been reinvented as a ski resort. Telluride Village, where the wealthy own homes and come to play, was built a number of years ago to bring money into the area. McEvoy and I hiked to the top of Bridal Veil Falls as part of one day's stay in the then-quaint little town.

Schoening owned a dog, named Uncle Spunky, who had a place in his old Jeep, which he liked to take into the high country over the old mining roads, especially the one named Black Bear that switch-backed below Bridal Veil Falls into and out of Telluride. One day Schoening and Uncle Spunky, who was referred to as the first dishing washing cycle because he licked all the plates clean before they were hand washed, took McEvoy and me on an adventure on Black Bear Road. At the top we stopped to view Bridal Veil Basin, LaJunta Basin, and Wasatch Basin before hiking to the summit of what Schoening called Wasatch Mountain, but no one has ever been able to verify this fact. Schoening's CJ-7 Jeep was never in the best of repair, so while ascending a steep slope the clutch slipped out. Schoening kept the brake on while McEvoy and I blocked the wheels with rocks; then, he scooted under the Jeep and fixed the clutch. We took away the rocks, and we were on our way. The knuckles on our hands were white from clutching the roll bar so tightly!

On our way home to Springfield, Missouri, we stopped at the old Climax Molybdenum Mine, where we went into a mountain. Molybdenum is a mineral used in hardening steel. We got to see the crushers in action and the rest of the refining process used to extract the mineral from the rock before it was shipped to steel mills around the world. While the Climax Mine has been closed for years, I remember it as my first venture into a mountain.

Those two weeks with McEvoy deepened our friendship, got McEvoy hooked on mountain climbing, and gave me confidence to think about backpacking to and climbing other mountains in Colorado. However, two years would elapse before I was able to return to the high country.

1978: Greg McEvoy 2

While we are making plans, life happens. This is true for me for the only year—1978—since 1975 that I have not been to Colorado! After getting to know McEvoy and his parents and sisters, he and I planned a three-week trip together in 1978 that bypassed the Colorado Rocky Mountains, but took us on a 6,618-mile road trip from Missouri to Albuquerque, New Mexico; Flagstaff, Arizona; Los Angeles, San Francisco, and Sacramento, California; Portland, Oregon; Seattle, Washington; Lethbridge, Alberta; Regina, Saskatchewan; Winnipeg, Manitoba; and Madison, Wisconsin, where we joined his parents and sisters who were visiting their grandmother in Evansville, Wisconsin.

On this trip I saw the desert—the Painted Desert and the Petrified Forest—for the first time. We crossed a major portion of it during the night because the car I owned had no air conditioning and, of course, it was very hot near the end of July!

This was also my first time to see the ocean—specifically, the Pacific. Both McEvoy and I were mesmerized by the ocean, spending parts of several days and one evening on the beach. In a poem simply called "Ocean," I compared it to "a famished beast / pawing the line of shore / roaring forth sand and salty brine." In another poem, titled "Ocean Delight," I wrote: "foamed lap / and a whale spewed spray / a nagging child / beating slave sand into submission."

McEvoy, who, as already mentioned was on his high school swim team, enjoyed the waves pushing him back to shore. The one evening we went to the beach he danced on his feet and his hands in the sand. Both of us wanted to experience the ocean through all of our senses.

We also spent a day at Disneyland, Universal Studios, and a few of the twenty-one California Franciscan Missions, which line the California coast from San Diego to Solano. Each mission was built a one-day horseback ride from the next. Other highlights of this trip included Crater Lake, Olympia Brewery, Space Needle, Treasures of Tutankhamun exhibit at the Seattle Art Museum, and backpacking, camping, and hiking in the Mount Rainier Backcountry before heading through Idaho into Canada.

Neither of us had ever been to Canada; thus, we had decided to cross part of the southern portion of the country before making our way back into the U.S. Of course, in those days no passport was needed; we just drove across the border, identifying ourselves to the Canadian border official as tourists.

The high point of the Canadian portion of the trip for me was visiting the Cathedral of St. Boniface in Manitoba. On July 22, 1968, the old Romanesque structure had caught fire and burned to the ground. What was left was the facade, the apse, and few sections of wall. Instead of tearing down the old structure, it was stabilized, and a new cathedral was built inside the ruins. One passed through the stone arches of the ruins in order to get into the new building. While I had always been interested in church architecture, visiting this unique melding of the old and the new piqued my curiosity as to what could be done with a little bit of creativity. Little did I know then that I would end up writing a book about Catholic Church architecture and furnishings and serve as a consultant on several church renovation projects.

While traveling on BART, the San Francisco Bay Area Rapid Transit subway system, McEvoy spoke one of those memorable sayings that has stayed with me my whole life. He said, "I like to look at things after I have already passed them." I had been asking him what he wanted to see in San Francisco, and he would usually answer me that he wanted to see something we had either already driven past or ridden past in the subway. I remember that proverb often, especially when traveling and thinking that maybe I should have stopped and seen something that I had just passed!

1979: Greg Eck, Greg McEvoy 3

Having circumnavigated the Rocky Mountains in 1978 for a road trip with McEvoy, I made up for it in 1979 with two trips to Colorado. The first occurred in March with Greg Eck, a tennis partner. Even though I was living in Joplin, Eck, who lived in Springfield, and I had stayed in contact with each other after I moved to Joplin. He wanted someone to travel with him to Denver to see his brother, Jim, who was working as an engineer there and living alone in an apartment in Aurora.

The highlights of the trip included the National Center for Atmospheric Research in Boulder, located at the base of the Flatirons, huge upthrust rock formations. After exploring the site, we drove through the snow-covered mountains, my first time to see them in winter.

Another highlight of this trip was my first attempt at skiing at El Dora Ski Resort. After taking the basic instruction class, I was taken to the top of a hill by a chair lift and told to ski down. I tried to come down, but decided that it was just too steep. Fear of falling and breaking an arm or leg got the best of me. Speed has never been an important part of my life, and speed on skis made it clear to me that it would probably never be! Later in my life, I would get hooked on cross-country skiing.

To commemorate my ski attempt, I wrote a poem, titled "Ski Attempt:"

> equipped with
> wooden barrel staves
>   hooked to my feet
> winter slick
>   covering earthen firmness
> sticks in hand
> filled with more fear
>   than inner courage
> lifted up to new heights
> I glide through the mountain breath
>   around a highway of obstacles
> to the starter
> and enough
> unequipped

One day, Eck and I went to Estes Park and hiked part of Longs Peak Trail in the snow. The sky was dark blue, and the snow was up to our waists when we turned around and headed back to the car. That was my first experience of hiking in the snow, and we covered eight miles.

This trip included visiting the Air Force Academy in Colorado Springs and the old Stapleton International Airport, Larimer Square, and the Zoo in Denver. However, it was the snow-covered mountains that got etched in my memory. In a poem, titled "New Vision," I tried to capture that experience:

slender lady-like aspen
shiver in the winter white

snow planted summits
quilt potential flowered color

coned fir and spruce
reach out to caress the blanket corners

and the wisdom of an older age
shines through with a transparency
into the inner core of being
for life already lived

The second trip to the Rocky Mountains in 1979 was with McEvoy in late July and early August. McEvoy was preparing for his first year in college; I was entering into full-time high school teaching. This 4,545-mile trip included a visit to Carlsbad National Park in New Mexico and the Grand Canyon in Arizona, before heading to the Rocky Mountains in Colorado.

Besides the excitement of touring Carlsbad Caverns, a "New Cave" was just opening; in order to follow the park ranger through it, one had to have hiking boots and a flashlight. After a mile hike in the Guadalupe Mountains, we met a ranger who took us through the cave, which did not have any illuminated walkways. With only a flashlight, I learned what true darkness is.

The next highlight of this trip was the Grand Canyon. McEvoy and I camped on the South Rim, then we backpacked seven miles on the Kaibab Trail to Phantom Ranch on the Colorado River. I remember standing in line to get information at the Phantom Ranch information desk, hearing a clerk cancel reservations for two people, and saying that I would take the reservations.

Overnight accommodates at Phantom Ranch consisted of a bunk bed in a dormitory with eight other men. It was cold-water evaporation cooled so I could sleep at night in the ninety- to one hundred-degree heat. It had shower and rest room facilities—all for the price of $8.24 per person! Dinner was available per person for $10.14, breakfast for $4.35—both served in the Dining Hall—and a sack lunch for $3.25. We bought the whole package.

After hiking down to the Colorado River early in the morning in order to avoid the heat of the day, as recommended by the park rangers, we spent most of the day relaxing in the river or in the shade. After enjoying the family style dinner, we wandered around for a while, showered, and went to bed. Early the next morning we enjoyed a family-style breakfast, picked up our sack lunch, and headed out of the canyon following the Bright Angel Trail for ten miles. The goal was to get to the South Rim by noon; otherwise, the 130-degree temperature would take its toll. Of course, lots of water has to be carried and consumed on the way out in order to avoid dehydration. I remember reaching the top after stopping repeatedly to give my knees a rest and being absolutely spent.

The desert beauty of the Grand Canyon left its imprint upon me. I wrote a poem to commemorate my first and only visit to that place. Called "Grand Canyon Ball," the poem was selected for publication in the 1980 *National Anthology of Poetry*. It states:

> six-storied ponderosa pines act as resined bows
> for the strings of the fir-branched violins
> as the fingers of the wind begin the canyon prelude
>
> with the sharpness of a newly honed tool
> prepared by the master tinker
> the river carves the butte steps of the canyon floor
>
> the sun discos across the sky in a familiar course
> as the moon pirouettes in her orbit from half to full
> the grasses perform bowed waltzes in their formal attire
> while winged creatures soar to the rise and fall of the melody

I always wanted to return to the Grant Canyon, but the mountains stole my heart. And that is where McEvoy and I headed after a night of recuperation in a motel. We took the East Fork of the Cimarron River outside of Ridgway and off the Owl Creek Pass Road. After backpacking seven miles we came to an old mining cabin that had served the Silver Jack Mine. The cabin, which was open, contained two old bed springs and an old wood cook stove. Instead of pitching a tent outside, we decided to put our sleeping bags on the bed springs and build a fire in the stove.

The goal was to climb Uncompahgre Peak (14,309 feet) in the San Juan Mountains. I had heard from friends about what an easy climb this peak was. So, McEvoy and I had decided to attempt it. After getting well above tree line the next day, we got caught in a forty-five-minute sleet storm. In order to protect ourselves from the ice pellets, we got as close as we could to some rock outcrops and covered ourselves with our ponchos. Once the sleet stopped, it began to rain. Of course, we got soaked. So, we abandoned the peak and headed back to the cabin, where we built a fire in the stove to dry our clothes. The next day we backpacked out of the area, making a firm resolve to attempt Uncompahgre Peak again the following year.

My poem "Mountain King" captures some of the experience of the adventure on Uncompahgre Peak:

> snow-bearded red face
> cloud-crowned majesty
> with cascading fir-folds
> in an ermine clad robe
> seated on a stone hewed throne
> commanding respect for endless distance
> with a wind-whispered voice

This third—and what was to be the last—expedition with McEvoy also included a stop in Denver to visit Jim Eck and, after traveling across Nebraska and Iowa, to Evansville, Wisconsin, to visit McEvoy's grandmother, who lived there, and his family, who were visiting there.

This trip remains in my memory because we went to the depths and the heights of the earth in a few days.

1980: Mike King

In the summer of 1978, I moved to Joplin and began to teach part-time in McAuley Regional Catholic High School. It was there that I met Michael (Mike) J. King, a freshman in high school. What attracted me to king was his intellectual ability. He was a critical thinker, and a very good one at that! In 1979, I became a full-time teacher of Religious Studies in McAuley, and King was in my classes on World Religions and Latin. Thus, in late July and early August 1980, I set out with a new travel partner: King, who was then a Junior in McAuley High School. Over the course of two years I had gotten to know him well. As a result, I had also gotten to know his mother and his grandmother, whom I visited on a regular basis. His father had died when he was a child, and I served that role during his high school years.

Travel plans took us to Albuquerque, Santa Fe, and Los Alamos, New Mexico, to visit my friends in those places, and, of course, to the Rocky Mountains in Colorado. The high point of the Colorado portion of the trip was a six-mile backpacking trip following the Middle Fork of the Cimarron River into the Uncompahgre Wilderness Area, located off Owl Creek Road outside of Ridgway.

After finding a suitable camping site, we pitched my red pup tent and prepared for the night. The goal for the next day was to climb Uncompahgre Peak (14,309) in the San Juan Mountains—the same peak I had tried the year before. After breakfast the next morning, we hiked about four miles to the Wetterhorn Basin. A familiar scenario began: Clouds began to come in, thunder could be heard in the distance, and we turned around and headed back to camp. After a little rain in camp, we broke camp and backpacked out. Thus, my second attempt to stand on the summit of Uncompahgre Peak was thwarted by the weather!

In Telluride, where we were staying at St. Patrick Rectory with Schoening, we greeted the arrival of Wildeman, Koetter, and Marvin Rush—all friends of mine from

Indiana. With them we hiked around Telluride and went on Jeep Rides on the Sheridan Cross Cut Trail and Black Bear Trail, stopping long enough to hike what Schoening called Wasatch Mountain.

King and I made stops in Aspen, Climax, and Denver before heading back to Joplin. Not only did this trip help to develop further my relationship with King and his with me, but I came to understand that prayer and mountain climbing are connected. Just as I could not dominate the mountain by climbing it, so prayer could not dominate God. Furthermore, just as I had to inhabit the mountain, all I could do was inhabit prayer. Both of these insights led me to further contemplation and the composition of "The Mountain Prayed:"

> as I climbed
> > the mountain bowed his white head in prayer
> and whispered a truth
> > older than eternity itself:
>
> I cannot be dominated or conquered;
> > I can only be inhabited and explored.
>
> My peak is only the beginning;
> > My foundation is the real end
> > where roots are sunk deep
> > into union with the Creator.
>
> To climb me is to descend;
> > To descend is to reach the peak of prayer.

By November of 1980, I had invested a lot of time, energy, and emotion in a friendship with King. I had gotten some response from him both inside and outside the classroom, but it was getting harder to find time for us to be together. After finally getting some time one evening, I explained to King that friendship demanded work; it was not just about me giving to him. I, too, had the need to share time, to be supported, and to be loved. He had refused my invitations to go to the lake, to see movies, or even to talk to me. I told King that I had observed a pattern in his relationships with women; he was reluctant to share himself with the women he dated because that meant relinquishing control. The same was manifested in his relationship with me; I wanted more from him, but he could not relinquish control. The pattern was found in class; during small group sessions, he could not relinquish control and take an exercise seriously. I explained that the pattern was also visible in his lack of participation in Mass; he couldn't relinquish control and join in singing hymns and answering prayers when he attended the Mass I celebrated in St. Peter the Apostle Church, Joplin, where I lived.

In the notes I prepared for that one-on-one meeting, I told King that if he didn't learn to relinquish control that his life would not be enriched by others. I told him that he had many gifts and much to share with and teach to others. Because of his intellectual capacity, he would need people to enrich his life.

In 1980, between Christmas and New Year's Day 1981, King notified me that he was not going with me on the March cruise upon which he had agreed to accompany me. He and several other students had been caught with beer on campus by the basketball coach. Being part of the full-time faculty, I stood with the rest of the teachers with the punishment decreed by the principal. This made King furious. So, he decided to renege on his promise to go with me. I had been looking forward to our time together; so, I was deeply hurt when he told me that he was not going. In my journal entry for December 27, 1980, I wrote, "I cannot be burned and hurt anymore. As far as I am concerned, this friendship is over!"

After King's grandmother, Minnie McSherry, could no longer come to Mass due to old age, I began to stop by the home where she lived with King, his mother, and her daughter. Minnie, who was called Cookie by almost everyone, and I would sit in a pair of rockers in a bay window and talk sometime for hours. I stopped by to see her on December 30, saw King, told him I was sorry for the way he felt, and he said nothing.

Once school resumed in January 1981, I told him, "The ball is now in your court. You make the next move or call the next shot." On January 15, I explained to King how he viewed all of life as a game that he played. Religion was a game he played with his mother. His friends existed to be used for whatever purpose he wanted. High school was a game to get to college, to get a job, to make lots of money. Because all of his life was a game, he never lived. He had no time for living. I told him, "I know a lot about you, but I do not know you." In my January 19 journal entry, I wrote: "I have been burned so bad and hurt so much that I don't dare even think about the cruise we were to take together. I am not investing anything anymore without some response." By February 16, 1981, King had declared the relationship finished. I made plans for the March cruise with John Brothers. On April 7, 1981, King came to tell me that he was sorry for what had occurred. We mended the relationship.

By July 22, 1981, we were relating well again. It took time to heal, but King was responding. Together we renegotiated our friendship and decided to get together on a regular basis to see films, to swim, to play tennis, etc. King and I did travel again together, but it was not to the mountains. A year later, we went to the World's Fair in Nashville, Tennessee, and from there to Miami, Florida, where we caught a ship and cruised around the Caribbean Sea for a week. In one of the special one-on-one moments, I told him, "You are like a son to me; if I ever had a son, I hope he would be just like you." In my journal I reflected upon how scared I was of this relationship because I was not in control of it; both of us were free and must remain so. By December 15, 1981, King was withdrawing again from home, school, and me. We maintained a friendship through 1982, when he graduated from McAuley High School and went off to college. I lost contact with him for a while, but as he grew more and more, got married, moved to Virginia, and had two children, he began to come by and see me in Springfield when he was visiting his mother and sister in Joplin.

For over the past thirty-five years, once a year or every other year King has made it a point to come and see me when he is in Joplin refurbishing the old home he and his wife bought there. From 1997 to 1998 we engaged in intensive philosophical e-mail discussions about films, family, relationships, and many other life experiences. Some years after the e-mail discussions came to an end, King suggested that we hand-write letters to each other in order to share our thoughts and lives; this process lasted for a couple of years. In both endeavors, which King suggested, he lost interest in the process and, due to his job and the travel associated with it, did not have the time to continue. But while the intensity of our relationship diminished, the basic friendship remains.

1981: Steven Vinyard 1

Steven Vinyard, a young man I had met at a church celebration who became a friend from Joplin, joined me for a two-week trip to Colorado in late July and early August 1981. We drove to the Nellie Creek Trailhead, backpacked a few miles, and set up camp. This was my third attempt to climb Uncompahgre Peak (14,309 feet) in the San Juan Mountains, and this third time I made it to the summit.

The successful ascent of Uncompahgre Peak was a watershed moment for me. Up to this point in time, I had climbed only mountains that others had chosen. I chose to climb this one, and, in the future, I would choose to climb many more. In other words, I began to plan my own Colorado climbing trips.

Uncompahgre is not a difficult climb; in one way it is an easy hike to the summit. What slows down most people is the altitude; it takes time to build up enough red blood cells to carry enough oxygen to the body's tissues to keep it functioning optimally. Once arriving on the summit, one sees a space the size of a football field with a small rise in elevation where the summit marker is located.

After Vinyard and I successfully made it to the summit of Uncompahgre, we broke camp and drove to Yankee Boy Basin to climb Mount Sneffels (14,150 feet), which I had climbed twice before. Again, we were successful, and this gave both of us the confidence we needed to explore more of the high country.

I commemorated these climbs with a poem, titled "Mountain Storm":

> thunderheads prospect peak boom
> besieging the orb of golden ray
> dropping their lode of nugget dew
>   —plenitude that produces soil riches
>   and air sparkles—
> then the cumulus retreat
> and the warming streams overflow anew

We spent a day exploring Mesa Verde National Park and the cliff dwellings left by a people who vanished over seven hundred years ago. For the first time, I took the Narrow Gauge train from Durango to Silverton; in 1981, a round-trip fare cost $18.50 per person. The D&SNG (Durango and Silverton Narrow Gauge) was marking its centennial. The steam locomotive leaves Durango and climbs the Animas River Canyon through the Needle Mountains and the Grenadier Mountains and arrives at the old mining town named Silverton, from which hundreds of tons of silver ore were once carried by the narrow-gauge train to Durango, from where it was shipped to refineries. The train often stops at Needleton, where backpackers can get on or off after exploring Chicago Basin and climbing any of the three fourteeners located there; the trail into Chicago Basin follows Needle Creek. I didn't know then that I would ride this train several more times to Needleton and backpack into Chicago Basin.

This trip with Vinyard also included my visit to what was then called Great Sand Dune National Monument (now Great Sand Dunes National Park and Preserve). We took a day and hiked in the heat and the wind and the sand to the highest dune. The sand dunes stand at the east end of the San Luis Valley. Mountain streams carry the sand to the valley, where the wind picks it up and carries it along until it hits the wall of the Sangre de Cristo Mountains. There, the sand falls and forms a desert. The wind shapes and reshapes the dunes in this National Park.

"Great Sand Dunes" is my attempt to capture the experience of climbing the highest sand dune:

> granules borne on whirl wings
> record a Heraclitan truth:
> only change is real
> nothing is
> all is continuous passing away
> a consuming movement of
> driven duned grit
> without form wind sketch

Vinyard, who died in 2013, and I would travel together to Colorado for several more years.

1982: Steven Vinyard 2

On August 1, 1982, Vinyard and I left Joplin with two high school students. Vinyard had joined the faculty of McAuley Regional High School in 1981, and, after consultation with him, we invited Peter Boever and Kyle Emrich, high school juniors, to join us. Boever was an athlete, but not necessarily a great student; Emrich was a great student, but not necessarily an athlete. We wanted to share our previous year's experience of backpacking and mountain climbing with two young men. This was the first time that I had ever led a group of three other people on a backpacking and mountain-climbing trip. Indeed, this was my first attempt to make plans to explore and climb mountains with more than one other person!

We made our way to Matterhorn Creek Road and backpacked into the high country for a few miles, until we found a place to pitch our tents near Matterhorn Creek. Vinyard pitched a two-man, easy-to-assemble, green tent, and I pitched my two-man, red pup tent. After establishing camp, we delegated responsibilities to gather fire wood, prepare food, and explore our beautiful surroundings. The next day we climbed the Matterhorn (13,590 feet) in the rain. After returning to our camp, we dried out and rested.

The next day we took off for Wetterhorn Peak, passing a canvas shepherd's tent situated in a valley surrounded by wild flowers in bloom. The white canvas contrasted with the purple, yellow, and red wild flowers. Then, we slowly made our way to the summit of Wetterhorn Peak (14,015 feet). Here, Vinyard took the lead and guided us over the near vertical final ascent. From the top of Wetterhorn, we could see clearly the Matterhorn we had climbed the day before and Uncompahgre, climbed the year before, not to mention countless other San Juan Mountains. Before we descended and got back to camp, it began to rain.

The next day we broke camp and moved it to the South Fork of Silver Creek. We wanted to climb Sunshine and Redcloud, two more fourteeners which are accessible from the South Fork of Silver Creek Basin. After backpacking a few miles, we found a good camp site, pitched tents, delegated camp responsibilities, and planned our strategy for the next day. After a good night's rest and a hearty breakfast, we took off for what we thought was Sunshine Peak. When we arrived at the summit, however, we discovered that it was an unnamed 13,432-foot peak, which we unofficially designated as Mt. St. Kyle in honor of our companion Kyle Emrich, who was most disappointed. After consulting our map, we discovered that we had misread it. But we determined that the altitude we had gained did not need to be lost.

As this point Vinyard calculated that we need only to hike the ridge from Mt. St. Kyle, and that would take us to the summit of Sunshine Peak, (14,001 feet). After eating a snack, we took off on the ridge and began to circle South Fork Silver Creek Basin. We arrived at Sunshine Peak, signed the register located in a cylinder, and hiked on to Redcloud Peak (14,034 feet). After signing the register there, we discussed our descent, and decided that all we needed to do was to drop down into the basin from where we were and we would be right at our campsite, which is exactly what we did. Of course, by the time we got back to camp, it was raining. So, we broke camp, backpacked out of the area, and drove to a motel, where we could spread out all our wet clothes and tents and dry them.

Our next stop was Ouray, Colorado, and a hike on Horsethief Trail. After a Jeep ride to Poughkeepsie Gulch by Schoening, we decided to climb Hurricane Peak (13,447 feet). Of course, it had been raining, and the rocks were slick. Furthermore, when sand and rock mixed together get wet, they have a tendency to form landslides. While climbing Hurricane Peak, which had no trail—so we were bushwhacking—I stepped into a small gully, where the rocks and sand turned into a mudslide. I grabbed a hold to the rock on my left and right and watched as the earth under my feet washed down the side of the mountain. Once the slide stopped and my heart stopped pounding in my chest, I lowered myself down, warned my fellow climbers around me of what might happen, and continued to the summit.

After getting back to Ouray, we rested and drove to Grand Junction, Colorado, where we visited friends and saw the Colorado National Monument. From there it was on to Denver and the usual sightseeing places there.

We managed to climb three fourteeners and three thirteeners in the rain! We traveled 2,506 miles that trip, and I discovered that I was becoming a mountaineer in skill and confidence. Even though I was not aware of it at the time, I was beginning to see mountaineering as a spiritual experience that would influence the rest of my life. My poem "Mountain Quietude" reflects this:

> in the highland mountains lofty alping
> wind breezes whisper poems
> branches creak spruce with age
> stones stand still for senility
> snows weep summer tears
> meadows grass lush waves
> blossoms flower sweet preserves
> hush hears silence spoken

All of us returned to Joplin as changed men because of our experiences of camping, hiking, and climbing in the mountains. Vinyard and I prepared for a new school year as teachers, and Boever and Emrich prepared for it as students.

1983: Steven Vinyard 3

For the third—and what was to be the last—time together Vinyard and I set out from Joplin for the Colorado Rocky Mountain on August 7, 1983, accompanied by Michael Lohkamp, a freshman in college in Springfield, and Robert Smith, a Junior in McAuley High School, where both Vinyard and I taught. Lohkamp was a member of a family with four sons; he was the oldest. When I lived in Springfield, I had spent a lot of time with the whole family, even babysitting at times for his parents. Smith and I had become bicycling companions; he was diabetic, so I had to learn all things diabetic from his mother before she permitted him to go backpacking and mountain climbing.

We began our backpacking in the desert below the Sierra Blanca, part of the Sangre de Cristo Mountain Chain, in south central Colorado. While there was a very rough Jeep road to Lake Como at eleven thousand feet, we had only a car. So, we backpacked the five miles to the lake, found a camping site, pitched tents, delegated camp duties, and explored the area in preparation for our climb the next day. Our goal was Blanca Peak (14,345 feet), the fourth highest peak in Colorado. Before leaving on this trip, I had purchased a three-man, green pup tent with yellow rain fly to replace my two-man, red pup tent. Because of the additional space it provided and the additional height, I came to call it my luxury tent and would often joke about my Lazy Boy recliner inside!

After a good night's sleep and a hearty breakfast, we took the trail to Blanca Peak. It was long and arduous, but all of us made it to the summit. We had to stop often to let Smith eat, as he was burning lots of calories and his blood sugar would drop. However, the view from Blanca Peak is seared in my memory. From there we could see the other fourteeners in that area: Little Bear, Ellingwood, and Lindsey, not to mention Lake Como below us and the San Luis Valley stretched out in the distance. We returned to camp in late afternoon, rested, fixed dinner, and prepared for the backpacking trip down to the car the next day.

Following the successful climb of Blanca, we headed to Handies Peak. We had planned on a short backpacking trip, camp, and climb. However, when we arrived at Handies, it was raining, and it looked like it was going to rain for a long time. We decided to forgo the backpacking and camping, stash our packs under an evergreen tree to keep them dry, and climb Handies in the rain. There was no thunder, so we were not afraid of getting hit by lightning.

Donning our ponchos, we headed toward Handies (14,048 feet). All the way to the summit it rained on us off and on. For a few moments the sun would break through the clouds, then the next shower would fall; the sun was warm, but the rain was cold. We completed the climb by reaching the summit, signed the register, took a few photographs with lots of clouds in them, and then headed back to where we left the car, picking up our packs on the way. We were soaked, of course. So, the next stop was a motel for the night where we could dry our clothes and packs. That backpacking and camping trip was abandoned.

After drying out, we headed to Durango, Colorado, to catch the Durango and Silverton Narrow Gauge train to Needleton, about halfway between Durango and Silverton. Needleton, an old mining village, is the drop off point for backpackers for the trail that follows Needle Creek into Chicago Basin. The train is the only way into the area and, consequently, the only way out. After backpacking about five miles, we found a good camp site very near Needle Creek, pitched tents, delegated camp responsibilities, and rested in preparation for the next day's climb. All that night, we slept to the gentle roar of the water in the creek smoothing the boulders in its path.

The trail through Chicago Basin was surrounded by wild flowers and flowing streams of fresh water. In those days, we would never hesitate to stop at a clear, flowing stream and fill our canteens or water bottles; today, such practice is no longer possible due to the number of people who now make their way into the backcountry and pollute the waterways. We made our way to Windom Peak (14,082 feet). The last few feet to the summit were over huge granite boulders and slabs of stone, but the view from the summit was spectacular, especially the other fourteeners located nearby: Mount Eolus (14,083 feet) and Sunlight Peak (14,059 feet). Furthermore, this was the first time I had ever seen mountain sheep—rams, ewes, and lambs—scrambling among the rocks and foraging on the tundra grasses and flowers in the high country.

After making our way back to camp from Windom's summit, we spent the remainder of the day resting and preparing for our backpacking trip to Needleton to catch the train out of the wilderness the next morning. We got up early, ate a hearty breakfast, and headed down the trail to Needleton to catch the train back to Durango; missing the train would have meant spending another night in the area. After two days in the wilderness without a shower, we were pretty grubby. I remember there not being room for us to sit in one of the passenger cars of the train, so we stood with our packs in the cargo car.

From Durango, we drove to Ouray, to meet Schoening, who was living there while work was being finished on his home in Norwood. We enjoyed two Jeep trips with him. One day he took us to the base of what he called Ajax Mountain (12,785 feet), which we climbed, and on another day to the base of what he called Telluride Peak (13,509 feet), which we also climbed. Several times with his CJ-7 he would cross a stream and drown the engine; I remember Lohkamp raising the hood, taking off the distributor cap, drying the contents, putting it all back together again, lowering the hood, and off we would go again. We could never be sure of exactly what mountain we were standing on, because the printed mountain guides and maps often disagreed with Schoening's name for a peak. The views, however, were outstanding!

We concluded our stay in Colorado with a hike along Bear Creek Trail outside of Ouray. Then, we headed back home to Joplin for Vinyard, Smith, and me and Springfield for Lohkamp. With having climbed so many more fourteeners in two weeks, I knew that I was becoming a real mountaineer, and my confidence in planning and executing climbs was itself climbing.

My friendship with Smith developed over bike riding. He had a ten-speed bike, and I had a three-speed bike; in the summers when he was in high school, we began to take short bike trips around Joplin in order to get into shape to take a much longer one before summer ended and high school began again. Often, our long trips would involve his mother coming to get us once we reached our final destination. Along the way, we would stop to drink the water and eat the food we carried with us in small bags attached to the seat and resting on the back fender of our bicycles. While I was living in a small white house on Indiana Street in Joplin, Smith would drop by to visit. He would sit in my living room, and we would talk about all manner of things that were important to us. Because of the relationship that we developed, Smith joined me on this trip to Colorado to mountain climb and on an ocean cruise after this. His favorite baseball team was the Chicago Cubs.

After he graduated and went to college to study writing, he began working for a newspaper in Arkansas. Then, he married for the first time and began to raise a daughter. After twelve years, he and his wife divorced, and it wasn't long before both of them married a second time. The last time I heard from Smith was around Christmas in 2006. I sent my annual Christmas letter to the usual address, and he replied by sending me an e-mail in which he recounted what had happened and his work in Lowell, Arkansas, at the *Arkansas Democrat-Gazette*. He narrated how his first wife did not understand what was important to him and his work, and how his new wife did. In my response to Smith's e-mail, I wrote, "I remember how important it was for you to be understood by me when we used to spend a lot of time together. I was interested in the real you that I got to know underneath the fake you that was on the outside that you used to protect yourself." Smith was a big man, who played high school basketball, and used his largeness to protect his feelings. When we were together, however, we disclosed who we really were to each other. In the e-mail Smith sent me, I noticed how articulate he had become as a writer, and I praised him for that. As in previous real encounters, the memories of our relationship remain with me.

1984: Darin Dankelson

In what was to be my last school year (1984–1985) of teaching in McAuley Regional High School, Joplin, Darin Dankelson, a student, and I headed to Colorado on August 5, 1984, for two weeks in the high country. Dankelson was the youngest of four brothers of a family that I had gotten to know while teaching at McAuley. We became good friends, and I had invited him to travel with me to Colorado before he began his senior year of high school. He was excited about going. Our first stop was a backpacking trip into the Sierra Blanca, where I had begun the year before. The two of us backpacked from desert to alpine for five miles and established our campsite below Little Bear Peak, one of the four fourteeners in this area, near Lake Como.

I had the grand idea of climbing Little Bear, one of the toughest ascents among the fifty-four fourteeners in Colorado. After a hearty breakfast we set out for a couloir, which would enable us to rock scramble to the ridge. The higher we got, the wetter the rocks were; it had rained and sleeted up high the night before, but it had only sprinkled at our campsite. We got to the ridge and began to move along it toward the summit when we met several climbers coming down. They told us that it was very slick with sleet and ice further ahead, making the ridge very treacherous. So, after some discussion between Dankelson and me and an evaluation of what the weather might do based on the clouds coming in, we decided to abandon the climb and head back to camp.

After abandoning the attempt to summit Little Bear Peak, we spent the day in camp resting and preparing to backpack out the next day. Early in the afternoon the rain clouds came in and began to drop cold water on us. We kept thinking that it was only the usual afternoon thunder showers that occur often in the high country. I think we stayed in the tent and played cards. When the rain finally stopped, we attempted to light a fire and prepare dinner; this was a few years before I invested in a camp stove. Of course, the wood was soaked. It wasn't long before the rain began again. Even though it was around 6 p.m., we decided that we did not want to spend the evening in the rain. So, we packed all our rain-soaked gear and headed back to the car. I remember telling Dankelson that we were going to have to hurry to make use of what natural light we still had. By the time we got to the car it was completely dark, and we had to use flashlights to see. We left the area and headed to Alamosa, where we found a motel and a place to dry our gear and ourselves.

From here we headed to Norwood, where Schoening had a home, which he named "The Hermitage." In the course of our time there, he took us to the trailhead for the Lone Cone (12,613 feet) in the San Miguel Mountains. We hiked the trail, crossed the boulder field known as the Devil's Armchair, and climbed the west flank to the summit. This was to be the first of many ascents of Lone Cone for me.

From the summit of Lone Cone, we could see more of the San Miguel Mountains, namely, the Wilson Massif, consisting of three fourteeners: Mount Wilson, Wilson Peak, and El Diente. We could also see the Dolores Massif: Dunn Mountain, Middle Peak, and Dolores Peak. And, of course, Little Cone could be seen from the summit of Lone Cone.

Schoening had a female wolf hybrid named Sneffels. Wolf hybrids were wolves that had been crossbred with Alaskan malamutes in an attempt to create a better sled dog. The experiment did not work, because when the wolf gets tired, it simply lies down and refuses to move forward, let alone to pull a sled! However, the 120- to 140-pound wolf dog became desirable to own as a pet, especially by people who lived on large tracts of land. The breed kept most of the wild wolf and little of the tame malamute. So, Sneffels had to be kept on a leash—or should have been kept on a leash—to keep her from chasing any other wild animals that she might smell, such as picas or marmots.

Schoening, however, loved to take her to the high country, where he would unleash her and permit her to roll around in a snow field. The wolf hybrid had the short, fine insulating hair under her longer external hair. She would get extremely hot in the sun; rolling around in a snow field would enable her to cool down. Once she was off the leash, it was close to impossible to catch her to put her back on it. She followed us across the boulder field to the ridge of the summit of Lone Cone on the other side. In a scrub spruce she found a porcupine, which she pursued until it placed a number of quills in her nose; then she came running to us howling in pain. Schoening tried to cover her eyes and remove the quills, but she would not let him even get close to her. So, he put her back on the leash and we continued to the summit of Lone Cone.

When we got back to the truck at the trailhead, he found a covering for Sneffels's eyes, found some needle nose pliers, and attempted to pull out the quills. He got one out, but that was all he was going to get out. She knew what was going to happen, and she wouldn't let him near her. A porcupine quill has a barb on the end of it, like a fishing hook. So, it causes a lot of pain when a person attempts to remove it. After struggling with the wolf hybrid for a long time, we headed back to The Hermitage, where Dankelson and I got out of the vehicle and Schoening took Sneffels to the veterinarian, who put her to sleep and removed the quills from her nose. Needless to say, she protected her nose for many days after this event.

On a hiking trip, we went to Woods Lake and the Navajo Lake Trail, enjoying more of the beauty of the San Miguel Mountains. Before getting home to Joplin, Dankelson and I drove to the top of Mount Evans (14,260 feet). Mount Evans has a paved road all the way to the top. Until 1979, when it burned, there was a summit house—Crest House—where one could buy a souvenir or get a cold drink; after it burned it was never rebuilt. All that remains are the four rock walls near the parking lot below the summit.

We returned to Joplin on August 18, after driving 2,505 miles across Kansas and through the Rocky Mountains. On this trip, most of our hiking and camping had to be cancelled because of the monsoon season. Despite the rain, I got a renewed awareness of the presence of God and made more connections between the experiences of God on mountain tops in the Old Testament, particularly in the Psalms. I came to a deeper appreciation of why the Hebrews, Israelites, and Jews believed that the LORD, their God, lived on mountain peaks.

1985: Richard Anderson

Richard Anderson, a student from McAuley High School and an avid Boy Scout, and I left Joplin on July 21, 1985, and headed to the Rocky Mountains. My relationship with Anderson was based on our mutual love for the outdoors. I had gotten to know him through teaching and working out at the same fitness center he attended after school. We went to The Hermitage, Schoening's home, located outside of Norwood, Colorado. Because the monsoon season had arrived, it rained almost every day. So, most of our backpacking and camping trips were cancelled, and we stayed with Schoening.

He, along with his female wolf hybrid, Sneffels, climbed the Lone Cone (12,613 feet) in the San Miguel Mountains. We also went to the Silver Pick Basin trail, hiking into the basin right below Wilson Peak and Mount Wilson in the San Miguel Mountains where we stopped at the ruins at what had one time been a miners' boarding house; all that remained in those days were a few stone walls and piles of lumber that had once served as a roof for the one-room structure. Of course, while eating lunch there, it rained on us!

We took the Black Bear Jeep Road into the basin and hiked to what Schoening called Telluride Peak (13,509 feet). Of course, while enjoying the view of Telluride below, the heavy black storm clouds assembled and rained on us. While we were with

Schoening, friends of his from Australia arrived for a few days; both were mountaineers and couldn't wait to get into the high country.

The best memory I have of this trip is sparked by a photograph I took of the moon. A full moon was peeking through the clouds at The Hermitage one evening. Because there were no city lights with which to contend, I set my old 35-millimeter camera on my car hood, aimed the lens at the moon beams streaming through the clouds, and guessed at the aperture opening time. I got fantastic pictures of the moon, of which the best one was made into an 8" X 10" print and framed.

After Anderson and I finished our 2,353-mile vacation and I got back to Joplin and he to Carthage, where he lived, on August 1, I finished packing and prepared for a move from Joplin to Springfield. I had finished seven years of teaching in McAuley Regional High School—religion and Latin—and I was asked by Leibrecht to work in adult education and assist the editor of the diocesan newspaper in choosing adult education articles for *The Mirror*. This was my last trip to Colorado with a high school student.

1986: Alone 1

The 1986 trip to the Rocky Mountains began June 29, and I went alone. My destination was The Hermitage outside Norwood, Colorado. Schoening had bred his female wolf hybrid with another wolf hybrid named Tonka from Ouray. Sneffels gave birth to many pups, and Schoening kept four of them. Thus, he had a pack of five wolf hybrids. He created what he called a harness for each of them; each harness consisted of several straps of leather that went over their backs and around their necks and was belted under their stomachs. To this harness was attached a leash in order to walk them and keep them from chasing anything that might cross the path or to keep them from pursuing every smell they caught on a breeze.

The first trip was to the snowfield on the east flank of Lone Cone so that the wolf hybrids could cool off by rolling in the remains of the previous winter's snow. While Schoening stayed at the snowfield with the wolf hybrids, I went on to climb the Lone Cone; this was my third ascent of the mountain in the same number of years.

The second trip was to Silver Pick Basin below Mount Wilson and Wilson Peak. Schoening stayed with the wolf hybrids at the ruins of the miners' boarding house while I attempted Wilson Peak. While I was making my way on the ridge, thick white clouds came in; I could hardly find the trail. The clouds continued to circle the mountain. To this day I do not know if I ever made it to the summit. I have a photograph of what looks like the chute to the summit that those who have climbed it speak about. They also talk about the register that was there, but I could not find it. And getting very concerned of what kind of weather the clouds might bring—lightning and thunder—I set the timer on the camera to take a couple of pictures of me sitting on what I thought was the summit, and headed down as quickly as I could. The thick cloud cover finally broke up, but I was well on my way down the trail when this occurred. Therefore, I do not know if I stood on the summit or not.

One day I went out exploring alone to the Dolores Massif. Because no mining was ever done there, there are no old roads or trails; the only way to get in is by bushwhacking, and that is what I did. Using the mountaineering skills I had learned over the past years, I worked my way through lots of willow brush and up a spine in the Dolores Massif. Once getting to a high point between twelve thousand and thirteen thousand feet, I saw that the ridge I was on dropped a lot of altitude before connecting to Dolores Peak; so, I decided to abandon the attempt and bushwhacked back to my car. After having enjoyed the views, I promised myself that I would return to attempt the three Dolores Mountains another day; that has never happened.

Through my repeated trips to Norwood, I got to know the Raabe family—Roy, Pam, Sonya, and their son, Matthew. Both Pam—who succumbed to a brain tumor—and Roy—who made it to his older years—are now dead, but I remember sharing delicious meals with them in their home in Norwood. One Sunday Matt—as he preferred to be known—and I climbed the Little Cone (11,981 feet). Matt was a freshman in high school, and both of us knew where the road was that got us to the end of where homes had been built on the Little Cone. We drove to the end of the road and bushwhacked the rest of the way to the summit. Because the Little Cone stands in the midst of the west end of the Sneffels Massif, the Dolores Massif, and the Wilson Massif, the view was breathtaking. We could even see the La Sal Mountains in southeastern Utah. We were almost surrounded by snow-covered peaks. This was a fitting end to my first trip to Colorado alone. After traveling 2,999 miles, I returned to Springfield on July 17.

1987: Alone 2

I usually give a trip a name. Thus, the trip to the Colorado Rocky Mountain for 1987 is titled "One Month in Colorado;" I was there alone from July 1 to July 27. My then-friend, Schoening, had become pastor of Sacred Heart Parish, Paonia, and St. Margaret Mary Parish, Hotchkiss, and I was going to spend a few weeks serving as the visiting pastor.

I arrived in Paonia to find that Wildeman, with whom I had first climbed Mount Sneffels in 1976, was there with a friend of his. They were meeting three more of their mutual friends from Indiana in a few days. After getting settled, Schoening, Wildeman, his friend, and I took off for a hike around Lost Lake Slough off of the Kebler Pass Road, a gravel/dirt road from the Paonia Reservoir to Crested Butte that is open only during the summer.

Schoening left after this and went to his home, The Hermitage, located outside of Norwood. I discovered that Wildeman and his friends were planning a climb of Mount Sneffels (14,150 feet) after camping in Yankee Boy Basin; Wildeman invited me to join them both for the car camping and the climb, and I did. The sky was a dark blue with the sun shining; the air was crisp, but not cold. All of us made it to the summit, where we could see for hundreds of miles in 360 degrees. This was my fourth time to stand on the summit of Mount Sneffels and sign the register there.

While staying in Paonia, I discovered that I was not far from the North Rim of the Black Canyon of the Gunnison. Most people see the Black Canyon from the South Rim since it is easy to get to, being located right off of a major highway from Gunnison to Montrose. I took several hours to drive around the North Rim, stopping at every sight-seeing pullout and photographing the beauty of the canyon. It left an impression on me that continues to this day, and I have returned many times to immerse myself in the austere beauty of this natural phenomenon.

Because this was an area of Colorado in which I had never been before, I took to exploring the mountains in the area. I found someone who took me to the Mount Lamborn trailhead, dropped me off, and picked me up a few hours later. Climbing Mount Lamborn—named because there used to be the image of a lamb formed in the rocks on the side of the peak—alone, I came to a deeper appreciation of my own skills in mountain climbing. Furthermore, I had never explored the West Elk Mountains before.

The trail to the summit of Mount Lamborn (11,395 feet) heads to the pass between Lamborn and Landsend—so named because it is the last of a chain of West Elk Peaks. After getting to the pass, the trail switchbacks up a tundra covered alp, then comes out on the ridge to the summit, which consists of several huge granite slabs with a cylinder containing a register—maintained by the Paonia Library—cemented into one of the granite pieces. Mount Lamborn was the first mountain that I had truly climbed alone. Yes, I had climbed the Lone Cone alone, but someone was waiting for me down the trail. Climbing Lamborn, I realized that there was no one waiting for me; all that was supposed to happen later in the afternoon is that I would be picked up by the same man who had dropped me off earlier that morning. I had no way of knowing if, indeed, he would do so. After this first ascent of Lamborn, I would go on to climb it a few more times in subsequent years.

More exploration of the area followed. After getting to know several of the families from the church, I began taking some of the boys with me. Joe Bear and Joshua Martin joined me in hiking the Beckwith Pass Trail (now called the Cliff Creek trail) off the Kebler Pass Road. The Beckwith Pass Trail offers a view of the Ruby Mountains that immediately caught my attention and would become my objective in subsequent years.

I made a short trip from Paonia to Norwood to join Schoening for a few days, taking along with me Tony Bear, brother of Joe. While there we hiked into Silver Pick Basin with all five of Schoening's wolf hybrids. We stopped at the ruins of the miners' boarding house and ate lunch. Back in Paonia, Joe Bear joined me for a hike into East Beckwith Bowl; we were looking for the true summit of East Beckwith, but couldn't find it amidst all the rocks.

Returning to The Hermitage, Schoening, the wolf hybrids, and I made a trip to the snowfield below the Lone Cone. While the wolf hybrids cooled off by rolling and playing in the snow with Schoening watching them and keeping them on their leaches, I made my fourth ascent to the summit of the Lone Cone. After Schoening returned to Paonia, I spent a few days in The Hermitage alone and figured out how to get as close as possible to the ridge that would take me to the summit of Groundhog Mountain (12,165 feet), which I climbed. From there I had fantastic views of the Wilson Massif, the Lone Cone, the Dolores Massif, the Little Cone, and the west end of the Sneffels Range.

After a few days of enjoying the silence of The Hermitage, I left to return to Springfield. I traveled 2,946 miles. I had begun to explore a new area of Colorado—the West Elk Mountains—as well as continuing to explore a previously hiked and climbed area—the San Miguel Mountains—and I was making plans to see what might exist on the other side of Kebler Pass, more specifically, the Ruby Mountains.

1988: Alone 3

As in 1987, I spent the month of July 1988 in Paonia, Colorado, where, with the growing confidence of the past year, I continued to explore the West Elk Mountains. My first climb was Landsend Peak (10,806 feet) alone. Before July 1988 I had bought an Isuzu four-wheel-drive vehicle to take to Colorado in order to get into the high country by myself; no longer would I be dependent upon others to get me to the high-country trailheads. The Isuzu had four cylinders and came equipped with skid plates so that any rocks on the old roads would not harm the oil pan, the transmission, or the gas tank.

After getting myself to the Mount Lamborn trail, instead of continuing to the left of the pass, I bushwhacked through fallen timber to the right of the pass in order to get to the summit of Landsend, named because it is the end of a chain of West Elk Mountains. At the summit and overlooking the North Fork of the Gunnison Valley is a memorial pile of rocks with one flat stone carved with the words: "In memory of Porter AZ Bowen 1946–1984."

A few days later, after doing some research, I took the North Smith Fork Road to a trail that paralleled Coal Mountain, another West Elk Peak. When I found a spot that I could bushwhack through, I headed for the long ridge that leads to Coal's summit. A little rock scrambling got me to the 11,705-foot peak from which I had views of Mount Lamborn, Landsend Peak, and several other mountains that I did not recognize at the time.

On another day I climbed South Saddle Peak (10,005 feet), a little higher than its neighbor North Saddle Peak. Collectively referred to as the Saddle Peaks because together from a distance they look like a saddle, this was another bushwhacking climb through desert and subalpine. After arriving at the summit of South Saddle Peak, I remember listening to the buzz of the bees as they pollinated the wild flowers which were blooming everywhere.

While I was living in Paonia, a friend named Art Hobbs from Joplin, Missouri, came for a visit. I took him for a ride on the Kebler Pass Road, a gravel/dirt road connecting the Paonia Reservoir and Crested Butte and open only in the summer. I had been on the road before, and I had noticed the Ruby Mountains, a chain of nine peaks in the Elk Range and very visible from the Beckwith Pass Trail which I had hiked before. Access to the southernmost peak, Ruby, is from Lake Irwin on the Crested Butte side of Kebler Pass. My friend and I had decided to explore Lake Irwin, when I got the urge, after walking along a trail below Ruby, to scramble through the rocks off the trail and attain—without much difficulty—the summit of Ruby Peak (12,644 feet).

At the time, I did not even know the name of the mountain I had climbed. It was there, and on the spur of the moment, I had decided to get to the top of it. When we got back to Paonia, I got out a map and discovered that I had climbed Ruby Peak, one of nine Ruby Mountains, so named because of the iron ore in the rock that gives off a dark red color when the sun shines on it. After attaining this information, I made a promise to myself to explore more of the Ruby Mountains.

After a few weeks in Paonia, I went to Norwood to spend a few days alone in The Hermitage. While there, I led Roy Raabe, a resident of Norwood, and Monica Odom, a resident of Nucla, to the summit of the Lone Cone. Both had become friends through my repeated visits to Norwood, and both had expressed an interest in climbing the Lone Cone. So, with them behind me we made our ascent of the peak; it was the fifth time I had stood on this summit in the same number of years.

1989: Alone 4, Bill Tembrock 1

July 27 to August 14, 1989, was a watershed in terms of mountain climbing in several ways. In 1988, I had climbed Ruby Mountain (12,644 feet), the southernmost peak of nine summits forming the Ruby Range, part of the Elk Range, and named because of the iron ore in the rock that gives off a dark red color when the sun shines on it. I had made a promise to myself to return to explore more of these summits off the Kebler Pass Road on the way to Crested Butte from Lake Irwin. While standing on Ruby Peak the year before, I had noticed that there was an old mining road/trail between Ruby and its immediate neighbor to the north, Mount Owen.

So, after arriving in Paonia I asked Joe Bear, a young former hiking partner, to join me in an attempt of Mount Owen. We drove to Lake Irwin and took the rough road to the old mining road/trail. With little difficulty we hiked the old road to Mount Owen (13,058 feet), the highest point in the Ruby Range. By this time, I was determined to climb the other seven Ruby Mountains. I began to do some research in order to determine the best routes to take in order to access the other Ruby Mountains.

While climbing Mount Owen, we encountered another mountain climber, named Brian Farmer, with whom we spent some time talking. Farmer was a sheep farmer, who brought his sheep to the high country in that area for grazing during the summertime. He had several shepherds who lived in huts or trailers near the sheep to watch and protect them. Farmer had been delivering supplies to his shepherds. Over the years he had become interested in the Ruby Mountains and had been climbing them when he finished delivering supplies to his shepherds. He and I exchanged telephone numbers and addresses and promised to stay in contact for a climb together in 1990. To further entice me to join him, Farmer sent me copies of photographs he had taken that day in the high country.

The year 1989 was also a watershed in mountain climbing because I made my first ascent of a mountain with William Tembrock, known to most people as Bill. Tembrock and his wife, Kathy (Kathleen), and three children were members of St. Margaret Mary Parish, in Hotchkiss, which I visited for Mass on Sunday while living in Paonia, about ten miles away. In the past several years I had seen and talked to the Tembrocks, but I did not know that Bill was a mountain climber; all I knew is that he ran an apple orchard, and Kathy was an elementary school teacher.

I had been asking parishioners both of Sacred Heart Parish, Paonia, and St. Margaret Mary, Hotchkiss, if they knew anyone who could tell me the way to the summit of Mount Gunnison, one of the West Elk Peaks that I had researched but was not confident to bushwhack on my own. Everyone with whom I spoke told me to talk to Bill Tembrock. So, I did. He told me that he climbed it once before a long time ago, but thought that he would remember the way. He was excited about climbing it again.

We set the date for the climb for August 7. Bill brought his son, Luke, and I brought Joe Bear. While we did not have a glorious beginning to the climb—driving to Beaver Reservoir but getting lost on a side trail that took us to Minnesota Pass and away from Hoodoo Creek—we recognized our mistake and bushwhacked over to Hoodoo Creek, which we followed up its steep gradient out of the valley to tree line. Once there, all four of us rock scrambled for miles until finally achieving the summit at 12,719 feet in elevation. After a snack, we began our descent, bushwhacking through aspen trees and fallen timber, and finally arriving at the Isuzu we had left at Beaver Reservoir twelve hours earlier!

This trip to the Rocky Mountains had introduced me to two fellow mountain climbers, Farmer and Tembrock, with whom I would share many future adventures.

1990: Alone 5, Bill Tembrock 2, John Kossler 1

Two major connections had been made in my 1989 mountain climbing expedition to Colorado. I had met Farmer, a sheep rancher, in the Ruby Mountains, and I had climbed Mount Gunnison with Tembrock in the West Elk Mountains. Furthermore,

I had determined that I was going to climb all nine peaks of the Ruby Range and continue to climb with Tembrock. All of this continued to develop in 1990.

For the fourth year in a row, I went to Paonia, arriving July 18, 1990. Before Schoening left for his home in Norwood, he took Matthew Taylor, a young friend of his, and me on the Crystal Creek Road between Crawford and the Black Canyon of the Gunnison to the Bald Mountain Reservoir and the trailhead to Bald Mountain. Taylor and I made our way over the trail, which was lined on both sides with wild flowers of every color. While the summit is only 11,787 feet above sea level, the view it affords of the West Elks is worth the five-mile round-trip hike to the top. It would be fifteen years before I would return to this beautiful place.

Since this was my fourth year in Paonia for several weeks, I had gotten to know the parish secretary, Denise Kossler, who was also a parish musician, playing the guitar. Denise had a twelve-year-old son, named John, who was too young to work on the cattle ranch her husband ran. One day she asked me, "Why don't you take John with you on a mountain climbing trip?" So, I asked John if he would like to climb Mount Lamborn, since he and his family lived below the peak on Lamborn Mesa. He was excited about doing it. So, Kossler and I climbed Mount Lamborn (11,396 feet), and began a friendship that would last for decades. This was my second ascent of Mount Lamborn in the West Elk Mountains.

Kossler and I got into a lot of trouble with his mother that summer. After climbing Lamborn together, we drove to Crystal Creek Road so I could take a photograph of Bald Mountain. We got back late for Kossler's baseball game. A week or so later, we took the Kebler Pass Road to Crested Butte, crossed the Slate River on an old bridge that connected a mining road to Gunsight Pass (11,922 feet), located below Mount Emmons. We scrambled over rocks, stood on Mount Emmons (12,392 feet), and headed back to Paonia; we were late for another of Kossler's baseball games! But what a view we had of the Ruby Mountains.

Making connections with Farmer, whom I had met on Mount Owen the previous year, I accompanied him on one of his resupply trips to his shepherds in the high country below the Ruby Mountains. Together, we climbed Purple Mountain (12,958 feet), the northernmost peak of the Ruby Range, from the old Yule Pass Road/Trail.

Making a connection with Tembrock, with whom I had climbed Mount Gunnison the year before, he and his son, Luke, and I explored the East Beckwith area above Lost Lake Slough off of the Kebler Pass Road on the Paonia side of Kebler Pass. None of us knew exactly which of the summits in the Beckwith Massif was East Beckwith. After scrambling over large boulders into the rock basin, I spotted a cairn on the top of a summit to which we had not been heading. Once that occurred, we immediately changed our approach and headed toward what was clearly East Beckwith Mountain (12,432 feet).

The year 1990 was a summer of keeping mountain climbing connections. I followed up with Farmer, and he and I climbed together. I followed up with Tembrock, and he and I climbed together. I made a new connection with Kossler, and he and I climbed several mountains together. During that July 17 to August 11 trip, I climbed four new mountains, and, while in Norwood at The Hermitage for a few days, made my sixth ascent of the Lone Cone (12,613 feet).

1991: Jim Reynolds 1, Kossler 2, Tembrock 3

Early in 1991 I invited Father James L. Reynolds to join me on my annual trek to the Rocky Mountains in Colorado. Reynolds and I had lived in the same house (rectory) for a year in 1976. Over the course of that year, we had become good friends and enjoyed getting together and talking about academic subjects. He had studied mathematics and I had studied theology in many of its various forms. We often got together and engaged in intellectual enlightenment, meaning we attempted to see as many sides of a topic as possible. This occurred not only in the areas of religion and theology and liturgy, but in the areas of science and mathematics as well.

Reynolds indicated that he was interested in joining me on vacation in Colorado. So, we made plans to travel together. Again, for the fifth summer I was headed for Paonia, where Reynolds and I would live for a few weeks before heading to The Hermitage in Norwood for a few days before coming home to Missouri. We arrived in Paonia on July 10 and, after picking up Kossler, who had hiked with me the year before, on July 11, we headed to Mount Lamborn (11,395 feet).

This was the first mountain that Reynolds ever climbed. Below the summit he stopped for a few minutes and stretched out on some flat rocks to rest. Kossler was fascinated by Reynolds, who is also remembered—he died in 2008 after a ten-year battle with colon cancer—for his famous sayings about himself in third person, such as: "Father is tired." Kossler, who was a quiet, thirteen-year-old, continues to tell the story of the priest who climbed Mount Lamborn and stopped on the way to the summit to take a nap!

After Mount Lamborn we got together with Tembrock, who had become a good friend, for a car camping trip before climbing Mount Elbert on July 17. Tembrock brought along his son, Luke, who was becoming a very good mountaineer. After building a huge fire in our camp, getting a good night's sleep, and eating a hearty breakfast, the four of us hit the trail to Mount Elbert, Colorado's highest summit at 14,433 feet. In fact, getting to Elbert's summit, we had to hike over other fourteen thousand foot-plus summits! We reached the top by noon, ate a snack, and then began our descent. The clear day was giving way to some clouds. "I can't believe I did this," was the memorable Reynolds's saying after reaching the top.

After Lamborn and Elbert, I figured Reynolds was ready for the Ruby Mountains, and I had my eyes focused on Purple Peak—not to be confused with the northernmost summit of the Ruby Mountains named Purple Mountain. So, after taking the Kebler Pass Road to Lake Irwin, we parked the Isuzu near the end of the old mining road and began to scramble through the rock bowl that connects Purple Peak and Mount Owen. It was a bright sunny day with a dark blue sky—perfect for mountain climbing. Reaching the ridge, we turned right and headed to Purple Peak (12,800 feet). All that Reynolds said upon reaching the summit was, "Oh, hell!" He had just participated in his first rock scrambling adventure!

Because I had climbed Mount Owen before, I knew there was an old mining road between Mount Owen and Ruby Mountain. So, I suggested to Reynolds that we head over to Mount Owen (13,058 feet), the highest point in the Ruby Range, and then take the road back to the Isuzu. It was an easy ridge walk to Mount Owen. Standing on its summit, Reynolds said, "Isn't God great to have made these mountains?" After sitting down and eating a snack, we continued on the ridge to the road between Owen and Ruby and began our descent. We could see further down the road that there was a huge snowfield blocking it, and we would have to cross it to continue.

When we got to the snowfield, I told Reynolds to let me go ahead and make some steps through it for him to follow. I had some experience of crossing snowfields and knew how to create a path through them, but he did not know this technique. I knew snowfields were dangerous, especially after having been in the sun all day; the sun softens the snow that has become crystallized into ice, and it begins to melt from underneath, turning loose of the rocks to which it is attached. I made my way across the steep snowfield, leaving deep footprints for Reynolds to follow.

Just as I took my last step, a portion of the snowfield turned loose and down I slid the rest of the snowfield and then tumbled through lots of flinty, sharp rocks until I came to an abrupt stop. My heart was pounding in my chest. With trepidation I managed to stand and to feel my arms and legs to see if anything was broken. I seemed to be OK, but blood was seeping out of my elbows and knees, which had been cut by the flinty rocks over which I had slid.

My first thought was to find Reynolds, who would have been high above me, and tell him to be very careful finishing his crossing of the snowfield. However, when I looked up, I could not find him, and began to wonder where he went. The sun was shining in my eyes, so I couldn't see clearly. I called his name, and got no response. I called it again, and from below where I was, he answered. He had continued to try to cross the snowfield after it turned loose, slid down the rest of it, and tumbled over the rocks just like I did—only he slid further down the mountain. He was walking towards me.

As he got closer, I asked him if he was OK, and he said he was except for a few cuts and bruises which were seeping blood. I noticed that he carried a rock in one hand. Not knowing what had happened to him at this point, I asked him why he had a rock in his hand. He answered me that his fingers were cold and the rock was warm. That immediately eliminated the fear I had that he was coming after me with a rock!

We found ourselves above Green Lake; if we would have continued to tumble down the mountain, we would have ended up in the half-iced, half-thawed lake. We looked at each other's cuts and decided that they were only scratches, but we would not be able to tell for sure until we washed them off. We were not about to do that on the side of a mountain; furthermore, we might reopen a cut that had already stopped oozing blood. We also knew that we had to keep moving to keep our muscles from tightening and get back to the Isuzu in order to get out of the wilderness and back to Paonia in case we did need a doctor's care.

As we slowly continued down the road, we spotted another vehicle near my Isuzu and three or four other mountain climbers standing around it. Once we reached them, they told us that they had watched us fall and, because one was a medic, had decided to wait and see if we were OK. We assured them that we were fine and able to get ourselves back to Paonia. Once we got back, the first thing on our agenda was a shower so we could see how deep were our cuts. After both of us emerged from showers, which attacked our skin like needles on our elbows and knees and anywhere else we had a cut, we determined that we were fine and all cuts were minor abrasions. That evening we joined Pete and Shirley Tulio, friends from Somerset, a coal mining town between Paonia and the Paonia Reservoir, for dinner. While eating a steak, Reynolds got choked, and we had to hit him on the back to dislodge the beef from his throat!

After a day of rest, we knew we needed to get back on the hiking trail. So, we headed back to Lake Irwin to hike Scarp Ridge, an above-tree-line area that offers mountain views of 360 degrees of the Ruby Mountains and more. Scarp Ridge, 12,212 feet high, was a perfect hike after sliding down a snowfield two days before. At the end of that day, Reynolds said: "Father is pleased. Father is happy. This was a beautiful hike."

No trip to Colorado would have been complete in those days without a climb of the Lone Cone. So, after driving to The Hermitage in Norwood, we climbed the Lone Cone (12,613 feet); this was my seventh ascent of the peak. At the top, Reynolds delivered another of his famous sayings: "Father has his first blister—on his big toe!" By the time we got back to Missouri, we had traveled 3,637 miles together, and Reynolds was hooked on mountain climbing.

To commemorate this first of several mountain climbing trips with Reynolds, I wrote a poem titled "Lost in the Mountains (for Jim Reynolds):"

> Seas of mountains over the skyline roll.
> > Peaks form hard waves of foamy-white snow fields.
> > Early morning rains drop, like salt spray, yields
> Pastel tundra flowers, floating the knoll.
>
> Windy whispers bring worship to the soul
> > And spin shirts and slacks into sails and shields.
> > Gray-streaked cotton cloud lightning bolt—flash!—wields
> Rumbles; echoes roar down the valley whole.

A pause for solitude: two climbers stop
    In-between the syllables of their word.
On the summit presence—awe!—they eavesdrop.
    The quiet song is louder than the bird.
Grace glides over rough rocks on the alp's top
    And the bright, full moon has spirit bestirred!

1992: Sabbatical, Alone 6

In 1992, I took a five-month sabbatical. Three months were spent in Alaska, one month was spent in Colorado, and one month was spent in Europe. The time in Alaska and Europe are documented elsewhere; here I will reflect on the month of September 19 to October 12 in Colorado. While in Alaska, I had been in contact with the chancellor of the Diocese of Pueblo, which comprises most of the southern half of the State of Colorado. We had been dialoguing about a month-long assignment for me, since Schoening had broken his ankle, went into retirement, and Sacred Heart Parish in Paonia and its mission, St. Margaret Mary Parish in Hotchkiss, had a new pastor. The chancellor sent me to Del Norte.

Holy Name of Mary Parish in Del Norte had two mission churches: Immaculate Conception, Creede, and Holy Family, South Fork. Holy Name of Mary had once been a Franciscan Center; the rectory was the former friary with many small rooms for the priests and brothers who lived there. The church itself was built in the Franciscan Mexican-American style of architecture. The pastor was Rev. Eugene Harden, the first black priest in the Diocese of Pueblo, who had just returned from several weeks of chemotherapy treatment for lymphatic cancer in preparation for a bone marrow transplant, which he received in November that year. However, in late September he was too weak to fulfill his ministerial duties to the three parishes for which he was responsible.

While on sabbatical in Alaska, Reynolds, whom I had introduced to mountain climbing the year before, had joined me for my last two weeks in that state and had accompanied me on the trip to Colorado by way of the Marine Highway. We had stopped along the southeast coast of Alaska, driving off of one ferry and spending a few days in Juneau, catching the next ferry to Sitka, spending a few days sightseeing and hiking, catching the next ferry to Ketchikan, where we did more sightseeing and hiking, and finally taking the ferry to Prince Rupert, British Columbia, Canada, from where we headed south to Colorado. When we arrived in Del Norte, Harden greeted us as "missionaries from Alaska."

The first weekend was easy, since Reynolds traveled to the mission parishes for Mass and I said Masses in Holy Name of Mary Parish. All that Harden was able to do was to visit with us and fix a meal every once in a while. Reynolds was supposed to spend another week with me, but after becoming restless, he asked me to take him to the Alamosa airport, where he made arrangements to fly home. That left me alone with Harden, who spent most of his days resting. I was determined to explore the area.

The first mountain I climbed was Del Norte Peak (12,400 feet). Del Norte Road took me to the trailhead from which I hiked to the summit of the bald mountain. I had never seen the mountains in late September, so this was my first time to experience the dried tundra grasses and the various hues of yellow, red, and orange of the aspen leaves. After a day of hiking and climbing, I would rest for a day in Del Norte, sometime seeing the town and other times writing. Harden was fascinated by my presence because he knew that I had written many articles for *The Priest* magazine, to which he subscribed. Often, he would come into one of my rooms (I had two or three that he told me I could use) and talk to me about writing and share some of his own feeble attempts at the craft. On my way back to Del Norte I stopped at Lookout Mountain, a Del Norte feature, which I climbed to the height of 8,475 feet.

After Del Norte Peak, I took the West Frisco Trail and headed to the summit of Bennett Peak (13,203 feet). In the high country, things were freezing during the night. The little pools of water on the trail were etched with ice crystals; the trail floor looked like someone had painted it with ice and red, yellow, orange, and brown aspen leaves. The beauty of the trail floor made me feel guilty walking on it.

In a few days I returned to the same area to explore an unnamed mountain 12,223 feet in elevation. After climbing it, I named it Harden Peak in honor of the pastor in Del Norte. I told him that I had unofficially named a mountain after him when I got back to the rectory where we were living. He was very pleased and flattered. In early October before I left, he was feeling well enough for some sightseeing, so we went to see the mountain I had named after him. Early in 1993, I got word that the bone marrow transplant had not worked, and Harden had succumbed to cancer and died.

The first week of October I spent in Hotchkiss at Tembrock Orchards. The apple harvest was well underway, so Bill was not able to get away for a hike. Kathy was busy teaching. And Luke was in school. So, I spent my days exploring the orchard, taking photographs, reading, and relaxing.

Upon returning to Del Norte, I climbed Poison Mountain (11,999 feet). After Harden began to feel better and he wanted to go on a short hike, we went to the Del Norte Window, a formation of rock that has a huge hole in the middle. We hiked to the rock formation and back, and this pretty much tired Harden.

I left Del Norte on October 12 to continue my sabbatical. Spending a month there gave me the opportunity to explore another area of Colorado, to hike its trails in the high country, and to climb its peaks. Other than the memory of the fall colors is that of Harden, a good man who left this world way too early.

Harden taught me how to see the presence of God not only in the mountains, but in the death and resurrection of Jesus and in our own daily dying and rising. He viewed his cancer as a gift from God to help him in his ministry to the Hispanic population of the San Luis Valley in which Del Norte is located. He was a very gentle man with great patience and great trust that his cancer could be held in remission. His death in early 1993 did not erase his trust; it finished tracing the paschal mystery of Jesus—death and, hopefully, resurrection—in Harden's life.

1993: Alone 7

I made two trips to Colorado in 1993, and neither of them involved any mountain climbing. In mid-June I traveled alone to The Hermitage, where Schoening was now retired. We took jeep and day hiking trips throughout the area. From June 19 to 20, I joined the Tembrocks and their children—John, Nicole, and Luke—on a backpacking trip into Little Elk Basin, where, after establishing our campsite, we enjoyed the West Elk Mountains that surrounded us. Back in Norwood, I led a hike on the Lone Cone Trail with three local women, but we did not climb the Lone Cone. And that was how I spent two weeks in June 1993 in Colorado.

In December, I returned to Norwood for ten days including Christmas. Instead of driving, I flew into Montrose, where Schoening met me and took me back to The Hermitage. Over the ten days I was there, Schoening taught me how to cross-country ski. Other than my feeble attempt at slope skiing in 1979, I had not attempted the sport again. Schoening had extra skis, boots, and poles that fit me. We went to the end of the plowed Lone Cone Road, where he showed me how to begin, and I fell in love with cross-country skiing that Christmas day in 1993. Almost every day after that we took the skis and went to a different area outside of Norwood to enjoy the winter wonderland of snow.

One day we went to Ouray to ski. After we finished, we went to the famous Ouray Hot Springs, where we exchanged our ski wear for swimming trunks and jumped in one of the hot springs' pools. The hot water emerges from the earth at a very high temperature. As it flows from one pool to the next, it cools. So, most people begin with the coolest pool and transfer in stages to the hotter ones. While we were enjoying the therapeutic waters, it was snowing. I will never forget the feeling of snow falling on my bare shoulders as I swam in the hot springs in Ouray.

1994: Luke Tembrock 1, Nathan Smith, Jim Reynolds 2

In early June of 1994, Luke Tembrock, Bill's and Kathy's teenage son, from Hotchkiss, Colorado, traveled to Springfield, Missouri, via Greyhound Bus. A day or two after his arrival, he went to work for a week at a local camp. When that week was finished, he joined the group I had put together for a hiking and climbing trip to Colorado.

The members of the group consisted of Reynolds, who had joined me for three previous trips to Colorado, and Nathan Smith, the teenage son of a person with whom I worked. Smith was about the same age as Tembrock. So, in late June the four of us headed to Horn Fork Basin on a backpacking trip with the goal of climbing Mount

Harvard in the Collegiate Peaks Wilderness Area. All of us except Smith knew that we had no altitude sickness problems.

After backpacking for miles, we made our way into Horn Fork Basin, found a very nice camping site, and proceeded to pitch both my large green and yellow three-man pup tent and my two-man orange pup tent. The larger tent was for Reynolds and me; the smaller tent was for Tembrock and Smith. After assigning various camp duties, we prepared dinner and relaxed around a huge camp fire.

After a hearty breakfast the next morning, Tembrock, Smith, and I headed up the Mount Harvard Trail, while Reynolds, who had been cultivating fly fishing, remained in camp, planning to see what he might catch in Bear Lake, not too far from our camp site. I continued to ask Smith how he was doing as we made our way to Mount Harvard. After getting way above tree line, he began to suffer from altitude illness, which is characterized primarily by a throbbing headache. Tembrock and I could not leave him on the trail and continue to Mount Harvard because we had talked about an alternate route down. We could not trust that he could find his own way back to camp, since this was his first time in the high country. So, the only option we had was to descend and get Smith back to a lower altitude. Once we got back to camp and gave him some aspirin, he lay down for a while in his tent, and, when he got up, his headache was gone. We had not given Smith enough time to acclimate to the altitude. After another night in camp, we headed to The Hermitage outside Norwood.

Schoening was leaving on a trip, and we were taking care of The Hermitage and the wolf hybrids that he owned. We cleaned the house, resealed the decks around it, and fed the wolf hybrids. When we were not doing that, I took Smith to the summit of the Lone Cone, making that my eighth ascent. He demonstrated that he had acclimatized and no longer suffered from altitude sickness. Reynolds spent a lot of time fly fishing in the various reservoirs and lakes in the area.

We also joined Bill and Luke Tembrock for an attempt of the summit of West Beckwith Mountain. However, when we got to the ridge, Reynolds, Smith, and I decided to stop because the ridge was composed of rotten and loose rock. The Tembrocks made their way slowly and carefully to the summit, while we waited and watched them inch their way to 12,185 feet. Our descent was what came to be known as a Tembrock experience—through downed-timber forest and yard-high brush and wild flowers.

Meeting friends from Nucla, Colorado, namely, Ida Vanderpool and her daughter, Heidi, and Monika Odom and her daughter, Rhonda, along with Smith, I led the five of us on a hike of the Blue Lakes Trail off the East Dallas Divide Road. We walked to the first Blue Lake, sat on the rocks, and ate lunch. The wild flowers were blooming everywhere; so, they occupied a lot of our viewing time. Reynolds and I also hiked the Lone Cone trail one day.

After Schoening came home, we traveled to the Great Sand Dunes, since neither Reynolds nor Smith had ever been there. We spent the greater part of July 6, 1994, hiking to the highest dune, getting coated in sand. After returning to the Isuzu, we drove to La Junta, where we found a motel room, showered, went to dinner in a Mexican restaurant, and got a good night's sleep before heading back to Missouri the next day.

I returned to Colorado for Christmas, December 20–30, staying at The Hermitage in order to engage in cross-country skiing. I flew into Grand Junction, where Schoening met me and took me to his home. Besides skiing with Schoening, one day I invited Bill, Kathy, and Luke Tembrock to come for a cross-country afternoon trip. Along with Schoening, we skied over miles of the unplowed Lone Cone Road outside of Norwood in the bright sunshine. When not skiing, I cooked meals, cleaned, and worked on writing projects that I had brought with me.

The year 1994 marked the second year in a row that I had not stood on the summit of a mountain that I had not climbed before. I was determined to change that for 1995.

1995: Luke Tembrock 2

In early June, Luke Tembrock arrived from Hotchkiss, Colorado, by way of a Greyhound Bus in Springfield and headed to a local camp to work for a week. Once he returned and got a few days of rest we went to see the cannon-firing demonstration of the Civil War re-enactment at Wilson's Creek National Battlefield, Springfield, on July 18. Two days later, we headed to Colorado to backpack into what Tembrock had named Ego Sum Basin, the area below Stewart Peak in the Northeast San Juan Mountains. By this time, the teenage Tembrock had become a very good mountaineer, and I was pleased to let him decide where we would backpack and climb on our way to taking him to Hotchkiss. He chose Stewart Peak because he and his father had climbed it the year before.

Once we got on the old mining road to Ego Sum Basin, the Jeep I was driving began to heat. We had to open the windows and turn on the heater to cool off the engine as we switch-backed our way to the basin. We backpacked for a few miles, found a camp site below Stewart, pitched my tent, and set up camp right at tree line. Tembrock built a large camp fire, and we fixed dinner.

After a good breakfast the next morning, we trudged through snowfield after snowfield to the summit of Stewart Peak (13,987 feet) on June 22. We signed our names on the register that was there, made our descent, broke camp, backpacked to the Jeep, and headed to Hotchkiss, where Tembrock's parents were happy to welcome us. A few days later, Bill, Luke, and I went to the Uncompahgre Plateau, specifically Cottonwood Creek Road, where we car camped June 24–25. Bill and Luke had begun the practice of spreading their sleeping bags on a tarp without pitching a tent. Thus, they found a place in the grass, spread the tarp, opened their sleeping bags, and climbed into them. I remember choosing to sleep in my sleeping bag in the back seat of the truck!

After traveling to Norwood, I spent a few days at The Hermitage, taking a trip with Monika Odom and her daughter, Rhonda, from Nucla. Our first stop was in

Paradox, Colorado, on June 30, where they showed me a whole series of Native American petroglyphs, carved into and sketched onto the sandstone rock. After this stop we continued on to Arches National Park in Utah where we hiked through mile after mile of desert landscape to view the natural rock arches that water once carved out of the solid rock.

I spent some of the days of Christmas at The Hermitage, cross-country skiing, cooking, cleaning, and writing, as I had the previous three Decembers. I had come to appreciate the beauty of the high country in winter, especially the warm sun, the clear blue sky, and the open ski trail.

I had kept the promise I had made to myself the year before. I had climbed a mountain whose summit I had not previously set foot on. I had also come to a deeper appreciation of the mountaineering skills of teenage Tembrock. And I was already making plans for the next summer.

1996: Alone 8, Bill Tembrock 4

For several years, I had wanted to get back to the Ruby Mountains and finish climbing the rest of the nine peaks that form that range. I had spoken about the Ruby Mountains to Bill Tembrock, and I got him interested in joining me. So, on June 23, after doing some mountain access research, Tembrock and I headed to Crested Butte, took the Slate Creek Road, and crossed Slate Creek onto the Oh-Be-Joyful Road which follows Oh-Be-Joyful Creek. We left the truck in front of the remnants of an avalanche from the previous winter which had deposited a huge pile of uprooted trees across the road. After preparing our gear, we backpacked to Democrat Basin, where we found a camp site just below tree line, pitched a tent, gathered firewood, made a fire ring, built a fire, and fixed dinner, after which we explored the basin for about an hour, planning our climb for the next day.

After a good night's rest and a hearty breakfast, we headed into Democrat Basin carrying ice axes because it was still covered in several feet of snow from the previous winter. Our goal was to climb to Oh-Be-Joyful Pass, where we would be on the north end of three of the Ruby Mountains on less than a two-mile stretch of ridge. Needless to say, it was slow going over the snowfields until we got into the rocks. Reaching the pass, we headed south to Hancock Peak (12,410 feet), upon whose summit we stopped long enough to eat a snack. From there we continued south to Oh-Be-Joyful Peak (12,400 feet), losing little altitude by having to scramble around rock outcroppings on the ridge.

On Oh-Be-Joyful Peak, Tembrock asked me if I was going to be able to get to the third peak. I had been getting tired, and my feet were hurting. I remember telling him that I knew that I would never get to this part of the high country again, so we had to get to the third peak. He had already stated that he wanted to get back to Hotchkiss that night. I told him that if I made it to the third peak, he would have to spend another night in our camp because I would not have the energy to walk out after all the climbing we had been doing. He agreed that we could spend the night of June 24 in Democrat Basin, and I agreed that I would make it to the third peak.

What was at stake was not only making it to the third peak. Once there, we had to come back over the same ridge that we had just traversed. There was no way to descend into Democrat Basin from the third peak. So, we would have to come back to Oh-Be-Joyful Pass and go back to our camp the way we had come. After finishing our discussion, we ate an energy bar and headed to Afley Peak (12,646 feet). Unlike the other two mountains, which differed only by ten feet in elevation, we would have to gain 246 feet to stand on Afley Peak. Upon arriving there, I remember Tembrock declaring that this was "a significant alpine experience."

We stopped for a while on Afley's summit to eat a snack and drink some water before beginning the climb back over Oh-Be-Joyful and Hancock. Once descending the trail to Oh-Be-Joyful Pass, we found ourselves in Democrat Basin, which had been exposed to the sun all day. In the late afternoon, the snow was soft. So, with every step we took we sank up to our knees in snow. We had to use our ice axes for balance. This made getting back to camp even more arduous and left us pretty wet. However, after ten hours of climbing and seven-miles of trail, we made it back to camp, where both of us dropped onto a log to rest before getting a fire built and diner prepared.

Immediately after dinner we crawled into the tent and into our sleeping bags. The next morning we broke camp, backpacked out of the Ruby Mountains, and headed to Hotchkiss, where we would narrate our exploits to Kathy. With these three Ruby Mountains, I had now climbed seven of the nine; only two remained.

After this significant alpine experience, I went to The Hermitage in Norwood for a few days. Schoening and I went to Telluride on June 29 to join the people of St. Patrick Parish, of which Schoening had been the pastor and which I had visited many times when he was the pastor there, in celebrating its centennial. I remember that we took one of the ski lifts above tree line above Telluride before the celebration and hiked around for about an hour. We got to the church, and I remember serving as Master of Ceremonies for the bishop, Arthur Tafoya, who was present for the centennial celebration.

1997: Jim Reynolds 3, Bill Tembrock 5, Luke Tembrock 3

Traveling with Reynolds again, we headed to Colorado on June 29. On July 1 we had driven to Lake City and taken the Henson Creek Road to Nellie Creek Road, from which we backpacked about four miles into the Big Blue Wilderness. After pitching a tent and setting up camp, we located fire wood, made a fire ring, and prepared for a restful evening in the wilderness. Our goal the next day was Uncompahgre Peak, a summit I had first stood on in 1981.

My Life of Ministry, Writing, Teaching, and Traveling

The four-mile climb to Uncompahgre Peak (14,309 feet) the next day was not too strenuous. Reynolds had been recuperating from colon cancer surgery and chemotherapy treatments, and he wanted to get acclimated on an easy trail before we tried anything requiring strong mountaineering skills that would zap him of his energy. I had suggested this summit, and he thought it was a good idea. We made our way to the summit with ease, joined other climbers who were already there, ate a snack, and descended back to our camp, where we spent the rest of the day resting. The next day we broke camp and backpacked out to the Jeep and headed to The Hermitage in Norwood for a few days before going to Hotchkiss to Tembrock Orchards to narrate our expedition to Bill, Kathy, and Luke.

While in Norwood, we made an expedition to the La Sal Mountains in Utah. I had seen the La Sal Mountains many times from the summit of the Lone Cone, and I was intrigued by them. I did some research and figured out how to get to them, also discovering that not one of the three had a trail to the summit. So, early in the morning of July 7, Reynolds and I left Norwood and headed for the La Sal Mountains in Utah. Our goal was to reach the summit of Mount Peale, the highest of the three peaks.

We followed the directions my research had yielded and found an old dead-end logging road that got us close to the east flank of Peale. We bushwhacked our way to the rocky ridge. Along the way to the summit, Reynolds began to tire and decided to stop and wait for me to achieve the summit. I got to the 12,721-foot peak, ate a snack, and headed back down the rocky ridge to meet Reynolds and head back to the Jeep. Estimating about where we needed to re-enter the woods in order to cross the dead-end old logging road, we left the ridge and began bushwhacking again.

After a while it became obvious that we had missed the logging road and had descended the peak too far to the west. There was nothing to do but to continue, hoping that we would cross a road and be able to connect with the logging road. Finally, we did come to a gravel/dirt road with a view of the valley and the road we had traveled over that morning. I pointed out to Reynolds where we had driven, the fork of the road we had taken, and how far we were now away from that fork that connected to the dead-end logging road. There was nothing to do but to keep descending into the valley on the road we were on until we came to the junction where the road divided and we could get on the road we needed.

Reynolds was concerned about having to spend the night in this area without a tent and with only the snacks we had in our day packs. I assured him that we would be fine. While we were discussing our options, I heard a truck coming up the road we were on. I stood in the middle of the road and waved the truck to a stop. I explained to the driver what we had done. He told us that he was a former Boy Scout Troop leader, who had once taken a group of Scouts to the summit of Peale from the same dead-end logging road that we had been on and had gone too far west and ended up one the same road we were on.

We asked him if he would be willing to take a detour from where he and his wife were heading—to a cabin on a lake to celebrate their fiftieth wedding anniversary—and bring us to the Jeep on the other side of the mountain. He told us to put our gear in the back of the truck and to climb into the cab. And off we went. It took him a good thirty minutes to go back to the main road junction, take the other fork, and then take us to the dead-end logging road. He knew the way since he had been there before. While taking us there, we discovered that he and his wife were Mormons from Moab, Utah. We told him that we were both Catholic priests. After that Reynolds and I spoke often about the two Moabites who rescued us that day. After dropping us off, we tried to offer him some money for gas, but he would not take it. He told us to do for others what he had done for us. He and his wife left us at the Jeep and made their way back to the junction and got on the road they were on when we met them; they were an hour behind schedule. We got back to Norwood early in the evening, tired but ready to tell our story about the friendly Moabites!

On July 9, Reynolds and I led a group of Coloradoans—Monika Odom, Roy Raabe, and Sonya Raabe—to the summit of the Lone Cone (12,613 feet); this was my ninth ascent of this peak. Being able to look over into Utah from the Lone Cone and see Mount Peale made me want to climb the other two La Sal Mountains.

By July 11, we had arrived at Tembrock Orchards in Hotchkiss. Bill, Luke, Reynolds, and I headed to Crested Butte, then the Slate River Road, and, after crossing the Slate River, into Poverty Gulch. At the wilderness boundary we parked the truck and proceeded to backpack toward Daisy Pass, looking for a wide bench to set up our camp. From there the next day we wanted to climb Augusta Mountain and Richmond Mountain. We made it to the summit of Augusta at 12,559 feet. Then, calculating where we were and looking at Richmond and the snow cornices on the ridge that we would have to traverse, we decided not to risk having the snow cornices turn lose with us on them. We headed back to our camp, where we took down the tent, packed up our things, and backpacked to the truck we had left the day before. This was the eighth of the Ruby Mountains that I had climbed; only one more remained, but it would have to wait another year.

For the first time after traveling over the Black Mesa and the Black Canyon of the Gunnison for years, Reynolds and I decided to explore it since we had access to the North Rim from Hotchkiss. After talking to the Tembrocks, we discovered that there was a trail few people ever took from the North Rim to the Gunnison River—named the SOB (Yes, it stands for Son of a Bitch) Trail. And, furthermore, it is aptly named. The trail is almost straight down, extremely vertical, and is best described as a washed-out area. Furthermore, it is lined with poison ivy and brush, disappearing quite often. Officials of the Black Canyon of the Gunnison National Monument do not recommend it. Of course, that did not stop Reynolds and me from hiking it.

It was a very hot day, so we carried plenty of water with us. We were in no hurry and didn't want to twist an ankle or break a bone. We made our way down the dusty, rocky trail to the Gunnison River, where we found a rocky beach and rested in the shade with the cool mist of the river falling over us. After a while, we pulled ourselves up the trail, often holding on to small trees or branches in order to get a foothold. By the time we emerged on the North Rim, we were soaked in sweat and very tired and ready to get back to Hotchkiss for a shower. This was my first and only traverse of the SOB Trail.

In December I made another trip to Colorado to spend Christmas in The Hermitage outside of Norwood. First, I headed to Hotchkiss to visit with the Tembrocks. One day Bill and I hiked four miles into the Dominguez River Canyon to see the Native American petroglyphs etched on the red canyon stone and to visit Bill's friend, Bill Rambo, who lived as a hermit deep in the canyon. Rambo, who had a degree in engineering, had escaped from the world and returned to his family's old homestead and orchard, where he lived alone in a shack, herded a few goats for milk and food, and made two annual treks out of the canyon into Hotchkiss or Delta to purchase beans and rice and any other supplies that he might need. In order to get across the Dominguez River, he had to cross an old rickety suspension bridge that looked like it would fall into the river at any moment. Even walking across it made it creak and moan, as it swayed in the breeze. Tembrock and Rambo had become friends, and Tembrock often brought him produce from the orchard, magazines, and other things that he thought he might be able to use.

Rambo had no electricity, heated with wood, and got his water from an old ditch that had at one time carried the precious liquid to fruit trees. The canyon was his desert, like the desert hermits in the early centuries of Christianity. After being introduced to him by Tembrock, he recounted to me how his family would pick the fruit from the orchard, box it, and haul it out of the canyon to the railroad tracks, where they would send it across the river on a line and pulley to be shipped to surrounding areas. When I accompanied Tembrock in visiting him on December 22, 1997, I readily understood why he wanted to live in such beautiful surroundings. The canyon had its own unique ascetic value, and here it was not too far from the mountains.

Tembrock had bought Rambo a small computer that ran on batteries that could be charged with solar energy, so he was able to keep up with news and other things going on in the world. As we sat outside in the warm December sun, we discussed politics and other world events for about an hour. Then, we decided it was time to leave and began our hike out of the canyon to the truck where we had left it.

After making plans for the Tembrocks to come to The Hermitage after Christmas, I headed to Norwood. The day after Christmas Bill and Kathy and their adult children, John and Nicole, came to The Hermitage for a cross-country ski trip. The snow was perfect, and we skied for hours on the Lone Cone Road with a clear blue sky and lots of sunshine all afternoon.

By the end of the year I was back in Springfield. I had been to the heights of the mountains and to the depths of the canyons, which I had experienced for the first time and was developing a deep appreciation for their beauty.

1998: Jim Reynolds 4, Bill Tembrock 6

In 1998, Reynolds joined me again in late June and early July for another Colorado exploration. I had my sights set on Mount Massive, the second highest peak in the Centennial State. We backpacked into the Mount Massive Wilderness, found an ideal camping site within view of a huge snowfield, pitched a tent, gathered fire wood, and settled in for the evening. The night was clear, and the stars were plentiful. Reynolds had bought a GPS device and spent a lot of time attracting satellites to it in order to determine our coordinates.

The next day we made our way toward the summit of Mount Massive. Reynolds, who was still in colon cancer recuperation, decided to stop and head back to camp. I continued to the summit at 14,421 feet over a snow-covered trail and ridge. The previous winter had witnessed a deeper-than-usual snow fall, so that even on July 23, snow was abundant in the high country. After getting back to camp, we gathered our gear and broke camp and backpacked out of the wilderness. Our destination was Leadville for a few days of rest and recuperation.

On June 25, we headed south from Leadville to Mount Antero, one of the fourteeners in the Sawatch Range. An old mining road leads the climber to within a half of a mile of the summit—if the mining road is not blocked by a snowfield. The mountain is known for its extensive deposits of aquamarine, clear and smoky quartz, and topaz crystals, all for which many people search. Reynolds and I could see that the road was blocked by a snowfield with several four-wheel drive vehicles stopped in front of it above tree line. We decided not to join that group because we would have to back down the old mining road in order to get off the mountain.

We found a turn-out area where we could park my Isuzu, gathered our day packs, and headed up the road to the summit. Along the way we met a woman and her son who were both exploring for minerals and climbing the peak. We exchanged greetings with them and moved on ahead of them. We hiked the road, walking carefully over many snowfields—remembering what had happened to us on a snowfield in the Ruby Mountains a few years before—and got to the end of the road. All that remained was the half of a mile ridge hike to the top of the pyramid-shaped summit. Slowly we scrambled over the rocks until we got to 14,269 feet, Antero's Summit, where we dug the register out of the snow and signed our names to it.

The view from Antero was spectacular. To the north were Princeton, Yale, and more of the Collegiate Peaks. To the south were Shavano and Tabeguache. To the east were the Arkansas River Valley and Salida. To the west were mountains whose names we did not know. And all of them were streaked with snow. Just to sit on Antero's summit and eat a snack surrounded by such beauty was a transforming spiritual experience for both Reynolds and me.

On our way down the old mining road, we encountered two climbers late in the afternoon attempting to reach Antero's summit. Each of them carried two metal hiking poles. In the distance, thunder could be heard; the bright blue sky had clouded over; the afternoon rain showers were coming in. I remember us telling them that it was not a good idea to continue, especially not with metal lightning-seeking poles at fourteen thousand feet elevation. They ignored our warning and continued on. We picked up our pace to get back to the Isuzu before it began to rain. I often wonder what ever happened to those two climbers.

Once down from Antero's summit and out of the wilderness area, we headed to a motel for a few days of rest and recuperation before traveling to The Hermitage in Norwood. While there, we answered a call from the La Sal Mountains to attempt a climb of Mount Tukuhnikiviatz, the second highest peak in Utah. Early on a bright sunny morning, Monika Odom from Nucla joined Reynolds and me for the drive to the La Sal Mountains. After having been there the year before to climb Mount Peale, we had a good idea where we were going and what kind of bushwhacking we would have to do to reach the summit. A very primitive trail led us through the basin, formed by the junction of all three La Sal peaks, to the long ridge to Tuckuhnikiviatz's rounded summit at 12,482 feet. I was the first to arrive, followed by Odom and Reynolds. Once again, the view into Colorado of the snow-streak San Miguel Mountains was spectacular.

The final climb of this year was with Bill Tembrock. Our goal was the last of the Ruby Mountain summits: Richmond Mountain. After getting to Crested Butte over Kebler Pass and taking the Slate Creek Road, we crossed Slate Creek at a low water area, and proceeded up the Oh-Be-Joyful Road to the Ruby Wilderness boundary. From there we backpacked into Democrat Basin, where we found a campsite and each of us pitched our own one-man tent in the midst of a babbling brook and tundra grasses and every color of wild flower imaginable. Everywhere there were snowfields; the mountains were streaked with snow. The beauty of the high country was enough to make us just stop and pause to absorb all of it.

After a hearty breakfast we began our climb to the summit of Richmond Mountain. I had been working at climbing all nine of the Ruby Mountains since 1988—ten years! I was about to fulfill a dream. Slowly we made our way over one snowfield after another; Reynolds and I were especially careful after our slide off the snowfield between Mount Owen and Ruby Peak. Once we got to the saddle, all that remained was a climb up the steep ridge to the summit. On July 4, we stood at 12,501 feet. I remember shouting for joy that I had now finished climbing all nine of the Ruby Mountains. I took photographs both south and north so that I would have a lasting record of these summits that had occupied my mind for ten years. After descending the peak back to camp, we gathered our gear and backpacked to the wilderness boundary and the truck, where I said goodbye to the Ruby Mountains for the rest of my life. I have never been back to that area.

On July 6, Reynolds and I went to Dominguez Canyon and hiked to the petroglyphs before stopping along the Little Dominguez River, eating lunch, and soaking our feet in the cool water. We also got to watch the herd of mountain sheep that make their home in the canyon.

A few days later we drove to Dinosaur National Monument on the Yampa River, where we toured the museum and enjoyed several days of canyon hiking before heading back to Missouri on July 10.

This trip further developed my own spirituality of mountain climbing. The high country was filled with wild flowers and snowfields. Our camping sites were near babbling streams with snow-streaked mountain peaks surrounding us. The beauty nourished my ascetic spirit. This trip was an undeserved blessing.

1999: Alone 9, Others, Matthew (Ver) Miller 1

In mid-July 1999, I arrived in Hotchkiss, Colorado, at Tembrock Orchards from which Bill, Kathy, and Luke Tembrock, Luke's friend Kata, Joyce Klava, a mutual friend, and I began a backpacking trip into the West Elk Wilderness. We took two vehicles because of the number of people and the gear we needed for the overnight trip. Bill and Luke led us over the trail and down to West Elk Creek, where we crossed and found a camp site below West Elk Peak. I had brought some old tennis shoes to put on in order to cross the creek and keep my boots dry. So, after exchanging my boots for the tennis shoes I walked through the stream to the other side. Some in our party crossed barefooted. Kathy attempted with her boots on. Some borrowed my tennis shoes so their boots would stay dry or to give them traction on the wet, slick rocks.

On July 22, it had been sprinkling on us and, before we could get tents pitched, it rained on us. However, after the rain, it began to clear. We got the tents pitched, a fire ring made, and gathered wood while wearing rain gear. A breeze began to dry our damp tents and clothing. While we dried, we enjoyed shrimp on ice that Klava had carried with her with a glass of wine that someone else had brought in! After eating dinner and spending time around the camp fire, everyone crawled into their tents in preparation for the next day's climb. During the night, it rained on us and soaked our camp.

After a hearty breakfast, all but Kathy began the climb to the summit of West Elk Peak (13,035 feet), the highest point in the West Elk Wilderness. We slowly climbed the rocky, tundra-covered mountain under dark blue skies sporting a few puffy clouds. After a short rest and a snack, we began our descent and arrived at camp by early afternoon. We broke camp and prepared ourselves for the backpacking trip to the vehicles.

Since we had gone down to camp by the creek, we had to climb out. The climbing out with backpacks was difficult. Because of the rain, the water in the creek was high and Kathy fell in when crossing it. Again, I was the only person who had brought along an old pair of tennis shoes to use to cross the creek in order to keep my boots dry. Some used them to cross, tossing them back across the creek after getting to the other side. Needless to say, the rocks were slick, and this made the crossing even more difficult with the higher water.

We seemed to be slowing down a lot, and I wanted to get back to the vehicles before it rained again. So, I told the group that I was moving on and would meet them at the vehicles. I picked up my pace, found my stride, and headed out. I had not paid too much attention when we were hiking in because Bill and Luke were leading; I was more focused on conversations with Kathy and Klava. So, when coming out I took what looked like the main trail. By the time it came to an end at a road, where I discovered a parked cattle trailer, I knew that I had missed the trail to the vehicles. Instead of going straight through some trees, I had continued to the right.

Furthermore, it was getting dark and hard to see. I turned around and began to retrace my steps in the hope of finding the trail I had missed. I knew that the rest of the group would be either coming along or just passed the trail junction, but I also knew that I would have to hurry to find them. My hike became a jog. I began to shout, "Bill, Bill, Bill." At first I got no answer, but after a while I heard a faint, "We're here," from Bill and Luke. They had already passed the trail junction, but they heard me and backtracked to find me. Needless to say, I was relieved that they heard me.

I explained what mistakes I had made—not paying attention to my surroundings hiking in and not staying with the group hiking out. They reminded me about how important it is to stay together in the wilderness and to pay attention going in so I could find my way out. By the time we got to the vehicles, it was very dark. We were tired and still had a trip ahead of us to get back to Tembrocks's home. When we got back, everyone took turns showering, while others fixed dinner. At some time before midnight, we ate dinner on July 23.

On July 25, I met Kossler, whom I had known for many years, in Paonia. From there we hiked to Overland Reservoir and Crater Lake. On July 27, I made the five-hour trip to Denver's airport to meet a former student who had become a good friend. After securing a room at a motel, I met Matthew Miller (now Ver Miller) at the airport. He had flown from Springfield to join me for two weeks of mountain climbing; this was his first experience of being in the high country.

The next day we took off for Kite Lake in the Mosquito Range. Northwest of Fairplay we went through the old town of Alma and headed northwest into Buckskin Gulch for seven miles to Kite Lake at twelve thousand feet. When we got there, a number of vehicles were in the parking lot, but most of the camping sites were open. We paid our fee, found a camp site, pitched my three-man pup tent with yellow rain fly, and prepared a fire from the split wood near the concrete fire pit. We got out our food and put it on the picnic table near the tent. While getting all this done, we noticed that most of the vehicles had left. By early evening the only people left in the area were Miller and I and a couple across the lake. What a beautiful high-country place in which to find solitude!

It got cold during the night at this elevation. The tent fly flapped like a flag in the wind that blew down from the fourteeners surrounding us. If we hadn't been in the tent, it may have blown away. By the time daylight arrived, both of us were ready to crawl out of our warm sleeping bags and begin the objective of the day: four fourteeners.

After breakfast on July 29 we followed the trail to Mount Democrat at 14,148 feet. After reaching the summit, we signed our names on the register there. We descended a short distance to the trail leading to Mount Cameron at 14,238, and climbed to its summit. Cameron is not counted among the fifty-four fourteeners in Colorado because it is too close to its three fourteener neighbors. After walking over Cameron, we headed to Mount Lincoln (14,286 feet), where we stopped to eat lunch. Then, descending from Lincoln, we took the trail to Mount Bross (14,172 feet). Since we had been going around Kite Lake—albeit at fourteen thousand feet—we needed only to drop down from Bross through the scree to our campsite, which we could see from all four summits. By the time we got back to camp, we had hiked about four miles and walked over four, fourteen thousand-foot peaks—and this was Miller's first time in the high country!

After breaking camp, we packed my Jeep, and headed to Paonia, where I was staying. A few days later, Miller and I went to see the Black Canyon of the Gunnison from the North Rim. On August 1, we joined Kossler for a hike on the Dark Canyon Trail along Anthracite Creek. The next two days we were in Grand Junction hiking trails through the Colorado National Monument. And on August 4, we were backpacking into Horn Fork Basin.

I had first visited Horn Fork Basin in 1994 on a backpacking trip with Reynolds, Nathan Smith, and Luke Tembrock. The goal of the trip was to climb Mount Harvard in the Collegiate Peaks Wilderness Area. We had not achieved that goal because Smith got altitude sickness above tree line, and we had to get him to a lower elevation before backpacking out. I knew that high altitudes did not bother Miller, since we had climbed four fourteeners together about a week before.

After pitching my tent and preparing our camp, we rested the afternoon of August 4. With a hearty breakfast in our stomachs, we set off on the morning of August 5 on the trail that leads to the summit of Mount Harvard. It was a cloudy day, but by noon we were sitting on the summit at 14,420 feet, the third highest mountain in Colorado. Harvard is different from the rest of the fourteeners in that the climber has to traverse from the ridge under the peak and finish the ascent over huge boulders on the other side. On the summit we signed the register, ate a snack, and watched as the clouds came in and covered us in fog. There was no thunder or lightning, but we knew the clouds meant rain at lower elevations and sleet at fourteen thousand feet.

Except for some sleeting on our way down, we got back to our camp without getting wet. We broke camp, backpacked to the Jeep, and headed to a motel for a shower and rest before driving home to Missouri.

For me 1999 was the year I decided to climb as many of the fourteeners as I could. I had been preoccupied in previous years with the nine peaks in the Ruby Mountains, but I had finished those. After five more fourteeners—four of which counted—I was ready to climb many more of them.

2000: Jim Reynolds 5, Bill Tembrock 7, Kathy Tembrock

For the millennium year, Reynolds and I headed west to Colorado, Utah, and Wyoming on July 16. We hiked seventy miles, and we drove 3,705 miles. On July 18, after spending a night in a bed and breakfast in Breckenridge, we headed outside town toward Quandry Peak. The trail through the basin below the mountain got us to a gentle-slopping ridge that led us right to the summit. Reynolds, who again had been recuperating from chemotherapy treatments for colon cancer, tired out quickly and returned to the Jeep to wait for me. Since the trail was well marked and well-traveled, we knew there would be no problem with us separating from each other and finding each other later. Furthermore, both of us were well-seasoned mountaineers.

I continued on to the 14,265-foot summit. While sitting there, I was able to see Mount Democrat, Mount Cameron, Mount Lincoln, and Mount Bross, the four fourteeners I had climbed with Miller the year before. The clear blue sky with bright sunshine made this a perfect day to sit on the top of such a peak. While getting lost in the scenery, a seventy-year-old-plus climber, who had gotten to the summit before I did, began to speak to me. We discovered that we had climbed a lot of the same mountains. After speaking for a while, we both began our descent, walking together and speaking about the spirituality of mountain climbing all the way back to where I had left the Jeep and where Reynolds was now napping. I cannot remember his name or where he lived, but I do remember that I wanted to be still climbing mountains when I got to be seventy or eighty years old.

July 20 found us hiking the Spud Pass Trail in the Raggeds Wilderness with Bill Tembrock. We had driven to Tembrock Orchards a day after I had climbed Quandry Peak. While traveling those sixteen miles that day, we passed wild flowers that just drew us into their beauty. The blue and green of the high-country lakes in the mountain basins reminded me of what paradise must have been like. While crossing one cold, flowing mountain stream, Reynolds spotted two bottles of beer in the gravel. We do not know if those were left there by someone recently or the year before and forgotten about. No matter the case, Reynolds and Tembrock retrieved them, opened them, and drank them on our way back to the truck. On a hot afternoon it was a perfect find.

On July 21, Reynolds, Bill and Kathy Tembrock, and I drove to the parking spot called Paradise Divide outside of Crested Butte and off of the Slate Creek Road and began an eight-mile backpacking trip to Yule Pass on the northern boundary of the Ruby Range in the Raggeds Wilderness. After climbing to the pass over the old mining road that was now the trail, we descended on the other side, found a camp site, and began to establish camp. Because Kathy was slower than the rest of us and Bill hung back to stay with her, Reynolds and I descended faster and found a camping spot that we thought would serve the four of us well.

Bill didn't like us getting ahead of him. So, when he and Kathy finally caught up with us, he told us that it was not a good idea for us to get so far ahead, especially when he couldn't see us in the trees. Of course, he reminded me of the incident the previous year when I had gotten lost coming out of the West Elk Wilderness. After looking at our chosen campsite, however, he had to admit that it was a perfect location.

Bill and Kathy had a tent, and Reynolds and I each had our own one-man tents. We had decided before this trip that each of us would get his own one-man tent and pack it wherever we went. This eliminated the need to carry my heavy three-man tent, and it gave each of us the option to pitch our tent as far away from others as we desired; this gave all of us privacy in the wilderness. After establishing a common fire ring and gathering plenty of wood, we explored the wild flower meadows surrounding us. The bright yellow mule's ear, the dark purple lupine, and the fire-truck red Indian paintbrush formed a painter's pallet. Following dinner and a good night's sleep, we arose the next morning to a clear blue sky, ate breakfast, and backpacked up to Yule Pass, descended to the truck, and headed back to Hotchkiss.

Meeting with Kossler on July 23, we hiked three miles around Lost Lake Slough, Dollar Lake, and Lost Lake off of the Kebler Pass Road. Here, the fire weed was in bloom. Fire weed is so named because it is one of the first plants to emerge after a forest fire and because at a distance its three-to-four-feet tall purple blossoms look like flames of fire.

After traveling to The Hermitage in Norwood, Reynolds and I headed to the La Sal Mountains in Utah on July 25. I had explored the La Sals in 1997 and climbed Mount Peal, and in 1998 climbed Mount Tukuhnikiviatz. The goal of this four-mile hiking trip was to finishing climbing the La Sal Mountains by ascending Mount Mellenthin's summit at 12,646 feet—which both of us did. We celebrated that evening with several glasses of wine over dinner in The Hermitage.

By the end of July, we were in Wyoming in the Wind River Range. Reynolds had wanted to go here, so he was also responsible for planning the hiking we would do. We had decided to find a motel room close to where we would be hiking and make that our home base instead of engaging in any backpacking. We found a little motel with wood-paneled walls, carpeted floors, and a bathroom for a very cheap price and made it our home for several days.

We hiked twelve miles on the Smith Lake Trail to Smith Lake and Middle Lake in the Popo Agie Wilderness, Soshone National Forest, on July 28. From here we went to the Jenny Lake Trail, the Cascade Canyon Trail, and the South Forks Falls on July

29 and hiked fourteen miles in Grand Teton National Park. On August 1, we hiked seventeen miles on the Pole Creek Trail to Eklund Lake and the Sweeney Lakes Trail to Upper Sweeney Lake, Middle Lake, and Miller Lake in the Bridger-Teton National Forest, Bridger Wilderness. It is trite to write that we were surrounded by rugged beauty, but we were. The high-country lakes were set within the evergreen forests. The trails to them were overgrown with wild flowers streaking yellow, red, and purple everywhere. The high-country beauty surrounded us, and we found it hard to leave it in order to return to our motel room for the night.

On our way home through Kansas, we topped off this trip by visiting the Cathedral of the Plains, better known as St. Fidelis Church in Victoria, Kansas. We had seen its twin sandstone towers from Interstate 70 many times, but we had never decided to explore it. This time, however, we marveled at the church's architecture and its interior Roman and Gothic designs. After a visit there, we returned to Missouri on August 4.

Even though I had only climbed two mountains in 2000, I had hiked seventy miles around high mountain lakes, through lush evergreen forests, over aspen-covered hills, and into and out of meadows of color. It was the most memorable trip that Reynolds and I took together before cancer claimed his life eight years later.

2001: Jeremy Stanton, Tembrocks 1, Others

After having finished the nine peaks in the Ruby Range, and after climbing Mount Elbert, Mount Massive, Mount Antero, and Mount Harvard in the Sawatch Range, I set my sights on the other eleven fourteeners in the Sawatch Range that, basically, runs north to south from Leadville to Poncha Springs, Colorado. For the 2001 expedition I invited a former student who loved the outdoors: Jeremy Stanton. He was twenty years old. I met Stanton in the fall semester of 2000 in a New Testament course I was teaching at SMSU (now MSU).

We left Springfield on May 28, rather early to be heading to the mountains, and arrived at the North Cottonwood Creek Trailhead and backpacked into Horn Fork Basin, my third time being there. The mountains were still covered in snow; in fact, our campsite was not too far from a huge snowfield—and that was well below tree line. Our objective was to climb Mount Columbia (14,073 feet), another peak in the Sawatch Range. Not only did we achieve that objective the next day, but we got back to our campsite in time to pack up and backpack out. There was snow everywhere; even on the summit we had to dig through the snow to find the register to sign our names on it. The clear blue sky enabled us to see and name other peaks in the area for miles around. Seeing all those snow-covered mountains gave me the impetus to continue to climb in the Sawatch Range.

On our way to Tembrock Orchards in Hotchkiss, we stopped at Lake Irwin off the Kebler Pass Road and below the Ruby Mountains. On June 1, the lake was still partially frozen and the mountains were snow covered. We also stopped at Lost Lake on the Kebler Pass Road for a short hike before arriving in Hotchkiss.

The next day, June 2, we joined Bill and Kathy Tembrock, John Tembrock and Amanda Woodward, Ethan Hemming and Nicole Tembrock, Luke Tembrock, and Grady Harper, a friend of Luke's, in a backpacking trip into Dominguez River Canyon, a place I had been to several times before. While Bill, John, Ethan, Luke, Grady, and Jeremy went exploring deeper into the canyon, Kathy, Amanda, Nicole, and me set up camp along the Little Dominguez River. There must have been a fresh hatching of gnats, because they were everywhere. We coated ourselves in bug spray as we relaxed in the shade near the river. After the others returned, we told them about the gnats, but they did not seem to be too concerned; they decided to go swimming further down the river.

Those of us left at the campsite began to discuss the possibility of leaving after they returned and heading back to Tembrock Orchards for the night instead of setting up tents and backpacking out the next day. The gnats were really beginning to aggravate us. As our conversation progressed, we agreed upon a strategy to convince the others that we would prefer to pack up, backpack to our vehicles, and go back to Hotchkiss. It took some doing, once the others returned—especially among those who had not been bitten by the gnats—but we managed to convince most that we needed to get away from the gnat infested area.

By the time we got back to Tembrock Orchards and began to get everyone through a shower, the gnat bites had begun to swell and itch. Some of us were covered with the whelps. A day or so later, I had to stop at a pharmacy and ask the pharmacist to recommend ointments to apply to the itching whelps. It took two weeks before the swelling went away and the itching stopped.

After getting back to Tembrock Orchards, everyone pitched in with fixing dinner, which we ate around 11 p.m. We decided where everyone would sleep, washed the dishes, and went to bed. I remember sleeping in a small detached room the Tembrocks called the Sanctuary. It contained a desk, a wood stove, and a couch. Through its screen door, the cool evening breeze came in, but the gnats could not!

A day or so after enduring the gnats, Stanton and I headed to The Hermitage. On June 5, I led Stanton to the summit of the Lone Cone, my tenth ascent. As it had been in Horn Fork Basin, the Lone Cone was covered in snow. There was snow on the lower trail; there was snow in the Devil's Armchair; there was snow on the summit. We had to wear gaiters in order to keep the snow out of our boots, especially on our descent after the snow had softened in the day's bright sunshine.

After this it was back to the Collegiate Peaks in the Sawatch Range. On June 7, we found ourselves car camping off the road that leads to the trailhead to climb Mount Princeton. Because we had announced this plan while we were with all those at Tembrock Orchards, Ethan Hemming had decided to join us. He showed up right before sunset, pitched his tent, and visited with us around our camp fire before climbing into his sleeping bag.

On June 8, after a hearty breakfast, Hemming, Stanton, and I headed up the road and found the trail to Mount Princeton. I remember the snow-covered high country. There were only a few wild flowers and the tundra grasses were just beginning their thirty-to-sixty day growing period. We hiked over numerous snowfields, as we slowly made our way to the 14,197-foot summit of Princeton. While enjoying the summit view, a low cloud came in and dropped hail stones the size of pennies on the trail below us; we didn't know that is what the weather was doing until we began our descent.

The views from Princeton were breathtaking. We could see its neighbors, Mount Antero and Mount Yale. We could see the Arkansas River Valley. We could also see the thick, dark afternoon clouds coming in, and we knew we needed to get back to our vehicles, break camp, pack up, and be on our way before the rain came in. Hemming headed back to Denver; Stanton and I returned to Springfield on June 9.

This had been the earliest I had ever been mountain climbing. However, I was now more determined than ever to stand upon the summits of the rest of the fourteeners in the Sawatch Range. It would take a few years before that dream would be realized, but I had only nine more mountains to climb.

Stanton and I connected on our mutual love for hiking and his quest to understand God in his life and become the best man that he could be. Our relationship grew through dinners together and one memorable hike through eight inches of snow, followed by time in the sauna in the fitness center to which I belonged and a meal at my house. For the spring semester of 2001, Stanton decided to participate in the university exchange program by attending Colorado Western University in Gunnison. He loved skiing, and Crested Butte, a famous ski area, was about forty-five minutes away. Once he went there, our relationship continued through e-mail. This form of communication enabled a different approach from face-to-face communication. In one e-mail I remind Stanton that he was a good man in many ways, but especially in the way he took responsibility for working on himself, learning how to reflect on his experiences, and learning how to articulate his feelings. The awareness work he was doing on himself further enabled growth in his relationship with God. Because he was such a willing mentee, I told him that I considered him to be a blessing in my life over the past months. He responded by telling me that the first time he had talked to me—he called it spilling his guts—that he knew I was a blessing to him.

During the semester he spent on the CWU campus, I continued to supply reflection questions for him to think and write about. Stanton needed to learn how to process his experiences through reflection upon them. The absent feeling he felt about moving to CWU was homesickness for family and friends. Likewise, while he was searching for God, he also needed to let God find him. I tried to help him awaken to this through journaling. In February, he narrated an aha moment communicating with a female friend who told him that he had become a man and was no longer a little boy. Stanton told me that what she said to him and what I had been saying to him about becoming a man echoed together. He named that as God's presence with him. Then, he thanked me for being there for him.

Throughout the semester, I continued to urge him to journal and to reflect. I encouraged him to look for the themes that God wove in his life and articulate them. I told him that he was a man, that he was still becoming a man, and that he was getting comfortable in a man's skin. He was understanding himself, defining himself, and shaping himself into the type of man he wanted to be. I shared with him the fact that two people in a healthy relationship put no boundaries on each other. Each one sets free the other one. The more each person sets free the other one to be who he or she is, the more each becomes who he or she is. The best way to kill a good relationship, I wrote to Stanton, is to lay claim to the other in some way.

For spring break, Stanton flew home after having a minor accident skiing—knocking himself out and getting a mild concussion with some short-term memory loss. We got together for dinner while he was home to get caught up with each other. It was then that I invited him to join me on the 2001 summer trip to Colorado. By April 2001, I could see that Stanton was entering deeper into reflection because he was writing poems and sharing them with me. After the trip to Colorado, we got together to share the photos we took and reflect verbally on the time we spent together. Stanton went back to CWU for another semester and graduated from SMSU (now MSU). After graduating and getting a job, we got together infrequently. He married in 2004, and, other than an occasional e-mail, and accidently seeing him after a night class I was teaching at SMSU (MSU) one time, I never saw him again.

2002: Alone 10, Tembrocks 2, Others

Because of teaching responsibilities, I had only one week to spend in Colorado in 2002, August 3–10, and I went alone to Tembrock Orchards. Bill and Kathy Tembrock had relatives from Minnesota visiting them. So, one day Tembrock and Terry, Alan, and Matthew Wermerskirchen, Kathy's brother and nephews, and I went to hike the Smith Fork Trail of the Gunnison River.

After they left a few days later, Tembrock and I went to Bailey Reservoir off Laroux Creek in the Grand Mesa National Forest to bushwhack to the summit of Green Mountain. Since there was no trail, we had to use trial and error to find our way through the rock formations to the top. We arrived on the 10,802-foot summit after walking through meadow after meadow of wild flowers with a silhouetted view of the West Elk Mountains shrouded in thick blue-tinted clouds.

Even though Green Mountain was the only summit I stood upon in 2002, I was making plans for 2003 and more of the fourteeners in the Sawatch Range.

My Life of Ministry, Writing, Teaching, and Traveling

2003: Jim Reynolds 6, Tembrocks 3, Matthew Ver Miller 2, Brian Prokes

For Spring Break, March 20–28, 2003, Reynolds and I made what would be our last trip together to Colorado. Our destination was Tembrock Orchards, from where we would head to Grand Mesa for cross-country skiing. I had cross-country skied several times before this trip, even buying my own skis, boots, and poles. This was Reynolds first attempt at a sport that I had come to love.

County Line Trail was our first destination on the Grand Mesa. Bill Tembrock was attending a meeting, so Kathy, Reynolds, and I traveled from Hotchkiss to the groomed cross-country trailhead. Kathy and I showed Reynolds what to do, taught him a few ways to stay upright, and led him off onto the trail. After falling several times, he was beginning to figure it out.

However, on this March 22 day, Kathy fell while skiing down a hill and hurt her foot. While she was able to ski back to the truck, she experienced pain in her foot, but, other than taking a pain killer, did nothing about it. It continued to bother her the next day, so a friend of hers, a physician's assistant, stopped by to look at the swelling; he concluded that he thought it was just a sprain and would mend itself. The next day while Bill, Reynolds, and I returned to the County Line Trail on the Grand Mesa, Kathy went to get an x-ray, only to discover that she had a fracture and needed a cast. When everyone got back to Tembrock Orchards, we got the news that Kathy would need to keep her foot elevated for as long as possible every day. That meant that the job of chief cook and bottle washer was mine.

Reynolds, who had not taken to cross-country skiing, decided to try snow shoeing. So, after renting a pair of snow shoes, he took up the sport of snow shoeing while Bill and I skied. Reynolds was very happy being on the snowy trails with snow shoes, and Bill and I were very happy being on the trails in cross-country skis. Kathy was not very happy being in a cast, but she continued to teach her classes—in the Hotchkiss School System and was not on break—while sitting in a Lazy Boy recliner that Bill had managed to find and bring to her classroom. It was on this trip that I began to call Kathy "queen" and "your majesty."

On this trip Reynolds and I made several more trips to the Grand Mesa to snow shoe and ski. Even I rented snow shoes for one day and joined him on a snowy high-country excursion. It was a wonderful way to mark our last trip together. Shortly after this, Reynolds' colon cancer returned; this discovery was followed by more surgeries, more chemotherapy, and more weakness. He fought the cancer with everything available, but on June 3, 2008, it took his life. He and I had traveled together in 1991—twice—in 1994, in 1997, in 1998, in 2000, and in 2003. We had backpacked into wilderness areas together; we had climbed mountains together; we had cross-country skied and snow shoed together. But beyond all that, we had become friends, who visited each other often and shared our dreams and thoughts. His death brought that friendship to an end in 2008. I still grieve his passing.

While Reynolds continued to fight cancer over the next five years, I continued to mountain climb. My second trip to Colorado in 2003 was August 4–15. Accompanying me were Matthew Ver Miller (note that Miller had legally changed his name before getting married the previous Christmas to reflect a part of his bride's name) and Brian Prokes, an avid exerciser and a former student who became a good friend. I met Prokes in a New Testament class in the fall semester of 2002 at SMSU (now MSU). We left Springfield on August 4 and arrived at our first destination on August 5: Denny Creek Trail. We backpacked into the wilderness for a few miles, found a good camping site, and proceeded to pitch tents, gather firewood, and take care of other camp chores.

After dinner and an evening of sitting around the camp fire, we crawled into our sleeping bags for a good night's rest in preparation for the next day's climb. Our objective was another of the Collegiate Peaks named Mount Yale. The next morning featured a clear blue sky. After breakfast, we prepared our day packs and headed up the trail to the summit. The trail led us through high meadows of fire weed in purple blossom and over babbling streams until we got into the high basin below Yale's summit. From there the trail went to the ridge, which enabled us to climb to the top. The three of us stood at 14,196 feet, enjoying views for a hundred miles at 360 degrees. I had climbed another of the fourteeners in the Sawatch Range, leaving only eight more to go. However, it would soon be only seven more to go.

After spending some time on the peak enjoying the views, eating a snack, and talking to others who had arrived before us and were arriving after us, we made our descent to our campsite. On the way back it began to rain enough for us to put on ponchos. After breaking camp, we backpacked to the Jeep and found a motel room for the night.

On August 8 we were hiking the Four Mile Creek Trail in the Mosquito Range. In previous years I had climbed Quandary Peak, Mount Lincoln, Mount Democrat, and Mount Bross. The only fourteener remaining was Mount Sherman. After a ten-mile gravel/dirt road trip to a locked gate, we began our ascent through a privately operated mine—which permitted hikers to trespass as long as they stayed on the road/trail—we hiked to the high mines, gained the saddle between Mount Sherman and Mount Sheridan, and headed to the summit of Sherman. We had reached the 14,036-foot summit by mid-morning; in other words, this was an easy climb.

I do not remember signing a register, but I do remember Prokes talking about a headache, which meant altitude sickness. Ver Miller and I had agreed that we wanted to walk over to Mount Sheridan (13,748 feet) while Prokes went back to the Jeep to rest. There was no way that he would get lost because we could see the Jeep—and other vehicles—parked below us.

All three of us headed down to the saddle between Sherman and Sheridan. Prokes continued his descent, while Ver Miller and I continued to the summit of Mount Sheridan, where the view of Sherman and the surrounding mountains and valleys made us stop and ponder in silence the beauty in which we were standing. Because some dark clouds had already begun to roll in, we began our descent, reached the Jeep, found Prokes sleeping, and decided to find a motel room and hang out for the rest of the day. It was just about noon when Ver Miller and I had made it back to the Jeep, and we had already climbed two mountains! Furthermore, I had finished all five of the fourteeners in the Mosquito Range.

On August 10, we drove to the new trail that the Colorado Fourteener Initiative (CFI) had built to the two southernmost fourteeners in the Sawatch Range: Mount Shavano and Tabeguache Mountain. We hiked a few miles of the Colorado Trail before getting on the Blank Gulch Trail that would take us to Shavano and, from there, to Tabeguache. After mountain climbing, specifically peak-bagging, took off in the 1980s and 1990s, the CFI was formed in 1994 to protect the high country. Its members attempt to mitigate the impact that hikers have on the routes and alpine basins and insure long-term sustainability of the trails on the fourteeners. In some cases, new trails have been created and old ones closed to prevent further erosion. In other cases, old trails have been supported with huge stones forming steps and timbers placed across them to prevent further erosion. The old trail to Shavano and Tabeguache took the hiker up a flank of Tabeguache, and from there he or she continued over to Shavano.

Prokes, Ver Miller, and I made our way on the well-traveled new trail to the summit of Mount Shavano (14,229 feet), where we met two other mountain climbers from Denver. They were enjoying a mid-day snack and attempting to decide whether they would head over to Tabeguache when they finished. Out over the Arkansas River Valley dark clouds were forming and thunder could be heard in the distance. It didn't take the three of us long to decide that Tabeguache Mountain would have to wait for another day. Our decision sparked the two weekend-climbing Denverites to join us in our descent. I had finished another fourteener in the Sawatch, leaving only seven more to climb.

Prokes and Ver Miller caught buses taking them to wherever they were headed next. I went to Tembrock Orchards to spend a few days with Bill and Kathy Tembrock. On August 12, Bill and I hiked the Anthracite Pass Trail (ten thousand feet) to get to the trail leading to Marble Peak (11,314 feet). It was an easy ten-mile hike with stupendous views of other mountains in all directions. Upon our descent, we hiked to the Yule Marble Quarry. Yule Marble is known for its 99 percent purity. It is still mined and transported around the world.

After a few more days at Tembrock Orchards, I headed back to Missouri on August 14, arriving on August 15. I was very pleased with myself. I had climbed three fourteeners, a thirteener, and an eleven-thousand-foot peak. Furthermore, I was even more determined than ever to finish the seven fourteeners that I had not yet ascended in the Sawatch Range.

Prokes, who sat in the front row of my fall 2002 New Testament course, was one of those people whom I wanted to get to know. He came to my office for an optional student interview, and that got the getting-to-know-each-other process started. I invited him to dinner one night, and he accepted. I discovered that he came from a family in Maryville, Missouri, and that he had brothers and sisters. They lived on a golf course, and Prokes was very much into golf. His father was a judge, and his mother was a homemaker as well as a writer of music.

For the Spring 2003 semester, Prokes was offered a scholarship to play golf for Central Missouri State University in Warrensburg, Missouri. Before accepting the offer, we discussed it; Prokes loved golf and thought this was a perfect fit for him. We continued our relationship through e-mail. Through the course of the semester, Prokes began to reflect on the lack of academic challenge at CMSU. He continued to tell me that academics were a joke there. Thus, while he enjoyed playing lots of golf, he knew that he was not being stretched academically. By the end of the semester, he had made up his mind to return to SMSU (now MSU). While stopping in for a visit in May 2003, he confirmed his decision to return to SMSU (MSU) for the fall semester. At that time, I invited him to come to Colorado with me in August. He was interested.

While on the Colorado trip, he had mentioned that he was looking for a place to live for the fall semester 2003. Off the top of my head, I mentioned that I had a guest room I would rent to him. Thus, when I got back to Springfield after the mountain climbing trip, Prokes contacted me and we got together to look at the possibility of him moving into the guest room and negotiating rent. Thus, in the fall of 2003, Prokes moved into my guest room. We had to do some adjusting in order to be able to fit his things and clothes in there, but the adjustments were made. I even cleared the second bay of the garage for him so he could park his car there. We had agreed to get together for dinner one night a week, but other than that we both did our own thing. Besides attending classes and working out on a daily basis, Prokes spent most of his time away; my house was just a place to sleep. I only asked that he locked all the doors when he came in at night; because he had lived on a golf course, this became an issue that began to raise other issues.

Prokes and I had talked about relationships, but it was mostly theory. However, after rekindling a relationship with a female from his hometown, he began to learn the truth about the freedom required for a relationship to grow. His female interest was attending SMSU (MSU); thus, he maintained residence with me in order to keep his parents happy, but he spent most time out of class and at night with his girlfriend.

Prokes was a member of the Missouri National Guard. Once a month he had to make a trip to his home town to spend it with his unit for the weekend. However, around Thanksgiving time, his unit got called to active duty, and he was required to report on December 1. I instructed him to go to his teachers and find out what he needed to do in order to finish the semester early and not lose credit for all the work he had done in his courses. He did.

He packed his things and, with the help of his parents, moved out of my guestroom before Thanksgiving. In other words, the National Guard called him to duty before I could tell him that he would not be living with me for the 2004 spring semester. After he left, I entered into a process of reflection on what had happened to me for four months in the autumn of 2003. I concluded that I had been used; I was a front for Prokes's parents so that they would not know that he was living with his girlfriend. Prokes was a little boy in an adult body; he was immature and trapped in his own dysfunctionality.

Not only did it take me months to convince him to lock the doors of my house, but when I asked him to pick up the mail and the paper while I was away for a weekend, I came home to find mail in the box, some doors opened, and my newspaper nowhere to be found. I found stains on the carpet, dirty pans in the cabinet, plastic bottles in the dishwasher, etc. He often left his car unlocked and parked on the street with his keys in the ignition; his clothes were scattered all over his room. After doing laundry, he merely threw them on the bed without folding them or putting them away. Prokes had no respect for me, my things, himself, or his things. He was living a life of pretend. I got too close to him and figured him out; that is when he stopped staying here and moved in with his girlfriend. He continued to claim that he lived with me because all his stuff was here. However, by the end of November 2003, he had not spent but one night since the middle of October 2003.

I also discovered that Prokes could not learn from his mistakes. He continued to get speeding tickets because he drove over the speed limit. Three thousand dollars were spent on a sleep study, but he continued not getting enough sleep by going to bed and getting up on a regular basis. What I had experienced in the fall of 2003 was that I could not trust him. Because he lived in a pretend world, in which everything was fine from his point of view, he could not admit that he was wrong. I had been trying to reason with one who was unreasonable, trying to reflect with one who was not reflective, attempting to guide one who didn't want guidance, and to love one who didn't want love. Prokes could not engage in reflection because to do so he would prove himself wrong and he would have to change. So, he avoided all self-reflection and focus on himself because that would mean change, growth, and development. My love for Prokes was authentic, but his love for me was an exercise in pretend, a ruse.

In January 2004, Prokes and his National Guard unit were deployed to Frankfurt, Germany, where he would stay for one and a half years. In March 2004, I received an e-mail from him in which he listed his schedule as the supply officer for his unit. In the e-mail I discovered that he had lots of time alone and had begun to keep a journal to help him bring what he was thinking to the surface. In other words, besides enjoying trips across Europe, he was beginning to reflect. During the summer of 2004, his girlfriend visited him, and they traveled to Italy for a few weeks. Upon returning to the base near Frankfurt, he sent me an e-mail telling me about their trip, but more importantly he wrote about their relationship: "We have had to work on our relationship continuously! We agreed to pursue individual aspirations first, and bring it back to the friendship. Most of all we are trying to support each other the best we can. You said something about freeing a person if you really love her; that is the goal: a freeing love."

Once the announcement was made that the deployment was going to be extended to April 2005, Prokes e-mailed me that he and his girlfriend had some serious discussion about the continuation of their relationship. He wrote: "We try on the communication thing, but we thought maybe it was the best thing to do and then we could see where we both were after the deployment. That lasted for about a week. It definitely opened up to a level needed to enable it to survive fruitfully though." I commented: "A long distance relationship takes a lot of work because you don't have the other person in your presence. That can be both good and bad. It is good because it makes you communicate thoughts and feelings that you would not otherwise do; it is bad because there is more to relating than just communicating. The two of you have to decide how—and if—you preserve it."

On August 27, 2004, I received an e-mail from Prokes that represented the growth that I had hoped for. He stated, "There is more time to contemplate and reflect." And that is what he did in that e-mail. "For the first two months in Germany I was bored out of my mind," he wrote. "I was trying to live the life I left behind. Whenever I finally did open up to the new environment, it seemed things started to fall into place better. This has been a big blessing in my life."

Then, came this paragraph: "I miss getting to spend time with you—mostly our talks while dinner was cooking and pushing me to be a better man, but also the rest of it too. Our contrast in lifestyles made me quite upset for a while. I may not be able to see fully where you were coming from, but I was out of control. Every time we would talk about locking the doors, cleaning up, etc. I thought you were insane. I probably absorbed about ten percent of what you were trying to get through my thick skull, but now there are guys over here going through the same responsibility difficulties and the other 90 percent you were trying to drive in is starting to sink in. Those lessons will not soon be forgotten. I miss talking with you more than anything. I know it was not said enough back then: Thank You for everything, Mark." I responded: "I enjoy watching people grow into who they are going to be—or at least the potential for whom I think they can be."

In January 2005, Prokes's girlfriend made another trip to Germany to spend time with him and travel a little. On January 22, 2005, he e-mailed me, writing, "It was apparent we both have continued to change, but since we agreed to have no expectations of the trip, we enjoyed each other's company." In March 2005, Prokes returned to the U.S. He was able to take several block classes at Ozarks Technical Community College before enrolling for the fall semester of 2005 at SMSU (MSU). In a March 1, 2005, e-mail, he wrote, "When we are once again residing in the same city, I propose we get together and catch up. That would be nice."

And that is exactly what we did. We processed our relationship and all that had happened in the past year and a half. Prokes informed me of his plans to major in entrepreneurship. Then, after living with some of his friends for a semester or two, he asked me if he could come back and live with me for the last semester of his senior year. I readily acknowledged that he could. After he graduated, I saw him a few times when he came to Springfield. Ultimately, he and his girlfriend, who pursued a doctorate in business, moved to Texas, where Prokes worked on a golf course. After they married, they moved to Florida, where Prokes became a golf professional, working on a golf course and playing golf most days with wealthy businessmen. We kept some contact with each other during those years, often calling each other. After he moved to Florida, I never heard from him again.

2004: Tembrocks 4, Adam Park 1

For Spring Break 2004, I traveled alone to Tembrock Orchards to join Bill and Kathy on one cross-country skiing trip to the Grand Mesa. Spring came early in 2004 to the Grand Mesa, and the snow was melting in March. That put an end to cross-country skiing! The rest of the time I spent with Tembrocks. I enjoyed the bright sunny days reading and working on projects I had brought with me. Also, I learned a new skill: burning ditches in the orchard. It took several people to watch the fire and keep it from spreading to the fruit trees while the brown weeds in the water ditches that carry the liquid to the fruit trees went up in smoke.

On August 1, I headed back to Colorado with a former student who loved the outdoors: Miles Adam Park, known as Adam to his friends. I had invited him to join me on this mountain climbing expedition, and he was excited about it. I met Park in a New Testament class I was teaching in the fall semester of 2003. On August 2, we were car camping on the South Fork of the Clear Creek Trail not too far from the ruins of the Baker Mine. Our goal was to climb Huron Peak, a fourteener in the Sawatch Range. It was a cold, cloudy day, but we made it to the summit at 14,003 feet, signed our names to the register there, and began our descent back to our camp. Park had climbed his first fourteener, and I had but six fourteeners to go in the Sawatch Range before finishing all fifteen of them.

Park did develop some mild altitude sickness on the descent. After telling me that he had a headache, I gave him some Tylenol, told him to drink lots of water, and to get out a snack and eat something. He told me he wasn't hungry; I replied that it made no difference. We continued to dialogue for a while, until he ate a snack. Within twenty minutes he was feeling better, his headache disappeared, and we were on our way to the Jeep.

After a day of rest in a motel room in Buena Vista, we headed to the Missouri Gulch Trail on August 5 for a day climb of Missouri Mountain (14,067 feet). Again, it was a cold, cloudy day, but, after making it to the summit, we signed the register, ate a snack, and patted each other on the back before heading back to the Jeep.

August 6 was a rest day in Buena Vista, but August 7 we were back on the trail. This time the goal was Mount Belford and Mount Oxford which are climbed together. It was a Saturday, and the weekend mountain climbers were out in force; from the higher elevations it looked like ants on a trail. We passed many of them on the trail to Belford at 14,197 feet. Then, after signing the register, we made our way to Mount Oxford (14,153 feet). In order to get back to the Jeep, we would have to go back the way we had come. That meant that after climbing Oxford, we would have to reclimb Belford in order to begin the descent. So that day we climbed Mount Belford twice. I had finished two more fourteen-thousand-foot summits in the Sawatch Range and, in so doing, finished all the Collegiate Peaks. I had only three more fourteeners in the Sawatch Range left.

On August 9, Park and I headed to the trail to Mount Shavano, which we would have to climb in order to get to Tabeguache Mountain. We left early in the morning and ascended Shavano easily to its 14,229-foot summit. On the way we noticed a camp site in a valley and later caught up with a lone, male climber. The three of us finished the climb up Shavano together, then he and I decided to climb Tabeguache Mountain, the reason I had climbed Shavano again. Park decided to stay around Shavano while the two of us descended to the Shavano-Tabeguache saddle, ascended Tabeguache, returned to the saddle, and re-ascended Shavano in order to hike out.

So, after signing the register on Shavano, the lone hiker and I made our way to Tabeguache Mountain. We signed the register on the 14,155-foot summit and then headed back to the saddle and back to Shavano, where I expected to find Park. However, he wasn't there. I decided that he must have begun his descent on the trail and that we would catch up with him. So, we made it over Shavano and began hiking down the trail. Finally, we did catch up with Park, who told us that he had gotten off the summit to rest and a mountain ram had attacked him. So, he ran down the trail to get out of his territory. While Park was escaping a ram, I was counting; I had only two more of the fifteen Sawatch Range fourteeners to go.

After Tabeguache, we headed to Tembrock Orchards for a few days. With Bill and Kathy Tembrock on August 11, Park and I hiked the Exclamation Point trail on the North Rim of the Black Canyon of the Gunnison. I had been to the Black Canyon many times, as had the Tembrocks, but we wanted to show it to Park.

On August 13, Bill Tembrock with Joyce Klava, a friend of Tembrocks and of mine, and Park headed to the South Fork Lake Creek Road for a ten-mile round-trip climb of La Plata Peak. Because of the distance and the elevation gain, it was a long and slow climb. Klava almost stopped several times, but Tembrock kept urging her on. Finally, all four of us stood on the summit at 14,336 feet, the fifth highest point in the State of Colorado. It was a clear-blue-sky day; thus, the views from La Plata, located near the middle of the Sawatch Range, were enough to keep us occupied for a long time. However, we didn't have a long time to stay on the summit; we knew we had a long hike to get back to the truck. So, after eating a hearty snack and resting for a few minutes, we began our descent. We made several stops to rest on the way down, and one time Tembrock, who had run out of water, stopped at a stream, filled up his water bottle, and added chemicals to it to kill any microscopic bugs. Once we got to the truck, we headed back to Tembrock Orchards.

The next day Park and I headed back to Missouri. Together we had climbed seven fourteeners—six never before climbed by me. I had stood on the summits of fourteen of the fifteen fourteeners in the Sawatch Range; I had but one more to go, and it would be a very long journey. This trip with Park convinced me that I had become a mountaineer. I had set my goal to climb the nine peaks in the Ruby Range and accomplished it. I had set my goal to climb the five fourteeners in the Mosquito Range and accomplished it. I had set my goal to climb the fifteen fourteeners in the Sawatch Range, and I was one summit away from accomplishing it.

Park was an interesting man who was an extremely poor student in high school, but had found his place in academics in college. We began to talk before and after class and discovered that both of us liked the outdoors. So, we began to go on hikes together and to share dinner at my house or at his. In those days, Park was living in a house owned by and being renovated by his step-father. A few times after hiking, Park prepared dinner for us there. We continued to get together regularly to talk about religious studies, in which Park had decided to major. After he graduated, he entered the master's program of the Religious Studies Department at SMSU (now MSU). After he finished his master's degree in religious studies, he moved to Florida, where he was involved in a doctoral program, and that is when I lost contact with him.

2005: Adam Park 2, Zach Kinler

I considered 2004 a very successful year for mountain climbing. The plan for 2005 was to have a repeat performance. The repeat performance began with a Spring Break cross-country ski trip to Tembrock Orchards March 28 to April 1 with Park. I had invited Park to join me after we had climbed so many mountains together the previous summer. Bill Tembrock, Park, and I spent several days skiing on the Grand Mesa and McClure Pass with clear blue sunny skies above and snow-covered branches of tall evergreen trees all around us.

On August 8, I arrived in Boulder, Colorado, to meet my then twenty-three-year-old godson, who was finishing his last years of college there. I had invited Zachary Kinler, originally from Joplin, Missouri, to join me on a mountain climbing trip while he was in high school, but he wasn't interested. However, once he got to Boulder and experienced mountain climbing, it was amazing how his interest changed!

Mountain Climbing and Colorado

After picking up Kinler and his gear, we headed to South Clear Creek Road, located eleven miles south of Georgetown. We drove to Guanella Pass, found a car camping spot, pitched a tent, and prepared for the next day's climb to the summit of Mount Bierstadt. The six-mile round-trip trail leads the hiker over a boardwalk, completed in 2001 by the Colorado Fourteener Initiative to prevent as much erosion as possible on the most over-used trails to the summits of the fourteeners. Once getting to the ridge, we made our way to Bierstadt's 14,060-foot summit, where we signed our names on the register, ate lunch, and began our descent to our camp. After packing everything, we headed to a motel room for the night and for some rest. The August 9 climb of Bierstadt was my first ascent of one of the six fourteeners on the Front Range.

On August 10, we headed to the Grays Peak Trailhead in the Arapaho National Forest. Our objective was to climb both Grays Peak and Torrys Peak, located on the Front Range. Earlier in the summer, Kinler had climbed both of these peaks with some of his college friends, but he wanted to climb them again with me. We found a car camping site and pitched our tents. Then, we explored the area, especially the ruins of Stevens Mine. On August 11, after a hearty breakfast, we began hiking through a high mountain meadow covered in every color of blooming wild flower imaginable. We made our way to the summit of Grays Peak (14,270 feet). Then, after a short rest, continued to the saddle between Grays and Torrys Peak and climbed to the summit of Torrys Peak (14,267 feet). After eating a snack and resting, we began our descent to the saddle and from there to the trail that had meandered through the wild flower meadows in order to get back to our camp at the trailhead. By the time we got back to our camp, we had hiked eight miles. We broke camp and headed to a motel for the night and a rest day.

I had but one more fourteener to climb in the Sawatch Range to be able to declare that I had ascended the summits of all fifteen of them. So, on August 13, Kinler and I began a ten and a half-mile climb of the Mount of the Holy Cross (14,005 feet). I had heard other climbers talk about this trail that took us over a pass, down into the valley, over a river, and up the ridge on the other side to the summit. Everything they said was true. The gaining of altitude, then the loosing of altitude only to gain it again wore us out on our ascent. Kinler kept urging me forward, telling me that I could make it, and I did.

I do not remember a register on the summit of the Mount of the Holy Cross. So, after eating lunch on the summit and resting for a long time, we began our descent to the valley and our ascent to Half Moon Pass on the other side. While hiking up to the last pass, I had to stop several times to rest. Again, Kinler coached me onward and upward. About all that kept me pulling myself up the final ascent was the fact that I had just finished climbing all fifteen fourteeners in the Sawatch Range.

As one goal was achieved, another goal was taking its place. Kinler and I had just finished climbing three of the six fourteeners in the Front Range. That meant that I had only three left—and two of them had roads to the summit: Mount Evans and

Pikes Peak. However, these summits would have to wait for another year. Kinler and I had our sights set on one of the fourteeners in the Elk Range, namely, Castle Peak.

August 15 found us hiking ten miles to the summit of Castle Peak (14,265 feet). Kinler was not only a good mountain climbing companion, he was great at trail finding. He led the way to Castle's summit, from which we had great views of not only the Elk Range, but many other massifs off in the distance. Having done lots of research, I had no intention of setting a goal for myself to climb all the fourteeners in the Elk Range because they were outside my skill set; most of them require a climbing helmet, a rope, and an ice axe.

After finishing Castle, we spent the night in Aspen in a very nice hotel room. Then, we headed to Hotchkiss and Tembrock Orchards. While Kinler went fly fishing—another skill he had developed while living in Colorado—Bill and Kathy Tembrock and I went on a three-mile hike/climb to the top of Bald Mountain (11,787 feet). I had climbed this mountain in 1990, but remembered that the trail to its summit was covered in wild flowers. While on our way up the trail, dark clouds blew in and falling sleet pellets forced us to find cover under some evergreen trees and put on rain gear. On this August 17, it got very cold. Once the sleeting stopped, we emerged from our protective den and continued to the summit of Bald Mountain. While it was cold enough to keep our rain gear on, the sun did shine, finally, and we sat down, ate lunch, and enjoyed all of the West Elks that we could see.

On August 19, Kinler and I left Hotchkiss and headed over Interstate 70 to Boulder, where I returned him to his apartment and then headed back to Missouri. I drove 2,547 miles on that trip, and I hiked/climbed thirty-eight miles. I came to appreciate Kinler's mountaineering skills and to trust his judgments. He and I had renewed our relationship, and we had talked about doing more of the same the next year. I had accomplished one mountain climbing goal—the fifteen fourteener summits in the Sawatch Range—and I had set a new goal—the six summits in the Front Range.

2006: Scott Hinkebein 1

On the next to last day of July 2006, I picked up Scott Hinkebein in Nixa, Missouri, and the two of us headed to Colorado. I had met Hinkebein in St. Francis of Assisi Catholic Church in Nixa. I learned that teenage Hinkebein was an avid outdoorsman; he loved canoeing, kayaking, hunting, camping, and backpacking. As we got to know each other better, I decided to invite him to join me for the 2006 mountain climbing trip to Colorado, and he eagerly accepted.

Our first stop was the Lily Lake Trail on the way to Mount Lindsey in the very rough Sangre de Cristo Range. We backpacked for about a mile, found a campsite, pitched tents, gathered firewood, and prepared for the night. The next day we attempted Mount Lindsey. We met four other climbers on the trail, and when we got to a very vertical area, one of them, who said he had been mountain climbing in Tibet, turned around; we decided that was a smart idea. We hiked and climbed about ten miles that day, but did not reach Lindsey's summit.

On August 2, we found a car camping place on South Colony Lakes Road and set up camp. This time our goal was Humboldt Peak, another of the Sangre de Cristo Range fourteeners. The next day we stood on Humboldt's summit at 14,064 feet surrounded by clouds. However, this time the twelve miles we hiked and climbed left us with the prize of Humboldt Peak.

On August 4, we found a car camping site right at the confluence of Stewart Creek and Cochetopa Creek at the trailhead for San Luis Peak in the San Juan Range. This may go down in history as the most beautiful camping spot I ever enjoyed. The campsite was covered in grass and surrounded by babbling streams on two sides. And, it was about fifty feet from the San Luis Peak trailhead. After pitching tents, it began to rain. Hinkebein joined me in my three-man green and yellow tent to play cards and read until the rain stopped.

The next morning was very chilly, but we began our twelve-mile hike and climb after warming up with hot coffee and a hearty breakfast. The trail to the summit of San Luis Peak is gentle, but long. On the 14,014-foot summit, we met a mountain guide and a whole group of people he had led to the peak. We participated in his commercial endeavor by holding his "San Luis Peak, 14,014 ft. Aug. 5, 2006" sign in front of the camera for a photograph. After returning to our camp, we packed everything and headed to Tembrock Orchards in Hotchkiss.

While visiting Bill Tembrock (Kathy was out of town), the three of us hiked the Gunnison Forks to the ruins of an old shepherd's stone cabin. Many years ago, someone had built a structure from the stones in the area. In the one-room cabin, there was a place to eat, a place for fire, and a place to sleep. The builder had also constructed a cistern for water storage. From here he could lead his sheep to pasture on the hillsides and bring them back to safety for the night.

After a few days in Hotchkiss, Hinkebein and I headed toward Snowmass Mountain, another fourteener in the Elk Range. After finding the Snowmass Creek Road and the Snowmass Falls Ranch with parking at the trailhead for Snowmass Mountain, Hinkebein and I began a nine-mile backpacking trip to Snowmass Lake at 11,000 feet. It is at the lake that the trail begins for Snowmass Mountain! Not only is there lots of vertical elevation, but two log jams have to be crossed along the way. If the elevation doesn't do in the hiker, then the careful balancing that must be achieved in order to move from one log to the next probably will!

We got to the lake after hours of backpacking, found a camping site, pitched tents, prepared dinner, and went to bed because we were very tired and we hadn't even begun the trail to the summit of Snowmass Mountain. The next morning after breakfast we began hiking the trail that we thought would take us to the top of Snowmass Mountain. However, we discovered that we had gotten onto the Trail Rider Pass Trail which was taking us to the pass and away from Snowmass. After re-examining the map, we saw that the Snowmass Trail took off from Snowmass Lake. It was difficult to find because it was covered by willow bushes. By the time we got off the Trail Rider Pass Trail and found the Snowmass Mountain Trail, it was too late in the day to begin a mountain climb. So, we decided to save it for the following year and enjoy our evening around Snowmass Lake. We had hiked an additional six to eight miles and gotten nowhere! And the next day we had a nine-mile backpacking trip ahead of us to get back to the Jeep.

The next morning, August 10, we broke camp and retraced our steps—all nine miles worth—to the Jeep. We packed it, and headed home to Missouri, stopping for one night along the way, and arriving home on August 12. Both of us were determined to return to Snowmass Mountain and stand on its summit.

This was my first backpacking and climbing trip with Hinkebein; we would travel together for two more summers. While he was a teenager in high school, I came to appreciate his outdoor skills and his endurance. On this trip, I also rediscovered my own endurance. Hinkebein and I backpacked/hiked sixty miles together.

2007: Scott Hinkebein 2

While Snowmass Mountain was still on our agenda, Hinkebein and I did not head there immediately on August 3, 2007. Rather, our first destination was Longs Peak in the Front Range. I had set a goal to climb all six of the fourteeners in the Front Range, and I had climbed three of them with Kinler. I didn't want to lose sight of that goal, so Hinkebein and I headed to a motel room in Estes Park where we stayed on August 4 after having found the Longs Peak trailhead earlier in the day.

Early in the evening Kinler arrived with the woman he was then dating. The next morning we left the motel room at 2:30 to meet Ver Miller from Denver at the trailhead. At 3 a.m. all five us with headlamps set out on what would be the one-day, longest hike/climb of my life.

Obviously, we began in the dark. Until the eastern light began to appear, we hiked for miles in the dark, consulting each other so that we agreed that we were still on the well-traveled trail. We climbed through forests and meadows and made our way to the above-tree line, flat rocky area called the key hole. Many tents were pitched in this area, as many climbers backpack to this area, spend the night, and make the climb the next day. We had chosen not to backpack to the spot due to the crowds and the fact that we would be above tree line where there was no wood for a fire and it would get very cold at night.

All of us made our way through the key hole and to the back side of Longs Peak, where the steep ascent continues. On and on we hiked, following the painted markings on the rocks called fried eggs because that is what they look like! By noon we had reached the 14,255-foot summit, where we celebrated for about an hour. After eating lunch, we began our descent along the back side of Longs Peak, through the key hole, and down the trail. On the descent we got to see the high country that we had passed through in the dark hours before.

We got to the parking lot fourteen hours and thirty minutes after having left it. The round-trip hike/climb was fourteen miles. And while all five of us were excited about having accomplished our goal, all five of us were also dead tired with sore feet on this August 5 day. Hinkebein and I went back to our motel room in Estes Park to shower and rest for a couple of days. Everyone else went back to where they lived. I had climbed another Colorado fourteener and now had only two left to achieve my goal of climbing all six on the Front Range. Furthermore, the final two had roads to their summits! It would be a few years before I got to these two peaks, however.

After a few days for rest and recuperation, Hinkebein and I headed to Snowmass Mountain, where we had gotten lost the year before. On the way there, we spent some time in Meeker at the St. Catherine of Siena Chapel and St. Malo Retreat Center. On August 8, we arrived at the Snowmass Mountain trailhead, parked the Jeep, prepared our backpacks, and began the nine-mile climb to Snowmass Lake. I remember crossing the two log jams that are a part of the trail with greater ease than the previous year. After getting to the lake, we found a campsite, pitched tents, gathered firewood, and prepared for a restful evening before taking off early the next morning to get to the summit of Snowmass Mountain by noon.

The next day featured a bright sunny morning with a clear blue sky—perfect for mountain climbing. We found the trail in the willow bushes along the lake and began our ascent above tree line. Because the trail switchbacks through a lot of high-country rock fields—which slide around from time to time—there are several sets of cairns—rock piles—that mark the way. Furthermore, since many people climb Snowmass before all the snow is melted, some cairns mark the trail around various snowfields, which, of course, were already melted by August 9. Hinkebein proved his mountaineering skills by going ahead of me and locating the most direct trail through all the markers.

Up and up we climbed. Finally, we came to a ledge with some huge rock slabs. I was getting very tired, but Hinkebein, who was still in the lead, coached me on until we stood on the summit of Snowmass Mountain (14,092 feet). It had taken us two attempts to get there, but we were there, enjoying the view of mountains for hundreds of miles in 360 degrees. After resting and eating lunch, we began our descent, again picking our way through the multiple cairns and trails that would get us back to the lake and our campsite. Once back to camp, we both crawled into our tents and slept before making ourselves get up earlier in the evening, fix dinner, eat, and go back to bed!

By the time we backpacked out of the area the next day, we had spent nineteen hours and fifteen minutes backpacking eighteen miles and hiking/climbing another ten miles. Both of us were wiped out. We needed a motel room, a bed, and several good meals before we were ready to backpack and climb again.

On August 13, we were ready. Arriving in Silverton, we caught the Durango and Silverton Narrow Gauge Railroad train that stops in Needleton, about halfway of the journey between Silverton and Durango. Leaving the Jeep in Silverton, we boarded the train with only our backpacks. After getting off at Needleton, we backpacked into Chicago Basin, following the Needle Creek Trail. The last time I had been to Chicago Basin was to climb Windom Peak in 1983. Our goal this time was Mount Eolus.

Needleton sits at 8,212 feet; Chicago Basin sits at 11,000 feet. Thus, backpackers must gain almost three thousand feet in elevation over six miles. I had noticed that backpacking was taking a toll on me in my older years, but I didn't realize how much of a toll until this trip with Hinkebein. It would be an understatement to say that I had to push myself to keep going until we got to Chicago Basin and found a camp site. I didn't have much choice, because we didn't have reservations to catch a trail out for two days. By the time we got to the basin, found a camp site, pitched tents, gathered fire wood, and prepared dinner, I was really tired.

The next morning, August 14, we took the trail toward Mount Eolus. At tree line we encountered a herd of mountain goats, males, females, and young. They were not all that frightened by our presence because they see so many people coming and going in Chicago Basin. They looked at us for a few minutes and then continued to munch the sweet tundra grasses upon which they were grazing.

By the time we got to North Eolus (14,039 feet), I was getting very tired. We encountered two other men on North Eolus, with whom we chatted for a while. One of them was ready to continue to the 14,083-foot summit, and one wanted to begin his descent. Likewise, Hinkebein wanted to continue, but I, knowing how long it would take to get back to camp and the six-mile backpacking trip awaiting me the next day, wanted to call it quits. So, we decided that one of the men would accompany Hinkebein and the other would join me in a slow descent. Thus, two could get to the summit and get caught up with the two who had already begun to get off the mountain.

The two of us below watched as the two above switch-backed their way through the rocks, got to the ridge, and made it to the summit. We made our way down slowly, giving the two above time to catch up with us. Then, the four of us continued our descent back to our camp; the other two men were camped further below us. After getting to camp, I remember being really wiped out—and there was still the six-mile backpacking trip the next day to get to the train stop. I spent the last part of the afternoon resting and contemplating how many more of these kinds of backpacking trips I could endure and climb a mountain the next day. The answer I wasn't yet willing to give to myself was not many.

The next morning, we ate breakfast, broke camp, stuffed everything into our backpacks, and headed down the Needle Creek Trail to Needleton, where the train stopped on its way from Durango to Silverton. We got on it, got to Silverton, put everything in the Jeep, and headed back to Missouri, arriving on August 17.

I had learned a great lesson from the six miles we climbed to North Eolus and the twelve miles we backpacked—all of which took fourteen hours and thirty minutes. I had learned that I needed to listen to my body; it was telling me that I could not do what I used to do. Of course, it would take a few more lessons before I finally learned it!

In 2007 Hinkebein and I had climbed/hiked thirty miles. We had backpacked another thirty miles. And we had driven 2,284 miles. I had stood on the top of Longs Peak, a mountain I never thought I would ever climb. I had returned to Snowmass Mountain and stood on its summit. I claimed North Eolus as a peak, even though it was not the summit of the massif. My excitement was clouding my vision of backpacking and climbing as I was facing my sixtieth birthday.

2008: Scott Hinkebein 3, Tembrocks 5

Hinkebein and I made our third and final trip together to the Colorado Rocky Mountains in 2008. We left Missouri on July 13 and arrived at the Lake Como Road on July 14. There, we met Ver Miller from Denver. Our goal was to backpack the three and a half miles to Lake Como on July 14 and climb Ellingwood Point on July 15. The last time I had been in this area was 1983, when I climbed Blanca Peak, and 1984, when I had attempted Little Bear Peak.

The road was impassable in 1983 except for a four-wheel drive vehicle. It was even more impassable in 2008; a four-wheeler was about all that could get over it. In fact, once we met Ver Miller and began backpacking from desert to alpine, a four-wheeler with several men on it passed us. We encountered them again further up the road/trail where their four-wheeler had tipped over while trying to maneuver over and through huge boulders in the road uncovered by the wash-out spring rains. Everyone was fine; they managed to right their vehicle and pass us again further up the road.

When we finally arrived at Lake Como at 11,700 feet, I noticed that a lot had changed since 1983 and 1984. There used to be private cabins all around the lake that were kept in usable condition. Now, all of them were ruins, either completely demolished or standing with open doors, broken windows, or blown-away roofs. I concluded that since the road was no longer passable, cabin-owners could not get to their property to take care of it. Furthermore, when those cabins had been built, the fourteener traffic had not yet begun.

We circled part of the lake to find a camping site everyone could agree on. Then, we began to pitch tents—everyone brought his own—and to find firewood to build a fire for the evening. After all camp duties were accomplished, we settled in for a relaxing evening around the fire while eating dinner. I remember that the men who had passed us in the four-wheeler had camped a good distance away from us, but stayed up most of the night making a lot of noise and drinking the coolers of beer they had strapped to their four-wheel vehicle!

The next morning, while camp was quiet, all three of us got up, fixed breakfast, and began hiking the trail to Ellingwood Point (14,042 feet). It was a clear day with a blue sky and plenty of sunshine. The trail led us around Crater Lake, still partially covered in ice and snow, to the ridge between Blanca and Ellingwood. This part of the high country was absolutely stunning. On the way, Hinkebein developed high altitude sickness; we stopped for a while with him and gave him some Tylenol. Once his headache went away, he decided he would stay at that spot while Ver Miller and I made it to the ridge and, finally, to the summit. We knew we had to descend the mountain the same way we ascended it, so Hinkebein would be safe and we would pick him up later. And so Ver Miller and I made our way to the 14,042-foot summit, enjoyed the view for about thirty minutes while eating a snack, and began our descent. We found Hinkebein, retraced our steps, and found ourselves back at our campsite in the very early afternoon.

Someone brought up the topic of breaking camp and backpacking out. The original plan was to spend that night at Lake Como, but because of the previous night's noise from the men on the four-wheeler, we agreed that it would be best to break camp, head back to the Jeep, and drive to Alamosa to find a motel room. I remember being very leery of trying to backpack three and a half miles after having hiked/climbed seven that day. The lesson I had learned from the previous year had not been learned as well as I thought. Since the other two wanted to backpack out, I joined in the decision.

A long way down the old road/trail, I began to get really tired. My backpack was getting heavier and heavier, my shoulders were hurting, my feet were sore, and I had to keep stopping. Finally, about a mile away from the Jeep, I informed the other two that I could not go any further. I was near exhaustion. I took off my backpack and sat on it; I said that we had to do something. Someone could go get the Jeep and come and pick me up, even though the rough road would certainly take a toll on the vehicle. Or, I could just leave my gear here and come back and pick it up the next day. Ver Miller asked me if I thought I could walk back to the Jeep if he carried my pack. So, he strapped my pack to his chest—he had his pack on his back—and we began walking toward the Jeep again. About a half a mile from the Jeep, I experienced exhaustion. Both Ver Miller and Hinkebein went on to the vehicles; Ver Miller drove my Jeep up the road to pick me up. Then, he took me back to his vehicle and Hinkebein.

After we got all our gear loaded into our vehicles, I asked Hinkebein if he thought he could drive the Jeep to Alamosa; he said he didn't think he could. That left only me! So, with me in the lead and Ver Miller following in his vehicle, we headed to Alamosa to find a motel room for the night. We stopped at the first motel we saw, found a room, and proceeded to bring in what we needed for the night. Ver Miller went to the restaurant to see how late it was open, as we had not had diner yet and it was getting close to 9 p.m. Hinkebein got into the shower.

Ver Miller returned with a menu; he had made arrangements with the restaurant to get room service if we got our food order to the cooks within a few minutes. I looked over the menu and quickly decided what I wanted. I told Ver Miller just to go into the bathroom, read the menu to Hinkebein in the shower, and find out what he wanted. After this was done, Ver Miller went back to the restaurant and placed our order.

By the time I finished a shower and Ver Miller followed me, the order was ready and delivered to our room. We were almost too tired to eat it, but we gathered around the small round table in our room and ate our dinner, going to bed almost as soon as we finished. I had relearned the lesson I had learned the year before: Ten miles of backpacking and mountain climbing in one day was too much for me!

The next morning Ver Miller got up and headed back to Denver. Hinkebein and I decided to stay in the motel for another night. However, since he had never been to the Great Sand Dunes, we spent some time there, hiking the trail for about an hour on very sore feet. We returned to the motel and enjoyed an afternoon of swimming in the pool and sitting in the sauna. After supper in the motel restaurant, we went to bed early in order to recuperate from the trip to Lake Como.

From Alamosa we drove to Hotchkiss. Bill and Kathy Tembrock had sold Tembrock Orchards and moved a mile away sometime over the past few years. After selling the property, they moved to the home they bought, but Bill continued to work the orchards and harvest the crop for the new owners. By 2008, however, they had fully divested themselves of the orchard and were living on Barrow Mesa.

Hinkebein and I drove to their home on Barrow Mesa. On July 19, the four of us went to the Crystal Trail on the North Rim of the Black Canyon of the Gunnison and hiked five miles. My feet were still sore and my shoulders and back muscles were very tight, but these five miles helped to get me prepared for the next adventure of this trip.

It had become a tradition that Bill and I—and whomever I brought with me—would plan a climb together. We would name a peak and determine the feasibility of climbing it. Early in 2008, we had settled on Treasury Mountain, a 13,462-foot peak north of the Ruby Range and off Yule Pass. So, on July 16, after Luke Tembrock, Bill's and Kathy's youngest adult son, joined us, the five us in two vehicles headed to Paradise Divide below Yule Pass to find a campsite and to car camp. We found a campsite on a grassy knoll that was surrounded by mountains. Bill and Kathy pitched a tent, Hinkebein pitched a hammock, and I pitched a tent—all within a relative short distance of each other. Luke had decided to sleep under the stars in a sleeping bag on a tarp. That night we enjoyed a roaring camp fire, around which we sat for hours.

The next day the four men headed up the road/trail to Yule Pass, from where we began our bushwhacking trek to Treasury Mountain. The first thing we encountered was a snowfield blocking the road/trail. Because of the steepness and hardness of the snow, we could not risk attempting to cross it. So, we lost a lot of altitude by dropping down below it and coming up on the other side of it to regain the road/trail. It wasn't long before we encountered another steep snowfield blocking the road/trail. This time we decided that we needed to scramble up the tundra mound to the ridge, where we could see our destination and avoid the other snowfields blocking the road/trail up ahead. Once we got on the ridge, we could see Treasury Mountain, and Luke led us around high-country snowfields right to it. So, by mid-morning we stood at 13,462 feet above sea level.

We had talked about maybe also climbing Treasure Mountain which shares a saddle with Treasury. When we got to Treasury's summit, we could see that there were more snowfields blocking the ridge, that we would lose a lot of altitude that we would then have to regain, and that the ridge was a lot steeper than we had thought. Hinkebein and I quickly decided that we were not attempting Treasure. Bill and Luke debated it and decided to give it a try. After they took off down the ridge, Hinkebein and I sat on Treasury's summit and enjoyed the views. It wasn't long before we heard the Tembrocks coming back up to the summit. They had gotten but a few feet and encountered another steep snowfield blocking the ridge. They determined that the time spent going around that snowfield and probably more after it was going to put them very late getting back to Hinkebein and me, and, consequently, getting back to our camp and Kathy, who was spending the day pressing wild flowers and reading. So, hiking in the high country until we were sure that we had bypassed all the snowfields on the road/trail, we made our way back to camp, packed up everything, and headed back to the Tembrock home for the evening. A few days later, Hinkebein and I headed back to Missouri.

This trip confirmed that my backpacking days were over, especially long backpacking trips into the high country. The work zapped my energy, so that I was not able to climb the next day. The whole point of backpacking was to get close enough to a mountain to be able to climb it without having to hike many miles, like Longs Peak. I had to admit to myself that my backpacking days were over; I had experienced exhaustion on the Lake Como Road. I was also getting close to admitting to myself that my days of the strenuous climbs of the fourteeners were coming to a close, too. However, there was still Pikes Peak and Mount Evans in the Front Range that I knew I could climb.

2009: Kinlers, Tembrocks 5, Kristopher Morehead 1

In 2009, I made two trips to Colorado. The first was a cross-country skiing trip during Spring Break. On March 19, I drove to Joplin and spent the night with my godson's parents, Karl and Sheri Kinler. They and their daughter and grandson were heading to Crested Butte to see Zachary Kinler, who worked as one of three key ski instructors in Crested Butte Village. They invited me to join them, and I did.

Because there was no cross-country skiing in Crested Butte in those days—only slope skiing—I made plans with Bill and Kathy Tembrock to come to Crested Butte, pick me up, and take me back to Hotchkiss. They did, and I enjoyed four days of cross-country skiing with them. The morning that Bill was going to bring me back to Crested Butte it was snowing. We tried taking the road over the Black Mesa, but it became impassable, and we had to turn around, go back to Hotchkiss, and take a more traveled highway to get to Crested Butte. Of course, it was the longer way to get there. After depositing me at the condominium where the Kinlers were staying, Tembrock headed back to Hotchkiss.

The Kinler van was planning to leave the next morning to head back to Missouri. However, a snow storm was coming through and both the authorities of Colorado and Kansas were predicting that the major roads would be closed. Sure enough, the next day's weather report indicated that eastern Colorado and western Kansas highways were covered in snow and shut down. We had no choice but to stay in Crested Butte for an additional day. This gave me an evening to take Zach to dinner and visit with him. The day after our dinner together the Kinler van was able to hit the road and head back home to Missouri. Indeed, a lot of snow had fallen in eastern Colorado and western Kansas; we saw downed power lines and snow piled many feet tall by snow plows on both sides of the highways.

My next Colorado expedition, which began on July 19, featured a new friend: Kristopher Morehead. I had met him in Nixa, got to know him through our Missouri hikes together, and invited him to join me on this trip. He was an assistant band instructor in the Nixa Public School system. We arrived at the Tembrocks on July 20, and he became an instant friend of Bill's and Kathy's.

So, on July 21 the four of us headed to the Washington Gulch Trail below Gothic Mountain outside of Crested Butte. After finding what Bill called the ideal campsite, we car camped, pitching tents, gathering firewood, and preparing for a long evening under the stars in the wilderness. The next day while Kathy pressed wild flowers and read, the rest of us took the trail that would lead us to Gothic Mountain's summit. We found the trail and hiked it for three or four hours; it was very steep, and that made our climb very slow.

After finally getting above tree line, we could see where we were, and we could see how much further Gothic's summit was from us. Due to the roughness of the climb to that point, all three of us concluded that climbing the last ridge to the summit would be too much for us. From the lesson I learned the previous two summers, I knew it would exhaust me. So, I was the first to declare that I was as far as I was going to go. By the time we got back to camp, all of us realized that we had made the right decision. By the time we broke camp and got back to Hotchkiss, we were dead tired.

A couple of days later, we went to the North Rim of the Black Canyon of the Gunnison and hiked some of the trails there. Morehead had never seen the Black Canyon of the Gunnison, but as he listened to Bill talk about the SOB Trail, he wanted to hike it. I had already hiked it one time with Reynolds, and I had the intention never to hike it again. So, the day after our visit to the Black Canyon of the Gunnison, Bill and

Morehead went back and hiked the SOB Trail while Kathy and I took care of domestic chores at home.

Bill wanted to get Morehead on top of a fourteener. So, after he and I discussed the possibilities, we decided that Handies Peak would be perfect. So, we planned another car camping trip to American Basin. We left Hotchkiss for the trip on July 24 with all our gear. We stopped in Lake City to eat lunch, and then continued to American Basin.

After finding a great car camping spot, we pitched tents, build a fire ring, and gathered fire wood. After dinner we walked the old road to American Basin, where we would drive to the trailhead the next day. Both sides of the old mining road were covered in wild flowers. The basin was covered in wild flowers of every color. It was like walking on a carpet of color.

Following the well-marked and easy-hiking trail the next morning, we made our ascent of Handies Peak, passing Sloan Lake, the color of turquoise, on the way. On July 25, all three of us stood on the 14,048-foot summit of Handies. I had been there only one time before in 1983. After signing the register on the summit and eating a snack, we began our descent, retracing our steps from the morning and arriving at the truck and Kathy, who had pressed wild flowers and read, by early afternoon. After driving to our campsite, we broke camp, packed the truck, and headed back to Hotchkiss.

On the way back to Hotchkiss, we got to witness one of those flukes of nature that can be seen occasionally in Colorado. As we were coming to the junction of two major highways, we noticed storm clouds on the top of the mountains through which we had driven. When the clouds cleared, the mountain peak was covered with sleet, so much that it looked like snow. This was July 25! While it was sprinkling rain on us below, it had been sleeting and snowing at the highest elevations, leaving a winter wonderland above and wet gear in the back of a truck below! After getting back to Hotchkiss, we spent a day resting and then headed back to Missouri.

I climbed no new mountains in 2009, but I was able to practice what I had learned the two previous summers, namely, that I could no longer undertake long backpacking trips. Car camping enabled me to get into the high country, where I could hike and climb without being worn out before even beginning. I took note of this for myself.

I had also further developed a spirituality of mountain climbing. Through the beauty of the wild flowers, the lakes, and the mountains, God breaks through. These are kingdom moments, not to be missed. However, when I was worn out because of backpacking many miles, I had been so focused on my sore feet, aching shoulders, and painful back that I was missing those kingdom moments. This trip got me back in contact with them.

2010: Kristopher Morehead 2, Matthew Ver Miller 3, Tembrocks 7

On June 27, Morehead and I headed to Colorado together for the second time. We arrived at Willow Creek Trailhead the next day. My good friend Ver Miller from Denver met us at the trailhead. Then, the three of us began backpacking and climbing to Willow Lake, from 8,600 feet to 11,564 feet in four miles. I should have known better than to have attempted this; I thought I had learned my lessons from the past three summer Colorado trips, but, sad to say, I needed to keep learning it. The excitement of getting into the high country blinded my physical abilities.

The goal, after reaching Willow Lake, was to climb Challenger Point (14,081 feet), not counted among the 54 fourteeners, but a mountain I thought I could climb in the rugged Sangre de Cristo Range. Of course, the backpacking trip exhausted me. We found a camping site, pitched tents, built a fire ring, gathered fire wood, and enjoyed what we could of the evening. The mosquitoes were everywhere when the wind was not blowing. They swarmed around us as we hiked in; they swarmed around us at our campsite; they swarmed around us on our climb the next day, around our campsite the next night, and around us on the way out the morning after that. They made us miserable, and no amount of bug spray seemed to keep them away for long. Only when the evening finally cooled down did they leave us alone.

On July 29, after a hearty breakfast and before the mosquitoes were active, we began our hike to Challenger Point, following the Willow Creek Trail, which had a tendency to disappear in places. I was still tired from the backpacking trip the previous day, but I was determined. After circling the lake and climbing up above it, we continued on the trail until it disappeared in what looked like a rock slide. Being exhausted, I told Morehead and Ver Miller that I was turning around and heading back to camp; they were free to continue on together. I sat on a rock and ate a snack, watching them make their way through the rocks, trying to identify the trail that would take them to the ridge and, finally, the summit. It wasn't long before I saw them coming back toward me; they could not find anything of a trail and decided to turn around. They concluded that there had been a rock slide, which wiped out the trail. So, the three of us descended to our campsite and spent the afternoon resting, walking, exploring, talking, and taking photographs.

I give myself some credit here for making it clear to my two companions that I would not be able to break camp and backpack to the vehicles at the trailhead. Ver Miller knew that I knew what I was talking about, since he had carried my pack and his for about a mile on the Lake Como Road a few years before this. Morehead just trusted that I knew what I was talking about.

After a restful afternoon, mostly staying in our tents in order to avoid having to swat mosquitoes, we built a fire, fixed dinner, and crawled into our sleeping bags for a good night's rest before breaking camp and heading down the trail the next day. All along the switch-backing trail, we fought mosquitoes with bug spray, handkerchief swats, and baseball-cap wavings. It was a relief to finally get to our vehicles, deposit our gear, and get inside and away from the whining pests. The mosquitoes on this trip reminded me of the gnats along the Dominguez River in 2001. Ver Miller headed back to Denver; Morehead and I headed to Hotchkiss to the Tembrock home.

On July 2, the Tembrocks, Morehead, and I took the Kebler Pass Road to the Cliff Creek Trail on the way to Beckwith Pass to see the wild flowers. We hiked for several hours through meadow after meadow of red, white, yellow, and blue. When we weren't looking down, we were looking toward the Ruby Mountains and naming the nine peaks that Bill and I had climbed together or with others.

On July 4, Bill, Morehead, and I went to hike the Dominguez Canyon. Our goal was to check on Rambo, the hermit who lived miles into Little Dominguez Canyon on his family's old orchard property. We found him and sat outside and talked with him for about thirty minutes. Rambo had sold his family's property to the Bureau of Land Management in 1988 and been granted a life estate lease, meaning that he could live there until his death, when the land would become part of the Dominguez Canyon Wilderness Area. Until he died, he had full use of the land and the road that led to his cabin. After discovering that Rambo was fine, we left him and went to explore the Native American petroglyphs in the Dominguez Canyon; Bill and I had seen them several times, but Morehead had not. After hiking in the canyon heat all day, we were ready to head back to the truck and a cooler place.

Morehead and I headed back to Missouri on July 7. I realized that for the first time in many years I had not climbed a mountain. I had backpacked and relearned that I was getting too old to doing much more of that. I had hiked in the high country and in the canyons, and knew I liked this as much as climbing. I was in a stage of transition—and ageing. I was getting close to giving up backpacking; I wasn't ready yet to give up hiking and climbing, and the next few years would confirm that I could still do both.

2011: Kristopher Morehead 3, Matthew Ver Miller 4, Tembrocks 8

I wrote the following poem, named "New Day," to commemorate the July 14–28 trip to Colorado with Morehead, our third time to travel together to the Centennial State:

> The yellow orb climbs over the rocky arches,
>   filling the shadows with golden beams
>   and awakening the day.
>
> Praise erupts almost immediately spontaneously
>   from the chorus of chirping birds and humming flies
>   and buzzing bees and whistling marmots and clucking ptarmigan—
>   all honoring their God.
>
> Stirring in my tent womb,
>   I zip open the flap and the new world enters in.
> Last night's fire still warms a few coals
>   buried under the ashes.
> Crawling out onto the thick composting soil of aspen and spruce,

Mountain Climbing and Colorado

I hear the hallow echoes bass boom of my own footsteps.

Hearing my own silence joins me to the quiet
  which is an unheard symphony of forest smells—
  earthy piney snowy dewy muddy leftover smoky—
  sensualizing activity in my brain.

Spirit stirs the aspen leaves making them quake.
  Spirit whispers through the spruce needles.
Spirit rustles the tiny wild flowers—asters, columbine, monks hood, orchid
  —to blossom.

The climb begins with a few soft steep steps
  on the ridge toward the rising sun.

After leaving Missouri and spending the night in La Junta, Colorado, Morehead and I headed to La Vita, Colorado, outside the Spanish Peaks area. We found a motel, built out of mobile homes, and rented a room (trailer) for a few days. The next day we began exploring the West Spanish Peak Trail, which we hiked for four miles. We got lost where the trail rises above tree line and begins its ascent through rocks. By the time we noticed that we were not on the trail, we had found the cairns that mark it, but it was getting too late in the day to attempt to climb the West Spanish Peak.

On July 16, we explored the East Spanish Peak Trail, called the Wahatoya Trail. After taking an unkempt, rough road, we found the trailhead and hiked for about five miles. On the trail, I saw a black bear coming down a section that we were getting ready to climb. As I was leading, I turned around to Morehead and pointed toward the bear; I didn't want to say anything, because the bear would have heard me and run off into the woods. I knew it wouldn't take long before the bear smelled us, which it did, and scampered off the trail and into the aspen grove. Morehead began to complain about his knee hurting, so we turned around and considered ourselves lucky to have seen a black bear. This was the only bear that I have ever seen in the wilderness in Colorado. I have watched several cross the road, but I was always in a vehicle. After returning to the Jeep, we went back to our motel room/mobile home to await the arrival of Ver Miller from Denver.

He arrived late in the afternoon. After sharing our bear story with him, we planned the next day's hiking adventure. Morehead made it clear that he was not up to hiking for a few days because of his knee. So, Ver Miller and I made plans to climb West Spanish Peak. On July 17, we got an early start, headed to the trailhead, and began our climb. I knew the way, since Morehead and I had been on the same trail two days before. It was slow because it was steep, but both of us made it to the 13,626-foot summit. I had seen and been interested in the Spanish Peaks for over twenty years, but I had never planned a trip to explore them. Now, I stood on the top of the highest of the two. We made our descent and returned to our motel room in the mobile home, found Morehead, showered, and celebrated with snacks and wine our five and a half-mile climb before heading off to dinner.

The plans for the next day were to head to Mount Lindsey, a peak I had attempted with Hinkebein several years before. However, the more I thought about the long, rough road to get to Lindsey and the steep trail that turned around Hinkebein and me, I proposed a change in plans to Ver Miller and Morehead. Furthermore, Lindsey would involve a backpacking trip, and I had definitely learned my lesson about that in the previous years' experiences.

So, after looking at maps and discussing possibilities, we decided to head to Humboldt Peak in the Sangre de Cristo Range. After taking the Colony Lakes Road, I recognized that a lot had been changed since I had been there in 2006. The road had been closed at a lower elevation, and a new parking lot had been created. Along the road campsites had been made, complete with level tent spots and metal fire rings. We found a turnout spot where we could park our vehicles with a camping spot right below it. We pitched tents, set up camp chairs, gathered fire wood, and settled in. A ranger came along and told us there was a fire ban. Then, it began to rain. So, we climbed into our vehicles to escape getting wet, spending the time the rain shower occurred in conversation. Once the sun re-emerged, we prepared dinner and went to bed.

The next morning we began our climb. When I had climbed Humboldt in 2006, vehicles were able to continue up Colony Lakes Road for several more miles to the trailhead. Since the road was blocked, we had to climb those miles. We walked the road until we came to the old trailhead and then began our climb to the summit of Humboldt; the Colorado Fourteener Initiative had been busy on this trail, putting in rock steps everywhere to stop trail erosion. By noon we sat on the 14,064-foot summit, enjoying the view of the other mountains in the area before beginning our descent.

After over seven miles, we returned to our camp, packed up everything, loaded our vehicles, and took off. Ver Miller headed back to Denver; Morehead and I headed to a motel room for the night and Hotchkiss the next day.

After arriving at the Tembrock home in Hotchkiss, we joined Bill and Kathy on a three-mile hike to Exclamation Point on the North Rim of the Black Canyon of the Gunnison. On June 22, we joined them for a five-mile hike to the summit of Bald Mountain (11,787 feet), which marked my third ascent of this peak. And a few days later, after their son Luke joined us, Bill, Luke, Morehead, and I planned a climbing trip to the summit of Mount Lamborn. Our first choice was to head to Crested Butte and take the Slate River to Yule Pass, but, after calling Kinler, who worked there, we found out that because of the previous winter's snowfall, the roads were not open. So, Mount Lamborn it was.

We did not take the usual route to the summit of Lamborn. Bill and Luke plotted a course that took us over rough dirt roads, rocky roads, and over roads that were so overgrown that we had to bend in the side mirrors on the truck to keep them from getting knocked off by brush! Once we parked the truck on a level rock slide, we began to hike the trail that often disappeared before our eyes. However, being the excellent trail-finder that he is, Luke led us through the trees and over the creeks until we got to the bottom of the huge tundra-covered alp that is unique to Lamborn.

We switch-backed our way to the summit at 11,395 feet. The wind was blowing, and the gray clouds were rushing in. We had all signed our names to the register when it began to sprinkle on us. We put on rain gear because we knew a storm was coming. Quickly we began our descent, switching-backing down. The wind picked up, and the sleet began to pelt us with no mercy. After the sleet finished, the rain fell in sheets. No amount of rain gear could have kept us dry. By the time we got off the alp and back to the trail through the woods we were soaked, but there was nothing to do except keep hiking and, hopefully, dry out.

If wasn't long before the clouds passed and the sun began to shine. We stopped to take off our rain gear and put it into our day packs. As we continued down the trail, our clothes began to dry. By the time we finished this eight-mile, June 26 climb by reaching the truck, we were dry and warm again. The only thing all of us wanted was to get out of the wilderness and back home to a warm shower and a good meal.

That was my fourth ascent of Mount Lamborn, the last having been ten years before. Morehead and I headed back to Missouri the next day. On the way home I reflected on the successes of this trip. No backpacking was involved. I had hiked/climbed over thirty-seven miles, and, while often feeling tired after a day in the wilderness, I never felt exhausted. Backpacking was definitely out; car camping was in. Hiking and climbing in the high country was still possible even in my older years.

2012: Jeremy Graddy, Matthew Ver Miller 5, Kristopher Morehead 4, Kosslers 1

Remembering what I learned over the past four or five previous years enabled me to plan a hiking and climbing trip to Colorado in 2012 that was adventurous and successful, but included no backpacking. I traveled with a former student, who had become a good friend: Jeremy Graddy. I met Graddy in a New Testament night class I was teaching in the fall of 2009 at MSU. One evening I invited him to hang around after class. We began to talk, and continued to do so for two hours! Both of us wanted to develop the relationship. Throughout the semester, we continued to get together not just for conversation, but also for some hikes and other activities. Once the course was finished, we maintained our relationship through e-mail and occasional dinners together. He was in post-graduate school, working on a doctoral degree in physical therapy, and had a week off of classes. So, on July 8, we left Missouri for Colorado. After a night in a motel along the way, we arrived in Denver on July 9 at the home of Ver Miller where we spent the night.

Early the next morning we headed south to Pikes Peak. Even though there is a road to the summit of Pikes Peak, I wanted to climb it; it was one of the two fourteeners that I had not yet climbed on the Front Range. We drove to the Devil's Playground on the Crags Campground Trail and hiked and climbed from there to Pikes Peak summit at 14,110 feet. The round-trip hike/climb consisted of five and a half miles. As a side note, The Devil's Playground, according to a sign at the site, is so named because of the way lightning jumps from rock to rock during a thunderstorm!

On the way back to Denver from Pikes Peak, Ver Miller's four-wheel drive vehicle began to lose power, and he had to pull off Interstate 25. He had failed to bring his cell phone with him, I did not have a cell phone, and Graddy's had little power left because of all the photographs he had been taking with it. Using Graddy's phone, Ver Miller contacted a towing service, but, because the phone's charge died, wasn't sure if he had given all the necessary information. He hiked up the hill in hopes of finding someone who would let him use a phone.

Graddy and I stayed with the vehicle. A few minutes later, a tow truck arrived and began to prepare the vehicle for transport to Denver. Ver Miller had not yet returned; so the tow truck driver went up the hill to hunt for him, found him, and squeezed all of us into the cab of his truck, telling us that he was calling a transport vehicle to come and get us, but while we waited he was getting out of the hot sun and into some shade. So, we got on the interstate and took the first exit, found a shade tree, parked under it, and waited for the transport vehicle to show up. After about thirty minutes it arrived.

Graddy and I got into it, and Ver Miller stayed in the tow truck cab to show the driver where he wanted the broken vehicle taken. We spent the next hour making our way through afternoon Denver rush hour traffic, finally depositing the broken vehicle and being taken to the Ver Miller home. Not only was the climb of Pikes Peak an adventure that day, but getting back to Denver was an experience as well!

After another night with Matthew, his wife Janna, and their sons Jazer, Josiah, and Trevor, Graddy and I headed north west to visit other friends of mine: John Kossler, his wife, Amy, and their two sons, Ethan and Jacob. They lived on the Bureau of Land Management boundary; so, there were hiking trails at their front door. They recommended that we hike the Elliot Ridge Trail on July 12. So, early in the morning we set off over the dirt/gravel road to the trailhead.

The Elliot Ridge Trail leads the hiker into the Eagles Nest Wilderness Area. It almost immediately takes the hiker above tree line and puts him on a ridge from where he can see for miles in all directions. We hiked twelve miles over one high grassy ridge after the next, soaking up the beauty of the wild flowers and the scenes of mountains that stretched out before us. We stopped in a meadow and sat on the grass to eat lunch. Then, we continued on the trail that crossed other trails until Graddy spotted something orange in a ravine in the distance. We made our way to the object to discover that it was a tent that apparently had been blown down into the ravine from further up the massif. Because it fell into the ravine, its owners couldn't see it. Over the winter it had collapsed from the snowfall. As the snow melted, we saw it. Graddy shook out the water in it—along with several water bottles and candy bars—dried it out, and folded it up, attaching it to his day pack to take home.

I was getting tired, but he encouraged me to continue to the next point on the ridge; it was obvious that it was a high point. So, we climbed to the top and found a cairn marking it as a summit, but we had no idea what summit it was. When we got back to the Kosslers, they immediately knew that we had climbed Meridian Peak (12,426 feet). From there we had a terrific view of Eagles Nest, the mountain massif that gives its name to the wilderness area.

After spending the night with the Kosslers, we headed back to Missouri on July 13. The original plan was to stop along the way, spend the night, and get back on July 14. However, Graddy was driving and decided that we could make it to Springfield on July 13. So, we arrived around 10 p.m. and unpacked the Jeep. He headed home, and I went to bed.

Graddy and I maintained contact with each for a long time. Before he finished his doctoral class work and practicum assignments, I sent him an e-mail on February 22, 2013, after we had enjoyed some time together over dinner and a bottle of wine. "I keep coming to a deeper appreciate of the openness that exists between us and the freedom that affords us," I wrote. "I want you to know what a special gift you are to me." On February 23, he replied, "Our openness is like connecting or speaking to God through one another. I think that is why I feel so peaceful and energized by our personal exchanges. It is like being in the presence of God and speaking to him as friend." After Graddy finished his practicum assignments around the U.S., he married his high school sweetheart and began a family. Even though he lives close, family and work keep us from seeing each other.

Earlier in 2012, I had traveled with Morehead to Hotchkiss to visit the Tembrocks over spring break and enjoy cross-country skiing. Morehead had never cross-country skied before, but caught onto it immediately. Beginning on March 18, we skied every day for four days successively the Ward Lake Trail on Grand Mesa, McClure Pass, Skyline Trail on Grand Mesa, and County Line Trail on Grand Mesa. After finishing on March 21, Bill took us to the Gunnison River Archaeological Area, where archaeologists continue to uncover Native American artifacts from thousands of years ago. After reading the interpretive signs at the site, Bill led us back to the truck through a desert slot canyon.

Bill and Kathy told Morehead and me that they had planned nothing else except cross-country skiing for the days we were going to be there. We left on March 22, spent the night in a motel along the way home to Missouri, and arrived on March 23.

To commemorate the four days of cross-country skiing, I wrote a poem, simply titled "Skiing":

> The yellow orb alarms the blue planet
> > leaving orange red gray brush strokes
> upon the clouds scattering glitter
> > over the evergreen tatting lacy scarves
> on the alpine meadow quilting patchwork blankets
> > stretching barren aspen into long dark shadows.
> A wind wisp shivers branches
> > and rustles flakes flitter sparkles
> along the groomed ski trails.

This cross-country skiing trip was the best that I had ever had, probably because it was devoted solely to skiing. Our daily schedule consisted of getting up, eating breakfast, packing our day packs, and taking off for that day's destination. After skiing for a few hours, we returned to the Tembrock's home, showered, fixed and ate dinner, played dominos, and went to bed in preparation for the next day's adventures.

I remember getting to the Ward Lake Trail on Grand Mesa and it began to snow. We skied for a few hours in the snow. The flakes were huge; the falling snow created a fog-like scene among the evergreen trees through which the trail wound. By the time we got back to the truck, snow covered the road and the snow fog made it difficult to see exactly where the road was. Of course, as we gradually descended from the eleven-thousand-foot mesa, it got warmer and the snow was melting. A further few miles down the road and there was no snow at all!

Both of these trips to Colorado taught me that I could enjoy Colorado hiking and climbing—without the backpacking that zapped my energy—and cross-country skiing for days without a lengthy period of recuperation. Only one more fourteener remained on the Front Range. Plans were to climb it in 2013.

2013: Kristopher Morehead 5, Matthew Ver Miller 6, Tembrocks 9, Kosslers 2

Only one more fourteener remained for me to climb in the Front Range, and that was the destination of Morehead and me on July 14, 2013. We arrived at the Ver Miller home in Denver on July 15, and with Ver Miller climbed Mount Evans from Summit Lake on July 16. Standing on the 14,264-foot summit not only enabled me to declare that I had finished the six fourteeners in the Front Range, but I had finished climbing the fourteeners. After spending a little time on the summit with the hundreds of people who drive to the parking lot near the summit and walk the rest of the way to the top, we hiked the road back to Summit Lake, having covered six and a half miles.

With the successful ascent of Mount Evans, I completed the six fourteeners in the Front Range: Longs Peak, Grays Peak, Torreys Peak, Mount Evans, Mount Bierstadt, and Pikes Peak.

In the Sangre de Cristo Range, I had climbed Humboldt Peak (twice), Blanca Peak, and Ellingwood Point. The other fourteeners require mountaineering skills that I did not have: Kit Carson Peak, Crestone Needle, Mount Lindsey, Little Bear Peak, and Culebra Peak, which is on private property and open only occasionally for climbing.

I've climbed all five fourteeners in the Mosquito Range: Quandry Peak, Mount Lincoln, Mount Democrat, Mount Bross, and Mount Sherman.

I've also climbed all fifteen fourteeners in the Sawatch Range: Mount of the Holy Cross, Mount Massive, Mount Elbert, La Plata Peak, Mount Belford (twice), Mount Oxford, Missouri Mountain, Huron Peak, Mount Harvard, Mount Columbia, Mount Yale, Mount Princeton, Mount Antero, Mount Shavano (three times), and Tabeguache Mountain.

I have climbed two fourteeners in the Elk Range: Snowmass Mountain and Castle Peak. The other four—Capitol Peak, North Maroon Peak, Maroon (South Maroon) Peak, and Pyramid Peak—are out of my mountaineering skills range.

In the San Juan Range, I've climbed eight of the thirteen fourteeners: San Luis Peak, Uncompahgre Peak (twice), Wetterhorn Peak, Redcloud Peak, Sunshine Peak, Handies Peak (twice), Windom Peak, and Mount Sneffels (four times). Sunlight Peak and Mount Eolus require a long backpacking trip from Needleton into Chicago Basin—which I cannot endure any more—and are beyond my mountaineering skills range anyway, as is Mount Wilson and El Diente. I do not know if I ever made it to the summit of Wilson Peak; at one point in my life I thought I had, but at another I didn't think I did. So, I do not know.

Thus, out of the fifty-four fourteeners recognized by the Colorado Mountain Club, I have climbed thirty-nine of them for sure, and maybe forty of them. I have also climbed several fourteeners which are not on the official CMC list, such as Mount Cameron (14,238 feet), North Eolus (14,039 feet), and several unnamed fourteen thousand or fourteen thousand-plus peaks on the way to a named summit. I have never had a goal of climbing all fifty-four official fourteeners, but after having reached the summit of thirty-nine or forty of them, I think that is pretty good for an Old Mines missionary from Missouri.

As I wrote in an article, "Mountains: Places to Encounter God," in the Summer 1995 issue of *The Critic* magazine: "[T]o experience God, one must climb [a] mountain." Later in the article, I added,

> After having experienced one mountain and the inner unity of the self, I find that I have been drawn back to the mountains to soak up their raw, massive, terrifying beauty over and over again. This . . . is what I call the spiritual experience of mountaineering. It is in the process of climbing the mountain, as well as standing on its summit, that I believe I have become aware of God's appearance, experienced his presence, and descended the peak as a changed person.

After investigating specifically named mountains in the Bible and explaining what events occurred on them—primarily a manifestation of God—I concluded the article by writing:

> By standing on the summit of a mountain, I have better understood the mountaineering experiences related in the Bible. I realize that I have had experiences similar to Moses who, after spending forty days and forty nights on Mount Horeb (Sinai), descended with the skin of his face having become radiant while he conversed with the Lord (Exod 34:29). I, like Moses, have been sunburned by God's presence!

The same experiences of mountain climbing—no matter if the summits were fourteen, thirteen, twelve, or eleven hundred feet—led me to write *Mountain Reflections: A Collection of Photos and Meditations*, a 100-page book released by Leavenhouse Publications (Springfield, MO) in 2011.

Being finished climbing fourteeners did not imply that I was finished with mountain climbing. I doubt that I will ever be finished with mountain climbing. I am finished with backpacking; I am finished with car camping. I intend to continue to mountain climb, maybe reaching the thirteen-thousand-foot peaks of all those mountains I have ignored on the way to the summits of the fourteeners. I will continue to hike in the high country with my day pack on my back, my water bottle stowed securely in my day pack, my walking stick in hand, and my nose pointed to a distant peak. There is always more of Colorado to see.

The day after climbing Mount Evans, all the Ver Millers—Matthew, Janna, Jazer, Josiah, and Trevor—and Morehead and I went to Roxborough State Park and hiked three miles among the red rocks foothills south of Denver. On July 19–20, Morehead and I, while visiting the Kosslers—John, Amy, Ethan, and Jacob—outside Kremmling, Colorado, hiked a total of eight miles on two separate days to Surprise Lake and Lower Cataract Lake in the Eagles Nest Wilderness Area. After this, Morehead and I headed to the Tembrock home in Hotchkiss.

The 2013 trip to Colorado featured another ascent of the Lone Cone (12,613 feet). Bill Tembrock, who has climbed all fifty-four fourteeners on the official CMC list, wanted to climb the Lone Cone. So, he, Kathy, Morehead, and I drove to the trailhead—I knew the way from my ten previous trips there—car camped and climbed it on July 23. I had not been to the Lone Cone in twelve years, but the road to the trailhead came back to me like flashbacks in a film.

The lower part of the trail was marked and in better shape than I ever remembered it. Because of the rock slides and the upheaval of rocks caused by freezing and thawing, the upper part of the trail was in the worse condition that I had ever seen it. Nevertheless, while Kathy read at our campsite, Tembrock, Morehead, and I bushwhacked our way to the summit. Even though the Lone Cone is only a little over twelve thousand feet tall, a register has always been kept on the peak; registers on summits are usually only associated with fourteeners. So, after eating a snack, all three of us signed the register and began our very slow descent. By the time we got back to the campsite, the afternoon showers were beginning. So, we hurried to break camp, pack the truck, and headed back to Hotchkiss, telling the stories of our struggles and triumph to Kathy all along the way.

On July 25, my godson, Kinler, drove from Crested Butte over Kebler Pass to Hotchkiss to join the Tembrocks, Morehead, and me for a three-mile hike to the Archaeological Site along the Gunnison River. This is the same place that Tembrock had taken Morehead and me after our cross-country skiing trips in 2012. Kinler was working in a fly-fishing store in Crested Butte and leading people on fly fishing expeditions in the Crested Butte area, and he had a free day. I hadn't seen Kinler in a couple of years, so it was good getting back in contact with him.

Once we got to the site, we discovered that there were archaeologists working there. We talked to one of them, who explained what they had been finding and to what period of history it could be traced. After this, we hiked to the Gunnison River, where Kinler engaged in some fly fishing while the rest of us sat under a tree in the shade. After we regrouped, Kathy went back up the trail upon which we had descended, while the rest of us followed Bill through the slot canyon. Kathy met us with the truck at the end of the slot canyon and took us to the other vehicle we had left in the parking lot.

After the hike, Kathy and I prepared dinner, while the other men took care of chores. Then, we all sat down together for the meal. Shortly after we were finished eating, Kinler headed back over Kebler Pass to Crested Butte; he had to work the next day. Morehead and I packed up the Jeep and left Hotchkiss on July 26, spending the night in Garden City, Kansas, and returning to Missouri on July 27.

I returned home, after my thirty-seventh trip to Colorado to mountain climb in thirty-eight years, knowing that I had achieved another goal, namely, the last of six fourteeners in the Front Range. However, I also reflected that I had reconnected with many friends—Ver Millers, Kosslers, Tembrocks, Kinler—and that while I had always thought about it and even written about it, I had never expressed it verbally to myself that friendship is also an experience of God. I had become aware that God shines through my many Colorado friends both on and off the summit.

2014: Zach Dumas, Alone 11, Matthew Ver Miller 7, Kosslers 3, Tembrocks 10

As I had done several times in the past, I made two trips to Colorado in 2014. The first was a cross-country skiing trip with Zach Dumas March 9–14. I had met Dumas in a freshman class—General Education Program 101 Service Leaning—I was teaching at Missouri State University; we became friends fast, and he often referred to me as his mentor. I invited him to join me, and I told him that I would teach him about cross-country skiing. I had my own equipment, and I knew that he could rent his from a shop I knew about in Cedaredge, Colorado, on the road to the Grand Mesa. Because he was an athlete, he caught on to cross-country skiing quickly. Because the Tembrocks were out of town, I rented an inexpensive hotel room in Delta, Colorado, from where we took off every day to the Grand Mesa and other places where I knew the skiing would be good. Dumas, who lives two blocks away from me with his wife and pets, stays in contact through walks and shared dinners. We spent a week getting up, eating breakfast, heading to a cross-country place, returning, resting, eating dinner, and retiring early to do the same thing again the next day.

I returned to Colorado alone in mid-July making my first stop in Denver. Ver Miller wanted to climb Grays Peak and Torrys Peak, so I agreed to accompany him as far as I was able. After making our way out of Denver and to the trail head, we began the hike through high country meadows colored in wild flowers. After getting above tree line I began to tire, so I explained to Ver Miller what happened to the trail in the higher elevations—because I had climbed those two peaks before—and, after telling him that I would meet him in the parking area, sent him on his way. As I began my descent to the parking area, I met a climber from Scotland. Discovering that we were both teachers, we hiked together to the parking area while talking about teaching all the way. I had no more than arrived at Ver Miller's four-wheel drive vehicle, and he showed up after having climbed both peaks. With two more of the Front Range peaks climbed, Ver Miller was peak-bagging!

From Denver I headed north to Berthoud to the house the Kosslers now called home. After arriving there, I explored Devil's Backbone Open Space alone, and joined John, Amy, Ethan, and Jacob in exploring Horsetooth Open Space. Both were wonderful hikes in the foothills of the mountains.

My next stop was Hotchkiss and the Tembrocks on the western slope. We hiked a trail along the south rim of the Black Canyon of the Gunnison. In all the years I had been going to that area, I had never explored the south rim. We also explored the Gunnison Tunnel and Diversion Dam. This 1904–1912 project consisted of building a 5.8–mile long tunnel which funnels water from the Gunnison River to an area that would be desert without it. This July 20 to August 2 trip was full of hikes. While I had hoped to join Ver Miller in his ascent of Grays and Torrys, I was remembering my recent past experiences in the mountains, and I had enough courage to admit to him and to myself that I could not climb fourteeners anymore. However, the next year would find me exactly where I didn't think I could climb.

2015: Alone 12, Matthew Ver Miller 8, Tembrocks 11, Kosslers 4

I marked my fortieth anniversary of travel to Colorado with a trip there July 15–31. My first stop was Denver and a few days with the Ver Millers. Matthew, Jazer, Josiah, Trevor and I enjoyed a day hiking in Mount Falcon Park. After that on July 19, I accompanied Ver Miller on his climb of Mount Bierstadt (14,060 feet). I had climbed the mountain with Kinler a few years before this, but Ver Miller had never attempted it. As I had done the previous year, I told him that I would accompany him as far as I could go, and then I would stop. We hiked slowly and took frequent rest breaks. I made it to the summit and received accolades from other climbers who had passed us on the way to the top. I didn't think that I had another fourteener in me, but I proved myself wrong.

From Denver and the Ver Millers I traveled to Hotchkiss and the Tembrocks. We enjoyed a hike to a place I had never been before: Kannah Creek Falls on the Grand Mesa. After parking the four-wheel drive vehicle, we hiked for a mile to the falls, where we found a grassy area with some large rocks for seats and ate our lunch. The falling stream served as background music for our meal. The wild flowers, blooming abundantly, presented a carpet of color for our table.

After leaving Hotchkiss, I headed to Berthoud and the Kosslers. On the way there, I drove through Rocky Mountain National Park, which was marking its one-hundredth anniversary. Here I bought my Senior Pass for future admission to all national parks without charge. While visiting the Kosslers, I also made a day trip from Berthoud to the park to hike the Lawn Lake Trail to Roaring River Falls, a distance of six miles.

2016: Alone 13, Tembrocks 12, Kosslers 5, Matthew Ver Miller 9

My first trip to Colorado in 2016 occurred in February. I had been asked to give a retreat in the two parishes—Sacred Heart and St. Margaret Mary—in the Paonia-Hotchkiss area. So, a few days before the retreat was to begin, I drove to Hotchkiss to stay with the Tembrocks and enjoy some cross-country skiing. That was the winter that the Tembrocks received so much snow that we could ski out their back door and through the fields! We also made a few trips to the Grand Mesa.

After the retreat I headed to Crested Butte for a few days to visit with my godson, Kinler, and his then-girlfriend (later wife), Elsa Kavajecz. They had met each other when Kinler was working as a ski instructor and Kavajecz was working as a snowboard instructor in Crested Butte Village. I enjoyed some meals with them and two cross-country ski trips with them before heading home to Missouri.

My second trip to Colorado in 2016 began on July 21 with a visit with the Kosslers in Berthoud. John, Amy, Ethan, and Jacob and I, using my Senior Pass, made two trips to Rocky Mountain National Park to hike the Ute Trail and the Glacier Gorge Tail. We enjoyed high country tundra, lakes, falls, and mountains. Before leaving Berthoud, I hiked the Ramsay-Shockey Open Space Shoshone Trail alone one day and enjoyed a lake, Ponderosa Pine forest, and mountains. From Berthoud I headed south to Denver to the Ver Miller home. From there Ver Miller and his eldest son, Jazer, and I headed to Culebra Peak, a fourteener which sits on private property. Ver Miller had investigated the process of getting admittance to the ranch which surrounds the mountain and paid the admission fee of one hundred dollars for adults and fifty dollars for his son. Because Culebra is located in the southern part of Colorado near the Colorado-New Mexico border, we spent the night in a hotel in the oldest town in Colorado: San Luis. The next morning we got up early and followed the directions we had been given to the gate, where we found other cars with climbers awaiting entrance. We listened to the orientation talk given by the ranch hand responsible for this part of the operation and then drove to one of the parking areas he had pointed out to all present. Then, after getting our gear ready, we began the hike through meadows to the ridge that would enable us to climb Culebra.

Once we got to the ridge and I saw what lay ahead, I told Matthew and Jazer that I was not able to continue. If I did reach the summit, I would not be able to descend and get back to the car. So, I decided to stay on the ridge near a rock pile while they went to climb to the summit. I sat in a comfortable place among the rocks for three hours using my walking stick to keep the marmots from getting too close and into my pack while they made it to the summit and back to me. Then, I joined them in the hike down the meadow to the car. I recognized then and still do now that that was the best decision I ever made when mountain climbing and hiking. While I regretted not being able to join them to the summit—and this was Jazer's first fourteener—I recognized that I had made the right decision after having learned how age was affecting my climbing abilities in previous years. After stopping at a Subway for some food, we headed back to the Ver Miller home in Denver and a victory celebration.

From Denver I headed to the Tembrock home in Hotchkiss. Once there, all got ready for a trip to Crestone, Colorado, to stay in the home of their son—John—and visit all the religious foundations that have settled there. Our first stop was at the Buddhist Tashi Gomang Stupa and Shrine. The next day we visited the Nada Hermitage Carmelite Spiritual Life Institute, the Haidakhandi Universal Ashram and Divine Mother Temple, the Shumei International Institute, and the Buddhist Retreat Center. Seeing all these religious places in one small town re-awakened my world religions degree and fostered writing using some of their sacred texts. After getting back to Hotchkiss, Bill and I enjoyed a hike along Fire Mountain Ditch. As we walked along the water that flows to the orchards and ranches in the area, Tembrock pointed out the various filtering systems employed by those who have rights to the water. After a couple of days, I headed back to Missouri.

2017: Alone 14, Tembrocks 13, Matthew Ver Miller 10, Kosslers 6

Adding together all my experiences of mountain climbing, I reached the conclusion that except for peaks that could be reached in short distances, mountain climbing was now a past part of my life. In 2017, either I gave away or sold in a garage sale all the equipment—tents, backpacks, cooking utensils, water purifiers, etc.—that I had been hauling to Colorado every summer for the past three years and never using. The chapter on climbing was closed, while that on continuing to go to Colorado and hiking was still open.

As in the previous year, in 2017 I made two trips to Colorado. The first was in April to give a retreat to the people in Sacred Heart Parish, Paonia, and St. Margaret Mary Parish, Hotchkiss. I decided to fly to Montrose, where I was met by the Tembrocks and taken to their home. Before the retreat, we enjoyed some cross-country skiing on the Grand Mesa. After the retreat, they dropped me off in Montrose at a hotel so I could catch an early morning flight from there to Denver, and from Denver to Springfield.

In mid-July I drove to Denver to spend a few days with the Ver Millers. We hiked in the Staunton State Park, located in the foothills, and Alderfer/Three Sisters Park, also located in the foothills. From there I headed to Berthoud, where I joined the Kosslers on a hike to Coyote Ridge and two hiking trips in Rocky Mountain National Park: (1) Nymph Lake, Dream Lake, Emerald Lake, and Bear Lake, and (2) Bierstadt Lake. Besides the lakes, along which we sat to eat our lunch, we enjoyed the snow-covered mountains, running streams, and wonderful trails. After such beauty, I headed home across the high plains of Colorado and the fields of Kansas.

2018: Alone 15, Bill Tembrock 8, Kosslers 7, Matthew Ver Miller 11

The first trip to Colorado in 2018 occurred in March. While there was little snowfall on the cross-country trails on the Grand Mesa, I did manage to get in a few days of skiing. This was the first time that I had ever been able to see the rocks through the snow because it was not very deep. However, one day after it had snowed a little the night before, Tembrock and I went skiing. He decided to cut across a dam by creating his own trail. I stood on the groomed trail and told myself that I should not follow him, but I did anyway! I got to the end of a hill and decided that it was too steep and I would pick up too much speed. So, I took off my skis intending to walk down the hill and put the skis on to continue the trip. Because the sun had been shining on the snow all day, it was very soft and I sank up to my knees. Not being able to lift up my feet because of the snow's depth, in order to get a foothold, I had to crawl back to the trail, scooting my skis and poles along the way. By redistributing my weight over hands and knees, I was able to stay on top of the snow and get back to the groomed trail.

My second visit to Colorado in 2018 occurred in the summer. I began by visiting the Kosslers in Berthoud. We made two trips to Rocky Mountain National Park in late July. We climbed Deer Mountain (10,013 feet)—a six-mile hike—and followed the Cub Lake Trail, which not only took us to the body of water, but led us through an area full of ripe, wild raspberries. We stopped along the trail and picked handfuls of the delicious fruit and ate until we were full and our hands were red from picking the fruit.

After a few days with the Kosslers, I headed to Hotchkiss to spend a few days with the Tembrocks. We made a trip to the Colorado National Monument outside of Grand Junction. On another day we hiked four miles of the Piburn Trail, where we found more ripe, wild raspberries. We stopped and picked handfuls and ate them joyously.

The third stop was in Denver at the Ver Miller home. We spent a few days in their vacation-rental home—Aspen Leaf Lodge at 11,200 feet—outside of Fairplay. There I enjoyed the cool air of the high country, some hikes, and some mountain views before heading back to Denver and then back to Springfield. By the end of the summer of 2018 I had firmly accepted the fact that the days of mountain climbing, except for lower elevations, were over. Now, however, I had many stories to tell about my days in the high country.

2019: Alone 16, Kosslers 8, Tembrocks 14, Matthew Ver Miller 12

The 2019 trip to Colorado began June 26, with a visit to the Kosslers in Berthoud and two trips to Rocky Mountain National Park. On the first trip, June 29, we hiked 6.8 miles to and from Fern Falls and Fern Lake. On the second trip, June 30, we hiked only 2.2 miles to Nymph Lake and Dream Lake. There was so much snow left over from the previous winter that we had to cross a snow field to get to Dream Lake! I would discover later than Colorado got one hundred thirty percent of its annual snow fall in the winter of 2018–2019. This meant that the mountains still had plenty of snow on them, the streams were running above normal due to the snow melt, and the falls roared as the water tumbled from higher levels to lower ones.

I have known John Kossler since he was twelve years old in 1990. His mother, who was Sacred Heart Parish secretary, asked me to take him with me on a climb. I was spending a month in Paonia, Colorado, celebrating Masses in Sacred Heart Parish and its mission, St. Margaret Mary Parish, Hotchkiss. Kossler was too young to work on the cattle ranch and had little to do that summer. I agreed to take him with me. He had lived below Mount Lamborn for twelve years, but he had never climbed it. So, that mountain was the first we climbed together. After that, we made a trip to Mount Emmons together. When I was in the area, I often contacted Kossler to join me on a hike or a climb. Once he became old enough to work on the cattle ranch that his father managed, he spent the summer herding cows. In high school, he was busy playing soccer, working, and deciding what to do with his life.

I don't remember exactly how the contact came, but he notified me that he was attending Creighton University in Omaha, Nebraska. Over the course of the four years that he was there, I travelled to Creighton to spend a weekend with him in the fall, and he came to Springfield for Easter. Through those visits, we renewed our friendship and continued to develop it in an adult manner. In my journal entry for March 31, 1997, I wrote, "I don't know when I have ever been so filed with hope as I have after John Kossler's four-day visit. The time I spent with him filled me and gave me new hope.

He shared his life and himself with me as I shared my life and myself with him. Our friendship fires turned into a bonfire!"

One topic of our conversation centered on the Myers-Briggs personality type indicator. I had shared with Kossler how it helped me know myself. On April 23, 1997, he sent me an e-mail, letting me know that he had taken it, and that he and I had only one letter difference. He was an S, preferring sensation, while I was an N, preferring intuition. Both of us were introverts (rather than extroverts), thinkers (rather than feelers), and judgers (rather than perceivers). In my e-mail response the next day, I wrote, "Our identical types (ITJ) also explain why we had such a good time together during your visit. By getting to know each other (again) on an adult-to-adult basis, we were also getting to know ourselves better, too. You revealed to me some aspects of who I am, and I hope I did the same for you."

In his e-mail to me, Kossler had noted that he had been accused of being cold and remote at times. I reminded him that was his introversion and not his inability to feel. "My guess is that you feel deeply, but don't trust your feelings, preferring to trust your ideas in your head. My introversion leads me not to trust myself with people until I'm sure of at least two things: I won't get hurt, and I'll get something in return." I added, "Relationships that we've established are important to us, and we'll do everything to preserve them for the same two reasons."

In his April 23, 1997, e-mail, he reflected on the end of the semester at Creighton. "I really want to go home, to see the ranch, the mountains, and everyone I miss, but I hate leaving, too, now that I'm settled in, know all the ins and outs, and have friends I won't see for three months. It's like moving back and forth between two different worlds." In my next-day reply, I advised him to taste and test both of the worlds in which he found himself. "Both are guides to your future. You'll figure out a way to bring them both together in time. You don't have to do it now. Just pay attention to the aspects of both that draw you toward them."

In my e-mail I also took the opportunity to raise Kossler's awareness about himself. He was well on a journey of self-discovery. "One of the most fascinating things that comes through your e-mail is that you are conscious that you are conscious. It's a sign of the depth of your thinking abilities. It means that you are always thinking ahead and figuring out what the outcomes of actions might be." I continued,

> One thing personality inventories have taught me is that the more I know myself, the better I can know others. The level of being conscious that you are conscious is not only a rare gift, but it is an indicator of how well you know who you are and how well you are comfortable being who you are. I sensed this when we were together. I picked it up several times while you were visiting and we were able to sit together in silence. It's what drives me to want to get to know you even better, because you can disclose to me aspects about myself that I am not aware of, and, hopefully, I can do the same for you.

Over the years we maintained contact through e-mail and occasional visits, as can be seen in the above narrative. Often when seeing each other, we enjoyed the silent communication between us. While attending Creighton, he met Amy, whom he married in 2005. I was privileged to witness their exchange of vows. "You've been a lifelong friend and mentor to me, and I'll never forget Easter in Springfield," he wrote in a card thanking me for coming to Colorado for his wedding. "I've learned much about friendship and my own spirituality from you, and I will always look to you as a teacher as well as a confidant."

After completing a Master's Degree at Colorado State University, John and Amy moved to a ranch in Kremmling, Colorado, where Kossler served as the environmentalist for land and stream recovery. There, they began a family: Ethan and Jacob. John worked on the ranch, and Amy raised their two sons while pursuing photography. After a number of years, they moved to Berthoud, Colorado, for the educational opportunities offered to their sons. While John continues to do some work for the ranch, he founded Western Meridian Resources in which he serves as an ecologist guiding individuals and businesses through the process of land and stream reclamation.

In 2012 and 2013, I visited the Kosslers, who were then living in Kremmling, Colorado. Once they moved to Berthoud, Colorado, in 2014, I visited them there. After I bought a Senior Pass to the National Parks in the United States, we began taking hikes in Rocky Mountain National Park in 2015, and we have continued to do so to 2019. Not only have I gotten to know John better, but I have come to know his wife, Amy, and I have watched his sons, Ethan and Jacob, grow into good hikers. I have known John for 29 of his 42 years!

From Berthoud in 2019 I headed to Hotchkiss to spend a week with Bill and Kathy Tembrock. With a friend of theirs, we hiked the Cliff Creak Trail toward Beckwith Pass on July 5, 2019. Because the snow had just melted in the high-country meadows, there were few wildflowers. It would be another two to three weeks before the meadows burst into color. Meanwhile, the view of the Ruby Mountains provided a winter scene of snow-covered peaks and brought back many memories of having climbed them in previous years.

The final stop for 2019 was at Aspen Leaf Lodge. I got there on July 9 and enjoyed two days alone in this high mountain paradise. Other than taking a walk every afternoon, I worked on a manuscript for a book, read, and relaxed. Ver Miller and his four children arrived on July 11, and on July 12 all of us set out to climb Pennsylvania Mountain. In 2018, while spending a few days at the lodge, we had hiked to a spot above tree line on the Pennsylvania Mountain Trail, and I said that I would be willing to try it in 2019. So, early on the morning of July 12 we set out. We met a Fairplay resident on the trail who told us that the mountain we could see in front of us was a false summit. We discovered that there was another one behind it. Finally, we got up high enough to see the tundra grass-covered mound ahead of us on the other side of an old mining road in a valley right below us. So, we headed that way. While the Ver

Miller boys made their way through a huge snowfield, Ver Miller, Kezia, his daughter, and I made our way over the old road until it disappeared near the summit. All of us met on the top of Pennsylvania Mountain (13,005 feet). There we joined three other mountain climbers on rocks dug out of a mining prospect hole. While eating a snack and discussing the wonderful day we were experiencing, we named other mountains in the area before descending to where we left our vehicle. On the next morning I left the lodge and headed back to Missouri. I hadn't climbed a mountain in four years. I discovered that the five miles of walking we did the day before left me sore, but it also left me knowing that I could still enjoy the views of the high country.

Because of the coronavirus (COVID-19) pandemic of 2020, I was not able to make a trip to Colorado. For forty-two continuous years I had enjoyed mountains, hikes, wild flowers, humidity-free days and nights, and lots of friends in the Centennial State; all it took was an invisible virus to cancel year forty-three!

10

Ocean Cruises 1979–1990

1979: Alone 1

On February 7, 1978, I got my first appointment letter as a cruise chaplain. During the summer of 1975 and the spring of 1976, I had lived with a priest who served as a chaplain on ocean cruise ships, and he had given me the necessary contact information. So, on January 6, 1979, I flew on Ozark Air Lines from Joplin to St. Louis, where I caught a TWA jet to Miami, Florida.

If all would have gone well, I would have arrived in Miami with time to spare before embarkation. However, after getting to St. Louis, where a wet snow was falling, the TWA employees could not get the cargo doors closed on the jet, because they had frozen open. After all had boarded the plane, the captain announced over the loud speaker system that we would be delayed while the workers outside attempted to get the cargo doors unfrozen and closed. He assured all the passengers that this should be accomplished in a very short time.

Nothing happened. Passengers waited and waited and waited. The captain told us that the outdoor crew was getting some kind of equipment to melt the ice so the cargo doors would close properly. After two hours of waiting, the indoor crew began to serve free alcoholic beverages along with soft drinks! Finally, after three hours the cargo doors were closed, and we were cleared for takeoff. There were a number of people on this plane headed to Miami to catch ships; again, the captain informed the passengers that he had contacted the ships and their captains had agreed to delay leaving Miami until we got there—which would be long past departure time.

When we arrived at the airport terminal, vans from Norwegian Caribbean Lines were waiting for us in the luggage claim area. Drivers held signs for the ship. I didn't know it at the time, but there were at least fifty passengers on that plane headed for the MS Southward, and that was the ship upon which I was assigned as chaplain. After getting us and our luggage loaded, the drivers hurried to the pier, where we were herded off the pier with our luggage in tow, directed up the gangplank, and greeted on the ship by some of the cruise staff who checked us in and sent us to our cabins. Meanwhile, the ship was leaving the harbor. All the usual embarkation procedures were ignored because all the offices were closed. Usually, after checking in, one's luggage was tagged with one's cabin number on it, and it was delivered to one's cabin. Usually, there was the opportunity to take pictures of groups of people sailing together. People had the opportunity to stand on the deck and watch the ship leave the harbor and head for the ocean. At this time of the day—it as around 6 p.m.—dinner was already being served in the dining rooms. Furthermore, all of us who had just boarded had missed the Coast Guard mandatory life boat drill.

I was given an inside cabin on the lowest passenger deck and shown where the crew dining room was. I was told to get to my cabin with my luggage, leave it there, go to dinner in the crew dining room, and get ready to be introduced to the passengers that evening. Since this was my first cruise and first time serving as chaplain, I was given information about what to do if I got sea sick—eat saltine crackers and stop fighting the ship's listing—and given a chaplain's schedule.

I liked eating in the crew dining room, because I could go to dinner any time I wanted. Other than eating, I could use any part of the public areas of the ship. I was introduced to the passengers by the cruise director during the welcome aboard festivities. Then, I went to my cabin, unpacked my clothes, and prepared for the week-long cruise.

All this had taken place on a Saturday. On Sunday the ship was at sea all day. I had Mass at 9 a.m. and a Protestant service at 10 a.m. in the cinema. Basically, I used the Scripture texts from the Mass for the Protestant service and preached the same homily. A collection was taken and sent to a charity of my choice. The tradition onboard the Southward was Mass was celebrated on days at sea and not when in port. So, on Tuesday, while the ship continued to the pier in Cozumel, Mexico, I got off with others at Playa Del Carmen for a trip to Tulum to see the Mayan ruins. After this, we went to Xelha National Park, where the ship provided us with a box lunch, then Playa Del Carmen Hotel, from where we were taken back to the ship.

On Tuesday the ship docked in Georgetown, Grand Cayman. I roamed around Georgetown, engaged in some shopping, and then attended the Galleon Beach Party at Galleon Beach Hotel for lunch, swimming, and sunbathing. After getting back on the ship, the Southward left Georgetown at 6 p.m. and sailed toward Ocho Rios, Jamaica. Arriving there on Wednesday, I took the Dunn's River Falls Tour. After being deposited at the bottom of the falls, we climbed to the top and walked through the straw market. Then, we were taken to Shaw Park Gardens in order to view the harbor and the anchored MS Southward. From there we were taken to Fern Gulley, and, finally, dropped off in the shopping area before heading back to the ship. By 8 p.m. that evening, we were on our way to Great Stirrup Cay, Berry Islands, Bahamas.

Because Thursday was a day at sea, I celebrated Mass in the cinema, then attended the debarkation talk. The rest of the day was spent reading in various public areas of the ship. At 7:15 p.m. I led a number of couples in a renewal of their marriage vows, a well-attended event on ship which even included a certificate of renewal given to each couple.

On Friday morning the ship anchored off Great Stirrup Cay, an uninhabited island used by Norwegian Caribbean Lines. Almost all passengers got off the ship to enjoy the privacy the island offered. Passengers could snorkel, toss horseshoes, sunbathe, swim, beach comb, eat lunch, etc. on the island. I noticed an old road a few feet beyond the palm trees and decided to explore it. It took me to an old army installation, an abandoned light house and home for the light house keeper, and ended on the ocean on the other side of the island. I remember enjoying the privacy of my own beach there!

Everyone had to be back on board by 2 p.m. The last tender, a small boat that could pull up to the ship and ferry people to and from the island, left the island at 1:30 p.m. So, at 2 p.m. the ship weighed its anchor and headed back to Miami. As ship's chaplain, I was responsible for helping the Jewish passengers prepare for and welcome the Sabbath at sundown. I remember getting to the cinema and asking some of those present how they wanted to proceed. They elected a leader from among themselves and conducted the Sabbath service.

We docked in Miami at 7 a.m. on Saturday while eating breakfast. Then, once the ship was cleared by customs officials, passengers began to debark, go to the customs' shed where their luggage had been placed (it had to be packed the night before and placed outside one's cabin door), claim it, and proceed through the customs' line, declaring anything on which taxes needed to paid, like more than the legal limit of alcohol or more than the legal spending limit.

After successfully getting through U.S. Customs, I caught a taxi and headed toward the Miami airport, hoping that my flight home would in no way resemble my flight there. This first cruise hooked me on sailing. Not only had I seen the Atlantic Ocean for the first time in my life, but I had sailed many miles on it to countries I had never been to before. I had enjoyed my free time reading and writing poetry. Many more cruises would follow.

1980: Alone 2

After a successful cruise on the MS Southward in 1979, I was ready to serve as ship chaplain again. This time I was assigned to the MS Starward, a sister ship of the MS Southward, both operated by Norwegian Caribbean Lines. This was a Saturday-to-Saturday cruise, February 2–9, 1980. After flying from Joplin to Miami and catching a taxi from the Miami airport to Dodge Island, the New Port of Miami, I went through all embarkation procedures and found myself on the MS Starward with none of the problems of the previous year.

At 5:15 p.m. I participated in the mandatory Coast Guard emergency boat drill, which consisted of finding the lifeboat assigned according to passengers' cabin numbers. At 6 p.m. the ship left Miami for a day at sea before arriving at Port Antonio, Jamaica, on Monday. At 10 p.m. I was introduced as the ship's chaplain to the passengers in a lounge. On Sunday at 9:30 a.m., I celebrated Mass in a theater, followed by a Protestant service at 10:10 a.m. The rest of the day was spent exploring the ship, reading, and attending various events onboard.

On Sunday afternoon the ship ran into a water spout, a tornado at sea, with eight- to ten-foot waves. The ship not only sailed up and down but listed from one side to the other. Many passengers were sea sick; that night at dinner, the dining room was very sparsely populated. Most passengers remained in their cabins.

After arriving at Port Antonio, Jamaica, on Monday, I took the tour that transported me and some of my shipmates along Red Hassel Road past dwellings and shops to the agricultural area of Cambridge and Sherwood Forest. We saw the famous Blue Mountain, Athenry Gardens, and Caves of Nonsuch. At one stop I remember buying Blue Mountain coffee. The tour ended with complimentary rum drinks at the Dragon Bay Hotel and a stop to shop for art and local crafts before returning to the ship. By 5:30 p.m. the ship was supposed to leave Port Antonio and sail to Ocho Rios, Jamaica, which I had visited the previous year. However, the wharf was covered with water from the high seas. So, we stayed an extra day in Port Antonio. Finally, on Tuesday afternoon we left Port Antonio and sailed to Port Au Prince, Haiti, where the ship docked at 8 a.m. Wednesday.

Since I had never been to Port Au Prince, I took a sightseeing tour by car to government buildings, the casino, the modernistic French institute, the iron market, the art center, and the old cathedral. We were also taken to Boutilliers, from which we could see the city below us and for miles and miles in all directions. The tour culminated with a stop at the Barbancourt Rum Factory, where we enjoyed complimentary rum samples and could purchase Haitian rum to bring back to the U.S.

All passengers had to be onboard by 1:30 p.m., because the ship set sail for Nassau, Bahamas, at 2 p.m. Thursday was a day at sea with all kinds of events taking place on the ship. At 7:15 p.m. I gathered with married couples who wanted to renew their marriage vows in the theater; the service I prepared consisted of a Scripture text, a prayer, the recitation of vows, and the signing of a certificate for the couple. This service was well attended. By 9 p.m. the ship was docking at Prince George Wharf in Nassau. Many people went to a nightclub or a casino. I waited until the next morning to explore the famous straw market.

On Friday at 11 a.m. the ship set sail for Great Stirrup Cay, Berry Islands, Bahamas, where we enjoyed an all-afternoon beach party. I got off the ship and found the old road through the palm trees that I had walked the previous year, retracing my steps and enjoying the beach on the other side of the island where there was no one. After an enjoyable hour or so on the beach, I rejoined the ship's passengers for food and drink, boarded the ship, and waved goodbye to the island at 6 p.m., when we headed back to Miami. Meanwhile, I assisted the Jews in preparing for Sabbath eve services at 7:45 p.m.

On Saturday, the ship docked at 7 a.m. in Miami. All of the luggage that passengers had packed the night before and put outside their cabin doors had been loaded onto huge baggage carts, which took it to the customs' shed. There, officials placed the luggage in rows with aisles in between the rows. Dogs could be seen walking between the rows and sniffing bags to detect drugs. Once this was accomplished and the ship was cleared by U.S. Customs officials, passengers debarked, went to the customs' shed, located their baggage, and carried it to a customs' official. Usually all the customs' official did was ask if one had anything to declare—meaning that the person had exceeded his or her exemptions—and accept the declaration card, allowing the passenger out of the customs' shed. If one had something to declare, then he or she went to a cashier to pay the duty, and was permitted to leave the shed after that.

I had enjoyed this second cruise with Norwegian Caribbean Lines. Now, I had been on two of its four ships: the MS Southward and the MS Starward. I had been to places I had never seen before in the Caribbean, and I was ready for more such experiences.

1981: John Brothers 1

In 1981, I was assigned as chaplain to the MS Southward, the ship I had sailed on in 1979. I was teaching in McAuley Regional Catholic High School, and I had invited Michael King, a student with whom I had been spending a lot of time, to join me on the cruise. I had discovered from Norwegian Caribbean Lines that as long as I shared my cabin with someone, there was only a minimal charge for the other person in addition to the air fare to and from Miami. However, after I had bought airline tickets, King and some of his friends had been caught on school property drinking beer. I, of course, sided with the faculty; this upset King, and he not only refused to talk to me, but also told me that he would not join me on the March 14–21 cruise. After giving him some time to reconsider, which he didn't, I invited John Brothers, a teenager and student with whom I was playing tennis and swimming on a regular basis. In school, we had begun to talk to each other and, then, to play tennis together and swim afterward. In Joplin, I had a friend who had a private tennis court and swimming pool, and she let me use both anytime I wanted. So, we often went there to play tennis and to swim afterward. While I taught Brothers the fine art of tennis, he taught me how to dive into the pool. Brothers and I continued our friendship and sporting activities, and these led me to invite him to join me on an ocean cruise.

Brothers and his parents were excited about the opportunity. They did not see any problem with him missing a week of school, as he could get his assignments from his teachers and do his homework on the cruise. I called the airlines and got the name on the ticket changed after paying a fee for doing so.

Brothers was a good young man. He was a good student, but not totally sure of himself. Because he was not always sure of himself and often needed to talk to me or others about decisions he was contemplating, the ocean cruise was ideal for Brothers.

He had many older brothers and sisters who had done well in life and only one brother younger than he. Because of his older siblings' success, he was usually scared of making a mistake. So, I spent a lot of time preparing him for this cruise, explaining how things worked on a ship, and boosting his confidence.

While he shared my cabin with me and we agreed to always have dinner together, he moved out of his comfortability zone in order to meet other people his own age on the ship and to get involved in shipboard activities. He loved the beach and the sun and spent a lot of time enjoying both. We got along so well that I invited him to join me on an ocean cruise a second time. After he graduated from high school, he went to college, got married, and raised children. I encountered him one more time at a class reunion at McAuley High School. Like many others, I have fond memories of our relationship.

Brothers and I flew to Miami, boarded the ship, and set sail at 6 p.m. on Saturday, March 14. After watching the ship sail away from Miami, we ate dinner and went to the lounge, where I was introduced as the ship's chaplain to the passengers.

Sunday was a day at sea. Sunday morning at 9:30 I celebrated Mass for all Catholics; this was followed by the Protestant service at 10:10. The rest of the day was spent reading while Brothers explored the ship. As he found his way around, he met other people his own age. And he began to spend more time with them and what they were doing, often looking to me to give my approval and encourage him to do so. By Sunday evening Brothers was making connections and moving out of his comfort zone.

On Monday we arrived in Cozumel, Mexico, and spent the day there. I remember us doing some shopping—Brothers had several gifts he needed to get to bring back to people in Joplin—and seeing some of the town. Once onboard the ship we usually went our separate ways, except for dinner when we made it a point to be together and get caught up with each other.

Tuesday was spent at Georgetown, Grand Cayman, where, after a bit of shopping, we spent a long time on the white, sandy beach. Brothers loved the sun; so when he was not stretched out on a deck chair, he was stretched out on a beach chair.

Ocho Rios was the ship's stop for Wednesday. I remember accompanying Brothers on the Dunn's River Falls trip. While he climbed the falls—I had climbed them two years before—I walked the path on dry ground. The afternoon was capped off with time on the Jamaican Beach right off the pier where the ship was docked.

While at sea all day on Thursday, I conducted the renewal of marriage vows for those couples wanting to do so in the cinema. Just like the two years past, I conducted a short service with a Scripture reading and prayer, renewal of vows, and the giving of a certificate provided by the ship. After this, I joined Brothers for the last formal dinner of the cruise and the show in the lounge. In the 1970s and 1980s, there were several formal dinners onboard cruise ships, meaning that men dressed in coat and tie and ladies wore evening gowns. After sitting at one's assigned table, waiters took orders by courses.

The passengers ordered an appetizer from several choices, a salad from several choices, a main entree, and a dessert. There was also a cheese tray that could be requested, and a wine steward could be summoned to place an order for a bottle of wine; if all the wine was not consumed in one evening, it would be re-corked and presented to the passenger the next evening.

It so happened that Thursday, March 19, was Brothers' birthday. I had asked the maitre d' of our dining room to provide a cake for him. Brothers didn't know about this. So, the waiter took his dessert order, but showed up with a birthday cake and several other waiters singing the Happy Birthday song to him.

That dinner was called a Vikingfest. Norwegian Caribbean Lines was owned by Norwegians, who supplied the captains and major ship crews for all NCL ships. This was my first experience of Aquavit, a liquor made from potatoes. During dinner, ships photographers roamed through the dining room, taking pictures of people who were traveling together. Later in the evening, the photographs were displayed for purchase. Brothers and I have a picture of us all dressed up for dinner and one with Brothers receiving his surprise birthday cake.

I usually went to bed after the evening show, while Brothers met his new friends for socializing and dancing until the early hours of the next day when I heard him enter our cabin. He enjoyed his birthday onboard the MS Starward.

The Friday all-day beach party was cancelled due to the weather. So, the ship took us to Nassau, Bahamas, where we took a tour of the island's old fortifications and did some shopping. I remember showing Brothers the famous straw market. I had to be back to the ship in time to help get set up for the Sabbath eve service for the Jews onboard. Then, it was pack suitcases, so they could be placed outside the cabin door in preparation for debarkation the next day.

We were back in Miami by breakfast time on Saturday, March 21. After the ship was cleared by U.S. Customs, we debarked, claimed our luggage, went through customs, got a taxi, and headed to the airport for our flight home. It was a trip both of us remembered for years. In 1982, we sailed together again.

1982: John Brothers 2, Michael King

From January 2 through January 9, 1982, I served as chaplain onboard the MS Starward, the same ship I had been on in 1980. Because John Brothers and I had gotten along so well in 1981, I invited him to join me on this cruise, and he accepted without even thinking about it. We drove to and from Miami, Florida, a round-trip distance of 2,815 miles. I met passengers at 4:30 p.m. with other members of the cruise staff after embarking earlier in the afternoon. Then, Brothers and I participated in the U.S. Coast Guard emergency drill—getting our life jackets from the cabin and going to the lifeboat station to be checked off by a ship's officer. Once that was complete the ship left Miami and headed to Port-Au-Prince, Haiti. Dinner followed with evening entertainment.

The next day, Sunday, January 3, was the Solemnity of the Epiphany of the Lord, and I celebrated Mass for a few hundred Catholics at 9:30 a.m. in the theater. That was followed by the Protestant service at 10:10 which I also conducted. The Starward carried three hundred crew members and had the capacity for 928 passengers. I always took a collection at both services; I used the funds to pay for the expenses of the trip and the fee the ship charged for Brothers to accompany me. What was left was donated to charities when I got home.

After the religious services, I listened to a travel talk and found a quiet place on the ship to read until it was time for lunch. Brothers found other young people his own age and got involved in onboard activities. Since he had been on a cruise once before, he was more confident meeting people and joining in shipboard activities. We had agreed to meet in our cabin around 5 p.m. to get ready for the traditional, formal captain's cocktail party before the formal welcome-aboard dinner. Evening entertainment finished this day at sea.

We docked in Port-Au-Prince on Monday, January 4, at 8 a.m. We stayed there until 4 p.m. Brothers and I got off and walked around, exploring in shops all the handmade items and artistic creations along with the bargaining that was involved in purchasing anything. I do not remember if it was this trip or another during which I bought Haitian paintings and wood cups. It was an experience asking sellers for the price and then beginning to offer less. This took time and patience to get the seller and the buyer to agree on a price. If the buyer couldn't get the price down to what he thought the item was really worth, then all he needed to do was to begin to walk away. The seller would follow and continue the bargaining in the hopes of still making the sale.

The evening was dubbed Country and Western, and that meant dinner was informal. After dinner, entertainment followed. Later, there was an ice-carving demonstration and an outdoor midnight buffet of barbecued ribs and chicken.

At 10 a.m. on Tuesday, January 5, the ship docked in Ocho Rios, Jamaica. Since both of us had been here before, we opted to walk around Ocho Rios and do some shopping. Since the ship didn't leave Jamaica until 11 p.m., the after-dinner entertainment consisted of the Winston Ferguson Calypso Revue, a local Ocho Rios group that came aboard to entertain the passengers every week. The group featured fire dances and calypso music among other things.

Wednesday, January 6, was a day at sea. Passengers were kept occupied with optional exercise classes, all kinds of sports activities, trapshooting, and more. It was Mardi Gras night onboard ship, so some passengers dressed in costumes or crazy hats for dinner. The evening entertainment featured the song styles of the cruise director, Chris Weaver. Bingo and horse racing followed, and the midnight buffet topped off the evening.

On Thursday at 1 p.m. the ship arrived at Nassau, Bahamas. Passengers got off the ship to shop in the famous straw market. The farewell dinner that evening was followed by the renewal of marriage vows service I conducted. There was no evening entertainment, because many passengers went to the nightclubs in Nassau or to the casino.

On Friday, January 8, the ship left Nassau and sailed to Great Stirrup Cay, Berry Islands, Bahamas, arriving at 11:15 a.m. for the all-day beach party. Brothers went snorkeling. I ate lunch ashore and then found the old road behind the palm trees that I walked to the other side of the island. While I did this for exercise, I also did it for the quiet. I remember stopping on the sandy road and picking up sea shells, which I also found when walking the beach later in the day. I helped the Jewish passengers mark the beginning of the Sabbath after dinner at 7:15 p.m. in the theater. The ship left the island at 8 p.m. and headed back to Miami.

Following dinner there was evening entertainment, and following that there was packing to do. Luggage had to be outside cabin doors by midnight so the ship's staff could collect it in preparation for debarking Saturday morning in Miami. By 7 a.m. the Starward was docked in Miami and U.S. Customs officials were onboard clearing the ship. Once we got off and claimed our luggage in the customs' shed, we found my car, and began our drive back to Joplin, Missouri. We stopped Saturday night in a motel, and arrived Sunday evening, January 10. The next day Brothers had classes to take, and I had classes to teach.

I remember having a very good second cruise with Brothers, who, basically, went to things that interested him on this cruise. I spent a lot of time reading and photographing sunsets. I had also begun a practice of keeping an empty wine bottle. After washing it and letting it dry, I would write a note, placing it in the bottle, put in the cork, and go out on one of the ship's decks and toss it overboard. On the note I would put my name and address and the name of the ship and the dates of the cruise. Over the course of the years I sailed, I got two responses to those message-in-a-bottle tosses. A couple found one along the east coast, and a man in Spain found one on a Spanish coast. After dinner our last night at sea, Brothers and I went to a deck and I let him toss the wine bottle with the note into the ocean.

After a few months in 1981, Michael King had gotten over his anger, and he was speaking to me again. One day he asked me if there was any possibility of him getting invited to join me on another cruise; I told him there was in June of 1982. After doing a little research, he discovered that the World's Fair was going to be in Knoxville, Tennessee, in 1982. So, we planned a road trip to both Knoxville and Miami.

We left Joplin on May 30 and headed to Mount Vernon, Kentucky, the closest town to Knoxville where we could find a motel room. I remember driving through Mount Vernon looking for a liquor store; I wanted to buy a six-pack of beer. When I couldn't find one, I stopped at a grocery store and asked why I couldn't find alcohol. The clerk told me that we were in a dry county; I had heard of such things, but this was the first time I had ever experienced it. I did without a beer that evening!

Ocean Cruises 1979–1990

From Mount Vernon, Kentucky, we drove to Knoxville, found the World's Fair grounds, parked the car, and explored the exhibits all day. When both of us were finally worn out from walking, we left the fairgrounds, found the car, and drove to Chattanooga, Tennessee, where we found a motel room and spent the night. Our next destination was the John F. Kennedy Space Center, just outside Titusville, Florida. Once we got there, we toured the visitor's center, listened to presentations about NASA's plans, and boarded a bus that took us around launch pads and other sites associated with rockets and flights into space.

From Titusville we drove to Miami, where, after spending a few days on the beach, we boarded the MS Skyward on June 6, 1982. I was assigned to be the ship's chaplain for a one-week cruise from Sunday to Sunday. This was my first time onboard the Skyward, another ship in the Norwegian Caribbean Lines fleet. And this was my fifth cruise with Norwegian Caribbean Lines.

After boarding the ship and participating in the U.S. Coast Guard drill of finding our life jackets in our cabins and putting them on and then finding our life boat, we were dismissed. At 5 p.m. the ship left Miami and headed to Playa Del Carmen, Mexico. After dinner King and I explored the ship until it was time for me to be presented as ship's chaplain at 10:15 p.m.

Monday, June 7, was a day at sea. The ship offered exercise classes, dancing classes, dive-in presentations on snorkeling, trapshooting, and more in addition to sun bathing on a deck chair. Monday evening featured the formal dress captain's cocktail party, a multi-course dinner, and a cabaret show.

The next morning we arrived at the Yucatan Peninsula of Mexico. King had decided to participate in the snorkeling program onboard ship; he would be taken snorkeling in all the ports of call. I, possessing a religious studies degree, opted for the Chichen-Itza tour, which left the ship at 6:45 a.m. Once the few of us taking this tour got to the air conditioned motor coaches, we were on our way for the four- to five-hour trip to Chichen-Itza. On the bus we were given information about the Maya ruins. Upon arrival an English-speaking guide directed us to the sacrificial well, the temple of Kukulcan, the observatory, the ball court, and more. We had time to climb the steps to the top of the temple and eat the box lunch the ship had provided for the trip.

All of the tourists were hot and tired by the time we got back into the motor coaches for the return trip to the ship. We arrived just in time to shower and go to the featured Mexican dinner and then the show starring dancers of the ancient Maya from Mexico City. Around 7:30 p.m. the ship left Playa Del Carmen and headed the forty nautical miles to Cancun, Mexico.

Basically, Cancun was a U.S. beach city transported to Mexico, complete with U.S. hotels and restaurants. There was a free tour of Cancun, and lots of time to spend on the beach of a hotel that catered to ship's passengers. Continuous tender service shuttled passengers to and from Cancun all day. I explored Cancun, while King went snorkeling.

At 4 p.m. the ship left Cancun and headed to Cozumel, Mexico, an island off the Yucatan Peninsula. After arriving at 7 p.m., the ship hosted a Sol Caribe Beach Party on the Sol Caribe Hotel Beach, a short walk from the pier. Food and drinks were served while passengers listened to music and danced in the sand. Around 10:30 p.m. there was a fireworks presentation.

On Thursday, June 10, the ship remained at Cozumel. Passengers could shop or participate in snorkeling or enjoy the beach. At 3 p.m. the Skyward set sail for Great Stirrup Cay, Berry Islands, Bahamas. Friday was an all-day at sea with plenty of activities onboard to keep passengers occupied. At 5:30 p.m. I performed my first duty as ship's chaplain by helping the Jews get ready for their Sabbath eve service.

By 9 a.m. on Saturday, June 12, the ship dropped anchor off the coast of Great Stirrup Cay. King went snorkeling, and I went hiking on the old road through the island by the light house and to the private beach on the other side. At 5 p.m. the ship weighed anchor to sail back to Miami. I had Mass for the Catholics at 5:30 p.m. in the cinema; that was followed by the Protestant service at 7:15 p.m. in the cinema. After the evening show, King and I packed our bags and put them outside our cabin door. He returned his snorkeling equipment.

When we woke up on Sunday morning, we had already docked in Miami. The usual procedure followed: U.S. Customs officials came on board to clear the ship, passengers disembarked to the customs' shed, turned in their embarking forms, paid any duty owed, and, in our case, went to my car and began the trip home, returning to Joplin on June 15.

Because King was self-motivated and secure in his own decision-making, he did what he wanted on the trip. When we both wanted to do the same thing, we did it together. He did a lot of snorkeling, but I was not interested in that. I did a lot of shopping and sightseeing, but he was not interested in those activities. We made it a point always to go to dinner together and to get caught up with each other.

This was the only time I would ever go to a World's Fair; my only regret was not spending more than a day seeing some of its exhibits. The high point of the trip was seeing the ruins at Chichen-Itza. A few years before, I had seen the ruins at Tulum. I had read about Chichen-Itza, but never dreamed that I would actually get there. The day was long and hot, but well worth the time and energy it took to explore the area.

1983: Arthur Hobbs 1, Sean Farley

In November 1982, I got my cruise assignment for the SS Norway for July 23–29, 1983. The SS (Steam Ship) Norway was purchased by Norwegian Caribbean Lines when she was the SS France. As the SS France, the ship had sailed for thirteen years, making transatlantic crossings and international cruises. However, with the greater use of airplanes for transatlantic crossings, the SS France was docked and awaited her fate. After NCL purchased her, she underwent renovation and refurbishment and joined the NCL fleet in Miami in 1980.

The SS Norway was the largest cruise ship in operation from and to the port of Miami in 1980. She was twice as big as any other cruise ship, more than three football fields long, thus, needing two of the usual piers to dock her. She just had enough room to turn around in the Miami harbor, and she could not dock at most of her ports of call. She carried her own tenders, which were lowered into the sea and took passengers to and from her to the shore. She stood seventeen stories tall. Because she carried more than three times as many passengers as the other ships in the NCL fleet, chaplains had to have gained experience on the smaller ships before they could be assigned to the SS Norway. Because she carried close to twenty-seven hundred passengers and crew, the SS Norway was considered a small floating city.

The Norway's crew numbered closed to eight hundred, and she was able to host 1,854 passengers. To feed so many people thousands of pounds of meat, fruits, and vegetables were loaded every time she came into the Port of Miami. Ten passenger decks provided sixty-five thousand square feet of open deck space. The ship contained an eighth of a mile jogging track, three swimming pools, and two tenders which could each carry four hundred passengers from the ship to the shore and back.

Arthur Hobbs, a friend from Joplin, Missouri, with whom I had played a lot of tennis, joined me for the drive to Miami and my first cruise on the Norway. Meeting us on the ship were other friends from Joplin: Karl and Sheri Kinler. After boarding at 1 p.m., Hobbs and I found the Kinlers and began to explore the huge ship until the mandatory U.S. Coast Guard emergency drill at 3:45 p.m., when we had to go to our cabin, find our life jackets, put them on, and proceed to our life boat stations, where our names were checked off of a clipboard by a ship's officer. Once this was done, the ship set sail for St. Thomas in the U.S. Virgin Islands at 4:30 p.m. I remember standing on one of the upper decks and watching this ship—the size of three football fields—leave its piers and head out to sea.

As chaplain, I was introduced to the passengers at the 8:30 p.m. and 10:30 p.m. cruise staff introductions. On the smaller NCL ships there was only one round of introductions, but, because of her size, there were two on the Norway. The cruise director told passengers always to consult the daily activity sheet, an 8 ½" X 14" white page, single-spaced, and printed on both sides. There were activities for children, young adults, parents, grandparents, etc. There was a bar on almost every deck; there were two huge dining rooms and many other places where food was served. Passengers could participate in shuffleboard, ping-pong, horseshoes, basketball, etc. There were fitness classes, arts and crafts demonstrations, fashion shows, lectures, a library, and a shopping mall.

On Sunday, I celebrated Mass at 9:15 a.m. for hundreds of Catholics in one of the bars. Mass was followed by the Protestant Service at 10 a.m. for hundreds of Protestants. By this time I had a standard line I used at all services: Only on a ship can you attend a religious service and sit at a bar at the same time! Catholics appreciated this more than Protestants, however. After the religious services, I joined Hobbs for a travel briefing, lunch, deck time, reading, and the formal captain's welcome aboard cocktail and dinner party before the shows and other activities of the evening.

Monday was a day at sea. I celebrated Mass at 9:15 a.m. for about thirty Catholics. The tradition on the SS Norway was that Mass was offered every day we were at sea, but not on days in ports. After Mass there was a tour of the bridge, followed by a shopping talk on St. Thomas, lunch, a movie, happy hour, evening entertainment, and more. If a passenger could forego sleep, he or she could be kept occupied around the clock and, of course, always find food available somewhere with no difficulty on this ship! The midnight buffet was a spectacle itself, usually featuring an ice carving eight to ten feet tall.

On Tuesday, July 26, the SS Norway dropped anchor in the harbor of Charlotte Amalie, St. Thomas, U.S. Virgin Islands, at 8 a.m. and proceeded to unload its tenders, fill them with passengers, and begin shuttling people from ship to shore. Since neither Hobbs nor I had ever been to St. Thomas before, we took the city tour. We saw Bluebeard's Castle, Drake's Seat, Megen's Bay, and the Mountain Top Hotel before being deposited in the shopping district. It was a full morning and afternoon. The last tender left Charlotte Amalie at 3 p.m., and the ship weighed anchor at 4 p.m. As soon as the ship was moving, all the onboard activities began again.

Wednesday, July 27, was another all day at sea. I celebrated Mass at 9:15 a.m. After that I further explored the ship, found a quiet corner to read, went to lunch, and with Hobbs attended the afternoon matinee live Broadway musical performance of "My Fair Lady." After that, we attended the ship's galley tour. At 5:45 p.m. I celebrated the renewal of marriage vows service for those couples desiring to renew their marriage vows. Dinner was followed by a concert by The Lettermen.

Thursday, July 28, was a half day at sea, and that meant Mass at 9:15 a.m. There was a debarkation briefing to attend, lunch, and finally, arriving at Nassau, Bahamas, at 12:30 p.m. Again, after dropping its anchors a short distance from Prince George Wharf, the SS Norway crew dropped the tenders off her hull and brought them to the gangplanks for passengers to board and be shuttled to and from Nassau.

Hobbs and I took the Ardastra Gardens tour. We drove past the British Colonial Hotel to Fort Charlotte, built in 1787 to protect the harbor from pirates. After touring its underground dungeons, we went to the Ardastra Gardens, where we viewed Caribbean Flamingos, Muscovy Ducks, Indian Peafowl, and more. We also saw the Aviary, filled with birds from around the world, and lots of other animals. The gardens, while containing lots of plants, leaned more to being a zoo. After some shopping and a visit to the straw market, we caught a tender and made it back to the ship before she sailed at 7 p.m. This was the evening for the farewell dinner, which meant formal attire. Dinner was followed by entertainment.

By 9 a.m. Friday, July 29, the Norway had dropped anchor at Great Stirrup Cay, Berry Islands, Bahamas. While there were plenty of activities onboard, there was a huge beach party on the island. Hobbs and I got to the island in time for lunch and a hike over the old road that took us by the abandoned light house and to the beach on the opposite side of the island. We returned to the beach party, got on a tender, and headed back to the ship. I had to help set up for the Sabbath eve services for the Jewish passengers at 5 p.m., and the ship headed back to Miami at 6 p.m. After a casual dinner, there were all kinds of evening entertainment before packing luggage and leaving it outside our cabin door for debarkation the next day.

The next morning the ship arrived in the Port of Miami. We stood on the deck and watched her turn around in the harbor. She had turbines underneath that enabled the captain to sit her in the middle of the harbor and turn one hundred eighty degrees before they pushed her to the two piers where she was tied. The usual procedure of U.S. Customs clearance followed by debarkation, claiming luggage, passing through customs, and finding our vehicle for the trip back to Joplin.

This was my sixth cruise with NCL, and it was delightful onboard the SS Norway. The multiple religious services satisfied my title as chaplain. I met Catholics from all around the world who often invited me to join them in a lounge before dinner for a drink. I wanted to come back and serve on the Norway again.

And that desire was confirmed by an assignment to serve as chaplain for the eight-day Christmas cruise, leaving Miami on December 23 and returning on Saturday, December 31. For this cruise, I invited a high school student and friend, Sean Farley, to share my cabin. Farley and I had become friends through classroom banter and several camping trips. Most teachers didn't know what to do with him, but I did. He was a very intelligent young man, and all he needed was someone who could challenge his ideas. I was able to do that. Furthermore, Farley was self-motivated and self-secure; I knew he would have no trouble making friends on the ship. His parents, who owned a local Joplin motel, had invited me to dinner several times, too. So, before I invited Farley, I spoke with his parents, who had no trouble with their only child being gone for Christmas.

Farley and I drove to Miami. Then, on December 23 we boarded the SS Norway. We got settled in our cabin, participated in the U.S. Coast Guard drill, ate dinner, and—for me—attended the two introductions as Catholic chaplain to the passengers. For the Christmas cruise, the SS Norway also carried a Protestant minister, who conducted a Protestant Christmas service. Farley had found a number of people his own age, and he was off to where they were gathering. During the extent of this cruise, I saw Farley usually only for dinner. He had the time of his life staying up late and enjoying the ship. I had planned on simply experiencing Christmas in a way different from all the years I had experienced it in Missouri.

Saturday, Christmas Eve, was an all-day-at-sea event, beginning with my celebration of the Eucharist at 9:15 a.m. The daily schedule was much the same as it had been in July. What was added to expand the usual seven-day cruise to eight days was another day at sea. Passengers had options for all kinds of sports, exercise classes, dance classes, travel briefings, arts and crafts demonstrations, snorkeling lessons, a live stage production, lectures, and more. There was an eggnog pour complete with Christmas caroling accompanied by the many bands onboard the ship. Florence Henderson was the evening's featured entertainment. After all this, I went to my cabin and went to bed. Farley crept in during the night and fell into bed.

After Mass on Saturday morning, a few people had approached me about celebrating the Sacrament of Penance with them during the day. I set up a time and place I knew would be private and told them to meet me there. The first couple of people showed up. Then, after them more and more; word had been passed around that I was hearing confessions before Christmas, and a number of people took advantage of this opportunity. I remember sitting in a quiet bar for about an hour celebrating the Sacrament of Penance.

Sunday was Christmas Day, and I celebrated Mass at 9:15 a.m. Onboard there were a lot of activities marking Christmas, like Santa's arrival, photograph time with Santa, a magic show, and more. I spent a lot of time in the sun on a deck reading, then I returned to my cabin to prepare for the captain's gala Christmas party before dinner, a formal attire requirement. Farley showed up in time to share with me how he had spent Christmas day, shower, and get ready for dinner.

When we got to the dining room, we discovered that we had a special Christmas menu from which to choose a six- to seven-course dinner. Most of the entries were associated with Christmas in some way. For example, from the appetizers one could choose hot spiced Christmas wine. The entrees caught my attention: golden crisp roasted Christmas goose, roasted tender Vermont turkey, baked sugar-cured ham with raisin sauce, and more. For dessert, we chose from among hot plum pudding, hot mince meat pie, Granny Smith green apple pie, and praline nougat Christmas torte. Christmas dinner was, indeed, a feast. And there was still evening entertainment before Christmas day was over.

On December 26, we arrived in Charlotte Amalie, St. Thomas, U.S. Virgin Islands. Farley participated in the dive-in program offered by the ship. Participants were taken to various areas at our ports of call where they snorkeled for several hours. While Farley did that, I took the tender to the shopping area and walked the streets looking for bargains. During dinner that evening I listened to an excited Farley narrate all he had seen snorkeling. The ship weighed anchor at midnight and set sail for Nassau.

Since Tuesday, December 27, was a day at sea, I celebrated Mass at 9:15 a.m. for a small group of Catholics. The usual onboard activities took place all day. At 5:30 p.m. I conducted the interdenominational renewal of marriage vows service for a large group of couples, giving each a signed certificate. An informal dinner followed during which I again got caught up with Farley on how he had spent his day onboard the ship—primarily playing sports on the decks.

The fifth day of this eight-day cruise, Wednesday, December 28, was another day at sea. I celebrated Mass at 9:15 a.m. for a small group of daily Mass-going Catholics, attended the debarkation briefing, got some exercise by walking the track, and wondering around the ship through all the Christmas decorations and watching people participate in various activities, such as Olympic games—in which Farley participated—dance, and a children's masquerade. Sometimes I just found a quiet place to read or to work on something else I had brought with me. After the informal dinner and evening show, I went back to my cabin and went to bed.

By 8 a.m. on Thursday, December 29, the ship was docked at Nassau, Bahamas. I remember spending a quiet day onboard the ship while everyone else got off to see the sights. I had been to Nassau many times before, and there wasn't anything else that I wanted to see or do. I even remember making suggestions to fellow passengers about what there was to see in Nassau, especially the famous straw market. Dinner required formal attire with evening entertainment. At 7 p.m. the SS Norway weighed anchor and set sail for Great Stirrup Cay, Berry Islands, Bahamas, where she arrived at 9 a.m. on Friday, December 30, for the usual all-day beach party. Farley was involved in the snorkeling program and other beach activities, and I, after eating lunch on the beach, took the old road to the other side. At 5 p.m. I helped the Jews set up for their Sabbath eve service, and at 6 p.m. the ship weighed anchor and prepared to bring us back to Miami on Saturday, December 31, New Year's Eve. At dinner I instructed Farley that he needed to pack his luggage and have it outside our cabin door before midnight—no matter what else he did. There was a roaring 1920s show in the evening to top off the last day of the eight-day Christmas cruise.

By the time we got up and went to the dining room for breakfast on New Year's Eve morning, the SS Norway was docked in Miami. It usually took a couple of hours for the ship to be inspected and cleared by U.S. Customs, which meant that the public areas on the ship were crowded with people ready to debark. Farley and I were among them. Once all was cleared, we went to the customs' shed, claimed our luggage, passed through customs, found my car, and began our trip back to Missouri. That New Year's Eve we spent in a motel halfway between Miami, Florida, and Joplin, Missouri.

What I most remember about this seventh cruise was the ease of traveling with Farley. He was a very low maintenance teenager. He made friends with many people his own age and had a good time with them. We had agreed to meet for dinner every night so we could get caught up on what each of us had done during the day. Sometimes we might pass each other coming to or going from our cabin. Most of the time I was in bed asleep, when Farley got to the cabin in the early hours of the morning, and he was in bed asleep, when I left for breakfast the next morning. Both of us were very independent, enjoyed the cruise in our own way, and did the things we wanted to do. Reflecting on this gave me more desire to invite others to join me on future cruises.

Also, this was my first Christmas at sea. In the past I had always spent Christmas in Missouri. Spending time in the sun on a deck and reading before enjoying a seven-course Christmas dinner was a new experience for me, and I liked it. I wanted to spend more Christmas Days at sea, and I would get my opportunity to spend both Christmas Day and New Year's Day in 1984.

1984: Arthur Hobbs 2

For 1984 I had back-to-back chaplain assignments for the MS Sunward II, a sister ship of the MS Southward, the MS Starward, the MS Skyward, and the SS Norway. The first was the Christmas cruise, December 24–28, and the second was the New Year's cruise, December 28-January 4, 1985. The Sunward II carried 857 passengers and three hundred crew members. It was much smaller than the SS Norway, upon which I had cruised two times previously, but I was excited about spending both Christmas and New Year's Eve at sea.

I invited my friend and tennis companion in Joplin, Hobbs, to join me on this cruise. He had been with me in 1983 on the SS Norway and was looking forward to sailing again. We drove his car to Miami and parked it on the pier. With this eighth Norwegian Caribbean Lines cruise, I was becoming a pro at embarkation. After settling into our cabin, Hobbs and I went to the cruise director meeting with passengers, during which I was introduced as the ship's Catholic chaplain; there was also a Protestant minister who was introduced as the ship's Protestant chaplain. The mandatory U.S. Coast Guard emergency boat drill followed, and at 4:30 p.m. the MS Sunward II set sail from Miami for Nassau, Bahamas.

After dinner, there were various onboard activities. I, however, had to get ready for Midnight Mass, since this was Christmas Eve. I remember not having all the supplies I needed for Mass; I had no Lectionary with the Scripture texts. I did have a worship aid that I had brought with me, and several other papers with some Roman Catholic prayers on them. I found a Gideon Bible, marked the Midnight Mass texts which I knew from memory, and decided that I could be creative. I got some Christmas carols—words only printed on sheets of paper—from the cruise staff. Before Mass began in the lounge, I asked for volunteer ministers—readers, eucharistic ministers, etc.—and we were ready to begin. I had to be finished in about 45 minutes, because many people attending Midnight Mass also wanted to attend the first Midnight Buffet onboard the ship.

On Christmas Day the ship arrived in Nassau, Bahamas, at 8 a.m. Santa made an appearance, and passengers went on tours—just like it was any other day for a cruise ship. While some shops in Nassau were closed in observance of Christmas Day, many more of them were open for business. Hobbs and I got off the ship and walked around Nassau, shopping and seeing some of the sights. Christmas dinner was preceded by the captain's cocktail party, then there were more tours to casinos and nightclubs in Nassau, where the ship stayed docked for the night.

At 6:30 a.m. on Wednesday, December 26, the Sunward II left Nassau and headed to Great Stirrup Cay, Berry Islands, Bahamas, where it arrived at 11:30 a.m. for the traditional breach party. I remember Hobbs and I eating lunch on the beach and walking the old road to the other side of the island. At 5:30 p.m. the ship sailed for Freeport, Grand Bahamas.

On Thursday, December 27, we arrived in Freeport, Grand Bahamas. I had never been to Freeport before, so this was an opportunity to see another area of the Caribbean. We took the glass bottom boat tour to the coral reef, where we could see the reef and colorful fish through the bottom of the boat. We were dropped off at the International Bazaar, the main shopping area of Freeport, where we wondered from shop to shop before returning to the Sunward II, which left Freeport at 6 p.m. and headed back to Miami.

While all other passengers were preparing for debarkation in Miami the next morning by packing luggage, Hobbs and I didn't have to do this. We had already been cleared to remain on the ship for the next cruise for which I was serving as chaplain. We were permitted to get off the ship in Miami through the crew exit, as long as we carried our boarding passes with us. Once all the passengers had debarked and the customs' shed had been cleared, we took a few hours to hike around the pier just to stretch our legs before setting sail again the afternoon of Friday, December 28.

My ninth cruise with Norwegian Caribbean Lines on the MS Sunward II was headed to Cozumel, Mexico. It was operating on a special holiday schedule and not following its usual route in the Caribbean. After all passengers had embarked and participated in the U.S. Coast Guard drill—going to one's cabin, finding the life jacket, putting it on properly, and reporting to the life boat station—dinner and welcome aboard introductions took place.

Saturday, December 29, was all day at sea. Passengers could participate in aerobic dance, purchase tour tickets for the various ports of call, attend the travel tour—consisting of information about shopping and customs—see a movie, play games, trap shoot, visit the casino, etc. The captain's formal cocktail reception preceded the evening's formal dinner, followed by the evening show called "Caribe Celebration."

Because the ship was docked at Cozumel, Mexico, on Sunday, I did not celebrate Mass until 7:30 p.m. Of course, very few people attended because they were just finishing their dinner or preparing to go to dinner. Over the course of the days I had been onboard, I learned that this ship did not usually have a chaplain; that explained why there were no church supplies. Again, I had to make do for Mass, but with the help of a Gideon Bible and the worship aid I had with me, I accomplished it.

The ship had weighed anchor at 4 p.m. and was on its way to Georgetown, Grand Cayman. Again, because this was not the ship's usual itinerary, the cruise staff often didn't know when to schedule various activities. Hence, the reason Mass on Sunday was not until 7:30 p.m. Competing with Mass was the evening entertainment.

Monday, December 31, New Year's Eve featured a tour of the MS Sunward II's wheelhouse before anchoring at 11 a.m. at Georgetown, Grand Cayman. Hobbs and I took the tender to the pier and walked around town after lunch onboard the ship. Many passengers did the same, while others had booked tours to see the island's sights or attend a beach party. Since I had been to Georgetown on previous cruises, I decided merely to walk around town

At 6 p.m. the ship left Georgetown and sailed to Montego Bay, Jamaica. Since this was New Year's Eve, dinner featured a special menu. There were both cold and hot appetizer selections, soups, entrees of leg of lamb, fillet of sole, roast goose, beef, salads, desserts, and cheeses. There was an evening show after each dinner sitting, another show at 11 p.m., and complimentary champagne served from 11:30 p.m. to 12:30 a.m. Passengers had been given funny hats to wear and horns to blow at midnight. Hobbs and I enjoyed a glass of champagne and went to bed. We had experienced New Year's Eve at sea

By 8 a.m. January 1, 1985, the MS Sunward II was docked at Montego Bay, Jamaica. At the same time, I celebrated Mass for the Catholics onboard, since this was a Holy Day of Obligation. Hobbs and I had agreed to take the three and a half hour tour of the Greenwood Great House, a home built in 1790 for entertaining the friends of the Barret Brownings of Wimple Street fame. After being transported by vans and busses the eleven miles from the pier to the house, passengers got to see most of the furnished house along with its outdoor gardens and swimming pool. The mansion's rooms contained original musical instruments, furniture, paintings, and a library in museum condition. The tour concluded with a complimentary drink and transportation back to the City of Montego Bay shopping district. Hobbs and I walked around the shopping district and boarded the tender that returned us to the ship, which sailed out of Montego Bay at 6 p.m. to Great Stirrup Cay, Berry Islands, Bahamas. New Year's Day evening featured an open casino, horse racing, jackpot bingo, a roaring 1920s show, and country and western evening.

We were at sea all day on January 2. The debarkation talk was followed by the Bahamarama Downs Horseracing and the usual onboard activities while at sea. There was musical bingo before dinner and a show after dinner.

We were back to Great Stirrup Cay by 11 a.m. on Thursday, January 3. While tenders took passengers to the island—named "Fantasy Island" by the ship's cruise staff—I remained onboard and read on one of the unoccupied decks. I remember Hobbs going ashore for a while. After dinner, we packed our luggage and put it outside our cabin door. There was not much to do on the ship that evening except to get ready to leave the next morning. On Friday, January 4, the ship was back in Miami by 8 a.m. Once U.S. Customs cleared it, we debarked, found Hobbs' car, and began the trip back to Joplin, Missouri.

We had spent eleven days on a ship and celebrated Christmas and New Year's Eve at sea. Because the MS Sunward II did not usually carry a chaplain, my duties were only to celebrate Midnight Mass on Christmas, Sunday Mass, and Mass on January 1. I had to be creative in terms of Mass supplies, because there were none on this ship, which usually did only three- and four-night cruises to Nassau, Great Stirrup Cay, and Freeport. These two back-to-back cruises made me evaluate eleven days at sea; my conclusion was that it was too long!

1985: Rob Smith

For 1985, I was assigned by Norwegian Caribbean Lines as chaplain on the SS Norway, June 29-July 6. I had invited Rob Smith to join me and share my cabin. In 1983, Smith had accompanied me on a mountain climbing trip to Colorado. Before that trip, I had to learn all about diabetes from Smith's mother because he was a diabetic. While teaching in McAuley Regional Catholic High School, Smith and I had gotten to know each other well. During the summer, we took bicycling trips together as often as possible to stay in shape and see sights in the greater Joplin area.

After flying to Miami, we boarded the SS Norway on Saturday, June 29, and joined in the fifth birthday celebration that the ship was marking. To celebrate the occasion, hundreds of balloons were released as the ship prepared to leave Miami. The cruise news for that day referred to the ship as the "queen of the cruise ships." After embarkation—getting our cabin assignment, picking a dinner table and a sitting time, and several other things—we went to our cabin, unpacked, and began to explore the ship. I gave Smith the quick tour and told him that he would have to explore the rest on his own. We went to one of the decks and watched others get on board until it was time to participate in the usual U.S. Coast Guard emergency drill—find our life jackets, put them on, and find our life boat station.

Some things had changed since the last time I had been on the Norway. Previously, almost every activity in the evening was doubled—it occurred once for the first sitting passengers and again for the second sitting passengers. This time there was only one round of cruise staff introductions during which I was presented to the passengers as the chaplain for the cruise. There were the evening shows and other evening entertainment and activities. I think Smith explored some of the teenagers' activities, but I went to bed because I had religious services the next morning.

On Sunday, June 30, I celebrated Mass for the Catholics at 9:15 a.m., followed by a Protestant service at 10 a.m. in a bar. It was nice to be back on a ship that had all the supplies I needed, unlike the last two cruises onboard the MS Sunward II where I had hardly anything. After the religious services, there was the usual travel briefing and the many activities offered on the Norway. Smith participated in some of the onboard sports opportunities, while I found a quiet place to read on deck. The evening featured the formal captain's cocktail party followed by the formal dinner and an evening show.

Monday was an all-day at sea, so I began the day with Mass at 9:15 a.m. for a small group of Catholics. The rest of the day was filled with sports program opportunities, arts and crafts classes, exercise classes, various demonstrations—pastry-making, ice-carving, etc., snorkeling instructions, and lectures. I attended the live stage production of the Broadway musical "Barnum." Dinner and a cabaret show followed.

Early on Tuesday morning the SS Norway dropped its anchors into the bay upon which Charlotte Amalie, St. Thomas, U.S. Virgin Islands, was located, dropped its two tenders into the water, and began taking people from ship to shore. I think Smith was involved in snorkeling; I waited until the crowds thinned out and wondered around the town for a while, coming back to the ship for lunch and spending the afternoon reading on one of the decks. There were few people around when the ship was in port, so it was easy to find an unoccupied deck chair and a quite place to read. At 3 p.m. the ship weighed anchors and sailed for Nassau, Bahamas. The usual dinner and evening entertainment followed.

As I had done on previous cruises, Smith and I agreed to meet for dinner every evening no matter what we had done during the day. While gathering in our cabin and dressing for dinner, we usually shared the events of our day and continued that through dinner. Because there were several other people assigned to the same table as we were, we also shared some of our day with them, and they with us.

Wednesday, July 3, found the Norway at sea. At 9:15 a.m. I celebrated Mass for a small group of Catholics. To keep the passengers entertained multiple activities were provided on the ship. The highlight of the afternoon was the SS Norway Olympic games, complete with military band opening and all types of team sports. Smith was involved with basketball, since he played the sport in high school. From an upper deck, I watched some of the games until it got too humid and went back in the air conditioned ship and read for a few hours. After dinner that evening, I conducted the interdenominational renewal of marriage vows for a number of couples.

Thursday, July 4, was Independence Day for U.S. passengers. I celebrated Mass at 8:30 a.m. for a small group of Catholics. The rest of the morning was filled with the usual onboard activities, including a debarkation briefing. At 12:30 p.m. the ship arrived at Nassau. Since I had been to Nassau many times, I waited until all the tour groups got off the ship and then got off and walked around for a while. The ship left Nassau at 7 p.m. While this was taking place, another balloon release was conducted to honor Independence Day. This was followed by a champagne pour for anyone who wanted to attend.

Dinner that evening featured a special July 4 menu printed in red, white, and blue. Passengers could choose from four appetizers, three soups, four main courses—poached salmon, baked ham, barbecued chicken, or sirloin steak—two salads, and more. Dessert featured cherries jubilee flambé on parade. It was a feast fit for Independence Day. Nightclub entertainment followed.

The next day, July 5, the SS Norway arrived at Great Stirrup Cay, Berry Islands, Bahamas, at 9 a.m. Smith was participating in the dive-in program, so he went snorkeling. Once the crowds thinned out, I took a tender to the island for lunch and hiked the old road to the other side of the island and enjoyed the private beach there. After about an hour I hiked back to the party area and caught a tender back to the ship. At 6 p.m. the ship weighed anchor and sailed to Miami. Smith and I caught up with each other for dinner; I attended the evening's 1920s show, while Smith joined his new friends for their last evening together.

This was the time that luggage needed to be packed and put outside our cabin door to facilitate debarkation the next morning in Miami. By 7 a.m. on Saturday, July 6, the SS Norway was docked at the new Port of Miami. After breakfast we gathered the few items we still had in our cabin and went to sit in one of the public areas awaiting clearance by U.S. Customs. Once that happened, we debarked, claimed our luggage, went through U.S. Customs, found a taxi, and went to the airport to catch our flight back home.

On this trip I took no tours, since I had taken all of them at various times in previous years. Furthermore, because I knew my way around the ports of call, I planned my own day's worth of activities rather than have a tour do it. I was spending a lot more time in quiet than I had in the past. As I reflect on these experiences almost thirty years later, I see how my spirituality was developing. Cruising took me away from the daily things and offered me new opportunities for reflection and growth. I loved sailing. I loved the sea. I experienced how small I was; no matter what the size of the ship, in the middle of the ocean—with water all around as far as I could see—the ship was very small. And these experiences were influencing my relationship with God. Indeed, how small I am from God's perspective!

I discovered that I was talking a lot more to passengers and telling them about the tours and what they would see. For some reason, passengers on the SS Norway were always more friendly to me as chaplain than on the smaller ships. I would get invited to join groups for a drink before dinner and discuss the day's activities or anything else that passengers wanted to talk about. I think the reason for the friendliness was that there were more Catholics onboard simply because the Norway carried more passengers. Because of my years of experience as a cruise chaplain, passengers trusted my opinion and sought it.

Smith and I enjoyed each other's company on this cruise. He was a low maintenance type of person who enjoyed playing sports, and there were plenty on the ship. Most of the time he did what he wanted, and I did what I wanted; we caught up with each other over dinner or walking the shopping districts of our ports of call. When all was said and done, this tenth cruise with Norwegian Caribbean Lines was declared to have been lots of fun by both of us.

1986: Alone 3

My assignment from Norwegian Caribbean Lines for 1986 was the Merry Christmas Cruise onboard the SS Norway. I chose to take this cruise alone. I had left McAuley

Regional High School, Joplin, in August 1985, and returned to Springfield after a seven-year absence. I was working in the field of adult education and living alone in a rented house. I caught a taxi to the Springfield airport on Friday, December 19, and flew to Miami. I spent the night in a motel not too far from the Port of Miami. I had learned that it was best to get to Miami a day ahead of sailing in order to avoid any snow or ice storms in Missouri—or any other connections that I might need to make—that might delay my plane from getting me to Miami on time.

After a leisurely morning in my hotel room, I got a taxi to the Port of Miami to await embarkation procedures for the SS Norway. This was my eleventh cruise with NCL, and I intended to celebrate. I had enjoyed my previous experiences at sea for Christmas, so I was looking forward to this one. Once the embarkation offices opened, I checked in, got my ticket and dining room assignment, and boarded with my luggage. I could never check my luggage, like other passengers did, because I never knew my cabin assignment until I got to the ship. After being asked if I needed help with my luggage several times, I made my way to my cabin and unpacked. This was another reason I liked carrying my own luggage onboard; I got to unpack it immediately and get settled. Other passengers had to wait until late in the afternoon before their luggage was delivered to their cabins. And, of course, sometimes luggage never appeared!

Since the year and a half that I had been on the Norway, the itinerary had changed; the island of St. Maartin had been added. That meant that I had a new island to explore. Furthermore, different tours had been developed for St. Thomas and Nassau. After looking over the possibilities, I knew this cruise would be filled with new opportunities.

More information about the SS Norway was provided. She had been sailing in the Caribbean for over six years. Her keel was laid in St. Nazaire, France, in 1957; she was launched May 11, 1960, as the SS France, and sailed until 1974, when she was moored in LeHavre. In 1977, Akram Ojjen of Saudia Arabia purchased her for twenty-four million dollars with the intent of creating a floating motel out of her, but that plan never came to fruition. NCL bought the SS France in 1979 for $18 million and sent her to Bremerhaven, West Germany, for renovation at a cost of $150 million. After this she was named the SS Norway, and made her maiden voyage out of Miami on June 1, 1980. In 1986, the SS Norway was still the largest passenger ship in operation, carrying 850 crew and cruise staff members and up to 2,400 passengers. Because the crew came from over thirty different countries, the Norway was the only commercial ship in the world allowed by the United Nations to fly the blue and white UN flag.

While there was only one captain, there were forty-nine deck officers, sixty engine officers, and seventeen pursers. Two doctors and three nurses cared for anyone found sick in any way. The dining room staff numbered 140 with 135 chefs and cooks. Add seventy-five bar staff, twenty-five gift shop staff, and 176 hotel staff along with almost one hundred cruise staff, instructors, technicians, musicians, and entertainers, and it's not hard to understand why the SS Norway was a small floating city. It was like a Las Vegas casino-hotel floating on the ocean.

The first activity before leaving Miami was the U.S. Coast Guard emergency drill. That was followed by dinner and cruise staff introductions. I joined the cruise staff two times to be introduced as the Catholic chaplain for the Merry Christmas Cruise. There was also a Protestant chaplain onboard for the cruise, and he would take care of the Protestant services, the renewal of marriage vows, and help the Jewish passengers prepare for their Sabbath service on Friday evening. This meant that I had fewer responsibilities.

Another thing that had changed was the incorporation of the religious services into the daily Cruise News. On all previous Norway cruises the religious services information was only listed on the back of the Cruise News at the bottom of the page. Now, it was incorporated into the daily list of activities; this made the information easier to find, and so more people came to the services.

On Sunday, December 21, I celebrated Mass at 9:15 a.m. in the Club Internationale for a few hundred Catholics. This bar had been the traditional place on the ship for religious services in all my past sailings on the Norway, and it remained so. I asked for volunteer ministers of all kinds and got them. Then, I proceeded to explain how we celebrated Mass in a bar. The SS Norway provided worship aids, so not only could we sing, but it was almost like Mass in a parish church. As soon as I finished, the Protestant minister conducted a service in the same place at 10 a.m.

The day at sea was filled with activities as only the SS Norway could provide them. In addition there was a travel briefing, lunch, an opportunity to see the live stage production of the Broadway musical "Barnum," and more. After lunch I grabbed a novel, found a deck chair, and read for most of the afternoon. The evening featured the captain's cocktail party followed by a formal dinner and the Suzanne Somers concert. On previous cruises I had gotten into the habit of walking the decks outside after the evening entertainment. There were never too many people outdoors in the evening, so it was always quiet. I enjoyed listening to the wash of water against the sides of the ship as she cut her way through the ocean. In some places, there was a hallow sound that could be heard as the smokestacks belched the remains of the oil the ship burned to create steam which powered her propellers. That is what the "SS" meant: Steam Ship.

Monday, December 22, was another day at sea. I celebrated Mass for a small group of Catholics at 9:15 a.m. Then, I listened to a shopping talk, ate lunch, and participated in a wine-tasting session for which I received a certificate of participation. I had been involved in numerous wine-tasting sessions at home, developing an appreciation for different types of wines from different regions of the world. This session furthered my appreciation. We tasted wines from six different countries. After dinner there was a cabaret show and all the many opportunities for dancing and listening to music that the Norway offered.

Early in the morning of Tuesday, December 23, the Norway dropped anchors in the Great Bay in front of Philipsburg, St. Maarten, Netherlands Antilles. I had chosen to take the Island Tour—Under Two Flags—after breakfast. The ship's tenders dropped off passengers on the pier, where we boarded buses that took us around the two-nation island. We traveled from Dutch Philipsburg to French Marigot, where we were given time to explore that port city with its open food market and fine French restaurants. Then, we traveled through the French St. Maarten and back to the Dutch side and a stop at Simpson Bay and a complimentary drink. The last stop was in the shopping area of Philipsburg. I wandered through the many shops and caught a tender back to the ship. While eating dinner on this country-fair evening, the ship weighed anchors at 7 p.m. and sailed for St. Thomas in the U.S. Virgin Islands.

On Christmas Eve the Norway dropped anchors at 6:15 a.m. at St. John, U.S. Virgin Islands. Only those passengers taking the St. John Island Tour were permitted to get off the ship. I took this tour because I had never been to St. John Island. I was driven around the island with stops to see Cruz Bay, Maho Bay, Whistling Cay, the British Virgin Islands, Coral Bay—the first settlement on St. John—and Caneel Bay overlooking the Rockefeller Plantation.

We also stopped at Annaberg Ruins, the last working sugar plantation on St. John. The sugar plantation began in the early 1700s and lasted until the early 1900s. In 1956, the ruins were put under the direction of the National Park Service to preserve them. They enable visitors to learn about sugar plantations, mills, slave labor, and more of two centuries ago when the island of St. John, like so many other islands, buzzed with activity, producing sugar, rum, and molasses.

After touring the Annaberg Ruins, we were taken to Cruz Bay, where we were dropped off and caught a ferry to St. Thomas, where the Norway had dropped anchors. After spending some time exploring the shopping area of St. Thomas—I had been here many times before—I caught a tender to the ship for lunch and spent part of the afternoon on a quiet deck with a good novel.

Dinner that evening was formal and was followed by a Christmas Eve Eggnog Pour, several evening shows, and some Christmas Eve Reflections at 11:25 from members of the cruise staff. At midnight an Interdenominational Christmas Eve service was held; it consisted of the singing of several Christmas carols before most people headed to the midnight buffet. I remember attending the midnight buffet and getting to bed early in the morning.

On Christmas Morning I celebrated Mass at 8:45 a.m. December 25 was all day at sea. Santa Claus made an appearance, there was a debarkation briefing, a tour of the bridge, all kinds of sports activities, the traditional Norway Olympic Games, bingo, and more. I chose to spend the afternoon outside on a deck chair with a good book, soaking up a little sun. Later in the afternoon I returned to my cabin to shower and dress formally for the captain's Christmas Day dinner.

There were cold and hot appetizers, three choices of soups, salads, and four entrees—roast Maryland Turkey, whole Dover sole, baked orange glazed Christmas ham, and broiled filet mignon—vegetables, desserts—hot plum pudding with rum, mince pie, yule log, fruit cake, ice cream and sherbet, and, of course, cheeses. What a feast! What a way to celebrate Christmas! It was hard to stay awake that evening during the cabaret entertainment.

On Friday, December 26, the Norway arrived at 11:30 a.m. at Great Stirrup Cay, Berry Islands, Bahamas, for the traditional beach party. NCL knew how to throw a beach party with constant shuttles from the ship to shore and from shore to ship. On the island, a picnic lunch was served—of course, if one stayed on the ship, lunch was served in several places—and games were played—volleyball, shuffleboard, horse shoes, etc. People could snorkel, walk the beach, rent various water equipment, and more. This went on all afternoon for those who wanted to participate. I remember staying onboard the ship and reading. The sky was overcast, and it looked like rain. A few showers did fall, but not enough to dampen most people's fun on the island.

At 6 p.m. the ship weighed anchors and sailed for Miami. After dinner there were all types of shows from which to choose along with the usual evening music and dancing. This was the evening to pack luggage and put it outside the cabin door in preparation for debarkation the next morning.

The ship arrived in Miami early in the morning on Saturday, December 27. In the past there had never been a Cruise News for the day the ship arrived in Miami. However, there was one for this cruise. It gave information about settling onboard credit, photo gallery hours, an immigration notice, a customs notice, and a farewell party—a new activity to draw passengers away from the public areas and keep them occupied while U.S. Customs cleared the ship. Once the ship was cleared, I found my luggage in the customs' shed, handed over my completed customs' form, got a taxi, and headed to the airport to catch my afternoon flight home to Springfield.

I loved this cruise. I loved sailing alone. I loved the new places I saw. I shared a table with a whole Jewish family. The family members made me welcome. They even celebrated Christmas! When I asked the parents why, they told me that they had just marked Hanukkah, but they are were on a ship celebrating Christmas and saw no reason not to exchange small gifts with each other. Sailing alone did not attach me to anyone, and this enabled me to accept invitations for a drink or a deck chair or a conversation.

1987: Arthur Hobbs 3

For the Happy Christmas Cruise of December 19–26, 1987, I invited my friend from Joplin, Missouri, Hobbs, to join me onboard the SS Norway. We flew to Miami from Springfield on Friday, December 18, got a motel room near the Port of Miami, and enjoyed the evening, knowing that we were boarding the largest passenger ship in operation the next day.

After walking around Miami for a while on Saturday, December 19, we took a taxi to the pier and prepared for embarkation after the offices opened. We got our room cabin assignment, dining room assignment, table assignment, and boarding pass and proceeded with our luggage to our cabin to settle in for the week. After a simple lunch on the International Deck, we opened our credit accounts on the ship and watched other passengers as they boarded. We participated in the mandatory U.S. Coast Guard emergency boat drill by finding our life jackets in our cabin, proceeding to our life boat stations, and being checked in by a ship's officer. After replacing our life jackets in our cabin, we got a cocktail and listened to piano music until it was time for dinner.

At 10:15 p.m. I was introduced as the ship's Catholic chaplain, and a Protestant minister, with whom I had sailed before, was introduced as the Protestant chaplain. I would be responsible for the Masses, and he would take the Protestant services, the renewal of marriage vows, and help the Jewish passengers on Friday evening.

On Sunday, December 20, at 9:15 a.m. I celebrated the Fourth Sunday of Advent Mass with several hundred Catholic passengers in a bar. After asking for volunteer ministers from their home parishes to serve as ushers, readers, eucharistic ministers, etc., we got started. The SS Norway always had up-to-date worship aids, and Mass was celebrated just like we were in a church. Since this was an all day at sea on our way to St. Maartin, there were all kinds of typical SS Norway activities onboard the ship. I enjoyed quiet places, reading, and working on a project I had brought with me. Hobbs, who had been with me on three previous cruises, did what he wanted, too. We joined each other for the formal welcoming dinner that evening with the captain's cocktail party preceding it. The evening entertainment was "42nd Street."

Monday, December 21, was another day at sea with Mass at 9:15 a.m. for a small group of Catholic passengers. Activities abounded. Early evening dinner was Italian, and the Kingston Trio entertained us after dinner, and there was still late-night entertainment of singing and comedy for those who wanted to attend. At midnight the traditional buffet was served for those who had not been able to get enough food throughout the day!

The ship arrived in St. Maarten on Tuesday, December 22, at 8:30 a.m. Hobbs went on a tour; I waited until the tender line thinned and went ashore to do a little shopping. I remember returning to the ship in time for lunch and spending the rest of the day on a deck chair in a quiet spot reading. We bade farewell to St. Maarten at 7 p.m. as the ship weighed anchors and sailed for St. John in the U.S. Virgin Islands. Dinner was informal, and the evening featured a roaring 1920s revue and country and western game booths, music, and dancing.

The ship arrived at St. John on Wednesday morning, December 23, dropped off passengers participating in tours, and continued on to St. Thomas, where it dropped anchors a short time later. Only twelve nautical miles separate St. John and St. Thomas. Hobbs participated in a tour, while I got off the ship to walk. At 6 p.m. the Norway weighed anchors and sailed for Great Stirrup Cay. An international casual dinner was served that evening, followed by a musical jazz tribute and a Broadway tribute.

Thursday, Christmas Eve, was a day at sea. I celebrated Mass for a small group of Catholics at 9:15 a.m. The debarkation briefing followed and then the usual SS Norway offering of activities, including horse racing, a Christmas pool party, the Olympic games, jackpot bingo, and more. After Christmas Eve formal dinner, there was a Christmas Eggnog Pour. The evening's entertainment consisted of Hollywood songs and dances. At 11:25 p.m. Christmas get-togethers were held in three different places on the ship, featuring caroling. I celebrated Midnight Mass and then attended the midnight buffet.

On Christmas Day I celebrated Mass at 9 a.m. for passengers who did not attend the Midnight Mass. The ship arrived at Great Stirrup Cay, Berry Islands, Bahamas, at 12:30 p.m. and passengers enjoyed the Christmas beach party until 6:30 p.m., when the ship headed back to Miami. Because it was Christmas Day, dinner was formal; this was not usually the case on the night before arriving in Miami.

Christmas Dinner, which was also the captain's farewell dinner, began with an option of appetizers: six cold and one hot. Passengers chose from three soups and three salads. The lean entree was steak tartar; the other entrees were roast Vermont Tom turkey, Scandinavian style Christmas ham, broiled rib eye steak, or sautéed fresh salmon. For dessert, one could choose from yule log, hot plum pudding with rum sauce, gingerbread soufflé, or mince pie. Also, there were ice creams and sherbets, cheeses, and fruits. Vocal music topped off the evening.

After getting back to our cabin, Hobbs and I took off our formal clothes, packed our luggage, and placed our bags outside our cabin door. There were activities throughout the night, including the Christmas buffet, 11:30 p.m. to 12:30 a.m.

By the time we went to breakfast on Saturday, December 26, the ship was docked in Miami. Announcements were made about immigration and customs. In order to organize the chaos of debarkation, passengers were asked to leave the ship only when their flight departure times were announced. This gave those who needed to catch an early flight an opportunity to claim their luggage, meet an airline representative for check-in, and get to the airport on time. Since Hobbs and I were not leaving until the next day, we waited until most passengers had debarked before claiming our luggage, getting a taxi, and going to a motel for the night. While this procedure added another day to our travels, it cut out a lot of hassle and worry about getting to the airport on time to catch a plane. The next morning we leisurely made our way to the airport, caught our flight, and returned to Springfield by way of Kansas City, Missouri.

I considered this twelfth cruise with NCL a relaxation cruise. I functioned as chaplain for the Catholics, but I also enjoyed simply being on the ship, working on projects, and reading. I had been to all the ports of call, so I was not interested in taking tours I had already been on. My goal was to come home refreshed, and that is the way I arrived in Springfield on December 27.

1988: Alone 4

Norwegian Caribbean Lines assigned me as chaplain to the MS Seaward, a new ship in the NCL fleet that had gone into operation in May 1988, for the 1988 Christmas

Cruise. Six hundred thirty-two crew members served her with the capacity for 1,534 passengers. I was excited to spend my thirteenth cruise onboard the MS Seaward.

I flew from Springfield to Miami on Friday, December 23, and, after spending the night in a hotel, embarked on the Seaward at noon on Christmas Eve, December 24. After getting settled in my cabin and meeting with some of the cruise staff, I participated in the U.S. Coast Guard emergency drill at 4:30 p.m. Thirty minutes later, the MS Seaward left Miami and headed for Great Stirrup Cay, Berry Islands, Bahamas. The bon voyage dinner was highlighted with eggnog and Christmas caroling in honor of Christmas Eve.

Like the daily Cruise News onboard the SS Norway, the Cruise News onboard the MS Seaward was printed on both sides of the 8 ½" X 14" sheet of paper. Among other activities onboard the Seaward was the Palm Tree restaurant, a very formal dining area requiring reservations and not included in the cost of the cruise. A full casino was onboard and open after dinner. During the welcome aboard festivities, I was presented to the passengers as the chaplain for the cruise. I celebrated a Midnight Christmas Mass for many Catholics in one of the lounges and joined many of them afterward for the traditional midnight buffet.

Sunday was Christmas Day. I celebrated Mass at 8:30 a.m. for Catholics who did not attend the Midnight Mass earlier in the morning. At 9:30 a.m. I held the Protestant Christmas Day service. While I was conducting religious services, the Seaward arrived at Great Stirrup Cay, Berry Islands, Bahamas, for the usual all-day beach party. Santa made an appearance on the island, lunch was served on the island and on the ship for those who didn't want to get off the ship, games were played, and there was a lot more to do on Christmas Day on an uninhabited island in the Caribbean. I remember thinking to myself that this was, indeed, a different way to spend Christmas Day. I walked the beach, collecting small sea shells; I walked the old road to the other side of the island and collected more small sea shells there. The ship left the island at 4 p.m. and headed to Ocho Rios, Jamaica.

The evening was strictly formal. The captain's cocktail party further emphasized that it was Christmas Day. The ship was decorated with trees and garland and wreaths everywhere. My traditional idea of Christmas—as being celebrated in cold weather—clashed with all the sun and warmth of the day. The dinner menu offered six cold and hot appetizers, three soups, a lean entree of sliced turkey breast, and four other entree choices: roast Vermont Tom turkey, lobster, roast prime sirloin of beef, and Scandinavian style Christmas ham. There were four desserts from which to choose, along with ice creams and sherbets, cheeses, and fruits. It was a feast!

Following dinner I went to the evening entertainment, sipping a Port wine while waiting for the show to begin. There were lots of other things going on after the cabaret finished, including late night comedy, but I was tired and went to bed. It had been a full day and a very Merry Christmas in the sun and on the beach.

Monday, December 26, was all day at sea. Activities abounded for passengers. There were exercise classes, sports of all kinds, a travel talk, casino games, an optional bridge inspection—in which I participated—ice carving, casino instruction class, wine tasting, a shopping talk, trapshooting, jackpot bingo, a fashion show—and those are only some of the highlights. I took my book, found a quiet place with a deck chair, and spent most of the afternoon reading.

Dinner was semi-formal. A roaring 1920s revue was presented by the members of the cruise staff and a few crew members as after-dinner entertainment. All kinds of opportunities for dancing brought passengers to the last activity of the day: the Italian style midnight buffet.

By 8 a.m. on Tuesday, December 27, the Seaward was docked in Ocho Rios. Once it was cleared by Jamaican officials, passengers went ashore, stopping in the Customs Building to change their U.S. dollars for Jamaican dollars. In times past, either form of currency was acceptable in Jamaica, but a new law had been passed that required all transactions to be conducted in the country's form of currency.

The first passengers off the ship were those on tours. The two or three tours that had been offered on other ships gave way to eight tours on the Seaward, including golf. NCL was offering passengers tours of Dunn's River Falls, plantations, yachts, rafts, gardens, and golf. In other words, there was something for everyone. I chose to get off the ship and walk through the shopping district for a while before returning to the ship for lunch and spending the afternoon on a quiet deck with a good book.

Those who stayed on the ship could learn how to fold napkins, how to mix exotic drinks, how to ballroom dance, or any other number of things. At 5 p.m. the ship left Ocho Rios for Grand Cayman, and at 5:15 p.m. I conducted the interdenominational renewal of marriage vows service, and went to dinner after that. The evening entertainment featured a singer. Late evening entertainment featured a 1950s and 1960s sock hop. By the time that got started, I was in bed.

By 8 a.m. on Wednesday, December 28, the ship was docked at Georgetown, Grand Cayman. Here, six tours were offered, including a trip around the island, rafting, beach partying, glass-bottom boat marine wildlife viewing, submarining, and golfing. Because I had been to Grand Cayman many times before, I chose to walk around the island, return to the ship for lunch, and spend the afternoon with a book on a quiet deck. At 4 p.m. the Seaward sailed for Cozumel, Mexico.

Wednesday's dinner was formal. Wednesday evening's entertainment featured "A Chorus Line." I had first seen this show in Kansas City, Missouri, with some high school students on a trip from Joplin to Kansas City. However, I enjoyed seeing it again on the ship.

Thursday at noon the ship anchored off the coast of Cozumel, Mexico. Before that, tours had departed for various places, including the one I was on to Chichen-Itza, when the ship anchored briefly in Playa Del Carmen, Mexico. I had been to Chichen-Itza once before in the early 1980s, and I had wanted to return and spend more time at the Maya ruins. This tour was limited to one hundred passengers, who were put on air-conditioned buses and driven to the ruins. Along the way, a guide explained Mayan culture and prepared us for the ruins. We got to spend three hours there along with eating the box lunch provided by the ship. At the predetermined time, we re-boarded the buses and were taken back to Playa Del Carmen, where we got on a ferry that took us to the MS Seaward.

This was a twelve-hour, all-day tour. By the time we got back to the ship, I had just enough time to shower and head to dinner. There were lots of other tours, such as those to Tulum and Xelha, Cancun, Cozumel, beaches, and golf. The evening entertainment came from Mexico City; the show was called Viva Mexico and featured all types of music and dancing. Late evening was Country and Western time with dancing and a barbecued midnight buffet. At midnight the ship sailed for Miami, Florida.

Friday, December 30, was all day at sea. Onboard activities abounded along with the debarkation briefing, sports, horse racing, casino, and more. The highlight of the afternoon was the Seaward Olympic Games. At 5:15 p.m. I helped the Jewish passengers get ready for their Sabbath eve service. Dinner was casual with entertainment that followed. Luggage had to be packed and placed outside cabin doors before 2 a.m. so that it could be gathered for debarkation the next morning. Lots of other activities went on until 2 a.m. However, I went to bed in order to prepare to head back home the next day.

There was a Cruise News for Saturday, December 31. The cruise staff tried to get passengers to stay away from gangways until the ship was cleared around 10 a.m. by providing a variety of activities. I conducted a Protestant service at 8 a.m. for a very small group of passengers. There was entertainment in several lounges and prize giveaways. The Seaward docked at 7 a.m., but the ship had to be cleared by U.S. Customs agents and all non-U.S. Citizens had to present themselves to immigration officials. Once we could debark, I claimed my luggage, got a taxi, and headed to the airport to catch my afternoon flight on TWA for St. Louis and from there to Springfield.

This, my thirteenth cruise with NCL, was the first cruise where the last event was not the all-day beach party on Great Stirrup Cay. I remember this as being a very relaxing cruise. I enjoyed my time alone, and I looked forward to sailing on this ship again in the future. Cruise opportunities had taken the form of a retreat for me. While I had responsibilities for religious services, I also had lots of time to pray, read, and relax.

1989: Chuck Granholm

I left Joplin in 1985 and moved to Springfield, where I had become the editor of *The Mirror* in 1987. I met (Charles) Chuck Granholm when he was in sixth grade in St. Peter Middle School in Joplin. The principle of the school asked me and the girls' volleyball coach to teach the sixth graders' sex education class. I took the boys, and the coach took the girls during our free periods at McAuley High School. Since the middle school was only a block down the street from the high school, the students came to our classrooms in the high school. After several sessions separately, we combined boys and girls for several sessions. Because of our openness about sexual biology, we got a lot of attention from sixth graders who were more than interested in the topic.

After he finished eighth grade, Granholm came to McAuley. While a teacher at McAuley Regional High School, I got to know Granholm well. We got together often to talk, to play tennis, and to swim. In high school he was an athlete, primarily playing basketball. By the time of the cruise, Granholm was in college at St. Meinrad College, St. Meinrad, Indiana. I had taken him there to see the place when he was a senior in high school and was looking for a college to attend. At that time, I thought he might have a vocation to priesthood. Not only did he like the academic challenge the Benedictine monks gave him, but the spiritual formation that went along with it. He developed an interest in counseling primarily because he was a very reflective person. He could sit quietly or poolside for hours contemplating whatever issue or idea had presented itself. In other words, he thought about his relationships. His first marriage didn't last very long, and the second one ended after his daughter was born and he had custody of her.

He settled in the Louisville, Kentucky, area, and we stayed in contact all through his college career and his counseling work. After he graduated from McAuley, he gave me a large card with the back page filled with a handwritten letter. He thanked me "for being a friend." He wrote, "You've helped me grow a lot over the past year, and I think I'm a little bit better person. You are a pretty smart guy, and when I have a problem I feel I can tell you and you'll understand." After thanking me for choosing to be a priest, who gives "pretty good sermons," he wrote: "I know at times you probably wonder what the hell you're doing teaching a bunch of high schoolers who think religion is crap. I don't know if many like your class, but they will someday realize how much it means to them."

Another activity that Granholm and I enjoyed was spending a few days together in a cabin a friend of mine owned in Forsyth, Missouri. The times we got there, we were able to talk, pray, and sleep a lot. He wrote: "I enjoy going to the cabin, talking things out, and beating you at tennis. Some of the conversations we get in are pretty wild. I don't know what I'll be someday, but thanks for helping me be it."

For one of my birthdays Granholm gave me a pamphlet card titled "What is a Friend?" On its twenty pages are pictures, poems, and reflections on friendship by various authors. What is important to me is what he wrote on the last page of the card: "Happy Birthday! You really are what this card says. Thanks for being there and helping me grow. Thanks for the little kick sometimes. I need it ever so often. Love, Chuck." It is important to remember that Granholm's birthday and mine are only one day apart. Granholm visited me one time in Springfield with his first wife about twenty-five years ago, but I have not heard from or seen him since. My memories of this human encounter remain.

On this fourteenth cruise with Norwegian Caribbean Lines, I was assigned as chaplain onboard the SS Norway for the Happy Christmas Cruise, December 23–30, 1989. This was my sixth cruise on the largest cruise ship in operation in those days. After getting to Miami on December 22, Granholm and I spent the night in a hotel. The next morning we caught a taxi to the pier, and we went through the embarkation process, getting our cabin assignment, choosing a dining room and table (we picked a table for two so that we could eat together and then leave without being rude to others at our table), unpacking our luggage, and touring the ship. At 4 p.m. the U.S. Coast Guard emergency drill was held. Dinner followed at 6 p.m. with a travel briefing after that. In typical Norway style, there were all types of activities during the evening. At 10:15 p.m. I was introduced as the ship's Catholic chaplain, and a Protestant minister, with whom I had sailed on the Norway before, was introduced as the ship's Protestant chaplain. Because the Jews were marking Hanukkah, there was a rabbi onboard, too, to lead the Jewish services. Granholm found people his own age and joined them for the evening.

Sunday, December 24, was all day at sea, the Fourth Sunday of Advent, and Christmas Eve. I celebrated Mass for the Catholics at 9 a.m. In the evening I celebrated a Mass for the crew of the ship. In between, there were opportunities for exercise, dance, gambling, bingo, seeing the bridge, attending "42nd Street," playing sports, swimming, and more. The welcome-aboard formal cocktail party and dinner was also Christmas Eve dinner. Following dinner, there was a variety of entertainment from which to choose. Then, at midnight I celebrated Mass in the theater for hundreds of Catholics, after which most went to the midnight buffet.

Christmas Day, Monday, December 25, began with Mass at 9:15 a.m. for those who did not attend earlier. Santa Claus came to the ship before that, and this being another day at sea meant that there were multiple opportunities for passengers. In addition, there were shopping talks on the ports of call. After lunch, I went to a deck, found a chair, enjoyed the sun for a while, and read. Granholm busied himself with sports and some quiet time in the sun on the deck, too.

Christmas Dinner featured the usual SS Norway menu of food choices. However, this year's menu looked a lot like the past several years' Christmas menus onboard the Norway and the Seaward. There were cold and hot appetizers, soups, a lean entrée—Kansas steak tartar—hot entrées—roast Vermont Tom turkey, Scandinavian style Christmas ham, broiled rib eye, and swordfish—desserts, ice creams, sherbets, fruits, and cheeses. While the menu was familiar, the food was the quality that I had come to expect from NCL. Granholm and I enjoyed our table for two, because we could talk about things that we did not want others to hear, as we shared how we had spent our day. All kinds of evening entertainment were provided including Dixieland music, a fashion show, a roaring 1920s revue, a sock hop, and other nightclub options.

On Tuesday, December 26, the SS Norway arrived at 8 a.m. in St. Maarten. Passengers had the option of choosing from seven different tours of the island, including golf. Granholm opted for the beach, and I chose to wander around the shopping district since I had been to St. Maarten before. Granholm and I caught up with each other in our cabin before dinner and shared our day while eating dinner. The ship left St. Maarten at 7 p.m. and sailed for St. Thomas. Lots of gambling opportunities were presented for the evening, such as the SS Norway lottery, bingo bonanza, and more. The evening show featured Broadway tunes, and that was followed by various nightclub options.

On Wednesday morning, December 27, the ship arrived at St. John, U.S. Virgin Islands, and stopped long enough to drop off any passengers on one of the three tours being offered. It then proceeded to sail to St. Thomas, U.S. Virgin Islands. Passengers had a choice of six tours in St. Thomas, including a day of golf. Granholm and I chose the Coral World tour, consisting of an underwater observatory of marine life. After the tour, we walked around Charlotte Amalie, and returned to the ship for lunch and an afternoon of sun and quiet onboard the SS Norway. The ship sailed for Great Stirrup Cay at 5:30 p.m., just as Granholm and I were preparing for the evening's Italian dinner. Following dinner, there were more opportunities to gamble, and since it was Country and Western evening, there were game booths, dancing, and other activities associated with the theme, including a chuck wagon midnight buffet.

We were at sea all day on Thursday, December 28, so I celebrated Mass for a small group of Catholics at 9 a.m. The multiple activities for a typical day at sea included exercise classes, sports, horse racing, and the afternoon Norway Olympics. Granholm spend most of his day playing sports and participating in the Olympics. Dinner featured the captain's formal farewell dinner, and a Hollywood show followed that. Passengers could listen to music or dance in several bars until 2 a.m.

Friday, December 29, began with Mass at 9 a.m. for Catholics. Following that was the usual debarkation briefing about leaving the ship on Saturday morning. At noon, the ship arrived at Great Stirrup Cay, Berry Islands, Bahamas. Granholm and I got off the ship and ate lunch on the island. While he was involved in sports, like volleyball and shuffleboard, I walked the old road to the other side of the island and picked up sea shells. At 6 p.m. the ship set sail for Miami. Dinner was casual, followed by evening entertainment and luggage packing before going to bed.

The SS Norway arrived in Miami on Saturday, December 30, early in the morning. After the usual immigration procedures and U.S. Customs clearance, passengers began debarking around 10 a.m. Granholm and I made our way to the customs' shed, found our luggage, handed in our arrival card, caught a taxi, and headed to the airport for our flight home.

I didn't know it at the time, but this would be my last cruise on the SS Norway. While I enjoyed being on this large ship for Christmas, I had been to all its ports of call many times. I would joke with passengers that I could give tours of the Caribbean islands, and I could. On this trip, I took no photographs; the only picture I have is the one I bought on the ship of Granholm and me eating dinner together. I enjoyed spending time with Granholm; he did what he wanted, and I did what I wanted.

Sometimes we did things together. We had agreed always to meet for dinner in order to get caught up with each other. I enjoyed spending Christmas at sea, since I had no other place that I had to be. I didn't know it then, but NCL would be undergoing a lot of change, and I would serve as chaplain only one more time before closing this chapter of my life.

1990: Arthur Hobbs 4

My fifteenth and last cruise with Norwegian Caribbean Lines was on the MS Seaward, the same ship I had been on in 1979. In 1989 NCL was undergoing many changes. The cruise programs/entertainment department contact with whom I had worked for almost a decade, Jeanne Camac, was replaced by Jeff Brown, manager of shipboard programs. Furthermore, NCL had been purchased by Kloster Cruise Limited, which also owned Royal Viking Line. Even the corporate offices had been moved.

Brown had contacted me in December 1989 about serving as chaplain onboard the Seaward in 1990. To secure my position, I had to complete a registration form and sign a letter of agreement (contract), supplying a photo and a curriculum vitae. Never in any of the fourteen previous cruises had I to complete such things. In the letter I sent Brown to accompany the above documents, I asked him to assign me to the MS Skyward for the Christmas 1991 cruise; this, of course, never materialized.

At the time all the paperwork had to be signed and returned, I had not yet decided to ask Arthur Hobbs to accompany me on the Seaward 1990 Christmas cruise. In March 1990 I notified Brown that Hobbs would be joining me. And so Hobbs and I flew to Miami from Springfield, arriving on Saturday, December 22, and spent the night in a motel in preparation to board the ship on Sunday, December 23. At noon embarkation began. After getting our cabin and table assignments, we found our cabin, unpacked, and went to an upper deck to each lunch. We participated in the U.S. Coast Guard emergency drill at 4:30 p.m. and watched the ship leave the pier and sail for Great Stirrup Cay at 5:30 p.m. Dinner followed at 6:30 p.m. After dinner the casino opened, there was a presentation on the tours at the ports of call, and at 10:15 p.m. I was presented to the passengers as the ship's Catholic chaplain; there was a Protestant chaplain onboard for the Christmas cruise, too, and he was presented as the Protestant chaplain. Earlier in the day I had found a letter from the senior hostess listing the services I would be conducting on the ship and instructing me to be present for the introduction at 10:15 p.m.

Monday, December 24, the ship arrived at Great Stirrup Cay at 9 a.m. for the all-day beach party. Over the years, NCL had bought the island and improved it with a picnic area complete with tables, shuffleboard courts, a volleyball court, bar huts, and even a home for several men who lived there and took care of the island, cleaning up after passengers left and repairing sports equipment, etc. The ship tendered passengers from ship to shore and back to ship all day. Because I had been to this island so many times before, I elected to stay on the ship and read and work on writing projects which I had brought with me. At 4 p.m. the ship weighed anchor and sailed for Ocho Rios, Jamaica.

Since this was Christmas Eve and the traditional captain's cocktail party, it was also a formal dinner evening. Eggnog was served during dinner, and formal portraits were taken by the ship's photographers. The formal dinner was followed by the Christmas Eve show, which featured Christmas carols both religious and secular. I celebrated Midnight Mass for a lounge full of Catholics and then went to the International Christmas Strolling buffet before returning to my cabin and going to bed.

Christmas Day was on Tuesday. Santa Claus arrived at 8 a.m., and I celebrated Mass at 9 a.m. for Catholics who had not made it to the Midnight Mass. Since this was a day at sea, all kinds of sports were available on the ship, along with a travel and shopping talk, a tour of the bridge, and many other activities. Hobbs, who had been with me on three previous cruises, chose what he wanted to do, and I did the same. As had become customary, we agreed to meet each other in our cabin and go to a lounge for a drink before dinner and eat dinner together.

The Christmas dinner menu on the MS Seaward was exactly the same as the Christmas dinner menu on the SS Norway in 1989; all that had been changed was the date! Under its new owner, Kloster Cruise Limited, NCL had found a way to streamline the menus on its ships in order to make more money by buying more food in bulk for its entire fleet. While Christmas dinner was excellent, the sameness spoiled the specialness of the day. The grand days of the Christmas cruise with each ship featuring a different menu were past. The Christmas evening show featured Broadway songs, and the Christmas Caribbean buffet was served outside on a deck under the stars.

On Wednesday, December 26, the ship arrived at 8 a.m. in Ocho Rios, Jamaica. Since I had been here many times before, I didn't get off the ship. I remember enjoying the quiet day on a deck reading and working on writing projects. At 5 p.m. the Seaward sailed for Georgetown, Grand Cayman. Dinner was informal, and a roaring 1920s revue followed. Much like the Christmas menu mentioned above, the roaring 1920s revue had become a standard feature on NCL ships. I had seen it so many times that I could almost join in the singing and dancing. Just like for the Christmas menus, the entertainment was becoming standardized on all the NCL fleet. For those enjoying late night entertainment, there was the sock hop.

At 8 a.m. on Thursday, December 27, the ship anchored at Georgetown, Grand Cayman. The usual tours were offered for those wanting to see the sights of the island or play golf. I remember getting off the ship to walk around the shopping district, but I came back to the ship for lunch. I spent most of the day on a deck reading and writing. The ship left Georgetown at 4 p.m. and sailed for Cozumel, Mexico. I led a small group of couples in renewing their marriage vows at 5 p.m. While on our way to Mexico and after dinner, Hobbs and I attended the Broadway musical "Anything Goes," which became a highlight of this cruise because it was the only thing that was different.

On Friday, December 28, the ship anchored briefly off the coast of Playa Del Carmen, Mexico, for those on the mainland tours to depart. Then, at noon it anchored in Cozumel, Mexico. The pier was a short taxi ride from San Miguel, the shopping area. However, I had chosen to take the Cozumel Island Tour. Lying eleven miles off Mexico's coast, Cozumel is only twenty-nine miles long and eight miles wide. San Miguel boasts a population of thirty-thousand inhabitants. What I wanted to see were the ancient Maya ruins at San Gervasio. Hidden in the heart of the islands tropical jungle, the ruins suddenly appear. I had seen the Maya ruins in Tulum on the coast and Chichen-Itza in the interior, and I wanted to see those on Cozumel. The bus tour also included a visit to a beach and the shopping district of San Miguel.

After the tour I came back to the ship to prepare for dinner. The ship stayed in Cozumel until midnight, when it set sail for Miami. This was Country and Western evening with music and dancing poolside. There was even a beer drinking contest and a hog-calling contest.

Saturday, December 29, was a day at sea. The usual many onboard activities were offered, including the debarkation briefing for the next day. The casino was open, sports activities abounded, and the Seaward Olympics were held. Gamblers could play jackpot bingo or engage in daily double horse racing. At 5 p.m. I celebrated Sunday Mass for the Catholics onboard. After the causal dinner, there was a cabaret-style show. Then Hobbs and I packed luggage in preparation for the next day's debarkation.

The ship arrived in Miami at 7:30 a.m. on Sunday, December 30. I remember it taking a long time for immigration and customs clearance because it was Sunday, and officials were not all that fast to get to the ship and do their various jobs. Finally around 10 a.m. passengers were able to debark, claim luggage, and head home. Hobbs and I had a late afternoon flight to catch at the airport. So, after getting a taxi, we headed to the airport, where we ate lunch and caught our plane back to Springfield, Missouri.

At the time, I didn't know this was my last cruise with NCL. As Kloster continued to make changes with NCL ships, the use of chaplains decreased and was gradually eliminated. I remember calling the office one time and being told that chaplains would pay half of the usual fare; I decided that I was not going to pay to go work!

I also remember getting assigned to work a NCL ship that docked in Puerto Rico by one manager of shipboard programs only to have that cancelled by the successor manager of shipboard programs. The cruising industry that I had participated in for almost a decade was undergoing radical change, and chaplains were no longer needed. Furthermore, the formal aspect of cruising was giving way to informality. And the cultural interest in all things sports was taking over shipboard activities. Gone were the days of elegant dining; coming were the days of shorts, T-shirts, and flip-flop dinners.

To this day I have never been on another ocean cruise ship. After fifteen cruises, many of them Christmas cruises, I decided that I had enjoyed spending Christmas on the ocean, but I was ready to find new ways to celebrate that feast. My spirituality had been enriched by spending time on the beach and on the ocean. I had written a number of books while at sea; now I sought new venues to inspire me and my craft.

While it took me a long time to find out what happened to the SS Norway, I discovered that in May 2003 a boiler explosion caused a fire that heavily damaged the ship. The ship that had been commissioned the SS France in 1962 and recommissioned the SS Norway in 1979 was towed from one place to another over three years until she ended up in India after being sold as scrap. From 2006 to 2008 she was taken apart piece by piece until she ceased to exist at the age of 44.

11

Other Travels

1969: Denny Schaab

OTHER THAN TRAVELING AROUND the Old Mines area and the high school trip to Springfield, Illinois, I never left the state until January 1969, when I went to Chicago with a group of seminarians from Cardinal Glennon College. Denny Schaab, Tom Doering, Bill Erker, Mike Pillick, and I headed to the Maryknoll Seminary in Glen Ellyn, Illinois, to visit with Pat Meehan, a high school classmate of the other four men.

Once I got to Cardinal Glennon College in 1968, Denny Schaab became one of my genuine human encounters. Schaab, who was in my class in the Autumn of 1968, had graduated from St. Louis Preparatory Seminary South. We seemed to connect with each other. Schaab came to my home during the winter break in 1969, and I spent a few days with him and his family in St. Louis after that. The last three days of the break we spent with the others named above traveling to and from Chicago.

On January 21, 1969, Schaab threw me a surprise birthday party, the first that I ever had. During the summer of 1969, we took a trip together to Silver Dollar City in Branson, Missouri. Since lunch was not served in the dining room in the seminary on Sunday, Schaab and I and several others began to eat soup and crackers together in our rooms, rotating every week from one room to another. Each of us had a hot plate and a pan in which to heat the soup and several bowls in which to serve it.

As the years went by at Cardinal Glennon College, 1968–1972, I began to make other friends and be accepted in other circles of friends. I remember one discussion with Schaab that centered on other people in our lives and how he felt that I was slipping away from him. I sensed possessiveness on his part. Thus, our friendship diminished, especially near the time of graduation, as I prepared to leave St. Louis and head to St. Meinrad School of Theology in southern Indiana, and he prepared to stay in St. Louis and attend Kenrick Seminary. After graduation in 1972, we did participate together in an eleven-mile float trip on the Gasconade River with two other classmates.

After arriving at Maryknoll in 1969, Meehan showed us where we were going to stay, and the next day we headed for Chicago with four Maryknoll seminarians. Our first stop was the aquarium, then the Museum of National Science and History with a tour through a submarine and a coal mine. After spending all day in the museum, we went to dinner in a Mexican restaurant in the loop named SuCasa. After getting tickets at Carnegie Theater, we saw the late showing of *Romeo and Juliet*, not getting back to the seminary until 2:30 Sunday morning! After attending the 9 a.m. Mass, we headed back to St. Louis. Thus, my first trip outside the state without adult supervision came to an end.

My next trip was not out of the state of Missouri but to the diocese for which I would be ordained a few years later: Springfield-Cape Girardeau. Schaab and I took a few days of vacation during the summer of 1969 to what-was-then called School of the Ozarks (now College of the Ozarks) and to Silver Dollar City, which was still in its infant stage. We stayed in a hotel on Indian Point after visiting the city in the late afternoon which enabled us to return the next day for free. I remember touring the grounds of the School of the Ozarks, seeing the carillon and other buildings, and visiting the various demonstrations of glass-blowing, iron-works, candy-making, etc. while enjoying the rides in the theme park where we had a great past ahead of us! I have fond memories of Schaab even though we have not had contact since 1972.

1973: Valerian Odermann

Near the end of May 1973, I took my first airplane flight from St. Louis to Bismarck, North Dakota, and from there to Richardton, North Dakota. I don't remember how I got to Richardton; most likely someone picked me up at the airport and drove me to Assumption Abbey in Richardton. On May 30 I held the book for the bishop who ordained Valerian John Odermann, a monk of Assumption Abbey, to the order of priest in the abbey church. I remember spending a few days before and after enjoying the monastery, seeing the sights, horseback riding, and resting. I knew Odermann from St. Meinrad School of Theology in which both of us were students. He was the teaching assistant who helped me outline and write the once-a-week church history paper I had due my first semester in St. Meinrad School of Theology.

1974: Michael Buttner 1

During the summer of 1974, I made a trip to Mary Help of Christians Abbey in Belmont, North Carolina, to visit a friend I had made in St. Meinrad School of Theology in 1972. James Buttner had decided to join Belmont Abbey after his first year of theology. So, he took a year off to become a novice in Belmont Abbey; as a novice, he was known as Michael. There were several other monks from Belmont Abbey who were attending St. Meinrad School of Theology, so I visited with them, too. Besides

My Life of Ministry, Writing, Teaching, and Traveling

attending the daily Morning and Evening Prayer and Mass, we went swimming in the pool of Belmont Abbey College—staffed by the monks. I also saw some of the sights while spending a week there.

1975: Jerome Martinez, Timothy Berg, Vernon Meyer 1

In early August of 1975 I left St. Louis, where I had been visiting friends, and flew to Albuquerque, New Mexico, to visit three friends there: Jerome Martinez, Timothy Berg, and Vernon Meyer. They took me on a tour of the city including dinner on top of the Sandia Mountains. We visited churches, went to a Pueblo to see the Corn Dance done by Native Americans, and then proceeded to Santa Fe to visit churches, the capitol, the Rio Grande Gorge, Taos Ski Valley, Los Alamos—where the bombs dropped on Japan were made—and eat at lots of Mexican restaurants. After four days in Mexico, Meyer and I headed to Colorado. This was my first trip ever to Colorado, and I immediately fell in love with the mountains.

Meyer, whom I had known from Cardinal Glennon College in St. Louis, had come to St. Meinrad School of Theology two years following my arrival there. He, like I, had decided to leave St. Louis and study for Santa Fe; in time that changed to Phoenix. Meyer, who was driving his car, took me to the Garden of the Gods, the Air Force Academy Chapel, and Pikes Peak (14,110 feet) in Colorado Springs. From there we went to Denver and, after joining a friend—Marian Bellotti—I made at St. Meinrad during the summer of 1974, we headed to a cabin in the Buffalo Springs area. We stayed there, along the Platte River, for a few days before heading to Mount Evans (14,264 feet) and Vail to attend the music festival. Then, it was back to Denver and a few nights at St. Thomas Seminary from which we visited museums, the capitol, and the mint. Before getting back home, I wrote a poem on August 3, 1975: "Amen! Colorado!"

> I heard the silence
> of the mountains!
> their black faces
> spoke words of age and wisdom
> of solidarity and change
> of grace and power.

After Thanksgiving in 1975 I made a five-day trip to Baltimore with several other St. Meinrad seminarians to attend the diaconate ordination of Doctor Terrance J. McGovern. While there, we visited the capitol in Washington, DC, the National Shrine of the Immaculate Conception, the Library of Congress, Catholic University, and other places. McGovern was a Christian Brother who attended St. Meinrad School of Theology in order to be ordained to the priesthood.

Other Travels

1978: Michael Buttner 2, Greg McEvoy

The year 1978 was filled with travel. The first stop was Mary Help of Christians Abbey in Belmont, North Carolina, for the ordination to the priesthood of Michael Buttner, OSB. I had been there in 1974 to visit with Buttner, who had joined the monastery. After spending a year in the novitiate, he returned to St. Meinrad to finish his theological studies. Then, he went back to the abbey to be ordained a priest-monk. It wasn't long before he became the registrar for the college sponsored by the Benedictine monks. After some years serving in that position, he left the monastery and became a diocesan priest and pastor of a parish.

After having been appointed to the Liturgical Commission of the Diocese of Springfield-Cape Girardeau by then-Bishop Bernard F. Law, I attended the Liturgical Workshop sponsored by the Catholic University, Washington, DC, the last week of May and the first week of June. I remember attending lectures and worship services. These were the days of implementing the changes in the liturgy mandated by Vatican Council II.

On July 23, Greg McEvoy, who was a high school senior from Springfield and with whom I had mountain climbed in the summer of 1977, and I left St. Mary Church, Joplin—where I had been assigned as of July 15—and headed to Albuquerque, New Mexico, to visit Meyer and Berg. The next day we continued our journey to Santa Ana, California, to visit McEvoy's aunt. On the way we took a side trip through the Painted Desert and the Petrified Forest in Arizona. This was my first time to see the Pacific Ocean, so we spent time on the beach. Because Santa Ana is a part of the greater Los Angeles area, we went to Disneyland, Universal Studios, the Chinese Theater, and Beverly Hills. After a few days we headed to San Francisco, stopping along the way at San Luis Obispo Mission, Carmel Mission, and Santa Barbara. We stayed in St. Patrick Seminary in Menlo Park. In Los Angeles we visited Fisherman's Warf, took a cruise on the bay, rode the cable cars, and toured the Civic Center and Chinatown.

From San Francisco we headed north to Portland, Oregon, taking a side trip to Sacramento to see the capitol and Crater Lake. Our next stop was Olympia, Washington, and the Olympia Brewery. After that we continued on to Seattle to go to the top of the Space Needle and see the Tutankhamun Exhibit, which was on tour from the Cairo Museum. We looked over fifty-five pieces of art—over three thousand years old—which were found in the tomb of the young pharaoh whose burial chamber was found by Howard Carter. From Seattle we headed to Mount Rainier, about seventy miles outside of Seattle, backpacked about a mile, set up camp, and enjoyed the beauty of the place before heading north into Idaho and then into Canada. We stayed one night in Regina, Saskatchewan, before heading to Winnipeg, Manitoba, where we saw the Pan-Am Swimming Pool, parks, orthodox churches, and Fort Garry.

After leaving Canada, we headed south to Evansville, Wisconsin, where we met McEvoy's parents, who were on vacation there visiting their relatives and friends. We played tennis, swam, rested, and made a day trip to Madison to see the capitol building. After this McEvoy and I returned to Springfield, and I headed back to Joplin. At that time, this was the longest vacation I had ever taken!

In October, I attended the Federation of Diocesan Liturgical Commissions Annual Meeting in Panama City Beach, Florida. The week consisted of workshops, lectures, and various presentations on the liturgy. Of course, there was plenty of time on most afternoons to enjoy the beach, which was located about a one-minute walk from the hotel where I was staying.

1979: Greg Eck

In March 1979, Greg Eck from Springfield met me in Joplin and we headed to Denver, Colorado, to visit his brother and my friend, Jim Eck. I had met Greg in Springfield and played tennis with him and his brother, Mark. Jim was an engineer in Denver, living in an apartment in Aurora, a suburb of Denver and not too far from the old Stapleton National Airport. We left early morning, March 23, and, after driving all day, arrived at Jim's apartment around 8 p.m. On Saturday we drove to Boulder and toured the National Center for Atmospheric Research. After that we drove and drove through mountains all covered in snow; this was my first time to see the mountains decked out in their winter attire.

On Sunday, March 25, all three of us went slope skiing in El Dora, a ski resort located between Denver and Estes Park. We got there around noon, took the basic instruction class, and then were taken to the top of a hill by a chair lift and told to ski down. Jim and Greg had skied before, but I had not. So, about half way down, I decided that was enough for me. My fear of falling, breaking an appendage, or running into a tree kept me from ever attempting slope skiing again. A few years later, I would learn how to cross-country ski, a sport I came to love.

While Jim went to work, Greg and I toured the capitol building and the Denver mint. Then, after doing some grocery shopping, we headed back to the apartment where I was serving as chef for the week. I prepared a meal for all of us once Jim got home from work. The next day Greg and I drove to the Longs Peak trailhead, located on the edge of Rocky Mountain National Park, and hiked through the snow for about eight miles until the snow was too deep. Little did I know in 1979 that one day I would climb Longs Peak.

On Wednesday, March 28, Greg and I drove to Colorado Springs to tour the Air Force Academy chapel. Then, we took the long way back to Denver, driving through the snow-covered mountains again. We ended the day with Jim at Sims Landing, a restaurant overlooking Denver in the foothills. While eating, we watch the planes lining up three- to five-deep to land at Stapleton Airport.

The next day Greg and I traveled to Stapleton International Airport, which used to be located within Denver before the new airport was built way out on the high plains. Greg had never been to an airport, so we spent time watching planes come in and go out. One of the landing strips was located over Interstate 70. While driving east or west on 70, it was easy to see a plane cross over the interstate. After a few hours watching planes and people, we went to Larimer Square, Denver's old town, where we went through the shops and ate lunch. Then, we took a trip to the Denver Zoo, and, after that, back to the apartment. On Friday morning we left Denver and, after driving all day, got back to Joplin around 2 Saturday morning. Greg headed back to Springfield Saturday afternoon.

In May of 1979, I went to Omaha, Nebraska, for the Region Meeting of the Federation of Diocesan Liturgical Commissions. The theme was celebrating the Word of God. This was a regional preparation for the national meeting that took place in Kansas City in October which I attended after giving a presentation at the Missouri Liturgical Congress in Jefferson City, Missouri, on "Sunday Sensuousness" to about one hundred people.

1981: Miscellaneous 1

Because I had the summer free while teaching in McAuley Regional High School in Joplin, I had the opportunity to attend several conferences in 1981. The first occurred during Lent in March. I went to Chicago to attend The Gathering. I got to hear then-current speakers, such as John Shea, Richard McBrien, Jose Hobday, Joseph Chaplin, and more. During the summer I made it to Notre Dame, Indiana, to participate in a workshop on Sunday Worship. I returned to Notre Dame in 1984 to attend the conference on Religious Education and Liturgy.

1985: Europe 1

I had always wanted to go to Europe, but I could never seem to save enough money to do so. Finally, the opportunity came when I offered to take a group of students from McAuley Regional High School in Joplin to Europe as part of an EF Program tour. On June 3, twenty-one high school students and two adult chaperons, in addition to me, drove to the Kansas City airport and boarded a plane for London. I had been in the process of organizing this trip since the fall of 1984. For two weeks we traveled to London, Paris, Lucerne, Florence, Rome, Venice, and Munich. Over all, everything went well as we traveled by motor coach from one country to the next. We toured cities, seeing important buildings and landmarks. In most places we had at least one free day.

My students were well disciplined. However, there are a few incidents that I remember. One occurred immediately after getting to our hotel in London. After I was sure that everyone was in his or her assigned room, one of the other adults—Hobbs—and I decided to go to the bar downstairs and drink a beer before going to bed. While we were sitting at the bar, a group of my students attempted to slip out of the hotel. I intercepted them and redirected them to their rooms upstairs. Another incident occurred a few days later in another city when I was being sure that everyone was in his or her room. We had a rule that no boy was to be in a girl's room, and no girl was to be in a boy's room. Any visiting was to occur in the hall. While walking down the hall, I saw a boy coming out of a girl's room, and he knew he was in trouble before I caught up to him. The punishment for breaking a rule was the forfeit of one's free day; instead of doing what one wanted, he or she had to spend the day with me going wherever I wanted. It took only that one incident to make all understand that the rules were to be obeyed. The only other problem that I remember on that two-week trip was that one girl left her suitcase in a hotel, when she was supposed to bring it to the bus. Thus, she left all her belongings in the hotel. Other girls helped her for the rest of the trip by loaning her clean clothes to wear. I think her suitcase arrived in Joplin a few weeks after we got home. It had been opened and items had been taken. This was to be the first of many educational travel experiences that I would enjoy in the next years.

1986: Mark Eck, Art Hobbs 1

The 1985 exploratory trip to Europe had whetted by appetite for travel. Such travel began in April 1986 to Plano, Texas, a town located north of Dallas, where I, Mark, celebrated the wedding of Mark Eck in St. Mark Church! I knew Eck from having played tennis with him in Springfield. While in Plano, I took the opportunity to visit South Fork Ranch, where the TV series *Dallas* was filmed, Six Flags Over Texas, and some friends from Joplin who had moved to Dallas.

In August I headed to Alaska for fifteen days. I had wanted to see Alaska for a long time. So, Hobbs from Joplin and I flew to Anchorage. After spending a few days exploring that city, we took the train to Fairbanks, then we stopped at Denali National Park and took the bus to see some of the features below Mount McKinley. We also took a tour that showed us glaciers, permafrost, and the famous Alaska Pipeline. We capped our Alaskan visit by attending the fiftieth state fair. This trip, while educational, gave me an understanding of the word *big*. The highlight of the trip was a small plane trip over some of the glaciers; the plane, owned by the Archdiocese of Anchorage, was flown by one of the priests of the archdiocese. This trip made me want to return to Alaska.

In September I flew to Craig, Colorado, to conduct a workshop on the western slope for the Archdiocese of Denver on Church, Ministry, and Spirituality. In October I was in a parish in Independence, Kansas, giving a weekend retreat/renewal weekend.

1987: Sean Farley

Early May of 1987 found me in Fresno, California, for ten days. I went to visit a former high school student, Sean Farley, and his parents, Dennis and Tieneke, who had moved there. After spending a few days with the Farleys, I rented a car and toured the Napa Valley and the Sonoma Valley, stopping often to taste wines. We also made a trip together to Yosemite National Park, which we drove through and stopped to enjoy lunch in a park restaurant.

Farley and I had become good friends while he was in high school. He was a very smart young man with whom most teachers did not know what to do. In my religion class he sat in the front row as close to me as possible. I remember one day when he was acting out that I looked at him eye-to-eye and said, "Sean Farley, I love you." From that day forward, I never had another problem with Farley. I also got to know his parents and would share dinner with them in their quarters of a motel which they owned in Joplin. Farley even joined me on an ocean cruise, and he often came with others to the cabin I used in Forsyth, Missouri. Other than the trip to Fresno, I have never seen Farley again.

Late May 1987 found me in Des Moines, Iowa, attending a Neuro-Linguistic Programming workshop. NLP, a process in which I had an interest, is a study of strategies that people create for themselves for living and dealing with problems in various situations.

In September, after being appointed editor of *The Mirror* in April, I traveled to New Orleans to see Pope John Paul II. About two hundred people rode buses there to stand alternately in the hot sun and pouring rain to get a glimpse of him. We had to be in our assigned areas—what I referred to as pens—in the morning, where we stood all day to await the pope's arrival. The sun scorched us. Then, the clouds began to gather. Then, it poured rain. Then, the sun returned. Finally, the pope raced by in the pope mobile. When Mass finally began, we could see the pope and other ministers who looked like they were about one-inch tall. After getting back to our hotel in early evening, I promised myself that I would never do any of that again. And I kept that promise.

1988: Catholic Press 1

I attended my first Catholic Press Association convention in Boston, Massachusetts, in May. I knew no one, and I had no idea what took place at a CPA convention. It was a new experience meeting Catholic journalists from around the United States and Canada, to see copies of their newspapers, to engage in dialogue with them, and to get a better idea of what I needed to do to bring *The Mirror* in line. After attending the awards ceremony, I wanted to win some of those certificates for my diocesan newspaper.

1989: Art Hobbs 2

The late May Catholic Press Association convention was in Baltimore, Maryland. After attending the convention's workshops and listening to its speakers, I took some time to visit Edgar Allen Poe's grave and the former home of St. Elizabeth Ann Seton, as well as seeing the Baltimore Cathedral. I also enjoyed time walking along Baltimore's restored inner harbor. I had learned that since my budget for *The Mirror* included attendance at the CPA convention, I might as well add a day or two to the trip and see the city!

From late June to early July, I toured Britain with Hobbs from Joplin. I had met Hobbs in St. Mary Parish in 1978 after a Sunday Mass. At the end of the Mass I had indicated that I played tennis and was looking for others who did the same. Hobbs told me that he played; so, we agreed on a time and place to play. We had also traveled together before. We spent time in London, Salisbury, Stratford-Upon-Avon, and York. Then, we went to Cardiff in Wales and Edinburgh in Scotland. It was on this second trip to Britain that I decided to visit the historic Gothic cathedrals in the country. I had a list of them in a travel book, and I began to be sure to stop wherever they were to see them. It was also on this trip that I visited Stonehenge, a place I had wanted to see since I was a little boy in grade school and seen pictures of it in a book. In 1989, a person could walk up to and around the stones; there was no barrier yet in place. Because I wrote a weekly column for *The Mirror*, I highlighted the cathedrals and Stonehenge in my articles. That column became a type of travelogue, not only telling others about my travels, but a record of where I had been.

1990: Catholic Press 2

In April I attended the annual Catholic Press Association convention in Nashville, Tennessee. Once every five years, the CPA paired with the Religious Education Congress. The five-day event featured all types of speakers and workshops. However, the best conference that I attended on newspaper work was the Society for Newspaper Design, which was held in San Francisco, California, in early October. I left San Francisco with many new and exciting ideas to bring back to Springfield and implement. The Communications Advisory Board that I had formed to advise me on updating *The Mirror* suggested that I join the SND and begin attending its conventions. The speakers and workshops were top of the line; at this convention I was introduced to the psychology of newspaper readers.

1991: Vernon Meyer 2

In late May of 1991, the Catholic Press Association convention was held in Phoenix, Arizona. *The Mirror* won third place in the local issue category for a story I wrote on the New Madrid Fault. The same story also won first place in the Associated Church Press competition for graphics. Another benefit of the Communications Advisory Board was its recommendation that I join and attend the ACP convention every year. After the conclusion of the ACP convention, I remained in Phoenix for a few days to visit with Meyer, a good friend who was ordained to the priesthood for the Diocese of Phoenix. We spent time visiting old mission ruins and seeing other sites around

Phoenix. In October I attended the Society for Newspaper Design convention in Boston. I brought home more ideas to use as editor of *The Mirror*.

1992: Darin Dankelson, Alaska, Steve Witek, Jim Reynolds, Europe 2

From May 22 through November 30, 1992, I was on a sabbatical that would influence me for many years. The sabbatical began with a wedding in Columbia, Missouri, of a former high school student from Joplin: Darin Dankelson. Dankelson was the youngest of four brothers. I had taught him in McAuley High School. He was an excellent student, who had been sick for a few weeks right before mid-semester grades were issued during his Sophomore year. I remember him standing in my office door asking me why he had a B in religion. I explained it was because of his absences and the work that he was missing. He was very upset because he was a straight A student. As tears filled his eyes, I explained that mid-semester grades meant nothing, and that by the end of the semester he would probably have an A. That experience led to a friendship between us. I remember joining Dankelson and his parents for dinner. I also remember him coming to my house for dinner. He accompanied me on one trip to Colorado to engage in some mountain climbing. It was because of our friendship that I was invited to celebrate his wedding.

The three-day affair of Dankelson's nuptials would end in divorce a few years later, but then it was a great experience of two families getting to know each other. A few years later, Darin would marry again and raise several children. To this day we maintain annual contact with each other through Christmas cards and letters.

After the wedding, I continued my traveling, making stops at Grand Teton National Park and Yellowstone National Park in Wyoming and Glacier National Park in Montana. Then, I entered Canada, driving through British Columbia and Alberta, following the Icefield Highway through the Canadian Rockies to Dawson Creek, British Columbia, where I picked up the Alaskan Highway, whose fiftieth anniversary of construction was being celebrated all along the way. I stayed on the Alaskan Highway all the way to Fairbanks, Alaska.

I took my time driving, usually covering no more than three hundred to four hundred miles a day. My brown Isuzu served me well all the way to Big Lake, a small community about fifty miles north of Anchorage where I arrived on June 8, after having driven 5,300 miles. Along the way I saw Fort Nelson in British Columbia, and Watson Lake and Whitehorse in what was then the Yukon Territory (now a province), with a side trip to Skagway, Alaska, from Whitehorse.

In exchange for a place to live, the archbishop of Anchorage assigned me to the circuit, a group of five priests who ministered to the parishes outside of the city of Anchorage. Most of the parishes outside of Anchorage did not have a permanent pastor; they were taken care of on a day-to-day basis by a pastoral administrator—a permanent deacon or a nun. A priest only came every other week or every third week to preside at Eucharist for the parish. On the alternate Sundays, the pastoral administrator presided over the Liturgy of the Word and a communion service. Every weekend I was sent to different parishes in Big Lake, Wasilla, Willow, Talkeetna, Trapper Creek, and Kenai. The Willow, Talkeetna, and Trapper Creek mission run was a 165-mile round trip from Big Lake. When I was finished with Masses, I got to sightsee and explore the Alaskan towns.

In Talkeetna I met Sister Louise Tibbets, the pastoral administrator of three parishes. She brought her gift of music to the people. Tibbets gave me refuge from Big Lake, after the permanent deacon there threatened me. After I arrived and met him, he and his wife informed me that I would be having dinner with them every night; I quickly made it clear that usually I would prepare my own meals. They insisted, but I insisted more! I knew there was tension between the three of us; the very first Mass I celebrated and at which the permanent deacon assisted, he stood in front of me for the Penitential Rite. Later, he told me that he would do the preaching at all the Masses; I reminded him that who preached at a Mass was up to me. Finally, after having cleaned the kitchen and mopped the floor of the parish hall—which I used—connected to my living quarters, some of his family brought their dogs in with their muddy feet. I was upset and let it be known. That is when he and his family threatened me. I packed up my belongings and went to Talkeetna, where Tibbets welcomed me to the use of the room off of the church and the parish kitchen for a month. Tibbets planned to stay in Talkeetna for three years while she discerned a possible call to ministry to native Americans in the Alaska bush—places one could get to only by plane.

While in Alaska for three months, I took three side trips. One trip was north over the Dalton Highway (400 miles of gravel road) from Fairbanks over the Arctic Circle to Prudhoe Bay and the oil fields and the Arctic Ocean. I traveled in a van with a few other people on a two-day tour. We spent the night half-way at a motel for truckers in Coldfoot, finished up the trip the next day, touched the ice-flowing Arctic Ocean on July 1, toured the oil fields, saw the beginning of the Alaskan pipeline, and flew back to Fairbanks from Deadhorse.

The second trip was to Dawson City, Yukon, over almost 300 miles of gravel roads, especially the Top of the World Highway. I drove to the Yukon River, crossed it on a ferry, and explored the heart of the Klondike Gold Rush for a few days. After watching a film on how cold it gets in Dawson City during the winter—cold enough for propane to freeze and the grease in a car to turn to jelly—I decided that I would not want to live there! While returning from Dawson City, I met another person who would influence my life: Steve Witek. He was a twenty-eight-year-old man from Massachusetts, who had moved to California and worked in construction—hanging ceilings—for five years before realizing that he did not know what he wanted to do with his life. He sold everything he had, including his truck, and with just the clothes that would fit in a backpack, hitchhiked to Alaska. I met him outside of Tok, where I had just bought four new tires for my Isuzu after having a flat on the Top of the World

Highway. I was singing a thanksgiving song to God for having protected me from not having another flat when I spotted Witek. I stopped, and he got in. We became instant friends and spent a number of days together three different times. I was on my way to Kenai, and Witek came with me for a few days. After he left, he came back a week later for a few more days. And on the way home, I found him on a ferry heading back to California. We stayed in touch for a few years, but then I lost contact with him; the memory of the good times we shared remains.

One particular memory concerns my reason for going to Kenai: to celebrate Masses on the weekend. After I picked up Witek, I told him that I was a university professor, which I was. That was fine until we got to Anchorage, where I told him that I was a priest heading to Kenai for Masses. After we got to Kenai, he came to the Saturday evening Mass. I looked out over the congregation, and there was Witek about mid-way in the church. On Sunday, after some sightseeing together, we went to the grocery store and bought some steaks and potatoes to bake for dinner. We forgot the sour cream. So, while I was cooking, I tossed the keys to my Isuzu to Witek and told him to go back to the grocery store and buy some sour cream. He looked at me in astonishment, and I knew why. He could not believe that I trusted him. He returned a few minutes later with the sour cream, saying that he could have left. I merely looked at him and said, "But you didn't!"

My third trip was to Nome, a small town on the Bering Sea, and to Kotzebue, a Native American village. The only way into Nome is by air, except during the summer when a few barges bring in a year's supply of groceries for those who have ordered them. Because Nome is located so far north—over the Arctic Circle—there are no trees. It is a very dreary place to live, but gold mining was still being done on the shore and in the tundra with dredges inland. Further north is Kotzebue, and it, too, is a dreary place to live. The natives of this small town had built a modern hotel in order to attract tourists to their arts, crafts, songs, and customs.

In mid-August, Reynolds, my best priest-friend who was then living in Joplin, joined me in Alaska for two weeks. After I picked him up at the airport in Anchorage, I took him to Talkeetna for a couple of days before he took the train to see Denali Park. Then, we traveled to Seward, Homer, and Kenai, where I had Masses for the last weekend I was in Alaska. Together we drove out of Alaska and into Haines Junction, Yukon, and into Haines, Alaska, where we caught the marine ferry going south. We made stops for a few days each in Juneau, Sitka, and Ketchikan. We stayed in bed and breakfast places, touring the towns and enjoying some hiking. We would drive off the ferry and drive onto the next ferry when we were ready to leave one town and head to the next. The southeastern panhandle of Alaska gets anywhere from eighty to 180 inches of rain a year; this means that it is a rain forest, and it rains every day.

We got off the ferry for the last time at Prince Rupert, British Columbia, and spent three days driving south through British Columbia, Idaho, and Wyoming, to Salt Lake City, Utah, where we toured the Mormon headquarters. After that we headed to Del Norte, Colorado, where I was assigned for four weekends to help the pastor, Father Eugene Harden, who was recuperating from a series of chemotherapy treatments for lymphatic cancer in preparation for a bone marrow transplant. He received the transplant in November, but died in February of the next year. Harden, who referred to Reynolds and me as missionaries from Alaska, saw his cancer as a gift from God to help him in his ministry to the Hispanic population in the San Luis Valley. After the first weekend in Del Norte, Reynolds flew back to Joplin, while I remained to help Harden. While living with Harden for four weeks, I served the mission parishes in North Fork and Creede. He recognized me as the author of the homily notes in *The Priest* magazine, and was thrilled to have a writer in residence at Del Norte.

I concluded the first part of my sabbatical with a retreat in Sacred Heart Jesuit Retreat House in Sedalia, Colorado. I spent six days there having my vocation confirmed and coming to some decisions about the next years of my life. After I finished the retreat, I headed home to Springfield for six days to put away five months of my life on the road. Then, I made a trip to England to spend two weeks touring sites—Tintagel, Glastonbury, Winchester—associated with the legendary King Arthur and seeing some of the major cathedrals and former abbeys in Sherborne, Exeter, Wells, Gloucester, Oxford, Winchester, and Chichester.

I crossed the English Chanel to France, where I spent two more weeks touring Rouen, Bayeux (seeing the famous tapestry), Toulon, Avignon, and Arles. In Bayeux I got so sick I could not get out of my hotel bed. The one clerk who spoke English called a doctor, who spoke very little English. However, we managed to communicate and he prescribed some medicine for me. The hotel staff went to the pharmacy for me and got it. After two days, I was feeling well enough to travel to Toulon, where I met Jim Paulson, a former student, and his wife, Genevieve, who took me to her doctor and translated back and forth between us. He was able to prescribe more medicine which actually cured me. The doctor sent me to get a chest X-ray to be sure I did not have pneumonia and to the pharmacy with prescriptions to be filled. Genevieve led me to all the places I needed to go and translated everything for me. I remember getting a hotel room—I had been staying with the Paulsons in their small apartment—in order to recuperate in my own room. After a few days of taking my medicine, I began to feel better enough to do some sightseeing.

I returned from France to Springfield on November 24, and I went back to work at *The Mirror* on November 30. This first sabbatical was one filled with new experiences, lots of learning, and the completion of four manuscripts. I remember driving across Montana and praying: "Lord, show me what you want me to do, and help me do it. Show me where you want me to be and help me to be there." That prayer was answered over and over again during the six-month sabbatical.

Other Travels

1993–1995: Europe 3, Catholic Press 3

After all the events of my sabbatical in 1992, 1993 was a calm year. I did travel to France for two weeks to visit cathedrals and shrines in Chartres, Orleans, Tours, Toulouse, Toulon, and Lyon. Likewise, in 1994 my travel consisted of trips to newspaper conventions. In May, I attended the Catholic Press Association Convention in Tampa, Florida, where *The Mirror* received a second-place award in the General Excellence category. From there I flew to Ashville, North Carolina, to attend the Associated Church Press Convention. And in October, I went to Kansas City, Missouri, to attend the Society for Newspaper Design Convention. The award *The Mirror* received confirmed the fact that I needed to keep contact with what others were doing in the world of newsprint. Other than my annual mountain climbing trip to Colorado, in 1995 I made a trip to San Antonio, Texas, to the Incarnate Word Motherhouse, where Sister Mary Ellen O'Connor, CCVI, a good friend, was beginning a sabbatical. During my six-day stay there, we visited the historic missions, including the Alamo, and made trips to Padre Island and Johnson City. On several trips we were accompanied by another Incarnate Word Old Miner, Sister Lorraine Bourisaw, CCVI, who was living at the motherhouse then. She died in 1996 after having a heart attack. I was privileged to fly to San Antonio, Texas, and celebrate her funeral and burial in the Incarnate Word Cemetery.

1996: Europe 4, Tim Vinyard, Catholic Press 4

My travels in 1996 began in Philadelphia, Pennsylvania, with attendance at the Catholic Press Association convention. Once the workshops were over, I saw the Liberty Bell, the State House, the mint, and several other important landmarks that are a part of U.S. history.

During the summer, I enjoyed a three-week trip to England and France with (Timothy) Tim Vinyard, who was then a junior high school science teacher in the Joplin School system. We began in London seeing "By Jebes," "Sunset Boulevard," "Miss Saigon," and "Cats." We also made it to the British Museum and several churches. Then, we traveled by train to Colchester, the oldest mentioned town in written literature in England and the place where William the Conqueror built his first castle in 1066. From there we traveled to Norwich, famous for its fifty-two churches, 365 pubs, and the cell of the mystic St. Julian of Norwich. Our next stop was Ely and the great Gothic cathedral founded by St. Etheldreda, a queen and abbess of a monastery for men and women. On to Peterborough we went to see another great Gothic cathedral, and from there to Cambridge to tour the various colleges that form the university.

After returning to London, we boarded the Eurotunnel (Chunnel) train to Paris. This four-hour trip found us reaching speeds up to 200 miles an hour. We spent two days in Paris seeing the Eiffel Tower, Notre Dame, and the Louvre in addition to some other sights. Then, we headed by train to Rheims, which was celebrating the fifteen hundredth anniversary of the baptism of Clovis, the first king of the Franks. We toured the cathedral where Clovis was baptized and the Basilica of St. Remigius, the bishop who baptized him. After Rheims, it was on to Troyes to see another cathedral, churches, and museums. Our next stop was Dijon, famous for its mustard, cathedral, churches, and museums.

The last days of this trip were spent in Toulon, where I visited Paulson, his wife, and their infant son. I had met Paulson in a New Testament class I taught at Southwest Missouri State University (now Missouri State University) in the fall semester of 1990. He was a good critical thinker, and we spent a lot of time outside of class discussing the philosophy and theology of biblical writers. We got together for dinner several times, and I learned that he had severe celiac disease, which meant that he could not eat gluten. I don't remember how he met Genevieve, who had taught French in Canada. She moved to Springfield, until he finished his degree at SMS (now MSU), and then they moved to Toulon, from where she came, married, and settled there. I visited them several other times.

This time Vinyard and I spent one day on the Mediterranean beach and one day getting ready for and participating in the baptism of Paulson's son. The baptism was followed by an eight-course meal in Genevieve's grandfather's garden with family and friends. Then, from Toulon we went back to Paris, from where we flew home. I always enjoyed Genevieve's family, especially her grandfather. My French was not that good, and he spoke no English. However, we would take a bottle of wine to the table in his backyard and sit and talk. He was very patient with me as I struggled through some French sentences. Another incident involving Paulson is narrated later.

The third weekend of October I flew to Indianapolis, Indiana, to attend the Society for Newspaper Design convention. After leaving the Springfield-Branson National airport, I arrived in St. Louis and boarded my flight to Indianapolis. After first being delayed because of a thunderstorm, the pilot instructed us to get off the plane and get something to eat because there were fifteen planes ahead of us waiting to take off and no planes were taking off and heading east because that was the direction the thunderstorm took. At 5:30 p.m. the flight was cancelled!

After standing in line for an hour and a half to see an agent, I was put on standby to catch the 6:40 p.m. flight to Indianapolis which had been delayed to 7:15 p.m. I boarded the plane. The plane left the gate at 7:15 p.m., taxied to the runway, and was put on hold until 8 p.m., when it finally took off. Halfway to Indianapolis the pilot told us that we were diverted to Dayton, Ohio, because the thunderstorm that went through St. Louis was now in Indianapolis. We landed in Dayton, refueled, took off, and arrived in Indianapolis around midnight.

I caught a cab to my hotel, where I had a confirmed reservation for a room, which I guaranteed with a credit card. The desk clerk told me that the hotel was overbooked and that I was being put in another hotel. There would be a room for me the next day. I remember asking the clerk if I had not been present if my credit card would have been charged for the room that I had booked even though the hotel staff had given it away. Sheepishly, he had say that it would have been. I remember asking him if he thought it was moral to get paid twice for a hotel room that had been used only once; he never answered me. In the other hotel, the air conditioning did not work. On the next morning I got a room in the hotel where the convention was being held after being offered a free breakfast for my inconvenience. The service at the hotel was poor, but the convention was good. On Sunday morning, the hotel had to call cabs to take people to the airport, as the man who was supposed to drive the shuttle overslept. Such was my last major trip of 1996!

1997: Catholic Press 5, John August Swanson

My travels in 1997 were not as exciting as those the year before, and they were minimal compared to those in 1996. I make a trip to Denver in late May to attend the Catholic Press Association meeting. And I made a trip to San Diego, California, in early October to attend the Society for News Design meeting. The high point of the trip to San Diego was meeting John August Swanson, an artist-friend from Los Angeles who met me at the airport in San Diego and took me to dinner with his friend, who taught in San Diego University. While serving as editor of *The Mirror*, I had requested and received permission from Swanson to use some of his prints as covers on the special issues of the newspaper. I very much liked his art. Because I exposed his work to a large audience, he sent me signed posters of his work and an original serigraph; all of his gifts are framed and fill the walls of my home to this day.

1998: Catholic Press 6

Travel occurred only in the U.S. in 1998. In May I went to New Orleans for the Catholic Press Association convention. While I had been there in 1987 to see Pope John Paul II, I did not have time to see the city. After the convention I spent time in the French Quarter, took the trolley to Loyola University, and saw other sights. Other than a trip to St. Louis, the only other places I visited were Fort Wayne, Indiana, where I gave a retreat on male spirituality to about thirty men, and Little Rock, Arkansas, where I presented a workshop on church renovation to members of Our Lady of the Holy Souls Parish who were preparing to renovate their church.

2000: Matthew Ver Miller

To mark the millennium, Matthew Miller (now Ver Miller) and I travelled to Europe in late May 2000, after he graduated from Southwest Missouri State University (now Missouri State University), and early June. His was the only graduation ceremony

I ever attended while teaching in the university for thirty years. I hosted his post-graduation meal for his family in the large house in which I was living at the time. After that, he wrote me a card: "Thanks for being part of my journey. It wouldn't have been the same without you! I look forward to the next leg of my journey and whatever it may hold. Thanks for your guidance and friendship."

I met Ver Miller in a Bible and Film class that I was teaching at SMSU (now MSU) in the spring semester of 1999. He began to drop by my office for help creating outlines and writing papers. Gradually those encounters blossomed into dinners together. Then, we went mountain climbing together. After that we began talking about a trip to Europe together, and the millennium was the perfect time to take it.

We visited England, France, and Switzerland. After spending time in London visiting the traditional sight-seeing places of the Tower, St. Paul's Cathedral, etc., we traveled by train to Nottingham, from where Ver Miller's grandmother came to the U.S. after World War II, to meet some of his relatives for the first time. Then, we went to York to see the walls and the cathedral and on to Durham to see the Gothic cathedral there. Once back in London, we took the train under the English Channel to Paris. After a few days in Paris, seeing the Eiffel Tower and the Louvre, we traveled by train to Claremont-Ferrand, where the first crusade was preached, then to Toulouse, to visit friends from Colorado who were living there, then Lourdes, Grenoble, and Chamonix-Mount Blanc—the most beautiful place in the world! Our last stop was Geneva, Switzerland, where we visited places associated with the Reformation, the World Council of Churches, and the United Nations. All that travel was a great way to mark the year 2000.

After Ver Miller graduated from Southwest Missouri State University in 2000, he enrolled in Springfield's Forest Institute of Professional Psychology from which he earned a doctorate in psychology a few years later. Throughout the time he attended classes at Forest Institute, we maintained our relationship by getting together for dinner one night a week. We also did some extensive work on a book that was ultimately published as *Human Wholeness*. At one point in our relationship, he appeared at my door one morning wanting to talk about his fiancée. He disclosed that even with wedding invitations already printed, he had decided that he did not want to marry her. I remember telling him that he was talking to the wrong person. He needed to see her and tell her that! He did break off the engagement, even though she kept showering him with gifts in the hope that he would reconsider and marry her. He never did.

Later in his life, he met Janna Ver Daught, a medical student. They began dating, and he began narrating all the positive experiences he was having with her. Ultimately, they decided to marry, but to change their names before they married so that the new name would appear on their doctoral diplomas. Thus, Miller became Ver Miller. I had the privilege of celebrating their wedding day on Christmas Eve 2001.

Once both of them completed their course work, they began their internships to finish the requirements for their doctoral programs. For a while they lived in

Springfield, then in April 2003, they moved to an apartment in Omaha, Nebraska. Janna interned at a hospital in Omaha, and Matthew at a center in Lincoln. I responded to an April 2, 2003, e-mail Matthew sent announcing their new address by writing, "After five years, I find it hard to believe that you have now moved." I added, "I'm glad you are getting settled and getting ready for the next stage of your journey." On April 3, 2003, Ver Miller wrote, "You aren't the only one who has had a hard time believing that I have moved." Then, reflecting on our five-year relationship, he wrote:

> I had a great five-year journey in Springfield. It has been a journey that has changed me dramatically. I have worked hard to grow, and I couldn't have grown to the degree I have without you. I give you a lot of credit for fostering much of this change that has taken place within me. Without you, I would still be years behind and the course of my life might have been extremely different. I like who I am, and I like where I am in life."

Ver Miller said that he would miss our frequent discussions, dinners, and movie nights, but he knew we would stay in contact through e-mails, telephone calls, and visits. He reminded me of a phrase he had once used to describe how, after meeting me, he wanted to get to know me: "You're not going to get away!" Then, he added, "The journey of our relationship will not end, but only change. So, as I begin this new journey in Omaha, so begins a new journey of our friendship."

After taking a little time to think about the five years I had spent with Ver Miller and remembering the feeling I had as he and the truck with his belongings pulled out of the parking lot of the apartment where he had lived and the waving of good-bye that both of us did that day, I wrote an e-mail to him on April 4, 2003. "I've spent some time reflecting on your leaving and the loss that I have felt in order to identify for myself what I've lost, what dying is taking place." I explained that I had lost discussions, dinners, and movies. But there was more. "I've been terribly (in a positive sense) altered by you—never again to be the same. And that's exactly what a journey is supposed to do—leave both of us changed." Then after mentioning that I had been changed by his views, struggles, and becoming, I wrote: "You're right; it is time for change for both of us. Journeys keep moving on."

As each of us continued our journey separately, we stayed in contact with each other, primarily through telephone conversations, and an occasional e-mail or visit. On February 15, 2005, as Matthew and Janna were preparing for a trip to South Africa, I received an e-mail from Ver Miller, stating, "You would be proud: I have been doing my own work, like I ask of my clients every day." He added: "I don't always like the things I discover, and many times I am amazed at how I get stuck on such simple dysfunctional thoughts. It certainly isn't easy to change; however, I have been able to make some good changes that have been quite rewarding."

The discussion continued in a February 20, 2005, e-mail. Ver Miller wrote: "I know I don't like change because it is difficult, uncomfortable, and sometimes scary, but it still amazes me how much I resist becoming and growing when that is the very thing I want to do. Much of the work I am doing now is implementing the change I know would benefit me."

On February 27, 2005, I received an e-mail from Ver Miller with an attachment of a reflection he sent to one of his former supervisors of his internship experiences. Before the attachment, there was a paragraph addressed to me:

> I am sure you are aware that others may describe you as abrasive at times, and I confess that was my perception the first few days in your film class years ago. However, as I got to know you, I learned to appreciate your honesty, genuineness, and straight-forward approach. In a world where there is such a focus on pleasing people, accepting the norm, not questioning our beliefs, and ultimately not "rocking the boat," it is easy to see how your class, as well as others, can be perceived as abrasive. A change has taken place, as things I once found abrasive and feared are now welcomed and perceived as refreshing. I am sure I sought you out because I knew there was much I could and needed to learn from you. You were very approachable due to the format of your class and personal interviews. You have taught me a lot about living a life based on personal conviction rather than societal expectations and fear.

On February 28, 2005, I responded to Ver Miller's e-mail, writing: "I like your metaphor of abrasive. An abrasive is used to get out stubborn stains! It goes deep and cleans away the crap with which many people surround themselves. Abrasive is prophetic. Abrasive makes one and others transparent so that we can see through them to the truth of who they are, and, consequently, who we are."

In the attachment, Ver Miller narrated his growth from thinking that he felt more comfortable socializing with people who were extroverts to his realization that what he was feeling was acceptance. "I have always felt more comfortable around people who are accepting and inclusive of others, confident in who they are and able to be themselves (genuine) without fear of what others or society might think." Then, applying what he had discovered about himself, Ver Miller concluded: "I am overly concerned about what others think and must temper my need to be accepted, approved of, and to please others." He became aware that he learned growing up that he got accepted because he pleased his parents. "This same message has been reinforced by religion, school, and society," he wrote. He realized that his learned and behaviorally reinforced pattern was inhibiting his personal, spiritual, and professional development, along with creating many fears. He wrote, "I understand now that to live as I have (bound by fear, seeking and gaining acceptance and approval from those of this earth) is death, and to die to that is gain."

On March 2, 2005, Ver Miller shared with me a longer two-page, single-spaced reflection on his insight. "Upon reflection I can now see that social anxiety has plagued me for as long as I can remember," he began. After he named areas which social anxiety kept him from pursuing, he wrote: "I have always known my functioning has been somewhat impaired, hindered, or inhibited in some way preventing me from living as optimally, as I believe I have the potential to do." Then, he recounted some of his experiences that led him to understand himself better. One of those was religion. "I have a great deal of frustration and anger toward religion," he wrote. He explained how the themes of pleasing others and God had become intertwined. He stated that a healthy relationship with God would be one of cooperation. He continued:

> Over and over again in my life, it has been drilled into me that there is only one way to God and heaven through Jesus Christ. I don't know if I believe this. All I have ever wanted to do was to know God more, and that is what I have been praying for since around the age of seven or earlier. I think the growth process in which I am engaged now and have been going through since 1998 is God answering my prayers. By the way, it certainly isn't the answer I expected, which is likely typical of God and certainly of Jesus in Scripture. I think I am being led to think and believe from a more pluralistic perspective, which would then allow me to embrace a revised theology and view of Christianity.

I replied to Ver Miller's reflection, writing, "The man I knew was in there is finally emerging to understand that the mystery of life is learning how to die well—and then practicing it repeatedly." I added:

> If we live our lives being who others want us to be, we never discover who we are. And what tragedy that life will be. We cannot control what others think about us; it is humanly impossible. We can only be ourselves, an ever-developing and ever-revelatory self. Integrity, genuineness, authenticity, honesty, whatever leads me (and you) to question everything about everything including ourselves—that's what I always refer to as "doing your homework" on your self. I don't think anyone can really LIVE if he or she lives in the confines of societal expectations and fears, trying to please others without first pleasing self.

I concluded my e-mail, writing, "Your statement indicates a breakthrough in self-understanding and knowledge. You are doing your homework." Ver Miller had indicated that he wanted to share the statement with me "because much of the reflection speaks of things we had addressed in some way at one point or another" during the years of our relationship.

Ver Miller and I stayed in contact primarily through e-mail and telephone conversations from 2005 until he and Janna decided to settle in Lakewood, a subsection of Denver, Colorado. He joined me for a day or two in mountain climbing expeditions from 2007 onward. After backpacking, climbing two peaks, and relaxing together in 2011, I sent him an e-mail on August 1, writing: "I really enjoyed seeing you and all the good conversations we had. You stirred up some good things in me, and I needed that. I found you more relaxed than ever; that means more comfortable being you!" He sent me an e-mail on August 2, stating: "It was great to catch up and, yes, the stimulating discussion were refreshing." He added, "Thanks for the feedback you provided. I agree that I am more comfortable than ever with who I am and continue to grow in that regard. It is good to know that it shows." I began to make a yearly stop in Lakewood to visit him when in Colorado beginning in 2012.

In January 2015, Ver Miller flew from Denver to Springfield so we could polish a manuscript we had worked on a few years before. Titled *Human Wholeness: A Spirituality of Relationship*, it was accepted for publication by Wipf & Stock. For several days we worked on language usage, grammar, and various subsections of the book. This visit became an annual January trip for Ver Miller, and it continues to this day. We use the time together to renew our friendship through discussions, meals, and walks. In a card in 2019, he wrote: "I thank God for you, the man you are, and what you share with this world. May the Lord bless you and keep you, my friend."

Matthew and Janna have two children of their own—Jazer and Trevor—and two they have adopted: Josiah from Ethiopia and Kezia from India. I continue to visit the Ver Millers almost every summer, and Matthew continues to come to Springfield every January to spend four to five days with me. This relationship continues to grow both of us.

2001–2009: Miscellaneous 2

The only trip I took in 2001, other than to Colorado, of course, was to Dallas, Texas, for the Catholic Press Association convention in late May. After leaving my job as editor of *The Mirror* on January 4, 2002, I bought a house on May 10, 2002, and, after having it renovated, I moved into it on July 20, 2002. Thus, in 2002 no major trip was taken except that of moving from the house next door! In late May 2003, I made a trip to the Incarnate Word Motherhouse in San Antonio, Texas, to join in celebrating the fiftieth anniversary of religious profession of my first-grade teacher, Sister Laura Magowan, and my good friend, Sister Mary Ellen O'Connor. I also joined Sister Ann Catherine Shaw, with whom I had worked in St. Louis when I was in college, in celebrating her sixtieth anniversary of religious profession. The five-days I spent there were filled with gatherings, meals, and liturgies.

In 2006, after founding St. Francis of Assisi Parish in Nixa, Missouri, and getting it up and running, I resumed some adult education work. In March 2006, I flew to Phoenix, Arizona, to give a weekend workshop on the passion narrative in Mark's Gospel. I spent the third week of July in Long Branch, New Jersey, about an hour's train trip south of Newark, participating in Seton Hall University's institute for priests. I gave a week-long workshop to twenty priests on understanding and preaching Mark's Gospel.

I made a trip to Almeda, Michigan, in 2009 to visit my friend, Hobbs, from Joplin. After he had retired, he had been spending his summers in an apartment there for a few years, but he was discontinuing this at the end of the summer. The town, located north of Detroit, offered trails for biking, which we enjoyed most of the days I was there. At the end of my week there, I loaded my Jeep with lots of Hobbs's things and headed back to Missouri.

Because I had bought a house that went through various stages of renovation, and I had founded a new parish—St. Francis of Assisi in Nixa, Missouri—which also went through various stages of renovation, I did not have the time nor the money to travel very far from 2001 to 2009. However, that changed with 2010.

2010: Europe 5

From May 24 to June 11, 2010, I traveled through Europe with my godson, Kinler, who was a ski instructor during the winter and a fly fisherman guide during the summer in Crested Butte, Colorado. For ten years I had wanted to get back to Europe, so I invited Kinler to join me. I had known Kinler since he was born. I knew his parents, Karl and Sheri, from my time in Joplin. They used to invite me to dinner frequently. After Zach was born, I thought they were going to ask me to baptize him, but instead they asked me to be his godfather. Until I left Joplin in 1985 to return to Springfield, I kept contact with Zach through dinners with him and his parents. However, after returning to Springfield, I began to lose contact with him, especially as he went through high school and then moved to Louisiana for college. Thus, in 2009 after thinking about a trip to Europe, I decided to ask Zach to accompany me. He calculated the best time for him to be gone from his job in Crested Butte, and we set the dates.

We saw Gothic cathedrals in St. Alban, Lincoln, and Litchfield, England. After taking the bullet train to Paris and seeing some of the sights there, we went to Taize for a day and a night. Then, it was on to Chamonix, where we hiked in the Alps for several days before taking a train to Geneva and catching a plane to Rome, where we visited some of the major churches with a day trip to Pompeii. From Rome, we flew back to London and from there back home.

While hiking in the Alps in Chamonix, located below Mount Blanc, I came across an older couple on a trail. She spoke only Italian. He spoke some French and some English, as well as Italian. With the little French I know, and the little French and English he knew, we were able to communicate with each other, switching often from English to French and back to English. While he and I were talking, he'd stop and translate what we were saying into Italian for his wife so she could join in the conversation. After she spoke, he would translate what she said either into French or English. While it took a long time to share an idea, we spoke to each other for about twenty minutes. It was an interesting experience of communicating, not only demonstrating the need to know other languages, but of interpretation of body language. Much of what we shared with each other was communicated not with words, but with actions. The couple was looking for a chair lift that would take them down to the trail from which they came. I explained that no chair lifts were operating in the skiing area in the summer time, and that they would have to walk back on the same trail they had taken. They were disappointed because they had a long walk ahead of them. As they went their way and I went my way, I reflected on how much we had communicated with each other, often not saying a single word!

I have kept some contact with Kinler over the years through my annual visits to Colorado. He had driven over Kebler Pass in the summer to share a meal with me at the home of the Tembrocks, to whom I introduced him a few years before. He also stopped by to visit me in Springfield several times while visiting his parents in Joplin. In 2018 he married the ten-year love of his life—Elsa—along the Gunnison River. I was pleased to attend and celebrate his special day. The setting was perfect for the fly fisherman he has become. A few years ago, he left his job as a winter ski instructor and went into full-time fly-fishing, working as a guide from a small outdoor supply shop in Crested Butte. After that he got into back-country skiing in order to check for potential avalanches.

2011–2014: Miscellaneous 3

Other than my annual trip to Colorado in 2011, I made a few-days trip to Eureka Springs, Arkansas, with a good friend, Jeremy Graddy. He and I had met in a New Testament class and became good friends. Our relationship began one night after class when he hung around for a discussion that went on almost to midnight. After that experience, we began to go to my house after class and discuss all kinds of things. Then, after that class was finished, we began to get together about once a month for dinner. After he graduated and before he began post-graduate work, we decided to see a town neither of us had ever been to before: Eureka Springs. We walked the streets, entering lots of arts and crafts shops, rode the train, ate at some good restaurants, tasted wine, and saw famous Thorn Crown Chapel.

Graddy and I maintained our relationship for many years. At one point he married the woman he had dated since high school, and she gave birth to a son and another child. A few times a year we continued to get together for a meal with a walk or hike preceding it. For a few years we e-mailed each other and tried to stay caught up on each other's activities. He earned a doctorate in physical therapy and works in the Springfield area. Besides Eureka Springs, we also traveled to Colorado for one week while he was in graduate school and before he got married. The genuine human encounter that sparked the beginning of our relationship continued for a few years, but the demand for time with his wife and children took precedence and the relationship was put on hold.

In April 2013, I traveled to Jefferson City, Missouri, to celebrate the sixtieth anniversary of religious profession of my first-grade teacher, Sister Laura Magowan, CCVI. We had time to visit on the day before and reminisce about first grade in 1956 in St. Joachim School, Old Mines, Missouri. Magowan was also present at my high school graduation in 1968 and my priesthood ordination in 1976. I considered it a privilege to preside at the Mass marking her sixtieth jubilee.

2015: Zach Dumas

On December 12, 2015, a former student and good friend, (Zechariah) Zach Dumas, and I left Springfield for a Viking Cruise on the Danube River. I had met Dumas in a required freshman course I was teaching at Missouri State University. On the first day of class of the fall semester I had introduced myself to the students, and he was the only person in the class who talked to me. At the end of the first class, he stayed behind to tell me that if he got on my nerves, I should let him know. Through the course of the semester, we continued to get to know each other. When the semester was finished, I invited him to my house for dinner and we shared what we liked to do in our free time.

One commonality was hiking. So, we began to schedule trips to the conservation areas around Springfield. After a few hours of hiking we would go to my house and share a meal and plan our next trip together. During those hikes and meals, we discussed deep truths of philosophy and theology. He is the only student I ever taught who ever referred to me as his mentor. Often, he shared with me his past experiences looking for my comments on them. At other times he shared what he was contemplating, seeking my input. His experiences of the women he dated were always topics about which he wanted my comments. After knowing Dumas for almost four years, and after having traveled with him on a cross-country ski trip to Colorado, I invited him to join me on a Viking River Cruise as a college graduation gift.

The problem we faced immediately was getting out of Springfield. After getting to the Springfield-Branson National Airport in plenty of time, we boarded the plane, and then were told that the plane had a fuel leak. We got off the plane and had to wait a few hours for another plane to arrive to take us to Atlanta, where we had already missed our connecting flight to Munich, Germany. Once the airline agent finished rerouting us, we ended up going to Amsterdam and then to Munich and a two-hour bus trip to Passau, Germany, where we boarded the ship, the Viking Mimir. We were supposed to have most of the day in Passau, but we just made it to the ship before it left its dock!

Once on the ship we enjoyed stops and tours of Passau, Linz, Salzburg, Melk, Vienna, Bratislava, and Budapest before flying home through Paris and Atlanta eight days later. I had always wanted to see that part of Europe and to see it at Christmastime. This trip satisfied both desires. I enjoyed the Christmas markets in most towns and the hospitality given on the Viking Cruise ship. The one-hundred passengers were divided into four groups and assigned an English-speaking guide for tours. We got home a few days before Christmas. The experience of the 2015 cruise made me anxious to take another.

I hosted Dumas's college graduation dinner with his parents, grandmother, and sister. He presented me with a mentoring gift. Then, it wasn't long before he got a job as a building inspector in Branson, Missouri. He moved there for about a year, and then, because he was continuing to work with the fraternity he had joined while at MSU, he moved back to Springfield. In between leaving Branson and settling into a home in Springfield, he lived in my guest room for about a month. In the meantime, he met Paige, and they moved into a home two blocks away from where I live, and they married in October 2019. Because of our close proximity, we see each other on a regular basis.

2016–2018: Retired, Corbin Cole, Shelbydog, Miscellaneous 4

After retiring from active ministry on February 1, 2016, I was free to travel more. And that is what I did in 2017 and 2018. I left Springfield on February 25, 2017, for an eighteen-hour plane trip to Australia. After flying to Dallas-Fort Worth and from there to LAX, I boarded a Quantas flight to Melbourne. I never experienced February 26 in 2017 because we crossed the International Date Line! Being one of thirty-four other tourists, I enjoyed seeing Melbourne, Hobart, Adelaide, Uluru (Ayers Rock), Darwin, Kakadu National Park, Cairns, Great Barrier Reef, and Sydney. The group flew to most destinations and was met with a bus that took us on sightseeing trips and to the hotels where we were staying. After three weeks of seeing all of Australia except for the Western State, I joined one-half of our group to continue in New Zealand, where I saw Christchurch, Mount Cook, Queenstown, Rotorua, and Auckland. My favorite part of the trip was touring the set where Peter Jackson directed *The Lord of the Rings* trilogy and the *The Hobbit* trilogy of films. I returned home on March 26, after being gone for a month of travel. The trip was made in honor of my good priest-friend, James Reynolds; he and I had talked about taking a trip to Australia, but he died in 2008 before we could do it.

The next trip in 2017 was to San Antonia, Texas, to the Incarnate Word Mother-house, to join Sister Pauline Nugent in celebrating her sixtieth anniversary of religious profession. I was joined by Kristopher Morehead, who had accompanied me there once before and who had joined me on several trips to Colorado.

After that few-day trip, the next one was onboard another Viking River Cruise Ship. This time Corbin Cole, a former student and good friend, joined me in December. On December 19, we flew from Springfield to Atlanta, Georgia, and from there to Amsterdam, The Netherlands, where, after a few days of sightseeing, we boarded a ship headed to Basel, Switzerland, on the Rhine River.

I met Cole in the second-to-last New Testament course I taught at MSU in the fall semester of 2016. There was something about him that caught my attention the very first day he entered my classroom. I decided that I wanted to get to know this guy. As I did with all my students, I interviewed him and found out a lot about him. The most important detail at that time was that he and his family celebrated Christmas in October before his grandparents went to Texas for the winter. He would drop by my office just to hang out and talk; that was an indication to me that he was interested in a relationship with me. Thus, after having known Cole for two months, I asked him if he was interested in joining me on a trip to Europe. He stated that he was, but he wanted to discuss it with his parents. I asked him to let me know that evening as I needed to make arrangements before the ship was sold out. He called me about 9 p.m. to tell me he wanted to go, and I called Viking to get the last available cabin on the ship, the Viking Eir!

In Amsterdam, we enjoyed the many canals and the Van Gogh Museum. I enjoyed the history lesson I got from a tour of Jewish Amsterdam, occupied by the Nazis during World War II. Once onboard the ship, we traveled to Kinderdijk to see some of the remaining windmills that pump water away from the soil so that it can be cultivated. The Gothic cathedral in Cologne, Germany, was our next stop on Christmas Eve, along with a tour of the city. On Christmas day we stopped with a tour in Koblenz. Then, it was on to Heidelberg, Germany, and the Romanesque cathedral in Speyer. From there we traveled to Strasbourg, France, the Black Forest in Germany, and Colmar, France, before landing in Basel, Switzerland, for a few days. The highlight of the visits to cathedrals was the large nativity scenes erected within them. The custom is to build Jesus' Nativity to reflect the city in which they are located. Some of the depictions were spread over a large section of the cathedral. In Basel, the highlight was visiting the antiquities museum and touring the reproduction of the tomb of Seti I, Pharaoh of Egypt at the time of Moses. Cole and I spent a number of hours walking through the reproduced tomb. Finally, we flew home from Basel to Paris, from Paris to Atlanta, and from Atlanta to Springfield.

The year between when I asked Cole to join me on that trip and when it took place, we continued to get together to discuss issues that really mattered to both of us. Once a week we would get together for dinner and sharing of ideas based on classes he was taking or I was teaching or on books and articles we were reading. During that year, he was working for UPS, but the early-morning work was killing him. I kept telling him to quit, but he kept saying that he needed to work. Finally, he got an offer to serve as the Contemporary Music Director of Kingsway United Methodist Church in Springfield. With that job, he was able to quit UPS.

After the good time we had traveling together in 2017, I invited Cole to join me on a trip to Russia in 2019. He accepted, and we had over a year to wait before that trip occurred. In the meantime, we had continued our weekly dinners and discussion sessions. When not discussing something, we began to play Pente, an ancient Greek game based on getting five stones in a row on a grid. We also began working on a book together. Cole named it *Love Addict*. It consists of reflections on the use of the Greek words for love in the New Testament. After that work got started Matthew Ver Miller joined us in completing it.

Another thing Cole did in 2017 was rescue a dog from the local Shelter. Her name is Shelby. He began to bring her with him to my house for our weekly gathering. At first, I was not too sure of having a dog in the house. I grew up in a time a place where the dog lived outside. What I began to discover was how smart Shelby was. She listened attentively to my commands and obeyed. I began to buy her some bones; I didn't realize how hungry she was until I watched her eat the bones. Then, I began to buy small bags of dog food to have on hand when she came to visit. Shelby—Shelby-dog, as I renamed her—is a Labrador-Boxer mix, brindle in color with streaks of dark red on her head and legs. Because of the red, she reminded me of the burning bush Moses experienced on Mount Sinai (Horeb). All was well as long as Cole lived with three other students, and there was always someone in the apartment with her.

However, after Cole and his girlfriend moved into a studio apartment together in May 2018, Shelby did not like the small living space and the lack of human companionship. She figured out how to break the bars of her kennel and get out in order to chew on the door frame, tear up a plastic storage container, and pee on the bed. I attempted to repair the kennel using chicken wire, but I could not outsmart her. While Cole was gone on a trip with his parents in the summer of 2018, I kept Shelby. Because she liked to climb and sleep on the furniture, I would put her in the back yard, which has a chain-linked fence, while I went to school to teach, come home at lunch time to let her in the house and feed her lunch, and then put her back in the yard for part of the afternoon until I came home from teaching. This worked well until she figured out how to push the back gate open even though it was locked! That I fixed. Then, she figured out how to climb the chain-linked fence in order to get out. That I could not fix!

When Shelby got out of the back yard, she made her way to the front steps, where she crawled as close to the front door as she could get and lay down on the step. A neighbor noticed her there one day and called another neighbor, who had a key to my front porch. She let Shelby on the porch. When this was discovered, we also found out that she had done no damage, but we were not ready to leave her there all day.

Once Cole knew that he could not leave her alone in the studio apartment, he began to ask me to take care of her for a day or two. So, she began to make frequent trips to my house. At first, knowing that she knew how to climb the fence and get out, we tried tying her to a tree in the back yard. I even took a Saturday and made her a house to get into in case it rained. She absolutely hated being tied. In fact, the first time I tied her it took her about twenty seconds to back out of her harness and get lose. It wasn't even an effort for her; she knew exactly what to do! So, I tightened her collar, tied her again, and watched from the window as she went into a fit, barking, tearing up plants, and chewing on her dog house. As I watched this take place, I realized that this was not the Shelby that I had come to know and love. I decided that I could not do this to her. So, I untied her and brought her into the house and left her on the front porch. She liked it there; the front porch was to her like having her own room. Through the glass door, she could watch the cars on a busy main street only a few feet away.

Other Travels

After I realized that Shelby wanted to stay inside and watch traffic, I began to give her house privileges. This meant that as long as she stayed off the furniture, she could be alone while I ran errands. However, it wasn't long until I came home one day to find the pillows off the couch and evidence that she had been on my bed. Thus, Shelby lost her house privileges and had to stay on the front porch when I was gone. As long as I was home, she never attempted to jump on furniture. One of the more interesting facts about Shelby is how smart she is. She listens to and obeys most commands. She also displays that she has done wrong when I get home; she approaches me with her head bowed very low to the floor. I discovered that all I have to do is to tell her how disappointed I am in her. She feels so ashamed that she puts her head on the floor and she will not even look at me! Later, she approaches me to make peace. So, after a couple of weeks she regained house privileges, and she has had them ever since.

Shelbydog and I bonded. I discovered that what she needed was love. Through experiences of having anything with a long handle on it (such as a broom, mop, or rake), I noticed that she would dunk as if getting ready to be hit. I surmised that she had been beaten by her previous owner. Also, when out for walks, if we encountered workmen, she would look at their boots. She kept a distance from anyone wearing work boots. I surmised that she had been kicked. She was also scared of water hoses; someone must have sprayed her with a hose at one time. Thus, I began to work with her by loving her and showing her that she was not going to get hit, kicked, or sprayed. As her trust of me grew, my love for her blossomed. She awakened not only compassion in me for one who had suffered like she had, but she became a living sign of the divine presence.

Basically, since 2018, Shelby has come to live with me. Yes, Cole came to get her and take her home with him for a few days. Then, he would bring her back to me. She fits into my daily schedule of prayer, writing, and walking. She likes living with me, going on walks two or three times a day, eating her meals on a schedule, sleeping in the sun on the porch, interrupting me for frequent belly scratches and acknowledgement, and going to bed when she wants. Over the course of incorporating Shelbydog—her pet name—into my monastic-like schedule, I have fallen even more in love with her. As she has gotten to know my way of life, I have gotten to know her and her way of life. Our bond is strong, and I intend to keep it that way.

In 2020, Shelby's owner, Cole, and the wife he married in September 2019, moved to Florida for work. Before they left, we had a discussion about what would be best for Shelby. They agreed to leave her with me, a good decision because she does not tolerate humidity well. After they left, with her veterinarian's help, I got Shelby's upset stomachs calmed down and cured. Likewise, her allergies were arrested with a drug developed for dogs. She lives with me; her room is the front, air-conditioned porch, except for her bed which is located next to mine in my bedroom. She has become my rascal companion.

My Life of Ministry, Writing, Teaching, and Traveling

The year 2018 was designated my year of travel. While it began in December 2017, it continued well into 2018. On February 1, 2018, I flew from Springfield to Dallas-Fort Worth, and from there to Madrid, Spain. There, I enjoyed a day at the Museo Nacional Del Prado before enjoying a two-week trip through Spain and Portugal with Trafalgar. After touring Madrid, we headed by motor coach to Valencia, only to have to pull off the road at a truck stop because of snow. Our tour director told us that it snowed in Madrid for twenty minutes every five years. However, this time it snowed for two days! After about an hour, the road was opened, and we headed to Valencia to see some of that city. Then, after a stop at *Habitat-Troglodita* in Guadix, Spain, where people live in caves carved out of the mud, we headed to Granada to see the Alhambra Palace, built by the Moors but taken over by the Christians.

In Cordoba we viewed the Roman bridge and the Cathedral Mosque of Cordoba, a Moorish mosque turned into a Christian cathedral. Our next stop was Seville, where we toured the 1929 Exposition Building, the Royal Palace with its gardens, the Cathedral, and the tomb of Christopher Columbus. After Seville we stopped at Jerez to tour the Sandeman Sherry distillery, complete with samples for tasting. Onto Cadiz we traveled and then to the Algarve Region of Portugal with frequent stops to enjoy the ocean and the statues it has carved out of the rock on the seashore. On the way to Lisbon, we stopped at the Monte Negro Ranch to view Lusitano Horses and enjoy lunch in the ranch house. In Lisbon, we toured the Hieronymite Monastery, Belem Tower, Suspension Bridge, and the Monument to Portuguese Explorers.

The high point for me was a stop at Fatima, Portugal. I had been to Lourdes, France, and I had always wanted to see Fatima, one of the many places where the Blessed Virgin Mary has appeared. I enjoyed seeing the Basilica Shrine of Our Lady of Fatima, watching a procession of pilgrims, and touring the New Church that was erected a few years ago to accommodate the large number of pilgrims who go to Fatima. On the way back to Madrid, we stopped outside Avila, made famous by St. Teresa of Avila, and an over-night stay in Toledo, touring the cathedral, and seeing St. Martin Bridge. I took a side trip to Segovia from Madrid to see the Roman Aqueduct and the Alcazar, a palace used by Spanish royalty.

In Segovia, one of the group of people, with whom I was traveling, decided to accompany me after we ate lunch around the city square. I spotted a table runner that I really liked. A gypsy lady came up to me, and I asked her how much it was. She spoke no English, and at first she did not understand me. I used the word *price*, and she immediately held up her ten fingers three times, indicating that it was thirty Euros. After shaking my head no and saying that the price was too much, I began to walk away. She came after me and offered the runner to me for twenty Euros; again, I shook my head no. She continued to follow me, and offered me the runner for ten Euros. I said yes and went back to her table to pay her. I paid no attention as she put the runner in a plastic bag, tied it shut, and accepted my ten Euros. My companion observed all this as we continued to walk around the square.

Other Travels

When we got back to the meeting place on the square, my companion decided to go and investigate the round table cloth she had seen on the gypsy's table. She asked me to accompany her. She asked the price for the table cloth, and the gypsy lady told her it was forty Euros. As we walked away, she asked for thirty Euros, but my companion said no. Then, grabbing a small table runner, she asked for twenty Euros for the two pieces. My friend agreed. After paying the gypsy lady for the two pieces, my friend opened the plastic bag to discover that only the table cloth was in the bag. She returned immediately and demanded her money back.

All this should have been a clue to me, but it did not register. I had put the table runner I bought in my jacket pocket. When I got back to my hotel room, I open the bag to discover that the table runner I had was much shorter than the one I thought I had bought. While I was not looking, the gypsy lady had switched the long runner for a shorter one. I wasn't all that upset, because ten Euros was a fair price for the runner I brought home. Furthermore, it was over an hour's bus ride to Segovia from Madrid.

On May 3, I left Springfield and flew to Chicago O'Hare, from which I flew to Copenhagen, Denmark, to begin a Trafalgar trip through Denmark, Norway, and Sweden. Copenhagen is a Hans Christian Anderson city, but more it is a city containing the National Museum and the National Gallery. Both are similar to other large national museums and galleries and well worth the time I spent in each before the official tour began. Once the official trip began, I saw the Opera House, the Christianborg Palace, the famous Little Mermaid statue—commemorating one of Anderson's tales—the Fredenborg Castle outside Copenhagen where I watched the changing of the guard, and Frederiksborg Castle, which contains the museum of National History. After this, we traveled to Odense, the birthplace of Anderson. While in Odense, I took time to visit St. Canute Church, which contains the reliquaries of the almost-complete skeleton of King St. Canute and his brother, Benedict, who were martyred in 1086. From Odense, I went to Bergen, Norway, after traveling on ferries and through tunnels under fjords, where the high point was seeing the home and writing cabin of Edvard Grieg, the composer of my favorite piece of music: "Pier Gynt Suite." I also took a funicular to the top of a mountain overlooking Bergen to see the city and the harbor at the end of a fjord.

From Bergen, the tour coach took us to Voss, Flam, Sogiefjord, and Leikanger, Norway, traveling in trains, ferries, and buses so we could see waterfalls, glaciers, and snow-covered mountains. Once arriving in Gieranger and seeing more of the same, we enjoyed spring in the high country of Norway: snowy mountain tops, green, high-country trees in blossom, rushing melt-water streams, waterfalls, and blue reflective fjords. The highpoint of the stop in Lom was seeing one of the few remaining stave churches, so called because they are made totally out of wooden staves. In Oslo, Norway, we saw the Vigeland Sculpture Park; there was a lot more to see, but time was limited.

The next day was spent in travel from Oslo to Stockholm, Sweden, built on fourteen islands connected by bridges or tunnels. The coach took us to Drottningholm, the home of Sweden's royalty, from where we caught a ferry that took us on a tour of the islands forming Stockholm. We also made a stop at the Vasa Museum to tour a ship—Vasa—that had sunk in the harbor in 1628 and raised in 1961. After it was raised and repaired—98 percent of the original remaining—it was towed to an area where a museum was built around it. Even though the tour ended, I remained for a few days to explore further. I spent time in the Riddarholmskyrkan, where Swedish royalty are buried, the Stockholm Cathedral, and the museum in the Royal Palace. On May 20, after traveling for about forty-five minutes outside of Stockholm, I arrived at the airport, where I boarded a plane to Chicago, and from there back home to Springfield. Denmark—more specifically Copenhagen—reminded me of Amsterdam; Norway reminded me of southeast Alaska, and Stockholm—more specifically Sweden's rolling hills—reminded me of the Missouri Ozarks. I would have liked to have spent more time in Oslo, seeing the city, and more time in Sweden seeing more than just its capital. Nevertheless, that trip to Scandinavia brought to a close my travel plans for 2018.

2019: Conyers, Georgia; Russia; Bohemia

My travels in 2019 began with a trip to Holy Spirit Abbey in Conyers, Georgia. That May 5 through 11 trip was in response from the Cistercian (Trappist) monks there for help in renovating their abbey church. The abbot had asked me to come and spend some time with the community and to give several presentations about Catholic architecture. After having my plane delayed at the Springfield-Branson National Airport for four hours for several different things, finally we took off and landed in Atlanta, where the abbot and his driver had been waiting for me. After a stop at a restaurant for dinner, we continued the thirty miles to Conyers.

The abbot gave me a tour of the abbey church and showed me to the suite of rooms that had been set aside for me in the monastery. I was given a choir stall and an alb and invited to join the community for all its religious services and to eat at the abbot's table in the refectory. Each monk and I ate breakfast and dinner privately and in silence, but the whole community ate lunch together in silence while listening to a reading being done from a desk in the refectory. While there, I met with the liturgy committee first, then I gave two presentations to the whole community with optional round-table discussions in the afternoon. I surfaced ideas for the monks to consider while renovating their church. All this was in conjunction with the third edition of my *The Liturgical Environment: What the Documents Say* book. I enjoyed thoroughly being a monk for a week, chanting psalms for morning, midday, evening, and night prayer. Mass was celebrated in different ways, and I enjoyed that very much. When I left at the end of the week, I left the monks a note that said how much I appreciated being a part of their community.

On June 6, Cole and I left Springfield for a Viking River Cruise in Russia. After the last Viking Cruise we had enjoyed together, Viking offered free airfare for the Russian cruise. I asked Cole if he was interested in traveling together again, and he gave me the affirmative. So, I made arrangements for us to fly from Springfield to Chicago, Chicago to Frankfurt, and Frankfurt to Moscow, arriving on June 7, two days before the cruise was to begin on the Viking Helgi. We enjoyed a guided tour of the Moscow Metro System. During Soviet times, the government not only built the metro system, it also built fantastic stations underground wherever two metro lines intersected. Each station is dedicated to a different theme and decorated in a different way. Thus, we saw stations with ceilings full of mosaics, paintings, stained glass windows illuminated from behind, crystal chandeliers, and brass statues. Each of the stations is a small art gallery.

We took a tour of the Kremlin, which is a Russian word meaning *fortress*. Thus, the Kremlin is a walled mini-city with multiple towers indicating where the gates are. Inside the Kremlin we saw the building where the government meets and where the president has his office. We entered the Russian Orthodox Dormition Cathedral, where many metropolitans are entombed. The many golden domes of the church can be seen from miles around. Also, in the Kremlin is the Russian Orthodox Archangel Cathedral, in which are entombed the bodies of the grand princes and tsars from Ivan I in 1325 to Peter II in 1730. Once outside the Kremlin, we saw the famous St. Basil Cathedral, which is a museum. Each of its many domes is constructed and decorated differently presenting a pastiche of colors. Once the Soviet regime began under Lenin, many of the churches were turned into museums. In modern times, they remain museums. However, in Moscow while the recently built Russian Orthodox Cathedral of Christ the Savior still displays the famous golden onion domes, the exterior walls display brass statues depicting various events found in the Bible.

After four days in Moscow, the Viking Helgi with its almost two hundred passengers sailed to Uglich, where we toured the Church of St. Dmitry on the Blood, where Ivan I's son, Dmitry, was found dead. Our next stop was Kuzino with a tour of the Kirillo-Belozersky Monastery, which at one time housed four hundred Russian orthodox monks. The museum with its collection of icons was our destination there. With only thirty monks now, the whole complex is being renovated and turned into a tourist destination after years of neglect. In Yaroslavl, our next stop, we toured the Church of St. Elijah the Prophet and the relatively new Dormition (Assumption) Cathedral. The white exterior of the cathedral is highlighted with six golden onion domes and a huge tile icon over one portal depicting the Dormition of the Virgin Mary. Unique to this cathedral are the brass statues depicting what is often referred to as the Hebrew Bible (Old Testament) Trinity. The icon was created by Russian painter Andrei Rublev in the fifteenth century; it is considered to be his most famous work. Russian Orthodoxy prefers icons to statues; that is what makes the setting with the statues outside the Yaroslavl cathedral so interesting.

After Yaroslavl we headed to Kizhi and the open-air museum of architecture that exists there. We walked around the island touring the Transfiguration Church, homes, windmill, sauna, and fences all constructed out of wood. Our next stop was similar to Kizhi; this was Mandrogi. The village, consisting of over fifty structures, houses handicraft workshops in which masters of multiple folk crafts create and sell artworks, such as woven fabrics, pottery, embroidered items, wood-carved items, glass blown items, enamelware, etc. This was one of my favorite stops on the river cruise.

After arriving in St. Petersburg, Cole and I took a trip to the Hermitage Museum to spend a large part of the day viewing hundreds of works of art which began as Catherine the Great's collection. We also traveled to Pushkin, outside St. Petersburg, to see Catherine's Palace, which was built to rival Versailles. We walked through room after room filled with windows and walls decorated in gold. Keeping in mind that Peter the Great moved the capital of Russia from Moscow to St. Petersburg in the eighteenth century in his attempt to westernize Russia, we toured the Peter and Paul Fortress with its Sts. Peter and Paul Cathedral. Under Peter the Great's influence, the church was built to resemble Roman Catholic Churches. In it are buried the tsars from Peter the Great to the last one, Nicholas II, who with his whole family was murdered after Lenin began the Soviet Revolution. In recent years, the Russian Orthodox Church canonized Nicholas II along with his wife and five children identifying them as martyrs for the faith.

There are three high points to this fifteen-day trip to Russia. The first was traveling with Cole again. While we did a lot together, we also took time to do what interested each of us individually. We made it a point to share dinner with each other every night. The second major highlight was the concert in Moscow we attended. The musicians played only native Russian instruments and entertained us for almost two hours. Finally, the third high point was seeing Swan Lake Ballet in St. Petersburg. I had seen parts of it, but never the whole ballet. Understanding the ballet was facilitated by the excellent tour guide we had. She informed us about the original ballet and how it had been changed under Stalin because he did not like the ending. She also knew all the variations that might occur during the dancing and, thus, prepared us to appreciate the ballet even more. On June 21, we flew from St. Petersburg to Frankfurt, Frankfurt to Chicago, and Chicago to Springfield.

I had always wanted to spend more time in European Christmas Markets. So, for my final trip in 2019 I took Cost Saver's Highlights of Bohemia Tour. I left Springfield's airport on December 4 and headed to the airport in Charlotte, North Carolina, where I was supposed to catch a flight to Frankfurt, Germany. Once I got to Charlotte, I was told that the plane that had landed had hit some birds, so another plane was being brought from the hanger for the trip to Frankfurt. Some passengers had to have their seats changed because the seats on the new plane were not the same as those on the plane we were supposed to take. All this took lots of time, of course; so, by the time this was done and we began to board, we were well behind schedule for takeoff. We were an hour late arriving in Frankfurt. By the time I got off the plane, went through passport control, and got information about the hotel where the tour was organizing, got a cab, and got to the hotel, it was 9:30 a.m., December 5. After resting a while, I ate lunch in the hotel dining room, and then explored New Isenburg, the suburb of Frankfurt in which the hotel was located.

In the afternoon of December 7, the other eighteen people on this tour and I met our director, who took us to the Christmas Market in downtown Frankfurt. Because this was a weekend, the market was so crowded that all I could do was move with the crowd. I explored a few of the booths, and then called it quits by going to the agreed-upon meeting place. I was cold and ready to be picked up and brought back to the hotel.

The next morning, we headed to Berlin on the autobahn. We went through lots of farm fields and villages, listened to our tour director explain various side excursions, and finally arrived at our hotel. The next day in Berlin we saw the Reichstag Building, the Brandenburg Gate, the Holocaust Memorial, remnants of the Berlin wall, and Checkpoint Charlie. Until this trip I had never understood how Berlin was divided between the allies after World War II even though the city was located in East Germany. All of my free time was spent in the Christmas Market, then a short rest in the Hilton Hotel, the agreed-upon meeting place to catch the coach back to our hotel.

On December 10, we left Berlin and headed for Warsaw, Poland. On the way we stopped in Poznan, Poland, the ancient capital of the country. The main attraction here was the Christmas Market all around city hall. After going from booth to booth in the market, I took up a spot in front of the city hall clock, which at noon features two goats emerging and butting heads twelve times. After arriving in Warsaw, a city almost totally destroyed during WWII but since rebuilt, we toured the Holocaust Memorial, the Old Town with its Christmas Market, and the Wilanow Palace at night. Everywhere there were lavish Christmas lights all along the major streets. However, in Wilanow Palace Gardens, we found a wonderland of lights, many of which were set to change colors as classical music was heard. It was a very cold and windy evening trapesing through the gardens, but the impression it left was well worth the chill.

On December 12, we stopped in Czestochowa, Poland, to see the icon of the Black Madonna. This was another Marian shrine that I had always wanted to see. Because it was winter, there were very few people there. I was disappointed that the gift shop was not open in order to buy a souvenir, but I was pleased that I had found a small icon of the Black Madonna in Warsaw and purchased it there. On December 13, I toured the grounds of Auschwitz and Birkenau. The brick buildings of Auschwitz are filled with museums which explain what happened there until WWII came to an end. The high point of Auschwitz was seeing the cell where St. Maximillian Kolbe died. The wooden buildings of Birkenau are ruins, but the brick ones still stand as a testimony to the Nazi murders that occurred there. It took away my breath to walk through the main gate—seen in many films—and walk the length of the compound along electrified, barbed-wire fences to the ruins of the places where Jews and others were gassed and cremated in the furnaces—destroyed by the Nazis at the end of WWII—to the Holocaust Memorial dedicated to all whose lives were taken and the plaques erected by various countries pledging that this will never happen again.

The nineteen of us on this tour talked about our experiences in Auschwitz and Birkenau on the coach to Krakow. Because we were a small tour group, each of us had two seats on the coach, giving us plenty of room to stretch out and to store our carry-on luggage and packs. Upon arriving in Krakow, we toured the castle and cathedral. Krakow had been the seat of government until a king moved it to Warsaw. The cathedral houses the remains of St. Stanislaus, a martyred Polish bishop. The high point of Krakow was a trip down into the Wieliczka Salt Mines. We were underground for a few hours walking through tunnels, seeing displays, and gazing upon sculptures made out of salt by the miners. Besides small chapels created by the Catholic miners, there was a huge church complete with statues, friezes, altars, etc. in place.

After emerging from the salt mines, we traveled to Budapest, Hungary, on December 14. I had been to Budapest before in 2015. On this trip I got to walk around Heroes' Square instead of being driven around it in a coach. I got to see again Fisherman's Bastion, the Church of St. Matthias, and the Parliament building on the Danube River. Of course, Christmas markets were located all over this area.

We arrived in Vienna, Austria, on December 16. I had been there in 2015, but this time I elected to visit Schonbrunn Palace, the summer dwelling place for royalty at one time in history. Not only did I enjoy a tour of the palace's first floor and the gardens—although there wasn't much to see in the winter except the many statues living the walkways—I learned that many ordinary people now live in apartments on the other floors of the huge building. And, of course, all around outside in front of the palace was a Christmas Market!

On December 18, we made a lunch stop in Brno, Czech Republic, before arriving at the capital: Prague. This is a city I had always wanted to see, and it is a city I hope to return to one day. We toured the Charles Bridge, Prague Castle, St. Vitus Cathedral, the Old Town Square with its Christmas Market, and the Jewish Quarter. Most of my time was spent in the Christmas Market. I enjoyed lunch in an Italian restaurant on the square while watching thousands of people walk through the Christmas Market. A feature of the town hall is its clock. At noon, statues of the twelve apostles parade through small doors, below which is an astronomical calendar displaying the month, day, year, and phases of the moon.

The highlight for me of this trip was the stop we made in Rothenburg, Germany, on our way from Prague back to Frankfurt. This still-in-tact medieval town with its walls still standing and its multi-colored half-timbered houses and narrow winding streets is a Christmas Market paradise! Everywhere there were booths with merchants selling food and wares. I saw as much of Rothenburg as I had time to see. Once I and my eighteen companions re-boarded the coach, we headed to Frankfurt. Many were leaving the next day, December 21. I, however, had booked one more night in the hotel. So, I did not head home until Sunday, December 22.

I had other travels planned for 2020, but the COVID-19 (coronavirus) pandemic caused me to cancel them and remain home, where it was safe.

12

Writing

Poetry

I HAD NEVER THOUGHT of myself as a published author, until I got my first poem printed in *Probe*, a publication of St. Meinrad School of Theology, in the September 21, 1972, issue. Two more poems were published in the September 28, 1972, and the January 11, 1973, issues of *Probe*. However, all three of those poems were written under the pen name of G. O. Thomas. I had created the pen name while I was in high school. The G came from my middle name—Gerard—the O from Our Lady (Mary) to whom I had a special devotion, and the T came from Thomas, my confirmation name.

After hearing about *Voices International*, a now defunct poetry quarterly, six of my poems were accepted for publication and printed on its pages. The first in the Fall 1978 issue was titled "Amen! Colorado!"

> I heard the silence
> of the mountains!
>
> Their black faces
> spoke words of age and wisdom
> of solidarity and change
> of grace and power.

Another poem titled "Wind" appeared in the same issue. The other four poems published in *Voices International* occurred in 1982. My favorite of those four poems was dedicated to and titled "Minnie McSherry." She was the grandmother of Mike King, a former high school student of mine and a companion on several trips. Often, I had visited McSherry in her home, which she shared with her daughter (King's mother) and King. I have vivid memories of sitting in a rocking chair opposite McSherry, whom everyone referred to as "Cookie," in a bay window and talking for twenty to thirty minutes on many Saturday afternoons.

in her fall ages of color
> she gazes out her pain
> viewing the panoramic prism of life

her strength is in the fiber of years
> life runged in her rocker
> and in her cane curve

sap runs full of wisdom
> rooted with wonder at the real of all
> witness worlds some seldom know

underneath living is more
> where fall is but the passing
> to complete the stuff of life

Because of my successful publication of poetry, I continued to submit poems. In the 1979, 1980, 1981, 1982–1983 *National Poetry Anthology* I had entries accepted. *The Joplin Globe* published five of my poems from 1981 to 1986 in a section of the newspaper called "Poetry Corner." The March 25, 1983, issue of *The Mirror* contained "Feet," a poem based on the narrative in John's Gospel about Jesus washing the feet of his disciples. A publication of Missouri Southern State College (now MSS University), titled *Winged Lion*, contained three of my poems in its Spring 1983 edition. Other poems appeared in the 1983 edition of *Our Western World's Greatest Poems*, the 1988 and 1989 *World of Poetry*, and the 1989 *World Treasury of Great Poems*, Volume II. Also, *The Daily News* published four of my poems in 1986.

Articles

While I was writing and publishing poetry, I was also writing articles. My first article, written under my own byline, appeared in the February 22, 1973, issue of *Probe*. Titled "Forum: Did We Sign the Papers?" it was a very strong, four-page critique of a liturgical conference that had occurred in St. Meinrad School of Theology. The only other article I wrote for *Probe* was a discussion of "Concluding Prayers" in the October 11, 1973, issue.

It wasn't until 1981 that I would have another article published, and this one was a long letter to the editor of *The Mirror* critiquing a movie review of "Raiders of the Lost Ark." That July 31, 1981, letter was followed by another one on November 29, 1985; this one critiqued a movie review of "Agnes of God." During the summer of 1985, I left Joplin and returned to Springfield to run diocesan adult education programs. That November 29, 1985, critique was the beginning of a series of articles that would be published in *The Mirror* in 1985 and 1986, many of which dealt with films.

Writing

While I was working on those articles, in 1986 I also wrote eight sample homilies for the "Renew" program and "Martin Luther King, Jr., and the Role of the Church in Making Peace" for the first and only issue of *Namaste: Country Reflection*. The first article for which I was paid was also written in 1986. For "The Gospel Book Controversy" in the August/September issue of *Liturgy 80*, I was paid $40!

Indeed, 1986 was a watershed year for article writing. "On What Level Do You Teach?" appeared in the September 1986 issue of *Eye Opener*, a publication of the Diocesan Religious Education Office, and "Using the Bible for Prayer" was printed in the October issue of the magazine. I also had an original prayer published in the October 19, 1986, *Together*, a publication of Families for Prayer, titled "For Columbus Day." Other articles appeared in *The Mirror, Eye Opener*, and *Together* through the end of 1986.

In the December 1986 issue of *The Priest*, I had my first article published nationally and was paid $100. This three-page article, titled "Exposition of the Blessed Sacrament Revised," marks my entry into writing for *The Priest,* a career that would last for many years. It was very quickly followed by "Joseph, A Man of Integrity," in *Markings: Homiletic Reflections for December 28, 1986,* which consisted of Scripture background, application, and discussion questions for the Feast of the Holy Family. Before *Markings* would go out of business, I would write twenty-eight of these four-page reflections from 1987 to 2002.

During 1987, I continued to get articles published in *Eye Opener, Liturgy 80, The Mirror*—of which I was named editor in July—*Together*, and *The Priest*. As editor of *The Mirror*, I wrote a weekly column titled "From the Editor's Desk" for fourteen and a half years. The November 1987 issue of *The Priest* contained the first installment of "Homily Backgrounds," which covered every Sunday and Holy Day in the liturgical calendar and which I would write for six years, getting paid $150 a month! That issue also contained a three-page feature article titled "Ending and Beginning the Celebration of Eucharist." All total, I would end up writing twenty-seven articles for *The Priest*, in addition to the six years of "Homily Backgrounds," and the twelve years of monthly book review columns from 2004 to 2016.

In subsequent years, I would have an article published in *Pastoral Life, Faith and Form, Catholic Digest, Worship*, and *The Critic*, a three-part article in *Queen of All Hearts*, five articles published in *Modern Liturgy*, four articles in *U.S. Catholic*, eight articles in *Environment and Art Letter*, two articles in *Design*, and two articles in *National Bulletin on Liturgy*.

Books

Day by Day through the Easter Season

In the April 24, 1987, issue of *The Mirror*, I began an eight week series of articles on "The Way of the Resurrection." The series consisted of fifteen stations of the resurrection of Christ modeled on the Stations of the Cross. When the series was finished, I sent a copy of the manuscript to Liguori Publications to see if the editor there might be interested in reprinting them. I got a letter from Father Thomas R. Artz, CSSR, Managing Editor of Liguori, on May 14 giving me "good news and bad news." The bad news is that the publisher was not interested in the material as a pamphlet. The good news was that they liked my writing style. "This is a gift that the Holy Spirit has shared with a precious few people," stated Artz in the letter. He went on to propose a book titled *Day by Day through the Easter Season*, a series of daily reflections covering the fifty days of Easter. On May 18, 1987, I accepted Artz's proposal and answered several questions he had posed in his letter. He responded on May 26. However, since his initial interest, I had been working on the project. So, by June 3, I had the book finished and sent it to him.

Artz replied with a letter on June 9, indicating that the manuscript looked good; it was "clear, concise, creative, practical—just what Liguori likes!" He wrote that other editors in the book and pamphlet department would be asked to read the manuscript and submit critiques. If all went well, then a contract would be issued. On July 20, I got another letter from Artz indicating that the book was accepted for publication. Julie Kelemen, an associate editor, sent me comments from the editors who had critiqued the manuscript. Kelemen wrote, "I was so impressed by [the manuscript] that I felt compelled to dash this note off to you." The comment sheet contained the statements: "Best manuscript I've read since being here!" "I can't imagine anyone who could not benefit from this book or fail to find it uplifting." On July 27, 1987, two copies of the "Royalty Agreement" contract were issued. I signed and returned one on July 31.

The book was released by Liguori Publications during the winter of 1988 with a copyright date of 1987, selling at $2.95, and it stayed in print until 1996; in 1994, the price was raised to $4.95 per copy. I dedicate the book to Arthur Lee Hobbs, a friend in Joplin with whom I played tennis, went to see films, and traveled. By the time the book went out of print, almost seventeen thousand copies had been sold. Furthermore, in 1992, the book had been translated into Chinese.

History of St. Joachim Parish: 1822–1972; 1723–1973

Of course *Day by Day through the Easter Season* was not my first book, even though it was my first nationally published book. My first book was *History of St. Joachim Parish: 1822–1972; 1723–1973*, published in 1972 by Yearbook House, Kansas City, Missouri. During the summer between the end of my junior year in college and the beginning of my senior year, I researched the history of my home parish, St. Joachim, in Old Mines, Missouri, while working as a part-time secretary in the rectory. After gathering information on the parish, I edited some material and wrote some in preparation to finish the project for the parish church's one hundred fiftieth anniversary celebration and the Old Mines area's two hundred fiftieth anniversary celebration.

Writing

I was paid with an office typewriter, which I used to prepare the text for printing by Yearbook House. I finished the layout in my free time once I got back to St. Louis to finish my last year of college.

The copies of the book arrived during the summer of 1972. The 200 8.5" X 11"-page book contains an introduction and conclusion written by me, pictures of the archbishop of St. Louis and his auxiliary bishops, and the pastor and associate pastor. Then follows a brief historical sketch of the Old Mines area, titled "We Are A People With A History." Archive photos, excerpts from the parish record books, pictures of the tombstones of prominent people who once lived in Old Mines, a list of the pastors and associate pastors who served the parish, the history of the schools, a list of graduates from the schools, a list of the nuns who taught in the schools, the parish census of 1890, and ads fill the pages. Only 1,000 copies were ever printed and sold.

Following the Star

With the experience of writing two books—one yearbook and one for a national publisher—I was ready for my next book. By March 14, 1988, I had finished a manuscript titled "Coming Soon: For Advent and Christmas," which I submitted to Alba House, Staten Island, New York, in the hope of acquiring another publisher. By March 25, 1988, the acquisitions editor, Father Victor L. Viberti, SSP, acknowledged receipt of the manuscript with a promise to get back to me as soon as possible. After burying his mother in Italy and marking his golden jubilee of ordination, Viberti sent his response to me on April 8, 1988. His letter began with these words: "Yesterday the members of our editorial board reluctantly decided to return your manuscript . . . for the single reason that we have already on hand several manuscripts on the same subject." He also included a copy of his favorable review of the work, recommending to the board that it accept my book instead of several others. However, the board disagreed with him. He did state, "Being now familiar with your style and polished writing, I optimistically expect that Alba House will be soon surprised by another manuscript from your gifted pen."

So, on April 15, 1988, I submitted the manuscript to Liguori Publications, receiving a postcard acknowledging receipt of the work and a statement that I should get a response in about eight weeks. On May 11, 1988, I got a letter from Artz, Managing Editor of Liguori Publications, informing me that Liguori was interested in publishing the work for Advent 1989. Two days later I responded that that would be fine with me. The Royalty Agreement contract arrived on June 14, and I returned a signed copy of it four days later. Nothing else was done on this project until the next year.

As the editor of *The Mirror*, I had attended the Catholic Press Association meeting in late May and met Artz and discussed the publication of this book. In the course of the discussion, he brought to my attention the fact that I needed to check the dates for the various cycles of Sunday Scripture texts. After I got home from the meeting, I checked the manuscript and discovered that, indeed, the dates were wrong. So, I set about fixing them, and by May 30, 1989, I had a list of corrections in the mail to Artz. The book was published in the Fall of 1989 with the title *Following the Star: Daily Reflections for Advent and Christmas*. I dedicated the book to my godchildren: Laura Kay Pashia, my niece, and Zachary Douglas Kinler, the son of friends in Joplin, Missouri. I didn't know it then, but Kinler would become not only a good friend, but also a companion mountain climber. *Star* sold for $3.95, until 1998, when the price was raised to $5.95. For the twelve years that the book was in print, almost thirty thousand copies were sold. Like its predecessor, *Day by Day through the Easter Season*, it was translated into Chinese in 1992.

Mystagogy

Because of the encouragement received from Viberti, I set to work on a book in which I thought Alba House would have an interest. However, before I got to Alba House, I attempted Liguori Publications because it had accepted two of my books for publication. I contacted Artz on August 3, 1988, and got a response on September 26, 1988, rejecting the manuscript. Artz gave several reasons why Liguori Publications was not interested in it, such as it was too much like other Lenten and Easter products, editors thought some sections might be beyond the understanding of lay readers, RCIA (Rite of Christian Initiation of Adults) leaders may not like it, and it had uneven chapter lengths. Artz asked me to contact Liguori should I prepare other manuscripts.

On November 8, 1988, I sent the manuscript to St. Anthony Messenger Press. Lisa A. Biedenbach, Managing Editor, sent me a letter rejecting the manuscript with six negative quotations from members of the editorial staff. She suggested revising the book, but I chose to send it to Wm. C. Brown Company Publishers on October 3, 1988. Sandra J. Hirstein, Editorial Director, wrote me on November 2, 1988, that while the book was "well-developed" and "well-written," Brown was "not the most appropriate publisher for it."

The manuscript's next stop on December 12, 1988, was Sheed & Ward. Robert Heyer, Editor-in Chief, replied with a form letter on December 16, 1988—obviously after not having read the manuscript—rejecting the book. On December 23, 1988, I sent the manuscript to Twenty-Third Publications. Stephen B. Scharper, Associate Acquisitions Editor, replied on December 29, 1988, writing that he found the manuscript intriguing, and enclosed three pages of guidelines. I revised the manuscript according to the guidelines and had it in the mail on January 11, 1989. On January 14, 1989, Scharper acknowledged receipt of the manuscript and told me that he would be back in touch within the next four weeks. He did on February 17, 1989. He told me that the "editorial staff found [my] work to be an admirable attempt to help form Christians in the liturgical paschal spirituality of Lent and Easter." He added: "The content is solid, and the style careful. The use of liturgical texts is also a welcome addition." And then, he wrote, "Unfortunately, however, we also found that the work lies a bit beyond our editorial ambit at this time." So, five book publishers had rejected the book, but there still was Alba House.

I sent the manuscript to Father Anthony Chenevey, SSP, who had succeeded Viberti as Editor-in-Chief, on February 27, 1989. Sometime between then and April 19, 1989, I received an undated letter from Brother Aloysius Milella, SSP, Editorial Coordinator, informing me that Alba House was accepting the manuscript for publication, and two copies of the Agreement contract (dated April 5, 1989) were enclosed. In his letter, Milella wrote: "We are happy to be associated with this manuscript. Our Editorial Board was unanimous in believing that it will fill an important current void in assisting people who are candidates in the RCIA programs or recently baptized. Thank you, Father Boyer, for the preparation and submission of this fine manuscript." Contrast those words with the negative words in the letter of Biedenbach above!

Because the manuscript quoted from various sources, copyright permissions needed to be secured. So, in July 1989, I began writing letters to copyright owners, some of whom were more cooperative than others. For example, the Confraternity of Christian Doctrine owned the copyright to *The New American Bible*. Charles A. Bugge answered my letter by requesting a copy of the manuscript so that he could "verify the accuracy of the selections and furnish proper acknowledgment information." On August 15, 1989, I sent him a copy of the manuscript with the selections from *The New American Bible* highlighted. On October 17, 1989, he returned the manuscript with corrections to be made and a license agreement to use quotations from *The New American Bible*. It was my responsibility to forward the corrections and the contract to Alba House, which I did on October 23, 1989. The CCD would take "1% of the retail cover price on each and every copy of each edition, including imprint editions," of the book. By the time Milella signed the contract, it wasn't until November 4, 1989, that Alba House received the contract granting permission for selections to be used. Milella wrote to me, "It would have been great to have his guidelines earlier, but we shall follow instructions for correcting and re-setting the quotations already in place in the text. . . ."

The International Commission on English in the Liturgy owned the material that I was using from the *Sacramentary*. My July 22, 1989, letter to Peter C. Finn, Associate Executive Secretary, was answered on August 9, 1989. Accompanying the letter was a form to complete; the form requested that every single paragraph and prayer that would be used in the book had to be listed. On August 30, 1989, Finn sent a letter to me informing me that he had sent a contract to Alba House. The Agreement contract stipulated the wording that the copyright notice in the book should contain and that "1.5% of the retail list selling price per copy sold" be paid to ICEL. On September 7, 1989, Milella informed me that he had received the contract and signed it.

Macmillian Publishing Company granted the permission needed as did Michael Glazier, Inc. No response was ever received from Costello Publishing Co., Inc., which owned the copyright to *Vatican Council II: The Conciliar and Post-Conciliar Documents*.

My Life of Ministry, Writing, Teaching, and Traveling

Mystagogy: Liturgical Paschal Spirituality for Lent and Easter was published in 1990. My fourth book had finally made it into print after going down a very twisting road. I dedicated it to the then-bishop of the Diocese of Springfield-Cape Girardeau, John J. Leibrecht, who seemed to support my success. Later, I would determine that this was a big mistake. From 1990 to 1998, when the book went out of print, 2,305 copies were sold. What I learned from this process would affect the rest of my writing career. I learned that some Catholic copyright owners could make book writing and publishing very difficult and were out to get a piece of the royalty pie. I also learned that the best approach was to write it myself instead of quoting it. Sometimes, rewriting in my own words was the best solution to avoid paying copyright owners out of my royalties.

Breathing Deeply of God's New Life

The original manuscript was titled "Preparing Spiritually for the RCIA: Resources." It began with a letter to Lisa A. Biedenbach, Managing Editor of St. Anthony Messenger Press in Cincinnati, Ohio, on May 29, 1990. I proposed a book "to help people to prepare for the spiritual dimension of the RCIA process." I proposed exercises for each stage of the RCIA. Each exercise would be based on a six-step process consisting of a Scripture passage, a quotation from the RCIA, a reflection, a meditation question, a prayer, and a journal question. On August 6, 1990, Biedenbach replied to my query offering me a contract and requesting a completion date. I responded on August 13, 1990, thanking her for the contract and telling her that the manuscript would be finished by February 28, 1991. The eight-page "Publisher-Author Agreement" arrived on August 16, 1990. After reading it, I signed it on August 22, 1990, and returned it to Biedenbach.

In her cover letter, Biedenbach welcomed me to the St. Anthony Messenger Press family. She told me that as soon as she got back the signed copy of the agreement that I would receive a $200 advance. I had never written a book for which I received an advance, so this was something new to me! The rest of the letter gave detailed directions about photocopying pages of the sources I would quote in the manuscript. I needed to deliver the manuscript by March 1, 1991, and be prepared to complete revisions by September 1, 1991. She wanted two hard copies of the manuscript or one copy and the files saved on a floppy disk.

Because I had been working on the book while all the correspondence was taking place, I sent two hard copies of "Preparing Spiritually for the RCIA" to Biedenbach on November 7, 1990, along with the photocopied pages of anything I had quoted in the manuscript. I informed her that I had written to the Confraternity of Christian Doctrine office and ICEL to get permission to use material from sources for which they held copyrights. After getting no response from Biedenbach, I queried her on January 24, 1991, about having received the book. Finally, on January 31, 1991, I got a response from Biedenbach. However, the response was to begin a period of nitpicking about the manuscript.

For example, Biedenbach did not like the use of church words, like "sacrament, homily, catechesis." She wanted the introduction to be clear that the book was to be used to prepare for the rites of the RCIA and not for the process. "You should assume a high school reading level at the most and keep this in mind when revising," she wrote. In other words, she wanted the work dumbed-down. On and on went the critique, even stating that "you" should be used for reflections. I set to work dumbing-down and revising the manuscript to suit the "conversational tone" Biedenbach wanted. I sent two copies of the revised work, titled "Preparing Spiritually for the RCIA: Resources" on June 6, 1991, thinking that I had addresses and solved all the issues raised by Biedenbach. On July 26, 1991, Biedenbach informed me that she had received the manuscript, but had been very busy with issues at work and with family. She asked for my patience over the next few months until the book editor could get to my work. She also enclosed my second advance check for $200.

I heard nothing about the book from July 26, 1991, to May 4, 1992. Susan Harper, Book Editor for St. Anthony Messenger Press, sent me a letter on May 4, 1992, informing me that she had finished editing my manuscript; she sent me seven pages she wanted rewritten. Of course, she also suggested exactly how they should be rewritten! I did what she asked and returned them to her on May 8, 1992. On May 12, 1992, I received another letter from Harper informing me that a Father Hilarion Kistner had given the *nihil obstat*—declaring it to be free of doctrinal or moral error—to the book with sixteen pages of suggested "changes or adjustments in some areas of the text." While I wasn't told that Kistner's suggestions needed to be followed, I knew that the book would never see the light of day unless I made them. So, on May 19, 1992, those changes were made and sent to Harper. In response on June 10, 1992, I got another $200 advance.

The galleys arrived on October 27, 1992. Biedenbach asked me to proof them carefully, to mark any changes, and to return the pages with changes to her by November 13 or sooner. If I had thought that the rewriting and rewriting phases of this book were finished, I was sorely mistaken. While there were very few changes that needed to be made, someone—I presume Harper—had changed the name of some Catholic Church documents. For examples, she had changed "Rite of Christian Initiation of Adults" to "Order of Christian Initiation of Adults." Then, throughout my book referred to the RCIA as the "Order." I told Biedenbach that this was "a serious error."

Also, all the prayers had been changed. I had used the liturgical style of prayer and indicated so in the introduction of the book. This meant that that section of the introduction had to be rewritten. The prayers had gone from liturgical to personal. I called attention to material that I had not written and did not follow the RCIA, missing sections, footnotes that did not agree, and quite a few other things. What I did like was the title given to the book: *Breathing Deeply of God's New Life: Preparing Spiritually for the Sacraments of Initiation*. While the serious changes were made in the galleys, I never received a letter from Biedenbach acknowledging that Harper did not know what she was doing when editing this book.

The book was published in 1993. It was dedicated to Mary Ann Ackerson, my "second mother," the person with whom I had lived for six years of my life. While I received a notice on April 15, 1999, that the book was going out of print, I received a royalty statement on March 11, 2002, indicating that 3,300 copies had been sold from 1993 to 2002. On July 2, 2009, I received a request from Xavier Society for the Blind to transcribe the book "into Braille, large print, and/or audiotape" for its library. I granted permission on July 9, 2009, and returned the document.

Writing *Breathing Deeply of God's New Life* had been a royal pain lasting for almost three years. However, I had learned a lot about quoting copyright material and working with editors. I had also learned that some editors ought to write the books they want themselves! The editors at St. Anthony Messenger Press changed, inserted, and deleted material from manuscripts without the writer's permission. Without careful analysis, an author could end up disagreeing with what he or she wrote!

Return to the Lord

While spending almost three years getting *Breathing Deeply* into print, I had worked on a book for the Season of Lent, titled *Return to the Lord: A Lenten Journey of Daily Reflections*. I had submitted the manuscript to Liguori Publications on February 28, 1990. On April 17, 1990, I received notice from Rev. David Polek, CSSR, Editor-in-Chief, that Liguori was not interested in the work. On April 25, 1990, I sent a query to Biedenbach at St. Anthony Messenger Press investigating if there was any interest in publishing *Return to the Lord*. On May 22, 1990, I received a letter from Biedenbach that there was no interest. In the meantime, I also sent a query to Robert Heyer, Editor-in-Chief at Sheed & Ward, on May 16, 1990. He expressed an interest in a letter dated May 21, 1990, and requested a copy of the entire manuscript, which I sent to him on May 25, 1990. On July 8, 1990, he informed me that the manuscript was not suited to the current needs of Sheed & Ward. "This is no reflection on the merits of your manuscript," wrote Heyer. So, on July 15, 1990, I sent the manuscript to Milella at Alba House. Viberti informed me that the manuscript had been received on July 24, 1990, and a decision of the editorial board would be forthcoming. On September 8, 1990, Milella informed me that Alba House was pleased to accept my manuscript for publication in January 1991. An Agreement contract was enclosed; I signed the contract and returned it with a letter expressing my happiness on September 15, 1990. I also informed Milella that the day before I had sent a copy of the manuscript to Bugge to get the necessary permission to use *The New American Bible* in the work. The galleys for the book arrived on October 19, 1990; I read them and returned them to Milella on November 5, 1990.

Writing

In my letter I called Millela's attention to inconsistent editing that had been done to my manuscript. I consistently used what is known as the Oxford comma, that is, in a series of three things, I insert the second comma. Someone had taken out some of them and left others. I put them back in. I also noted that someone had changed "my third person nouns to 'we all.'" I wrote to Milella, "Now, this might be fine for the Ozarks (where I live, we refer to this as *Ozarkese*), but it is very poor grammar and sentence construction to appear in a book." I changed them to "all of us." Finally, I noted that *The New American Bible* copyright permission did not appear in the galleys. I received a letter on November 15, 1990, from Father Edmund C. Lane, SSP, Managing Editor, acknowledging receipt of the galleys, promising to make the corrections I suggested, and informing me that permission for the use of the Scripture texts had come through. On January 23, 1991, I received complimentary copies of the just published *Return to the Lord*.

It took only from July 15, 1990, to January 23, 1991, to get that book into print! I dedicated it to my double uncle and double aunt, Thomas A. and Thelma A. Boyer, my godparents. Alba House, which became St. Pauls, has kept the book in print since 1991. From then through 2012, 2,510 copies have been sold. Getting *Return to the Lord* in print taught me that it didn't have to take three years to get a manuscript into a book. It took Alba House six months!

The Liturgical Environment

Another writing project in which I had been engaged while waiting for *Breathing Deeply* to be finished was *The Liturgical Environment: What the Documents Say*. Originally titled "The Liturgical Environment: Theology and Praxis," I had written this book early in 1988. On June 1, 1988, I had sent a copy of the manuscript to Viberti at Alba House, but received a letter from Anthony Chenevey, SSP, Editor-in-Chief, on June 22, 1988, that Alba House was not in a position to undertake publication of this book. On July 1, 1988, I sent the manuscript to Paulist Press, receiving confirmation of receipt from Donald F. Brophy on July 13, 1988. Because I had received no reply, on January 22, 1989, I wrote to Brophy, asking him about the manuscript. I got a reply on February 2, 1989, from Robert M. Hamma, Editor, stating: "Your work is very well done, clear, and comprehensive. I think liturgical committees would find it very readable and quite helpful. I'm afraid, however, that it doesn't fit into our plans at this time."

On February 14, 1989, I prepared a prospectus, consisting of a summary and outline of the manuscript, and sent it to Father Michael Naughton, OSB, Director of The Liturgical Press. Naughton replied on February 17, 1989, with a strong interest in the project. He requested a copy of the entire manuscript. He promised to review it and get back to me with a decision in a few weeks. "I would enlist several readers of the manuscript—theologian, liturgist, liturgical design consultant—who will probably scrutinize the thing more than you ever wished!" he wrote. He also requested other information, which I sent to him on February 22, 1989, with the entire manuscript. Naughton acknowledged receipt of the manuscript on February 24, 1989. I waited for a response, but when none came, I wrote to him on October 9, 1989, seeking information. He replied on October 25, 1989, saying that he needed to "light a fire under" the reader to whom he had given my manuscript.

Naughton called me sometime during the first week of November to discuss the possibilities of the manuscript. On November 6, 1989, he wrote that he was enclosing a critique of the manuscript, but no critique was enclosed! He did agree that the book should stand alone, and suggested that it be called *The Liturgical Environment: What the Documents Say*. "The idea of having all the references in a single volume can be of great help to those who are planning new churches." He added: "One of the reviewers found the subject matter 'exciting.' He said it was a good collection, 'a reference tool to placate the wary.' I'm not at all sure that that was your intent, and I think the book can be a very helpful reference even if one is not wary." He suggested that the book contain photographs of successful environments. He asked me for a decision as to proceeding. In a two-page response on November 12, 1989, I explained that the book should stand alone, that I was not interested in lots of photos, but would be happy to take a few for illustration purposes, that I liked his suggestion for a title, and that I would need to revise some of the manuscript in light of liturgical publications that had been issued since the manuscript had been first written.

On November 30, 1989, Mark Twomey, Managing Editor of The Liturgical Press, sent me a publishing contract for the book. In the cover letter, he told me that the goal was to publish it in late 1990, that an editor would be working with me, use of the electronic means available then for submitting the completed manuscript, and the use of photos. Several forms were included that needed to be completed. All were completed and returned to Twomey on December 11, 1989. Twomey acknowledged receipt of the contract and other materials on December 14, 1989. He also wanted a copy of the Systel System 300 disks to see if he could get the manuscript off of the huge floppy disks in order not to have to re-enter the text of the book. On December 12, 1989, I had sent him a page of corrections that needed to be made to the paper copy of the manuscript that he had before it went to an editor. On December 19, 1989, I sent him the floppy disks with the manuscript on them and the corrections that needed to be made.

In the meantime, the manuscript had been given to a copy editor named Bette Montgomery in Woodbury, Minnesota. She contacted me on March 11, 1990, with a letter explaining some editorial issues I needed to consider, such as changing the arrangement of some of the content, inserting subheads in a few places, supplying documentation, and fixing several footnotes. My work was done by March 25, 1990, and returned to Montgomery. In her communication with me, she had included a copy of a letter sent to Twomey from Msgr. Alan F. Detsher, Associate Director of the United State Conference of Catholic Bishops' Secretariat for the Liturgy, dated February 2, 1990. Apparently, Twomey had asked Detsher to review my manuscript. He criticized the "repetition in the text, especially the material at the beginning of each chapter." He didn't like the title of chapter 4, the Chair of the Presider, and wanted it changed to Presidential Chair. He also didn't like my recommendation that ministers other than the priest and deacon did not need to wear an alb. Knowing that Detsher could derail this project, I changed the name of chapter 4 and removed all material about the alb except for mentioning that it was worn by the priest and deacon.

While all this was going on, I needed to secure the permission of many different copyright owners to quote their material in my book. If the book was to be what the ecclesial documents say, those documents needed to be quoted, but the quotes were all copyrighted. Thus, I began another tiresome journey down the copyright road. The largest block of quoted material came from books whose copyright was owned by the International Commission on English in the Liturgy. I wrote to Peter C. Finn on December 12, 1989, and he sent a contract to Naughton on January 4, 1990. I never received a copy of that contract. The next largest block of quoted material came from copyrighted works owned by the National Conference of Catholic Bishops. I wrote to the NCCB Copyright Permissions office on December 12, 1989. I got a request from Charles A. Bugge for a copy of the manuscript, which I sent to him on January 6, 1990. On January 31, 1990, Bugge send a license agreement to Twomey. In that letter, Bugge informed Twomey that Detsher wanted "to review it again before sending it on to" him. I'm sure he wanted to review it to be sure that I had made the changes he wanted. I never received a copy of the license agreement.

Other publishers of copyrighted material responded quickly to my December 12, 1989, letter. Costello Publishing Co., Inc., responded on December 16, 1989, sending me a study edition of *The Conciliar and Post-Conciliar Documents* of Vatican II with revisions and corrections of typos and a promise to get in contact with Twomey. Eleanor Bernstein, CSJ, from the Notre Dame Center for Pastoral Liturgy, replied on December 18, 1989, requesting more information, which I sent on January 6, 1990, and she granted permission on January 16, 1990. Because Paulist Press had published *The Code of Canon Law*, I wrote to Paulist on December 12, 1989, requesting permission to quote from one canon. After not getting any response, I wrote again on February 9, 1990. Kathleen Doyle, Rights and Permissions for Paulist Press, replied by sending me an undated letter she had sent to Rev. Edward Pfnausch of the Canon Law Society of America, who owned the copyright to the book. On February 14, 1990, Doyle wrote again to Pfnausch. On March 5, 1990, I wrote to Pfnausch. Finally, on March 1, 1990, Pfnausch answered my letter and granted me permission to cite canon 964 in my book.

While this was taking place, I was taking black and white photographs to be used in the book. The altar, ambo, bishop's chair, baptismal font, tabernacle, and ambry from the then-recently-renovated St. Agnes Cathedral in Springfield, Missouri, were photographed and used in the book. The paschal candle stand was in Holy Trinity Church, Springfield; the chasuble with overlaid stole was designed by and featured me wearing it; the pottery cup and plate were from my own collection; and the banner was one of my creations from St. Mary Church, Joplin, Missouri. The photographs were sent to Towmey on February 3, 1990.

On August 29, 1990, Twomey sent the galley proofs to me for my review, asking me to finish them by mid-September and forward my corrections to Montgomery, who would collate any corrections that she noted with those I sent to her. On September 6, 1990, I forwarded my corrections to Montgomery. On December 5, 1990, Twomey asked me to look over the page proofs one more time. I did and returned them to him on December 18, 1990. On March 11, 1991, ten complimentary copies of *The Liturgical Environment: What the Documents Say* arrived. I had dedicated the book to my parents—Jesse Lee and Verna Marie Boyer—and my brothers and sisters: Jane Marie Pashia, Michael Jerome Boyer, Diane Marie Maxwell, Joseph Lee Boyer, and Jeffrey Allen Boyer. On September 3, 1991, after reading the book, I notified Twomey that some text had been omitted from one page when the book had been printed. Twomey promised to fix the text if the book were reprinted.

On October 2, 1997, after having received my royalty statement from The Liturgical Press, I noticed that most of my royalties went to ICEL and the USCB for use of copyrighted material. As noted above, I had not received copies of the contracts that The Liturgical Press had entered into with either of them. In my letters to ICEL and USCB, I noted that from June 1, 1966, to June 30, 1997, a total of 465 copies of *The Liturgical Environment: What the Documents Say* had been sold by The Liturgical Press. The total royalty at ten percent of all books sold came to $315.39. After ICEL took its cut of $161.94 (51 percent), I was left with $153.45. Then the USCB took its cut of $92.54 (29 percent), which left me with a total royalty of $60.91. The contract stated that ICEL and USCB got a percent based on the list price of every book sold, no matter what The Liturgical Press sold it for. Thus, The Liturgical Press might sell a book at $3.98 even though it was listed at $9.95. This meant that ICEL and USCB got a percentage of $9.95 even though the book only sold for $3.98. It wouldn't take long for me to be in deficit royalties!

"I wish to pose this question to you," I wrote: "Do you think that this practice is moral? I know that it is legal; a contract was signed. But do you think this is moral? Do you think it justice that I get $60.91 to represent the total royalty of sales of my book for a whole year? I ended up with 20 percent of the royalties due to me." In my letter, I wrote:

> I think it is important to pay royalties for copyrighted material which I used, but the method of figuring that royalty (based on the list price of the number of books sold) is not just when it leaves me with little of what is due to me. If I were rich or getting rich from publishing Catholic books, that would be a different story. However, I am not—not at $60.91 a year. I am appealing the way the royalty is figured and suggesting that it be calculated as a percent of the total royalty owed to an author, such as 1 percent total royalty.

Writing

The last paragraph of my letter to both ICEL and NCCB stated:

> We talk a lot about justice in the Roman Catholic Church, but we seem to practice little of it. We are much better at consumerism than justice. In my estimation, this is clearly a violation of justice which needs correction. I urge you to do something about it immediately and return what is justly owed to others, including myself. This question is addressed in the U.S. Bishops' document *Economic Justice for All*. Here's a fine opportunity for us to practice what we preach.

I sent copies of both letters to Twomey, and he acknowledged receipt on October 9, 1997.

On October 22, 1998, I received a three-page response from Peter C. Finn on behalf of ICEL. He blamed The Liturgical Press for not having informed me about the contract it signed with ICEL. He argued that ICEL needed the money to fund its work. He promised to get a copy of the book from The Liturgical Press to see if, indeed, the royalty had been calculated too high. Basically, he patted me on the head and told me to go away. He did not address the issue of the morality of the practices of ICEL.

The letter I received on October 1, 1998, from Mary Elizabeth Sperry, Permissions Manager for the Publishing and Promotion Services of the USCC, consisted of only one page. She, too, foisted the problem onto The Liturgical Press, without addressing the real issue I raised. She did inform me that the CCD was reviewing its royalty structure. And that was that.

It was after reading those two responses that I promised myself that I would never quote directly from another church document of any kind in order to avoid paying royalties. It was also at this time that I came to understand that the very institution that promoted justice—the Roman Catholic Church—did not give it! I, a Roman Catholic priest, had been cheated by the very institution I served. I was determined to right this wrong.

Despite what ICEL and NCCB (USCC) did, *The Liturgical Environment: What the Documents Say* sold over 5,000 copies. However ICEL and NCCB took more than half of the royalties due to me. I had no control over the payment of royalties because both organizations required the publisher to pay them before they paid me. However, I had an idea for the second edition of the book that would eliminate ICEL and NCCB from the process.

So, during the summer of 2003, I set out to prepare a second edition of the book after conferring with Twomey at The Liturgical Press. Because the first edition had been written on a system that was not compatible with desktop personal computers, I began by entering each chapter of the text in a word processing program that could be opened by The Liturgical Press. I had retitled the book "Liturgical Catechism: A Handbook for All Involved in Worship," but when Twomey sent me a contract, he wanted to keep the same name for it in order to "capitalize on the familiarity of that title in the marketplace." I agreed with him, and returned the signed contract on December 18, 2003.

Because revised and new documents had been issued by the Catholic Church since the publication of the first edition in 1991, some material needed to be revised and new material needed to be added to the second edition. Once I had each chapter entered on my personal computer, I set about putting everything in my own words—thus, eliminating almost all quotations—and turning footnotes into references where the reader could go to find the exact notation. I also added questions for reflection and discussion to every chapter. The 188-page work was typeset by late January 2004 and in print by July 2004. The list price was $17.95, and I dedicated it to the sixteen Sisters of Charity of the Incarnate Word who had taught me during elementary and high school in St. Joachim School, Old Mines, Missouri. No permissions to use copyrighted materials needed to be obtained; no contracts needed to be signed. And all the royalties generated by the book came to me. At last, I had learned that the best way to write a book was to rewrite copyrighted material and merely reference it. ICEL and USSB were now out of the loop.

The second edition of *The Liturgical Environment: What the Documents Say* remained in print until 2014, when, due to revised and new Church documents being issued, a third edition of the book needed to be prepared. In the intervening ten years, Twomey had retired and administrative changes had taken place at what was now known as Liturgical Press. While I worked with a number of people for the third edition of the book, my contact was Barry Hudock, Publisher, Parish Market, and all correspondence was done through e-mail. Once the contract was signed on May 14, 2014, I began work on the manuscript. I promised the manuscript by September 30, 2014, in order to facilitate the publication of the book early in 2015. New chapters were added, and revisions were made based upon then-current Church documents. The 279-page third edition, dedicated to Chris Haik, a long-time friend and church decorator, was released on May 6, 2015. Just like the second edition, no copyrighted material was quoted. Thus, no permissions were required from anyone, and no percent of royalties would have to be paid to anyone except me! That book won second place in the liturgy category in the 2016 Catholic Press Association Book Awards competition!

Mary's Day

No writer sits idle while awaiting a book's publication. There is always another book in the process of being written or in the process of finding a publisher. Such is my case. While getting the first edition of *The Liturgical Environment* into print, I had been working on a manuscript titled *Mary's Day–Saturday*. Before finally being published by The Liturgical Press in 1993, this manuscript made its way from one publisher to another. After completing the manuscript in 1990, I sent it first to Liguori Publications, where it was rejected in a month because of the plethora of Marian material already on hand. Next, Alba House reviewed the manuscript during the month of July 1990, and found "that the effort came up short, in spite of the appealing format."

Writing

Milella did not see the book "cutting new ground." The next stop on the publishing train was Daughters of St. Paul, which responded within two weeks with a form rejection letter. After this, I sent a query to New City Press, New York, which responded with a three-sentence letter on October 5, 1990, stating that the manuscript "does not seem to fit one of our current series." The next stop on the publishing train was Our Sunday Visitor Press. I queried OSV on October 15, 1990, and got a response on November 9, 1990, requesting the whole manuscript, which I sent on November 14, 1990. I got no word from OSV until March 24, 1991, and that was a rejection letter. While waiting on OSV, on November 3, 1990, I queried Ave Maria Press, thinking that it would be interested in a book about Mary. However, on November 13 I was told that it would be hard to market, and, therefore, Ave Maria Press was not interested.

After finally getting a response from Our Sunday Visitor Press, I queried American Catholic Press on March 27, 1991, and got a response on April 1, 1991, stating: "You are indeed widely published. We are fortunate to have you write to us. I regret that right now we are not in a position to publish a book on meditations for Marian celebrations." The letter was signed by Father Michael Gilligan, Director. On April 6, 1991, I queried Paulist Press, which requested a copy of the manuscript on April 11, 1991. I sent it on April 16, 1991, and got a rejection letter on April 24, 1991. The only stop left on the publishing train was The Liturgical Press; on May 2, 1991, I queried Mark Twomey, who responded on May 16, 1991, with a request for the entire manuscript, which I sent to him on May 20, 1991. On July 8, 1991, he responded with a letter telling me that The Liturgical Press was pleased to offer me a contract to publish the book in late 1992 or early 1993. On August 3, 1991, I returned the signed Agreement contact to him.

Because the book used biblical quotes from *The New American Bible*, permission from the CCD needed to be gotten. I wrote to Bugge and sent him a copy of the manuscript. He never replied to me, but sent a letter to Twomey with the corrections and a contract for Twomey to funnel off some of the royalties to the CCD office. To this day, while almost all other Bibles permit the free use of five hundred verses without written permission of the copyright owner, *The New American Bible: Revised Edition* permits only five thousand words. After noting this, I quit using *The New American Bible*, and began to use the *New Revised Standard Version* in my writing.

After clearing up several questions the editor of my book had asked, I received the printer proofs on October 29, 1992, and, after reading them, returned them on November 30, 1992. Another set of page proofs arrived on January 15, 1993; I returned this final set on January 25, 1993. Twomey wrote to me on March 30, 1993, and sent me complimentary copies of *Mary's Day–Saturday: Meditations for Marian Celebrations*, which I had dedicated to Jon, Jan, Greg, Suzy, and Julie McEvoy, friends living in Springfield.

Twomey wanted to publish this book because The Liturgical Press was also publishing the *Collection of Masses of the Blessed Virgin Mary*. According to Twomey, "the volume that you propose would parallel these volumes of official texts." On March 12, 1997, Twomey wrote to me and enclosed a copy of *Compostella: Messale per la vita cristiana*, the Italian version of the *Collection of Masses of the Blessed Virgin Mary*. That volume contained a portion of my *Mary's Day–Saturday* book for which I was paid a one-time use fee of $200! The book has never been declared to be out of print, even though royalties stopped arriving many years ago. *Mary's Day–Saturday* was my eighth book. However, I was nowhere near finished with the publishing world. I still had a lot of ideas that I wanted to see put into print. And my next book was going to be about suffering in the gospels.

Why Suffer?

Even though the author of a book gives it a title when he is finished writing it, that does not mean that that is the title it will have when it is finally printed. Such is the case with *Why Suffer? The Answer of Jesus*. This book was published in 1994 by the Pastoral Press, Washington, DC, even though no date appears on the copyright page! I have no idea why no copyright date was placed in the book; it is probably an oversight by an editor.

This book began as "Suffering—Powerful Powerlessness: A Guide through the Paschal Mystery." On November 11, 1991, I sent a query to Mark Twomey at The Liturgical Press; he expressed an interest on December 4, 1991. I sent the manuscript to him on December 9, 1991, and he replied on March 10, 1992, with a rejection letter. On March 14, 1992, I sent the manuscript to Milella at Alba House. Milella replied on July 27, 1992, stating "that we do not find the text suited to our current publishing schedule."

After letting the manuscript sit on my desk through the summer of 1992, I queried St. Anthony Messenger Press on October 26, 1992, received a response wanting a hard copy on November 2, 1992, sent it on November 27, 1992, inquired about it on February 18, 1993, and got a rejection letter on March 18, 1993. After waiting for months for a response, I decided to query several different publishers simultaneously. So, on March 27, 1993, I sent inquiry letters to HarperSanFrancisco, The Thomas More Association, Sheed & Ward, Paulist Press, and Ave Maria Press. HarperSanFrancisco replied on June 11, 1993, stating "that this is not a project we could publish with success." The Thomas More Association never replied. Sheed & Ward requested a copy of the manuscript on March 29, 1993, and I sent it on April 5, 1993, and received a rejection letter on May 13, 1993. Donald F. Brophy, Managing Editor of Paulist Press, responded on April 7, 1993, with the following: "The development sounds interesting, but I'm afraid we have several books on the topic of suffering at the present time and would not be able to consider another." Ave Maria Press answered with a telephone call on April 8, 1993, stating that it was not interested in the work.

Not being a person who is easily derailed, I sat down on May 15, 1993, and wrote another set of query letters. These went to Thomas Nelson Publishers, Abbey Press, The

Crossroad/Continuum Publishing Group, Orbis Books, ACTA Publications, Catholic Book Publishing Corporation, and The Pastoral Press. Thomas Nelson replied on May 18, 1993, indicating that my proposal would be reviewed on "three areas," namely "the nature of the material, . . . the author's credentials, . . . and the author's writing ability." On June 30, 1993, I received a letter from Mark Roberts, Editor, Biblical & Religious Reference; he wanted to review the book, which I sent to him on July 12, 1993. He acknowledged receipt on July 19, 1993. I wrote to him on February 4, 1994, requesting the return of my materials because The Pastoral Press had accepted the manuscript for publication. He returned my materials on February 24, 1994.

Abbey Press never responded to my query letter. Crossroad responded on June 18, 1993, requesting a copy of the manuscript, which I sent on July 6, 1993, and received a rejection letter on August 2, 1993. Orbis Books requested a copy of the manuscript on May 19, 1993, which I sent on May 24, 1993, and I received the following response from Robert Ellsberg, Editor in Chief, on July 13, 1994: "This is really a very fine treatment of an important theme, and your writing is clear and effective. Unfortunately, we have concluded that this would not really be quite right for our specialized program." ACTA responded on May 18, 1993, requesting a hard copy of the manuscript, which I sent on May 24, 1993, and got a response from Gregory F. Augustine Pierce on June 10, 1993, stating that my manuscript was "excellent work, but I'm sorry to report that it does not fit our publishing plans for the foreseeable future." He added, "I hope that we will be able to meet when I am in Springfield this August." One door closed with ACTA, but another door opened! Catholic Book Publishing Co. responded on June 14, 1993, expressing no interest in the manuscript. However, as indicated above, Virgil C. Funk of Pastoral Press responded on June 4, 1993, writing, "of course we are interested in seeing a copy of your manuscript." I sent it on July 6, 1993, and received a reply from Lawrence Johnson, Director of The Pastoral Press, on September 1, 1993, stating: "We would be happy to publish it if you are willing to replace the last chapter with a short chapter summing up, as it were, the New Testament message in regard to suffering." On September 8, 1993, I wrote to Johnson, indicating that I was agreeable to rewriting the last chapter and getting it to him by the end of September. It was in the mail on September 17, 1993.

On September 23, 1993, Johnson acknowledged that the manuscript and floppy disk had arrived in Washington, DC. He enclosed a copy of The Pastoral Press's "standard publishing agreement." He wrote: "Our usual procedure is to issue the agreement once the manuscript is edited and copy is sent back to the author for any corrections before typesetting is done. However, if you prefer to have an agreement earlier than this, there is no problem. Just let me know." He also stated that any royalties requested by USCC would be paid out of the royalty that would be paid me. He finished by discussing the title for the book, writing, "The challenge with your book will be to begin the title with positive words—words that contain relatively few syllables—words that can be easily remembered." On September 29, 1993, I wrote to Johnson explaining that

I was content to follow the usual process for getting the book in print, that I understood the royalty issue, and that I was open to the possibility of another title for the book.

In the meantime, on September 17, 1993, I had written to Bugge to request permission to use quotations from *The New American Bible*. After I rewrote the last chapter, I had changed the title to "Suffering—Powerful Powerlessness: A Guide through the New Testament." I sent Bugge a copy of the manuscript, knowing from previous experiences that he would want it. And I asked him to forward it to Johnson at The Pastoral Press when he was finished with it. I received a letter from Richard J. Nare, who had succeeded Bugge. Nare informed me that he had changed the procedures for getting permission to use the biblical translation and needed more information. I responded with what he needed on November 26, 1993. I also wrote to Johnson, informing him what Nare wanted to know. Other than providing some marketing information for the book, I did not hear from Johnson again until March 9, 1994, when he sent me the publishing agreement for the book. He informed me that he was sending the necessary pages to USCC in the hopes that my use of *The New American Bible* would fall under fair use provision. On March 16, 1994, I returned the proof pages that Johnson had sent me, noting the corrections that needed to be made. In that letter I also recommended that "we use the NRSV—Catholic Edition translation—since it grants free use of five hundred verses on the back of the title page. When I wrote the book on suffering, the NRSV-Catholic Edition did not yet exist.

In my letter to Johnson, I also stated:

> Furthermore (and I write this in all honesty and sincerity), I have never worked with a publisher who has kept me so informed before. I have books that have been published by four publishers, but not a one has taken as much time to keep me involved and informed of the publishing process as The Pastoral Press has. That is a feather in your cap! I want to "Thank You" and the rest of the staff at The Pastoral Press for your help and work in getting this book—and I hope other books—into print. Most likely, it is the smallness of your staff which enables you to be so concerned about and with the author.

On May 1, 1994, Johnson informed me that the book would be titled *Why Suffer? The Answer of Jesus*. I heard no more from him until December 1, 1994, when he told me that the book was at the printer, that he had taken my advice and changed the biblical translation from *The New American Bible* to *The New Revised Standard Version*, and that ten complimentary copies of the book would be arriving shortly. He also notified me that The Pastoral Press was "in the midst of a reorganization," but he did not specify what that meant. On December 9, 1984, I wrote to Johnson asking him what that meant. He had two other manuscripts that I had written, and I didn't want those to get held up for years in reorganization proceedings.

On February 1, 1995, Virgil Funk, President of the National Association of Pastoral Musicians, wrote to me "to inform [me] that the assets of the Pastoral Press which govern 'my' royalties have been sold, effective February 1, 1995." He explained that for the past two years the NAPM had underwritten the Pastoral Press for more than $200,000, and that could not continue. The Pastoral Press had been sold to Trinity Music, Inc., and moved to Beltsville, Maryland. While Johnson was staying with the Pastoral Press, Mindie Santi was the new owner; thus, full responsibility for inventory, rights, and royalties to my book had been signed over to her. On October 4, 1995, I received a letter from Santi stating that the Pastoral Press was undergoing a cash flow problem, and royalties could not be paid for January-June 1995. On April 8, 1996, Santi wrote again, sending royalty statements for all of 1995, but no check. She explained that while things were looking up, the Pastoral Press still had a cash flow problem. On July 7, 1998, Santi wrote a letter informing me that "all assets pertaining to The Pastoral Press [were] transferred to Oregon Catholic Press" as of July 8, 1998. If any royalties were owed, they were paid. Honestly, I had no idea and cannot tell from the statement form if I was ever paid any royalties from Santi; the statement form is so complicated that it is impossible to tell! Thus, as far as I can tell, before The Pastoral Press was sold to Santi, I was paid seventy-eight dollars in royalties. I am unsure if she paid me anything.

On July 8, 1998, John J. Limb, Publisher of Oregon Catholic Press, informed me that OCP had acquired all the products and assets of the Pastoral Press. On August 13, 1999, Lynn Heringer, Contract Administrator for Oregon Catholic Press, sent a royalty statement covering July 1998 through June 1999. She wrote, "If a royalty payment is due, it will be included with this statement; however, if the amount earned in a particular quarter is less than twenty-five dollars, it will be held until the payment due reaches such amount." I received no check. Since 1998 when OCP bought the Pastoral Press, I think I received two royalty checks amounting to a little over $50! It took from 1991 to 1994 to get this book in print. Then, The Pastoral Press was sold twice. While Santi was enthusiastic about getting it on its feet, she did not achieve her goal. Once OCP bought it, most of its merchandise was lost in the OCP focus on worship aids. I had dedicated the book to my then-friend, Father Sylvester Schoening, who had experienced repeatedly the powerful powerlessness of suffering. The fate of the book was to parallel the fate of our friendship. In 2017, after writing letters to OCP and getting no response, I spent a lot of time on the phone getting to someone who could tell me the fate of the book. It was declared to be out of print.

Entertaining Angels

If the reader thinks that getting *Why Suffer?* in print took a lot of energy, getting *A Month-by-Month Guide to Entertaining Angels* in print took even more effort. The 1980s and early 1990s witnessed an angel craze. Many books had been written on angels; angel figurines could be found everywhere. As I wrote on May 17, 1993, to Twomey at The Liturgical Press, the topic of angels "has arisen in the secular world and seems to be doing well in terms of the book market. Since I haven't seen anything on the Catholic market yet, I thought it was a topic worth exploring." In 1992 and early 1993, I had been researching and writing my own book on angels. Twomey requested a copy of the manuscript, but declined publishing it on September 30, 1993. In the meantime, I had written to Servant Publication on July 17, 1993, but Servant informed me on August 27, 1993, that it was not interested in the book.

As I had done with *Why Suffer?* instead of waiting months for a response from a publisher, I decided to send three query letters on July 19, 1993, one each to Orbis Books, Sheed & Ward, and Paulist Press. Orbis informed me on September 14, 1993, that it was not interested in the book, likewise Sheed & Ward on July 27, 1993, and Paulist on July 21, 1993. Paulist's Managing Editor Brophy wrote: "The topic interests us, but we had in mind a different kind of book on angels and have even talked to some people about writing it." On August 14, 1993, I sat down and wrote four more query letters. Saint Bede's Publications regretted to inform me that it was "unable to consider it for publication" on September 23, 1993. In a form, undated letter Lion Publishing checked the box: "It does not fit Lion's publishing plans." On August 24, 1993, David J. McGonagle, director of The Catholic University of American Press, wrote, "[T]he topic is just not right for our list." And the undated form letter from Beacon Press informed me that it would not be pursuing the project for publication "as it is too far afield from [its] current list to enable [it] to publish it successfully."

After writing to Blue Dolphin Publishing on August 24, 1993, I got a form letter response dated November 22, 1993, stating that the book did not fit into its publishing plans. On August 30, 1993, I wrote to Joseph Fessio at Ignatius Press in San Francisco, California. He called and requested a copy of the manuscript, which I sent to him on September 7, 1993. He informed me on September 24, 1993, through Mary Beth Bonacci, Project Manager, that he liked the book, but Ignatius Press was not able to publish it. I was determined to get this book in print. So, during the month of October 1993, I wrote to fifteen publishers attempting to get at least one interested in publishing the work. In October and November I received "not interested" letters from Oxford University Press, Doubleday, Peter Li Education Group, Religious Education Press, William H. Sadlier, Inc., and University of Notre Dame Press. The following didn't even reply to my query: Augsburg Fortress, Georgetown University Press, Fordham University Press, and Trinity Communications. The letters to Trinity Communications and New City Press were returned to me unopened!

However, out of my October 1993 queries, four publishers had requested that I send a hard copy of the manuscript. On October 29, 1993, I sent it to Christian Classics; John J. McHale responded on January 17, 1994, writing that "while the work seems to be very comprehensive, we feel that in the final analysis a heavy amount of editorial work would be necessary to make the material publishable in book form." Crossroad, too, requested a copy of the manuscript on October 20, 1993. I wrote to Crossroad on August 22, 1994, after having heard nothing for almost a year, requesting an update. I got a letter on September 12, 1994, informing me that Crossroad was not interested in the work. In my August 22, 1994, letter I had requested the return of the manuscript. On February 6, 1995, Michael Leach, Publisher, wrote: "A thousand apologies. Someone found your manuscript on top of a file cabinet. I return it with a red face." St. Paul Books & Media had requested a copy of the manuscript, but no answer was ever given to me about it. After receiving a telephone call from Dimension Books, I sent a copy of the manuscript to Thomas P. Coffey, President, on October 25, 1993. He responded with a hand-written note on December 13, 1993: "Thank you for the benefit I derived from reading your book. It is an excellent work. After some careful study of the market for it through our resources, however, we decided we could not distribute a sufficient number to please you or cover our costs." Thus, while some publishers liked the work, I could not find one to get it into print.

During most of 1994 I put the manuscript away and told myself that it would probably not ever be published. However, I had an idea after that to try one more time. I took the lengthy survey of angelology from the beginning of the book and turned it into a brief introduction and brief survey of angelology. I sent it to Pierce at ACTA Publications. He signed and sent me a contract to publish it on March 30, 1995. The book was published later that year. Pierce even got John Shea to write a foreword for it. I dedicate it to "Father James L. Reynolds, friend, messenger, fellow traveler, 'angel' in disguise." From when it was published to the end of 1995, 3,686 copies were sold. While it remained in print to 2001, another 742 copies were sold. Such is the tale of my tenth book.

Male Spirituality

Because of the great interest in male spirituality in the last decade of the twentieth century, I decided to write my eleventh book based on biblical men. Originally titled "Reflections for Men Only: Male Spirituality," I pitched the idea to Lisa Biedenbach, Managing Editor of St. Anthony Messenger Press, on April 17, 1992. She replied on June 3, 1992, expressing interest in the work. "Several editors wondered if you explore fatherhood and 'husbandhood' in the reflections," she wrote. "They are concerned that the book may reflect too much of a celibate male's thinking and experience and not enough of fathers' and spouses'." On June 25, 1992, while on sabbatical in Big Lake, Alaska, I wrote to Biedenbach, informing her that I had not begun work on the book yet. I also asked her for some minimal assurance of publication before I began work on it. In her reply of July 17, 1992, she asked me to send some samples of what I was proposing. Because I was on sabbatical, I did not get to work on the manuscript until February 1, 1993, when I sent the samples Biedenbach requested. On February 9, 1993, she wrote to me that St. Anthony Messenger Press had decided against publishing it because it would compete with another male spirituality book that SAMP had already published.

So, with a completed manuscript on hand, I wrote to Ave Maria Press on February 18, 1993. Frank J. Cunningham, Director of Publishing, requested a hard copy from me on February 27, 1993, which I sent on March 8, 1993, and which he declined on April 8, 1993, stating that he did not believe that AMP "could reach a large enough market with it to justify the risks of publication." I also wrote to Paulist Press on February 18, 1993, got a letter requesting a copy of the manuscript on February 22, 1993, sent it on February 26, 1993, and got an undated reply shortly thereafter praising some aspects of the book, but declining an interest in publishing it.

On February 18, 1993, I also wrote to Twomey at The Liturgical Press. Twomey requested a copy of the manuscript on March 12, 1993; I sent it to him on March 23, 1993. On June 28, 1993, Twomey wrote to me that the manuscript was still in a state of being reviewed. On August 6, 1993, he got back to me with an offer of publication if I was agreeable to making some revisions. He stated that the editorial committee wanted the book to be addressed to women readers, too, "indicating that both feminine and male aspects make up the spirituality of a person of either gender." He asked me to work through the manuscript and make it more inclusive. He also told me that it needed a new title. Once I made the revisions, he would issue me a contract. On August 30, 1993, I replied that I would make the revisions and get the new manuscript to him by Christmas.

I had the revisions done by September 22, 1993, when I sent the manuscript to Twomey. I had retitled it "Reflections about Men: Male Spirituality," but indicated that I was open to other possible titles. I also informed Twomey that I had sent a copy of the manuscript to Bugge in order to get permission to use *The New American Bible* translation for Scripture quotations. On September 30, 1993, Twomey sent me the standard agreement contract, which I signed and returned to him on October 11, 1993.

I had written to Bugge on September 22, 1993, following his usual process for getting permission to use selections from *The New American Bible*. Nare, who had taken over Bugge's position, replied, requesting more information that Twomey could give. I received the page proofs for the book on November 3, 1995, along with notification of the title: *Biblical Reflections on Male Spirituality*. I returned those on November 15, 1995, with corrections. In January 4, 1996, another set of page proofs arrived, and those were returned on January 12, 1996. The book was published on April 10, 1996. It was dedicated to Stephen Witek, a man-friend on a journey. I had met Witek while I was on sabbatical in Alaska in 1992. The first year 847 copies were sold. Out of the $496.42 royalty, CCD took $160.20. The use of *The New American Bible* was over. Other Bibles were granting free use of five hundred verses without written permission, and I was going to use the *New Revised Standard Version* in future books.

Writing

"Seeking Grace with Every Step": The Spirituality of John Denver

While I was on sabbatical in 1992, I worked on a book about John Denver. Before heading to Alaska, I had made cassette tapes of all Denver's vinyl records so that I could listen to the tapes and transcribe the lyrics of songs that were not printed on record sleeves. Those sleeves that had the lyrics printed on them I copied so that I would not have to take the records with me. Once I had all the songs that Denver had written on paper before me, I began to categorize the images he employed. As I examined the stacks of paper I had created, seven major themes had emerged, and they would become the chapters in my book.

After finishing the rough draft of the book, I wrote a letter to Denver on July 8, 1992, after getting an Aspen post office box number from The Windstar Foundation—an environmental non-profit organization founded by Denver—in 1990. After explaining what I was doing in the book, I asked Denver for an interview anytime between September 17 and October 17, when I would be in Colorado. I told him where I would be and offered to take him hiking. I got no response to that letter. So, on October 22, 1992, I wrote another letter, again requesting an interview, indicating that I was willing to fly to Aspen in order to get it. I got no response to that letter.

After completing the sabbatical, I returned to Springfield and polished the chapters of the book, which I had titled "'Seeking Grace with Every Step': The Ecological Spirituality of John Denver." In early 1993, I began to write to publishers in an attempt to get the book in print. Maybe I was naive, but I didn't think that it would be that hard to find a publisher for a book about a musical star like Denver. From March 1993 through the end of 1994, I wrote to forty-three different book publishers, most of whom had no interest in the book and some of whom did not even bother to answer my query! Some replied with form letters; some praised the manuscript idea; but no one was interested in publishing it except Meriwether Publishing in Colorado Springs, Colorado. Arthur L. Zapel, Executive Editor, answered my query letter of September 20, 1993, on September 23, 1993, asking if I had "clearance and a written release from John Denver or the copyright holder of the lyrics and music [that] would have to be reprinted...." I replied on September 29, 1993, telling Zapel that I had written to Cherry Lane Music Co., Inc., and requested information concerning the use of lyrics to Denver's songs in my book. I never received a response to the letter I sent to Zapel.

However, I did receive another response to my September 20, 1993, letter to Distinctive Publishing Corporation in Plantation, Florida. In an undated form letter, Charles Pierson, Editorial Assistant, expressed an interest in the manuscript and enclosed a set of manuscript guidelines. After implementing the guidelines, I sent the manuscript on a floppy disk to Pierson on October 13, 1993, only to get another form letter dated October 15, 1993, informing me that Distinctive Publishing Corp. no longer accepted manuscripts on disks; Pierson wanted a paper copy. On October 28, 1993, I sent one to him. On December 28, 1993, I received a letter from Alan

Erdlee, Publisher, informing me that the editors had made a careful analysis of my work. "Although your work does not fit our needs in our traditional purchase plan," wrote Erdlee, "there are alternative programs for which we should like to consider it." He referred to a brochure which outlined "the Partnership In Publishing program and the Author Pre-Purchase program." After thinking about Erdlee's proposals, I wrote to him on January 8, 1994, requesting more and specific information on both programs. After getting no response, I wrote to him again on February 4, 1994, and again on October 21, 1994. I did not receive a response to any one of my three letters. So, by the end of 1994, two years after having finished the book, I still did not have a publisher for it. However, Erdlee had planted the seed of an idea that would germinate throughout 1995 while I worked on other writing projects and the folder with the John Denver manuscript sat at the back of my file cabinet.

On September 29, 1993, I had written to Cherry Lane Music Co., Inc., requesting permission to use some of the lyrics of some of John Denver's songs in my book. I included a complete list of Denver's albums and the songs from which I wanted to quote. After getting no response, I wrote again on February 4, 1994. After getting a phone call requesting a list of the songs from which I wanted permission to quote, I sent the same list I had send before to Paula Becker on April 21, 1994. I got a response on June 7, 1994, from Paula Becker, Rights and Permissions. She wrote: "Fee for such use will be determined pending negotiations between us and your publisher. Please let us know when you have acquired a publisher so that we might know more particulars such as number of copies to be printed, retail selling price, territory of distribution, and date of first publication." Because I did not have a publisher, I could not answer her letter.

On April 25, 1996, after I had decided to publish the book myself (see below for that part of the story), I wrote to Becker again, informing her that I was having five hundred copies of the book printed, that copies would be given away as gifts, and that some copies would be sold for $12.95. I expressed my hope to hear from her soon so that I could finish negotiations for getting the book in print. Of course, no response came. So, I wrote again on June 10, 1996, only to discover that Colin Jones had taken over Becker's responsibilities at Cherry Lane. So, on June 13, 1996, I answered the questions he asked in a FAX of June 12, 1996, also sending copies of the letters exchanged between Becker and me. On June 19, 1996, I received two copies of the license with instructions to sign both copies and send one back for signatures there, then one would be returned to me. My copy of the license finally arrived on November 25, 1996, from Victoria Mifsud, who had taken over Jones's position. I could not wait forever to move on with this project.

After doing some research on book printers, I had found Rose Printing Company in Tallahassee, Florida, and, in March 1996, requested an estimate for printing what the company called short-run books. After deciding on specifics in terms of the number of books to be printed, the size of the book, the use of color, etc., I received a "Quotation" on April 19, 1996. After another telephone call to Rose Printing negotiating a contract, I signed the contract and returned it on May 19, 1996, authorizing Rose Printing to print and bind five hundred copies of the manuscript. In between April 19, 1996, and May 19, 1996, I had set about typesetting, that is, making the manuscript camera ready, and designing a four-color cover. Everything necessary for the production of the book was included with my May 19, 1996, letter.

In early June the proof pages arrived for any final corrections. On June 20, 1996, I informed Rose Printing to proceed with production. I received two copies of the printed book in early August, and replied with directions where to ship the rest of the books. By the end of August the books had arrived and were stored in my garage. The cost for printing 594 copies of what was now titled *"Seeking Grace with Every Step": The Spirituality of John Denver* was $2,928.73, including shipping and delivery. I published the book under the name of a company I created, namely, Leavenhouse Publications. I chose the word *Leavenhouse* because in the ancient world leaven was considered to be corrupt; ancient people did not understand how leaven—what we today know as yeast—worked. So, for the holiest of celebrations, like Passover, unleavened bread had to be used. The word *house* in the title referred to my home. Thus, I hoped that the words of the book that was written, polished, and published from my home would corrupt its readers with new information!

The book was copyrighted 1996 and dedicated "to all my friends in Colorado, both the living and the deceased, especially the Cluffs, the Farmers, the Heckers, the Hoffmans, the Kosslers, the Lunds, the Odoms, the Raabes, the Tembrocks, the Thomases, the Tullios, and the Vanderpools. Every book was signed and numbered by me. After giving away copies of the book for Christmas 1996 I sold copies in the local Catholic bookstore and through mail order until I was contacted through e-mail by an Internet Bookseller in Atlanta, Georgia, who sold all I had on hand through his website. Because only 594 copies were in print, by 2015 copies of the book were being resold for $19.95, $300, and $900 a copy around the world.

By the time Cherry Lane Music had returned a copy of the contract I had signed on June 19, 1996, on November 25, 1996, the book was already in print! According to the contract, I needed to send two complimentary copies of the book to Cherry Lane; I did that on December 1, 1996. Later, I sent two checks in the amount of $485.62 to cover the cost of using the copyrighted lyrics. Thus, ends the tale of publishing my twelfth book.

Home is a Holy Place

Book thirteen, originally titled *How to Pray in Your Home: The ABCs of Domestic Spirituality—An ABeCeDarian of Reflections*, began circulating from one publisher to the next on April 14, 1992. From then until November 15, 1993, I sent it to fifteen different publishers, each of whom rejected it. Included in the list were some of the publishers of my previous books: St. Anthony Messenger Press, Liguori Publications,

The Liturgical Press, and Alba House. My last effort was directed at ACTA Publications in Chicago. I had met the editor, Pierce, at a workshop he conducted in Springfield in August 1993, as part of a larger pastoral gathering. We talked about the types of books in which he had an interest. So, on September 29, 1993, I sent a query letter about "How to Pray in Your Home" to Pierce and got a response on November 3, 1993, requesting a hard copy of the manuscript, which I sent to him on November 15, 1993. In a telephone conversation that followed, I had informed him that I had used *The New American Bible* translation, but with the issuance of *The New Revised Standard Version Bible: Catholic Edition* and the free use of five hundred verses with no copyright permission required I was willing to remove the NAB and replace it with NRSV. In an Agreement contract dated January 21, 1994, with ACTA, the book had found a home. I returned the signed contract on January 27, 1994, and set to work changing the biblical quotations. The revised manuscript was finished and sent to Pierce on February 11, 1994. It was scheduled to be published in 1997.

In November of 1996, the proof pages of the book arrived. The new title was *Home Is a Holy Place: Reflections, Prayers, and Meditations Inspired by the Ordinary*. I corrected the proof pages and returned them to Pierce on December 6, 1996. He had heavily edited the manuscript, especially the introduction because he had changed the title. Almost all the entries in the book had been shortened. However, I wanted the book in print, and ACTA was about to accomplish that goal. So, in 1997, *Home Is a Holy Place* was published. During the next five years almost 3,000 copies were sold. After that sales diminished to an average of about 30 copies a year. In 2014, at the National Association of Catholic Family Life Ministers conference in Dayton, Ohio, the last of the copies were sold, but the demand for more was so great that Pierce designed a new cover for the book and reprinted it the same year. In addition, the book was translated into Italian by Alessandro Frigerio in 2000 and published by Piemme as *La Casa e un Luogo Santo: Esercizi di Meditazione Domestica*. In 2001, it was translated into Spanish by Jose Lopez Ballester and published by Narcea as *Mi Casa, el Primer Lugar de Oracion*. The book was dedicated to "Sarah Osia, my great-grandmother, who taught me to find God in the simple things of life." I dedicated it to her because the first reflection in the book on "Apron" reminded me of her.

Day by Ordinary Day

Now here begins a tale of woe that develops into a tale of happiness and back to a tale of woe. My books fourteen, fifteen, and sixteen, titled, respectively, *Day by Ordinary Day with Mark*, *Day by Ordinary Day with Matthew*, and *Day by Ordinary Day with Luke*, were born during 1989, and rejected in January 1990 by Liguori Publications and Ave Maria Press. After this, I queried Milella at Alba House on January 30, 1990. He requested the manuscripts for all three volumes on February 10, 1990, and I sent them to him on February 15, 1990. In a letter dated February 21, 1990, he acknowledged receipt of the three manuscripts. On April 9, 1990, he sent me an acceptance letter of all three manuscripts, writing, "High on substance and timeliness, most of all scriptural in a teaching and qualitative degree, this threefold set earned high marks from all of us on the staff." He enclosed three contracts, one for each book, to be signed and returned. "We're delighted to be the publishers of this trilogy," he wrote. I signed the contracts and returned them on April 16, 1990. In his letter acknowledging receipt of the contracts, dated April 23, 1990, he told me that he expected the first of the volumes to "see the light of print sometime next Spring, possibly earlier." That meant the first volume would be published in 1991.

Because I had used *The New American Bible* translation, Bugge needed manuscripts and contracts to be signed by Alba House. I had been down this road before and knew the steps to take. On May 1, 1990, I printed all three volumes of manuscripts and sent them to Bugge, who contacted me on June 7, 1990, stating, "I wish to commend you on the accurate use of the scripture selections. I found very few corrections to be made." He added, "I enjoyed reviewing the manuscripts; the content was easy to read, very practical and yet challenging. I think the books should do well." On the same day, he sent the license agreements to Alba House. I thought that the hardest hurdle to jump over was accomplished.

After inquiring in February 1991 about the publication of the first of the manuscripts, I got a reply dated March 21, 1991, from Milella, who wrote: "Both Father Ed Lane and Brother Frank Sadowski of our staff believe there are compelling reasons for issuing *Day by Ordinary Day with Matthew, Mark, Luke* as a compact single volume. Toward this end, they are working on areas of the manuscript where abridgement would benefit content flow, and tighten the overall text. We feel that a single volume edition would be more attractive to the buyer and a more viable presentation." He added: "You will have the chance to review the edited version of your trilogy when the galley proofs are relayed to you. We mean to work with you in tuning the continuous copy of this connected text."

After having heard nothing from Alba House for the rest of 1991 or 1992, on February 18, 1993, I wrote to Milella "to inquire as to the status of the publication" of my trilogy. After having gotten no response, I wrote again on March 23, 1994, and again received no response. I wrote on September 5, 1995, again. By now I was upset. I wrote: "We talk and write a lot about justice in Catholicism. Indeed, I have noted in Alba House's catalogues that the Society of St. Paul has published a number of books on the topic. However, we seem to be slow in practicing it. I think that after five years that I deserve some explanation or some statement as to what the status is of my manuscripts. Another publisher would have had them in print by now." I reminded him that I had three signed contracts from Alba House. Again, no response was made to my letter.

On January 8, 1996, I received a letter from Edmund C. Lane, SSP, announcing the royalties to be paid on my two previously published titles by Alba House. On January

13, I wrote to Lane, explaining that "for five years I have written to Brother Aloysius Milella about contracts I signed with Alba House in 1990, and I have never received an answer to one of my letters." I narrated the process in which I had been engaged since 1990, seeking information as to the status of my trilogy of manuscripts. Sometime in between January 13 and February 5, 1996, Lane called me and explained that when he took over Milella's position, he was not informed about the trilogy. He offered to buy out the contracts by estimating the sales, in-print life, and royalties of the three volumes. I declined his offer, preferring to get the manuscripts in print. On February 5, 1996, he wrote to me to explain that he had established a schedule for publication of the three books; he hoped to have the first volume in print by late 1996 or early 1997. He also discussed the copy of the manuscript that he had on file, how it was printed on both sides of a page, and how that was impossible to scan into the computer.

On February 12, 1996, I attempted to help Lane straighten out this mess. In my letter to him I explained that the original copy of the manuscript had been sent to Milella in 1990, the second carbon copy had been sent to Bugge, who sent his copy to Milella with the licensing contract. The only other copy of the manuscript that I had was the third carbon copy. The book had been written on a by-now old word processing program, which was not compatible with any computer system, and would take days to print out a copy! I also sent Lane copies of all the letters I had related to this project in an effort to help him find the original manuscripts. I included new biographical information. I asked him not to hold this project against me in the future, as I may want to publish another book with Alba House. I ended my two-page letter by thanking him for picking up this project and running with it. He replied on February 24, 1996, informing me that he could not find the original manuscripts and would be working from the marked up copies that he had, speculating that those may have been those that someone had begun to edit years ago. I promised to be in contact with me in the Fall of 1996.

Because all the text of all three manuscripts had to be re-entered, I did not begin to receive page proofs until early 1997, but they arrived sequentially every other month. I returned the last set in May 1997. Since I had received an Alba House catalogue and noticed that the trilogy was not advertized in the catalogue, I wrote to Lane on September 27, 1997, requesting an update. I wanted to know what Alba House was doing. On October 1, 1997, Lane wrote, telling me that all three volumes were at the printers. He added, "We share with you your eagerness to see these volumes in print; it shouldn't be too long now." He also apologized for not having kept me better informed. Finally, on November 6, 1997, I received my author's copies of the three new books. In his letter, Lane expressed his "sincere apologies for the long delay in getting these volumes into print" and his "congratulations on a job well done." It had taken seven years for this tale of woe to be turned into a tale of happiness! More happiness, however, was to come at a much later date.

In the meantime, Alba House sold the books both as individual volumes and as a set of three books. For the first five years, that is 1997–2001, the *Day by Ordinary Day with Mark* volume sold 1,302 copies; the *Day by Ordinary Day with Matthew* volume sold 1,274 copies; and the *Day by Ordinary Day with Luke* volume sold 1,197 copies. For this type of book, those were phenomenal sales. From 2002 to 2006, 395 additional copies of the Mark volume were sold, 393 copies of the Matthew volume, and 372 copies of the Luke volume. Despite my expectations, Alba House continued to keep the books in print and advertise them in its catalogues. So, from 2007 to 2011, 195 copies of the Mark volume were sold, 201 copies of the Matthew volume, and 189 copies of the Luke volume. From 2012 to 2014, 311 copies of the Mark volume were sold, 290 copies of the Matthew volume, and 299 copies of the Luke volume. Thus, as of the writing of this book in 2020 (for which I do not have any sales figures), the Mark volume has sold over 2,203 copies, the Matthew volume has sold over 2,158 copies, and the Luke volume has sold over 2,057 copies. How's that for going from woe to happiness? And that is not the end of the story of Alba House, now known as St. Pauls, keeping the book in print for over twenty years!

The official titles of the three books are: *Day by Ordinary Day with Mark: Daily Reflections for Ordinary Time Weeks 1–9: Volume 1*; *Day by Ordinary Day with Matthew: Daily Reflections for Ordinary Time Weeks 10–21, Volume 2*; and *Day by Ordinary Day with Luke: Daily Reflections for Ordinary Time Weeks 22–34: Volume 3*. I dedicated volume 1 "to my mentor and teacher, Bernard Brandon Scott, whose great love for the Scriptures has leavened me." Volume 2 was dedicated "to the staff of *The Mirror*, newspaper of the Diocese of Springfield-Cape Girardeau," for which I served as editor: Karla Essner, Leon Gibbar, Leslie Hunter Eidson, Marilyn Vydra, and Joan Ward." And volume 3 was dedicated "to the members of the 'Old Study Group': James & Dorothy Askren, Jerry & June Beck, Thomas & Raamah Crim, Edward & Julie Rice, and Olive White; and to the members of the 'Jackson Church' group: Arthur Hobbs, James & Brenda Jackson, Leigh-Ann Long, Timothy & Laura Vinyard, Mary Wieman, and Keith & Robin Zeka." As the titles of the volumes indicate, only the gospel passages assigned by the Roman Catholic Lectionary were reflected upon for every day of the thirty-four weeks of the Season of Ordinary Time.

In 2008, I began work on a project in which I hoped St. Pauls would have an interest. After thinking about writing volumes on the first readings for the weekdays of Ordinary Time, knowing that I would have two cycles with which to deal, I began working on reflections following the same format as the three previously published volumes. I originally conceived of the Year I reflections in three volumes, following the format of the gospels, weeks 1–11, 12–24, and 25–34. After having finished the three volumes in July 2009, I sent a three-page query letter to Lane on July 11, 2009, sending a hard copy of all three volumes. Lane responded on July 21, 2009, stating that his "initial impression is that it looks very good and has come at a very good time." On September 25, 2009, Lane wrote, "All of us here are eagerly looking forward to publishing your latest series of reflections on the daily readings, and so I am pleased to send you at this time two copies of our Standard Agreement form for the publication of 'Day by Ordinary Day: Daily Reflections, Year One' (3-volume set)." He added, "May I say how happy I am that we will be working together on this venture." I signed the contract and returned it to him on September 30, 2009. On March 2, 2010, he informed me that at a joint meeting of St. Pauls editorial and marketing staffs, it was unanimously decided to combine all three volumes into one, called *Day by Ordinary Day: Daily Reflections for Year One*. I responded on March 6, 2010, stating that I agreed with the decision and suggesting that "First Readings" needed to be added into the title. The page proofs arrived on April 29, 2010, with the book title of *Day by Ordinary Day: Daily Reflections on the First Readings, Year 1*. It was identified as volume 4. I dedicated the book to three good friends: Wesley Dowler, Jeremy Graddy, and Kris Morehead. I returned pages that needed correcting on May 10, 2010, calling attention to several typing mistakes and other issues. Lane acknowledged receipt of the corrections by e-mail on May 14, 2010. My author's copies arrived on October 4, 2010. In the nine years since it was published, over 500 copies have been sold.

On July 24, 2010, I sent the completed manuscript for *Day by Ordinary Day: Daily Reflections on the First Readings, Year 2* to Lane. He responded on August 23, 2010, with a standard Agreement contract to publish this fifth volume in my series. I returned it on August 30, 2010. The page proofs arrived on March 25, 2011, and, after reading them carefully, I returned them with corrections on April 25, 2011. Volume 5 was dedicated the staff of the St. Francis of Assisi Parish in Nixa, Missouri: Sue Brohammer, Sheri Duncan, Debbie Durham, and Leigh Sisk. I had founded that parish on August 22, 2004. My author's copies arrived on October 2, 2011. In the eight years that volume 5 has been in print, over 500 copies have been sold. Thus, what began as a woe in 1990—taking seven years to get the original trilogy into print—turned into a happiness in 2011—the publication of the fifth volume in the "Day by Ordinary Day" series.

According to all Alba House/St. Pauls contracts, royalty statements for the previous year are to be sent to the author by the end of January of the next year and checks sent by the end of March. In 2019 this did not occur. In May 2019, I began calling the publisher to find out why royalty statements and checks had not been issued. None of my electronic messages were ever answered. When I did speak to a representative on the telephone, I was told that someone would return my call, but no one ever did. I made several more calls in July 2019 attempting to secure the royalties owed me for 2018, but all I ever received was a promise that someone at Alba House/St. Pauls was working on them. The issue of justice that I have raised repeatedly with Catholic book publishers remains. Finally, on September 24, 2019, I got an e-mail informing me about my royalties for 2018. The e-mail stated, "For this year, no check will be sent to you because the amount is less than seventy dollars." I replied to that e-mail, writing:

There is nothing in my signed contracts about not receiving a check if the amount is less than seventy dollars. When I signed contracts with St. Pauls, I signed them in good faith that they would be adhered to both by me and by you, the publisher. I have adhered to them. Not only have you broken the contract—which says that the amount of royalties due will be announced by the end of January of the next year for the previous year—but you have not supplied the royalties according to the contract which says that they are to be paid by the end of March following the January announcement. And now there is another thing that is not in the contract: that the check must be for more than seventy dollars.

Therefore, I am left with no recourse. If a check is not received at my address by October 1, 2019, I will be filing a case in small claims court. I don't want to have to do that, but—personal issues aside—you leave me with no choice. You are drawing interest on my royalties, no matter how small they may be. Not only is that illegal, but it is blatantly unjust."

Within the week my royalty check arrived. However, neither a statement at the end of January 2020 nor a check at the end of March 2020 for royalties due me from 2019 were received from St. Pauls. Thus, ends the tale of woe that turned into a tale of happiness only to revert to a tale of woe!

Baptized into Christ's Death and Resurrection

After finishing work on the first three *Day by Ordinary Day* volumes in 1995, I began work on a book of reflections based on the Scripture texts in the *Order of Christian Funerals*. In one volume, I presented reflections on every Scripture text used in funerals for adults and children. By April 22, 1996, I had finished the manuscript and sent a query to St. Anthony Messenger Press; at that point the book did not yet have a title. I got a rejection letter on May 14, 1996. In the meantime, on April 22, 1996, I had written to Twomey at The Liturgical Press, explaining the project that still did not have a working title. On April 30, 1996, he requested a hard copy of the manuscript as soon as I finished it. On June 20, 1996, I sent the finished manuscript to Twomey with the title "Baptized into Christ's Death and Resurrection: Preparing to Celebrate a Christian Funeral." Sometime between June 20, 1996, and January 1997, Twomey contacted me and then sent me the nine-page critique of the manuscript; it recommended that The Liturgical Press print the work, but that it be published in two volumes, one on funerals for adults and one on funerals for children. Some of the critique was right on target and needed to be addressed by me. However, some of the critique was mere nitpicking or the dislike of the anonymous reader; he or she did not like the use of etc., and such phrases as Matthean Jesus, Markan Jesus, etc.! Taking all such things into consideration, I divided the manuscript into two volumes, rewrote the introduction to volume one and wrote an introduction to volume two, and made several changes as indicated by the anonymous reader's critique. By January 15, 1997, both volumes were ready and in Twomey's hands.

On March 3, 1998, I received a letter from Twomey with the second critique of the editor who had prepared the first critique. Enclosed was eight pages of nitpicking. Whoever this editor was, he or she did not like the use of certain words, like "slave," and wanted it replaced with "servant." He or she rewrote some of my sentences so that they were the way he or she wanted. I remember being very angry at some of the directions, like "reduce by half or more the use of 'he or she,' 'him or her,' 'his or hers,'" etc. There was one positive sentence: "I congratulate the author on having so thoroughly addressed what was written after the first reading." What that really means is that I changed what the reader thought should be changed. Twomey wanted an annotated list of the readings that provided a one-sentence summary of each reading at the end of the book. Three other forms needed to be completed. I sent those to Twomey on March 17, 1998, and got to work on getting the two manuscripts finished.

On March 25, 1998, Twomey sent me two copies of the two contracts for the books. One copy was to be returned to him, and one was to be kept by me. I signed the contracts and returned one copy to Twomey on April 1, 1998. On May 8, 1998, I sent him both hard copies and copies on floppy disks of *Baptized into Christ's Death and Resurrection: Preparing to Celebrate a Christian Funeral, Volume 1: Adults* and *Baptized into Christ's Death and Resurrection: Preparing to Celebrate a Christian Funeral, Volume 2: Children*, which he acknowledged receiving on May 12, 1998.

Nancy McDarby in St. Joseph, Minnesota, wrote to me on July 30, 1998, informing me that she was the editor of my two books. She enclosed a copy of the manuscript for volume one. I do not know if McDarby was the reader who submitted the two previous critiques, but she didn't hesitate to make changes in my work. In her letter she indicated that she had made "many alterations . . . [that] are not real corrections, but modifications that I judge make a sentence clearer or less heavy." She continues, "The change of 'just like' to 'just as' is, I must admit, strictly a matter of my taste—I simply think it 'sounds' better—and some other restyling falls into the same category." Using the old psychological method of saying something nice, then critiquing, then saying something nice, she concluded her letter, stating: "I really like the book and think it should appeal to a fairly wide audience. It is pastoral to the core—it faces death squarely but is at the same time profoundly gentle and full of hope and encouragement."

In my three-page response to McDarby, I indicated, "I prefer what I wrote," but "I have accepted [some] of your changes." However, I did state that I wanted the subjunctive mood to stay where I had used it. I also indicated that I did not like splitting up compound verbs with adverbs. And there were a number of changes she wanted which would have changed the theological meaning of the sentence. I wrote: "Personally, while I don't have problems with a female holy Spirit, Rome does. And I don't want to provoke any comments from across the ocean." I also made it clear that I did not like sentences that ended in prepositions, I disagreed with her use of the ellipsis, the word *church*, and that I would take out all the quotes from the *Order of Christian Funerals*, except for those used as epigrams, so as not to need a license from ICEL. I was determined not to have any of my royalties going to ICEL or CCD, because I had used the NRSV which did not need permission for five hundred verses or under.

On August 25, 1998, McDarby replied to my letter with a five-page e-mail using the manipulative psychology indicated above: write something nice, attack the writer, write something nice. In it she defended the changes she had made in my manuscript that I had rejected, even going so far as to attack my style, and inform me that she was overriding some of my corrections, but I would have the opportunity to change them on the proof pages. On August 27, 1998, she sent me three more pages which indicated changes I had made but she was overriding.

The page proofs for volume one arrived on November 16, 1998, and I fixed them the way I wanted them to appear under my name. Twomey had determined that I had used 1,218 words from the *Order of Christian Funerals*, and that I needed to contact ICEL for a license. He also wanted me to verify that I had used no more than five hundred verses of the *New Revised Standard Version*. I returned the page proofs on November 25, 1998. In my letter to Twomey, I stated: "I have further edited the quotations from the *Order of Christian Funerals*. I do not want to pay any of my royalties to ICEL. So, if more editing needs to be done in order to satisfy what you consider to be 'fair use,' let me know and I'll edit further or just remove [the quotations] completely." I also informed him that I had used only 324 verses of the NRSV—and some of those were only partial verses. As a result, all the quotations from the *Order of Christian Funerals* were removed from the book except for those that functioned as epigrams at the beginning of each part of the book. Where the quotations had been used, the phrase "*Order of Christian Funerals*: par. (number)" appeared. A final set of proof pages arrived on December 11, 1998, and I returned those shortly thereafter; there were three major mistakes that needed attention along with the insertion of capital letters at the beginning of the Scripture quotations either alone or in brackets. I did not want a quotation that was a complete sentence to begin with a lower case letter. Around the middle of January 1999, I received a final set of proof pages which I corrected.

I do not remember what happed with volume 2 and McDarby; I have no copies of correspondence between the two of us. On February 1, 1999, I received the proof pages for volume two; those were read and back in the mail on February 4, 1999. On June 21, 1999, Twomey wrote to me to be sure that I had received my author's copies of both volumes of *Baptized into Christ's Death and Resurrection: Preparing to Celebrate a Christian Funeral*. Volume 1 was "dedicated to those members of my family whose deaths have taught me the meaning of dying: Sarah Osia, Charles & Meade Boyer, Jeffrey Allen Boyer, Ernest J. & Margaret M. Boyer, Jesse L. & Verna M. Boyer, Mary Ann Ackerson." Volume 2 was "dedicated to Samantha Gail Pashia-McElyea, November 30-December 28, 1995, my first great-niece, who in twenty-eight days of life taught the paschal mystery to her parents, to me, and to hundreds of friends."

The Liturgical Press did not keep the books in print very long. By 2008 they were out of print, even though each volume sold over six hundred copies. I sold the last copies I had on hand on August 20, 2008, and later granted the same buyer to reprint as many copies as he wanted for use with the Carmel Mission Bereavement Ministry in Carmel, California. The director of the ministry wanted to use the books "to provide opportunities for education and spiritual development of twenty-four ministers so they can better serve [the] parish families at the time of the death of their loved ones, and also so that they . . . can enhance their own spiritual growth." Since that was the purpose of writing the books, I saw no reason not to grant the director freedom to reprint whatever he needed from them. Unlike ICEL and CCD I chose not to charge a reprint or use fee!

The Greatest Gift of All

On April 5, 1998, I signed an Agreement with ACTA Publications to publish my "Home for Christmas: Scriptures, Reflections, Prayers, and Memories," which was published as *The Greatest Gift of All: Reflections and Prayers for the Christmas Season* in 1999. The book, dedicated to Karl and Sheri Kinler and their children, Amy, Dory, and Zachary," friends in Joplin, was written in an abecedarian format of forty-two entries on the things of Christmas. Each entry consisted of a title, a biblical passage, a reflection, a meditation question, a biblical prayer from a psalm, and a memories section for personal record-keeping. In other words, the last part of each entry provided space for the reader to record personal stories about the people and things of Christmas in his or her home. The book was designed to be used over and over again throughout the years.

By July 13, 1999, I had received the proof pages and made corrections. By September 13, 1999, the book was in print. During its very short in-print life it sold over 2,500 copies. However, by July 30, 2001, Pierce informed me that ACTA was soliciting no further orders and paying no further royalties on it. In his letter declaring the book out of print, Pierce indicated that he wanted a larger market for the book. In 2001, something from the book was used by J.S. Paluch in the Christmas Edition of its parish bulletin series; while I never saw what was used, a payment of a few dollars was forwarded to me.

Meditations for Ministers

After speaking with Pierce on the telephone and listening to what he was saying, I proposed a book of short reflections for all types of Christian ministers—both lay and ordained. I began work on the book in 1998, and I sent sample reflections and a general outline to Pierce on August 22, 1998. He responded with a telephone call, asking me to revise the samples according to his specifications. Accordingly, on September

28, 1998, I returned the revised samples to him along with dividing the material into chapters, providing an introduction to each chapter, and presenting a one-verse quotation from Scripture at the end of each reflection. On January 5, 1999, he issued the standard Agreement contract to me. By April 13, 1999, I sent him the completed manuscript of "Daily Meditations (with Scripture) for Busy Christian Ministers"—both hard copy and files saved on a floppy disk. The book contained 366 reflections, one for each day of the year.

The book, finally titled *Meditations for Ministers*, was published in May 2000. I dedicated it to my "sister," Rosalie Digenan, DC, "friend, co-worker, confidant, supporter, minister, fifty years as a Daughter of Charity." I had worked with Digenan for many years as the editor of our diocesan newspaper and as an adult religious education teacher. Pierce, as I had learned before with other writing projects for ACTA, was known for cutting material from manuscripts. This book demonstrated that. My 366 reflections had been trimmed to a few more than 300! Some of the nineteen chapters in the book had been reduced to but a few of the original reflections that populated it. ACTA kept the book in print for about ten years, selling around 1,000 copies.

Waiting in Joyful Hope

During 1993, I had worked on a manuscript titled *Waiting in Joyful Hope: Daily Reflections for Advent and Christmas*. The book, based on the Scripture texts for every day of the Advent and Christmas seasons—including all three Sunday cycles—provided a seven-part exercise for each day: a title, a list of the biblical texts assigned for the day, a few verses from the gospel text assigned for the day, a selection from the writings of one of the Fathers of the Church, a reflection, a personal meditation question, and a summarizing prayer. Like other volumes in my writing repertoire, this one began its trip on the publishing train on January 24, 1994, at Mystic, Connecticut, with a query letter to Twenty-Third Publications, which passed on my offer on January 28, 1994, because it had just accepted a similar book for publication. On January 24, 1994, I had also sent a query letter to St. Anthony Messenger Press, which passed because it was already selling a similar book. Basically, on January 24, 1994, I had sent seven inquiry letters to various publishers. Sheed & Ward replied with no interest on February 25, 1994; Orbis Books replied March 2, 1994, expressing that such a work was outside the range of its program. Neither Alba House nor Our Sunday Visitor Press bothered to answer my inquiry letters.

Virgil C. Funk from The Pastoral Press expressed an interest in seeing the manuscript on February 10, 1994. I sent it to him on February 17, 1994, but never received a reply. A similar story concerns Liguori Publications, which requested a copy of the manuscript on February 1, 1994; I sent it on February 7, 1994, and got a rejection letter on March 16, 1994, explaining that Liguori was overstocked on Advent products. The Editor-in-Chief, Robert Pagliari, did recommend four other publishers which might be interested in the work. He concluded his letter by telling me that if I wanted the manuscript returned, I needed to send him $2.90 for postage! That was after he had requested me to send it to him!

The publishing train pulled into the station and stopped for a while after this in order to recalculate what it was going to do with this manuscript. I had other writing projects that needed my attention. Finally, on January 31, 1995, I got back to "Waiting in Joyful Hope: Daily Reflections for Advent and Christmas" and sent three query letters. Two received no response. The third one from Liturgy Training Publications instructed me to write to its senior acquisitions editor, even though David Philippart, editor, stated that LTP would probably not publish it. On February 11, 1995, I queried Victoria M. Tufano, Senior Acquisitions Editor, who did not respond until September 4, 1995, and who told me that it was "outside the direction" LTP was "taking in seasonal materials."

While attending the Associated Church Press meeting in April 1995, I had the opportunity to meet and chat about this manuscript with Christopher Humphrey, Senior Editor of Novalis in Ottawa, Canada. On May 8, 1995, after getting home, I queried him about his interest in the manuscript. In a May 18, 1995, letter he requested a copy, which I sent on May 24, 1995. I had my hopes that I had finally found a home for this book. Michael O'Hearn, Director of Novalis, wrote to me later in 1995, informing me that I was "a very fine writer, and [he] liked what [he] saw in 'Waiting in Joyful Hope.'" Informing me that the next editorial meeting was not until the last week of August, he promised to get back to me with a decision after that. My hopes were dashed on December 13, 1995, when O'Hearn informed me that Novalis had decided not to accept the book for publication. "The editorial committee discussed your manuscript at length," he wrote, "Some members felt that your manuscript was not as sensitive as it might be to female voices and images. Others had some questions, from a liturgical point of view, about the notion of the 'third coming.' Still others remarked on the lack of connection to liturgical action and about the way you see the notion of sign. And one member of the jury found your material a bit too moralizing in tone." After explaining that none of those were major problems "in and of themselves," he closed the rejection letter with wishes for a holy and blessed Christmas!

On March 18, 1996, I sent query letters to five more publishers and got no response to three of them. On April 2, 1996, Servant Publications expressed an interest in receiving a proposal; the two pages of guidelines were enclosed. I duly prepared a five-page proposal and returned it on April 11, 1996. On June 12, 1996, Heidi S. Hess, Managing Editor, called me to talk about the book. But on June 26, 1996, she wrote to tell me that while she "would like to have worked with [me] on this project," the committee "felt the writing was not 'popular' enough." She continued: "While I think your writing style would appeal to the conservative Catholic (who are generally the ones who would purchase this type of book anyway), I was not able to change their minds. I'm sorry."

Writing

In response to my March 18, 1996, letter to HarperSanFranciso, I received the pre-printed postcard indicating that the book did not fit Harper's current publishing needs. And while I received a response from the letter to Oxford University Press on March 26, 1996, requesting that I send a copy of the manuscript to the religion editor, which I did on April 18, 1996, I received a rejection letter on May 9, 1996. I also received a request from Forest of Peace Publishing requesting a copy of the manuscript on March 20, 1996; I sent the manuscript on March 25, 1996. I received a letter confirming receipt of the manuscript on April 16, 1996, and a rejection letter on October 2, 1996. In his letter, Thomas Skorupa, Editor, wrote that he enjoyed reading the manuscript and appreciated its intention and message. He also wrote: "[I]t's solid theology, comprehensive, well-organized, and well thought out." It just did not fit with the publishing schedule. He also wrote, "We affirm the value of your work. We also appreciate your very professional presentation, as well as the care with which you addressed your topic." After inquiring publishers about this book for three years, mailing manuscripts to many, and receiving rejection letters from most, I was just about to put the manuscript in the "never to be published" drawer of my file cabinet when Mark Twomey of The Liturgical Press came along.

Thus, just before giving up on getting the book in print, I wrote to Twomey on September 20, 1999, offering him the manuscript, but informing him that I had used the NRSV biblical translation for all Scripture quotes in order to avoid paying any royalties to use the NAB. While expressing a desire that the quotes be taken from the recently-published *Lectionary for Mass*, he was open to other possibilities once I sent the manuscript, which I did on November 23, 1999. On February 16, 2000, Twomey wrote to inform me that The Liturgical Press was going to publish the manuscript, but wanted to do it "in three booklets, one for each liturgical year." Year A would be published in 2001, Year B in 2002, and Year C in 2003. This meant that the manuscript would need to be taken apart and more daily reflections would need to be written. In a book, only one weekday reflection needed to appear. However, in three books three daily reflections would need to appear. The Sundays were in good shape since I had covered all three cycles in the book; they needed only to be divided into three booklets. On February 28, 2000, I wrote to Twomey with the information he had requested before issuing a contract, which was dated March 2, 2000. The use of the Lectionary texts was still an issue, but I signed the contract for *Waiting in Joyful Hope: Daily Reflections for Advent and Christmas*. I made several proposals to Twomey as to how to avoid paying any royalties for use of biblical texts. He replied on March 13, 2000, suggesting that I make the biblical texts only one verse long, then "the authorities in Washington would not charge an extensive fee for such minimal use of the texts." I accepted his solution in a letter dated March 18, 2000. I finished the manuscript for the first booklet and sent it to Twomey on June 26, 2000. He acknowledged receipt on June 30, 2000.

If there is one thing I have learned in the book publishing world, the contract only applies to the writer; the publisher is free to change it. On September 22, 2000, Twomey wrote, telling me that "because of marketing concerns, we have decided to publish the Advent and the Christmas reflections in two volumes, each of which are to be no longer than 64 pages." He added, "Thus, would you please look at these [enclosed] proofs in that regard, and rather than mark the proof, send a revised disk that has each book separately." What The Liturgical Press had decided to do was "to publish for 2001 copy that pertains only to the respective season for 2001, and in the case of Christmas for 2001 and the first days of January 2002." Twomey asked me to give some thought for the Christmas booklet, but thought "Waiting in Joyful Hope" was good for the Advent booklet.

This new development received my reply on October 2, 2000. I suggested "Filled with New Light" as the title for the Christmas booklet. I also raised a number of editorial changes concerning ellipses in Scripture quotes that I had put in and were not removed along with indents that were in the manuscript and now removed. Since there were to be two books, I requested a contract for "Filled with New Light." By dividing the books into two booklets, I informed Twomey, fair use would dictate that no permission would be necessary from biblical copyright owners. Twomey followed up on my letter on October 5, 2000, with a replacement contract for both booklets. The first set of page proofs for both booklets arrived on October 16, 2000; I returned them on October 23, 2000. The final page proofs arrived on January 4, 2001; after reading them, I return them on January 11, 2001.

Because *Waiting in Joyful Hope 2001: Daily Reflections for Advent* had become a seasonal offering, this meant that it had an in-print life of only one year. However, it sold almost 12,000 copies. I dedicated the booklet "to the priests who supported my vocation to the priesthood: Anthony J. Jansen, James M. Moll, Edward J. Schramm, Bernard A. Suellentrop, Richard H. Suren." *Filled with New Light—2001: Daily Reflection for Christmas*, dedicated to my friend, Matthew S. Miller (now Ver Miller), did not do as well, selling only 4,400 copies. I knew the future of the Christmas booklet was in danger when compared to three-times the sales of the Advent booklet.

And I was correct! I sent the manuscripts for the two booklets to be published in 2002 on May 12, 2001. On May 17, 2001, Twomey acknowledged receipt of them. Page proofs arrived on January 24, 2002. "We decided just this week to combine the two booklets into one because of the disparity in sales between the Advent and Christmas booklets during this past season for 2001," wrote Twomey. Now, I needed to adapt the introduction and make other editorial corrections in order to combine what had been one book, then two booklets, back into one book. According to Twomey's letter, "we sold 11,904 copies of *Waiting in Joyful Hope* and 4,752 copies of *Filled with New Light*. The reason to combine the booklets into one was the hope for "better overall sales." A new title had been given the book; it would be called "Waiting in Joyful Hope: Daily Reflections for Advent and Christmas 2002 and 2003." After working on combining the booklets into a book, I returned the page proofs on March 22, 2002. The book, titled *Waiting in Joyful Hope 2002–3: Daily Reflections for Advent & Christmas*, was dedicated "to my friend, Sister Mary Ellen O'Connor, CCVI, fifty years in ministry, and "to my friend, Chris Haik, one in whom I place great trust." It was published in September 2002 and sold over 8,000 copies.

It had taken two years to get some of this book into print. However, at this two-thirds-of-the-way point, I was fairly confident that the third book would be the easiest. On August 2, 2002, I sent *Waiting in Joyful Hope 2003–4: Daily Reflections for Advent & Christmas* to Twomey, receiving a letter confirming receipt on August 12, 2002. Page proofs arrived and were returned through early 2003, when the book was published. I dedicated it "to my 1956 first-grade teacher, Sister Laura Magowan, CCVI, who for over fifty years has continued to serve as a teacher in the Church." Over 30,000 copies were sold. The word *waiting* in the title aptly summarizes the history of this book from 1993 to 2003. In other words, it took ten years to see this book published in four booklets! I began this annual booklet that continues to be written by others and published by The Liturgical Press for almost twenty years.

Lent and Easter Prayer at Home

Lent and Easter Prayer at Home was published by Ave Maria Press, Notre Dame, Indiana, in 2002 and "dedicated to my great nephew, Zachary David Ingram, and my great niece, Rebecah Jane McElyea." However, the book that was printed was not the book I had written. After finishing the manuscript of what was titled "Home for Lent and Easter," I had queried St. Anthony Messenger Press on May 9, 2000, got a request to see the manuscript on June 9, 2000, sent it on June 19, 2000, requested a response on December 18, 2000, after not having heard a word, and did not get a negative response until May 1, 2001. "We are returning it to you because of our doubts on whether we could successfully market it," wrote Jeremy Harrington, Publisher. In other words, he was not sure the book would make a lot of money! A year had passed from the writing of my inquiry letter and a definitive response from St. Anthony Messenger Press.

After not having heard anything from SAMP, I sent a query letter on February 16, 2000, to Pierce at ACTA Publications; Pierce requested a copy of the manuscript through an e-mail. I sent the manuscript on March 2, 2000, but because he feared that a Lent and Easter book would have a small market and sales window, Pierce was not interested in publishing it on May 4, 2000. In other words, the main issue was making money again!

On May 12, 2001, I queried Frank J. Cunningham at Ave Maria Press who passed my letter to Robert Hamma, Editorial Director, who on June 11, 2001, requested a copy of the manuscript, which I sent on June 13, 2001. After discussing several things about the book with Hamma, I received a Publisher-Author Agreement, dated July 24, 2001, for Ave Maria to publish the book. I had no idea of what would follow. After a telephone discussion with Daniel Driscoll, Editor, about rearranging the contents of the book, I set to work reorganizing the abecedarian style into a structure of entries under one of three chapter titles: Lent, Holy Week, Easter. I sent the rearranged contents on July 23, 2001. I remember thinking to myself that this was not the book that I had written, but it was the book that was going to be published by Ave Maria Press. On August 15, 2001, Hamma sent me an e-mail, telling me that the title of the book had been changed to "Lent and Easter Prayer at Home." On August 28, 2001, I received "a clean edited copy of [my] manuscript" to be read over and corrected. Not only had Hamma edited material in the book—both to conform it to house style and to rearrange the contents—but he had done "some editing" to a number of the entries. In his two-page letter, he listed all the general and specific changes he had made. The only thing not touched was the last section of blessings for things (ashes, cross, candle, water, etc.) and food during Lent and Easter. Again, this manuscript kept looking less and less like the one that I had written.

On December 6, 2001, I received two author's copies of my book. While Driscoll was very pleased with what he had created from my manuscript, I was not pleased at all. The playful tone of my book had been replaced with a seriousness of the one published by Ave Maria. On August 18, 2006, not even five years after it was published, Hamma declared it to be out of print. In its short life, 3,888 copies were sold.

Using Film to Teach New Testament

Dedicated to Gerrit J. tenZythoff, the founder of the Religious Studies Department at Missouri State University, Springfield, who gently encouraged the completion of the book, I set out to write a book that demonstrated a technique that I had been using in my New Testament class: *Using Film to Teach New Testament*. TenZythoff, who was retired, but teaching a course or two, had attempted to hire me in 1978, when I was on my way to Joplin to teach in McAuley Regional High School. After returning to Springfield in 1985, one of tenZythoff's successors as head of the Religious Studies Department, James Moyer, did hire me to teach New Testament in 1989. After attending a summer adult education course taught by Bernard Brandon Scott, a former seminary instructor, I learned how to use film to demonstrate biblical themes. As I continued to look for more and more films that would help me communicate key themes in New Testament books, I developed a repertoire of films that I associated with many New Testament books. Gently urged to write a book about this method, and after having heard Scott speak about how not to become a living dinosaur, I got to work on writing the chapters that would become *Using Film to Teach New Testament*. Besides dedication the book to tenZythoff, I also dedicated it to Scott.

I had read about University Press of America's program to publish textbooks, and I concluded that what I was writing was, indeed, a textbook. So, during the summer of 2001, I submitted a proposal to University Press of America. On August 6, 2001,

Writing

Diana Lavery, Associate Editor, sent me a letter informing me "that the board has agreed to publish *Using Film to Teach the New Testament*." Enclosed was a contract to sign and return along with a number of other documents. UPA required camera-ready copy, what today would be known as typeset pages. Sample pages had to be approved by UPA's production editor before the final copy could be submitted. I had everything signed and completed by August 11, 2001, and in the mail to Lavery, noting in particular that, as a newspaper editor, I knew all about camera-ready pages, which would be ready by January 1, 2002. Lavery responded on September 5, 2001, with my copy of the publishing agreement and a number of sheets of directions to follow. By September 21, 2001, I had the camera-ready pages done. I sent a set of sample pages, according to the agreement, received immediate confirmation, and sent the rest of the camera-ready pages by early November 2001. I received confirmation of their receipt by UPA on November 9, 2001. On December 14, 2001, I responded to an e-mail, indicating that the title was *Using Film to Teach New Testament*.

The book was published in 2002. Two author's copies were sent to me on February 19, 2002. However, the printed copies arrived with a statement from "The Rowman & Littlefield Publishing Group (formerly known as University Press of America)." The office had moved from Lanham, Maryland, to Blue Ridge Summit, Pennsylvania. In other words, UPA had been sold while my book was in production. That information was also found in a pre-publication notice issued by UPA; a small line of type read "A member of The Rowman & Littlefield Publishing Group." The Fall 2002 UPA catalogue contained a listing of the book, but, again, UPA was listed as a member of R&L. The book was also listed in the Spring 2003 and Fall 2003 catalogues.

As part of the agreement with UPA, I had to purchase ninety-five copies of the book at the pre-publication price of $41 less 20% or $32.80 plus shipping charges. "The purpose of a pre-publication order is to cover the start-up cost of printing your book," stated the required agreement. If the pre-publication agreement was not signed, the book would not be printed. My ninety-five copies cost over $3,000. I sold some copies to students in courses I taught at much less than what I had paid for them. I also sold some to other people. In 2015, I was selling them for ten dollars in an effort to reduce my inventory. I never received a royalty from UPA or R&L. The book never appeared in another catalogue, and it was never declared to be out of print. It just disappeared off of the books-in-print radar.

Reflections on the Mysteries of the Rosary

My next book did not originate with me. While working with Twomey at Liturgical Press on the second edition of *The Liturgical Environment: What the Documents Say*, in a July 24, 2003, letter, he asked me, "Would you be interested in writing a booklet-length manuscript on the rosary—a short reflection on the mysteries, including the Mysteries of Light?" He explained: "We wish to publish a booklet of sixteen to twenty pages that is a reflection on the mysteries. The length of the reflections should be similar to what you did for the Advent and Christmas booklets. If you are interested in this project, please send a couple samples of these reflections for our review." I had a reputation for getting manuscripts finished and polished ahead of deadlines, and Twomey knew that.

Not wanting this offer to get away or be given to someone else, by July 28, 2003, I was ready to send three samples of the type of reflections I proposed for the rosary book. I asked Twomey to critique them and to get back to me. On September 12, 2003, he informed me that the acquisitions committee liked the samples and was offering me a publishing contract. He wanted the manuscript by March 1, 2004, in order to publish it in 2005. He also informed me that the readership he wanted to reach was "the popular pastoral market of the people in the pew." I returned the signed contract on September 19, 2003, along with other necessary forms and promised to have the manuscript finished by March 1, 2004, if not sooner.

Once I had accepted this writing project, I knew to whom I wanted to dedicate this book: Msgr. Jerome Neufelder, 1929–2002. He was a priest of the Diocese of Evansville, Indiana, who had served at St. Meinrad School of Theology as my spiritual director and friend. He, I, and a couple of other students met almost every morning of the school year for breakfast together. One of his favorite prayers was the rosary. So, while it was not my favorite prayer, I decided that it was most appropriate to dedicate the book to him.

Because the book was to be small, I set to work immediately on the reflections and sent the completed manuscript to Twomey on October 31, 2003. Twomey acknowledged receipt of the manuscript on November 7, 2003. Twomey wrote: "We will typeset *Reflections on the Mysteries of the Rosary* as time moves forward. If it is feasible to publish it in our fall season next year, rather than in our spring season 2005, we will do so. We are delighted to have the Rosary manuscript well in advance of the due date for it."

I heard nothing from Twomey, until October 19, 2004. He wrote: "The Little Rock Scripture Study in Arkansas with whom the Liturgical Press has a partnership is planning a new study program on the Rosary and would like to use your *Reflections on the Mysteries of the Rosary* as the text for it. The LRSS office will prepare a Study Guide, Answer Guide, a series of Audio Lectures, and a Video on the Rosary, which we will market to our LRSS customers. The Study Guide and your *Reflections on the Mysteries of the Rosary* will form the 'Study Set' that each participant in this new study will use." I was excited about this possibility. But then came the next paragraph about Cackie Upchurch, director of LRSS, who wanted me to make "a few adjustments in the copy" of the book, because she felt that they were "essential if the booklet is to be used in the program." In other words, she was blackmailing Twomey and me by eliminating the prospect of good sales if I didn't make the changes. In a copy of an e-mail she had sent to Twomey and which he sent to me, she stated: ". . . I'm sorry to say we have some concerns. If these concerns were to be addressed before publication, I think we could still use it; otherwise, we'll need to consider another option." Twomey said as much in his letter, stating, "The potential sales of the text used in the study is from five thousand to ten thousand copies annually."

I read through her list of concerns and omitted the use of "Hebrew Bible (Old Testament)" and "Christian Bible (New Testament)" the one time each was used in the manuscript. I made it clear that in a program that was dedicated to educating adults about the Bible, it seemed strange to me that such common usage among writers was to be removed. Another of her concerns was about the reflection on the Assumption and Coronation of Mary. Upchurch said they "repeated the same information." I explained how one doctrine built on the next, and "I repeated only where necessary to keep myself out of heresy." I urged Twomey to read them himself and see how different they were.

Upchurch's third issue was with the reflection on the Transfiguration, which I rewrote. Likewise, I rewrote the entry on the Resurrection. I also changed a few words which Upchurch didn't like in the manuscript. All was returned on October 25, 2004, to Twomey, who responded with an e-mail on October 28, 2004, informing me that there was "no further need for change in the proofs." However, he copied my letter to him and the corrected pages and sent them to Upchurch, who sent me an e-mail on November 3, 2004. In typical manipulative style, the opening paragraph and the concluding paragraph praised my work, and the rest of the two-page e-mail attacked it!

Upchurch wrote, "I have the definite impression that you resented our concerns and I do apologize if you found them petty or uninformed." Well, the fact of the matter was I did find them petty and uninformed. This sparked Upchurch to defend her knowledge of Scripture and present a list of reasons why she wanted the changes made. She went so far as to write, "If you feel very strongly and feel that changing the designations is an intellectual problem in your manuscript, then by all means keep it as you have it." What she didn't write was that if I did not change the manuscript, it would not be used by LRSS!

On and on she argued with me in the e-mail about the changes. In my response to her e-mail, I reminded her that the changes had been made. There was nothing to argue about! To this day I still stand back in utter amazement. First of all, I am amazed that a director of a biblical program did not want to make use of current biblical scholarship. Second, I am amazed at the psychological manipulative chess game one person was able to play and checkmate the editorial director of a major publishing company. Third, I am amazed at how petty and uninformed anyone in such a position could be.

On April 13, 2004, I received the initial proof copy of the book, and returned the pages needing correction on April 16, 2004. Final page proof arrived on June 8, 2004; they needed only three corrections, which I sent through e-mail on June 13, 2004. On January 10, 2005, Twomey sent my author's copies and informed me that the booklet would be used in the Little Rock Scripture Study program as the text of a new study of the rosary in the Fall of 2005. He also informed me that 10,346 copies had been printed. The book was translated and published in Spanish on August 8, 2007. In the ten years after the English edition was published, 25,626 copies of the book were sold. However, in the six years after the Spanish edition went on sale, only 1,019 copies were sold.

During the Fall of 2006 and Winter of 2006, I worked on a second edition of *Reflections on the Mysteries of the Rosary*. I queried Liturgical Press on March 30, 2007, but got no reply until September 11, 2007. Twomey had retired and been replaced with Hans Christoffersen. In his e-mail to me, he wrote that he had talked with Upchurch and sent her the manuscript proposal. That's all I needed to read; I knew that she would never consent to publishing a revised edition. He wrote: "We both agree . . . that it is too early to revise the current edition; for we have 4800 unsold copies in the warehouse, and the Spanish edition has only recently become available." He said that he needed to wait a couple of years before considering an expanded version.

I waited two years and e-mailed Christoffersen about the possibility of a second edition of the book on June 12, 2009. He replied on June 18, 2009, with an e-mail indicating that a revised edition would cost too much for those participating in the LRSS program. Therefore, Liturgical Press could not support the production of an expanded edition of the book. In 2014, I removed the contents of the first edition and gave the manuscript a new title. I offered it to four other publishers—ACTA, Ave Maria, Our Sunday Visitor, and Pauline Media—but no one was interested in it. I made one more attempt in 2015 to get it published by Liturgical Press, but got the same reply about not wanting a second edition.

So, imagine my surprise in May 2017 when *Hail Mary, Holy Bible: Sacred Scripture and the Mysteries of the Rosary* by Clifford M. Yeary arrived on my desk. Within a couple of days, May 31, 2017, to be exact, I e-mailed Hudock at Liturgical Press reminding him that I had submitted a second edition of my rosary book three times. I ask him, "Why was I not asked to submit [the second edition] for publication? This book is now in competition with my book." Nine or ten minutes later, I got a reply: "The decision was made by Little Rock Scripture Study (with our agreement) to replace *Reflections on the Mysteries of the Rosary* with Cliff Yeary's *Hail Mary, Holy Bible*." Upchurch, who now worked for Liturgical Press, knew about the second edition of my book, but she found a way to derail it.

After giving myself time to think about all this, I e-mailed Hudock on June 2, 2017. I acknowledged that legally Liturgical Press had every right to accept, reject, and revise whatever it choose to publish. I wrote:

> However, I want to raise a Catholic moral question: Does Liturgical Press have any obligation to its authors who, in my case, had already indicated that I wanted to write and publish a second edition of the rosary book? Not knowing that I had a second edition of the book would have removed all moral culpability; however, knowing that I had submitted the second edition three times to Liturgical Press would seem to indicate that I may want to revise the book,

don't you think? Minimally, would Liturgical Press have no moral obligation to contact me to see if I were interested in where it and Little Rock wanted to go? Furthermore, not even talking to me about the project would seem, to me, to carry some moral culpability on the part of Liturgical Press, wouldn't it?

Hudock was furious. He replied:

Unfortunately, your suggestion that our decision to publish a book of rosary reflections from another author, twelve years after the publication of yours, represents a moral failure on our part is difficult to understand. Why the willingness of an author to revise his or her work would entail a publisher's moral obligation to publish the revision, or why a publisher would be morally obligated to consult an author before publishing a book on a similar topic as the author's, is unclear.

It was very clear to me. From my perspective, Hudock and Upchurch knew about the revised edition, and Upchurch had somehow blackmailed Liturgical Press into not publishing it, not even having the common courtesy—let alone any moral (not legal) obligation—to notify me of what was about to happen.

I replied to Hudock, writing: "I'm merely raising the question of what moral responsibility Liturgical Press has to its authors. In Catholic moral thought, we begin with what is good for the other and attempt to balance it with what is good for the individual, or, in this case, Liturgical Press. If Liturgical Press has no moral responsibility to confer with its authors, then that is Liturgical Press's position."

I also explained to Hudock the broader view of Catholic ministry in my June 2 e-mail:

As a writer of books for thirty years, I know that publishers are out to make money; so are writers of books! However, there is more to Catholic publishing than making money, or at least my Church tells me there is. On my end, writing is a ministry for the common good. My gift is to be used for the building up of the body of Christ. My primary objective is not to make lots of money; in fact, I've learned that is impossible in Catholic publishing. What is Liturgical Press's ministry, other than making money? Is there a moral dimension to it? What care should Liturgical Press show to its authors? Is it not the case where sometimes a book needs to be published for the common good, regardless if it makes money or not? Does Liturgical Press have any moral obligation to contact an author of a book it already published when another author is offering something similar? On a business level, the answer is probably NO. However, on a Catholic moral level, I think there is a different answer that must be given.

Hudock replied: ". . . [Y]our suggestion that our aim is to make money, ahead of the common good or Catholic moral teaching, is unfortunate and troubling." My response was this:

> Whether you want to acknowledge it or not, making money has been a discussion of every book Liturgical Press has published that I wrote. When negotiating with you about *A Spirituality of Mission* (see below), that was one of the first issues you raised with me. How many copies will it sell? How many copies will parishes buy of a book based on the Easter Season? I'm not debating the importance of making money; all of us need to do that to survive. Asking the making-money question is very important. I'm raising a question as to what is the motivating or underlying agenda for a Catholic book publisher based on my experience. My conclusion is based on my experience. If my experience is one-of-a-kind, then I'm wrong. Please show me how I'm wrong and, again, I will owe and give Liturgical Press an apology.

I never received any response to my challenge.

In my June 2 e-mail, I told Hudock that I now found myself in a moral bind: "Do I violate the contract [I signed with Liturgical Press] and move forward with another publisher for a second edition, or do I let the first edition die for another few years until Liturgical Press declares it out of print, if ever?" Even though all the contracts I had ever signed with Liturgical Press indicate that the publisher will declare when a book is out of print, Liturgical Press had never declared any book I had written out of print even though most of them were! I told Hudock: "I have never received a notice that any [of my books] were going out of print, and I know for a fact that they have." Hudock replied on June 5, 2017, with a letter declaring my book "out of print." He added: "Should you wish to republish this title with another publishing house or on your own, you are free to do so. Permission for use of your material may be granted without further obligation to Liturgical Press."

Hudock also offered me at no charge the remaining eighty copies of my book that Liturgical Press had in its warehouse. I accepted his offer, thinking that I could sell them when giving retreats and talks for $5 each. As the reader will discover below, I slightly revised the second edition of the book, wrote a new introduction for it, and got it published in 2018 as *Rosary Primer: The Prayers, The Mysteries, and The New Testament* by Wipf and Stock Publishers. The introduction explains how to pray the rosary and lists the four sets of mysteries. Each of the four chapters presents four biblical reflections for the reader's choice for each of the five mysteries. Thus, the second edition of this book did not end up being placed in a file box with other manuscripts that would never see print in book form.

Loose-Leaf Lectionary

Because of the work I had done with Twomey at Liturgical Press, Twomey gave my name to Daniel Durken, the editor of the *Loose-Leaf Lectionary*, an annual publication of the Liturgical Press. After presenting the Scripture texts for every day of the liturgical year, a short reflection followed. Durken wrote to me on April 5, 2004, after having telephoned me before that, informing me that he was pleased that I had accepted this assignment and giving the specifics for this work. By April 21, 2004, I had the first three-month batch of reflections in the mail to Durken. These, of course, would not appear until 2005. The process of getting the liturgical calendar from Durken, writing three-months of reflections, sending them to him, and getting a check in the mail a few days later continued until November 1, 2005, when I had finished two liturgical years of weekday reflections.

From February 1, 2005, to January 31, 2007, my reflections for the weekdays of the liturgical year appeared in *The Loose-Leaf Lectionary*. I got paid seventeen dollars per reflection, submitting them in three-month batches. I estimate that I wrote over six hundred, 175–200-word reflections during that two-year period. While the reflections were not technically gathered into a book, the pages of two years of reflections with the Scripture texts for every day of two years fill over three magazine boxes.

During that time, Durken received several letters from subscribers which he forwarded to me for answering. These either dealt with biblical fundamentalism or with doctrinal issues. I spent some time explaining that Catholics are not fundamentalists and that later doctrinal teachings are not found in biblical texts written long before the doctrine was defined. For example, one priest wanted me to find transubstantiation in one of Paul's letters. Another writer wanted to find the doctrines of Mary's perpetual virginity and Assumption in Matthew's Gospel. A deacon did not like the use of modern biblical scholarship because it raised questions about the three endings of Mark's Gospel. Basically, subscribers wanted to be told what they thought they already knew! It was then and remains now a fascination of mine: how uneducated many people—clergy and laity—are when it comes to the Bible, a collection of books upon which they base their faith without ever examining the contents.

A Christmas Sermon

On July 7, 2006, I received a letter from Malaika Adero, Senior Editor of Atria Books, a division of Simon and Schuster, Inc., requesting that I submit my "most thought-provoking Christmas sermon" to be included among "those of the most recognized preachers in America." Before the July 21, 2006, deadline, I submitted my Christmas homily from December 25, 2005, which I titled "Christmas Past, Present, and Future." By September 1, 2006, I received a copy of how the homily would appear in the collection with the permission form authorizing Atria Books/Simon & Schuster to use my work in its anthology. My payment was twenty complimentary copies of the book. I signed and returned the contract on September 12, 2006, along with the corrected copy of my homily. My copies arrived in November 2006 when the book went on sale. The book was titled *Joy to the World: Inspirational Christmas Messages from America's Preachers*. It was edited by Olivia M. Cloud, and, in addition to my homily, it contained forty-eight Christmas sermons of ministers from a variety of Christian denominations. A biographical sketch appears at the back of the book for every minister, and there is a note that indicates that every sermon is copyrighted in the name of the minister who wrote it. This was the only time I was asked to contribute to such a volume of work.

When Day is Done

The manuscript titled "Bedtime Prayers" made only one stop—The Liturgical Press—on the publishing train before it found a home at Twenty-Third Publications. I sent a query letter on November 10, 2005, and got an e-mail reply from the editorial director, Mary Carol Kendzia, on December 1, 2005, requesting that I submit a formal book proposal, which I sent on December 5, 2005. Kendzia acknowledged receipt of my proposal on December 13, 2005, with an e-mail and a promise to present it to the acquisitions committee meeting during the first week of January. She notified me through e-mail on February 2, 2006, that my book was accepted for publication by Twenty-Third Publications. The formal letter arrived on February 6, 2006, with a request to add "an introduction to compline, and an outline for use in the home." She also informed me that the book would be published in the Spring of 2007. The Publishing Agreement arrived on February 17, 2006, along with other forms needing to be completed and returned. On February 25, 2006, I sent the manuscript for the book and all other completed forms. On December 7, 2006, an e-mail announced that Bayard, Inc., which published books under the Twenty-Third trademark, was in the process of reorganization.

On February 12, 2007, Dan Smart, Vice-President of Twenty-Third Publications, sent a letter indicating that as of the previous September, Twenty-Third had hired "Bret Thomas as Publisher and President of Bayard, Inc." He also stated that Kendzia had left in December 2006, and Dan Connors was appointed Editorial Director of Books. I had been down this road before. When one company buys another one or an editor leaves for a new job, the manuscript easily gets lost.

However, on February 28, 2007, the galleys for the book arrived. It was now titled *When Day Is Done: Nighttime Prayers through the Church Year*. I returned the galleys a few days later, and the final set arrived a few weeks after that. The book was published on March 15, 2007, selling at $12.95, and remained in print until July 6, 2015. In the course of its short shelf-life, over 1100 copies were sold.

Take Up Your Cross and Follow

If a book can be reincarnated, then *Take Up Your Cross and Follow: Daily Lenten Reflections* wins the prize for the most reincarnations. The tale behind this book begins on January 30, 1993, when I queried Liguori Publication about a manuscript titled "101 Stations of Life's Journey: A Pilgrimage with Jesus." My query letter was answered

Writing

by Paul J. Coury, Editor-In-Chief of the Print and Electronic Media Department. He wrote, "It sounds like an interesting book that would fit our market." He requested sample chapters and the completion of a formal book proposal, all of which I sent to Audrey West, Managing Editor of Books and Pamphlets, on March 15, 1993, according to Coury's directions in his letter to me.

On April 28, 1993, Kass Dotterweich, Associate Editor of Print and Electronic Media, sent me a two page letter, stating that my writing was strong, my content was solid, my purpose was well-executed, and my audience was tight. She wrote, "Liguori would like to work with you to bring this material to our readership." Before she was to present my manuscript to the publishing committee, she proposed some modifications. She wanted to change the motif of stations to pilgrimage, and turn the manuscript into four booklets instead of one book. She wanted a brief introduction to each booklet. Once that was done, she would present the manuscripts to the publishing committee. After thinking about her proposal, I wrote to her on May 3, 1993, informing her that I agreed to the modifications. I would have the manuscript broken into four booklets by the end of May 1993. It did not take as long as I had anticipated the reincarnation of the one manuscript into four manuscripts. In fact, on May 9, 1993, I had the four manuscripts in the mail to Dotterweich, who replied on May 19, 1993: "With pride and satisfaction I come to you with an informal acceptance of 'A Pilgrimage with Matthew's (et al) Jesus.' A formal acceptance and contract will follow the June publishing meeting." On May 23, 1993, I sent all the completed paperwork Dotterweich had requested along with a floppy disk with the four manuscripts on it. Dotterweich acknowledge receipt of all materials on May 26, 1993.

On June 21, 1993, Coury wrote to thank me "for all the effort and work" I had put into working on the reincarnation of the manuscripts. The four booklets had been submitted at the June 17 publishing meeting and rejected. While Coury listed a multitude of reasons in a fourteen-line paragraph, the bottom line was sales! On July 3, 1993, I wrote to Dotterweich, expressing my disappointment "especially after all the extra work I did on this project." She replied on July 7, 1993, expressing her own disappointment, but marketing and business did not agree. She stated, "At such times, I ask myself, 'Do we publish only books that will "sell," or are we committed to the Word?'" She also recommended several other publishers which, she thought, might be interested in my book. The reincarnation of the book to four booklets meant that one reincarnation was down; there were several more to go!

On July 3, 1993, I queried Heyer at Sheed & Ward, and received a July 12, 1993, reply indicating no interest in this book. I also queried Pierce on July 3, 1993, and got a no from ACTA Publications on September 16, 1993. An inquiry letter went to Emilie Cerar at Resurrection Press on July 3, 1993; she responded with a telephone call on July 5, 1993, and a request to see the whole manuscript, which I sent on July 7, 1993. Her reply on August 13, 1993, states that she was "unable to accept [my] title for publication." Neil Kluepfel at Twenty-Third Publications responded to my July 3, 1993, letter with his own on July 7, 1993, requesting a copy of the manuscript, which I sent on July 12, 1993. He responded on July 19, 1993, informing me that he had "read in entirety several chapters of the book" and was "impressed by [my] writing skills and Scripture scholarship." He made several suggestions as to how he would like to have the material in the book re-arranged "better to fit the Lenten season." I wrote to him on August 12, 1993, stating that I liked his suggestions, but would prefer that the book cover both Lent and Easter. His response on August 17, 1993, was that he didn't want a book that covered both Lent and Easter because he had found "that there is very little interest in Scripture meditations for the Easter-Pentecost season." He added, "We realize there should be, but that's not the case in our experience." He further emphasized his desire that I reorganize the material for Lenten use. He also expressed the problem he saw in reusing already-written material into a new product. He wrote: "I wish there was some way that I could assure you that the time you will spend creating this new Lenten product will receive an enthusiastic reaction from the editorial/marketing people here. I just don't know until I see how the Scripture passages hold together and whether the Scriptural Way of the Cross can become the skeleton for the booklet." On August 25, 1993, I wrote to Kluepfel, expressing my understanding as to what he wanted; I informed him that I had been working on and revising my original manuscript. On September 3, 1993, before I could get the revised manuscript to him, he wrote to me: "I'm sorry to advise you that the general consensus is that this would not be a product that we could count on for strong sales." The bottom line was sales! Thus, the third incarnation of the manuscript didn't even leave my house before it was rejected.

On July 3, 1993, I had queried Lisa Biedenbach at St. Anthony Messenger Press. She requested a copy of "101 Stations of Life's Journey: A Pilgrimage with Jesus" on July 29, 1993. I sent the entire manuscript on August 12, 1993, and, in typical Biedenbach style, received a negative answer on September 24, 1993. Biedenbach wrote: "We have reviewed your manuscript . . . and have decided not to publish it. Our staff thinks that the meditations don't offer much fresh insight and that the structure of the book isn't unique." She also listed two examples of reflections that she didn't like.

On September 18, 1993, I wrote to Aloysius Milella at Alba House, but got no reply. I also wrote to Orbis Books and got a no reply on October 1, 1993. On September 22, 1993, I wrote to Paulist Press and got a no reply on September 24, 1993. My query on September 22, 1993, to St. Paul Books and Media offering the manuscript in either book form or four-pamphlet form brought an October 15, 1993, reply from Sister Mary Mark, Editorial Director: "Although we are not accepting many manuscripts at this time, we are interested in reviewing yours. We would appreciate it if you would send us a printed copy of both versions." I sent the book and pamphlet materials to her on October 22, 1993. It was not until February 24, 1994, that she sent me a reply indicating that St. Paul Books and Media was not accepting either the book or the pamphlets for publication.

Writing

My letter of September 22, 1993, to American Catholic Press got no answer, while the same letter sent to Pastoral Press brought a request for the manuscript from Funk on October 4, 1993. I sent the book version of the manuscript to Funk on October 11, 1993, and he confirmed receipt on October 20, 1993. No further correspondence was made. I put away the folder containing the manuscript so that I could focus on other writing projects during 1994. On January 31, 1995, I queried Ave Maria Press, and got a no response on March 7, 1995. I queried Our Sunday Visitor Books on January 31, 1995, and got no response. On the same day, I queried The Liturgical Press, and got a no response on March 10, 1995. A year went by. On March 19, 1996, I queried Abby Press, and got an undated form letter response stating "we are not accepting outside material." Also, on March 19, 1995, I queried University Press of America with a no response on May 22, 1996; The Pilgrim Press with a no response on April 18, 1996; and Vantage Press and Viking Penguin, neither of which bothered to even answer my letter.

So, for three years—1993–1996—I tried to find a publisher for a book that had undergone three incarnations. From the Spring of 1996 until the Summer of 1999 the manuscript rested in its manila file folder in my file cabinet. I took it with me on retreat during the Summer of 1999 and tweaked the book form of the work. I retitled it "Your Life's Journey: Stations of the Cross." Each of four chapters contained fifteen Stations of the Cross. Each station consisted of a title, an invitation to prayer, a Scripture quotation, a reflection, a meditation question, and a prayer. On August 25, 1999, I queried Alba House about this fourth incarnation of my manuscript, and I received a request for the book on floppy disk on September 1, 1999. I sent the disk on September 7, 1999, got an acknowledgment of receipt on September 11, 1999, and a rejection letter on September 27, 1999. On November 8, 1999, I queried Templegate Publishers and received a negative response on November 26, 1999. On November 8, 1999, I also queried The Plough Publishing House and received a negative response on November 13, 1999.

The manuscript went into hibernation from 1999 through 2008. During the winter and spring of 2008, I got out the manuscript and brought it to its fifth reincarnation, titled *Take Up the Cross and Follow: Daily Lenten Reflections*. On April 10, 2008, I sent four query letters. A negative response was received on May 22, 2008, through e-mail from the Liturgical Press and from Ave Maria Press on April 30, 2008. No response came from either Twenty-Third Publications or St. Anthony Messenger Press. On June 27, 2008, I queried Edmund C. Lane at St. Pauls/Alba House. He replied with a request to see the manuscript on July 15, 2008. In his letter he referred to the book as *Take Up Your Cross and Follow: Daily Lenten Reflections*. On July 28, 2008, I sent him the manuscript with the title page changed from "the" to "Your." On August 15, 2008, Lane notified me that St. Pauls/Alba House was going to publish this book. He enclosed the standard contract and requested the final revision of the work "in a single computer file in one or another of the more popular word processing programs" sent to him by way of e-mail. I returned the signed contract on August 23, 2008, and sent the e-mail with the manuscript on August 26, 2008. The page proofs arrived on October 21, 2008, and I returned them on October 31, 2008, with the corrections that needed to be made. On January 6, 2009, my author's copies arrived. It had taken fifteen years and five incarnations to get this book in print!

These Thy Gifts

After finishing a manuscript titled *Simple Meal Prayers* in 2008, I began looking for a publisher for it. By 2008, many book proposals were done online; this meant that few letters were written. I submitted proposals to World Library Publications, Oregon Catholic Press, Twenty-Third Publications, Paulist Press, and St. Pauls/Alba house. All either sent rejection letters or didn't bother to reply to my proposal. However, on April 25, 2008, I did get a favorable reply from Andrew Yankech, Assistant Vice President of ACTA Publications. In his e-mail to me, he wrote, ". . . [B]ased on the strength of the sample chapters you sent, ACTA would like to accept your proposal and offer to publish your book." He continued: "The earliest that we could publish is late 2009 or early 2010, depending on how our publication calendar plays out. We could offer you a 12% royalty." On June 4, 2008, I got an e-mail from Yankech, asking me about the offer he had sent to me. I had not received the original e-mail. I replied the next day informing him that the book was still available, that he should send me a contract, and that I was pleased to publish with ACTA again. He replied in the affirmative and asked about sending the manuscript to him on a floppy disk; this I did on June 6, 2008. On June 10, 2008, he e-mailed me to let me know that he was able to open the files on the floppy disk. The contract arrived on June 17, 2008; I signed and returned it on June 20, 2008.

I heard no more about this book until August 2, 2010, when I received the edited version of the manuscript, now titled *These Thy Gifts: A Collection of Simple Meal Prayers*. I read through the manuscript and sent changes to be made to Yankech on August 3, 2010. By September 15, the book was in print. However, while the book was published in 2010, it bears a copyright of 2009. Almost six hundred copies were sold.

Mountain Reflections

After self-publishing my John Denver book in 1996, fifteen years later in 2011, I decided to publish a signed and numbered limited edition of *Mountain Reflections: A Collection of Photos and Meditations*. Only 102 copies of the 100-page coffee-table-size book were printed by Entourage Yearbooks in Princeton, New Jersey, at a total cost of $2,846. After signing the contract in February 2011, I received the layout materials from Entourage and submitted the complete layout on February 28, 2011. By April 21, 2011, the books had arrived.

The book's cover featured a four-color photo of mountains reflected in Willow Lake in the Sangre de Cristo Range in Colorado, a presentation page with the number of each book recorded on it, and page after page of reflections based on a biblical quotation about mountains on the left hand page, and a four-color photo of a mountain on the right hand page. Most of the copies of the book were given away as gifts—especially as Christmas gifts in 2011—although a few were sold at the local Catholic bookstore. *Mountain Reflections: A Collection of Photos and Meditations* was my thirty-sixth book, and it is out of print.

Nature Spirituality

What was published by Wipf and Stock as the 135-page *Nature Spirituality: Praying with Wind, Water, Earth, Fire* in 2013 began as "Flaming Out, Like Shining from Shook Foil: Finding God in the Elements of Nothingness, Wind, Water, Earth, Fire" in 1997. Like the book *Take Up Your Cross and Follow: Daily Lenten Reflections*, this book went through several incarnations before it made it into print. After finishing the work on the manuscript in the Spring of 1997, I wrote a query to Twomey at Liturgical Press on April 6, 1997. It was not until March 8, 1998, that I got a negative response. Knowing how long the process of submitting a proposal and hearing from a publisher might take, I learned to cut down on the time by submitting proposals for the same book to several different publishers. On April 9, 1997, I began my all-too-familiar process with Lisa Biedenbach at St. Anthony Messenger Press. On April 14, 1997, she requested an outline and two sample chapters, which I sent on April 21, 1997. Having received no response, I wrote to her on June 11, 1998, getting a reply on July 27, 1998, that an assistant sent me a letter on March 17, 1998—which I didn't receive—informing me that SAMP was not interested in publishing the book.

On April 9, 1997, I also queried Pierce at ACTA Publications in Chicago. However, it was not until January 2, 1998, that I sent the manuscript to him. It took him only a few days to indicate that he was not interested in it on January 13, 1998. No response was ever received from my April 9, 1997, query to Ave Maria Press.

On March 12, 1998, I queried Paulist Press. Kevin A. Lynch requested a copy of the manuscript on March 20, 1998. I sent the manuscript on March 24, 1998, and received a rejection letter on May 14, 1998. Also on March 12, 1998, I queried Jeremy Langford at Sheed & Ward; he requested a copy of the manuscript, which I sent to him on April 26, 1998. I received no response from him. New City Press in New York responded to my March 12, 1998, query letter on April 2, 1998, stating "it does not fit into our publishing program at this time." Rowman & Littlefield responded to my March 12, 1998, letter on April 27, 1998, stating that "it would not be right for Rowman & Littlefield." Prometheus Books in New York responded on March 17, 1998, stating: "Prometheus Books is a secular, humanist, free-thought press. We are the world's largest independent publisher of biblical criticism and critiques of traditional religious claims. Your project would probably be better served with a publisher more sympathetic to these traditional views." No response was ever received from Pilgrim Press in Cleveland, and Oxford University Press merely returned my letter.

From 1998 to 2002 the manuscript went into hibernation. After so many rejection letters I thought that it would never see the light of day. However, in the spring of 2002 I reworked the book, and on March 13, 2002, I queried Crossroad Publishing, but the letter was returned to me. I also queried Thomas More Publishing, from whom I received no answer, and Servant Publications, from whom I received no answer. Twenty-Third Publications said no, and, while Oregon Catholic Press expressed an interest, the editor was not interested. On April 19, 2002, I send a query to Loyola Press, Chicago, for whom I prepared a proposal, which was rejected on September 9, 2002. Likewise, Zondervan rejected the work on April 4, 2003, as did Paraclete Press on June 25, 2003, and as did New Leaf Press, Morehouse Publishing, and Eerdmans. The later did so in August 2005, when I had sent out another inquiry letter. Again, the book went into hibernation in a file cabinet with no hope of ever being published.

In 2013 I read a book published by Wipf and Stock Publishers, Eugene, Oregon, and that gave me an idea. I visited the website, read about the types of books Wipf and Stock published, and prepared a book proposal for what I was now calling *Nature Spirituality: Praying with Wind, Water, Earth, Fire*. I submitted the proposal electronically on June 20, 2013. On August 3, 2013, Christian Amondson, Assistant Managing Editor, e-mailed me that Wipf and Stock had accepted my proposed book for publication under its Resource Publications imprint. The contract was signed on August 5, 2013, and by the middle of September 2013 the book was in print. Of course, I did not know it then, but Wipf and Stock and I would be partnering on a number of future publishing endeavors. It had taken sixteen years and several incarnations to get this book on ecology into print.

Even though Wipf and Stock asked me to invest in the publication of the book—by paying $2 per type-set page and editing the manuscript or having it edited by another person—I liked working with the staff in Eugene, Oregon. So, with all that experience I set out on my next writing project with a view of getting it published by Wipf and Stock.

A Spirituality of Ageing

Yes, the word *ageing* can be spelled that way or *aging*. Both are acceptable ways to present the word in print. I chose *ageing* because I wanted to emphasize the *age* aspect of the word. And in academic work, *ag* without the *e* refers to agriculture. In 2013 I had chosen to work with some of the literatures of world religions. I had a degree in World Religions, but seldom used anything that I had learned because I taught courses in the Bible and film at Missouri State University. Most of the time I found myself immersed either in the Christian Bible (New Testament), the Hebrew Bible (Old Testament) or a movie. I began researching the literature of world religions with the goal of presenting a universal view of ageing. After completing my research, I decided to organize it as a workbook using the five stages of denial, anger, bargaining, depression, and acceptance. The last chapter functions as a synthesis of the reader's thoughts after having read the book and worked through its exercises.

After finishing the manuscript, I submitted a proposal to Wipf and Stock on Saturday, January 18, 2014. Matthew Wimer, Assistant Managing Editor, informed me that it had been accepted for publication under the Wipf and Stock imprint on March 17, 2014. The Wipf and Stock imprint requires authors to submit manuscripts to a professional copy editor. Since I was a professional copy editor, I informed Wimer that I would be editing my own book and saving some money in the process. The contract was issued and signed on March 18, 2014, and by the middle of 2014, the book was in print. This was one of my most rewarding experiences of getting a manuscript into print. There were no multiple proposals; there were no years of waiting for a reply from a publisher; there were no years of waiting for a manuscript to become a book. *A Spirituality of Ageing* was in print within six months from when it was submitted as a proposal. I was learning from Wipf and Stock that there are others ways to get a book published than the laborious and expensive process in which I had been engaged for years.

Caroling through Advent and Christmas

However, I was still not yet finished with the old process. In 2011, I worked on an Advent and Christmas book of reflections using hymns and Christmas carols as the starting point instead of the Scripture texts. The first query e-mail I sent was to Mark Zimmermann at Creative Communications on February 1, 2012. I proposed the title "Caroling through Advent and Christmas." He replied the same day, stating that he had already published something similar a few years before; therefore, he was not interested in my proposal. On February 18, 2012, I sent the proposal to Twenty-Third Publications. On February 27, 2012, I received an e-mail from Paul Pennick, Acquisitions for Twenty-Third Publications owned by Bayard, stating that its "seasonal booklets follow a very specific pattern, which has brought . . . consistent sales." As I had experienced this before, sales was the top consideration, not to mention the inability to change the pattern! "Your proposal format," he continued," would change that formula considerably, and our marketing people did not want to acquire a very different product."

Next, I tried Pierce at ACTA in Chicago on February 29, 2012. On March 1, 2012, Pierce e-mailed me that he liked the idea, but it would have to wait until the Fall of 2013. I responded the same day, telling him that I was willing to wait and to change the dates in the manuscript for 2013–2014. However, Pierce never answered my e-mail, and that was the end of it with ACTA.

In the meantime, on March 10, 2012, I sent a proposal and the manuscript to Liguori Publications, Liguori, Missouri, thinking this might be a suitable publisher for this book. Having heard nothing about my proposal, I inquired Liguori on July 31, 2012. I received an e-mail reply telling me that it was "still under consideration." There was a suggestion that taking out the specific dates would make the book useful for any year. Then, there was a lengthy paragraph about all the work the editorial staff was doing and how far behind the members were. This should have alerted me to the slowness that was ahead, but it didn't. Finally, on September 24, 2012, I received an e-mail from Christy Hicks, Acquisitions Editor, expressing an interest in my book and desiring to speak to me about it through a telephone conversation. We spoke with each other the next day. I agreed to remove the dates and, then, to send her the whole manuscript. She replied by saying she would speak with her marketing partner and get back with me in a few weeks. I did not hear from her again until December 20, 2012, when I received a two-page e-mail with her suggestions for tweaks. She wanted the introduction rewritten; however, she basically rewrote it the way she wanted it in the e-mail she sent to me! She didn't like some of the Advent hymns I had chosen and wanted more familiar hymns; the same was true for the Christmas carols. She wanted reflections "enhanced," but did not explain what that meant. On and on the suggestions went. If I made the changes, then she would present the book to the acquisitions committee. I responded to her e-mail on January 4, 2013, indicating that I would make the changes and get them to her by the end of February. However, I finished the changes and sent them to her on January 18, 2013. She did not reply until January 31, 2013, telling me that the process was moving forward.

On May 2, 2013, Susann Fields, Director of Finance and Business Operations for Liguori, sent me a contract for the publication of the book, which I signed and returned the next day. On August 1, 2013, Hicks send me an e-mail informing me that she was leaving Liguori for another job as of August 13, 2013. I had been here before. I knew that this meant trouble. And, indeed, it did.

I heard nothing more from Liguori until April 7, 2014, when Mary Brockgreitens, Liguori's publicist, informed me that she was changing the title of my book to "Caroling through Advent and Christmas: Daily Reflections on Familiar Hymns." There was also a long paragraph about marketing. I replied by stating that the subtitle should not be "on" but "with." On April 15, 2014, she informed me that I was correct. Then, she made corrections in the biographical information I had sent. "Given the nature of your book and its audience, we believe people will connect more readily with your pastoral experience than your academic experience," she stated. She rewrote my biography to suit her own needs.

On May 29, 2014, I received an e-mail from Julia DiSalvo, Acquisitions Editor, who sent me "the latest draft" of my book to be turned over to production in a week. She had added material to the work and rearranged lots of it. I informed her that she could not change what the Church's books presented in terms of Scripture texts and antiphons. I heard nothing more until October 2, 2014, when I received an edited draft of the book. After I looked over the mess that my book now was, I responded to DiSalvo on October 3, 2014, stating: "I cannot tell you how disappointed I am with it. I hate to write this, but I have to. After all the discussion we had about a subtitle, the subtitle does not appear. The dedication lines are not lined up the way I sent them and make no sense with one word on a line. I didn't write some of the introduction which confuses the A, B, C cycles that I had explained very carefully. Whoever made these changes does not understand the difference between Lord and LORD—and there is a big difference. An introduction to the First Sunday of Advent about cycles is further confusing. The lines of the first hymn, 'Go Tell It on the Mountain,' are not in correct order."

I went on to explain that whoever had edited my book did not understand how the liturgical year works, because, if he or she did, the person would not have made the changes he or she did. I also explained that my style had been radically altered or entirely dismantled. By October 2, 2014, my book looked nothing like I had submitted. I was ready to cancel its publication when it was taken away from DiSalvo, whom I suspect is the person who had changed it, when another editor at Liguori contacted me, sent me the proof pages, and asked me to go through them in a couple of days and restore what I had originally written. No one knows how much work this is until he or she begins it. I knew that my original material was accurate; now I had to compare what was on the proof pages to what I had originally written, and, in many cases, remove it or correct it.

This process had already been an exercise in frustration in March 2014. DiSalvo had informed me that all the hymns I had used in the book were in the public domain except one. It was my responsibility to obtain permission to use the material. On March 6, 2014, I wrote to the copyright owner, but received no response. I called on April 9, 2014, and the person in charge of granting permission to use copyrighted material didn't even know what I was talking about. The man I spoke to informed me that he was going to charge a fee to use the lyrics of the hymn. That means that four entries in the book needed to be rewritten. Of course, those were the four that Hicks had wanted changed. Now, I was putting back what I had taken out!

This book was rushed into production in October 2014 for the Advent-Christmas market of 2014–2015. For me the book represents not just frustration with people who know nothing about the liturgical calendar or how it works, but it also represents disappointment at the incompetence of those who were supposed to make the work look good. Even though I proposed one more book to Liguori, I made up my mind not to put myself through this ever again. It was back to Wipf and Stock for me!

Weekday Saints

In 2011, after having finished *Day by Ordinary Day: Daily Reflections on the First Readings, Year 2 (Volume 5)* for St. Pauls/Alba House, I set to work on a sixth volume titled "Day by Ordinary Day: Reflections on the Saints." The last volume of the series was to contain reflections on the proper readings for weekdays that interrupted the usual assigned Scripture texts. Also included in the last volume was a guide to the reflections on the readings for all the solemnities, feasts, and memorials that were scattered through the other five volumes. On July 1, 2011, I sent the volume to Edmund C. Lane, presuming that he would want it for St. Pauls/Alba House to complete the series. He confirmed receipt of the manuscript on July 7, 2011, and wrote on October 13, 2011, that it would not fit into the current publishing program. In other words, he was rejecting the work.

After a few days, I set to work dismantling the manuscript as volume 6 of a series and reassembling it as a stand-alone volume of reflections on the Scripture texts assigned for celebrations of saints that occurred only on weekdays. After reassembling the material, I noted anything missing reflections—those that were contained in the five volumes that St. Pauls/Alba House had published—and any other reflections that could be included in a stand-alone volume. After making an inventory, I began to write new reflections to replace those already published and to write reflections for Scripture texts that I had never considered before. By the time I was finished, I had a new book titled *Weekday Saints*.

I sent the manuscript to Liturgical Press on August 8, 2012. Trish Sullivan Vanni, Publisher of the Parish Market, replied the same day indicating "a positive reception" and requesting sample entries. Since the manuscript was finished, I sent those to her the same day. She e-mailed me on October 24, 2012, explaining that because of travel and a log-jammed acquisitions process, she would take my book to the acquisitions committee at the end of November. Having heard nothing from her, I e-mailed her on January 30, 2013, requesting information. After beginning the e-mail with an apology with all kinds of excuses for not communicating with me, she informed me that the book was rejected on January 31, 2013.

The next day I submitted a proposal to Franciscan Media. Mary Carol Kendzia, Product Development Director, responded with a rejection e-mail on March 15, 2013. On March 18, 2013, I sent a proposal to Twenty-Third Publications (Bayard). Paul Pennick, Acquisitions, requested parts of the manuscript, which I sent, and he informed me on March 22, 2013, that at an acquisitions meeting the committee decided not to accept the work for publication. I queried Joe Durepos at Loyola Press, Chicago, and sent the manuscript to him. While he was away, Vinita Wright, Senior Editor, read the work and rejected it on May 21, 2013. After submitting a twenty-page proposal to Our Sunday Visitor Press on June 20, 2013, Jacquelyn Lindsey, Acquisitions Editor, e-mailed a rejection letter to me on July 19, 2013.

On July 30, 2014, after letting the manuscript sit for a year in a file, and after having success with two previous books, I completed a proposal and sent it to Wipf and Stock. To my amazement, Wimer informed me that *Weekday Saints: Reflections on Their Scriptures* was accepted for publication by Wipf and Stock on August 4, 2014. The contract for the book was issued the same day! By late October 2014, the 154-page book was in print!

Writing

Human Wholeness

From 1997 to 2000 I participated in New Orleans' Loyola Institute for Ministry Extension Program, commonly referred to as LIMEX. The cohort of eight people took ten courses, each consisting of ten sessions over ten weeks, earning thirty credit hours and graduating with a Master's Degree or a Master of Religious Education Degree. As part of two courses, I wrote twenty-page papers that eventually evolved into the book, *Human Wholeness: A Spirituality of Relationship*. At the same time as I was involved in LIMEX, I was also cultivating the friendship of a student I had taught at Southwest Missouri State University (now Missouri State University). Matthew S. Miller (now Ver Miller) had been in one of my courses, and, through our dialogue and discussion of his work, we had become friends. Once the course was finished, we began to get together weekly for dinner, either in my home or in his apartment. After he graduated from SMSU in 2000, he continued to stay in Springfield and attend Forest Institute of Professional Psychology, taking courses toward earning a Master's and then a Doctorate in Psychology. We continued to get together for meals and began to share some ideas on a psychological and philosophical understanding of friendship. One evening I proposed the possibility of writing a book based on our discussions. We would have to record what we were talking about and translate it into written English. He agreed, and, so for a year, we worked on individual sections of an outline I proposed and we refined together. The basic process was discussion, followed by my writing of what I heard, and our critique of what I tried to put into words. By the time we were finished, we had a book titled "You're Not Going to Get Away: A Theology of Relationship."

On May 16, 2000, I sent the first of what would be twenty-five query letters for this manuscript. Twenty-Third Publications Co-Publisher Gwen Costello responded with an e-mail, requesting a hard copy of the manuscript, which I sent to her on July 11, 2000, after having traveled around some of Europe with Miller. On August 7, 2000, she wrote to inform me "that the decision to publish is negative." On August 11 of the same year, I queried Paulist Press, got a reply requesting a proposal, sent the proposal on August 21, 2000, and on August 28, 2000, received a letter stating that my manuscript did not fit in with Paulist Press's publishing program. On September 7, 2000, a letter was sent to Servant Publications; a senior editor responded with an undated form letter with one line checked about the manuscript not fitting the current publishing plans. Pierce did not ever respond to my October 2, 2000, query to ACTA. Thomas Skorupa at Forest of Peace Publishing did respond to my October 23, 2000 query. I submitted the manuscript to him on November 13, 2000, but he did not reject it until March 21, 2001. On October 23, 2000, I had also queried Ave Maria Press, but got no reply until February 17, 2001, from Frank J. Cunningham, Publisher. After getting an e-mail reply from him requesting a copy of the manuscript, I sent it to him on February 21, 2001, only to be told on April 2, 2001, that he had "decided against publication."

My Life of Ministry, Writing, Teaching, and Traveling

On April 10, 2001, I queried Orbis Books, receiving an April 19, 2001, letter informing me that it didn't fit into the "specialized program" there. Also on April 10, 2001, I queried Ambassador Books and received a May 22, 2001, rejection letter. An inquiry letter also went to Sheed & Ward on April 10, 2001. Jeremy Langford, Co-Publisher, sent an e-mail on April 20, 2001, requesting a copy of the whole manuscript, which I sent on April 25, 2001. On August 20, 2001, I sent him an e-mail, asking for an update on the status of the work. On September 26, 2001, he sent me an e-mail stating that Sheed & Ward "would love to publish it." He added, "As things look, it would fit nicely into our spring 2002 list." I responded that I would be delighted if Sheed & Ward published the book. All I needed was a contract. On October 1, 2001, I received an e-mail from Stephen J. Hrycyniak, Co-Publisher of Sheed & Ward, with a Marketing Questionnaire attached. Miller and I completed the materials and enclosed a black and white photograph of each of us, and sent everything to Hrycyniak on October 10, 2001.

On October 5, 2001, I got an e-mail from Langford stating that the "editorial advisory board members . . . decided not to contract [my] book on the grounds that it does not fit [Sheed & Ward's] list." Thus, as quickly as hope for publishing the manuscript arose, so did it quickly fade! On October 8, 2001, I wrote to Langford:

> I am very disappointed, especially after all the trouble and time spent preparing the promotional material and getting black and white photos done. I have other things to do than waste my time working on useless promotional materials. Furthermore, the co-author took a lot of time from his doctoral studies to prepare his side of the promotional materials. Why did you tell me Sheed & Ward was accepting the book for publication if, in fact, it had not been fully accepted? Doesn't that border on deceit?

On April 10, 2001, in addition to the publishers mentioned above, I also queried Liguori Publications, received a request to see the manuscript, and sent it on July 18, 2001. However, on September 28, 2001, I received a letter from John J. Cleary, Assistant Editor, informing me that the book was "not suitable for [Liguori's] publishing program at [that] time. . . ." My query to Thomas More on October 9, 2001, got a few scribbled lines on my letter indicating no interest. The October 9, 2001, query to Morehouse Publication fared no better, getting a form letter stating that the material did not meet the publishing needs. Likewise, Johns Hopkins University Press on October 19, 2001, responded to my October 9, 2001, letter, stating that "this project does not appear to fit the needs of our publishing program at present." Jossey-Bass declared on November 12, 2001, that my query of October 9, 2001, was not a project it could take on at that time. Chalice Press sent a rejection letter on November 30, 2001, and, while Crossroad Publishing sent me an e-mail, no other response was ever forthcoming.

After all my October 9, 2001, queries had failed, on December 21, 2001, I tried again. I began with St. Pauls/Alba House, and got a January 7, 2002, letter from Lane stating that it could not be worked into the publishing schedule. Resurrection Press requested a hard copy of the manuscript, which I sent on December 29, 2001, and which was rejected January 30, 2002. Twomey at Liturgical Press waited until February 1, 2002, to indicate he was not interested in the book.

On April 22, 2002, I queried A.R.E. Press and got an e-mail on April 26, 2002, with a brochure attached that explained the type of books published; this book did not fit the type. On April 22, 2002, I also queried Broadman & Holman Publishers, Nashville, Tennessee, and received a letter indicating that the book did not fit the publisher's needs. Standard Publishing, Cincinnati, Ohio, responded with a form letter with two of the seven points checked, namely, that the publisher was not looking for this type of material and the book did not fit its line. InterVarsity Press sent an e-mail on June 18, 2002, indicating no interest. St. Martin's Press replied with a form letter indicating that a literary agent had to submit a book proposal for consideration. Other publishers were also contacted, and no response, either letter or e-mail, was received. Thus, from 2002 to 2011, the manuscript lived in a file.

In May 2011, I discovered New World Library. I completed a proposal online on May 28, 2011, and submitted it. I had changed the title of the book to "Friendship: A Mystical Experience of God." I inquired about the proposal through e-mail on July 6, 2011. A response came through e-mail on July 18, 2011, informing me that New World Library was not interested in pursuing the project. After having contacted every publisher I knew existed, on August 22, 2011, I submitted a proposal to Eerdmans online and received a September 27, 2011, e-mail rejecting the book. At this point I was satisfied that this manuscript would never be published.

While visiting Ver Miller in Denver during the summer of 2014, I mentioned my success with book publishing with Wipf and Stock. He asked me if he thought that our book might be sent there. I told him that I would think about it. After I got home I found the manuscript and read it. I made some changes in it, gave it a new title (*Human Wholeness: A Spirituality of Relationship, Basis for Friendship, Basis for Mystical Experience*), and prepared a proposal for it with Wipf and Stock on September 10, 2014. On November 14, 2014, Wimer, Assistant Managing Editor at Wipf and Stock, informed me that the manuscript had been accepted for publication under the Wipf and Stock imprint. I notified Ver Miller the same day and explained to him the process of getting this book into print. Some things he could do from Denver, but other things meant that we would have to agree to get together and talk about the material in the book. The first thing that had to be done was to sign a contract, which would specify when the final manuscript would be delivered to Wipf and Stock. We agreed that we would have the project finished by January 31, 2015. Then, we signed a contract with Wipf and Stock on November 17, 2014, to publish the book. After working separately, but communicating frequently, Ver Miller came to Springfield mid-January 2015, and we finished the manuscript. By February 25, 2015, the book was in print. It had taken only fifteen years to get this 72-page book into print! The title we finally agreed on was

Human Wholeness: A Spirituality of Relationship. This was the first book I ever wrote with another author.

A Simple Systematic Mariology

After having published four books with Wipf and Stock, I decided to send a proposal for a book on Mariology to Wipf and Stock. I had worked on the manuscript of *A Simple Systematic Mariology* in the Summer and Fall of 2014. I had sent a proposal to Ignatius Press on October 25, 2014, and received a rejection letter on December 16, 2014. But spurred by the negative response, I prepared the Wipf and Stock proposal and submitted it on December 20, 2014, being pretty confident that it would be accepted for publication there. On February 3, 2015, Wimer sent me an e-mail stating that the book had been accepted for publication under the Wipf and Stock imprint. He asked me to increase the word count before submitting the final manuscript for publication. The contract was issued February 4, 2015. I had the final manuscript ready and sent to Wipf and Stock on February 26, 2015. On March 3, 2015, Wimer contacted me about some copy editing that needed to be done on the manuscript. I assured him that I would have it finished in a few days and that I was not hiring a copy editor to do what I knew how to do. I had always been suspicious of this part of the process. Generally, copy editors were paid $400. Because I copy edited my own books, Wipf and Stock did not get that $400 from me. However, as more and more books were accepted for publication, more and more e-mails began to arrive about copy editing. I continued to work on the manuscript, refusing to hire a copy editor, and, of course, risking not having another book accepted for publication by Wipf and Stock.

A Simple Systematic Mariology—my fifth Wipf and Stock title—was published April 8, 2015. It was only 63-pages long, but unlike previous books that often took years to get into print, this one took only about a year from the time I began to research the material and write it until the time the finished product appeared.

Praying Your Way through Luke's Gospel and the Acts of the Apostles

I had written *Praying Your Way through Luke's Gospel and the Acts of the Apostles* in 2010–2011. There are two major themes that hold together Luke's Gospel and the Acts of the Apostles. The first is eating, and the second is praying. Several books have been written on the eating theme; I chose to write a book on the praying theme, since no one had ever developed that thesis. After researching and writing during the Fall of 2010 and through the Winter of 2011, I submitted an e-mail proposal to Liturgical Press on March 8, 2011, and got a negative response on September 2, 2011. On the same day, I also e-mailed St. Pauls/Alba House and got a negative response on May 21, 2011. Next up was Paulist Press on September 3, 2011, which replied with a no on November 15, 2011.

Writing

I did not think that it would be hard to get into print a book like this. So, on December 5, 2011, I e-mailed Orbis Books; the editor replied the same day with a negative response. I prepared an online proposal for Franciscan Media on December 21, 2011, send the manuscript on January 20, 2012, and got a negative response on February 10, 2012. I also got a negative from ACTA on February 11, 2012. On March 12, 2012, I sent a query to Our Sunday Visitor Press, and got a no response on July 24, 2012. My query to Eerdmans on July 31, 2012, received a no response on August 22, 2012, and my query to Ave Maria Press on August 22, 2012, got a no response on October 17, 2012. I queried Fortress Press on October 26, 2012, and got a no response on November 1, 2012. Next up was Pauline Books and Media. After sending a query e-mail on November 10, 2012, I got a response asking me to complete a formal proposal on January 30, 2013, but a negative response came on February 6, 2012.

After all these negative responses, I put the manuscript away for a year. On February 6, 2013, I contacted Loyola Press, but got a no on April 2, 2013, after sending the whole manuscript on February 13, 2013. Twenty-Third Publications (Bayard) rejected the book on April 11, 2013, as did Chalice Press on February 22, 2014, Liguori on July 1, 2014, and several other publishers. As a friend said to me, "It shouldn't be this hard to get this book into print." And while I agreed with him, my experience was narrating a different story.

Based on my success with Wipf and Stock, I decided to send a proposal to Eugene, Oregon, on February 27, 2015. By April 8, 2015, the book had been accepted for publication by Wipf and Stock and a contract (Memorandum of Agreement) had been signed. By May 31, 2015, the manuscript was in the hands of the Wipf and Stock staff, and it was published on September 16, 2015. It was my sixth Wipf and Stock title.

While it took only five years to get this book into print, I was learning that the bottom line for Catholic publishers has nothing to do with the dissemination of information in book form. It has everything to do with money, selling books, making a profit—even though many Catholic book publishers are not-for-profit organizations! Wipf and Stock makes money and pays royalties, but has found a way to cut expenses. For example, the author is responsible for either copy editing his or her work or paying someone to do the copy editing for him or her. Also, the author pays Wipf and Stock $2 a page to offset the cost of typesetting. Finally, Wipf and Stock does not print hundreds or thousands of copies of the book; in fact, books are not printed until they are ordered. This means that there is no standing inventory and no need to rent space to store inventory.

Daybreaks

While working on *Caroling through Advent and Christmas* for Liguori Press, Theresa Nienaber, Acquisitions Editor, e-mailed me in early summer 2014, asking if I was interested in writing *Daybreaks: Daily Reflections for Advent and Christmas* and *Daybreaks:*

My Life of Ministry, Writing, Teaching, and Traveling

Daily Reflections for Lent and Easter. The Advent and Christmas Daybreaks would be published in 2015, and the Lent and Easter Daybreaks would be published in 2016. I was not familiar with the *Daybreaks* series. So, I asked for some sample copies, and, after looking over them, agreed to write both.

I had lots of freedom as to the subject matter within the context of the liturgical seasons. Whatever I wrote had to be short and fall within the guidelines that Nienaber sent me. For my theme I chose the people and things of Advent and Christmas and the people and things of Lent and Easter. With a little work on this project every day, it took me about a month to complete both writing projects. Nienaber e-mailed me on August 2, 2014, to tell me that she had given me some erroneous information about the Lent and Easter Daybreaks. I went through the manuscript and fixed it according to the mistaken guidelines she had sent to me.

While both writing projects were finished, I had received no contract. So, I held on to both of the manuscripts. On October 24, 2014, the contracts arrived, I signed them, and returned them. A few days later, I sent Nienaber the manuscripts. On January 24, 2015, I got the proof pages for both, and noticed immediately that the *New Revised Standard Version of the Bible* that I had used had been changed to the *New American Bible: Revised Edition*. That meant that every biblical quotation was now altered and, in many cases, did not now fit the context into which I had placed it in the manuscript. I spent a lot of time going through and fixing what had been altered. When returning the corrected page proofs, I asked Nienaber why the biblical translation had been changed; I had used the NRSV in *Caroling through Advent and Christmas*, and it was not changed to NABRE. Her response was that the NABRE was house style, and she was not sure why *Caroling* did not use it. I guessed that it was because it was so late getting into print that no editor took time to look at it!

In my e-mail, I also questioned the use of ellipses in brackets, a very strange construction I had noticed in the proof pages. I explained that putting ellipses in brackets was redundant. An ellipsis, consisting of three periods, indicates that something is missing in a quote. A bracket around a letter or a word indicates that something has been added to the quote to help the reader understand. For example, a quote using a pronoun will often have the noun inserted in brackets in place of the pronoun in order to tell the reader that the writer has inserted it. As I explained all this, I asked myself: How could an editor not know this? I did get an e-mail response on January 26, 2015, in which she wrote, ". . . [Y]ou were 100 percent right on this one."

The point that greatly disturbed me more than the use of ellipses in brackets was the addition of reflections to the Advent and Christmas Daybreaks. She wanted four full weeks of reflections, even through, because of the way the liturgical calendar is arranged, Advent only lasts a few days of the fourth week. If Christmas is on Tuesday, then the fourth week of Advent lasts only two days (Sunday and Monday). I explained to her that because of the variance in the liturgical year, there was no way to put extra reflections. I wrote them, anyway. The extra reflections were inserted after the specific December 17–24 series of Scripture texts to complete a full Fourth Week of Advent, even though there wasn't such in 2015 with Christmas being on Friday! The reflection I had titled "Virgin Sign" is "Nature," which has absolutely nothing to do with the topic of the reflection! The focus of the booklet is on Advent and the first week of the Christmas Season. The second and third weeks of Christmas have no reflections. In other words, the season of preparation, Advent, has little to recommend for celebration (Christmas). It is obvious that the focus of the booklet is on making money. Furthermore, there is nothing in the contract I signed about translating the English booklet into Spanish, yet it was done. There is no doubt in my mind that this is a move to boost sales, too. The reader needs to know that no royalties are earned on the sales of these booklets; the writer is paid a stipend; the publisher can print and sell as many as it wants.

On February 20, 2015, I went through the Lent and Easter Daybreaks, noting that the word "LORD" had been changed to "Lord" in all the biblical texts that had, again, been changed from NRSV to NABRE. LORD is used in the Hebrew Bible (Old Testament) as a substitute for Yahweh, since neither Jews nor Christians call God by name. Lord is used in the Christian Bible (New Testament) to refer to Jesus. Changing LORD to Lord means that the reference has been changed. After bringing this to Nienaber's attention, I fixed what I could and sent the proof pages back to her. After it was printed, I never did examine it closely to determine what changes were made after I had submitted the final proof pages.

What I learned from writing Daybreaks is that the editors at Ligouri were interested in only the bottom line. Many of them didn't understand the liturgical year or some basic editing uses. While the layout of both booklets was very nice, it was geared only to marketability. The focus, as I learned through e-mail and telephone discussions, is not on reflecting on the liturgical year; it is on getting Catholics to consume items containing reflections on the days of the seasons of the liturgical year. And, even more upsetting, there is very little focus on Christmas and Easter; the focus is on Advent and Lent because people buy a lot of pamphlets during Advent and Lent!

A Spirituality of Mission

Before I escaped from Catholic publishers I had one more experience of getting a book in print that focused only on making money. In 2014, I had worked on a book on the spirituality of mission. At the end of June 2014, I sent a query letter to Lane at Alba/St. Pauls; he responded on July 7, stating that the editorial staff had determined that they "simply could not fit this work into [their] present publishing program." On July 12, I queried American Catholic (previously Franciscan Media) and got a not-interested response on August 13 from Kendzia, Product Development Director: "The books are not jumping off the shelf, despite the Church's persistent emphasis on the importance of evangelization, a point made clear by Popes John Paul II, Benedict XVI, and now,

Francis. There is no doubt it is a key charism of Catholic discipleship; getting people to 'buy in,' especially with books and other resources, seems to be a challenge, however."

On August 2, I e-mailed New World Library, which never did respond to my submission except with an automated reply e-mail informing me not to respond to the message. After waiting the stated twelve weeks, I presumed that the answer was no. So, on February 9, 2015, I queried Hudock at Liturgical Press by sending him the entire manuscript. He responded with an e-mail on February 25, indicating that he had some interesting conversations about it with his colleagues. Then came the question: "Would you consider revising this project to frame it as a daily companion during the fifty days of the Easter season?" He explained, "The aim would be to develop the reader's awareness, day-by-day through the season, of their (sic) own spirituality of mission.... If we went this direction, it might be worth considering connecting the section for each day to the day's gospel reading, but that might involve a bit more revision."

I responded the same day with an e-mail indicating that I would consider revising the book "with the assurance of a contract to publish it." I added, "In other words, I'm not doing the revising and then having Liturgical Press tell me that it won't publish it. After forty-one books in print, I've learned my lesson on that one!" After I thought about this for a few hours, I e-mailed Hudock stating that there was no way to connect the entries in the book to the Easter Season readings, but that I was interested in developing a book of reflections for the Easter season based on the Scripture texts assigned for those days. Hudock replied: "We're unsure whether there would be a . . . receptivity to Easter daily reflections. Can you imagine parishes buying these in bulk as they do the other two products [of Advent and Lenten reflections]? What do you think?" I replied that I thought parishes would buy them if they were offered to them. Hudock stated that he would bring my book to the acquisitions committee at its next meeting on March 17 in the form in which I submitted it; if the members supported it, he would offer me a contract. After the March 17 meeting, Hudock contacted me to tell me that the acquisitions committee had accepted the book with, of course, some modifications. The contract was signed on April 2, 2015.

The committee wanted more material about the use of the book in the introduction along with several tracks alongside each entry for possible use. I provided three tracks: one began with Ash Wednesday; one began with Palm Sunday; and one began with the First Sunday of Advent. I sent these changes to Hudock on June 4. He replied on June 11 indicating that he wanted to stick to the Holy Week and Easter track; so I went through the manuscript and erased the other two tracks. On July 2, Hudock accepted the revised manuscript and passed it on to the managing editor, Andy Edwards, who informed me on November 1, 2016, he had done "some minor redacting to get each reflection down to a two-page spread in order to reduce the total page count to 160 pages. Edwards provided me with a list of fifteen reflections for me to go through in order to make them fit on two pages. The book was published in January 2017 as *A Spirituality of Mission: Reflections for Holy Week and Easter*. From the time of writing to the time of publication, three years had elapsed. My experiences with Wipf and Stock were pointing me away from Catholic publishers and toward a company that could get a book in print in a timely fashion and without all the hassles. As I found myself escaping the woes of Catholic publishing, I noticed my creativity returning and my stress level dropping. I had more ideas than I could keep writing about.

To top it all off, I noticed in the Liturgical Press 2019 catalogue that there now was listed a book for the Easter Season! It was like the annual one for Advent and Christmas (the series that I started) and like the annual one for Lent. I couldn't believe it! I had recommended the annual Easter Season book, but I was never contacted to write it!

Wipf and Stock

By the end of 2015, Wipf and Stock had published six of my books: *Nature Spirituality: Praying with Wind, Water, Earth, Fire* (2013); *A Spirituality of Ageing* (2014); *Weekday Saints: Reflections on Their Scriptures* (2014); *Human Wholeness: A Spirituality of Relationship* (with Matthew S. Ver Miller, 2015); *A Simple Systematic Mariology* (2015), and *Praying Your Way through Luke's Gospel and the Acts of the Apostles* (2015). The publishing process was simple: submit an online proposal, get a response within a few weeks, sign a contract, prepare the manuscript according to directions, and have a book published. As I looked toward my publishing future, I decided that this was the road to travel.

So, following the process, and after engaging in much research—demonstrated in four pages of bibliography—in order to incorporate my background in World Religions, Wipf and Stock published *An Abecedarian of Animal Spirit Guides: Spiritual Growth through Reflections on Creatures* in 2016. This book's entries are in alphabetical order. Each entry begins with a quote from a sacred text, which is followed by a reflection on the animal mentioned in the text, journal/meditation questions, and a prayer. It's companion volume, *An Abecedarian of Sacred Trees: Spiritual Growth through Reflections on Woody Plants*, was also published in 2016.

Also published in 2016 was *Overcome with Paschal Joy: Chanting through Lent and Easter—Daily Reflections with Familiar Hymns*. I had offered this book to Liguori Publications as a companion volume to my *Caroling through Advent and Christmas* book, but the editor had no interest in it. A little book that I had written many years ago which could not find a Catholic publisher was titled *Taking Leave of Your Home: Moving in the Peace of Christ*. Wipf and Stock published it in 2016. This book of reflections on moving from one house to another caused by health, age, death, job transfer, or disaster was rejected in 2003 by Ave Maria Press, ACTA Publications, Liturgical Press, St. Anthony Messenger Press, Pauline Books and Media, Paulist Press, Forest of Peace Publishing, and Resurrection Press. After letting the manuscript sit in my file for five years, Inner Traditions International/Bear & Co. and Liguori Publications rejected it in 2008. In between 2003 and 2008, several query letters received no response.

In 2017, Wipf and Stock published another researched book that I wrote about the Hebrew Bible (Old Testament). Titled *Divine Presence: Elements of Biblical Theophanies*, the book presents twenty-one natural elements employed by biblical writers in manifestations of God. The last chapter presents ways that modern people might understand and update the use of these elements. Also, in 2017, Wipf and Stock published my whimsical book *Fruit of the Vine: A Biblical Spirituality of Wine*. This volume shows how the transformation of grapes into wine parallels the transformation of people through their sharing of a glass of wine.

Names for Jesus: Reflections for Advent and Christmas, another book based on biblical texts, was published by Wipf and Stock in 2017. Each of fifty entries contains a Scripture quotation, a reflection that explores the meaning of the name, a journal/meditation section, and a short concluding prayer. Finally, in 2017, Wipf and Stock published my *Talk to God and Listen to the Casual Reply: Experiencing the Spirituality of John Denver*. This is the revision and updating of my previously self-published book *"Seeking Grace with Every Step:" The Spirituality of John Denver* (1996). I wrote *Talk* to commemorate the twentieth anniversary of John Denver's death on October 17, 2017.

Christ Our Passover Has Been Sacrificed: A Guide through Paschal Mystery Spirituality—Mystical Theology in The Roman Missal was published in January 2018. This book began as "A Guide through the Paschal Mystery" in 1993, when I queried Alba/St. Pauls and got a response that declared the manuscript to be "well written and readable," but not something Milella was interested in publishing. In contradiction to Milella, Twomey rejected the manuscript writing: "Our reviewers judged that the manuscript is too dependent on quotations as the basic message. The manuscript lacks extensive commentary on the scriptural and liturgical readings and prayers that are quoted." Tabor Publishing rejected the manuscript in 1994, along with St. Anthony Messenger Press and Liturgy Training Publications. In 1995, Resurrection Press rejected the manuscript after requesting a copy of it; Cerar, Publisher, charged me $2 in postage to have the hard copy of the manuscript returned to me! Other publishers rejecting the manuscript in 1995 included Servant Publications, Sheed & Ward, and Liguori Publications ("Although the manuscript received many positive comments, I'm sorry to say that the publisher has decided to forgo this project," wrote Anthony F. Chiffolo, Associate Editor). In 1996, publishers rejecting the manuscript included, Paulist Press, Our Sunday Visitor Press (". . . [A]t present, this is not the kind of material we need," stated Jacquelyn M. Lindsey, Acquisitions Editor), Orbis Books, and Ave Maria Press. In 1997, Jossey-Bass, Inc., Publishers, rejected the manuscript.

In the course of this manuscript's twenty-five years existence, it spent most of its time in a file cabinet. Also, the third edition of *The Roman Missal* was issued in 2011; this meant that the whole manuscript needed to be revised in light of the latest edition. I had already removed all NAB and NABRE Scripture material and substituted NRSV.

Harry Hagan, Associate Professor in St. Meinrad Seminary and School of Theology, endorsed the book, writing: ". . . Mark Boyer, standing in the great liturgical tradition of Adrian Nocent, Louis Bouyer, and others, unfolds the richness of the prayers, ritual, and readings during the celebration of the paschal mystery from Palm Sunday to Pentecost. . . . Boyer's work will help people recognize the wonderful and life-giving gift offered to us in the liturgies of Christ's paschal mystery." Paul Turner, pastor of the Cathedral of the Immaculate Conception in Kansas City, Missouri, stated that I "offered a pathway to clarity through a meditation on the paschal mystery."

Christ Our Passover Has Been Sacrificed: A Guide through Paschal Mystery Spirituality—Mystical Theology in The Roman Missal was my fifteenth Wipf and Stock title. It was followed later in 2018 by *Rosary Primer: The Prayers, The Mysteries, and the New Testament*, the second edition of my *Reflections on the Mysteries of the Rosary* already narrated above. Also, in 2018, Wipf and Stock published my *From Contemplation to Action: The Spiritual Process of Divine Discernment Using Elijah and Elisha as Models*. This original composition employs the ninth-century BCE prophets Elijah and Elisha as models. Their stories are embedded in the First and Second Book of Kings. Both of them are seers, messengers, and heralds of the LORD. They appear in activity when they are needed, and they disappear into solitude and silence when they are not. Each entry presents a Scripture text, a suggestion for reading more of the story from the books of Kings, a reflection, a journal/meditation question, and a concluding prayer. This book was my seventeenth Wipf & Stock title.

Another book published in 2018 is *All Things Mary*. This is a revised and expanded edition of my 1993 *Mary's Day—Saturday*. With the completion of the four-volume Lectionary from 1998 to 2002 and the issuance of a Supplement volume in 2017 along with the issuance of the *Collection of Masses of the Blessed Virgin Mary: Lectionary* in 2012, over two hundred biblical texts were presented for use in Masses honoring the Blessed Virgin Mary throughout the liturgical year and on special occasions. *All Things Mary* presents a reflection on every biblical text—along with a cross reference of its use—and a journal/meditation question and prayer. This was my nineteenth Wipf and Stock title, and it brought my published library to sixty volumes.

My eighteenth book was one written with Matthew S. Ver Miller, with whom I wrote *Human Wholeness*, and Corbin S. Cole, a former student, in 2019 and published by Wipf & Stock. Since I know Greek, I researched the use of the three of four Greek words for love in the Christian Bible (New Testament). Then, after grouping similar uses into chapters, I used modern technology to send groups of Scripture notations to my co-authors, who, along with me, reflected upon and e-mailed their ideas to me. I sifted through the ideas and wrote the book, *Love Addict*.

Also published by Wipf & Stock in 2019 was *Shhh! The Sound of Sheer Silence: A Biblical Spirituality that Transforms*. The goal of this volume was to help readers nourish their spirituality through their observance of silence and to be transformed through it. Each of the entries in five chapters contains a biblical quotation, a reflection, a journal/meditation question, and a prayer. By engaging in the process of reflecting on biblical accounts of silence, the reader can be transformed through his or her experience of being quiet.

The last book published by Wipf & Stock in 2019 was *What is Born of the Spirit is Spirit: A Biblical Spirituality of Spirit*. In over a hundred entries divided into nine chapters, I examine the use of the Hebrew word *ruach* and the Greek word *pneuma*—both words can mean breath, air, wind, or spirit. The premise of the book is that God's Spirit connects to our human spirit, and that is spirituality. By reading and reflecting on biblical texts and then applying them to our own lives, we foster biblical spirituality for ourselves and others with whom we come in contact.

In 2020, Wipf & Stock published *Very Short Reflections—for Advent and Christmas, Lent and Easter, Ordinary Time, and Saints—through the Liturgical Year*. The short paragraph for each day presents a theme found in the Mass texts instead of the Scripture texts. Also, before publishing this autobiography, Wipf & Stock published *Living Parables: Today's Versions*, written in cooperation with Cole. This book—*My Life of Ministry, Writing, Teaching, and Traveling*—is my sixty-fifth book.

In my early years, I had never thought of myself as a published author, until I wrote the history of my home parish and, after that, saw my first poem published. I had dabbled in poetry writing in high school and college, and I had some poems published during my post-graduate work. I wrote poetry for myself, to record my thoughts and feelings. After getting a few poems in print, and after getting a taste for writing for *The Mirror* before I became its editor, I did not yet know the thrill of seeing my name on a book. Thus, after my first poem, then my first article, then my first book, I was convinced that I had something to say. I did not contract to write a book; I always wrote the book I had in mind and then tried to find a publisher for it. After seeing sixty-five of my books in print, I am convinced that a book publisher somewhere is looking for what I have to say!

Endorsements

On the back cover—or infrequently on the first or second page under the front cover—a reader often can find endorsements. An endorsement is another reader's public support of a book. The reader providing the endorsement has credentials that support his or her opinion expressed in the few sentences of the endorsement. Thus, if I am writing a book on the Hebrew Bible (Old Testament), the publisher looks for an endorsement from a biblical scholar, who affirms what I have written. The scholar receives the typeset manuscript to read before the final proofreading is done and a cover is created for the book. Most publishers ask authors to submit five or more possible readers who might be willing to provide an endorsement for the book. Some reply to the publisher's request, and some do not.

Writing

The person who holds the record for the most endorsements of my books is Sister Pauline Nugent, CCVI, a member of the Modern and Classical Languages Department in Missouri State University, Springfield. She has enthusiastically endorsed fourteen of my sixty-five books. Second place is tied; Victor Matthews, Dean of the College of Humanities and Public Affairs at Missouri State University, Springfield, has endorsed six of my books, as has Vernon Meyer, a long-time friend and pastor of Sun Lakes United Church of Christ, Sun Lakes, Arizona. Third place for the most endorsements of my books is also tied; my good friend Matthew S. Ver Miller, a Licensed Psychologist and Board Certified Coach in Lakewood, Colorado, has endorsed five of my books, as has another good friend, John Kossler, an ecologist with Western Meridian Resources, Berthoud, Colorado.

Robert Hodgson has endorsed three of my books. A friend in Nixa, Missouri, Kristopher Morehead, has endorsed two of my books, as has Charles W. Hedrick, Jeremy Graddy, Harry Hagan, and Paul Turner. Stephen C. Berkwitz, Head of the Department of Religious Studies at Missouri State University, Springfield, also endorsed two of my books. Single endorsements of books have come from Janna D. Ver Miller, Lora Hobbs, J. Friedel, Mark Given, Luke Tembrock, Leslie Baynes, John Strong, Corbin Cole, Will Chiles, and Rita Thiron. This last group represents doctors, ministers, teachers, and former students. I acknowledge their contributions to the success of my writing.

13

Genuine Human Encounters

THROUGHOUT THE SEVENTY YEARS of my life, I have experienced what I call genuine human encounters. These are not acquaintances, nor are they simple friendships. They begin as acquaints, move into friendships, but then become genuine human encounters. They presuppose respect for the other person as other. They also presuppose integrity and trust that evolve into love. Some folks refer to such people as their best friends. I see potential in others; sometimes they don't see it in themselves and need me to awaken it. I've been privileged to have many of these best friends, and each one's story needs to be told. Some have lasted for only a few months; some have made it through many years. Some of my human encounters have already been narrated in the various chapters on mountain climbing and other travels. In my experience, time and place often separated me from the people I encountered genuinely. However, the memory of those relationships remains. In the order in which I made these genuine human encounters, I present the stories of some of them whose lives crossed mine.

Ted Agniel

A genuine human encounter occurred during my years attending Cardinal Glennon College (1968–1972). Theodore (Ted) Agniel, who was from Jefferson City, had attended the high school seminary in Hannibal, Missouri, before coming to Cardinal Glennon College. Because both of us were outsiders to the majority of our insider classmates, we gravitated toward each other. One year I enlisted Agniel to assist me in teaching sixth grade religion on Saturday mornings at St. Sebastian Parish in St. Louis. Incarnate Word Sister Ann Catherine Shaw was the director of religious education there. I would meet with Agniel before Saturday morning to make a lesson plan, from which he often strayed!

Because I was very much involved in my home parish, St. Joachim, for Holy Week, I invited Agniel to join me for the Palm Sunday celebration in 1971. I had carefully planned the Palm Sunday procession and Mass with the pastor's permission, and

I had counted on Agniel helping. He scheduled a workshop! I didn't know it then, but he was planning on leaving Glennon at the end of the year, the year before we were to graduate. In my journal, I recorded my hurt and disappointment, but I also noted that I would always forgive him. It was through Agniel that I came to understand God's forgiveness. I wrote that I loved him, but I did not think that he knew how to love yet. That year, 1971–1972, I was the head of the library student crew, and Agniel worked for me. I liked picking at him. I often found reasons to visit him in his room and hang out with him. Agniel left Cardinal Glennon College at the end of our Junior year in 1971. I remember him telling me that he had decided that the seminary was not for him. I do remember him finding me one time and visiting with me during the time I spent in St. Eustachius Parish, Portageville, Missouri, 1975–1976.

Noah Casey

At St. Meinrad School of Theology in 1972, I met a monk of St. Meinrad Archabbey who was a member of my class. His name was Noah Casey. Casey and I really didn't get to know each other until we attended Indiana University, Bloomington, together for the spring semester 1974. And even then, we got to know each other with the other two students from St. Meinrad who were participating in the program. Casey served as one of the deacons for the Mass during which Law ordained me to the priesthood in 1976. It was not until both of us were ordained priests and made Marriage Encounter together in May 1977 that we really encountered each other.

While Marriage Encounter was designed for married couples, priests often made the weekend with another priest. Instead of answers to specific questions being addressed to one's spouse, the priests addressed the people of God when sharing with each other. I knew about marriage encounter from couples who had made it in my home parish and St. Agnes Cathedral Parish, Springfield, where I was stationed as associate pastor. Casey and I spent a weekend in May 1977 writing and then sharing our responses to various questions. Our dialogues opened us to each other and gave us a deeper appreciation for each other. I came home and joined a marriage encounter group in Springfield, and then one in Joplin, for a few years.

Casey was a spiritual director in St. Meinrad College; after ordination to the priesthood he earned a Doctor of Ministry Degree in Spiritual Direction from Weston School of Theology in Cambridge, Massachusetts. Then, he returned to St. Meinrad College to continue his ministry in spiritual direction of college students. While I visited him at St. Meinrad a few times, neither of us really got any more involved in Marriage Encounter due to time spent in other ministries. He often joked during our visits that we had a relationship which just picked up wherever we had left it the last time we saw each other. Eventually, after St. Meinrad College closed, Casey left the monastery and became a priest in the Archdiocese of Indianapolis in 2007; he died there of colon cancer in 2015.

My Life of Ministry, Writing, Teaching, and Traveling

Mary Caroline Marchal

Another genuine human encounter occurred at St. Meinrad; this one took place during the summer of 1974. During the six-week summer school session, I got to know Sister Mary Caroline Marchal, who had attended summer school before and was functioning as activity director for the 1974 summer session. Her job was to get as many of the fifty-eight people (fifty nuns, three priests, one layman, and four seminarians) as possible to attend swim parties, picnics, and other such gatherings. Marchal and I quickly became friends and spent time recreating and discussing various topics. When she would come for visits later in 1974 and 1975, she would make it a point to stop by my room and see me.

I remember making a trip to Cincinnati, Ohio, where she lived and worked and meeting her brother. During the Christmas season, I flew to Cincinnati to see *Nutcracker* at the Cincinnati Music Hall. Marchal attended both my diaconate ordination in 1975 and my priesthood ordination in 1976 in Old Mines, Missouri. She also sewed several chasubles and stoles for me, made from cloth I purchased and sent to her. Sometime in the late 1970s she wrote me a letter indicating that she did not like the fact that I served as chaplain onboard cruise ships, and that she did not have the same ability because she was not ordained. Because of that, she decided to break off the relationship, and I never heard from her again.

The Lohkamps

When I first got to St. Agnes Parish, Springfield, as associate pastor in 1976, I met Wanda Lohkamp during vacation Bible school. She invited me to join her and her husband, Albert, and their four sons—Michael, Steven, Daniel, and Thomas—for dinner one evening. I accepted the invitation and drove the ten miles to their home in Republic, Missouri. Ultimately, I became a member of the Lohkamp family; Al and Wanda even referred to me as their son. On my day off every week, I joined them for dinner, and, because they had a pontoon boat, often joined them for outings on a lake and camping experiences. I was also found in their home for Christmas and Easter dinners, even for years after I left St. Agnes Parish and moved to Joplin.

Before I left St. Agnes Parish in 1978, I had to take leave of the Lohkamp household. I still have a card from them that begins, "Dear Son, We were so proud to be a part of your celebration. We would like you to know that we offer you us, our love, prayers, support, and great admiration, and most of all our home—your home! If [we] could really pick another son, it would be you. That's how [we] know God sent you to us." The card ended with the words, "May time and years never separate us." Of course, time and years did separate us, but my memories of sharing meals, babysitting, and hanging out with the Lohkamps remain. On a wooden desk pen/pencil holder, which I still have, on a piece of paper glued to the back, Wanda wrote: "Son, you touched us. We grew." Under those words are the names, "Al, Wanda, Michael, Steven, Daniel, Thomas." One year Michael joined me on a mountain climbing trip to Colorado.

Steve Lockhart, John Kennedy, Jared Fields

I met Steve Lockhart in the fall semester of 1997; he was a student in the New Testament class I was teaching. In the spring semester of 1999, he was enrolled in a film class I taught at Southwest Missouri State University (now Missouri State University). Along with John Kennedy, to whom I had taught New Testament in the fall of 1999 and who took my film class in the spring of 2001, and Jared Fields, who had also taken the film course in the spring semester of 2002, we formed a study group who wanted to continue to build on what we learned in the class. So, on a monthly basis, Lockhart, Kennedy, and Fields came to my house for dinner, then we watched a movie and discussed it. Sometimes our film critiques were short, and at other times they went on for a while. In that Bible and Film course, Lockhart became a very good critical thinker; he graduated with a degree in religious studies. After he graduated from college, he went to live and work in St. Louis, where I met him for lunch a few times when I was in the city.

In 2003, Lockhart took a job in Maine working with children. During the one year he was there, we exchanged many e-mails as he reached the conclusion that he didn't like working with children. So, in 2004, he returned to St. Louis. While living in an apartment in Maine, however, Lockhart wrote about how much he liked being alone and developing skills to take care of himself. Lockhart, along with Kennedy, attended my twenty-fifth priesthood jubilee in 2001, and, when he came back to Springfield to see his parents, he stopped in to see me once or twice. In 2002, he, along with Kennedy, helped me move. After that I lost contact with him. Lockhart was a gentle man, an eager student, who did not know he belonged in the world. Yet, he was a great contrast to Fields, who was married and preparing to move to Indiana to attend a seminary, and Kennedy, who had a girlfriend in Mexico to where he moved to marry her after getting his master's degree in Religious Studies. The last communication I had from Kennedy announced that he and his wife were parents.

Bradon Massey

I met Bradon Massey in a New Testament class in the fall of 1998 at SMSU (now MSU). I surmised quickly that he was a good critical-thinking student whom I would like to get to know. He accepted my invitation to come to dinner, and the relationship got started. The next semester, spring 1999, he enrolled in a Bible and Film course I was teaching, and continued to display his critical-thinking abilities. Massey, who was from Lebanon, was interested in exploring both human relationships and divine relationships. We talked often about both and how they were connected. When he came to my house, it didn't take us long to move from surface discussion to in-depth sharing. I helped him reflect upon what mattered to him to discover meaning, and he challenged me to reflect more upon what mattered to me.

Because he was working in his hometown area, during the summer of 1999, we exchanged some ideas through letter-writing. In a June 8 letter, he asked, "Why do you think faith is individual?" After asking the question, he described the mystical experience that led to the question:

> While I was thinking about [the question], I thought about the usual things. Then, I thought that faith would not mean as much, but then I got a couple seconds of the next level of understanding in my faith. To me it is like grasping the idea for a second and then opening your hand to look at it again in amazement only to have it fly off leaving you with nothing. I found it to be totally amazing.

In that letter he went on to describe how God spoke to him clearer when he was younger, but as he grew, he discovered that he heard more of the world and less of the Holy Spirit. "This might not seem like much," he wrote, "but when God shows me something, lately I have been overjoyed." He concluded by asking, "Wouldn't it be nice to sit beside God in his state of being (physical, spiritual, whichever works) and just converse as old friends or father and son?"

In my June 11, 1999, response, I explained that I thought faith was individual because each of us is a unique, unrepeatable, one-of-a-kind individual through whom God works and reveals himself. Each person deserves respect because he or she is a manifestation of God. Then, I explained that faith is also communal. It is nurtured by family and church. Other believers help us understand our faith even while we are helping them do the same. I explained that what he referred to as the next level of understanding in faith was an experience of God's kingdom. I explained how God breaks through our daily routines and finds us, but just as quickly as we are found, the experience dissolves.

"I think God is at work in your life in a big way and neither you nor I know where God is going to take you," I wrote. "All you can do is to be open to the experiences now and see what pattern they form in your life. By understanding the pattern, the direction will become clear to you." I wrote, "What I have liked about you since the first day I met you is your strength of character. You are a determined person who has an agenda for his life. God made you a strong character. Just be careful that your strength does not become your weakness and get in the way of listening to what the divine is telling you." I concluded my letter, writing, "Instead of only focusing on your immediate goal to finish college and get a good job, focus on your lifetime process of cooperating in your relationship with God."

I had no doubt that God was very important to Massey. In a July 1999 letter, he wrote to me: "God has revealed himself to me many different times throughout my life. Most of the time it has been when I look back at my life, and he gently reminds me that he was making my path straight. This is a quite large source of encouragement to me." In response to that statement, I replied on July 9: "There is more depth to you than you are disclosing, and it is in the depths of ourselves where we discover not only who we are, but who others are and who God is." I urged him to reflect on his relationship with his girlfriend and to identify the degree of that relationship. Then, I urged him to explore if the degree of that relationship influenced the degree of his relationship with God. In a similar vein, I urged him to look through his major life experiences and to notice the theme(s) that ran through them. I noted that all major life experiences are those of being saved by God. I explained, "By uncovering who you are, you identify your uniqueness, and that is a reflection of God." Because Massey had experienced living and was reflecting deeply upon it with my prompts, I knew that he wanted more out of life. Because he wanted more of it, I reminded him that was what drew me toward him.

Because he was a very responsible young man, I asked Massey to live in my house and water the plants while I was gone for two weeks one summer. He was working in Springfield, and he was delighted to have a place to stay with no one else around. We continued getting together every four or six weeks until he graduated from college, got married, and settled in the Lebanon area with a good job. I saw him a few times at Hammons Hall for the Performing Arts when I volunteered to work there for twenty years. We would chat for a few minutes, but I was working and needing to pay attention to the patrons of the hall. After those brief encounters, I never saw him again. Massey is one of those very good men, whom God had graced with multiple experiences of his divine presence. Massey's recognition of those experiences and his ability to reflect upon them for meaning served to enrich his life.

James Cox

I met Jim Cox in Fort Wayne, Indiana, on October 24, 1998. He was one of the thirty men who attended a retreat I gave on male spirituality. His father, James M. Cox, had contacted me in March 1998 about giving the retreat based on the *Male Spirituality* book that I had written. Because I was staying with the older Cox for the two days I was in Fort Wayne, I enjoyed dinner with Jim at the elder Cox's home. A connection between Jim and I occurred. Thus, after getting home a few days later, I sent him an e-mail asking him what he had experienced during the dinner.

On November 4, 1998, Cox replied, "I have never had a male friend seek me out as a spiritual accompaniment. I am flattered and intrigued." He expressed his disappointment in the past with men, labeling them as "superficial encounters." He wrote, "I hunger for the opportunity to drop all the careful, polite, thinking-of-others feelings to really let my soul's hair down, so to speak. This opportunity is one I would not like to pass up." In my November 9, 1998, reply, I told Cox, "There's so much more there that I'm not experiencing." I asked him, "Who do you desire to be? The answer to that question is predicated on knowing who you are now. And knowing who you are is equivalent to knowing who God is for you. It's all intertwined."

Both of us were hungry for the male spirituality that each possessed. However, the first hurdle we had to jump over was the culture's taint of male-male relationships. I wrote, "Men I've discovered don't trust each other too fast. Part of it is the homophobia of our culture that confuses intimacy with sexuality. All intimacy does not involve sex." I explained that I didn't think most men could distinguish the difference between intimacy and sex. I ended by asking Jim, a married man, to explore the difference between intimacy and sex. In an e-mail on the same day, Jim confirmed my thoughts, writing, "The idea of not trusting men oozes from the fears of knowing another man's personal matters." On November 10, 1998, I got another e-mail from Cox in which he answered my question, "Who do you desire to be?" He began his answer by noting all the roles he had played in the past and all that he had wanted to be. Then, he wrote:

> My most current me is "I am in progress," a work unfinished. That is a hard concept to grasp. I want things finished, to feel complete. I have very few instances when I have exhausted my defenses and have exposed myself. I have come to unlearn all the self-condemning messages that so easily come to my mind. I am most exposed when the defenses come down and the courage is up to open the door and shine light on the shame, sadness, and losses of my life. I know few who have ever lived long enough to take the plunge inside and surface and then realize that there are other men like they who have done it and need to talk about it the way they do.

On November 13, 1998, I responded to Cox's e-mail. "I don't think many men can handle who they are and prefer to present the façade or role since they are stuck in identifying or defining themselves by it." I commented on his idea of being a work in progress, writing, "That is the source of real living, of touching the depths of life, which I think is what you hunger for." I shared with him the role of son I had played until both of my parents died. "I had always been the son of my parents, but now that both of them were dead, that couldn't be any more. I was free to define myself in any way I wanted."

Then, based on what I had experience at the end of October, I wrote to Cox: "You have a great degree of security in yourself. Somewhere and somehow you overcame your fear to share yourself with other men. Deep down inside we know that in sharing or exposing ourselves we die and that that is exactly where authentic life, the fullness of living, is discovered. Isn't your yearning deep down to be so open that you can live off of the life of another shared with you?" I explained that neither of us was alone.

> I've died, and I need to share it with someone who knows what the hell I'm talking about. To know that I'm not alone gives me the support I need to keep doing it. I can learn from your dyings how to do it better, and you can learn from mine in the same way. What we discover is that this is the very mystery of Christianity. The more you die, the more you live.

I concluded by writing, "Living, I've discovered, is mostly made up of dying. How true is that for you?"

On November 16, 1998, I got an e-mail in which Cox expressed stress in his workplace caused by those who worked there. He wrote about seeing "people quickly close up, the spirits close, wall up, or shut down. The stress that it causes me is in the silence, the deafening silence. It's like I can feel the pain of these people crying out, and I feel this deep woundedness." In my November 18, 1998, reply, I noted that I called that deafening silence "deadly death" because it zaps one of energy and strength.

On November 16, Cox had written that he had no tolerance "for people who don't have the guts to apologize, acknowledge, forgive, and better themselves." On November 18, I wrote, "Not being able to handle people who don't want to grow is what makes you different." I explained that many people have a tendency to get stuck and satisfied with where they are and who they are. Cox was not like that; he had a self-definition that was growing and expanding, and he couldn't understand why everyone else did not share that self-definition.

On December 4, 1998, the e-mail from Cox narrated his relationship with a good friend from college and how they had been experiencing distance in their relationship. He had felt it at a reunion, and later he told him about his feelings; he discovered that his friend felt the same. Cox called him to check out what he was feeling. He narrated, "He complimented me for my ability to put difficult feelings and situations into words that helped the situation instead of blaming. That sounds nice to hear." Later that same day, I replied, writing: "If regular contact is not maintained, then people start drifting apart. Relationship is work. If there is no mutual diminishment and enrichment, people drift away, looking for it elsewhere."

In a previous e-mail, I had written to Cox that I needed his insights. In my December 7 e-mail, I explained, "You help me articulate what I think and feel from your point of view. My experiences are similar to yours. When you articulate your experiences, I am enabled to articulate mine." Cox wrote, "I love this opportunity to share." And I replied, "You are one of those blessings that is a surprise to me." Then, tying the e-mail back to the retreat, I wrote, "This is the kind of connecting that more men need to do, but they usually don't know it or fear it because our culture doesn't give them the opportunity to exchange with each other any type of intimacy."

In my December 16 e-mail, I wrote: "Both of us already are wise because we reflect on our lives and want to share the fruit of our reflection with each other. We understand each other and hunger for sharing the revelation of the depths we have experienced in living and reflecting on it."

In a series of e-mails before and after Christmas briefly we discussed death. I had written Cox about the death of an older female cousin due to cancer. Cox wrote, "Death is an interesting topic in that it is feared and rarely validated for the process and healthy opportunities it presents. The corporate America three days off and then back to work doesn't work for the human spirit." I replied, "I think your comments are right on target about death. I have to think through my own thoughts concerning life and death. What hit me this time is that she, my cousin, was just a few years older than I."

On January 21, 1999, Cox wrote about "moments of sheer joy." He had a mystical experience, a taste of the kingdom of God, while working out on the treadmill. "I had pure joy wash over me," he wrote. "Apparently, it was not mine to keep, but to experience. It seems to me this is how life usually is: Moments that leave us with fond memories not to be recaptured."

On February 20, 1999, he wrote that he didn't think he was "becoming the person God meant him to be." He felt "lost and worthless, like God was disappointed in him." He wrote, "My deepest fear is the fear I won't be the person God meant me to be and my life will have been lost. Nothing cuts me deeper." In my response four days later, I reminded Cox that he processed his life experiences through his emotions. "To be aware that you do this can be freeing and help you know yourself even better," I wrote. "You feel first and then struggle to articulate or intellectualize how you feel later." I continued, "Once we reach the level of awareness of how we are—and how we are is just how we are and this is OK or good—we realize that we don't have to prove anything to anyone but ourselves. All God asks is that we are always in the process of becoming who we are. We will never know all that we can become until we have become it."

I urged Cox to look to his past and to map his journey using what he considered to be the key moments of it. By looking back, he could get a perspective on how he got to where he now was. I reminded him, "Fearing that we won't be who God wants us to be is a healthy fear, one that keeps us from getting stagnant." I added, "God is constantly surprising us, revealing who God is in our own process of becoming." Thus, I concluded, "The better we know ourselves, the freer we are to reach out and invite others into our lives." In another e-mail on February 26, 1999, I gave him an example of a student I had helped as a result of our e-mail conversations. I had spent two hours with a student discovering "that I had to feel the way he did in order to be able to help him." A couple of days later, he came back to tell me how much I had helped him. I wrote to Cox, "I stand back in wonder when that happens and realize how much all of us are connected to each other."

In his March 9 e-mail, Cox had asked me, "How do we reconcile the Old Testament with the New when God was killing everyone in the Old and healing in the New? Did God change his mind or are the stories just that, stories?" I replied that we cannot reconcile the testaments. I told Cox that we have to keep in mind that people wrote biblical books. "The writings do not reflect God's understanding of God; they reflect people's understanding of God. And, of course, that is always lacking. People can only understand God to the degree that they can understand themselves." I explained that the Bible is not history.

> It consists of stories full of truth. A story does not have to be true in order to communicate truth. Before we read the Bible, we have to learn about the people who wrote it—their culture, their worldview, their problems, their lives.

Only then in that context can we begin to understand it. We can't presume that the Bible was written to us like the daily newspaper is. To understand it, you have to understand its intended audience. Otherwise, we can misread it or make it mean anything we want.

On March 11, 1999, the next e-mail from Cox arrived. He wrote that he had shared some of my thoughts with a good friend of his who was struggling. Cox concluded his e-mail by stating that he had been drawing well from our personal friendship. "You're a good man, and I'm glad to be your friend." The next day I sent Cox a brief e-mail, stating, "What I've learned, and what I think you're learning, is that we can't help anyone. What we can do is give one the resources to help himself or herself. We call it relationship, that which frees us to be who we are becoming."

After taking some time to reflect on what Cox had written, On March 15, 1999, I replied that I had thought more about his words. "You are a self-reflective person," I wrote, "who keeps catching his problems and probing them and working with them."

On March 17, 1999, Cox sent me a copy of an e-mail he had sent to a friend of his on the topic of grace. His reflections on grace summarize who Cox was becoming:

> Grace seems to be the strength to do what is right. In and of itself it won't do anything; it is what you do with it. I don't believe it will make you better. I think it is strength, insight, and personal freedom to do what you know in your heart God has meant you to do. And when you do it, you are rewarded with joy because you are following the path that God has led you down, and it's magic. It's freedom—true freedom to think what you want and freedom to be the person you are, as well as the person you are becoming.

He summarized it this way: "Grace is the freedom to be and the freedom to become, without any strings attached. This is the freedom to let what is inside of you be and become what is naturally there, that is, to let the God inside of you out." I replied on the same day, writing, "I prefer to think of grace as the action (a verb) of God sharing who God is with us in relationship. Grace is the Holy Spirit, that invisible force in our lives that keeps pushing us to become, to become who we are."

On the same day, I wrote:

> The church understands grace to be a gift from God that strengthens people in their lifetime pilgrimage to God. It is freely given. In fact, it is given so that we can respond to it. Notice how the verbs given and respond work. God offers God's self to us every day in hundreds of ways and especially through sacraments. So, my understanding of grace is right in line with the church's understanding. Just keep in mind that it isn't a thing, but the action of a relationship. The more you accept and give the more you receive, and the more you receive the more you give away.

My Life of Ministry, Writing, Teaching, and Traveling

Cox wrote: "My goal in life is to tell people every day what is right with them. Hardly anyone is doing this ministry; it is mine. It feels amazing to do it."

In my May 3, 1999, e-mail, I commented on his statement about not taking responsibility for anyone's pain. I added, "I can't take responsibility for anyone's happiness either." I continued:

> For me, self-knowledge reveals that the only person who makes me suffer is me, and the only person who makes me happy is me. We can never know another like we know ourselves. Self-knowledge, for me, is the key. To be gentle with myself means that I am always in the process of change and development. There is always a part of me that is constant and part of me that is not like me yesterday. To stand back and see the ongoing process of development in my life enables me to see the big picture—the one in which I impose pain or let someone else impose it on me, or I impose happiness or let someone else impose it on me. By impose, I mean that I consciously choose one or the other. Some people are better at choosing one or the other.

Then, I offered my own reflections on Cox's view of his work as ministry. I wrote:

> As you delve deeper and deeper into yourself, your ministry is to share your broader world view with others and to let them share theirs with you. As you keep getting broader and broader, you will invite others to push back their own boundaries and see their lives in new light, like you keep seeing your life. I call this enrichment and diminishment. Every time we share who we are and our thoughts with each other, we are both enriched by the other and diminished. We are more of who we are and we are simultaneously less because we gave some of self away in order to receive more. For me, those are the kinds of relationships that last—and take lots of work.

I continued:

> Giving self away has made me more and more aware and helped me feel the process ever more deeply. As I see it, the basic problem in our culture is that most people do not see the long-range picture of where their lives are going. I think that the process of really living and learning and delving deeper into me and into others and which opens us to others to greater and greater degrees has to be understood in a long-range view. I'm on a journey of living, always changing, always becoming more of who I am, and, hopefully, helping others to do the same. Then, every moment of pain and happiness seem to run together and are headed toward the end of the journey, when I will have become all I can become.

Our next e-mail exchange took place in late July. Cox's wife was preparing to enter the Catholic Church. Her questions to him became his questions to me. On the top of the list was the following: "Is the creation story true? Is the story of Noah true?

Is there a hell?" He noted that her fundamentalist beliefs came from her Lutheran background. He stated, "Stories may have truth in them but not be true necessarily." What he meant is that a story does not have to be historical to contain truth. He explained that he thought "evolution took place in some degree." That did not exclude God. He reasoned that if we didn't come from the garden with one couple—Adam and Eve—then there is no original sin and no need for baptism. He understood baptism as forgiving original sin and claiming people for Christ and the church. His next stop was the Noah story; using reason he concluded that all races on the earth could not have come from Noah's line, and all the world's animals could not have fit on an ark. Next came his reflections on hell. "I believe in evil," he wrote, "but I do not believe in an entity called Satan." He stated that Satan was created to make people scared of doing something wrong. "As for hell," he wrote, "I don't see a place that is fiery and hot. It seems a state of mind or being." He employed a very good analogy, writing, "Hell is where we lock the door from the inside and lock God out of our lives. All we need to do is unlock the door and receive all that is offered, knowing that we can never earn it." In other words, God forgives all sins.

The final question in this e-mail was this: "Why did Jesus die?" He began to answer his own question, writing, "I believe Jesus and the Father are supportive and loving and give me all I need to live in accordance with the path that is mine and what will bring me the most joy in my life and do whatever it is that I am supposed to do." He asked, "Am I on the precipice of understanding?" He concluded his e-mail, writing, "I want you to know how freeing it is for me to share this with you. I have no other person filling this void in my life that I can fully share this with. You are a valuable person and a great friend."

After thinking about Cox's e-mail for a couple of days, I responded. First, I addressed his biblical interpretation. "We do not believe in stories but in the truths that the stories are attempting to communicate," I wrote. "Belief in stories is called fundamentalism." I explained that the question one needs to ask when reading a biblical text is this: "What did the text mean to the people to whom it was written. We have to find out what the context was and the meaning at the time any text was written." I explained that academics call this myth. "Myth does not mean 'not true.' Myth is a system of stories that a culture puts together to answer the question: Where did people and creation and all other things come from?" I explained: "The creation stories in Genesis represent how ancient people imagined how all that exists came to be. It is not a scientific treatise; it is a myth written during the Babylonian captivity in dialogue with the Babylonian mythology. It was the Jews's way of saying that their God was greater than the Babylonian gods."

I explained that the Noah story is a second creation story. "Every ancient culture has a flood story. Along the Nile, where ancient culture developed, there is a flood every year." The biblical account assigns meaning—the flood washes away people who sin—to the story. Then, I went on to Adam and Eve, writing, "Original sin has nothing to do with Adam and Eve. Original sin is the human condition, the ability not to do what is right, to do evil. Baptism does not remove original sin, but it initiates us into a community of struggling believers—people who try to do good instead of evil. We need the support of the community, so we are initiated into it. Baptism does claim us for Christ, but only from a Christian point of view." I explained that people of other faiths cannot be excluded because they are not baptized. Jesus gave us a lifestyle; he showed us how to live with our humanness.

In regard to his comments about Satan, I explained that such a character is very late on the biblical scene. I referred him to Elaine Pagels's book, *The Origin of Satan: How Christians Demonized Jews, Pagans, and Heretics*. Then, I commented on hell, writing, "Hell is a Christian invention—the opposite of good. It is best understood as the absence of God. The experience of evil that all of us have is given a proper name, like Satan or Devil." Then, I added, "God does forgive all. If God didn't, then God would not be God. It is God's nature to be merciful. God loves us even when we don't love ourselves."

I addressed Cox's question about why Jesus died. "Jesus died because he was a troublemaker," I wrote. "He disturbed too many people. The best way to deal with someone who upset people in the ancient world was death by crucifixion to make an example for others to see. God is not vindictive and doesn't need to prove power. God is love, says the Scripture." I concluded by writing, "Your analysis is right on target. Keep working with it and help your wife to see the Catholic point of view. Biblical stories get tricky if we think they are written to us, which they aren't. We have to attempt to understand them in the context in which they were written." I urged him to "keep thinking and examining and figuring things out. That's where life and faith are located." On August 10, 1999, I received a short e-mail from Cox, stating, "You have affirmed me."

The next e-mail from Cox arrived on August 19, 1999. This one contained a list of questions. I answered the questions the same day. Cox asked, "If God is loving and not punitive, then why did he exact a price from his Son for sins against him?" I replied: "God didn't exact a price for sins. The only gospel that says that Jesus died for sins is Matthew, the second one to be written. To say that Jesus died for sins is only one answer to the question. There are many more or other interpretations of the meaning of his death. For example, Mark says that Jesus died as an example of how God is present with us even when we feel abandoned. Luke says that Jesus died an innocent martyr, an example of how to push on despite what might happen to us. I think one of the best answers is to say that Jesus died because he upset many people, who wanted to get rid of him. Basically, he was a religious trouble-maker. He called into question too many things that leaders of the time couldn't handle."

The second question followed the first one: "If God is loving and didn't exact his price from Jesus' death, why did he die?" I replied:

Jesus died because he upset the status quo. Jesus proclaimed that God was present here and now, working in people's lives. Jesus died because he was in the wrong place at the wrong time and upset the wrong people. What he showed us was how to live and how to die—cooperating with what God wants of us. Most of the time we prefer to isolate God away from us instead of realizing that we are in God. God is nearer to us than we ever realize. When we see the bigger picture, we are able to accept everyone and every religion as a manifestation of God or a way that God works through people to accomplish what God wants.

Next question: "If God is as loving and forgiving as I believe him to be, how could he ask for his Son's life?" I responded to that question, writing:

> God didn't ask for his Son's life. That is a popular notion with no biblical or doctrinal foundation. What God asked for was that Jesus cooperate with God—show people how to live in relationship with God. Jesus did that all the way to the cross. The cross, the logical outcome of upsetting too many leaders, shows Jesus cooperating with God—even though others refused. It is Jesus' faithfulness through death that we admire and try to imitate.

The next question came from his wife: "If the Catholic view is that the Old Testament is stories written to explain, then how do we know what stories are true? Who determines what is true and what is just a story? And if we take that question into the New Testament, is it true, with all its inconsistencies?" My response was this:

> We don't know what stories are true. In fact, such an interest is a fundamentalist question. Catholics don't care if stories are true or not. We're interested in the truth the story is trying to tell or convey. Most stories in the Old Testament attempt to convey the notion of a loving God, who chooses a group of people as his own and leads them out of slavery to freedom. When they are oppressed, God saves them repeatedly. God is with them through thick and thin, even when they sin or turn away. For me that offers a lot of consolation and hope.

I continued:

> The New Testament stories are the same. I don't think half of them ever took place, but that is not the point. The point is that God, who is always up to something, chooses all people through Jesus, who is the example for all people of how to live in relationship with God. There are tons of inconsistencies in both the Old Testament and the New Testament. Why? Because the human authors told stories to get to the truth. They never thought that later generations would believe the stories rather than believe the truth the stories were trying to convey.

Next question: "Did God truly exact a price from his Son for us to be able to join him in heaven?" Next answer:

> Of course not. God works through many avenues to get people to respond to him or her. There was no price to be paid for sins. God takes care of people's failures and sins immediately—usually before people do—since God created us the way we are. We cannot be perfect; we weren't created that way. So, God takes us as we are, works with us, in us, through us, and accomplishes the divine will if we cooperate. If we choose not to cooperate, then we're off on our own. But God will still search us out and try to get us to work with him. If you explore this idea in your own lives, you will discover how successful you've been and how you've failed. But both keep leading you forward as you cooperate with God through work, marriage, career, friends, etc.

I concluded by response to Cox's e-mail with a specific application to him:

> What is happening with your questions is you are growing into a deeper faith, a deeper trust of the God who has been at work in you for a long time. Deeper trust of God means that God is taking away some more of our crutches—those things we lean on for proof instead of just trusting that God knows what God is about. Keep questioning and God will lead you not to answers, but to more questions, more depth, more insight, more trust.

On the same day, August 19, 1999, I got a short e-mail replay from Cox. He explained that what I told him he had known in his heart to be true, which was like an itch in the back of his mind. He was happy that I was with him during this latest growth spurt. He wrote: "What really happened is that God just came to us to be with us and show us the way to the Father, and all this false interpretation is a moot point. Look to the truth that is always there, what Jesus called the spirit of the word, or law, not the words themselves." He ended by stating, "Thank you for validating what truth was emerging in my mind."

I heard from Cox again on November 28, 1999. In his very long e-mail, he narrated his "feelings of desperation." By that he meant the eternal questions: What are we? What am I doing? What is the point? He also relayed that he had not long ago marked his thirtieth birthday. "I have had the feeling of not going anywhere before. I work, eat, sleep, all week, take the weekend off, and then repeat. Where am I going? Nothing I do is giving me the fulfillment I desire. My feelings often shut me down intellectually and further mire me in the quagmire of my emotions."

A few days later I responded, "From my own experience and living, I think we go through a re-evaluation of our lives every ten years or so. You are at one of those points in your life. You went through this once you turned twenty or twenty-one. You'll go through it again when you turn forty and fifty." One thing Cox did understand was the need to take time for himself, quietly, alone and with someone who could really hear him. He wrote, "At the present time, you are it, my friend."

After those words of support and my reply, Cox posed his next question about indulgences.

> Sins are forgiven and absolved from eternal punishment, but temporal punishment or retribution is still needed. What I hear said is that the effects of our sins on earth need correction, or repayment, or fixing. If this is true, where do these concepts of correcting the earthly repercussion of the sin come from, and how do you know you have repaid the debt in full? What measuring stick do you use to gauge the progress?

In my reply, I presented my take on indulgences, writing:

> An indulgence is nothing other than a good deed. We are doing good deeds all the time, so why begin to count them now? Furthermore, anytime we begin to talk about post-death, we are, by definition, talking about that which we know nothing about. In my wildest dreams, I cannot imagine a God who forgives us and then says we must pay for what we've done wrong. That contradicts what Paul says over and over again: we are set free to cooperate with God. We fail, but we are forgiven and get moving again.

I urged him not to put too much emphasis on this one, small piece of Catholicism, to which even the church did not pay much attention.

Next question: "Why do you belong to a church that doesn't have all the answers? The Bible does. What more do you need?" I told Cox: "I usually respond that nothing or no book has all the answers to questions that hadn't been asked yet. We are people in process, not finished yet. So, a collection of books can only answer the questions people were asking when the individual books were written. It can't answer our questions today. It might offer some direction to find an answer, but it can't offer the answer. The church can't have all the answers to questions because it doesn't yet know all the questions."

In a January 5, 2000, e-mail, Cox referred to our friendship as serving like a compass, giving each other help and direction in finding our way through life. I told him that I liked that image very much.

The next e-mail I have from Cox is dated October 15, 2000. In that correspondence, he narrates attending a Christ Renews His Parish weekend. "The process of men sharing their lives and pain and supposedly their spiritual journey was more like a twelve-step process than much spirituality," Cox wrote. "Men have no idea what that is; I am convinced."

The once-a-week e-mail dialogue with Cox had gradually become a once-a-month exchange, then the e-mails had disappeared. The next e-mail I received from him was dated December 19, 2002. Granted there may have been some between 2000 and 2002, but I didn't save or print them because they did not cover anything in as much depth as previous e-mails had done. Cox's e-mail began, "I have thought of you from time to time. Today I was driving to work and you came to mind." He went on to announce the birth of his son five month previously.

The last e-mail I have from Cox is dated January 7, 2003. He said that his anxiety over several issues we dialogued about had been lifted, and he felt at peace with God again. I commented: "God loves us when we face the tough decisions in our lives and realize that God is there guiding us through them. Also, all our issues pale in importance to our relationship with God. Your experience of God at work in your life confirms that your relationship with God is healthy and growing. That's all you need."

Over the course of almost five years, Cox and I dialogued through e-mail on many and various topics that are not narrated here. I have presented the highlights of our dialogues in these pages. I concluded this important chapter of my life. I had helped another human being become free. Through this e-mail relationship in dialogue with Cox, I put into words my thoughts on many issues. Those words were used over and over again in ministry to others who found themselves in the same or similar situations.

Tom Kriegshauser

I met Tom Kriegshauser in a New Testament class in the fall semester of 2000. He needed to fulfill a humanity requirement, but ended up with an incomplete at the end of the semester. He finished the missing work, and that is what set the stage for our friendship. He enrolled in my Bible and Film course in the spring semester of 2001, but withdrew from the class a few weeks after it began. After he graduated he went to Finland to teach English. In a September 3, 2003, e-mail, after spending time traveling around Europe, he wrote:

> My trip really helped me realize many things about myself and also tested some of my abilities. After going on this adventure I know for sure that I can handle any challenged I am faced with. I also realized that my patience was much better than I thought. By hopping from place to place I have seen how flexible I really am. I have been able to understand more about my truths than ever before.

He added that in his international business, politics, and relationship course students had helped him with some of his own truths. That had been the focus of much of our discussions together. In his words, he told me "to keep helping people understand their truths." In my reply on the same day, I wrote, "It is difficult, but rewarding, to plop ourselves into other cultures and have to figure out what to do (and not to do) and what to say (and not to say). I don't think I'll ever get enough of travel because it helps me both to understand other people and to understand myself better." By the end of 2003, the last time I heard from Kriegshauser, he was on his way back to the U.S. and taking a job in Chicago.

Walter Watkins

In the fall semester of 2000, I was teaching a New Testament class when I first met Walter Watkins. He was sitting in the very last row of seats in the classroom on the right end. When I called his name and asked him to tell me something about himself, he explained that he was from Alaska; his parents were missionaries in the outback, and, after growing up there, he decided to move to the lower forty-eight states to attend college. All Watkins had to say was "Alaska," and I was interested. Eight years before I had spent three months of my sabbatical living there and seeing all the regions of the state except for the Aleutian Islands. Needless to say, we hit it off quickly. During the semester, we began to get together for dinner. We shared story after story about Alaska. I met Walter's friend Randy, who joined us for one memorable Easter Sunday dinner during which I served leg of lamb.

Often, we went on hikes together. We stayed in contact while Walter dated and broke up. Finally, one day he called me to meet him at a Panera Bread to discuss his latest break-up and another young woman in whom he had an interest. I remember telling him to ask her out. He did. And after several years of dating, they married. I remember attending their outdoor wedding. Even after he moved, we stayed in contact for a few years; he often visited me when he was in town. Ultimately, I lost contact with him once he, his wife, and son moved to Texas for work.

Scott Stewart

I met Scott Stewart, the son of a Springfield pastor, in my Spring 2001 Bible and Film course. Stewart was a very good student, and I invited him to dinner after the course was finished. He loved to discuss movies he had seen. So, for over a year we would enjoy dinner while discussing some of the latest films or a series of films that both of us had seen. After he graduated from SMSU (now MSU), Stewart married Jennifer, and the two of them moved to St. Louis for purposes of work. For a while Stewart and I exchanged e-mails, then for a few Christmases we exchanged cards and letters. Then, I lost contact with him.

Betty McKean

Betty McKean moved into the house next door to me a few years while I was living on South National Avenue. She was a lively elderly woman, who was moving back to Springfield from the lake country south of Springfield in order to be closer to medical care and to her son, who lived in Springfield. We got to be good neighbors and friends. When she would call me, she would begin the conversation by asking, "What the hell are you doing?" She once told me that she had married and buried three husbands, I think. I don't remember where she met Will Binge, but after a short time of dating she invited him to move in with her. He played saxophone in a band, and they went often to concerts in which he was participating. He had a couple of daughters who lived in Arkansas.

McKean had inherited and run a second-hand shop for a long time, and then made her living from rental properties she had all over the city. After a short amount of time, Binge asked McKean to marry him, and she said yes to his offer. They asked me to officiate in their living room with their adult children and a few friends present. After exchanging vows, he broke out into song for her. They made several trips together until the toll of age kept them home except for short trips around town. Almost every Sunday afternoon around 4 p.m. I made my way to their back door and kitchen where we sat around the table and had a glass of wine while discussing almost anything. This continued even after they moved to a house that had no steps in it and I had to drive to see them, and from there to yet another house where I had to drive to see them. When I moved to the house next door, Betty and Will supervised the moving of furniture out the door of the previous house in order to protect doors, door frames, walls, and floors. McKean died of a stroke, and I lost track of Binge after that. They were good neighbors and friends to have around.

(Jo)Nathan Allen

I met Nathan Allen in a New Testament summer session course in 2003. He was a college junior who e-mailed me the third day of class with his reflections on the question: Who founded Christianity? Allen revealed that he had once been an atheist, but had become a Christian. His past experiences enabled him to engage in discussions that would cause great consternation for many people because they would read it as an attack on their beliefs. Since Allen had chosen Christianity, he was open to investigating it. And because he was an excellent critical thinker, he possessed the intellectual tools to do so.

In that first e-mail of June 11, 2003, he argued, "Whether Jesus was resurrected or not doesn't matter as much as that he convinced people that he did." He continued, "We cannot prove any more that Jesus was resurrected than we can that the reason the Roman government established Christianity as its religion was because it had a change of heart after crucifying the Son of God." In class we had discussed the possibility that the Roman Emperor Constantine had started Christianity. Allen stated, "The claim of dying and being resurrected is one of the most difficult claims to make, especially in our increasingly skeptical society."

I responded the next day with an e-mail indicating that there are many different and correct answers to the question: Who founded Christianity? "It just depends on how you see the question and how you go about attempting to prove your point." I explained, "The best way to see any question is to entertain as many answers as possible and see which appeal to human experience the best. The answer you choose—Jesus, his followers, Constantine—depends on the degree to which it appeals to your human experience."

I explained:

> Belief in the resurrection, the experience of Jesus after he was crucified, is the basis for the New Testament. You can't write a book about Jesus if you don't believe that God raised him from the dead—whatever that means. Jesus didn't enable people to believe; their experience of Jesus alive after he was dead enabled them to believe. They, in turn, appealed to others' experiences and interpreted them according to their own point of view. Notice that the claim that God raised Jesus from the dead needs some human evidence, experience, to support it. Stories about Jesus appearing are metaphors which try to capture that experience in words (which, of course, as you well know, is quite impossible to do adequately) in a generic way. In the New Testament, stories are grounded in other biblical stories (Old Testament ones) to appeal to Jews. In that way the stories reshape the Jewish box sometimes. Ultimately, however, the whole Jewish Christianity thing fails and Gentile Christianity takes off. It's a movement that cannot be explained other than to say that it spoke and interpreted human experience and gave hope to those who came to believe it.

Because I surmised that Allen was attempting to reach a definition of faith, I wrote, "Faith, then, is a point of view (a mythology) which is both shaped by New Testament books (and personal experience) and which shapes New Testament books (and personal experience)."

As we delved more and more into the course material, Allen continued our intellectual discussion through e-mail. We had established that gospels were not biographies, but faith documents; I often referred to them as propaganda literature. In class I had explained the difference between the Jesus of history and the Christ of faith. Because the gospels do not always agree on who the Jesus of history was, they provide little information on him as an historical person. They are concerned with fostering belief in Christ. Allen wrote, "If Jesus lived today, it would be easy to have every second he was alive recorded on video and preserved so that there would be even less discrepancy as to what truly happened. The problem with the life of Jesus is that we can't rewind and catch parts we missed the first time."

In my e-mail response, I told Allen that ancient people were not interested in history in the same way that we are. Ancient people just lived their lives and died. They were not concerned about what went before and what came after them. Even though we could capture material on video, the interpretation of the material would differ. I explained that gospels are faith documents, which are biased by the writer's own faith. I continued, "If a story a writer knew didn't illustrate his brand of faith, he left it out or altered it in such a way that it did."

Allen moved on in his e-mail to the topic of reflections on science and religion. He wrote:

> I do believe that science, while good in that it promotes a higher standard of living and understanding of things around us, does enlarge our box and shoves some things out entirely. Science could be considered a religion as much as Christianity, and I only rate religions good as determined by whether their followers become better people through practice. People who worship the same God as I [but] who are not improved and do not become better people by practice are practicing the wrong religion.

My response emphasized how "science often provides the opportunity to really believe; it takes a lot of stuff and pushes it away. Authentic faith has no crutches, no proof. If faith enables a better life, then I think it is good. If it becomes a burden or doesn't engender growth and development, then it is time to move on."

Because Allen possessed the ability to reflect (critically think), he was already doing what I would teach the class to do. I explained, "It is through the process of reflection of experience that we assign meaning to something." Allen had been doing this for a long time; what I wanted him to do was to discover that it never ends. I explained, "As we get older, the meaning we assigned to an experience changes because we change and see it differently. Life is rich in experiences which are waiting to be reflected on and assigned meaning, but most people never take the time to do it. You fascinate me because you do it all the time."

Allen's June 16, 2003, e-mail contained some questions. First, he asked, "How do you remain open minded while coming to a conclusion?" I answered, "You acknowledge that your conclusion is one answer to the question and that there are other answers. The answer you have now will serve you well until you need to revisit the question." Constant re-evaluation is the way to growth and development, I told him. Second question: "Does the choice of an answer matter for any reason other than personal?" I replied, "Yes, it matters beyond the personal. The meaning you assign to your experience affects your wife and your children (some day). It affects anyone with whom you come in contact."

Allen's third question was about the occupations of the gospel writers. He listed occupations that had been used by novelists. I explained, "We do not know the occupations of the gospel writers. Although that hasn't stopped a lot of novel writers from pretending like we do. Remember, the gospels tell us more about the audience than the writer, although we do learn a lot about the writer, too." Allen was also interested in the meaning of biblical numbers, such as forty indicating a long period of time, three indicating a theophany, four indicating the earth, seven indicating wholeness, six indicating incomplete, and eight indicating perfection.

Allen continued to become aware that what was portrayed in film and told in Sunday school classes was not what the biblical text actually stated. He used the example of the Reed Sea instead of the Red Sea. I explained that contrary to Cecil B. Demille's *The Ten Commandments* with high walls of Jell-O, Reed Sea was probably more historically accurate. I explained how stories keep growing as they are told and retold over many years. "The Hebrews are on foot and could get through the marsh of reeds, but the Egyptians were in chariots and their wheels got clogged in mud."

My perspective had always been that stories in the Bible represent Hebrew, Israelite, and Jewish cultures; in other cultures, we should expect to find similar stories. The best example is the great flood story in Genesis. It is an example of a universal theme. Every culture has a flood story. As I explained to Allen, "Biblical literature reflects universal themes. It is not that they are unique to the Bible; it is that they are unique to all people." I explained to Allen: "If others have a faith that works for them, leave them alone. We have no way of knowing what God might be doing. I think God has a great sense of humor with all this religious stuff. Our task is to hold onto a faith that helps us grow and become better people, while at the same time acknowledging that there are other ways."

By June 23, 2003, Allen was reflecting on how living in the gray area of life—what we called holding on to Christianity while acknowledging other religions—enabled him to stand outside his secure box and question himself and his own beliefs. In high school he had been a debater; this enabled him to understand other possible perspectives. In other words, Allen had learned how to live with ambiguity. Allen acknowledged that converting from atheism to Christianity occurred when "he let go of some inner hate and hurt and tried to live as someone ever so slightly less selfish." He had negative experiences with missionaries, "who wanted to share their point of view with him, but not the other way around." He continued, "I support those who are trying to help others find a better life. I don't support those trying to convert those who are happy and good."

Living in the gray brought Allen "into conflict with some in his own church who felt that although God is a loving, kind God, he is also a religious and devout God who will not let non-believers into the kingdom of heaven." When it comes to Christianity, Allen wrote, "I think that Christ was trying to say that if someone truly followed in a Christ-like lifestyle, he or she would suffer due to what it asked of him or her. I think that it is impossible to avoid suffering no matter how close a Christian is with God. Suffering is inevitable."

Allen's June 28, 2003, e-mail was six pages long with reflections and questions. Because Allen learned best through dialogue, I explained that he arrived at truth that way. He had referred to it as debate. I explained:

> Dialectical philosophy says that one arrives at truth through authentic dialogue. Dialectic thought implies that one suspends everything one knows about something in order to investigate it on its own terms. One enters into dialogue with another in order to truly understand what he or she is saying or thinking in order to understand the other person on his or her own terms instead of trying to make him or her fit into one's own point of view. One has no hidden agenda of trying to make the other think like me. You are a master at it.

As an example, I recalled Allen's ability to seek answers to problems that are not addressed in the Bible. I reminded him that that he was updating the Bible. "You look at its basic principles and then say, 'What would this look like in the twenty-first century?' And your answer to that question (notice the dialectic) tells you what you ought to do. I call this navigating through life. Instead of getting stuck in the ancient biblical world, you take the core truths, update them to fit our world, and find a good way to live." Allen's perspective, which was no different than my own, was that Christianity made him a better person by what it did for him, and, thus, what it caused him to do for others."

Allen narrated his reflection on his conversion: "When I first changed, there was truly a physical calm that came over me, and that also caused me to release (most) of my previous inner hate and hurt. This change was viewable by those who would have had no idea that I had made an inner change. The time that it took place from the time it started to full conversion was multiple times faster than any change I could have subjected to on my own." I explained that he had experienced wholeness (holiness): "Once wholeness is tasted, we want more; and we will do anything to get it over and over again. It happens quickly and then it's gone. I equate that sense or feeling of wholeness with Jesus' proclamation that the kingdom of God is near or here. The desire to get it means that we change; we have to change in order to have it."

Allen also narrated his reflections on how his changing affected others. He lost some family and friends "since they did not like the person he became." I explained: "Some people cannot handle others changing because they can no longer control them. Every one of us takes a person and fits him or her into our neat categories; when that person no longer fits or changes, then we don't know what to do with him or her." Allen explained that he had never been one to try constantly to convert people to his way of thinking. I told him that my goal was to enable others to convert themselves to their way of thinking.

The next topic in the e-mail was science and faith. "Faith to me is answering the unanswerables," wrote Allen.

> Science causes me to search for the reason why things are or why things work the way they do. Some would argue that being a logical person rules out being able to believe in God. However, I think that the two can be combined and it is even possible to prove God logically with our limited human wisdom, language, and reasoning skills.

I replied by calling attention to Allen's dialectic skills. Then, I wrote:

> Through the dialogue of science and Christianity, the truth begins to emerge. The two ends of the continuum are not opposed; they are the extreme of what may be the truth, but the real truth exists somewhere in the middle or along the continuum. And that truth will continue to change as the dialogue

continues, as science learns and reveals more and as our experiences of God continue to add up.

After this Allen revealed his reflections on unmoved mover theology. He used Newton's law that says that an object at rest stays at rest until moved by an object in motion. He wrote:

> Now if we trace the history of the universe backwards through the infinite number of chains of events that put us where we are today, eventually we will get to a point where there is a single object as rest. Something had to be able to break our human law and be moving without something else putting it into motion. Something had to both exist and not exist simultaneously. This to me is God.

Noticing Allen's mystical bent—not to mention the continuum—he had established, I reflected on the possibility that things may have always been in motion. I wrote:

> Just because I or you experience everything as having a beginning and an end, including ourselves, does it necessarily follow that the universe had to have a beginning and an end? I think the universe has always existed and will continue to infinity. Some things never had a beginning and never will have an end. That means that some things have always been and will always be.

In other words, some things have always existed because God has always existed.

After this we dialogued about free will. He used the film *Bruce Almighty* to argue free will. Bruce (Jim Carey) is granted God's power by God (Morgan Freeman); he has to abide by the rule that he cannot affect free will. Allen wrote, "Free will is allowing humans to choose whether or not to follow God, but I think it goes farther than that. The ability to destroy all known life that is created without intervention is free will. We aren't just dolls; God loves us freely." He went on to explain how he often got into trouble in his church because he said, "God loves Satan; God created Satan. Sin was created when God created free will." I responded by writing:

> I think God is big enough to let people follow whatever religion, faith, or practice that enables them to become all they can be. I think God is more interested in people reaching their full potential (wholeness) than what faith they belong to. All whole living flows from the wholeness of God. Furthermore, God has to love Satan in order for God to understand God's own free will!

Selfishness is a byproduct of free will. "Like any freedom/privilege that is granted, it is first abused before it is respected," stated Allen. "I do believe that (most) people can overcome this and behave in a more civil manner and respect the freedom that they were given." I agreed with him, stating, "For me selfishness is free will gone amuck! Selfishness is free will either out of balance or out of control."

My Life of Ministry, Writing, Teaching, and Traveling

The e-mail moved on to acknowledge that all is not well in our lives or the world. I stated:

> It is a realization that we are not integrated or whole. So, we need to work on what will make us whole. For some people going to church and meeting the other members of the community of faith and being enriched through song, prayer, a good sermon, coffee, doughnuts, etc. assists many—but not all—people on the path to wholeness. Community mediates the experiences of God that other people have had and keeps everyone questioning, investigating, and reflecting upon their experiences.

I continued, "Personal experience dictates where we begin our theological and philosophical investigation. If we think people are basically good (because that is how we have experienced them), we begin there. If we think people are basically bad (because that is how we have experienced them), we begin there." I appealed to the continuum image with good on one end and bad on the other end. Through dialogue, I told Allen, we enable each other to see both ends and to realize that the truth lies somewhere on the line in the middle.

The e-mail dialogue ceased for a while once summer school was finished. The next e-mail I received was dated September 28, 2003; Allen was taking two classes in the fall semester while working. He apologized for taking several months to get back to me, but stated, "I wanted to let you know the impact of your class on me." One impact he narrated was seeing "how the preacher takes only pieces of the Bible out and talks on them, and how sometimes the sermon is taken out of the Bible's context to fit what people remember, rather than what they are reading." I responded by telling him that it was good to hear that his critical-thinking skills were still at work.

Then, Allen proposed what he called a moral dilemma:

> Is it better for a preacher to keep his job and tell people what they already believe in order to keep the congregation from leaving, while attracting new members (the business aspect of the church), or does a preacher have a responsibility (is it better for the church?) to point out to people what they are really reading and what it means even if it disrupts things in the church (a change to using the Bible as a textbook rather than a holy book)?

I answered his question by writing, "I thinking telling people what I know is more important than protecting them from ideas. I treat adults like adults, people who are capable of understanding ambiguity. I think this is a process. I don't give them everything at one time. It is important to give a little every Sunday instead of the whole thing the first time." I explained further: "I take a text (supplied by the Lectionary), place it in its context—sometimes even teaching its context—and then offer some possibilities of what it might mean today and how we might live the text in this century."

Allen wrote:

> Recently, I have spent many hours going over what I learned in your class over and over again, making sure I remember the class, and trying to piece more together. When this happens, I usually get excited about it and wish that I could take your class and break it down into chunks for teaching a Sunday School class at my church. I realize that this is probably a disaster waiting to happen, but I feel that your class really helped me to begin to think for myself and look at what the Bible was saying, rather than what I thought it was saying, and I can't thank you enough for that.

I replied, "You have to assess the readiness of your audience. In school, I have a captive audience: people who want to learn what I have to teach. Furthermore, I am in a department that specializes in critical thinking and contextual thinking." I wanted Allen to see that Sunday School was a different environment from an academic setting. "Some people cannot separate the historical-critical work from doctrine," I wrote.

> So, while you might be a disaster waiting to happen, you may be a light for some people who need to be set free from biblical baggage that keeps them from believing. As you have discovered, faith is not about what the Bible says; it is about living a healthy and whole lifestyle in relationship and in cooperation with God. God makes that simple; people, as they always do, want to complicate that.

I complimented Allen on seeing that change is the stuff of life. He was one of those rare people who had discovered that truth, while many people could not handle it. I explained to him that he, a person who had fallen in love with change, belonged to a church that seemed to thrive on not changing! He explained that he enjoined keeping in contact with me outside of class because I continued to spark change in him. I explained that he had sparked my thinking, too. These e-mail dialogues were enriching for me.

Allen was preparing to graduate in December 2003. In a subsequent e-mail, he expressed some unhappiness about graduating from college. I told him:

> Graduation puts you into another process of self-discovery, reflection, critical thinking, and self-definition. You have done this work several times in the past, and now you will have to do it again. Of course, now you have more experience, but it doesn't make it any better. Being the smart man that you are, ask yourself what you want to be this time, then work toward it.

I did not hear from Allen for almost two years! On February 22, 2005, I got an e-mail from him. He had moved to St. Louis, where his wife, who had finished a master's program at SMSU (now MSU) in 2004, was enrolled in a PhD program at St. Louis University. He was investigating the law school program at the same school. He explained how all that came about and mentioned several people I knew with whom he had come in contact. He expressed a desire to resume the e-mail dialogue.

My Life of Ministry, Writing, Teaching, and Traveling

I explained what had been going on in my life and told him that I was interested in resuming the e-mail dialogue, too.

So, on February 25, 2005, a two-page e-mail arrived from Allen. He began with a reflection on the word *old*. In the subject line of his previous e-mail, he had written, "Old Discussion Partner?" I asked him who was he calling old? He explained that he meant the word *former*. "This would bring up the question," Allen wrote,

> that if you and I, both native English speakers using even the same dialect can have two interpretations of the same written word with only hours difference in reading them, how can anyone be certain of the original meaning [of words] in the Bible, since it was written by many authors and has been translated many times by many people into many languages over more than one thousand fifty years?

He added, "I think that if this is not enough reason for people to be open and understanding to various interpretations, I'm not sure what would be." I responded by writing about the importance of context when interpreting biblical books. I stated:

> We can never be 100 percent certain of what something means, but at least we are closer to it than if we make it mean whatever we want by interpreting in our context. But to say that it has various interpretations threatens a person's point of view. Most people cannot handle plurality of thought. They want THE answer because it makes life easy to live. Most questions have several good answers. Making choices is what life if really about. It is easier to have someone else make the choices for us, telling us exactly what the Bible means.

On a lighter note, I had asked Allen if he was worried about being corrupted by the Catholic spin on things at SLU. He replied, "I'm not sure I have ever heard another Catholic put it that way. If corruption at SLU is like the corruption I have received from other Catholic professors, and it leads to me being more open minded and forces me to look at information in a new way, that is something I would be open to." In a side note, Allen stated, "I'm not sure I have ever really expressed how much I enjoyed your class. Although I'm not as fresh as I once was, I have all of my notes from the class and go over them after hearing a sermon to get to the other side of the story."

On March 3, 2005, Allen sent me his next e-mail, which, other than one major question, was a few comments about his job offers, the change in name from SMSU to MSU, and the books he had been reading. The major question was this: "Can you tell me how close to an original exists for the different books of the Bible? I know that it existed originally as spoken tradition, but how close does a version exist from when it was finally written down?" I responded:

> We have no originals. All we have are multiple copies of copies of manuscripts which differ in both lesser and greater degrees. What began as oral tradition, got written. But everyone doesn't copy exactly the same way, mistakes get

made, new things get added, something not readable gets left out. Biblical scholars take all the variants in manuscripts and create from them what they think might have been an original Greek text. That text gets translated into English. That's how we get the Bible today. That's why when someone says something about what the Bible says, if one checks the variants, one might discover that is says the opposite, too. We can never know exactly what an original written text actually said.

In his March 28, 2005, e-mail, Allen discussed belonging to a church. He had discovered his wife's need to be surrounded by other believers. He wrote, "I have this need, too, but I don't feel it is fulfilled in church." He explained, "In church there is a single man who tells you his interpretation of the Bible. The only interaction with the congregation that occurs is the singing of hymns or Scripture readings. The biblical interpretation done by the preacher is not open to questions or outside interpretations." He continued his reflection by noting the importance of Sunday School, but faulted it for the large group of people, the fact that only one person, instead of open discussion, answered questions, and the focus on one correct answer. Then, anticipating my next question, he wrote, "Now you may be asking how I fulfill my needs of sharing with other believers. Well, I've found myself growing closer to God recently through reading or listening to other people's ideas about God and reflecting on that with others who have read or listened to the same material. The closest thing that I can compare it to is a book study with a small group of three or four people." He concluded by asking me a question: "Would you tell me what role you think the structure of the traditional church plays in today's society?"

In my April 4, 2005, reply, I stated:

> Some people do need a church to support their faith. Faith comes before church; church is a vehicle for expressing and sustaining faith. Belonging to a body of believers enables a person to grow in faith and understanding of the Bible, the church, and what it teaches and stands for. Other people do not need a church; they have faith, but the institution gets in their way; it hinders their growth and development. That may be what you are experiencing. Also, some people grow out of a church and into another. If you think that the one you have belonged to is too much of the same, then experiment. Attend a variety of churches and see if any one suddenly grabs you or meets your needs again.

After that reflection, I also wrote, "Because you are a married man, you have another issue to consider. You are not making this decision in isolation; you have a wife to consider. Both of you have to reach a decision that supports where both of you are. You may need to go to church to support her; she may need to read what you are reading and discuss it with you to support you."

Then, I answered his question about the role of a traditional church in modern society.

> The role of a traditional church in society remains what it has always been: to bring the individual believers into a whole, to create a community. The body of Christ is not made up of individuals, but of a community of believers who need each other to continue their growth in faith and understanding. Different communities (denominations) accomplish that in different ways. Choosing the way that fits both you and your wife is an important decision not to be taken lightly. I don't think people belong to a church because they agree with everything that church teaches; they belong because it enables them to express their faith.

In Allen's April 15, 2005, e-mail, he told me, among other things, that he and his wife had decided to start going to different churches together until they found one they liked. Also, his wife was going to try to read the books that he did so that they could discuss them together. In my April 18, reply, I said:

> I think the best thing is for both of you to find a church that is good for both of you. Then, you can share the experience and the discussion. Reading and discussing books will help, too. Since every marriage is unique, the two of you have to work out the spiritual and the intellectual aspects of your marriage and make it work for the two of you.

The rest of his e-mail was a narrative of what he had been doing and the books he had read or was getting ready to read. The rest of my e-mail reply was also a narrative of what I had been doing and reading.

In his May 23, 2005, e-mail, Allen informed me that he and his wife had bought a house and were getting ready to move into it. He noted that they had found a church they liked, but discovered that many of the members possessed "anti-Semitic views." He reflected, "Although the Jewish population is hardly a majority, it isn't small by any measure. It is surprising for me to see something like that here in St. Louis." In his June 20, 2005, e-mail, he noted that they were settling into the new home. He was busy at work, not reading because of work on the house, and anticipating a busy summer with attendance at a wedding and several groups of guests. In my June 24, 2005, reply, I merely commented on the joy of finishing unpacking.

Allen's August 5, 2005, e-mail continued the discussion about joining a church. He wrote that he and his wife had been trying to figure out with what denomination of church they wanted to associate. He explained that when they were discussing this topic, his wife mentioned that she was resentful of a lot of the practices of the Southern Baptist Church, and she was surprised that he wasn't also. He wrote: "As we've talked about it, we've decided the difference has to be how early in life you were indoctrinated." His wife was a cradle southern Baptist; he didn't start going until he was seventeen years old. His wife felt betrayed when she found out that you could drink without getting drunk or that other religions (Muslims, Hindus, Buddhists) weren't evil; whereas he was able to take what worked for him and discard what he knew was crap!

Then came the question: "Do all people show resentment for their initial indoctrination, and, if so, how do you stop or at least lessen the effect?"

I answered Allen's question in my August 6, 2005, reply:

> I hear a lot of people complain about their formation in a church structure that doesn't tell them the whole truth. What that usually means is that a church deceives people into thinking that it is giving the people all the information to help them make the "right" decisions, when, in effect, only the information is given that will lead people to reach the decision the church wants them to reach. I think that formation in a church structure of some kind is important because it communicates values which one can't get anywhere else. However, I think it has to be done with some sense of openness and dialogue with the culture in which one lives and not just with the Bible. If the broader approach is taken, then there is less reaction as adults.

I continued:

> I think most people resent being treated like little children—being told that all drinking leads to drunkenness, etc. Instead of teaching people how to drink—which is the duty of parents and churches, in my opinion—good things (like wine and beer) are demonized. Later, when people discover they aren't demons, they resent what they were told earlier because they were lied to. All of us, somewhere in our lives, learn how to think for ourselves and decide whether or not we will stay in the church we are brought up in. I wish churches wouldn't paint the gray world so black and white using the Bible; it gives it a bad rap.

The last e-mail I received from Allen was dated September 18, 2005. In it he supplied a link to a story he had mentioned in a previous e-mail and narrated an auto accident his sister had been in. In my September 19, 2005, response, I merely narrated that I had checked out the link and gave him updates on six recent occurrences in my life. That e-mail never received a response.

I have attempted to narrate the high points of my spiritual and physical journey with Allen over the course of a few years. This narrative represents many conversations I've had with students from SMSU and MSU over thirty years of teaching the New Testament. Most of the conversations were never recorded, and I cannot recall them now. However, this one was recorded through the printing of e-mails. I printed and kept my e-mail exchanges with Allen because I wanted to review them after a few days of sending them. Also, they contained a lot of what I thought and wanted to write about more.

Eric Rogers

Another class-related relationship I had was with Eric Rogers, whom I met in the summer session 2003. We began our friendship with dinner one evening and discovered that both of us liked hiking. So, we enjoyed spending time hiking in conservation areas and talking the whole time! In a February 2, 2004, e-mail requesting a letter of recommendation, he wrote:

> Giving a brief introduction to how we met and the friendship that quickly spawned would seem to set the general tone. I thought you would do a wonderful job because you are so similar to me that I get a little worried sometimes! When you talk to me, I feel as though you have access to the files of my heart and know what I am all about. If you share that knowledge of me, I am sure it will accurately depict my character and morals.

I responded to his e-mail by telling him that I had sent the letter of recommendation. Then, I commented, "If I have access to the files of your heart because of our similarities, you have access to mine as well. I share that worry; it's what I referred to as transparency. I marvel that you know yourself so well and are willing to be so transparent; it took me twice as long to get to where you already are." Then, I reflected on our relationship: "After I invited you into a relationship, I said to myself that the risk would be worth it because we only win from this friendship. We can only come to know ourselves better. The downside of that is that we might discover areas we don't like or know we need to change or whatever, and we both know that we hate dealing with such, right? So, let's see where this takes us. I find it exciting, and you are good for me."

Will Chiles

In the fall semester of 2003, I was teaching my Bible and Film course. Enrolled in that class was Richard (Will) Chiles. He came to dinner one night at my house, and we discussed films we had seen in class and outside of class. We discovered that we both like hiking, so over the course of the next few years we met to hike either in a conservation area or along one of the trails in Springfield. We continued to share a meal now and then and to enjoy the outdoors together over the years. In 2017, Chiles moved to Nashville, Tennessee, for a few months to pursue writing music. Before that he spent a lot of time at a Lutheran renewal center in Chelan, Washington, known as Holden Village, where he worked in a variety of jobs. He endorsed my *Talk to God and Listen to the Casual Reply: Experiencing the Spirituality of John Denver* book in 2017, identifying himself as a singer-composer. Our relationship is what I refer to as a casual one; this means that we stay in contact with each other, even if we don't see each other but every year or so.

Genuine Human Encounters

Brant Horacek

I first met Brant Horacek in the fall semester of 2003 in a New Testament class. I remember wanting to get to know him because of his academic abilities. He had a methodical mind that was able to digest information and apply it. For several years I reprinted his exegesis of a biblical passage in my syllabus as an example for my students. In the spring semester of 2004, he enrolled in my Bible and Film course. Horacek was an excellent student, and that became the basis for our relationship. We talked often, got together for dinner often, and even enjoyed a hike or two while he continued his undergraduate and master's work. I remember talking to him about many different issues, including his heart condition. When he wasn't working on academics, he spent a lot of time on the internet learning the art of gambling, even getting a job working in a casino for a while. Ultimately, he began work on his doctorate, and that is when I lost contact with him.

Marilyn Cox, Thelma Reid, Pauline Katsfey

I met Marilyn Cox and Thelma Reid in the spring semester of 2004. Both of them, retired, were auditing my class. Cox and Reid were former elementary teachers. Immediately, I noticed that they contributed to class discussions and emerged as leaders for small groups. In other words, I knew I had two more teachers in my classroom. They enjoyed my class and came back for the fall semester of 2004 to audit my Bible and Film course. Because I changed the films frequently in that course, they audited it again in the spring semester of 2005 and in the fall semester of 2006. In 2007, Reid died; I remember attending her wake and meeting members of her family, who spoke to me about how much she enjoyed attending my classes.

After Reid's death, Cox continued to audit my courses. Technically, she had used up the free audit hours offered by MSU to retired people, but I permitted her to come because she was an asset in my classroom. So, she came to my New Testament course in the spring semester of 2007; the film course in the summer of 2007; the winter intersession 2008 course on Star Wars and the Bible; the fall intercession 2008 film course; my fall semester 2008 Old Testament course; the winter intersession 2009 Shymalan course; my spring semester 2009 New Testament course; my fall 2009 film class; my winter intersession 2010 course on Christmas; my winter intersession 2012 course on the Holocaust; my spring semester 2013 Lord of the Rings and Bible class; my summer 2013 film course; and my fall semester 2015 Hobbits class. All-in-all Cox audited more about 40 credit hours of courses that I taught. She facilitated small group discussions and helped many students write their papers. She died in 2016 after suffering a number of issues with her back over the years. She was 79 years old.

Cox also influenced Pauline Katzfey, whom she met at morning swim aerobics. Katzfey, a retired nurse, came to my fall semester 2007 New Testament course. Then, with Cox she attended the winter intersession 2008 Star Wars course, the fall semester 2009 film course, and the winter intersession 2010 course on Christmas. Because of her age, she was getting very feeble. However, she, Cox, and I often would go out to dinner together to stay in touch with each other when I was not teaching anything new. Cox loved to make the arrangements, pick up both of us, take us to dinner, and bring us home. Katsfey left her home and moved into an extended living center, where she died in 2018.

Even though all three of these women came to my courses as students, they ended up being teachers. Students admire older adults in a class; and older adults not only share their experiences of living with traditional college students, but they also assist them with developing critical-thinking skills, surfacing topics for papers, and helping with the writing of papers. I enjoyed having these three women in my classroom.

Bryan C. Hunter

I met Bryan Hunter in the fall of 2005. After he had stopped by my office at MSU a couple of times to talk about relationships in early November, he sent me a very reflective e-mail on November 25, 2005. He began by stating that he had the day to himself and had spent a lot of time walking. "I find it one of the best ways to truly think." I commented that I did my best thinking when jogging and walking around the track at the fitness center. "My mind is figuring out things that are important or looking at ways to solve problems," he wrote. Then, he got to the heart of our previous conversations.

"As we talked about relationships the other day, the idea of freedom was a common thread throughout," he wrote. I replied, "I don't think there can be a relationship if there is not freedom on the part of both people. If there is no freedom, then one person is in charge and the other is doing what he or she wants. In other words, without freedom there is manipulation." Hunter wrote, "For this freedom to be, each person must exist independently of the other." My response:

> I don't think one can have a real relationship with another until one can exist alone or independently. A person cannot need another; needing implies dependency. Independence brings one face to face with his or her aloneness or uniqueness in the world. In fact, there is no one exactly like me in the world; there is no one exactly like you in the world. We may share some similarities, but we are still, basically, alone. I think that scares most people away from independence to dependency. Being totally alone in the world is overpowering the first time we look at it, but it is true.

Hunter continued: "For a relationship to exist there must be a bond between the individuals. This bond must be strong enough that the two individuals have a reason to return to each other." I replied:

The bond must be there, but it must be freely chosen. You and I entered into a bond because we both said to ourselves that this relating might be worth the time and energy it will take, meaning that we can preserve our free independence and still give ourselves away in the hope of getting ourselves back changed and altered and be better because of the relating. I think that the reason people return to each other is that they find nourishment in order to be themselves. Ideally, relationships should set us freer to be ourselves. The bond cannot limit; it commits us to each other.

Hunter: "This is the fine line or balancing act that must be maintained to keep the relationship going." Me: "I call it commitment. Two people are committed to the relating. Both are dedicated to the giving and receiving required for a relationship. I think I prefer the word *dedicated* to the word *bond* simply because bond has the connotation of being tied down. To me, relating sets us free." Hunter: "In every bond, equality is not essential. One object may greatly overpower the other and the two objects will still be attached. However, in this situation, the more powerful of the two objects ends up defining the other." Me:

> Equality, to me, is a myth. No one of us is equal to another; we can't be. The reality of personal experience is too vast for any one of us to be equal to another. So, every relationship is based on inequality, and that is what makes the relationship an adventure into the unknown. You've experienced life that I can't due to time and place and everything else. I've experienced life that you can't for the same reasons. That inequality is what fuels our relationship; we want to drink deeply of each other's life in order to expand our view of the world and life. The more powerful of the two objects does not have to end up defining the other. It only happens if the two people in the relationship let that happen. If they keep checking it, it won't happen. That's where the work comes into the relating. It means that even in the act of relating both people must also be reflecting on the act of relating to be sure that no one is manipulating or taking control of the relationship. Such brutal honesty is the substance of relating.

Hunter continued his reflections: "I think that in relationships this is often the case because one person is either too insecure about his or her self or is too caught up with the idea that his or her partner is perfect for him or her. Both conditions can cause a person to hold on too tightly. These insecurities or infatuations may cause one person to smother the other, and as we said, essentially kill the person he or she should be trying to enhance." I replied:

> Yes, that is exactly what happens. Without a self-definition, no one knows who he or she is (even though that definition is always in flux). If, however, you begin at the other end and say that no one is perfect for anyone, then you won't hold on too tightly. Insecurities and infatuations have to be dealt with out in the open; I think they have to be named and talked about. Otherwise,

one person does end up smothering the other. Only the two people relating can know when that line is crossed, and they have to be so committed to each other that they are honest when they detect it being crossed. They owe each other the obligation to check it out. I think that two people in a relationship have to be brutally honest with each other and transparent to each other in order to keep the relationship from deteriorating. Both people have to be strong enough to confront each other; both people have to empower each other with the freedom to confront each other.

Hunter continued his e-mail, writing: "It seems that you must in the end find a person who is not perfect, but perfect for you. His or her strengths must be able to enhance you, and his or her imperfections must be acceptable to you. This way, he or she is not overshadowing you, and you are not trying to change him or her to erase the imperfections." I continued, writing:

This is where the picture gets really big. If you follow through with what you have written, you have to say that you can relate to every person. However, every person may not be the right person to nurture you, and you may not be the right person to nurture him or her. There can be no manipulation in a relationship. To manipulate another is to say that something is wrong with him or her and needs to be fixed. It also implies that the manipulator knows what is best for the other. I don't know about you, but I have enough trouble figuring out what is good for me, let alone knowing what is good for anyone else.

Hunter: "Beyond equality in personalities, there should not be a concept of ownership in a relationship." Me:

I don't think there is equality in personalities; I think there is equality in commitment to relate. We also relate unequally because there are never two people who are exactly alike. I do agree that no one owns the relationship. The two people in the relationship set each other free to relate to others in order to come back together in order to bring the fruit of that relating to their own relationship and enhance it. When a time of relating is finished, both people retain their freedom.

The depth of this e-mail conversation continued. Hunter wrote: "One should not say that 'he or she is mine,' but rather say that 'we are together.' This will allow both parties to go out into the world and live in accordance with their desires, while at the same time maintaining the bonds of the relationship." I replied: "Yes, this is where I put the commitment to the relationship idea. I have nothing to fear from you being free and vice-versa. I can only benefit from your freedom and you from mine." From here, Hunter went "to the thought of being with someone who is your twin. People often get so concerned with finding someone who is just like them that they forget to look at people who may add character to their life. In a relationship, and life in general, you need more than agreement. There must also be understanding of the differences." I responded:

> I don't think there is a twin. Even twins are not twins in terms of personalities and likes and dislikes. For me, openness to others does not imply that I will have a deep relationship with every person I meet. It just means that I am open to the potential for it until the person gives me reason to think or understand that it is not possible, or that I don't want it. I'm sure there are people who choose to relate to you, but you chose not to relate to them. For a variety of reasons, we make decisions about whether or not to enter a relationship. On Monday afternoon you made a move towards me; I responded to you. I could just as well as told you no and we wouldn't be e-mailing now. I responded to you because I detected a depth in you that I don't usually see in people and I want to see it. I want more of you because that more of you can enhance me. You said that you moved toward me because I asked about your book and where you were going to school. Both of us decided that relating might be a good thing, and we were right. We could have decided not to relate. I'm not looking for a twin; I'm looking for someone who is as reflective and interested in integrity and transparency as I am and is not afraid to talk about it in brutal honesty so that I can grow in freedom; you are he.

After not hearing from Hunter, I sent him an e-mail before Christmas. He had expressed an interest in Buddhism, and so I inquired about that topic. "I continue to reflect on the conversations we shared a month ago," I wrote, "and the depth of insight contained in them." He replied on January 12, 2006, narrating that he had read Descartes *Discourse on Method*. He wrote:

> I found that it paralleled Buddhist teachings. I find that Descartes is stripping away all of his beliefs, attempting to find purity. He goes along and questions everything that he has learned or, rather, taken as a truth without first questioning it. This seems similar to the idea of living mindfully, where one must have intent within each action for it to be worth doing. By stripping away all preconceived notions of the world, one can rebuild a stronger sense of reality.

Hunter continued:

> At the same time Descartes gives a lot of credit to common sense. And from what I've gathered, he ends up recreating, basically, the same philosophical framework that he had originally formed. Maybe it has something to do with the idea that God is internal, so even if you strip away everything else, the basic framework for life is still God. And, even if you try to second guess every minute detail, you will find that it was arranged in a certain manner for a reason.

On January 14, 2006, I wrote to Hunter: "I used to think that I found God in the mountains, but I have come to think that God finds me in the mountains, where there are no distractions and little noise. I find the mountains always to be refreshing." Then, I commented on his reflections on Descartes:

> In order truly to believe, we have to suspend or question all our preconceived beliefs and our preconceptions. The preconceptions are the hardest to suspend because we don't know what all of them are. That's where the mindfulness comes into play. I also think that that is where the self-knowledge comes into play. The more we know ourselves—really know ourselves, like knowing our ways of doing things, our preconceptions, our biases, etc.—the more mindful we can become because we can get all that out of our way. Then, we see reality. I think this is a gradual process that lasts a lifetime. In every year of our lives we come to see reality better. Seeing and knowing and being conscious of my reality enables me to let you enter into my reality and accept you the way you choose to be.

I continued by reflecting more on reality. "Being human, we are bound by systems of reality; they help us organize the chaos (the unknowns) of the world. So, in order to avoid getting stuck in one system of reality, which is what many people do, we have to question it often and mercilessly. Thus, while we have a system, it is always in the state of flux or change." Then, I added:

> I think we always come back to the God within. I think that God has left a bit of divinity in each of us deep down inside ourselves where only we go and no one will ever get there. That special place is where we confront our deepest selves and where we, simultaneously, meet or confront God. Because God is so much greater even in the little divinity placed within each of us that we are, we are challenged or pushed to be always in the process of becoming who we are, knowing ourselves. As we know ourselves, we see the patterns that have emerged in our lives over the years. By patterns I mean the threads that are constant, like our likes and dislikes, our ways of thinking, the types of people to whom we are attracted, etc. Not only do such things enable us to know ourselves, but they also enable us to know God who lives deep within us. In both Judaism and Christianity that presence of God is called the indwelling of the Holy Spirit. Notice that it is called spirit, which is exactly what we touch in ourselves deep down within. We are most human when we touch our divinity; we are most divinity when we know our humanity.

On February 15, 2006, I heard from Hunter again. He mentioned that he was getting near to graduating; he had gotten near before and decided to change something to postpone it. "I have been thinking a lot about life, religion, and the actions that we should do," he wrote. He narrated his attendance of philosophy club debates at the college he was attending in St. Louis. But it wasn't the topic of the debates upon which he reflected; it was "the manner in which it was discussed." He wrote: "I'm rarely offended by others' beliefs. I do not hold my beliefs to any higher importance than the next person, and I only prefer mine on a personal level. They work for me (or they are at least beginning to form a structure that will someday work), but I do not expect anyone else to adopt them." Then, he told me about two debaters. One of them was unbelievably calm; this one he admired. The other seemed to have a disdain for people who could not admit that God exists. Hunter's question was this: "How can someone who claims to be so sure of his faith be so cruel at the same time? It is not as if he is offering an open invitation to help people find faith in God and Jesus, but that he wants to do it by making non-believers look foolish. It seems to me that his faith, although strong, has created bold ignorance where acceptance should be held."

Hunter continued his e-mail by tying together learning and doing. "I am still struggling with what to do with my life," he wrote.

> I still feel that teaching would be a great fit, but I don't know what I would like to teach. Also, it is hard for me to say that I want to study religion, because I don't know what I would do in the event that I didn't get a position teaching. I know that that is a choice I will have to make, and one that must be made in faith, not in certainty. I think that one of my great struggles is in the learning vs. doing. I feel that education is important to me, but so is helping others.

Then, he narrated three options about volunteering abroad into which he was looking after graduation: a Peace Corps-like program, the Peace Corps, and teaching English in Japan or Thailand. "I think that this would be a great way to experience other cultures and religions."

A couple of days later I responded to Hunter's e-mail. I reminded him that turning points in life, like graduation, can spark in us a fear of completion because we have not decided what the next step will be. "We like to stay comfortable where we are instead of taking steps in a new direction not knowing where we are going or where we will end up." Besides fear of completion, I also reminded Hunter that he was a man who wanted to serve others; two ways kept surfacing in our conversations: teaching and police department. "You need to remove, as far as possible, all the cultural baggage that you have accumulated, like making money, instantly being gratified by getting what you want instead of learning that life is a process, and having to be what others think or want you to be. When you go deep down inside yourself to that place where only you go, what do you see or feel or hear?" I asked him.

> That's where you are most honest with yourself; that is where you are most you. What is it that keeps your fire burning? I'll guarantee you that it is something that will take a lot of risk on your part. Instead of being focused on the risk, focus on the joy and happiness that can be yours because you take the risk and walk through it instead of trying to figure out a way to get it without having to take the risk. I'm all for security, but taking the next step in our lives always means taking a risk.

I continued:

What is God asking of you? I think God is a very important part of your life, and you and he have been locked in a battle for a long time. What gifts has God given to you to enable you to take the next step? If you take an inventory of your personal gifts, you'll know immediately (however, I guess that you already know) what that next step is. From biblical literature it seems that God tends to choose people who know how to fight back; God likes strong men because they can stand up to God—and God can take it! Stop trying to find ways to get around taking the next step.

I suggested that attending the philosophical discussions may have been a way to determine what God was asking of him. I also told him that I agreed with his analysis of the two debaters. "We do not awaken people to God's presence by shouting at them," I wrote. "We simply help them name what may be an experience of God in their lives, because we have had a similar type of experience. It's always a question: Could that have been God? Yes? No? Maybe?"

In his e-mail to me, Hunter had asked me if I thought changes in the Catholic Church had hurt it. "I hear a lot of people saying that they are reformed Catholic, meaning they no longer practice," he wrote. I replied:

Roman Catholicism, like any other church, has to continue to change in order to meet the needs of its members. The changes flowing from Vatican II in the 1960s didn't hurt the Catholic Church. What has hurt it more is that its members have adapted the values of U.S. culture instead of the values of the Church. It is easier to follow the culture and play soccer on Sunday than it is to follow the teaching that one must be at Mass on Sunday. The individualism of U.S. culture continues to attack the community focus of Roman Catholicism. Those who no longer practice have so bought into U.S. cultural values that the Church can no longer get through to them and show them another way to live their lives in relationship with God and each other as a community (church). See, they have bought into Protestantism, which stresses the individual because Protestantism makes itself appealing to U.S. citizens by identifying itself with the values of U.S. culture. Those values, however, are not always biblical values.

I explained to Hunter that I, as a minister, spend most of my time calling people to conversion, calling them to adapt the values of their Church instead of the culture. I wrote:

The real members, those who believe in God, those who have experienced God at work in their lives, those who have discovered that the best way to be free is to be committed to a relationship with God and a community, never stop converting (changing) or growing. Their lives are an adventure cooperating with God. The barrier that has to be broken through in our culture is individualism, that idea that the only person who matters is me, that I am the center of the universe, that I have to take care of me, that in every situation I am correct.

In his e-mail, Hunter had apologized for the delay in e-mailing. "The best bonds are those that can part and join again without any hard feelings," he wrote. I replied: "I respect who you are and who you are becoming; you respect who I am and who I am becoming. If we can assist each other on the way, why not serve each other?" I never heard from Hunter again.

Joni Lauf and Lucas Bond

In the spring semester of 2008, I met Joni Lauf in a New Testament class I was teaching. I didn't know it at the time, but she, being a very good student, was dating Lucas Bond. She recommended my course to Bond, who enrolled in my Bible and Film class in the fall intersession of 2008. Bond, an outdoorsman, who loved hunting and hiking, found common ground with me soon. He continued to enroll in my courses, taking my winter intersession 2009 course on M. Night Shyamalan and World Religions, my summer intersession 2009 Jesus in Film course, and doing at independent study in 2009 in film. All throughout that time, we got together for dinner and hikes.

Once both Lauf (with a teaching degree) and Bond (with a film media degree) graduated, they moved to Jefferson City and married. I attended their wedding. She is a business teacher, and, after working as a reporter for a TV station and in several jobs for the state of Missouri, Lucas finally got his dream job of working for the Conservation Department of Missouri, putting to use his degree in film by making videos on various and sundry topics concerning wildlife, hunting, fishing, and conservation. They are the proud parents of three thriving children. Bond continues to hunt deer, and we get together minimally once a year for a venison feast. If he is in town, he makes it a point to stop by to visit; if not, I see him and Joni and their children once a year in Jefferson City. Bond and I stay in touch through e-mail exchanges three or four times a year.

Josh Durham

I met Josh Durham in St. Francis of Assisi Parish in Nixa. He was a drummer in the band led by his mother, who prepared music for Sunday Mass. I really met Josh Durham in 2008 on a fall bike trip. He was a twenty-year-old college student, the oldest child of three siblings—two brothers and a sister. While we biked over the trail, he began to talk about his desire to claim his life in terms of making his own decisions, establishing a workout program for himself in a local fitness center, and making a move out of his family's home.

His mother, the dominant, controlling matriarch of the family, kept all the members' schedules, did all the cooking, shopping, and laundry, planned all family trips, etc. This fostered the total dependence of her teenage children on her. As a result, none of them knew how to plan, make decisions, cook, shop, or wash clothes. There was a lack of self-confidence on the part of each child because of his or her inability to take care of himself or herself to any degree. The father, who acquiesced to his wife, fostered her dominance to the point of telling his eldest son that it was not a good idea for him to leave home, because it would upset his mother too much!

By the time I entered into dialogue with Durham, he already believed the truth propagated by his mother's dominance and manipulation. He was scared to claim his own life, because it would upset his mother. He was dependent upon her, because he knew nothing about the basics of human existence, such as grocery shopping, food preparation, doing laundry, cleaning his room, etc. Because he could not take care of himself, he was dependent upon her. Therefore, he needed to live at home instead of moving into an apartment near the campus where he attended college.

Emotionally he was very sensitive, but his feelings had been so manipulated by his parents that he suppressed them as an effort to block the hurt he felt. His parents had used his sensitivity against him, telling him that he could not make good decisions and that he could not take care of himself because he had learned no basic life skills. As a result, he could make no plans to move away from home. He wanted to break out of the manipulation of his parents but didn't know how to do it without hurting from the emotional turmoil it would cause and the emotional abuse he would receive.

Durham's parents were more than willing to give him whatever he needed. So, all things—car, insurance, gas money, credit card, cell phone, clothes, food, etc.—were provided by his parents. To leave those things would have disappointed his parents and demonstrated his ungratefulness. So, he willingly accepted this parental manipulation, under the cover that they were taking care of him and making themselves look good.

They even rewarded him for good behavior, meaning that when he did what they wanted him to do, they gave him freedoms his siblings did not enjoy. He was able to come and go when he wanted. He was able to stay out later than his siblings. He was able to be gone for a weekend. This system of reward further clouded the manipulation he was experiencing. While it didn't feel right, he was not able to recognize totally what was happening to him. I remember asking him, "What college student would need his parents' permission to come and go or stay out late or visit friends on campus?" He was a walking case of dissonance that was easily detected by others outside his family.

I first detected this dissonance when he would say one thing to me, but never enacted his words. He talked on and on about joining a fitness center and getting in shape, yet he never did it. He spoke about staying home one Christmas instead of traveling hundreds of miles to see relatives he didn't care about, yet he went with his whole family on the trip. Endlessly he confided that he had plans to leave home, get an apartment with some of his college friends, and take care of himself, yet he was still living at home during his senior year in college. He always found a way or a reason not to put into action any plan he had because he lacked the self-confidence to do so. And if his parents disapproved in any way, the plan was immediately abandoned. He was not living his life; he was living the life his parents—primarily his mother—had planned for him.

What I discovered as I listened more and more in between the words he spoke is that he hated his family. His behavior indicated such, since he stayed away from home as much as possible. He considered his home as a place merely to sleep, shower, and eat. As I analyzed his situation and presented my summary to him, he rejected all of it, because he had to protect the family—it was all he had. My analysis of the family's dysfunctionality was seen as a threat. He shut down all communication with me.

As I wrote page after page in my journal in an attempt to understand Durham, I kept running into a rock wall. In other words, the dissonance was so loud, I couldn't hear myself. I had attempted to help him see himself. As I probed the frustration he felt, more and more information began to tumble out. He spoke about his high school friends, whom his parents had judged as not people with whom he should be associated and how they had seen to it that he broke off those friendships. While he had been permitted to date when he turned sixteen, he had to bring his date home so she could be approved by his parents. Even learning to drive lasted for over two years; he was not permitted to drive by himself until he was almost eighteen because his parents did not trust him.

A few days after the discussion, I pointed out to Durham how his family was dysfunctional, asking him to reflect upon the families of people his own age, hopefully, to compare how he was controlled with how much they were controlled.

I pointed out that he was not free, that he was, in fact, manipulated. His frustration came from having been programmed by his parents always to feel guilty about any decision he made, because it was not the decision they wanted him to make. They gave him choices; after he choose what he wanted and revealed his feelings about his choice and his reasons for making that choice, they told him he was wrong. He felt guilty and attempted to please them by doing what they wanted—even though he didn't want to do it; it wasn't his choice.

Sitting together on a park bench on a break during our first bike trip, he had asked me to go home with him and to explain to his mother that she should not control his life. I told him that he was taking control of his life; he told me that every time he took some control that he had friction about it because it was always the wrong choice.

He kept trying to figure out how to think his way out of making the wrong choice, but this was impossible to do. He could not think his way out of this because it was not about thinking. It was all about psychological control; it was all about his parents using his feelings against him; it was all about manipulation. It was not his fault that they controlled him. He could not change them; the only person he could change was himself.

I told Durham that his parents' pattern of manipulating him would not change unless he made a decision to change it. After becoming aware of the ways they controlled him, he could then stop feeling guilty for his decisions or his inability to live up to their expectations. The feelings of guilt are what manipulated him. The parents used those feelings of guilt to control him. If he began to live his own life the way he wanted, this would cause all types of friction because he would be changing the pattern; they would attempt to exert even more control.

While joining his family for a ten-day trip, he told me that he shared with his parents some of what we had talked about. They listened to him and told him that they heard him; then, they began to use what he said to control him. When I talked with him after the trip, I knew that we were back to October on the park bench. They used his growth and development to make him feel guilty for wanting to claim his own life. He was back to the beginning of the struggle to claim his life.

Whatever he shared with his parents enabled them to exercise even more control over him because he shared his feelings with them. He told me that they didn't want him to make a trip he had contemplated, and I explained that that was because they would have no control over him. They found more ways to keep him at home, telling he would suffer from the potential money he could have earned if he were working; he needed to get into an internship program, he needed to save money, etc. If he didn't choose what they wanted, he would be made to feel more guilty, which only added more fuel to their control. This was dysfunctional family at its best.

He did not know who he was when his parents controlled and manipulated him. I related several examples to help him see my point that he was controlled as to what decisions to reach. Even during time with me, he was controlled through telephone calls from his mother, who had to check in with him and find out where he was.

I pointed out to Durham that when he cooperated with this pattern, he added to the dysfunctionality of his family. He contributed to the dysfunctionality by not stopping the abuse. I also indicated that he could not change his parents; rationality, logical arguments, would not work. They were not using reason; they were using a pattern of dysfunctional psychology. However, he could change himself and his living situation.

Durham shared with me some of the ways that he was attempting to take responsibility for his own life. He was buying the gasoline he put into the van he drove. He had earned some money from taking care of the pool in his neighborhood over the summer. And he was earning a little money from another job. However, he said that he got no affirmation for that, no recognition, from his parents.

I pointed out that for them to give affirmation or recognition would be to say that he had made a good decision without their help (control), and that would set him free. They could not do that; they must be in control of every decision he made—either obviously or subtly. On the park bench during the bike ride, he had asked me to be his guide, and that implied following my lead. He kept saying to me that he wanted to be an independent man, but he enjoyed all the dependencies of a boy at home. I kept getting cognitive dissonance because I heard him say one thing (independence and responsibility) but his actions said the opposite (dependence and irresponsibility).

In other words, Durham's inner and outer reality did not coincide. And they never did coincide. After three months of growth, Durham returned to his former boyhood ways. He was still living at home as a senior in college. He still did not know how to shop for groceries, cook a meal, wash his clothes, clean his room—basically take care of himself. His mother treated him like a little boy, and he responded accordingly. I learned that after he finished college he moved away and got married. After he broke off the relationship with me, I never spoke to him again about what really mattered to him.

Wesley Dowler

I first met Wesley Dowler in an intersession class I taught on Jesus of Nazareth in Film in May 2009. He was a very quiet student during the whole week-long-class, but through his body language and the paper he wrote for the class, I concluded that I would like to get to know Dowler. So, on the last day of class I invited him to come to my house for dinner, and he accepted. That first dinner began a five-year friendship. The discussion during that first meal featured two critical thinkers exploring a variety of topics. I wanted to have more evenings like that, so we began to get together every four to six weeks for dinner and discussion of many varied topics.

Dowler was very much engaged in his church. He served as a teacher, and he was interested in religious studies. So, over the course of the years, we explored a lot of the Bible and church doctrine and practice. I watched as Dowler reached decisions based on reason rather than on church practice. He discovered that having an alcoholic drink did not make him a bad person. He and his friends often got together to smoke a cigar, and he discovered that occasionally smoking a cigar did not make him a bad person. Evening after evening he would bring up topics to explore; some of these came from his attendance at church and some of them came from his attendance in his classes at Missouri State University. Because he was not sure of what he wanted to major in, he spent his first two years of college taking a variety of courses from all across disciplines.

While he and I never travelled together, Dowler did travel a lot. For a while he worked in a Subway Restaurant and then for City Utilities. There may have been several other places he got a job in order to save his money for travel. He lived at home with his siblings and did not spend money on non-essentials. Other than the summer after his first year in college when he took a road trip to the western U.S. with a high school and church friend, he usually flew to Europe and spent the summer exploring countries other than his own. When he would return before the fall semester would begin, we would get together, and he would narrate tales of his travels, like sleeping on a sidewalk, sleeping in a hostel, meeting a young woman with whom he became a very good friend. Because I had seen a lot of Europe, we were able to connect on the same places and enter into lively discussions. As soon as he got home before the fall semester was to begin, he resumed work in order to make and save money for the next summer's travels.

My Life of Ministry, Writing, Teaching, and Traveling

After graduating from MSU with a major in science and a minor in religious studies, immediately he began work on a Master of Science Degree in Chemistry. While pursuing graduate courses, he was hired as a Teaching Assistant, a job he kept for a number of years. He loved being in charge of the laboratory and introducing freshmen to science. After finishing his thesis, he graduated from MSU with his master's degree at the end of the summer of 2014. He had already been looking at possible schools at which to pursue a doctorate. He was very happy when he got word that he would be working on the degree at the University of Utah in Salt Lake City. Thus, in the fall of 2014, he and his girlfriend, Chunling Cao, headed west.

I figured that all was well. I received an e-mail or two which explained that they had found an apartment, and she had found a job. They were getting settled, and he was excited about the chemistry program. But then the e-mails stopped. I kept sending them, but I got no replies. I left messages on his cell phone, but got no replies. I concluded that he was very busy. However, that was not the case at all.

Finally, over winter break I made contact with him by calling his cell phone. I invited him to come for dinner, but he was heavily booked with family and friends. So, we agree to get together for lunch on December 26, 2014. He arrived for lunch around 10 a.m., and we began to get caught up with each other. It was then that he filled me in on what had happened to him. After getting to Utah, he had experienced severe depression, something he admitted he had had for a long time. He told me that all of his travels were a way he tried to run away from it. By keeping himself busy in college and post-graduate work, he kept himself distracted from it. It had gotten so bad that his girlfriend had urged him to see a doctor, which he did. He checked himself into a hospital to be treated for severe depression, and the hospital would not let him check himself out. His parents had to go to Utah, check him out, and bring him back to Springfield. He told me that he had a doctor here who put him on medication to help him cope. He assured me that he was doing fine and that in a few days he and his girlfriend were heading back to their apartment in Salt Lake City; he hoped to renegotiate the doctoral work with his professor at the University of Utah. As we usually did, we covered lots of other topics until he had to leave. I figured all was well, he was getting medical treatment for depression, and he was ready to get back to living his life.

Imagine my shock one morning in late January when I stopped by the Religious Studies Office Manager's desk to say hello and she asked me if I had heard about the death of a former religious studies minor. I said that I had not. Then, she said his name, and I almost fainted. I remember saying, "What? I just had lunch with him a few weeks ago." I explained to her that we had been friends for five years, and I had no idea that he had died. In disbelief I went to my office and searched for his obituary on my computer. And there it was. Wesley Dowler had died on January 23, 2015. I just sat alone for a long time. I had thought everything was fine. I thought Dowler was back in Utah. I realized that I had missed his funeral on January 26, 2015. I needed a moment to catch my breath.

I decided to call his parents. I had never met them, but I wanted to find out what had happened from December 26, 2014, to January 23, 2015. His mother answered the phone, and, after I told her who I was, she asked me to hold while she put his father on the line. I told Dowler's father that we had been friends for five years, and I just had found out about his death. I expressed my sympathy to the whole family. His father explained that the depression had gotten bad again, and Dowler had not returned to Utah. They wanted to keep him at home in order to continue to see his doctor and monitor the prescription drugs the doctor had given him. On the night of January 22, 2015, intentional or not intentional he had overdosed and died. They found him in his room on the morning of January 23. I cannot begin to express what a hole I felt in my life. My relationship with Dowler was friend and mentor, and, at first, I felt like he had abandoned all we had put into that relationship over the years.

In part, his obituary read:

> Wesley traveled the world. He went on several mission trips to various places doing different works. He enjoyed skiing, hiking, caving, and exploring the world through travel. Wesley was always a kind, generous, and caring person. He never thought of himself better than anyone else and truly believed in helping others. He will be greatly missed by all who knew him.

After reading those words, I remembered the stories he told me about mission trips. He and I had done some hiking together, but mostly we were discussion partners exploring the depths of truth. We explored the world together through the stories we told when we returned from trips and got together over wine and food. Indeed, Dowler was kind, generous, and caring, especially when he was teaching. He lived frugally; one year he went through all his clothes, books, and other things and gave away all he didn't need. He told me he kept only the bare essentials in order to live a simple life. Even five years later, I still miss him, but I treasure the memories of all the dinners and discussions we enjoyed together.

Thomas (Tom) Pesek

I never taught Tom Pesek; I was asked by his father to see him and talk with him while he was still in high school. He was enrolled in a strenuous academic program in a high school and very much interested in philosophy. We began meeting in a sandwich shop in the fall of 2010. After the third session, on November 20, 2010, I sent Pesek an e-mail telling him how much I enjoyed our time together. When we first began to meet, I made it clear that whatever relationship developed between us was mutual. "I left [our third session] feeling very full," I wrote; "that's what a great man-to-man relationship does. Thanks for all the growing you have done that enables this to take place."

I receive a reply e-mail on November 22, 2010, from Pesek. He wrote about appreciating my feedback, but asked for more than positive feedback. "I know you have the capacity to take a much more scrutinizing eye to my character, since you know me well, and I tell you everything worth hearing." We had worked on eliminating Pesek's procrastination, and that was being eliminated gradually, giving him more time to read. "I see you as a professor and advisor of men and also one very learned about classical and contemporary things that matter," he told me.

> Though we are on a closer man-to-man relationship now and see more eye to eye, could you put more pressure on me about random things? Perhaps hold me to a higher standard or even require me to write you reflections on things? Because of the non-formal nature of our relationship, you've taught me a different way than most teachers would. Conversation is a powerful tool, but written responses act as a mirror.

He ended that e-mail by stating that he was hungry and felt that much more remained to be learned.

The next day I responded to Pesek's e-mail, writing:

> My positive feedback is because your growth is positive. I have been focused on the positive because most things negative trigger rebellion in you, and I wanted to avoid adding that layer to get to the real Tom. I've been waiting to hear that you are able to handle anything negative; in order for me to give that kind of feedback, we have to be able to approach each other as equal men—and you have been responding as an equal man for the past couple of months. Also, deep trust of each other is what grounds us in this process and sparks the desire in us for more.

I continued by telling Pesek that I wanted to hear his ideas.

> I'll attempt to push back the boundaries of [your ideas]. Your ideas flow from who you are. There are always holes or inconsistencies—that's why growth takes a lifetime—and we need each other to point them out. We are always in the process of change through ideas and through the physical and the spiritual and the emotional and the sexual and the psychological. So, reflection has to circle back around and around and around, going deeper and deeper every time.

Then, I posed these questions to Pesek: "How many roles can you play at exactly the same time? Can you be my professor, writer, and advisor (teacher and mentor and friend) as I am your professor, writer, and advisor (teacher, mentor, and friend)? Can we set each other free to the degree that we are free from freedom?" I continued: "I think that is the pressure you really seek and the higher standard to which you want to be held. In order for me to do that for you, you have to do the same for me. See, I'm hungry, too. It's time to start feeding each other from the depths of our storeroom."

I received a short response from Pesek on November 23, 2010: "Thanks for understanding where I'm coming from." In our previous e-mails, we had talked about getting together to go for a hike. I presented several scenarios to Pesek on November 24, 2010. He responded on November 25, 2010, telling me that we could take an afternoon hike; then he would need to get back home to complete homework. I don't remember all we talked about, but I do remember enjoying the conservation area with Pesek.

With our regular Saturday meetings, I had fostered the idea that Pesek keep a journal. On January 21, 2011, we could not get together for some reason, so he sent me a four-page entry from his journal and asked me to comment on it. The next day, I commented on several ideas presented in the entry. Pesek had written, "I've never been good at keeping myself personally accountable for something that only matters to me." I wrote: "What is important to you is important to you unless you renege on yourself. Sometimes what we think is important is not important; what we say is important is a defense, a way we protect ourselves from others (maybe even our true selves). It can also be the false self we want to project to others so they cannot get into our lives." Pesek wrote, "I suppose I steer away from making those personal goals because I know I have trouble completing them." I replied: "I don't think that is true. I think your personal goals are too easy and, therefore, they present no challenge to you. If there is no new challenge—because you have already met it—there is nothing to prove to yourself. You need personal goals that will require you to reach down into the depths of yourself in order to complete them; that is what you thrive on."

I also noted to Pesek that praise permeated his journal entry. "You really do want to be praised, complemented, etc., but it scares you to admit it to yourself and to accept it because you think it may be manipulation. I think this is based on past experiences of praise manipulating you. Some praise, however, is authentic, and it has no strings attached to it. The task is to determine which one is authentic praise, and it is not easy to do."

Pesek's journal entry contained words about his future. "I would love just simply being a high school English teacher." My response began with a question: "What's your passion?" Then, I wrote:

> From what I've heard from you, I think it is teaching. It may be teaching English, but I think it is teaching philosophy, especially philosophical literature, and writing about it. You are a good writer; you have the ability to take your thoughts and put them in print. You have the potential to be an excellent writer with a little work on English grammar! You enjoy learning, and you enjoy facilitating it, making it happen for others.

Then, with some deeper reflections, I continued: "I think that what scares you about the future you have is that it requires commitment to it, and commitment limits you. You need to commit to your own future. What keeps you from doing that? Fear? Fear of the unknown? Fear of success? Fear of sharing yourself until your drained? We can only be fully filled when we have been totally emptied. So, get busy emptying yourself of yourself so you can be filled."

Another question Pesek had asked in his journal entry was this: "Why do I like stirring up trouble so much? Not trouble, just doing enough to have someone look at me." He considered himself a decent student, a decent conversationalist, and a possessor of decent social skills. He also thought of himself as having an amazing life, having a girlfriend he could only see at school, and being cool and different. I told Pesek:

> You like stirring up trouble in order to be noticed. Somehow this became a pattern imprinted upon you—a default mechanism that got your attention. Most of us fall into a pattern; some people do good things in order to get praise; some stir up trouble in order to get attention. You like living on the edge, and the edge is often a place where trouble breeds. However, the edge can also be a place of exploration and learning. I think you can make that transition. I also think that you only want to be noticed when you want to be noticed; it is not a great desire on your part, but it is a human need. The task is to learn how to live within the continuum and/or to create a comfortable, nourishing place for yourself, like your room.

I concluded my reflections on Pesek's journal entry, writing:

> You are a good man, a good critical thinker, a decent philosopher, a person with the ability to explain himself, a man with a girlfriend and a relationship that, despite lots of struggle, you have managed to keep alive. The only person you have to impress is yourself. And if you do a good job impressing him, all the rest will come into place. You can impress him with the fire I've seen burning inside you; fire warms and lights as well as burns. It's not accidental that you are a decent philosopher and that your spiritual, awakened side complements the other. Both need to be developed; they are not opposed. Trust both of them, and see where they take you. It is out of the spiritual that you have matter for philosophizing, and it is out of philosophy that you are sent to the depths of the spiritual to test its truth.

We continued to meet at a local sandwich shop on most Saturdays to discuss various things in which Pesek was interested. On one Saturday I shared with him what I considered to be the six aspects that make us human—intellectual, psychological, emotional, physical, sexual, and spiritual—to which he added the aesthetic. I had to admit that he was right, and that aspect got incorporated in a 2015 book Matthew S. Ver Miller and I wrote: *Human Wholeness: A Spirituality of Relationship*. Pesek and I dialogued about the meaning of the aesthetic aspect of human wholeness for several weeks.

On February 16, 2011, I sent an e-mail to Pesek because I had not received the reflections he had promised to send. I had been reflecting on Pesek and the frustration I felt with the lack of change in him.

> I think there is a pattern traced in you of not finishing what you start. I don't see you acting on what you learn about yourself; I don't see you implementing the change, making the change. For example, you tell me you spend too much

time online, but you don't stop spending time online. You tell me you want to take responsibility for your life, but you don't act on it, that is, make the change. You see that your first response to change is rebellion, yet such awareness is not implemented so you stop some of your patterned rebelling. Where is the commitment to yourself? The only person who can be committed to change in you is you. Yes, it is hard, but it is not impossible. You have all the resources you need to do it. Why can't the pattern be altered? What's keeping the process of change from occurring?

In the e-mail response I received on February 18, 2011, Pesek wrote: "I completely agree that I have made next to no progress of seeing off this procrastination and all the other problems we've uncovered. I have late work in every class. I do things on my own time, apparently. Regardless, looking at my situation objectively, one would say that I've fallen off the deep end." He went on to narrate that in order to get caught up on his high school work, he had been reading in the car, but he knew that he would be back in the pattern of late work again. "I have no idea where to direct myself to keep the ball rolling, so to speak," he wrote. "It's only something I can do on my own, obviously. Yet, it is all we talk about. I have no answer, but I'm not about to stop trying."

In the next paragraph of the e-mail, he answered my question about not replying in a timely fashion.

> For me, I feel as if I must attain a certain equilibrium in order to devote to lengthy replies to things, such as this and things even my girlfriend sends me. But I have not felt that I have met that level stage for more than two weeks, so not much gets done. I have a predetermined unconscious order in which I do things, and to complicate it that order is constantly interrupted by distractions and things that I add to the mix based on temporary feelings and modulating interests. Though as I type all this, and it makes sense to me because it is coming directly from reflections on my actions, or lack of actions. I can't help but know that the observing eye will see this and will mark through it with a red imaginary correction pen and note next to it 'excuses'. That may be, but I cannot justify myself by any other means. I have no one to hide behind, and I ask for no one to take the job.

Pesek continued with a reflection: "Today I discovered that in the face of oppression, insult, or just disagreement, I tend to be conscious of my own offense, but I play it off as something I do not care about, as a way of retaining some sense of dignity. We have gone over this before as rebellion, but I think this is a closer description."

On February 19, 2011, I replied to Pesek's e-mail. I wrote:

> You can be whoever you choose to be; I have no intention of changing you. I understand your desire to preserve your dignity. I don't think you don't care; otherwise, you wouldn't have responded to my e-mail. But here is where I am lost: What are you asking of me? I agree; we keep going around in circles, and

> I fully understand that you are ready to stop trying to try. In my definition of help, help implies some desired change on the part of the person seeking the help; once the change is made, then more help can be given to aid more change. If you don't want help to change, what are you asking of me? I'm very frustrated not knowing what my role is.

The next part of my e-mail served as a summary of where the two of us had been over the past month. I wrote:

> We tried discussing philosophy, but that seemed to pass away. We've tried reading an article and discussing it, but that seemed to die. We've tried getting together only every two weeks, but that seems to have died, too. We've tried changing your procrastination, but little or no change has been achieved. I don't want to keep pushing you to change your procrastination if you don't want to change it. That makes me a broken record, and I don't like being that way. What are you asking of me? Maybe you are not asking anything of me, and I'm very comfortable with that. I've very comfortable being your friend, meeting with you as often as you want, listening to you, supporting you, giving you a good experience of a younger man-older man relationship, going hiking with you, enjoying the same things together. From my perspective, what I want takes second place to what you want. If that presupposition is wrong, then please let me know. Maybe we just need to sit down together and tell each other what we want from each other. I am committed to you and our relationship; I'm not giving up. I just need some sense of direction.

I have no e-mail reply to my words. We may have gotten together and talked after I sent that e-mail; I cannot remember. What I do remember is that I have not seen Pesek again. I learned from his family that he had graduated from high school and college—changing his initial major in philosophy to business—and married.

Connor Allwood

I met Connor Allwood in the fall semester 2013 New Testament course I was teaching in which I also met Anderson (see below). He was a very likeable young man and a very good student. He was majoring in criminal justice, but did not know what he wanted to do with it. I invited him to dinner one night, and he was very much focused on the brotherhood of his fraternity. He found that he needed the support that his brothers gave him. He talked a lot about joining the marines after graduation. In fact, he had contact with a recruiter, who continued to guide him in physical fitness in order to get into the marine corp. We developed our friendship throughout his stay at MSU. After graduating, he moved back home to the Kansas City area to await his call to basic training. I don't remember what job he had, but that gave way with moving to the Washington, DC, area for basic training. We stayed in contact through e-mail.

However, after making it through basic training, Allwood began to face some mental health issues that he had sublimated for a long time. After reaching a crisis point one night, he began to get help, and that help led him out of the marines almost as fast as he had entered. He realized that the brotherhood he thought he would get was not what he needed. So, he moved home for a while, got a job, and then got an apartment with several of his friends. He continues to stay in contact with me through e-mail and the occasional visit.

Allwood introduced me to one of his friends, Brian Hamm, who was a student at MSU majoring in education. He accompanied Allwood to dinner at my house on several occasions, and after Allwood entered the marines, Hamm came alone a few times. Hamm was focused on biblical fundamentalism, which put restraints on his life. I attempted several times to set him free from his literal interpretation of biblical accounts, but he couldn't let it go. The concern that occupied him the most was his brother, who grew marijuana in Colorado. The last time I saw and spoke to Hamm, he was contemplating marriage. Later, I learned that he had married and got a job teaching.

Chase Anderson

In the fall semester of 2013, I was teaching a New Testament class, and I met Chase Anderson in it. He and Connor Allwood (see above) caught my academic attention. I invited Anderson to dinner, and he accepted. He told me that he had never been invited to dinner by a professor, so he accepted in order to find out what it was like. Anderson was pursuing a degree in criminal justice, but he did not know what he wanted to do with it. We would often sit in my living room after dinner or lunch and discuss possibilities. He told me that after graduation he could enroll in a police academy, but he had spent a summer riding along in police cars in St. Louis and didn't want to do that as a job. So, I asked in what else he might have an interest. He told me he might be interested in being a firefighter.

After hearing this, I suggested that he volunteer at a firehouse and find out what such a career might be like. He began to look and call around, and a firehouse in Strafford, Missouri, welcomed him with open arms as a volunteer. They gave him jobs to do and took him on calls. At one point, he even got a bed and spent some nights there, while he was continuing his college education. When the chief announced a firefighter training class, Anderson signed up for it and passed it with little trouble. He could not work full time because he was in school. In the meantime, he was enrolled in my 2014 winter intersession course on the Lord of the Rings and the Bible, and my spring 2014 course on Hobbits and the Bible. This meant that we saw each other on a regular basis both in the classroom and out of it.

I don't remember all the other firefighter programs Anderson enrolled in after college graduation, but I know he passed test after test and got certificate after certificate in order to become proficient in emergency medicine. Ultimately, he got a job as a firefighter in Joplin, Missouri, while still living in Springfield. He did not mind the commute every few days, since he was on for several days and then off for several days. When I was visiting my friend, Art Hobbs, in Joplin one time, Anderson invited us to the firehouse and gave us a tour of it and a fire truck with all his and its equipment. For over an hour he named each piece of equipment and identified its use. After that experience, I knew he had chosen the best career for himself.

My role in Anderson's life was counselor. During his last semester (spring 2014) at MSU, his father died; the man had a bone-marrow transplant which didn't work. Anderson left MSU for two weeks to attend his father's funeral and burial. When he returned, I met with him after class one evening. He informed me that he intended to drop the courses he was taking and finish in the fall semester of 2014 instead of the spring semester. I told him that he was not doing such a thing! I advised him to go see each of his professors and tell each of them what had occurred. Then, he was to ask them what he would need to do to make up the work he had missed in each of his courses. All his professors presented him with lists of the work he needed to do in order to finish his courses. He spent part of the summer of 2014 getting all the work done. Then, he received his diploma in August when the summer graduation ceremony was held.

As Anderson's plans for his future continued to develop, I functioned as co-planner, helping him set a course in order to attain the next goal. The ultimate goal was to finish several certification requirements for firefighters and pass state tests in order to return to St. Louis and get a job as a firefighter. In 2017, Anderson was ready to move back to St. Louis. He enrolled in the firefighting academy there, passed it, and got a job as a firefighter. He and I stayed in contact through e-mails. After living with his mother for a while, he got his own apartment and set new goals for himself. He learned that goals are achieved patiently by breaking them down into smaller parts, accomplishing the smaller part, and moving on to the next step. When in Springfield, he shared dinner with me one evening in the fall of 2019. Early in 2020 he transferred from one firefighting district to another one in which he desired to work. He did that only after performing his first rescue from the second story of a burning building and saving a woman's life. I stay in contact with him through occasional e-mails.

Jaret Scharmhorst

I met Jaret Scharmhorst in a New Testament class in the fall semester of 2017. Out of thirty-four students in that course, he shone as an outstanding academician. I liked to get to my class early, and he usually showed up early; thus, we began a dialogue from one day to another. I notice he had a stack of library books one day, and I asked him about them. I told him that I hadn't seen a student with books for research for a very long time. He told me what he was working on and the thesis he was going to develop for a history class he was in. I also learned that he was majoring in history. Once the semester was over, I invited him to dinner, and we spent the evening talking about a variety of topics. I discovered that Scharmhorst was able to handle himself with the skill of a learned man. Both of us enjoyed our time together. We continued to get together for dinner and evening discussions about every two months until he began a job in Jefferson City in January 2020. He got married in June 2020, and the last I heard from him through a telephone call, he and his wife were living in Jefferson City and he was working at the capitol.

Others

While I was attending St. Meinrad School of Theology (1972–1976) and spending the summers serving as a secretary in my home parish of St. Joachim in Old Mines, Missouri, I enjoyed a relationship with Bret Merseal. I don't remember much of our conversations, but Merseal dropped by to see me occasionally and discuss a variety of topics.

In St. Agnes Cathedral Parish (1976–1978), I met Edward Rippee. At one point in his life he was interested in the priesthood. I joined him and his family for dinner several times over the two years I was living in St. Agnes Rectory. I remember one snowy evening trudging through the snow to get to their home. I also remember going to a cabin his family owned on a river for a few days of rest. Not only was Rippee a good student, but he was an excellent critical thinker. After high school, he went to college, and after that he married.

Another person in whom I had an interest was Greg Marino. He was a first cousin to the Eck clan; I witnessed the marriages of four of the Eck brothers: Andy, Jim, Mark, and Greg. At one time I had asked Marino to join me on a trip to Colorado to mountain climb, but he was not interested. After he graduated from high school and college, I ran into him at a birthday celebration I was attending for one of his grandmothers. We began talking. I invited him to dinner at my house. He came, and we discussed lots of issues. We repeated that scenario throughout one whole summer. Through dialogue with him, I began to develop what ultimately became the book *Human Wholeness*. We saw each other a few times after that, and I attended his wedding. He and his wife moved to Houston, Texas, and I visited them there one time. Then, they moved around the country for work, and I lost contact with him.

While I have narrated friendships established while I was teaching in McAuley Regional High School (1978–1985), I have not mentioned Thomas Soetaert. Soetaert joined me a few times when I took groups of young men to spend a weekend in a cabin of a friend in Forsyth, Missouri. We also spent time in discussions in my office. After I moved back to Springfield in 1985, I remember him coming to visit me one time. He was home in Joplin on leave from the Navy. I remember listening to him tell me all about his travels around the word as a member of the armed forces.

When in active ministry after 1985, I got to know Rob Haik, the son of a good friend with whom I gave church environment workshops. I remember one time helping Haik type a paper after he had injured his hand. We sat at the kitchen table in his house, and he dictated what he wanted to write, and I typed it on a word processor. Before that, his mother, Chris, had taken me home with her for a few days to care for me when I had fallen on some ice and bruised my hip. I was renting a house from her and had called her to take me to the emergency room of a local hospital. Later, Rob moved into another one of Haik's rental houses next door to me. He took care of my mail and plants when I was gone on sabbatical in 1992 for six months.

I met Nathan Essner through his mother, whom I hired as a reporter when I was editor of *The Mirror*. While we never travelled together, he asked me to witness his marriage in St. Louis University Church. I maintain contact with him and his wife through our annual Christmas cards and letters.

While editor of *The Mirror*, for a number of years I went to St. Joseph the Worker Parish, Ozark, for Christmas, Ash Wednesday, and Holy Week celebrations. Being editor, I edited a column from the Diocesan Director of Worship, Father Paul McLoughlin, who was the pastor of the Ozark Parish. Serving as Master of Ceremonies for most of those above-mentioned occasions, I met Nathan Laurin, an altar server. Laurin was excellent at his craft, so I often made him my assistant. He could think on his feet and anticipate what needed to be done next. He served as the Master of Ceremonies for my twenty-fifth jubilee celebration.

I lost contact with him for a while, but after I founded St. Francis of Assisi Parish in Nixa, he began to attend Mass there. We renewed our friendship. One summer, while I was gone on vacation, he house sat for me. He knew how to run a chain saw, and so he helped me cut some rail-road ties to fit in a flower garden I was preparing. In the meantime, he was studying to be a nurse. His goal was to work on helicopters that transported people to hospitals. After he decided to marry, I met with him and his fiancé to help them discuss their feelings about church. While I opted for each of them continuing to attend his and her church as an enrichment to their marriage, they were set on picking a neutral church which they could both attend together. After that discussion, I never saw Laurin again.

Jonathan Myles was another altar server I got to know in St. Joseph the Worker Parish. In some ways he was Laurin's successor. His mother would bring him early to services so that I could teach him what to do. He had an older brother named Kevin. Together Jonathan and Kevin took me fly fishing one afternoon; that was a singular occasion, as I have never been fly fishing again. They and their mother came to my house for dinner one time. After I stopped going to Ozark, I lost track of them until their mother died, and I saw them at her funeral. Kevin has become a very good stonemason.

Another person I got to know in Ozark was Brian Love, the son of a LIMEX classmate, Cyndi Love (now Berry). I had seen and spoken to Brian several times, especially when going on family hikes and sharing dinner with him, his parents, and his brothers. Brian, very much an extrovert, graduated with a degree in English and got a job as a dispatcher for a local trucking business. He married, bought a house, and then they divorced. I remember him spending a lot of time with me as we worked through the break-up of his relationship with his wife. After a time of healing, he married again, and they moved. The last time I saw him was at his father's funeral many years ago.

When I look over my class lists of thirty years of teaching, I find other names of students that I got to know to some degree. For example, I met Troy Earwood in my first Bible and Film class in the fall semester of 1995. For a while, we got together for dinner and discussions, but Earwood, after graduation, was having trouble making plans to move out of his family home and be on his own. While I enjoyed talking with him, he seemed to be unable to make the changes in his life that would enable him to be independent. I remember being frustrated, and gradually stopped inviting him to my home.

There was also Dwayne Isgrig, whom I met in the fall semester of 1996 in a Bible and Film course I was teaching. Isgrig was a very good writer. Since I was the editor of *The Mirror* at that time, I used to hire him to cover stories. He enjoyed writing, and I enjoyed having a part-time reporter.

Likewise, I met Jonathan Goss in a New Testament class in the fall semester of 1998. I discovered that he, too, was a very good writer. So, I employed him as a reporter to attend events and write stories. Goss liked the fee paid by *The Mirror* for his reporting. Ultimately, he moved to Kansas City, married, and enjoys a big family. I keep contact with him annually through our Christmas card and letter exchanges.

Another reporter was Daniel Rice, whom I met in a New Testament class in the fall semester of 1999. He was an excellent student and a good writer. His plan was law school after graduation. He won a journalism award for a story I assigned him to write. He worked as a cook at a local Italian restaurant for a while. So, when I went to dinner with friends, I usually made it a point to eat at his place of work.

Friendships developed between me and Brent Wilkinson, whom I met in a fall semester 1999 New Testament class. We saw each other regularly at the fitness center where both of us worked out. For a few minutes we often discussed something that had been said in class.

In the spring semester of 2003, I met Aaron Donnell in a New Testament class. We got together a couple of times for dinner and some discussions. He was a good man, but was not sure of pursuing a relationship with a professor.

John Thomas took three of my courses: in the spring semester 2014, he was in my Hobbits and the Bible course; in the fall 2014 semester, he was in my Bible and Film course; and the spring 2015 semester, he was in my Spirituality course. I invited him to dinner somewhere along the line, and got to know the depths of him. He was a very good critical thinker; he reflected regularly; and he had plans for his future. I enjoyed sharing a meal with him every four to six weeks until he graduated. After that I lost contact with him.

I met Daniel Pattyson in my spring 2014 New Testament class. I discovered that he was a musician, who taught guitar playing, and a home repair man. I hired him to do several jobs around my home, like putting tar around the chimneys, cleaning the gutters, repairing a light, etc. He took my Spirituality course in the spring semester of 2015. He would often drop by my office to talk about his work, his college courses, and his plans for the future. I hired him a second time to take care of some home repairs. He sent me an e-mail announcing that he and his wife had a baby. After he graduated, I lost contact with him.

In the fall semester 2015, I taught a second block course on The Hobbits and the Bible. We watched Peter Jackson's Hobbit films in class, and I drew parallels between them and biblical stories. One student in that class was Eli Wohlenhaus, who happened to be the editor of the MSU student newspaper, *The Standard*. Because I had served as an editor for over fourteen years, editing became a topic before class discussions. I discovered Wohlenhaus to have excellent critical thinking skills and to be a good writer. Once that class was concluded, he returned in the spring semester 2016 to participate in my The Lord of the Rings and the Bible second block class. Because we already knew each other, we continued to discuss the organization required to run a newspaper. I invited him to my home for dinner one night, but he told me that he didn't think he could share dinner with one of his professors; so, he declined my invitation. Wohlenhaus was getting ready to graduate with a degree in journalism. After he graduated in 2016, he headed to Washington, DC, where he had some connections. I heard from him a few times through e-mails, which he used to narrate his search for jobs to pursue his skills. My last e-mail in 2019 never received a response.

In the same New Testament class that I met Corbin Cole in the fall semester of 2016, I also met Isaac Shaw, David Gonzales, and Brandon Williams. Cole and I began a life-long friend relationship that also turned us into travel companions. Isaac Shaw, a home-schooled freshman, was what I considered a manipulated young man. His parents used a variety of psychological techniques to control him without teaching him how to survive on his own. He longed to leave home, but he could not take the steps necessary to do so. I invited him and Cole to dinner at my house one evening in order for Cole to help him understand what he needed to do to survive. The result was that he left college because his parents told him it was not good for him!

On December 8, 2016, I received an e-mail from him in which he mentioned that he was not doing well. He narrated: "After leaving MSU, I quit my job at the request of my parents who didn't like the late shifts I was doing. They promised me work to do at home, but there wasn't any. I have ended up wasting all my time doing nothing and have become quite depressed." He explained that he was finding it difficult to function and that he missed college. The arguments with his parents had become worse, and his mother told him that he was no longer allowed to live at home, but she also was not allowing him to take the car he had used as his own! I responded the same day, writing:

You are being manipulated by your parents. Quitting your job left you with no recourse to income. It was a psychological move to control you. You need a full-time job with an income that enables you to live on your own. Taking away your car and throwing you out of the house strips you of all your human power. It leaves you totally dependent and vulnerable. How can you not live at home if you have no vehicle to go somewhere else?"

I urged Shaw to marshal his resources and to go live with a family member or a friend temporarily, to get a full-time job so he could support himself, and to become self-sufficient and no longer dependent on others. "As long as you keep playing into your parents' hands, they have control, and you do not," I wrote. "You can wallow in depression or you can do something about your situation."

I received a response the same day. Shaw wrote, "I understand now more than ever that I need to make a change or the situation will only get worse if I let it. Truth be told I am rather afraid of leaving home, and I am afraid of leaving my comfort zone. My parents understand this as well as I do. Their position has become clear to me. They do not want an equal relationship, but obedience." In the same e-mail, he asked me if my offer in the previous September of my guestroom still stood.

The next day I had to tell Shaw that my guestroom was not going to be available until April 2017. I was going to be mostly out of town for the next three months. I urged him to search for housing near the MSU campus. However, I told him that he needed to have a job to support himself before he left home. I urged him to leave home on his terms and not to run away from home on his parents' terms. He had to work through leaving his comfort zone behind and work through the fear of being independent. "Your parents know your fear and they use it against you," I wrote to him. "Fear is most deadly because it controls people. The opposite of fear is trust which engenders healthy adult relationships in which people respect each other's positions without attempting to manipulate them to their truth."

In that e-mail, I helped him lay out a plan of action. He had a job beginning in late December. I explained that he needed to stand up to his parents and tell them that he was using the car to get to work with no conditions. For a couple of months, I urged him to save his money so he could then find a place to live, preferably close to work. Then, he could move himself and his things out of the house and return the car to his parents. Setting a date as to when to move out provided a goal to be achieved while avoiding parental manipulation. I urged him to demonstrate that he could manage his life. That way he would be moving out on his terms. "When they threaten you, you walk away because a threat is a manipulation," I wrote. "Then you demonstrate your adulthood, while keeping in mind your plan of action. You can be the independent person you want to be. But you have to avoid the manipulative confrontations."

I ended my e-mail by pledging my support if any way that I could. "You just have to be the man you envision yourself to be by gradually becoming him," I wrote. "It's a lot of growth and work, but if you want it bad enough and are willing to suffer to get it, you can achieve it." I told him that if he wanted to talk, we could arrange a time and place. I never heard from Shaw again.

While all the drama was taking place with Shaw, I watched David Gonzales, another freshman, grow by leaps and bounds during that semester. He excelled in the academic pursuit of the New Testament, and he learned how to relate to me and his peers in the academic setting of the classroom. Even though he came to my home a couple times for dinner, we never developed anything beyond a student-professor relationship. He was still learning how to pursue study and friendships when I last saw him at the end of the semester.

The young man who did know how to relate to me as an adult was Brandon Williams. Williams was an excellent student, who would drop by my office to talk about his life. He was struggling with taking some time off from college to explore other possibilities. I encouraged him to do so! He felt lots of pressure from his family to stay in college until he graduated. During one summer, he began to come to dinner, usually with Cole. He shared his plans to join the Air Force. After telling his parents what he intended to do, he discovered that they were supportive of his move. Before he left for basic training, he came to dinner one more time with Cole at my house. We wished him well in his new endeavor. I never heard from him after he left.

I do not remember where or when I first met Patrick Murphy. Our friendship grew when he was in St. Meinrad School of Theology. We would gather for dinner and for discussion of various theological topics. At one point he left the seminary after discerning that priesthood was not for him. For a number of years, he taught religious studies in Springfield Catholic High School. When I was editor of *The Mirror*, he also functioned as a part-time reporter for the diocesan newspaper. After I founded St. Francis of Assisi Parish in Nixa, I asked him to be the Director of the Rite of Christian Initiation of Adults for the new parish because he had the theological background to lead discussions with those seeking to join the Catholic Church. He served for a few years in that capacity. Then, he returned to the seminary for a short time before coming back to Springfield and getting a job taking care of the buses for the Springfield Catholic School System. I gradually lost track of him except to see him in public.

Groups

Old Study Group

After I was ordained and assigned to St. Agnes Cathedral Parish in Springfield in 1976, I was introduced to what ultimately became known as the Old Study Group. The previous associate pastor, Father Fergus Monaghan, had been their leader, and that responsibility now fell on my shoulders. James and Dorothy Askren, Jerry and June Beck, Thomas and Raamah Crim, Edward and Julie Rice, and Olive White where the members of the group who studied Scripture. After agreeing on a biblical book to read, we would meet and discuss it. The discussion would flow into a happy hour and dinner at the home in which we were meeting. We would rotate the host's home among the members, meeting monthly except during the summer. I served as the leader of this group from 1976 to 1978, when I left Springfield to go to Joplin. After I left the group stopped gathering.

Jackson Church

In 1979, I became a full-time high school teacher in McAuley Regional Catholic High School. Because Sisters of Mercy taught in the school, we decided to create a chapel on the second floor of the building known as the old convent. There was an empty room there into which we brought a large statue stand, which served as an altar, and a lecture stand, which served as an ambo. Chairs were placed on both sides choir style. Besides the nuns, several other people came to the daily Mass I celebrated during that first year, 1979–1980, because of the convenience of the time of day. Gradually, the sisters' attendance fell off and the attendance of others' waned. So, at the end of the school year, I announced that I would not be celebrating a daily Mass in the chapel over the summer nor during the next school year.

From the small group of other non-school-affiliated people who came, a small group formed led by James and Brenda Jackson. They invited me to their home to celebrate a Saturday evening Mass with some of their friends. Thus, was born what became known as the Jackson Church group. Members included Arthur Hobbs, James and Brenda Jackson, Leigh-Ann Long, Timothy and Laura Vineyard, Mary Wieman, and Keith and Robin Zeka. Those were the usual participants, but there were many others who joined us once or five times or for a few years before moving on to something else. The group always met in the Jackson home on Saturday evening. Its focus was on the Scripture texts for Mass, with dessert and drinks that followed. For the first few years I prepared worksheets for the Sunday Scripture texts for the monthly Saturday evening meetings. These consisted of quotations from the biblical texts, questions for reflection, and other materials that fostered the spiritual growth of the members. I would prepare materials about a month in advance so members would have plenty of time to complete the worksheets and bring them with them to the meetings.

By the time I moved from Joplin to Springfield in 1985, I had taught the members of the group to prepare the worksheets on a rotation basis. As each couple or individual took turns preparing for our monthly gathering, those doing the preparation could have it ready to give to the members at the previous meeting, mail it to the members, or take time to complete it during the meeting. This continued to be the mode of operation of the group until I could no longer drive to Joplin because of Saturday evening pastoral responsibilities in 2003.

Around 1982 the Jackson Church members began to gather for Holy Week services. We met on Saturday evening before Palm Sunday to mark the Passion of the Lord. We met on Holy Thursday first to celebrate a Christianized version of the Passover Meal followed by foot washing and Mass. We honored the cross on Good Friday as a small group. And after dark on Holy Saturday we gathered for an all-night Easter Vigil. We built and blessed a fire and kept it going all night. We prepared a large candle, and lit small candles that we used all night instead of turning on the electric lights. After each reading was proclaimed, a different person led us in an application of the text, a response, and a prayer. Sometimes those parts were interspersed with silence. On and on the process went throughout the night. We blessed water and renewed our baptismal promises, wearing white to indicate that we were among the baptized. We brought the vigil to a close at sunrise with the first Mass of Easter, sitting around the Jackson dining room table, where we had eaten our Passover Meal only two days before. By the time daylight was filling the sky, we had completed our vigil. Then, we went out to eat breakfast together. The vigils over the years were spiritually and mutually nourishing. The only reason we stopped them was because my pastoral responsibilities kept me from going to Joplin to be with the group. From time to time over the years, various members have hosted once-a-year soup suppers or met to go out for lunch; at those gatherings are discussed the religious experiences of the past.

Robin Zeka

I met Robin Zeka during the years (1979–1983) I lived in St. Peter Rectory and celebrated a single Mass almost every weekend. She and her husband Keith were members of St. Peter Parish. I also knew Robin through McAuley High School (1978–1985), which their four daughters attended. Zeka discovered that I was an avid tennis player, and she invited me to play tennis with her. As we did that occasionally, we got to know each other, and I invited her and Keith to come to the Jackson Church group meeting. They came, and they stayed. After I left Joplin in 1985, I stayed in contact with Robin through the monthly gathering of the Jackson Church group, whose meetings I continued to attend for many years.

Zeka and I also engaged in e-mail exchanges. She listened to me talk about using films to teach New Testament at SMSU (now MSU), and decided to use movies to develop her spirituality. In an October 2, 2000, e-mail she expressed wonderment about "what life experiences lead us to our fate." Zeka was growing out of organized religion. "I have shattered most of my church illusions and severed the blind cord that binds," she wrote. She wasn't angry; she just was not getting what she needed from organized religion. "I am hungry and am not fed. I think there comes a time when religion becomes God's biggest obstacle," she wrote. Developing her spirituality, wanting to be herself, she referred to herself as "this weird woman who seems to flourish in fallowness and delight in this divine mystery that constantly flutters beside me."

I responded to Zeka's e-mail the same day, writing, "We grow into and out of community (organized religion) as we make our journey. It's OK to grow out as long as you leave open the possibility to growing in. Sometimes when we are not fed, we have to take responsibility to feed ourselves." I reminded her that weaving into and out of organized religion was a search for better nourishment. My comments got her to think about how often she had done this in the past. "I have been doing this my entire adult life," she wrote. "You have helped me clarify the need to remain open to being once more where I have been before." The next day, I added, "We can close a door as long as we remain open to the possibility of opening it. We have no idea what old door might need to be reopened." I also reminded her that, as a church, we have a rich history of non-community people, some called hermits or anchorites, who lived alone and did their own thing. I also explained: "I had to balance community with aloneness for myself. I can't take too much community. I like being alone, living alone, staying at home alone. I enjoy small communities, like the Jackson Church, because I am fed as well as feed the members."

She asked me, "Do you really think that Divinity has a divine plan?" I responded in the affirmative. I exhorted her to feed herself with Scripture, reading books on spirituality, praying, journaling, etc. She wrote about going to church and sitting in a pew and wondering why she was there. I wrote that I had often experienced the same thing. "I want to be fed too," I wrote. "So, about once a month I go with Matthew Miller to Second Baptist to be nourished by John Marshall, the pastor there. He is the best preacher I've ever heard. He fills me with what my own church cannot. I think God is always ironic in this way, pushing back boundaries, making life dangerous." Zeka responded on October 6, 2000, writing, "Life breaks us, and we are stronger at the broken parts."

The next e-mail I have from Zeka is dated January 24, 2001. In that correspondence, she writes, "The further I move from the church of my choice the closer I get into the sacred. I find myself in the middle of gratitude or in the middle of a prayer without putting myself there." I responded, writing, "It is the difference between praying and being prayed, between saying thanks and being thanksgiving, between reading a book and being all the characters in the book. It's the difference between saying I'm alive and being alive." I reminder her that many great people had found themselves outside of the very place they began looking for God. I concluded: "I am convinced that the more we get out of the way—and this also means not letting the institution get in the way—the more God is able to do as God wills. As long as you remain true to yourself, you are true to God. As long as you are faithful to yourself, you are faithful to God. What a risk! Yet, what a life!"

On the same day in a different e-mail, Zeka asked: "What if my perseverance leads not to fruit showing up on my path, but to another path and then another and then a matrix of paths leading here, there, and who knows where?" I responded: "Fruit shows up wherever God wants it to show up. Perseverance means that we trust God more and more." I added:

> There comes a point when we must do what we believe (trust) is right and whatever that may be does not break our relationship with God, but, on the contrary, makes it grow even stronger. We cannot violate our deepest selves. To do so would be to violate the relationship with the Divine, who makes us who we are and calls us to become more of who we are every day until we see clearly and remain faithful.

I told Zeka that we may see fruit where we did not expect to see it.

> Institutions (like the church) have a tendency to get in the way of this taking place because an institution wants to control what God is doing instead of being led by God. Institutions (and those who lead them) get stuck in the very thing that should set them free to explore even more. Without critical thinking the institution kills the spirit and life of its members, except for those who are strong enough to hold on and still move forward. Sometimes that means turning loose and moving forward.

On February 9, 2001, Zeka wrote: "My estrangement with the church is at an end. Church as magisterium, church as bureaucracy is no longer critical to my spirituality, no longer the determinate, no longer the seat of wisdom, no longer the example of compassion or Christian. How good it feels to arrive at this point. I travel light." I replied: "I'm convinced that we have to set ourselves free from the institution. Faith is always bigger than the institution."

Zeka continued to grow. The next e-mail I have preserved from my correspondence with her is dated December 31, 2003. In it she asked for any advice I might give her "for letting go of guilt." She explained that she felt guilty for her mother's suicide, which had occurred a few years before. She stated that the guilt was about not having done more. And she added that it was destructive. I responded the same day, writing:

> Sometimes, guilt is the result of claiming responsibility for someone else's actions. We cannot be responsible for what an adult does. The illusion is that we are in control of another's life. Thus, when that other commits suicide, we must be responsible for it. The fact is that we are not in control of another's life, and we are not responsible for it. The hardest part, I think, is facing the fact that we are not in control and letting that go.

I explained that was hard to do because "we have to admit to ourselves that there was an actual situation that we did not control." I continued: "You did not control your mother's death. And if there is one thing that really leaves us feeling out of control, it is death. My advice is to face your presupposition that you were in control and raise your awareness that you were not. If you do not consciously let it go, it will continue to be destructive."

The conversation continued on the same day. Zeka wrote that she had not considered control. Then, she asked me to help her move out of it. She also asked, "Is this another form of control?" I replied: "The only way I know to give up (some) control is to practice doing it. Practice letting go. When the thought that you are guilty (responsible) for your mother's death comes to mind, get rid of it by telling yourself that you are not guilty and that the feeling is not appropriate." I reminded her that the culture in which we live tends to operate on feelings instead of evaluating a situation rationally. "We don't act on every feeling we have," I wrote. "We carefully evaluate feelings and determine which ones we will act on and which ones we will not. Apply that to your current situation. Refuse to act on the feeling of guilt."

This conversation flowed over into January 1, 2004. Zeka thanked me for discussing this with her. She said she knew she had work to do on herself about the issue of her mother's suicide, which was tearing her apart, harming her self-esteem, and hurting her relationships with others. She wrote, "I cannot deal with the events of that day and put her to rest until I can release myself from the necessity to crucify myself continually." I replied: "The hardest work to do is the work we must do on/for ourselves. The only person who can release you from your claim of responsibility for your mother's suicide is you." I urged her to realize that having control is an illusion.

On February 3, 2004, Zeka wrote about having more questions than answers concerning her mother's suicide. "Perhaps I must learn to be content and hope the questions are in fact the answers. The questions, I come to think, hold the key to my transformation. I am entering a space or place where I am unsure of being. I trust my doubt is not an obstacle and my hope is a grace." I replied the next day, writing:

> The only person who has the answers to the questions you have is your mother, and she did not reveal the answers. Since the questions are not yours, why not just be content that you have recognized them and then let them go? You cannot continue transformation with some other person's questions; you can only continue transformation with your own questions by seeking answers to them. The unsureness of being where you are is that you are trying to live someone else's life which you cannot do. Your doubt is your uneasiness in being where you are now; so, leave there. Letting all that go will free you to re-enter the transformation process, and grace will flood your life.

The last saved e-mail from Zeka I have is dated September 16, 2007. In it she discussed what she referred to as "bad ritual." What she meant by that term is poor liturgy: lack of participation by those in attendance and lack of preparation by those who lead it. She asked me if I found it difficult to preside over liturgy in which people did not participate. I told her that it was very difficult for me because I was prepared and I wanted to celebrate, but in my experience few people cared; all they wanted was to get Mass over. Zeka wrote: "Without organized religion in one's life, one must live a self-disciplined life. Organized religion provides that discipline/direction for its members." I responded, writing: "I would have made a much better hermit, but I long for a community that wants to pray, sees it as a priority, and actually does it. I long for a community that can transcend itself."

"Since leaving organized religion, I have created ritual in quietly personal ways," wrote Zeka. "It brings pleasure, meaning, and growth." I replied: "Ritual is important to most people, unless they prefer chaos." Zeka: "Without aware, secure, and educated individuals, community is doomed. There must be a balance here, a space for the Divine to slip through, a place where the individual and community meet, where I am me and you are you." Me: "Each person has to know who he/she is before being willing to give that person away in community. I don't see many people who know who they are, so they do not know how to form community." Zeka went on to reflect how she didn't think she needed community except in small doses. I replied, writing, that I didn't need much community either, except when it comes to support in ritual prayer. I wrote: "I have trouble understanding those who have to have a fire lit under them or patted on the back every time they lift a finger to do something. I cannot begin to give what people want of me because most of the time I get nothing in return. That means that I am always drained. In a real community, there is mutual giving and taking."

That was the last e-mail exchange I printed and kept. While we have communicated over the years through e-mail and continue to exchange Christmas cards and letters and birthday greetings, we no longer delve into the deep things that matter. We have gone our separate ways, found our own support systems, and developed our spiritualities according to the place, time, and age given to us.

Old Study Group

After moving from Jopling to Springfield in 1985, the members of the Old Study Group contacted me; they wanted to reconvene. So, we had an organizational meeting in the home of one of the couples and discussed how we wanted to proceed. I began by asking them what they wanted to do. The basic response was that they wanted to do some studying and some fellowshipping. So, I agreed to see what I could find for the studying part and help them organize the fellowship part: drinks and dinner.

Over the next years, we read articles and books. I looked for series of adult education materials that I could use for a short session with the group. After a while, they asked me to add Mass to the schedule. So, by the time we stopped because of the ill health of the members, a typical Sunday afternoon began with Mass, was followed by study and discussion, then drinks, then dinner. We rotated homes, meeting monthly. By the middle of the first decade of the twenty-first century, the members were getting older, and the group disbanded. Members began to die. Now, in 2020, only three of us remain.

Genuine Human Encounters

Partners in Performance

A third group to which I belonged was named Partners in Performance. This was a group of volunteers who served Juanita K. Hammons Hall for the Performing Arts. Hammons Hall opened in the fall of 1992 while I was on sabbatical. I joined the two hundred-plus volunteer force one year later and went through the required training. For every show in the 2,222-seat Hall, a large group of volunteers was needed to take tickets, to give directions to patrons, to guide people to their seats, to manage coat-check, to sell concessions, and other duties that may be unique to a specific show. Once the volunteer completed his or her job, he or she was able to sit in the seats in the back of the theater and watch the show. Once a year when the season was finished—usually May—a banquet was held for volunteers, who also got to sit in the theater and watch some entertainment before the volunteer of the year was announced and five-year service pins were awarded. Every five years a volunteer got a pin to put on his or her name badge. The first pin (five years) was black on gold, the second pin (ten years) was black on silver, the third pin (fifteen years) was all gold, and the fourth pin (twenty years) was red on yellow. The first three pins were circular; the fourth one was a rectangle.

A few years after I joined Partners in Performance a house manager—Chris Williams—was hired who recognized my organizational abilities. Because I was usually present for my assignments early, he invited me to help him check in volunteers to be sure that everyone who was assigned a position was present; that set him free to take care of tasks only he could handle. Once he saw that I could accomplish that easily, he began to delegate the responsibility to assign volunteers to the various positions needed for a show. Once he gave the pre-show briefing, he would turn to me and ask about positions still needing volunteers; I would tell him, and he would fill them with any extra volunteers we may have or move someone from one place to another.

One January, after I had assisted him for a year or more, Chris was bedridden with the flu during a week when there was a show almost every night. He called me and asked me to take his place at the Hall. I was responsible for assigning volunteers to the various positions, checking the list to be sure I had every position covered, and taking care of any other details. Every night for a week I went to Hammons Hall for the Performing Arts and organized the Partners in Performance. Once all volunteers took their places and the show began, I would walk around to be sure everything was functioning as it should and then head back home. That year at the end-of-the-season banquet, I received the Best-Imitation-of-Chris Award for my service to the Hall. It consisted of a plastic flash light—one used by volunteers—attached to small piece of a stage floor board that had warped when a water pipe burst and flooded the stage. The inscription on the metal plate attached to the wood stated, "Best Imitation of Chris."

After a number of years Chris left to go work in another venue in another state. Instead of a house manager, the Hall was run by students who attended Missouri State University and were majoring in entertainment management. The Partners in

Performance were managed by a Volunteer Coordinator. I continued to volunteer in all the various positions, even being chosen for special positions when needed. While students worked with volunteers, they did not have the authority nor the experience that any other volunteer would have had. I even offered to help them several times over the years, but they always declined my help. After a few years of having no Volunteer Coordinator, the Hall manager asked a faithful volunteer to take over the position. I referred to her as a new pharaoh, because that is how she treated volunteers. She began to make changes to a process that had worked for many years. The major change that I objected to was the prohibition that volunteers could no longer sit on the steps.

All volunteers had to be present an hour and half before a show was scheduled to begin. Upon arrival, one checked in at the desk to let the Hall manager know he or she was present. Then, all waited for the briefing done by the Hall manager, usually ten- to twenty-minutes after check-in. Once the briefing was finished, all volunteers went to their assigned stations; usually we were there over an hour before the show began and often more than thirty minutes before the doors of the hall opened. So, we would sit on the steps. I brought student papers to read and grade or a novel to read. Other volunteers did the same. Some just sat and talked about the weather, politics, or religion. Because all of us were older people, who knew what standing on their feet for several hours was like, we sat on the steps. The new volunteer coordinator didn't like that and forbade it.

I had been thinking about it for about a year before I decided to test it. So, my last evening working, I had a stack of student papers needing to be read and graded. I brought the papers with me, and, after getting my assigned station, proceeded to sit on the steps and read them. A student worker came alone and told me that I could not sit on the step. When I didn't get up, she went to the volunteer coordinator, who came to see me. I told her that there was no one around—no patrons in the Hall—except volunteers, and sitting on the steps was hurting no one. She told me to get out, and so I got up to leave. I had been contemplating leaving in May anyway. She asked me, "What do want?" I replied, "My twenty-year pin." As I walked out of the theater for the last time as a volunteer, I doubted if I would ever see that pin. But a week later, it arrived in the mail. That was in April 2013. I had finished serving as a Partner in Performance for twenty years.

In the beginning, I greatly enjoyed working at the Hall. Volunteers were appreciated and treated with respect. During the time Chris was Hall manager, I had suggested that he get folding chairs and put them inside the theater for all the volunteers at doors into the theater. I explained to him that older people could not stand through a two-hour show. Folding chairs could be put in place once the show began and easily removed for intermissions and the end of the performance. He accepted my recommendation, and folding chairs were provided at all entrances into the theater. As time elapsed, more and more stringent guides were put in place. We were told that we could not leave our position for any reason, even to use the bathroom, until we were dismissed by a student worker. Likewise, ticket takers had to count all the tickets in their box and bundle them in groups of fifty before they could leave after the show began. Student managers treated volunteers as if they were children instead of respecting their experience and wisdom. Before I quit volunteers were treated as if they were pawns on a chess board. Somehow or other those in authority had forgotten that they were volunteers.

14

Three Major Incidents and Memorable Retreats

Duped

I MET FATHER SYL Schoening during the summer of 1976 in Telluride, Colorado; he had been pastor of St. Patrick Parish there since 1969. After that initial meeting, I continued to visit him almost every summer thereafter. I saw him a few more times in Telluride; in St. Margaret Mary Parish, Cortez, 1981–1986; in St. David Parish, Ouray, where he stayed for a while, and in Sacred Heart Parish, Paonia, and St. Margaret Mary Parish, Hotchkiss, 1986–1991. In 1982, he had built a home on forty acres of property he owned outside of Norwood; he named the home "The Hermitage." Because he was still in active ministry, he could not live there, but he did go and spend time there off and on until he retired in 1991. After The Hermitage was built, he bought an additional ten acres that bordered his property. It was an unusual sale, since lots in that part of Colorado had to consist of forty acres. However, after an old ranch was divided into forty-acre parcels, there remained one ten-acre parcel, which Schoening bought. Upon seeing the ten-acre plot, I asked him if I might buy it from him in order to build a home for me upon it.

He told me that he did not want to sell it because it was a good buffer for his property. However, he told me that he had been thinking about what to do with his home and property once he died, and, since he had no heirs, he wanted to know if I was interested in it. He wanted it to be maintained as a hermitage. I told him that I was very much interested in it, and that I would, indeed, be willing to maintain it as a hermitage. I told him that it would be hard for me to pay the high real estate property taxes, and he advised me that he was creating a trust for the house and property which would include funds to pay the taxes.

From 1983 I began to spend some time at The Hermitage almost every summer for a few days or a week or more. In 1987, I began serving as a priest substitute for Schoening in the parishes in Paonia and Hotchkiss, while he spent a month at The

Hermitage, where I would visit with him for a few days. I liked spending time in Paonia and Hotchkiss and got to know a lot of people over the five years that I did this. I also became acquainted with very good friends who enjoyed mountain climbing as much as I did. While spending time at The Hermitage, I often engaged in clean-up projects, hauling away piles of things that Schoening left everywhere, cleaning the refrigerator, and doing some heavy house cleaning. Almost every-other summer, I put sealer on the decks. Schoening was not one to keep things clean, and I could not stand all the stuff piled around. Over the years, I invested lots of time into the upkeep and repair of The Hermitage.

I went to Colorado to spend Christmas with Schoening in December 1993. One day we went to the Tisdel, Hockersmith, & Burns Attorney at Law office in Ouray, Colorado, to meet with Richard P. Tisdel to prepare the proper papers naming me as Schoening's General Power of Attorney and other necessary paperwork to ensure that I was the inheritor of the house and property. On March 10, 1994, I received copies of Schoening's General Power of Attorney, Trust Agreement of the Hermitage Foundation, Last Will of Sylvester Herman Schoening, and Living Will of Sylvester Herman Schoening.

In the General Power of Attorney, Schoening appointed me as his attorney "in fact and agent" in his name and for his benefit, giving me, among others, the powers to collect funds due him and pay his bills, to acquire and sell, to manage his affairs, to bank, etc. Schoening had signed the document on March 3, 1994. I needed to sign the original copy and return it to Tisdel; a copy was provided for my file. In the Trust Agreement of The Hermitage Foundation, "the real property known as The Hermitage" was put at my disposal "to use in any manner which [I] consider[ed] appropriate during 'my' lifetime. . . ." If the trust assets and income were not sufficient to pay the bills, then I could liquidate all or any portion of the real property assets. I was also named "successor trustee" in the document. In other words, upon Schoening's death I would inherit his home, property, and everything else associated with the trust he had created. Furthermore, I would have the final decision over everything. This latter document was also dated March 3, 1994.

Also on March 3, 1994, Schoening signed the "Last Will of Sylvester Herman Schoening." In it, he left everything to the trustee of The Hermitage Foundation, that is, I. Anything left over was to be given to the Christian Foundation for Children and Aging in Kansas City, Kansas. I was appointed as his personal representative and given all the powers necessary to carry out the provisions of his will. In the "Living Will of Sylvester Herman Schoening," also dated March 3, 1994, he expressed his desire to die with dignity, having no extraordinary means, including artificial nourishment, keep him alive.

As I had done before, I continued to visit Schoening during the summer and sometimes spending Christmas at The Hermitage. During the summer, I continued to perform repair work and cleaning; during the winter visit I often cooked Christmas dinner to which Schoening invited some of his friends. Over two different summers, once Schoening was retired, I spent over two weeks each time house sitting the place while he traveled. This meant not only cleaning and repair work, but also taking care of the many wolf-hybrids Schoening raised and had in runs on the property.

I had introduced my good friend James Reynolds to Schoening, and Reynolds visited him from time to time. After returning from a visit, Reynolds came to visit me and told me that there was something going on with The Hermitage. Schoening had asked him if he was interested in it. Reynolds knew that it was to be mine upon Schoening's death. He told me that he told Schoening that he was not interested in it. This occurred in 2001.

Over the course of the years of visiting there, I had bought a storage cabinet and put it in the room I used upstairs in The Hermitage. Since the drawers of every dresser was full of Schoening's stuff, I needed a place to put my things, especially for long stays. I also brought some clothes that I used only for mountain climbing or cross-country skiing there and left them in the cabinet I had. Before I did this, I had asked Schoening if this would be OK, and he had indicated that it would.

Another incident occurred that was not related to The Hermitage. While visiting my good friends, Bill and Kathy Tembrock in Hotchkiss one summer, Reynolds and I listened as they explained the renovation that was going to take place of their parish church. As we listened, Reynolds asked them several questions and pointed out that they were not following guidelines. He recommended to them my book on the liturgical environment. In the course of the renovations, they read the book and got others to read it. The result was a change in the original renovation plans, which upset some of the pillars of the church. Those people visited Schoening, told him what was going to happen, and got him involved in the renovation issue even though he was retired. He blamed me for the strife that resulted from the renovation.

Furthermore, Schoening did not like the Tembrocks, who were my very good friends. When I was staying in The Hermitage during one two-week stretch, I had invited Kathy to come and spend a few days, and she did. When I was there for one Christmas, I had invited them to come for a day of cross-country skiing, and they did. A few Christmases later, I invited them again, and they and some of their adult children and spouses came. On one occasion, Schoening told me that he did not think that it was a good idea that I befriended the Tembrocks. I remember not replying to his remark and thinking that no one was going to tell me who my friends would be.

During the summer of 2002, I met Reynolds at The Hermitage; this was to be my last visit there. While Reynolds, Schoening, and I were eating the dinner I had prepared one summer night, Schoening told me that I needed to take my things out of the cabinet I had upstairs and leave. He handed me some money to pay me for the cabinet. Both Reynolds and I left the next morning. We knew that we were no longer welcomed there. Schoening had changed his mind about leaving The Hermitage to me. He no longer needed me. I had been duped, but I continued to hope that he would not go to the lawyer and have anything changed. I was reminded of the prophet Jeremiah, who accused God of having duped him (Jer 20:7).

In December 2004, I sent him a Christmas gift of a fruit cake and some nuts. In a card dated December 12, 2004, he informed me that he had tried to make The Hermitage a retreat center for the Cistercian (Trappist) monks from St. Benedict Monastery in Snowmass, Colorado, but they were not interested. He tried the Benedictine monks at St. Meinrad Archabbey in St. Meinrad, Indiana, but that fell through, too, even though two monks had visited him to look over the place. I answered that letter, asking about what was prompting the change in plans.

On Tuesday, January 4, 2005, Schoening sent me an e-mail, explaining that "one of the main considerations [for his change in plans] was the five-fold increase of the assessment value of The Hermitage over the original cost basis leading to tax problems and the advisability of an exempt organization receiving it. Then, the stability offered by a monastic entity for the intended use of The Hermitage as a hermitage/retreat [was the other consideration]." The e-mail contained a promise for a future letter, which arrived January 13, 2005. He began the letter, writing: "You, indeed, were in mind of the old hermit for the future of, and would have been so should I have died meantime, the hermitage, and as of March 3, 1994, my personal representative. Due to some—actually very many, practical complications—the Tisdal law firm assumed that burdensome task on August 6, 1998." This was news to me; for the past five years he had bypassed the documents he had executed without informing me.

In the letter-card, he reiterated the rise in taxes and his desire "to consider a tax-exempt entity via a 'living-estate' type of arrangement less The Hermitage become [the] victim of [an] immediate sale to meet obligations." He added: "Then, too, over later years it seemed your great involvement and such amazing organization abilities would make your leaving the Springfield area highly unlikely. Also, you have at least another ten years, perhaps longer, before retirement." He continued:

> And, there is a twenty-year difference in our ages. Ergo, ... it was difficult for us to communicate being oriented in different ways of temperament. It was greatly affected by the Hotchkiss church (renovation) events and seeing so many really good people "trod over" (my opinion) in what happened there. The moving in of personal property on a long-term nature without asking first hurt me just as you were subsequently hurt.

He concluded by stating, "Yes, times and circumstances change, but the recall and presence of friendship do not."

Another part of a card was inserted into the letter-card as a postscript. It read: "With appreciation, always!, for your fixing, cleaning, walks with the good wolves, filling in here at The Hermitage, at Telluride, Paonia, and for all the good hikes, times, before my life-changing event of 1989, the initial leg trauma, and the 1991 . . . bone infection . . . and operation of 1996, re-fracture of 1999." In 1989, Schoening had fallen off his bicycle while riding it to the wolf den he kept in Paonia; he broke his ankle and leg. The doctors used pins to put the pieces together, but his body rejected the metal and a bone infection resulted. The ulcer on his leg would not heal. Finally in 1996, a doctor recommended that the metal pins be removed; all but one was taken out. In 1999, the other one had to be removed and the leg re-broken and re-set. Until he died in 2012, he fought bone infections.

I answered the card-letter with a two-page letter on January 24, 2005. In my letter, I told him that the property was his, and he was free to do with it whatever he wanted. "All I wanted to know," I wrote," was why [he] once told me [he was] going to leave it to me and then changed [his] mind as early as 1998 without telling me." In the next paragraph, I stated:

> See, Syl, I think I was duped. And I am angrier with myself for letting you dupe me than I am with you. When you bought the additional ten acres out by the road, I asked you about buying that ten acres from you for myself. That's when you told me that I was the only person who had shown an interest in The Hermitage and that you wouldn't sell me the ten acres, but you were going to leave it to me. I took you at your word.

I continued:

> With that understanding, I invested several summers substituting for you in Paonia and Hotchkiss. I cleaned the place. I sealed the deck many times, and fixed things—taking care of The Hermitage when you were gone to Europe. I took care of the wolves. I invested time and energy into what I thought was my future, only to be kicked out and told that other plans have now been made. In other words, I've been duped. If I had no future there, I wouldn't have invested in it.... The future in which I had invested the past twenty years no longer existed.
>
> My long-range plans were always to retire in Colorado at The Hermitage. I truly love the place. I've written many of my books there. It's a place of inspiration and prayer. It would have been a perfect place for retirement.... I just want you to know that my commitment was sincere. Until two weeks ago, when I removed it, I had a picture of The Hermitage sitting on the bookshelf of my living room. I took that picture and had it framed after you told me you were leaving the place to me. I have now removed it, since that dream or future no longer exits.

I also addressed the other issues he raised in his letter-card, such as difficult communication between the two of us, the consulting I did with the people in Hotchkiss about the renovation of their church, the fact that I had asked him about putting a cabinet in the room I used, and several other issues. I concluded my letter by asking him why he thought he needed to control The Hermitage from the grave?

Here is my concluding paragraph:

Syl, it has been nice knowing you. You taught me a lot about the mountains and the high country. You gave me a great appreciation for Colorado. And for that I will always be grateful. You gave me a love for mountain climbing and taught me some skills that I continue to use today. But real friends don't dupe their friends or attempt to manipulate them, even if they disagree with them. The word of real friends is true no matter what comes their way; they are faithful. I was faithful. As far as I am concerned, all that is over now. I'm in the process of making peace with myself for letting you use me and making peace with you and your decisions.

On January 29, 2005, I got another letter-card which added nothing more to the discussion, except to say that he had changed his mind because I had not visited him since 2002, when he had told me to take my things and leave. In the card was a check for $550 in honor of my fifty-fifth birthday. On February 4, 2005, I returned the check to Schoening, telling him in a one-page letter that I could not be bought or appeased with money. I also told him that the reason I had not been there since 2002 was because he had kicked me out. I wrote: ". . . I have closed that chapter of my life." That was my last communication with Schoening. I do not know what he did with The Hermitage and its property. As indicated above, he died in 2012, and he was buried on the property. I never returned to The Hermitage. To this day it reminds me to be careful that I am not duped again!

Accident and Court Case

On January 19, 2006, I left my driveway and turned right, headed east for a few feet, stopped at the Stop sign at the corner, saw that the right hand lane was clear of traffic, and turned right onto National Avenue. I drove south on National Avenue for sixteen feet until I was hit by a van driven by Carol Pendergrass from Ozark, Missouri. She was on her cell phone and had not seen me enter National Avenue. She not only hit me; she pushed my blue 2000 Jeep Cherokee onto the curb and across the sidewalk into the front yard of a house on National Avenue. She did not stop until sixty-five feet later, where she pulled into a driveway. Within twenty minutes a Springfield Police Officer arrived; Pendergrass had called the police immediately because she had her cell phone out.

The officer, Eric Hawkins, parked his police car with its lights blinking between her car and mine. After arriving between 6:05 and 6:15 p.m., he conducted no investigation of the accident, and he asked only one question about it. He asked Pendergrass what happened; she told him that I ran into her. He did not ask me what happened. I told him that I was driving onto National Avenue when she hit me. Then, he asked why he was called; both of us told him that we needed a police report for insurance purposes. Then, he asked for our driver's license and proof of car insurance. I already had mine in my hand and gave it to him. Pendergrass only had her driver's license, but said that she had insurance but could not find the proof of insurance card. Hawkins told her that it was OK before going to his patrol car to complete the accident report. I couldn't believe that I heard a police officer tell a person that it was OK not to have the proof of insurance card in the car with you since it is Missouri law. Meanwhile, Pendergrass went to her vehicle and went through the glove compartment and, finally, found her insurance card and gave it to Hawkins, who got out of his patrol car to go get it.

While waiting for Hawkins to arrive, I asked Pendergrass to exchange names, addresses, insurance companies, agents, telephone numbers, etc. with me. She was reluctant, but after I gave her my information, she wrote some of her information on a small piece of paper. She did not know the name of her insurance agent or telephone number and couldn't find the information in her car door or glove compartment. I had to ask her for her address and telephone number.

Pendergrass went to her 2002 Black GMC Envoy, and I went to my Jeep, while we waited for Hawkins to complete the accident report. After a long wait, during which members of her family began to arrive, park on side streets, and come over to her vehicle—which meant that she had made more telephone calls—Hawkins got out of his patrol car; he gave Pendergrass the blue referral information card and told her she could leave. He walked over to me and gave me the same; then, he said that he was giving me a ticket. I asked him why I was getting a ticket. He told me that I had failed to yield. He walked with me to my Jeep and I showed him where her van hit my Jeep. I told him that I did not deserve a ticket. He said to me, "Tell it to the judge."

So, that is exactly what I attempted to do on February 15, 2006. I arrived at the Municipal Court Building well ahead of my 9 a.m. appointment. I sat in the courtroom and watched the judge conduct business. Before I could make my plea of not guilty, I had to listen to a pre-plea offer from an assistant prosecuting attorney. I don't remember all the elements of the deal, but it did involve taking a defensive-driving class, paying a fine of around $130, and not getting a ticket within the next ninety days. I told her that I was not guilty, and I wanted to tell my story to the judge. I was not paying money for something I did not do. All I did on that February morning is tell the judge that I was not guilty. I was told that I would get a summons as when next to appear in court. A couple weeks later, the summons to the hearing arrived; it was scheduled for March 27, 2006. Again, the assistant prosecuting attorney offered me a plea agreement, which I refused. This time, I think, the defensive driving class was still in play, but the fine to pay had dropped below $100. I refused the plea agreement, the judge listened to me tell him again that I was not guilty, and I was told that I would receive a date for my trial in the mail.

The trial was set for May 17, 2006, at 2 p.m. As I had done before, I got to the courtroom early to watch the judge deal with his cases. And as before, I was required to attend a pre-trial conference; this time the plea deal consisted only of paying a fine around $30. I rejected the plea agreement, telling the assistant prosecuting attorney that I was going to tell the judge my story. She threatened me; she told me that if I lost my trial, she would tell the judge to impose a maximum fine with other consequences. I couldn't believe what my ears heard. Nevertheless, I rejected her plea agreement, and after a wait, my trial began.

The judge asked me if I were representing myself, and I acknowledged that I was. He turned to the assistant prosecuting attorney and asked her if she were representing the city, and she acknowledge that she was. Then, he invited her to call her first witness, Hawkins. She asked him to relay what had happened on January 19, 2006, and he told her that I had failed to yield at a Stop sign and ran into Pendergrass. The judge asked me if I wanted to cross examine. I said that I did. So, I asked Hawkins, "Did you at any time ask me what occurred at the accident on January 19, 2006?" And he replied, "I did not." I said, "So the account of the accident as reported on the ticket reflects only what Pendergrass told you; is that correct?" And he replied, "It is." I told the judge that I had no more questions.

The attorney called Pendergrass to the stand and asked her to narrate the events of the accident on January 19, 2006. She told her that I had run the Stop sign and ran into her. She disclosed other information about where she was going. After the attorney was finished asking her questions, the judge asked me if I wanted to cross-examine her. I said yes. I had but one question, "Were you on your cell phone when the accident occurred?" And she replied, "Yes." I told the judge that I had no more questions.

The judge then asked me to present my defense. I told him that the ticket says that I failed to yield, but that is not true. The accident occurred at 5:43 p.m. on Thursday, January 19, 2006. I explained that I had stopped at the Stop sign. I had to wait for a long line of traffic to get through the light at Sunshine and National, two blocks further south, before I could turn right onto National Avenue. At rush hour the traffic backs up two to three blocks from Sunshine on National. A truck was about a half of a block down the street in the right lane. I turned onto National in front of the truck. I had no more than completed my turn onto National when I was pushed up onto the curb on the right side by Pendergrass, hitting my Jeep on the left side. I had already claimed the lane when she hit me. If I were still turning, she would have pushed me onto the curb and into a lamp post that is there on National. The lamp post is sixteen feet south of the curb. She pushed me up onto the curb south of the lamp post. She was talking on her cell phone and paying less attention to traffic than she should.

Furthermore, after she pushed me onto the curb, she did not stop. She continued to drive down the street to the first driveway into which she pulled. That driveway is sixty to seventy feet south of where she hit me. There was no signal light flashing on her vehicle, indicating that she was changing from the left to the right lane. Probably, she looked in her side view mirror and saw the truck—the same truck I saw—coming slowly down the street, but she did not turn her head and look to see if a vehicle (mine) was in her blind spot. She presumed that the lane was open; that is when she hit me. Thus, I was not guilty of failure to yield.

I told the judge that I had a diagram of the intersection to draw on the blackboard in the courtroom. He told me to go ahead and draw it. I pointed out the distances that I had spoken about. I also told him that by the time I stopped my Jeep on the curb, where she pushed me, and walked over to where Pendergrass had stopped, she had already called the police on her cell phone. That led me to speculate that she was on the cell phone or at minimum had it out while she was driving. When I asked her if she were OK, she told me that both she and her baby (who was in a car seat in the back seat) were fine. I told the judge about her reluctance to exchange names, addresses, telephone numbers, insurance companies, agent names, agent telephone numbers, etc. I also told him about all the people she called immediately after the accident. I told him that the child was sick, and she was taking it to the emergency room. I did not know how sick the child was, but with all the other people arriving someone could have taken it, but that never happened.

I explained to the judge that if Hawkins had thoroughly investigated this case, he would have discovered that I was not guilty of failing to yield. I had already completed my turn onto National Avenue before I was hit by Pendergrass. If I had still been turning, Pendergrass would have pushed me into the lamp post located there instead of further south of the lamp post where I landed. I also explained to the judge that Hawkins did not provide the correct information about tickets; he had told me that all I needed to do was to pay the ticket, when in effect I had to make a court appearance.

When I finished my defense, the judge asked the assistant prosecuting attorney if she wanted to cross-examine me. She asked me one question: "Do you have any qualifications for reconstructing accident scenes?" I answered her, "I am able to use a tape measure." The judge looked in her direction, and said, "You have to do better than this," picked up the ticket, and tore it into two pieces! He said to me, "You are not guilty. All court costs will be paid by the prosecuting attorney's office. You are free to leave."

After I got home on that spring May afternoon, I reflected upon how much time it took to work my way through the judicial system. I also reflected on the plea agreements offered to me and how this system is interested only in getting money out of the citizens. Most citizens would have plead guilty, paid the ticket and court costs, and been done. I, however, wanted to experience how the judicial system worked. It was a revelation to me. Nevertheless, I was proud to say that I had represented myself and won my case. I called my insurance company agent and told her that my rates had better not go up as a result of this accident, since I had been declared not guilty. She couldn't believe that I had won my case, and she wanted a copy of the court record. I got a copy a few days later and sent it to her.

Landscaping

On January 22, 2019, Tony McIntosh appeared at my front door with his Asplundh truck parked in front of my house. He wanted to know if he could bring the truck up the driveway to the garage over which hung the oak tree that City Utilities wanted trimmed to keep the branches from getting into the electric lines that were strung on two sides of it. Knowing that the tree trimmers were coming, I told McIntosh to go ahead after asking him to be very careful.

This was the third time that City Utilities had come to trim the oak tree. The first time I did not grant permission for the truck to pull into the driveway; the driver merely put it there. I went outside and asked the workers not to drop branches onto the roof of the garage or onto the roof of the potting shed attached to the back of the garage. They ignored my request and punched a hole through one of the corrugated fiberglass panels of the potting shed roof. I didn't know it at the time because no one said anything to me about it. However, later in the day I went to the potting shed and found a brick sitting on the roof covering the hole. A day or two later, one of the men who had punched the hole in the roof called me and told me he was coming to fix the hole. He brought a small piece of corrugated fiberglass with some kind of glue and patched over the hole that had been made. I did not like how the hole had been fixed, knowing that the patch would turn loose, blow away in the wind, and the things I stored in the shed would get wet. I wrote a letter to the person in charge of tree management for City Utilities of Springfield explaining how the men had shown up at my house, driven onto my driveway without asking, got out of the truck and crushed out a cigarette on my driveway, and never bothered to pick up the butt. She called me, apologizing for the cigarette butt, and came to visit me with her assistant. I showed her what had been done along with the inadequate patch. She told her assistant to go buy a sheet of corrugated fiberglass that matched the color of what I had, remove the damaged panel, and replace it at no charge to me. I thanked her, and her assistant showed up the next day and took care of the problem. As I had explained to her, I did not have a hole in the roof before; therefore, I should not have a hole in the roof now.

The second time a crew arrived from City Utilities to trim the oak tree, I reminded them of what happened the first time. After I was asked, I granted permission for the truck to pull onto the driveway. I told them not to drop any branches on the roof of the garage or on the potting shed. This time I had a crew of adults acting like children, who kept sneaking up behind each other and goosing each other! I couldn't believe the behavior I was seeing. Because they had started late in the afternoon, they came back the next morning to finish the job they had started. The same behavior was evident. I had to run an errand, but when I got back, they were gone. However, a new green metal rake lay sprawled in the driveway. I had to get out of my car and remove it before I could get into the garage. So, I picked up the rake, thinking someone was going to return to get it, but after a few days when no one claimed it, I added it to my tools.

The third time for the oak to be trimmed featured McIntosh with Asplundh. Before he could even get the truck into the driveway, he ran it over the corner of the landscaping stones forming the retaining wall across the front yard of my house. Not only did the truck dislodge some of the stones, it also broke a few of them. McIntosh backed the truck out of the driveway and parked it on the street. He apologized to me. A few minutes later three other men showed up; they were a part of the crew being led by their foreman Ray Holliday, who promised me that the stones would be replaced and the retaining wall would be fixed in a couple of days. The crew went on to trim the oak tree, letting branches fall onto the garage, even though I asked them not to let that happen. They failed to clean off the roof, even though I asked them to do so. Also, the branches that fell in my back yard were not raked or gathered, so I picked them up to keep them out of the flower gardens.

A week after the stones were broken, McIntosh appeared in my front yard examining what he had done. He and his wife were in a car. He got out and promised me that all would be taken care of within a week. His wife thanked me for being understanding about this. I got his telephone number so that I could contact him if I needed to. He had asked me for the name of the person who had installed the retaining wall, and I gave that and his number to him. He told me that that business was no longer doing landscaping. I told him to look through the telephone book or go online to find someone who knew how to cut the stones and fix the corner. Of course, he did not do anything, because he did not want to have to fix the damage; Holliday had a policy that if a workman damaged anything, he was responsible for fixing it.

As I found out from McIntosh's co-workers, McIntosh was not supposed to be driving a truck in a driveway without the assistance of the other members of the crew. Winter continued; it snowed; it sleeted; it rained. On March 1, I called Holliday and explained that nothing had been done about the broken stones on the corner of my retaining wall. Nothing happened as a result of that call. On March 29, 2019, I called McIntosh to inquire about when my retaining wall was going to be fixed. No one answered the phone, but I left a message that was never answered.

After searching for Asplundh online, I discovered on the company's home page a place to notify the business about damaged property. So, on April 10, 2019, I e-mailed Asplundh. I explained what had happened and what had been promised. "Here I am almost three months later, and nothing has been done about this," I wrote. "Everyone hopes that I will just forget about this or get it fixed myself." I continued:

> While this is a moral or ethical issue insofar as my property should be fixed by those who damaged it, I am getting ready to take this to small claims court if something is not done, if I am not contacted with a definite date of when my property will be fixed, within the next few days. I really don't want to have to take this to court. Asplundh should do the right thing, the right moral thing, and see that my property is fixed. Since I have exhausted other means, small claims court is the only one left to me.

On the same day that I sent the e-mail in the morning, I got a reply in the afternoon from Holliday. He wrote that he had followed my instructions to McIntosh about wanting the same man who had installed the retaining wall to fix it. I never gave those instructions; I only gave the name of the man who had installed it to McIntosh. Holliday narrated that McIntosh had contacted that man, who told him that he no longer did that kind of work. Then, Holliday narrated that McIntosh took my next suggestion, another landscaper I found in the telephone book, and he told him that the job was too small. This e-mail made me aware that Holliday was making me responsible for finding someone to fix the stones which McIntosh broke. I kept telling McIntosh and Holliday that it was not my responsibility to find a repairman; it was theirs. "Now it is apparent this route will not satisfy the situation," wrote Holliday. "So, I have instructed McIntosh to take the bricks [he bought] and have them cut and install them. This should be done no later than April 17, 2019."

On April 13, 2019, McIntosh showed up at my house. He told me that he was taking the broken stones so he would have a pattern to have the new stones cut to fit the places where they belonged. It was a Saturday, and it began to rain before McIntosh got back. He brought the wrong color and the wrong thickness of stones with him. I watched from the window as he stood in the rain and piled stones on top of stones without leveling them or being sure that there were no cracks in between them. Then, I watched as he poured sand into the cracks between the stones to fill in the spaces before driving away!

The next day, April 14, 2019, I left an e-mail message for Holliday. I explained what McIntosh had done and how bad it looked. I invited Holliday to come and see the job his worker had done. On April 15, 2019, Holliday called me from his bed in the hospital; he had fallen on some sticks and punctured a lung; he was not able to investigate this. I told him that the plan had been changed. I had had enough of this fooling around. I was getting a stone mason I knew to fix the retaining wall, and Asplundh was going to pay for it. Holliday asked me to let him know when the stone mason was going to fix the wall so he could be here. I contacted Kevin Myles, a young man I had known from St. Joseph the Worker Parish, Ozark, and whom I had seen recently tuckpointing a chimney of a neighbor. Myles told me when he could be here in a couple of days; I called Holliday, who showed up right after Myles did. Holliday asked Myles how much it would cost to fix the corner of the retaining wall, and Myles told him $450. I told Holliday that I was paying Myles once he found the right size of stones for doing the job that day and cut them to fit. The next day Holliday presented himself with $450 in cash and counted it out to me to be sure it was all there. He apologized for this taking so long. I remember telling him that if responsibility would have been assumed immediately, none of this would have happened. The threat of small claims court is what put the repair work into motion. The tree trimmers hired by City Utilities have no respect for the property upon which they are working. Three times this has been demonstrated to me!

On January 23, 2020, at some time during the night, someone ran a car onto the curb and hit the corner of the retaining wall, knocking it out of alignment but not breaking any of the stones. I do not know if someone was attempting to turn around by pulling into my driveway and missed the driveway, or if someone was attempting to get even for having had to pay $450 for the damages he did a year before. While I have no proof that McIntosh ran into the stones, noting that it was almost exactly to the same date when the damage was done, I cannot help but think that this was his revenge. On January 24, 2020, I filed a police report, knowing that nothing would be investigated concerning this issue. In that report, I mentioned McIntosh's name as a suspect.

Memorable Retreats

While I have made many retreats over the years—some of them privately and some communally—there are four that stand out in my life. The first occurred during the summer of 1978. I went to the cabin in Forsyth, Missouri, offered to me by Ruth Hamilton, for a few days of quiet to ponder what had happened to me over the previous two years of parish ministry and to prepare for my move to Joplin for part-time parish ministry and part-time chaplaincy in McAuley Regional Catholic High School. I prayed and sought guidance from the Holy Spirit.

In two years after priesthood ordination I had had two very different pastors. One was team oriented, and one was not. One was frugal, and one was not concerned about collections. One preferred a housekeeper, and one didn't think such a person was needed. One would have had the broken air conditioning fixed in an instant, and one was satisfied that it was not working and saving money. I was realizing gradually that I did not like many aspects of parish ministry, like hospital visitations, endless meetings, fund raisers, people who would not stop pushing issues, etc. I found all that draining of precious human energy. Furthermore, there was little room for me to use my gifts of teaching, organizing, environment design, etc. So, the purpose of the private retreat was to help me make a transition from full-time parish ministry to part-time parish ministry and part-time school chaplaincy and teaching. I left that retreat with the promise to myself to use the year to discern the next step in my life. At the end of that year, I went into full-time teaching ministry.

Another memorable retreat was made at the Heartland Center for Spirituality, Great Bend, Kansas, run by the Dominican Sisters of Peace. It was called a Parables Retreat, and it was supposedly open only to Dominicans. During the last few years when I was teaching at McAuley High School in Joplin, Missouri, the principal was a Dominican. She had given me the brochure about the retreat, and it looked interesting to me. So, I paid my deposit and went. As I remember, there were no other men but me and the retreat director! While he used the parables as the basis for the five-day retreat, he also guided the retreatants with reading material. One aspect of one article he gave us to read and discuss was the ability to see better in the dark. I had always presumed that dark was bad and light was good. However, as I began to reflect upon all the times I had seen people better in the dark, I gained a new appreciation for sitting with friends around a campfire or in front of a fireplace, eating a meal in dimmer light or in candlelight, taking a walk at dusk either alone or with another, etc. Exploring the spirituality of light enlightened me.

The third outstanding retreat took place during a week at Sacred Heart Jesuit Retreat House in Sedalia, Colorado. It marked the end of the first part of my 1992 sabbatical and served as a transition to the next part. I had been editor of *The Mirror* for five years, and there was lots of friction between me and the bishop-publisher. The question I had posed to myself was this: Do I continue as editor when I return? Or do I look for another ministry? I remember sitting outside on a bench in a garden, being quiet, and pondering what was before me. After having spent three months in Alaska helping in weekend parish ministry and one month in Colorado doing the same, I knew that I did not want to go back to full-time parish ministry, and I enjoyed college teaching, which I had been doing part-time for four years. But I needed some confirmation about continuing as editor of the diocesan newspaper. As I sat on the bench not yet having an answer, I prayed. I remember feeling dry, tired, and frustrated. I remembered the prayer of the prophet Ezekiel and I adapted and prayed it: Come from the four winds, O breath, and breathe upon me (Ezek 37:9). A few seconds later, a very light breeze blew over me, and I knew that was my answer to stay the course.

One summer I travelled to Easton, Kansas, to make a week's long retreat in Shantivanam House of Prayer, a retreat center founded by Ed Hayes. I arrived on the specified day of the week, got my cabin-hermitage assignment, met the three or four people who lived in individual hermitages on the retreat property and ran it, and unpacked my car with groceries and clothes and whatever else I would need for the week. My hermitage, without air conditioning, consisted of two rooms: a kitchen-dining-room-sitting area with a desk and a bed room with an attached bath. Also, there was a small screened-in porch, which I went through to get to the front door of the hermitage. I liked the solitude provided by what was called the Forest of Peace. There were trails for walking and discovering shrines and lakes along the way. There was an imitation miniature version of Stonehenge, where I remember going to say Mass one day. One evening during the week a community dinner was provided in the main dining room, and prayer was said several times a day in the chapel with the altar that stood on the ground in the middle of the floor. That experience of solitude—reading, writing, praying, cooking, walking, etc.—in silence remains with me to this day. Sad to say, but the original Shantivanam House of Prayer was later changed into Christ's Peace House of Prayer in order to remove the universal religious aspect of the center and turn it into a Catholic retreat center.

Taking time every year or several times a year to stop and reflect on the direction my spiritual journey was taking and continues to take is important to me. I remember traveling through Montana in 1992 and seeing Big Sky Country, which brought me to pray: Lord, show me where you want me to be and help me to be there. Guide me with your Spirit. That prayer has been answered time after time during simple and memorable retreats. Since retirement, I live a daily retreat with Shelbydog.

15

Conclusion

THIS AUTOBIOGRAPHY DOCUMENTS MY history of ministry, writing, teaching, and traveling, so this life of an Old Mines missionary will not be forgotten. This autobiography has been composed from the selection of e-mails, letters, and cards I have saved over the past seventy years. If I would have kept everything like those, I would need several storage units to house all of it!

I have not found it easy to present my life in a book. It is difficult to take seventy years of living and translate them into words. Certainly, everything cannot be put into print or digitized, and yet some can capture the essence of who I am. Daily things, like eating, sleeping, showering—basic care of self—are not unimportant, but pale when compared to the extraordinary experiences of living and human encounters. These latter give my life meaning, reveal my not-yet-finished tapestry, and give a glimpse of the trajectory my life has taken. I chose to manage the threads woven into my tapestry by exploring them through ministry, writing, teaching, and traveling with all the tangents and twists and turns they contain. Many threads cross each other; some appear and quickly disappear; some are broken; and some are still being woven in. As I mentioned in the introduction, I have found out who I am and I continue to discover who I am because I know I know myself with and through others.

Ministry

I am not one of those people who state that he or she would not change a thing of the past if his or her life could be lived again. I regret not investigating options for priestly ministry in the Church. If I had, diocesan priesthood would not have been my choice. I would have joined a monastery or entered the Jesuits, gotten a doctorate in Scripture, liturgy, or theology, and spent my life teaching in an institution of higher learning. I didn't consciously discover that I didn't like secular, diocesan ministry until 1979, when I realized that I was born to teach in some manner. I now know that diocesan priests and others, along with bishops, are only focused on parish ministry. Men who do not fit that focus often become outsiders to diocesan priesthood.

I was in awe with the traditional idea of being a priest, but that was not the reality I experienced in 1976. Furthermore, I realized that it wasn't primary for me; writing, teaching, and traveling took priority. That hierarchical understanding was impossible for bishops and other priests to grasp, especially in a time of personality cult in Roman Catholicism. In my naiveite, I did not explore the freedom I was asked to relinquish with ordination, the conferences and clergy days I was required to attend, and the bishops and pastors who considered it their responsibility to impose their wills upon mine without ever considering my needs or wants. Nevertheless, with Paul, in his letter to the Philippians, "I am confident of this, that the one who began a good work among you [—me—] will bring it to completion by the day of Jesus Christ" (1:16).

Writing

This is my sixty-fifth book, but it is not my last one. I have a book on the spirituality of journey outlined. And I have plans for the fourth revised edition of *The Liturgical Environment: What the Documents Say* to work on. Another book may be one on the sacraments; that ideas is in its conception stage. It needs to germinate a while longer before it can develop, be born, and grow into a book. I have no preternatural knowledge of what idea may present itself after all that.

Teaching

Teaching—high school, college, adult education—runs through my blood. If the opportunity presents itself to teach, to give a workshop, or to conduct a retreat, I will take it. I love seeing people understand something new or delve into a new insight which leads them to deeper truth and crutch-less faith.

Traveling

I have seen a lot of the world, but there is always more to see. As long as I can, I intend to travel to other places both on this continent and to others. I find it exciting to see how other people live, what they eat, and how they work. And until I am not able to travel any more, I will continue to explore this world.

The End

I have lived a very full life. It has been rich in many ways. Even as a young boy, I saw the world from a different perspective than my parents and elders did. I was a free spirit. I remember after being disciplined by my parents with a switch (part of tree branch), a fly swatter, a belt, or made to kneel by my bed, saying and promising to myself that if I ever got old enough to leave the French ghetto of Old Mines, that I would do so and not return except to visit family and relatives. In other words, because my parents could not understand my point of view, I dreamed of escape to a world that could. I have kept that promise.

I travel the rest of my years in good health. I've worn glasses since I was a college freshman. Because my father was red headed, I've inherited his skin with rashes, precancerous carcinomas, and moles—all monitored by my dermatologist. After double hernia surgery I lost my immunity to the virus that causes warts on hands and feet. I found a very good dermatologist who prescribed a compound that taught my body to kill the wart virus. While I've had some hearing loss in my left ear, my audiologist and physician's assistant restored the total loss—caused by ear plugs—with steroids. I've passed two colonoscopies. I suffer all the time from allergies, a condition I inherited from my mother, who also passed on bad teeth. Of course, as a child, I had no regular dental visits. I was taken to the dentist only when I had a toothache, which no folk remedy could stop. Before entering the college seminary, I underwent a full dental regiment under the care of a dentist in DeSoto, Missouri. He pulled a few molars, whose cavities could not be filled, after administering anesthesia, and he filled more without anesthesia! I once asked for it, and he said no. I've had to explain that to my dentist when she sees me fearful of whatever the next procedure may be. Despite the fear, I have kept a regular teeth-cleaning schedule with visits to the dentist, discovering in the process that my teeth are very hard to anesthetize—which explains why I felt so much pain in the past. Now, whereas one or two doses of anesthesia will work for most people, I need three or four for fillings, crowns, and a bridge. My allergies are being treated by an experienced physician's assistant; he listens, advises, and offers remedies.

I know that longevity was not in my parents' genes, but it was in my grandparents'. Both of my parents died in their seventieth year of life. I know I will die someday in the future. In the meantime, I hope to make it to eighty, and I will consider anything beyond that to be bonus years. Often, I remember my mortality when praying Psalm 39:5: "You [, LORD,] have made my days a few handbreadths, and my lifetime is as nothing in your sight. Surely everyone stands as a mere breath," or Psalm 144:3-4: "O LORD, what are human beings that you regard them, or mortals that you think of them? They are like a breath; their days are like a passing shadow." In other words, I am like a puff of air or a shadow in a campfire. With Mark Nepo, who writes a column titled "Our Walk in the World," which appears in *Spirituality & Health* magazine (22:5 [2019] 74–75),

> . . . I can affirm . . . that once you've lived the work and done the work, you are the work. And going public with the work is about casting seeds and seeing which will sprout in the world. Regardless of which seeds come up or not, the truth we serve drips like medicine beyond our dreams and needs. . . . Each time we give our full being, a small miracle issues forth beyond our control.

Conclusion

I have straddled two centuries—the twentieth and twenty-first. I've straddled pre-Vatican II and post-Vatican II Roman Catholicism. I've found it a challenging, yet a privileged time to work, to be alive, to cast seeds, and to dream. In this book, I have presented my life of ministry, writing, teaching, and traveling as a missionary from Old Mines, Missouri.

Indices

(Mountain) Basins

American, 258
Chicago, 199, 202, 252, 267
Democrat, 222–23, 228
Ego Sum, 221
Horn Fork, 219–20, 231, 234–35
Little Elk, 219
Silver Pick, 206–7, 209
South Fork of Silver Creek, 200
Wasatch, 190
Wetterhorn, 195
Yankee Boy, 183, 189, 198, 208

Bible Translations

NAB, 378, 389, 420
NABRE, 416, 417, 420
NRSV, 370, 378, 385, 389, 416, 417, 420

Books

All Things Mary: Honoring the Mother of God—An Anthology of Marian Reflections, 421
A Month-by-Month Guide to Entertaining Angels, 371
An Abecedarian of Animal Spirit Guides: Spiritual Growth through Reflections on Creatures, 419
An Abecedarian of Sacred Trees: Spiritual Growth through Reflections on Woody Plants, 419
A Simple Systematic Mariology, 414
A Spirituality of Ageing, 406–7, 419
A Spirituality of Mission: Reflections for Holy Week and Easter, 398, 417–18

Baptized into Christ's Death and Resurrection: Preparing to Celebrate a Christian Funeral: Vol. 1: Adults, 383–85
Baptized into Christ's Death and Resurrection: Preparing to Celebrate a Christian Funeral: Vol. 2: Children, 383–85
Biblical Reflections on Male Spirituality, 374
Breathing Deeply of God's New Life: Preparing Spiritually for the Sacraments of Initiation, 359

Caroling through Advent and Christmas, 407–8, 415–16, 419
Christ Our Passover Has Been Sacrificed: A Guide Through Paschal Mystery Spirituality—Mystical Theology in The Roman Missal, 420–21

DayBreaks: Daily Reflections for Advent and Christmas, 415–17
Daybreaks: Daily Reflections for Lent and Easter, 415–17
Day by Ordinary Day: Daily Reflections on the First Readings, Year 1, 382
Day by Ordinary Day: Daily Reflections on the First Readings, Year 2, 382, 409
Day by Day Through the Easter Season, 353–54, 356
Day by Ordinary Day with Luke, 378, 381
Day by Ordinary Day with Mark, 378, 381
Day by Ordinary Day with Matthew, 378–79, 381
Divine Presence: Elements of Biblical Theophanies, 420
Filled with New Light: Reflections for Christmas 2001–2002, 390
Following the Star: Daily Reflections for Advent and Christmas, 355–56
From Contemplation to Action: The Spiritual Process of Divine Discernment Using Elijah and Elisha as Models, 421
Fruit of the Vine: A Biblical Spirituality of Wine, 420
The Greatest Gift of All: Reflections and Prayers for the Christmas Season, 386

History of St. Joachim Parish: 1822–1972; 1723–1973, 62, 75, 354
Home Is a Holy Place, 377–78
Human Wholeness: A Spirituality of Relationship, 187, 332, 336, 411, 413–14, 419, 421, 472, 477

Indices

Joy to the World: Inspirational Christmas Messages from America's Preachers, 399

Lent and Easter Prayer at Home, 391–92
The Liturgical Environment: What the Documents Say; *The Liturgical Environment: What the Documents Say* (second edition); *The Liturgical Environment: What the Documents Say* (third edition), 158, 172, 346, 361–62, 364–66, 393
Love Addict, 341, 421

Mary's Day—Saturday: Meditations for Marian Celebrations, 366–68, 421
Meditations for Ministers, 386–87
Mountain Reflections: A Collection of Photos and Meditations, 268, 404–5
Mystagogy: Liturgical Paschal Spirituality for Lent and Easter, 356, 358

Names for Jesus: Reflections for Advent and Christmas, 420
Nature Spirituality: Praying with Wind, Water, Earth, Fire, 405–6, 419

Overcome with Paschal Joy: Chanting through Lent and Easter—Daily Reflections with Familiar Hymns, 419

Praying Your Way through Luke's Gospel and the Acts of the Apostles, 414, 419

Reflections on the Mysteries of the Rosary, 393–94, 396, 421
Return to the Lord: A Lenten Journey of Daily Reflections, 361
Rosary Primer: The Prayers, The Mysteries, and The New Testament, 398, 421

"Seeking Grace with Every Step": The Spirituality of John Denver, 375, 377, 420
Shhh! The Sound of Sheer Silence: A Biblical Spirituality that Transforms, 421

Take Up Your Cross and Follow: Daily Lenten Reflections, 400, 403, 405
Taking Leave of Your Home: Moving in the Peace of Christ, 419
Talk to God and Listen to the Casual Reply: Experiencing the Spirituality of John Denver, 420, 454
These Thy Gifts: A Collection of Simple Meal Prayers, 159, 404

Using Film to Teach New Testament, 112, 392–93

Very Short Reflections—for Advent and Christmas, Lent and Easter, Ordinary Time, and Saints—through the Liturgical Year, 422

Waiting in Joyful Hope: Reflections for Advent 2001; *Waiting in Joyful Hope: Daily Reflections for Advent and Christmas 2002*; *Waiting in Joyful Hope: Daily Reflections for Advent and Christmas, 2003*, 387–91
Weekday Saints: Reflections on The Scriptures, 409–10, 419
What is Born of the Spirit is Spirit: A Biblical Spirituality of Spirit, 422
When Day Is Done: Nighttime Prayers through the Church Year, 400
Why Suffer? The Answer of Jesus, 368, 370–72

Cities/Towns/Villages

Adelaide, Australia, 340
Alamosa, CO, 205, 218, 254–55
Albuquerque, NM, 181, 188, 190, 195, 318–19
Alma, CO, 230
Almeda, MI, 336
Amsterdam, Netherlands, 339–41, 346
Anchorage, AK, 322, 325, 327
Arles, France, 328
Ashville, NC, 329
Aspen, CO, 182, 196, 248, 375
Atlanta, GA, 339–41, 346, 377
Auckland, New Zealand, 340
Auschwitz, Poland, 349–50
Avignon, France, 328
Avila, Spain, 344

Baltimore, MD, 318, 323–24
Basel, Switzerland, 340–41
Bayeux, France, 328
Belmont, NC, 317, 319
Bergen, Norway, 345
Berlin, Germany, 349
Berthoud, CO, 270–71, 273–74, 276, 423
Big Lake, AK, 325–26, 373
Birkenau, Poland, 349–50
Boston, MA, 71, 80, 323, 325
Boulder, CO, 192, 246, 248, 320
Branson, MO, 95, 144–45, 316, 340
Bratislava, Slovakia, 339
Breckenridge, CO, 232
Brno, Czech Republic, 350

Indices

Brown Hollow, MO, 9, 22–23, 31
Budapest, Hungary, 339, 350
Buena Vista, CO, 245
Buffalo Springs, CO, 318

Cabool, MO, 115, 132, 135, 138–39, 143, 170
Cadiz, Spain, 344
Cairns, Australia, 340
Cambridge, England, 329
Cambridge, Jamaica, 281
Cambridge, MA, 425
Cancun, MX, 287–88, 308
Cardiff, Wales, 324
Carthage, MO, 207
Cedaredge, CO, 270
Charlotte Amalie, VI, 290, 292, 298, 311
Charlotte, NC, 348
Chamonix-Mount Blanc, France, 332, 337
Chartres, France, 329
Chattanooga, TN, 287
Chicago, IL, 316–17, 321, 346–48, 378, 405–7, 410, 440
Chichester, England, 328
Christchurch, New Zealand, 340
Claremont-Ferrand, France, 332
Climax, CO, 190, 196
Colchester, England, 329
Coldfoot, AK, 326
Colmar, France, 341
Cologne, Germany, 341
Colorado Springs, CO, 192, 318, 320, 375
Columbia, MO, 325
Concordia, KS, 78
Conyers, GA, 172, 346
Copenhagen, Denmark, 345–46
Cordoba, Spain, 344
Cozumel, MX, 279, 283, 288, 295, 307–8, 313–14
Craig, CO, 322
Crawford, CO, 213
Creede, CO, 217, 328
Crested Butte, CO, 208, 211, 213, 222, 225, 228, 232, 236, 256–57, 262, 269, 271, 337–38
Crested Butte Village, CO, 256, 271
Czestochowa, Poland, 349

Dallas, TX, 322, 336
Dallas-Fort Worth, TX, 340, 344
Darwin, Australia, 340
Dawson City, YT, 326
Dawson Creek, BC, 325
Dayton, OH, 330, 378
Deadhorse, AK 326
Del Norte, CO, 217–18, 328

Delta, CO, 226, 270
Denver, CO, 183, 189, 192, 195–96, 201, 230, 236, 240, 250, 253, 255, 258–59, 261–64, 266, 268, 270–74, 318, 320–21, 331, 335–36, 413
Des Moines, IA, 116, 323
DeSoto, MO, 2, 7, 17, 22, 508
Dijon, France, 330
Durango, CO, 199, 202–3, 252
Durham, England, 332

Edinburgh, Scotland, 324
Ely, England, 329
Eureka Springs, AR, 338
Evansville, IN, 59, 183, 186, 394
Evansville, WI, 190, 195, 319
Exeter, England, 328

Fairbanks, AK, 322, 325–26
Fairplay, CO, 230, 274, 276
Fatima, Portugal, 344
Flagstaff, AZ, 190
Flam, Norway, 345
Florence, Italy, 321
Forsyth, MO, 73, 309, 323, 477, 504
Fort Nelson, BC, 325
Fort Wayne, IN, 331, 429
Frankfurt, Germany, 242–43, 347–50
Freeport, Bahamas, 295, 297
Fresno, CA, 322–23

Garden City, KS, 269
Gaudix, Spain, 344
Geneva, Switzerland, 332, 337
Georgetown, CO, 247
Georgetown, Grand Cayman, 279, 283, 295–96, 307, 313
Gieranger, Norway, 345
Glastonbury, England, 328
Glen Ellyn, IL, 316
Gloucester, England, 328
Granada, Spain, 344
Grand Canyon, AZ, 193–94
Grand Junction, CO, 201, 221, 231, 274
Great Bend, KS, 504
Grenoble, France, 332

Haines, AK, 327
Haines Junction, YT, 327
Hannibal, MO, 55
Heidelberg, Germany, 341
Hobart, Australia, 340
Homer, AK, 327

513

Indices

Hotchkiss, CO, 173, 208, 212, 217–19, 221–26, 229, 233–35, 238, 248–49, 255–59, 262, 265, 268–74, 276, 492–96

Independence, KS, 322
Indianapolis, IN, 41, 330

Jefferson City, MO, 29, 75, 321, 338, 424, 463, 477
Jerez, Spain, 344
Joplin, MO, ix, 76–78, 80–81, 83, 116, 118, 170–71, 174, 188, 192, 195–96, 198–99, 201, 203–4, 206–7, 211, 246, 256, 278, 280, 282–83, 286, 288–89, 291, 293–94, 296–97, 300, 303, 307–8, 319–25, 327–29, 336–38, 352, 354, 356, 364, 386, 425–26, 476–77, 483–84, 488, 504
Johnson City, TX, 329
Juneau, AK, 217, 327

Kansas City, KS, 493
Kansas City, MO, 62, 76, 305, 307, 321, 329, 354, 421, 474, 479
Kenai, AK, 326–27
Ketchikan, AK, 217, 327
Kinderdijk, Netherlands, 341
Kizhi, Russia, 347
Knoxville, TN, 286–87
Koblenz, Germany, 341
Kotzebue, AK, 327
Krakow, Poland, 350
Kremmling, CO, 268, 276
Kuzino, Russia, 347

La Junta, CO, 221, 261
Lake City, CO, 223, 258
Lakewood, CO, 335–36, 423
La Vita, CO, 261
Leadville, CO, 227, 234
Lebanon, MO, 119, 427, 429
Leikanger, Norway, 345
Lethbridge, AB, 190
Lincoln, England, 337
Lincoln, NE, 333
Linz, Austria, 339
Lisbon, Portugal, 344
Litchfield, England, 337
Little Rock, AR, 172, 331
Lom, Norway, 345
London, England, 321, 324, 329, 332, 337
Long Branch, NJ, 336
Los Alamos, NM, 195, 318
Los Angeles, CA, 190, 319, 331
Louisville, KY, 69, 186, 309
Lourdes, Frances, 332, 344

Lucerne, Switzerland, 321
Lyon, France, 329

Madison, WI, 190, 320
Madrid, Spain, 344–45
Mandrogi, Russia, 347
Marigot, St. Maarten, 302
Marshfield, MO, 118–19
Maryville, MO, 241
Meeker, CO, 251
Melbourne, Australia, 340
Melk, Austria, 339
Menlo Park, CA, 319
Miami, FL, 197, 278, 280–89, 291, 293–97, 299–301, 303, 305–6, 308, 310–12, 314
Moab, UT, 225
Montego Bay, Jamaica, 296
Montrose, CO, 209, 219, 273
Moscow, Russia, 347–48
Mount Cook, New Zealand, 340
Mountain Grove, MO, 115, 132, 135, 138, 140, 143, 170
Mount Vernon, KY, 286–87
Munich, Germany, 321, 339

Nashville, TN, 197, 324, 413, 454
Nassau, Bahamas, 281, 284, 286, 290, 292–93, 294–95, 297–98, 300
Needleton, CO, 199, 202–3, 252, 267
New Isenburg, Germany, 349
New Orleans, LA, 127–28, 323, 331, 411
Nixa, MO, 115, 143–45, 149–51, 153–54, 157–58, 163, 248, 257, 336–37, 382, 423, 463, 478, 482
Nome, AK, 327
North Fork, CO, 328
Norwich, England, 329
Norwood, CO, 203, 205–9, 211, 213–14, 216, 219–21, 223–26, 228, 233, 492
Notre Dame, France, 329
Notre Dame, IN, 321, 363
Nottingham, England, 332
Nucla, CO, 189, 211, 220–21, 228

Ocho Rios, Jamaica, 279, 281, 293, 285, 306–7, 313
Odense, Denmark, 345
Old Mines, MO, ix, –xi, 1–3, 9, 29, 38, 42, 44–45, 56–57, 62–63, 68, 70–71, 74–75, 80, 157, 267, 316, 338, 354–55, 366, 426, 477, 506, 508–9
Olympia, WA, 191, 319
Omaha, NE, 274, 321, 333
Orleans, France, 329

514

Indices

Oslo, Norway, 345–46
Ouray, CO, 200–201, 203, 207, 219, 492,–93
Oxford, England, 328

Panama City Beach, FL, 320
Paonia, CO, 173, 208–14, 216–17, 203–31, 271, 273–74, 492–93, 495–96
Paradox, CO, 222
Paris, France, 321, 329–30, 332, 337, 339, 341
Passau, Germany, 339
Peterborough, England, 329
Pevely, MO, 44, 68
Philadelphia, PA, 329
Philipsburg, St. Maarten, 301–2
Phoenix, AZ, 71, 318, 324–25, 336
Plano, TX, 322
Playa Del Carmen, MX, 279, 287, 307–8, 314
Pompeii, Italy, 337
Port Antonio, Jamaica, 281
Port-Au-Prince, Haiti, 281, 285
Portland, OR ,190, 319
Potosi, MO, 3, 16, 22, 28–29, 38, 40, 46, 57–58
Poznan, Poland, 349
Prague, Czech Republic, 350
Prince Rupert, BC, 217, 327
Prudhoe Bay, AK, 326
Pushkin, Russia, 348

Queenstown, New Zealand, 340

Regina, SK, 190, 319
Rheims, France, 330
Richardton, ND, 317
Ridgway, CO, 194, 195
Rolla, MO, 37
Rome, Italy, 71–72, 134, 321, 337, 384
Rothenburg, Germany, 350
Rotorua, New Zealand, 340
Rouen, France, 328
Sacramento, CA, 190, 319
Ste. Genevieve, MO, 75
St. Alban, England, 337
St. John, VI, 302, 304, 311
St. Louis, MO, ix, 30, 32, 37–38, 40, 42–43, 45–48, 50, 55–57, 60, 63, 80, 145, 181, 278, 308, 316–18, 330–31, 336, 355, 424, 427, 441, 449, 452, 460, 475–76
St. Meinrad, IN, ix, 57–60, 63–64, 66–70, 181, 309, 318–19, 425–26, 495
St. Petersburg, Russia, 348
St. Thomas, VI, 289–90, 292, 298, 300, 302, 304, 311
Salida, CO, 227
Salisbury, England, 324

Salt Lake City, UT, 327, 468
Salzburg, Austria, 339
San Antonio, TX, 4, 329, 336
San Diego, CA, 191, 331
San Francisco, CA, 190–91, 319, 324, 372
San Gervasio, MX, 314
San Luis, CO, 272
San Luis Valley, CO, 199, 202, 218, 328
San Miguel, MX, 314
Santa Ana, CA, 319
Santa Barbara, CA, 319
Santa Fe, NM, 66, 181, 188, 195, 318
Seattle, WA, 190, 319
Sedalia, CO, 328, 505
Segovia, Spain, 344–45
Seville, Spain, 344
Seward, AK, 327
Shell Knob, MO, 115, 165, 167, 170
Sherborne, England, 328
Silver Dollar City, MO 316–17
Silverton, CO, 199, 202, 252
Sitka, AK, 217, 327
Skagway, AK, 325
Sogiefjord, Norway, 345
Somerset, CO, 216
South Fork, CO, 217
Speyer, Germany, 341
Springfield, IL, 37
Springfield, MO, ix, 49, 56, 69–70, 73–74, 80–81, 83, 88, 91–92, 94–95, 108, 117–18, 120, 127, 129–30, 132, 143–45, 157, 165, 170, 172, 174–76, 179, 183, 190, 192, 198, 201, 203, 207–8, 210, 219, 221, 227, 230, 234, 236, 239, 241, 244, 265, 268, 273,274, 276, 300, 303, 305–6, 308–9, 312, 314, 316, 319–22, 324, 328, 330, 332–33, 336–41, 344–48, 352, 363, 367, 369, 375, 378, 392, 411, 413, 423, 425–27, 429, 441, 454, 468, 476–77, 482–83, 488, 495
Stockholm, Sweden, 345–46
Strasbourg, France, 341
Stratford-Upon-Avon, England, 324
Sydney, Australia, 340

Taize, France, 130, 337
Talkeetna, AK, 326–27
Tampa, FL, 329
Telluride, CO, 183, 189–90, 195–96, 206, 223, 492, 495
Telluride Village, CO, 189
Tiff, MO, 47
Tintagel, England, 328
Titusville, FL, 287
Tok, AK, 326

Indices

Toledo, Spain, 344
Toulon, France, 328–30
Toulouse, France, 329, 332
Tours, France, 329
Trapper Creek, AK, 326
Troyes, France, 330
Tulum, MX, 279, 288, 308, 314

Uglich, Russia, 347
Uluru (Ayers Rock), Australia, 340

Vail, CO, 318
Valencia, Spain, 344
Venice, Italy, 321
Victoria, KS, 234
Vienna, Austria, 339, 350
Voss, Norway, 345

Warrensburg, MO, 38, 241
Warsaw, Poland, 349–50
Washington, DC, 57, 61, 318, 319, 368, 369, 474, 480
Wasilla, AK, 326
Watson Lake, YT, 325
Wells, England, 328
Whitehorse, YT, 325
Willow, AK, 326
Winchester, England, 328
Winnipeg, MB, 190–91, 319

Yaroslavl, Russia, 347
York, England, 324, 332

Countries

Australia, 207, 340

Bahamas, 279, 281, 284, 286, 288, 290–91, 293–96, 298, 303, 305–6, 311
British Virgin Islands, 302

Canada, x, 188, 191, 217, 319, 323, 325, 330, 388
Cayman Islands, 279, 283, 295–96, 307, 313
Czech Republic, 350

Denmark, 345–46

England, 328–29, 332, 337

France, 300, 328–29, 332, 341, 344

Germany, 242–43, 300, 339, 341, 348–50

Hungary, 350

Italy, 134, 242, 355

Jamaica, 279, 281, 283, 285, 296, 306–7, 313

Mexico, 181, 279, 283, 287–88, 295, 307–8, 313–14, 427

Netherlands Antilles, 301
New Zealand, 340
Norway, 345–46

Poland, 349
Portugal, 344

Russia, 341, 346–48

St. Maartin, 300, 304, 310–11
Spain, 286, 344
Sweden, 345–46
Switzerland, 332, 340–41

Courses Taught

The Bible (in) and Film, 175–77, 180, 332, 406, 427, 440–41, 454–55, 463, 479
Christmas in the Bible and Film, 177
Death and Afterlife, 177
English in Upward Bound, 179
Generation X: Religion and Spirituality, 177
The Hobbit and the Bible, 178
The Hobbit, The Lord of the Rings, and the Bible, 178
The Holocaust in Film, 177
Introduction to University Life, 175–76
Jesus in Film, 177, 463
King Arthur and Magic Merlin, 177
Lions in the Bible and Film, 177
The Literature and World of the New Testament, x, 174–76
The Literature and World of the Old Testament, 175
The Lord of the Rings and the Bible, 475, 480
The Matrix and the Bible, 177
M. Night Shyamalan and Religion, 177, 463
Sacred Journey, 177
Spirituality in the Bible and Film, 177
Star Wars and the Bible, 177, 455–56
Superheroes in Film, 177
Virtue in Film, 177

Indices

(Water) Falls

Bridal Veil, 189–90
Dunn's River, 279, 283, 307
Fern, 274
Kannah Creek, 271
Roaring River, 271
Snowmass Falls, 249
South Forks, 233

Gulches

Buckskin Gulch, 230
Poughkeepsie Gulch, 200
Poverty Gulch, 225

Hotels

British Colonial, 290
Dragon Bay, 281
Galleon Beach, 279
Mountain Top, 290
Playa Del Carmen, 279
St. Nicholas, 38
Sol Caribe, 288

Lakes/Reservoirs

Bailey Reservoir, 237
Bald Mountain Reservoir, 213
Bear Lake, 220, 273
Beaver Reservoir, 212
Bierstadt Lake, 273
Big Lake, 325–26, 373
Blue Lakes, 220
Bull Shoals Lake, 94

Crater Lake, 191, 230, 254, 319

Dollar Lake, 233
Dream Lake, 273–74

Eklund Lake, 234
Emerald Lake, 273

Fern Lake, 274

Green Lake, 215

Kite Lake, 230–31

Lake Como, 201–2, 204, 253–56, 259
Lake Irwin, 211, 214, 216, 234
Lost Lake, 233, 235

Lost Lake Slough, 208, 213, 233
Lower Cataract Lake, 268

Maroon Lake, 182
Middle Lake, 233–34
Miller Lake, 234

Navajo Lake, 206
Nymph Lake, 273–74

Overland Reservoir & Crater Lake, 230

Paonia Reservoir, 208, 211, 216

Sloan Lake, 258
Smith Lake, 233
Snowmass Lake, 249–51
Summit Lake 266
Surprise Lake, 268

Table Rock Lake, 165

Upper Sweeney Lake, 234

Watson Lake, 325
Willow Lake, 259, 404
Woods Lake, 206

Mines

Baker Mine, CO, 244
Climax Molybdenum, CO, 190
Old Mines, MO, ix–xi, 1–3, 9, 29, 38, 42, 44–45, 56–57, 62–63, 68, 70–71, 74–75, 80, 157, 267, 316, 338, 354–55, 366, 426, 477, 506, 508–9
Silver Jack Mine, CO, 194
Stevens Mine, CO, 247
Yule Marble Quarry, CO, 240

Mountains

Afley Peak, 233
Ajax Mountain, 203
Alps, 337
Augusta Mountain, 225

Bald Mountain, 213, 248, 262
Bennett Peak, 218
Blanca Peak, 202, 253, 267
Blue Mountain, 281

Castle Peak, 248, 267

Indices

Challenger Point, 259
Coal Mountain, 210
Collegiate Peaks, 220, 227, 231, 235, 239, 245
Capitol Peak, 267
Crestone Needle, 267
Culebra Peak, 267, 271

Deer Mountain, 273
Del Norte Peak, 218
Dolores Peak, 205, 208

East Beckwith Mountain, 209, 213
East Spanish Peak, 261
El Diente, 205, 267
Elk Range, 211, 248–49, 267
Ellingwood Point, 253–54, 267

Front Range, 247–48, 250–51, 256, 264, 266, 269–70

Gothic Mountain, 257
Grays Peak, 247, 266, 270
Green Mountain, 237
Grenadier Mountains, 199
Groundhog Mountain, 210

Hancock Peak, 222
Harden Peak, 218
Handies Peak, 202, 258, 267
Humboldt Peak, 249, 262, 267
Hurricane Peak, 200–201
Huron Peak, 244, 267

Kit Carson Peak, 267

Landsend Peak, 209–10
La Plata Peak, 245–46, 267
La Sal, 208, 224–25, 228, 233
Little Bear Peak, 204, 253, 267
Little Cone, 205, 208, 210
Lone Cone Peak, 205–7, 209–11, 214, 216, 219–21, 224–26, 235, 268
Longs Peak, 250, 253, 256, 266
Lookout Mountain, 218

Marble Peak, 240
Maroon Bells, 182
Maroon (South Maroon) Peak, 267
Matterhorn Peak, 200
Meridian Peak, 265
Middle Peak, 205
Missouri Mountain, 245, 267
Mosquito Range, 230, 239–40, 246, 267
Mount Antero, 227, 234, 236, 267

Mount Belford, 245, 267
Mount Bierstadt, 247, 266, 271
Mount Blanc, 332, 337
Mount Bross, 231–32, 239, 267
Mount Cameron, 231–32, 267
Mount Columbia, 234, 267
Mount Cook, 340
Mount Democrat, 231–32, 239, 267
Mount Elbert, 214, 234, 267
Mount Emmons, 213, 274
Mount Eolus, 203, 252, 267
Mount Evans, 182, 206, 247, 256, 266, 268, 318
Mount Gunnison, 212–13
Mount Harvard, 220, 231, 234, 267
Mount Horeb (Sinai), 268, 342
Mount Lamborn, 209–10, 213–14, 262–63, 274
Mount Lincoln, 231–32, 239, 267
Mount Lindsey, 248, 262, 267
Mount Massive, 227, 234, 267
Mount McKinley, 322
Mount Mellenthin, 233
Mount of the Holy Cross, 247, 267
Mount Owen, 211–13, 215
Mount Oxford, 245, 267
Mount Peale, 224–25, 228
Mount Princeton, 235–36, 267
Mount Rainier, 191, 319
Mount St. Kyle, 200
Mount Shavano, 227, 240, 245, 267
Mount Sheridan, 239–40
Mount Sherman, 239–40, 267
Mount Sneffels, 183, 185, 188–89, 198, 208–9, 267
Mount Tukuhnikivatz, 228, 233
Mount Wilson, 205–7, 267
Mount Yale, 227, 236, 239, 267

Needle Mountains, 199
North Eolus, 203, 252–53, 267
North Maroon Peak, 267
North Saddle Peak, 210

Oh-Be-Joyful Peak, 222–23

Pennsylvania Mountain, 276–77
Pikes Peak, 182, 248, 256, 264, 266, 318
Poison Mountain, 218
Purple Mountain, 213–14
Purple Peak, 214–15
Pyramid Peak, 267

Quandry Peak, 232, 267

Redcloud Peak, 200, 267

Indices

Richmond Mountain, 225, 228
Rocky Mountains, 172, 182, 190, 192, 193, 195, 206, 207, 212, 214, 253
Ruby Mountains, 209–16, 222–23, 225, 227–29, 232, 234, 260, 276
Ruby Peak, 211, 228

Sandia Mountains, 181, 188, 318
Sandia Peak, 181
Sangre de Christo Mountains, 181, 199, 404
San Juan Mountains, 189, 194–95, 198, 200, 221
San Luis Peak, 249, 267
San Miguel Mountains, 205–6, 210, 228
Sawatch Range, 227, 234–37, 239–41, 244–48, 267
Scarp Ridge, 216
Sierra Blanca, 204
Snowmass Mountain, 249–51, 253, 267
South Saddle Peak, 210
Stewart Peak, 221
Sunlight Peak, 203, 267
Sunshine Peak, 200, 267

Tabeguache Mountain, 227, 240, 245, 267
Telluride Peak, 203, 206
Torrys Peak, 247, 270
Treasure Mountain, 256
Treasury Mountain, 255–56

Uncompahgre Peak, 194–95, 198, 200, 223–24, 267

Wasatch Mountain, 190, 196
West Beckwith, 220
West Elk Mountains, 209–10, 212–13, 219, 237
West Elk Peak, 210, 229
West Spanish Peak, 261
Wetterhorn Peak, 200, 267
Wilson Peak, 205–7, 267
Windom Peak, 203, 252, 267
Wind River Range 233

Newspapers

Arkansas Democrat-Gazette, 204
The Independent-Journal, 29, 57
MCC Messenger, 98–100
The Mirror, 84–86, 89–99, 101–10, 112–15, 117–20, 128–29, 131–33, 135, 170, 174, 207, 308, 323–25, 328–29, 331, 336, 352–53, 355, 381, 422, 478–79, 482, 505
The Torch, 36–37, 41–45

Oceans

Arctic, 326
Atlantic, 280
Bering Sea, 327
Caribbean Sea, 197, 295, 300, 306
Mediterranean Sea, 330
Pacific, 191, 319

Other/Miscellaneous

Algarve Region, Portugal, 344
Altar Servers, 14–15, 66, 69–70, 75, 130, 140–41, 151–53, 158–59, 478
American Catholic Church, 108
Archives, Archdiocese of St. Louis, 63
Asplundh, 500–504
Associated Church Press, 89, 92, 114, 115, 324, 329, 388
Assumption Abbey, Ava, MO, 172
Assumption Abbey, Richardton, ND, 317

Bachelor of Arts in Philosophy, 57
Bachelor of Science in Education, 80
Bantam Chickens, 21
(San Francisco) Bay Area Rapid Transit (BART), 191
Boundary Questionnaire, 116–17
Boys State, 38–39
Byzantine Chapel, 65

Call to Action, 107–8
Cardinal Glennon College Library, 51–52
Carmel Mission Bereavement Ministry, 386
Catholic Press Association, 89, 91–92, 114, 115, 323–24, 329, 331, 336, 355, 366
Chicago O'Hare Airport, 345
Christmas (at Sea) Cruise, 291, 293, 294, 299, 301, 303, 310, 312, 313, 314
Christmas Fireplace, 19
Christmas Market, 339, 348, 349, 350, 409
Christmas Nativity Scene, 20
Christmas Tree, 19–20
Cincinnati Music Hall, 426
City Utilities, 467, 501, 503
Colorado Fourteener Initiative, 240, 247, 262
Colorado Mountain Club, 183, 189, 267
Communications Advisory Board (CAB), 88, 91, 94, 95, 99
Confirmation, 10, 12, 149–51, 153, 156, 170, 351
Conley Hall, 186
Contemporary Music Director of Kingsway United Methodist Church, 341
Corn Dance, 318

Indices

Diocesan Development Fund, 90, 169
Durango & Silverton Narrow Gauge Railroad (D&SNG), 199, 202, 252

Easter Baskets, 18
Easter Chicks/Ducks, 18–19
Easter Eggs, 17–18
Easter Water, 19
Eigemann Hall, 64
Encyclopedias, 17
Ecumenical Center, 83
Enneagram, 116
Excellent in Scholarship, 46

Faithful Service, 46
First Communion, 7–8, 12
First Mass, 70
Flower Gardens, 21–22

Good Citizenship, 46

Herff Jones, 41
Holy Spirit Abbey, Conyers, GA, 172

International Date Line, 340

Jackson Church, 381, 483–85
Journalism Awards, 114–15
Juanita K. Hammons Hall, 489

Kingston Trio, 304
Knights of Columbus, 67

Lamarques in Old Mines, 74
Lamb Cake, 17
Lawnmower, 21
LAX, 340
The Lettermen, 290
Little Rock Scripture Study, 394, 395, 396
Lois St., Springfield, MO, 120
Lusitano Horses, 344

Marriage Encounter, 425
Master of Arts in Religious Studies, 64, 80
Master of Ceremonies, 41, 44, 75, 170, 181, 223, 478
Master of Divinity, 70
Melkite Rite, 76
Mercy (St. John) Hospital, 118
Missouri Supreme Court, 29, 75
Missouri Lifetime Teaching Certificate, 80
Missouri National Guard, 241–42
Minnesota Pass, 212
Municipal Court Building, 498

Myers-Briggs Type Indicator, 115, 275

National Honor Society, 44
Neuro-Linguistic Programming (NLP), 116
New Madrid Fault, 324
Newman Hall, 59–60
New Year's (at Sea) Cruise, 293–94

Old Mines Area Historical Society, 80
Old Study Group, 381, 482, 488
Ordination to Diaconate, 63–68
Ordination to Priesthood, 68–69
Ouray Hot Springs, 219
Outstanding Teenager of America, 43
Ozark Air Lines, 278

Palm Sunday, 19
Parish School of Religion (PSR), 43–44
Partners in Performance, 489–91
Pente, 341
Pier Gynt Suite, 345
Powersite Dam, 74
Priestly Formation Program (PFP), 54–55
Proficiency in Bookkeeping, 46

Rabbit Cake, 21
Reformation, 332
Regents Scholarship, 46
Religion News Service, 95, 103, 104
Religious Education Congress, 324
Retirement, 126, 171–72, 505
Ring Day, 41
Rural Parish Workers of Christ the King, 70

Sacred Heart Retreat Center, 328
Sabbatical, 109, 112, 131–32, 174, 217–18, 325, 328–29, 373–75, 441, 478, 489, 505
St. Joachim School Song, 44
St. Michael House, 70
St. Thomas Aquinas Chapel, 60
Sanctuary, 235
Shelby City, 38
Shelby(dog), 340, 342–43, 505
Sherwood Hall, 60
Silver Jubilee, 128–29, 131, 157
Society for Newspaper Design, 89, 92, 102, 324, 325, 329, 330, 331
Society for the Propagation of the Faith, 165, 170–71
Spelling Bee, 13
Springfield-Branson National Airport, 330, 339, 346
Swan Lake Ballet, 348

Indices

Televised Mass, 42–43
Textbook Covering, 27
Trans World Airlines (TWA), 278, 308
Teaching Assistant, x, 61, 65

Uncle Spunky, 190

Valedictorian, 45
Viva Mexico, 308

Washington County Library, 9, 16
Washington County Memorial Hospital, 57
Western Auto, 35
Western Meridian Resources, 276, 423
Winston Ferguson Calypso Revue, 285
White House on Indiana St., Joplin, 81–82
Whole Community Catechesis (WCC), 146, 148, 152–53
World's Fair, 197, 286–88

Parishes

Holy Family, Shell Knob, MO, 165–66, 170
Holy Family, South Fork, CO, 217
Holy Name of Mary, Del Norte, CO 217
Holy Trinity, Marshfield, MO, 119
Holy Trinity, Springfield, MO, 363

Immaculate Conception, Creede, CO, 217
Immaculate Conception, Springfield, MO, 95, 117, 130, 144, 170

Newman Student Center, Fayetville, AR, 172

Our Lady of Sorrows, Nucla, CO, 189
Our Lady of the Cove, Kimberling City, MO, 173
Our Lady of the Holy Souls, Little Rock, AR, 172, 331
Our Lady of the Lake, Branson, MO, 144
Our Lady of the Ozarks, Forsyth, MO, 73

Sacred Heart, Mountain Grove, MO, 132, 135–37, 139, 142
Sacred Heart, Paonia, CO, 173, 208, 212, 217, 271, 273–74, 492
Sacred Heart, Webb City, MO, 81
St. Agnes Cathedral, Springfield, MO, 69–70, 73–74, 77, 80, 85, 129, 145, 170, 363, 425, 477, 482
St. David, Ouray, CO, 492
St. Elizabeth Ann Seton, Springfield, MO, 81, 83–84, 144, 172
St. Eustachius, Portageville, MO, 67–68, 70, 425
St. Francis de Sales, Lebanon, MO, 119

St. Francis of Assisi, Nixa, MO, 143–45, 152, 154, 156–59, 162, 172, 248, 336–37, 382, 463, 478, 482, (St. Clare of Assisi Chapel, 158)
St. James, Potosi, MO, 46
St. Joachim, Old Mines, MO, 1–3, 12, 24, 29, 31–32, 35–36, 41–42, 44–46, 56–57, 62–63, 66, 69–70, 75, 338, 354, 366, 424, 477
St. Joseph the Worker, Ozark, MO, 144, 156
St. Margaret Mary, Cortez, CO, 492
St. Margaret Mary, Hotchkiss, CO, 173, 208, 212, 217, 271, 273–74, 492
St. Mary, Joplin, 77–78, 81, 116, 174, 319, 324, 364
St. Meinrad, St. Meinrad Archabbey, St. Meinrad School of Theology, St. Meinrad College, St. Meinrad, IN, 57–61, 63–64, 66–72, 74, 76, 81, 128–29, 181, 185, 187, 309, 316–19, 351–52, 394, 421, 425–26, 477, 482, 495
St. Michael, Cabool, MO, 132, 135, 139–42
St. Patrick, Telluride, CO, 189, 195, 223, 492
St. Peter, Jefferson City, MO, 29
St. Peter the Apostle, Joplin, MO, 78–79, 81–82, 118, 188, 196, 484
St. Philip, Evansville, IN, 186
St. Sebastian, St. Louis, MO, 56
St. Stephen, Bentonville, AR, 172

(Mountain) Passes

Beckwith, 260

Daisy, 225

Guanella, 247
Gunsight, 213

Half Moon, 247

Kebler, 208, 210–11, 213, 228, 269, 338

McClure 246, 265
Minnesota, 212
Oh-Be-Joyful, 222–23

Trail Rider, 249

Yule, 213, 233, 255, 262

People

Ackerson, Mary Ann, 11–12, 16, 20–21, 27–29, 31, 39–40, 48–50, 58, 66, 69–70, 360

Indices

Adam, Jean, 78–80
Adero, Malaika, 399
Agnew, Francis, 541
Agniel, Ted, 56, 424–25
Allen, (Jo)Nathan, 442–53
Allwood, Connor, 474–75
Amondson, Christian, 406
Anderson, Chase, 474–76
Anderson, Hans Christian, 345
Anderson, Richard, 206–7
Armstrong, Donald & Theresa, 162, 164
Artz, Thomas, 354–56
Askren, James & Dorothy, 129–30, 381, 482
Avila, St. Teresa of, 344

Ballester, Jose Lopez, 378
Ballew-Gonzales, Christine, 108–12, 131
Banasik, Michael, 86–88
Bandler, Richard, 116
Battreal, Donnie, 66
Baum, William, 56–57, 61, 170
Bauer, Sylvester, 76
Bear, Joe, 209, 211–12
Bear, Tony, 209
Beck, Jerry & June, 130, 381, 482
Becker, Paula, 376
Bellotti, Marian, 318
Berg, Timothy, 66, 69–70, 181, 318–19
Berkwitz, Stephen, 175, 177, 180, 423
Bernstein, Eleanor, 363
Berry (Love), Cyndi, 128, 130–31, 478
Biedenbach, Lisa, 356–60, 373, 402, 405
Bird, (Rose) Carol, 41, 43
Bishop, Margaret, 130
Bishop, William, 107
Biskup, George, 61
Boever, Peter, 199, 201
Bonacci, Mary Beth, 372
Bond, Lucas, 463
Bone, Joey & Barb, 66
Bone, Timothy, 69
Bosso, Melissa, 129, 131, 143–44, 146, 148
Bourisaw, Lorraine, 69, 329
Bourisaw, Marjorie, 13
Bourisaw, Mary Lou, 5
Boyer, Alberta, 1
Boyer, Charles & Meade, 1, 27, 385
Boyer, Dennis, 66
Boyer, Diane Marie (Maxwell), 2, 364
Boyer, Ernest & Margaret, 1
Boyer, Francis & Lena, 1
Boyer, Jane Marie (Pashia), 2, 19–20, 28, 131, 157–58, 364
Boyer, Jeffrey Allen, 2, 364, 385

Boyer, Jesse Lee & Verna Marie, 1, 69, 126–27, 364
Boyer, Joseph Lee, 2, 364
Boyer, Juliette, 1
Boyer, Loreda, 10
Boyer, Martha, 6
Boyer, Michael Jerome, 2, 364
Boyer, Patricia, 47
Boyer, P. Gregory, 66, 157
Boyer, Thomas & Thelma, 1–2, 10–12, 70, 157–58, 361
Boyer, William (Bill), 1
Brockgreitens, Mary, 408
Brohammer, Sue, 382
Brophy, Donald, 361, 368
Brothers, John, 197, 282–86
Brown, Jeff, 312
Brug, Theodore, 69–71
Bryan, Kevin, 69, 71
Bucher, Phillip, 75, 95
Buechlein, Daniel, 61
Bugge, Charles, 357, 360, 363, 367, 370, 374, 379–80
Bugnitz, Achille, 67
Burghoff, Clement, 46
Buttner, (James) Michael, 66, 69–71, 317, 319
Byrne, John, 56

Canute, St., King, 345
Capazzi, Joseph, 14
Carberry, John J., 55, 66
Carr, Ephrem, 61, 65, 69–70, 72
Carter, Howard, 319
Casey, Mrs. Larry, J. 16–17
Casey, Noah, 64, 69, 71, 425
Casteel, Troy, 91
Castrillon-Hoyos, Dario, 134–35
Catherine the Great, 348
Cerar, Emilie, 401, 420
Chaplin, Joseph, 321
Chenevey, Anthony, 357, 361
Chiffolo, Anthony, 420
Chiles, Will, 423, 454
Christoffersen, Hans, 396
Clarke, Julie, 151
Clarke, Michael, 153, 159
Cleary, John, 412
Cloud, Olivia, 399
Clovis, King, 330
Coffey, Thomas, 373
Cole, Corbin, 340–43, 346, 348, 421–23, 480, 482
Coleman, Michael, 45
Coleman, Rose Ann, 27, 29
Coleman, Tim, 66

Indices

Columbus, Christopher, 344, 353
Camac, Jeanne, 312
Connors, Dan, 400
Conway, Chrysostom (Daniel), 64
Costello, Gwen, 411
Courtway, Agnes, 26–27, 29
Coury, Paul 401
Cox, James, 429–40
Cox, Marilyn, 455–56
Crim, Thomas & Raamah, 130–31, 381, 482
Crites, Michael & Emily, 146
Cunningham, Frank, 374, 391, 411

Dankelson, Darin, 204–6, 325
Dant, Joseph, 69–71
Davis, Thomas, 35
Declue, Jerry, 45
De'Clue, Juliette, 37, 43
Degonia, Yvonne, 26
Denver, John, 183, 186, 375–77, 404, 420, 454
Derryberry, Nancy, 129
Detsher, Alan, 362, 363
Detten, Pam, 131
Dewig, Eugene, 186
Dietz, Rachel, 75–76
Digenan, Rosalie, 132–33, 142–43, 387
DiSalvo, Julia, 408–9
Doering, Tom, 316
Dolan, Mark, 62
Donnell, Aaron, 479
Dotson, Mitchell, 159
Dotterweich, Kass, 401
Dowler, Wesley, 382, 467–69
Doyle, Kathleen, 363
Driscoll, Daniel, 392
Duchaine, R. Mark, 66, 72
Duffner, Ralph (Jake), 90
Dumas, Zach (Zechariah) & Paige, 269–70, 339
Durepos, Joe, 410
Duncan, Sheri, 146, 154–56, 382
Durham, Debbie, 382
Durham, Josh, 463–67
Durham, Tyler, 152, 158–59

People (*cont.*)

Durken, Daniel, 398–99
Dvorscak, James, 64
Dyer, Wayne, 117

Earwood, Troy, 479
Eck, Andy, 477
Eck, Greg, 156, 192, 320, 477
Eck, Jim, 195, 320, 477

Eck, Mark, 322, 477
Edwards, Andy, 418
Eftink, Glenn, 172
Ehrich, Tom, 103–5
Eidson, Leslie (Mayes, Hunter), 88, 100, 102, 109, 131, 381
Ellsberg, Robert, 369
Emrich, Kyle, 199–201
Erdlee, Alan, 375–76
Erker, Bill, 316
Essner, Karla, 110, 115, 381
Essner, Nathan, 478
Etheldreda, 329

Farley, Dennis & Tieneke, 322–23
Farley, Sean, 288, 291–93, 322–23
Farmer, Brian, 212–13
Fessio, Joseph, 372
Fields, Jared, 427
Fields, Susann, 408
Fifelski, Constance, 80
Finn, Peter, 357, 363, 365
Flaming, Wade, 123–26
Flesch, Norbert ,77, 80
Foley, Mary Sheila, 35
Fowler, James, 117
Francis Clare, 10
Frigerio, Alessandro, 378
Funk, Virgil, 369–70, 387, 403

Gardner, Robert, 53
Gaydos, Francis, 53–54
Geeser, Sue, 143
Gibbar, Leon, 381
Giel, John, 66, 69, 71
Gilligan, Michael, 367
Given, Mark, 129, 423
Gonzales, David, 480, 482
Goodson, Eleanor, 79
Goss, Jonathan, 479
Graham, James, 52
Granholm, Chuck (Charles), 308–11
Gray, Melissa, 107, 110
Gladiaux, Marybeth, 52
Glennon, Stephen Marie, 34–35
Graddy, Jeremy, 263, 338
Grinder, John, 116

Hagan, Harry, 421, 423
Haik, Chris, 118, 131, 366, 391, 478
Haik, Rob, 477–78
Hamilton, Alexander, 74
Hamilton, Ruth, 73–74, 504
Hamm, Brian, 475

523

Indices

Hamma, Robert, 361, 391–92
Hanson, James, 70–71
Harden, Eugene, 217–19, 328
Harper, Grady, 235
Harper, Susan, 359–60
Harrington, Jeremy, 391
Hart, Mary Hood, 110, 115
Hartigan, Ambrosia, 15, 27, 33
Hawkins, Eric, 497–500
Hedrick, Charles, 130, 423
Hemming, Ethan, 235–36
Henderson, Florence, 292
Heringer, Lynn, 371
Hermann, Lou & Kay, 166
Hess, Heidi, 388
Heyer, Robert, 356, 360, 401
Hicks, Christy, 408–9
Higginbotham, Robert, 60
Hinkebein, Deb, 147, 150–51, 153, 155–57
Hinkebein, Scott, 248–56, 262
Hirstein, Sandra, 356
Hirtz, Daniel, 138
Hobbs, Art(hur), 82, 171, 211, 288–91, 294–96, 303–5, 312–14, 321–24, 336–37, 354, 381, 476, 483
Hobbs, Lora, 423
Hobday, Jose, 321
Hodgson, Robert, 115, 129, 423
Hoffman, Pat, 76
Holden, (Margaret) Alice Marie, 35–37
Holliday, Ray, 502–3
Holtmeyer, William, 68
Horacek, Brant, 455
Howard, Helen, 75
Hrycyniack, Stephen, 412
Hubner, Jody, 135–36
Hudock, Barry, 366, 396–98, 418
Huelsing, Justin, 135
Huelsman, Faye, 77
Humphrey, Christopher, 388
Hunter, Bryan, 456–63
Hyland, Rosita, 35, 37, 39–40, 42–46

Ingram, David & Laura, 131
Ingram, Zach(ary), 391
Isgrig, Dwayne, 479

Jackson, Jim & Brenda, 131, 381, 483–85
Jackson, Peter, 177–78, 340, 480
Jansen, Anthony, 33, 35, 37, 41, 43, 45, 66, 71, 390
Jewell, Ronald, 50, 55
Jogues, Isaac, 54
Johnson, Lawrence, 369–71

Johnston, James Vann, 151, 158, 163–65, 167, 169–70
Jones, Colin, 376
Julian of Norwich, 329

Katsfey, Pauline, 455–56
Kavajecz, Elsa, 271, 338
Keene, Jack, 137
Kelemen, Julie, 354
Kennedy, John, 427
Kennedy, Joseph, 45–46
Kennedy, (Ita Patrice) Patricia, 34. 37
Kendzia, Mary Carol, 400, 410, 417
Keusenkothen, Jim, 105–6
Kiefer, Thomas, 119
King Arthur, 328
King, Jeremy, 66, 71
King, Michael, 195–98, 282, 284, 286–88, 351
Kinler, Karl & Sheri, 130, 256–57, 289, 386
Kinler, Zach(ary), 131, 246–48, 250, 256, 262, 269, 271, 337–38, 356
Kistner, Hilarion, 359
Klava, Joyce, 229–30, 245
Kluepfel, Neil, 401–2
Knetzke, Jerry & Sallie, 157
Koetter, Paul, 70, 72, 182–83, 189, 195
Koevenig, Marian, 56
Kolbe, St. Maximillian, 349
Kossler, Denise, 213
Kossler, John & Amy, Ethan, Jacob, 130, 212–14, 230–31, 233, 264, 274–76, 423
Kovacs, Julie, 159
Kriegshauser, Tom, 440
Kurtenbach, Joseph, 135, 137–39, 141–42

Lambert, (Catherine) Evelyn, 43
Lambert, Mary, 167
Lane, Edmund, 361, 379–82, 403, 410, 412, 417
Langford, Jeremy, 405, 412
Lauf, Joni, 463
Laurin, Matthew, 130
Laurin, Nathan, 130, 158, 478
Lavery, Diana, 393
Law, Bernard, 62, 65–69, 71, 75–78, 80, 82, 170, 319, 425
LeBlanc, Steven, 66, 69, 71
Leibrecht, John 80–81, 83–86, 89–109, 111–14, 118, 122, 126–27, 129, 131–35, 138, 141, 143–45, 147, 149–50, 154, 158, 170, 207, 358
Leveillee, Roger, 69, 71
Lewter, Pat, 77
Libasci, Peter, 66, 69–71, 187
Liebeck, Maria, 56

Indices

Lincoln, Abraham, 37–38
Lindsey, Jacquelyn, 410, 420
Linzee, Clementine, 52
Leach, Michael, 373
Lee, Robert, 84–86, 92
Leonard, Sebastian, 60
Limb, John, 371
Llewellyn, John, 175, 180
Lockhart, Steve, 427
Lohkamp, Al(bert) & Wanda, Michael, Steven, Daniel, Thomas, 201, 426–27
Lohkamp, Michael, 201, 203
Long, Leigh-Ann, 381, 483
Love, Brian, 478–79
Lynch, Kevin, 405

Macip, Glenn, 66
Magowan, Laura, 4–8, 46, 130, 336, 338, 391
Mahler, Allegra, 121
Maloney, Charles, 61
Marchal, Mary Caroline, 65, 70, 426
Marino, Greg, 477
Mark, Mary, 402
Marshall, John, 485
Martin, David, 66, 71
Martin, Joshua, 209
Martinez, Jerome, 66, 71, 181, 318
Mary Mark, 402
Massey, Bradon, 427–29
McAuliffe, Michael, 56
McBeath, James Joseph, 37, 43
McBrien, Richard 97, 321
McDarby, Nancy, 384–85
McDevitt, Michael, 83–85, 117
McDonald, Jack, 38
McElyea, Bill & Audrey, 131
McElyea, Rebecah, 391
McIntosh, Tony, 500–504
McEvoy, Greg, 188–95, 319–20, 367
McEvoy, Jon & Jan, Greg, Suzy, Julie, 367
McGonagle, David, 372
McGovern, Terrance, 318
McHale, John, 372
McKean, Betty, 441–42
McLoughlin, Paul, 126–27, 478
McNicholas, Joseph, 56
McSherry, Minnie, 197, 351
Meehan, Pat, 316–17
Mifsud, Victoria, 376
Miller, David, 165, 169
Melito, Ignatius, 54–56
Merseal, Bret, 477
Meyer, Vernon, 63, 66, 69–71, 181–82, 318–19, 324, 423

Milella, Aloysius, 357, 360–61, 367–68, 378–80, 402, 420
Moll, James, 66, 69–71, 390
Monaghan, Fergus, 74, 81, 482
Monaghan, Justin, 81
Monseur, Ted & Susan, 78
Montgomery, Bette, 362, 364
Moore, Mrs. Mark H., 17
Morehead, Kristopher, 257–63, 265–66, 268–69, 340, 382, 423
Morrison, Thomas, 61, 65–66, 69, 71
Moyer, James, 174–75, 180, 392
Murphy, Patrick J., 131
Murphy, Patrick H., 482
Myles, Jonathan, 478
Myles, Kevin, 478, 503

Naes, Vincent, 42
Nare, Richard, 370, 374
Naughton, Michael, 361–63
Nelsen, Michael, 69
Nelson, Thomas, 368–69
Nepo, Mark, 508
Neufelder, Jerome, 60, 63, 394
Nienaber, Theresa, 415–16
Nugent, Pauline, 130, 340, 423

O'Connell, Anthony, 55
O'Connor, Mary Ellen, 63, 131, 329, 336, 391
Odermann, Valerian, 317
Odom, Monica, 211, 220–21, 225, 228
Odom, Rhonda, 220–21
O'Hearn, Michael, 388
Osia, Glen, 70
Osia, Oliver, 11–12
Osia, Sarah, 12, 20, 27–28, 378, 385
Osia, Zeno, 28
Owensby, Hunter, 130

Pagliari, Robert, 387
Park, (Miles) Adam, 244–46
Pashia, James, 24, 45
Pashia, Laura, 356
Pashia, Matthew, 131
Pashia, Pap & Jane, 131
Pashia-McElyea, Samatha Gail, 385
Pattyson, Daniel, 480
Paul, Gale, 6
Paul, Thomas, 48
Paulson, Jim & Genevieve, 328, 330
Peck, M. Scott, 117
Pendergrass, Carol, 497–500
Pennick, Paul, 407, 410
Pesek, Ken, 129

Pesek, Tom, 469–74
Peter the Great, 348
Pfnausch, Edward, 363
Philippart, David, 388
Pierce, Gregory, 369, 373, 378, 386–87, 391, 401, 405, 407, 411
Pierson, Charles, 375
Pillick, Mike, 316
Pinkston, Carol Jean, 139–41
Pinson, Martin & Theresa, 157
Poe, Edgar Allen, 323
Polek, David, 360
Politte, (Evangelista) Rose Mary, 29–30, 32, 34
Politte, Janet, 3
Politte, Joan, 13
Politte, Mary Ann (Pratt), 38–40, 45, 57, 62
Politte, Ronald, 3
Pope John Paul II, 323, 331
Portell, Angela, 13, 15
Pratt, Freda, 45
Pratt, Wayne, 39–40
Prokes, Brian, 238–44

Raabe, Roy & Pam, Sonya, Matthew, 208, 211, 225
Rambo, Bill, 226, 260
Reicher, Barry & Diana, 151–57
Reid, Thelma, 455
Reidy, Thomas, 69, 72, 82, 84–85, 100, 112, 133–34, 143, 147, 149–50, 154, 171
Reitzer, Melvin, 56
Reker, Val, 75
Renault, Philippe Francois, 62
Reynolds, James, 75–76, 108, 111–12, 122, 124, 131, 214–17, 219–20, 223–25, 227–29, 231–34, 238–39, 257, 325, 327–28, 340, 373, 494
Ricar, Paul, 44
Rice, Daniel, 115, 479
Rice, Edward M., 67–68
Rice, Edward & Julie, 131, 381, 482
Rippee, Edward, 477
Risse, Richard, 63
Ritter, Joseph, 10
Roberts, Mark, 369
Robling, Katy, 159–62
Rochford, William (Bill), 79, 81, 118–19
Rogers, Eric, 454
Ross, Raymond, 53
Rublev, Andrei, 347
Runge, Fenton, 55
Rush, Marvin, 195
Ryan, Joseph, 46
Rynish, John, 61

Sadowski, Frank, 379
Santa Claus, 7, 20, 302, 310, 313
Santi, Mindie, 371
Schaab, Denny, 50, 63, 316–17
Schaefer, Dennis, 66
Scharmhorst, Jaret, 476–77
Scharper, Stephen, 356
Schneider, Steven, 64, 66, 69, 71, 75
Schramm, Edward, 57, 66, 71, 390
Schoening, Sylvester, 189–90, 195–96, 200, 203, 205–10, 213, 217, 219–21, 223, 371, 492–95, 497
Scott, Bernard Brandon, 129, 381, 392
Seti I, 341
Seton, Elizabeth Ann, 323
Seyer, James, 68
Shaw, Ann Catherine, 56, 336, 424
Shaw, Isaac, 480–82
Shea, John, 321, 373
Sherba, Girard, 69, 72
Shibley, Amel, 67–71, 76
Shikany, Paul, 69–70
Sisk, Leigh, 382
Sisney, Jill, 103–4
Skorupa, Thomas, 389, 411
Smart, Dan, 400
Smith, Candy, 99–100
Smith, Janet, 90, 120, 129
Smith, Nathan, 219–20, 231
Smith, Robert (Rob), 201–4, 297–99
Smullen, Cronin, 24–26
Sobaski, Eric, 164
Sobaski, Gina, 162–65
Sobaski, Megan, 163–65
Soetaert, Thomas, 477
Sperry, Mary Elizabeth, 365
Stanislaus, St., 350
Stanton, Jeremy, 234–37
Steensland, Craig & Mary, 157
Stewart, Scott, 441
Strong, Frank, 38
Strong, John, 423
Suellentrop, Bernard, 2, 29, 37, 41–45, 66, 70–71, 390
Suren, Richard, 57, 62–63, 66, 69, 71, 390
Sutton, Tony, 102–3
Swanson, John August, 331

Tafoya, Arthur, 223
Taylor, Matthew, 213
Tembrock, Bill (William), 211–14, 219–23, 225–30, 232, 234–35, 237–38, 240, 245–46, 248–49, 255–57, 260, 262, 265–66, 268–74, 276, 338, 377, 494

Indices

Tembrock, John & Amanda Woodward, 219, 226, 235
Tembrock, Kathy (Kathleen), 212, 219, 221, 226, 229–30, 232, 234–35, 237–38, 240, 245, 248, 255–57, 259, 262, 265–66, 268–74, 276, 338, 377, 494
Tembrock, Luke, 213–14, 219–23, 229, 231, 235, 255–56, 423
Tembrock, Nicole & Ethan Hemming, 219, 226, 235
Tembrock Orchards, 218, 224–25, 229, 232, 234–35, 237–38, 240, 244–46, 248–49, 255
tenZythoff, Gerrit, 77, 174, 392
Thebeau, Kevin, 66
Thomas, Bret, 400
Thomas, G.O., 351
Thomas, John, 479
Tibbets, Louise, 326
Tisdel, Richard, 496
Tolkien, J.R.R., 37
Treml, Cece, 146–50
Trosley, Anthony, 69, 71
Truman, Harry, 2
Tscherne, David, 66, 69–71
Tufano, Victoria, 388
Tulio, Pete & Shirley, 216
Tully, Henry, 66, 69, 71
Turner, Paul, 421, 423
Twomey, Mark, 362–68, 371–72, 374, 383–85, 389–91, 393–96, 398, 405, 413, 420

Upchurch, Cackie, 394–97

Vanderpool, John & Ida, 220, 377
Vanderpool, Heidi, 220
Vanni, Trish Sullivan, 410
Ver Daught, Janna, 332
Verkamp, Gabriel, 70
(Ver) Miller, Matthew, 130, 187, 229–32, 238–40, 250, 253–55, 258–64, 266, 269–74, 276–77, 331–36, 341, 390, 411–13, 419, 421, 423, 472, 485
Vetter, (Mary of the Assumption) Frances, 34
Viberti, Victor, 355–57, 360–61
Villmer, Natalie, 131
Vinyard, Steven, 198–203
Vinyard, Tim & Laura, 130, 329–30, 381
Vydra, Marilyn, 75, 80, 85, 88, 90–92, 109, 381

Ward, Joan, 113–14
Watkins, Walter, 441
Weaver, Chris, 285
Weber, Lawrence, 100
Wermerskirchen, Terry, Alan, Matthew 237
Werne, Janet, 61

Wessel, Frances, 143, 145
West, Audrey, 401
Westhues, John, 70, 73, 75–79, 145
White, Olive, 381, 482
Wickersham, John, 56
Wiedelman, Sharon, 131
Wieman, Mary, 381, 483
Wildeman, (Richard) Dick, 65–66, 69–71, 182–83, 185–87, 189, 195, 208
Wilkinson, Brent, 479
Williams, Brandon, 480, 482
Williams, Chris, 489
William the Conqueror, 329
Wilson, John, 69
Wilson, Thomas, 70
Wimer, Matthew, 407, 410, 413–14
Witek, Steve, 325–27, 374
Wittry, Mary Beth, 130
Wohlenhaus, Eli, 480
Wright, Vanita, 410

Yankech, Andrew, 404
Yeary, Clifford, 396

Zapel, Arthur, 375
Zatina, Gregory, 117
Zeka, Keith & Robin, 130–31, 381, 483–88
Zimmermann, Mark, 407

Periodicals

Catholic Digest, 353
The Critic 267, 353

The Daily News, 352
Design, 353

Environment and Art Letter, 353
Eye Opener, 353

Faith and Form, 353

Liturgy 80, 353
Loose-Leaf Lectionary, 398–99

Markings, 353
Modern Liturgy, 353

Namaste: Country Reflections, 353
National Bulletin on Liturgy, 353
National Poetry Anthology, 352

Our Western World's Greatest Poems, 352

Pastoral Life, 353
The Priest, 218, 328, 353
Probe, 351–52

Queen of All Hearts, 353

Reader's Digest, 46

Together, 353

U.S. Catholic, 353

Voices International, 351

Winged Lion, 352
World of Poetry, 352
World Treasury of Great Poems, 352
Worship, 353

Places

Air Force Academy, 192, 318, 320
Alamo, 329
Alaska Pipeline, 322
Alcazar, 344
Alhambra Palace, 344
Annaberg Ruins, 302
Arctic Circle, 326
Ardastra Gardens, 290
Aspen Leaf Lodge, 274, 276
Assumption Abbey, 317
Athenry Gardens, 281
Ayers Rock, 340

Baltimore Cathedral, 324
Barbancourt Rum Factory, 281
Barrow Mesa, 255
Basilica of St. Remigius, 330
Basilica Shrine of Our Lady of Fatima, 344
Belem Tower, 344
Berlin Wall, 349
Beverly Hills, 319
Black Forest, 341
Black Madonna, 349
Black Mesa, 225, 257
Blessed Virgin Mary Shrine, 15–16
Bluebeard's Castle, 290
Brandenburg Gate, 349
British Museum, 329
British Virgin Islands, 302
Brown Hollow, 9, 22–23, 31
Buddhist Retreat Center, 272
Buddhist Tashi Gomang Stupa and Shrine, 272
Bush Stadium, 43

California Franciscan Missions, 191
Caneel Bay, 302
Cardinal Glennon College Library, 51
Carmel Mission, 319
Carmel of St. Anne, 93–94, 117–18
Cathedral Mosque of Cordoba, 344
Cathedral of the Plains, 234
Catherine the Great's Palace, 348
Caves of Nonsuch, 281
Charles Bridge, 350
Checkpoint Charlie, 349
Chichen-Itza, 287–88, 307, 314
Chinatown, 319
Chinese Theater, 319
Christianborg Palace, 345
Church of St. Dmitry on the Blood, 347
Church of St. Elijah the Prophet, 347
Church of St. Matthias, 350
Civic Center, 319
Coral Bay, 302
Coral World, 311
Cruise School, 50
Cruz Bay, 302

Del Norte Window, 218
Denver Zoo, 321
Diocese of Jefferson City, 55
Diocese of Springfield-Cape Girardeau xi, 56–57, 61, 64, 66–67, 69, 72–73, 78, 127, 134, 319, 358, 381
Disneyland, 191, 319
Dodge Island, 280
Dormition Cathedral, 347
Drake's Seat, 290
Drottningholm, 345

East Beckwith Bowl, 209
Edvard Grieg Home, 345
Eiffel Tower, 329, 332
Eigemann Hall, 64
English Channel, 328, 332
El Dora Ski Resort, 192, 320
Exposition Building, 344

Fern Gulley, 279
Fisherman's Bastion, 350
Fisherman's Warf, 319
Fort Charlotte, 290
Fredenborg Castle, 345
Frederiksborg Castle, 345
French Quarter of New Orleans, 331

Garden of the Gods, 318
Great Barrier Reef, 340

Indices

Great Stirrup Cay, Berry Islands, Bahamas, 279–81, 286, 288, 291, 293, 295–98, 303–6, 308, 311–12
Greenwood Great House, 296
Gunnison Tunnel and Diversion Dam, 270

Habitat-Troglodita, 344
Haidakhandi Universal Ashram and Divine Mother Temple, 272
Heartland Center for Spirituality, 504
The Hermitage, 205–8, 210–11, 214, 216, 219–24, 226, 228, 233, 235, 348, 492–97
Hermitage Museum, 348
Heroes' Square, 350
Hieronymite Monastery, 344
Holocaust Memorial, 349
Holy Spirit Abbey, 346

Illinois State Capitol, 37
Incarnate Word Motherhouse, 4, 32, 329, 336, 340, 366
International Bazaar, 295
Jewish Quarter, 350
John F. Kennedy Space Center, 287
Kakadu National Park, 340
Kirillo-Belozersky Monastery, 347
Klondike Gold Rush, 326
Kremlin, 347

Larimer Square, 192, 321
Liberty Bell, 329
Library of Congress, 51, 318
Lincoln Grave Site, 37
Lincoln Home, 37
Little Mermaid, 345
Louvre 329, 332
Maho Bay, 302
Mary Help of Christians Abbey 317, 319
Megen's Bay 290
Monte Negro Ranch, 244, 344
Monument to Portuguese Explorers, 344
Moscow Metro System, 341
Museo Nacional Del Prado, 344

Nada Hermitage Carmelite Spiritual Life Institute, 272
Napa Valley, 323
National Center for Atmospheric Research, 192, 320
National Gallery, 345
National Museum, 345
National Shrine of the Immaculate Conception, 318
New Port of Miami, 280, 299, 303

New Salem State Park, 37
Notre Dame, 321, 329, 391

Olympia Brewery, 191, 319
Opera House, 345

Padre Island, 329
Painted Desert, 190, 319
Pan-Am Swimming Pool, 319
Paradise Divide, 232, 255
Parliament Building, 350
Peter and Paul Fortress, 348
Petrified Forest, 190, 319
Petroglyphs, 222, 226, 229, 260
Phantom Ranch, 193
Prague Castle, 350
Prince George Wharf, 281, 290

Reichstag Building, 349
Riddarholmskyrkan 346
Rio Grande Gorge, 318
Rockefeller Plantation, 302
Roman Aqueduct, 344
Royal Palace, 344, 346
Russian Orthodox Archangel Cathedral, 347
Russian Orthodox Cathedral of Christ the Savior, 347
Russian Orthodox Dormition Cathedral, 347

Sacred Heart Jesuit Retreat House, 328, 505
St. Basil Cathedral, 347
St. Benedict Abbey, 495
St. Boniface Cathedral, 191
St. Canute Church, 345
St. Catherine of Siena Chapel, 251
St. Fidelis Church, 234
St. Joachim Church, 1–2, 12, 42, 45, 62. 66
St. Joachim High School, 31–32, 35–36, 42, 45
St. Joachim School, 24, 29, 42, 44, 46, 63, 69, 338, 366
St. Malo Retreat Center, 251
St. Martin Bridge, 344
St. Meinrad Development Office, 81
St. Patrick Seminary, 319
St. Paul's Cathedral, 321, 332
St. Pius X Abbey, 44, 68
Sts. Peter and Paul Cathedral, 348
St. Thomas Seminary, 318
St. Vitus Cathedral, 350
Sandeman Sherry Distillery, 344
San Luis Obispo Mission, 319
Schonbrunn Palace, 350
Seattle Art Museum, 191
Shantivanam House of Prayer, 505

Indices

Shaw Park Gardens, 279
Sherwood Forest, 281
Sherwood Hall, 60
Shrine to Blessed Virgin Mary, 15–16
Shumei International Institute, 272
Silver Dollar City, 316–17
Sims Landing, 320
Six Flags Over Texas, 322
Sonoma Valley, 323
South Fork Ranch, 322
Space Needle, 191, 319
Stapleton International Airport, 183, 192, 320
State House, 329
Stockholm Cathedral, 346
Stonehenge, 324, 505
SuCasa, 317
Suspension Bridge, 226, 344

Taos Ski Valley, 318
Thorn Crown Chapel, 338
Tower of London, 332
Transfiguration Church, 347
Treasures of Tutnkhamun, 191, 319

United Nations, 300, 332
Universal Studios, 191, 319

Van Gogh Museum, 341
Vasa Museum, 346
Vigeland Sculpture Park, 345

Whistling Cay, 302
Wieliczka Salt Mines, 350
Wilanow Palace, 349
Wilanow Palace Gardens, 349
World Council of Churches, 332

Yucatan Peninsula, 287

Poems

"Amen! Colorado!", 318, 351

"Colorado Reflections", 182

"Grand Canyon Ball", 194
"Great Sand Dunes", 199

"Lost in the Mountains (for Jim Reynolds)", 216

"Minnie McSherry", 351–52
"Mountain King", 194–95
"The Mountain Prayed", 196
"Mountain Quietude", 201

"Mountain Storm", 198

"New Day", 260–61
"New Vision", 192–93

"Ski Attempt", 192
"Skiing", 265–66

"to be Coloradoed", 183–85

"Wind", 351

Public Lands

Alderfer/Three Sisters Park, CO, 273
Arapaho National Forest, CO, 247
Arches National Park, UT, 222

Black Canyon of the Gunnison National
    Monument, CO, 209, 213, 225, 231, 245,
    255, 257, 262, 270
Big Blue Wilderness, CO, 223
Bridger-Teton National Forest, WY, 234
Bridger Wilderness, WY, 234
Bureau of Land Management, 260

Carlsbad National Park, NM, 193
Collegiate Peaks Wilderness, CO, 231
Colorado National Monument, CO, 201, 231,
    274
Coyote Ridge, CO, 273

Denali National Park, AK, 322 327
Devil's Backbone Open Space, CO, 270
Dinosaur National Monument, CO, 229
Dominguez Canyon Wilderness, CO, 229, 260

Eagles Nest Wilderness, CO, 264–65, 268
Estes Park, CO, 192, 250–51, 320

Glacier National Park, MT, 325
Grand Canyon, AZ, 193–94
Grand Mesa National Forest, CO, 237–38, 244,
    246, 265–66, 270–71, 273
Grand Teton National Park, WY, 234, 325
Great Sand Dune National (Monument) Park
    and Preserve, CO, 199, 220, 255
Gunnison River Archaeological Area, CO, 265

Horsetooth Open Space, CO, 270

Mesa Verde National Park, CO, 199
Mount Falcon Park, CO, 270
Mount Massive Wilderness, CO, 227

Indices

Mount Rainier Backcountry, WA, 191, 319

Popo Agie Wilderness, WY, 233

Raggeds Wilderness, CO, 232–33
Ramsay-Shockey Open Space, CO, 271
Rocky Mountain National Park, CO, 271, 273–74, 276, 320
Roxborough State Park, CO, 268

Soshone National Forest, WY, 233
Staunton State Park, CO, 273

Uncompahgre National Forest, CO, 188
Uncompahgre Plateau, CO, 221
Uncompahgre Wilderness, CO, 195

Wilson's Creek National Battlefield, MO, 221
West Elk Wilderness, CO, 229, 233

Xelha National Park, MX, 279, 308

Yellowstone National Park, WY, 325
Yosemite National Park, CA, 323

Publishers

Abbey Press, 368, 369, 403
ACTA, 369, 373, 378, 386, 391, 396, 401, 404, 405, 407, 411, 415, 419
Alba House/St. Pauls, 355, 356, 357, 360, 361, 366, 368, 378–83, 387, 402, 403, 404, 409–10, 412, 414, 417, 420
Ambassador Books, 412
American Catholic Press, 403, 417
A.R.E. Press, 413
Attria Books, 399
Augsburg Fortress, 372, 415
Ave Maria, 368, 374, 378, 391, 396, 403, 405, 411, 415, 419, 420

Bayard, 400, 407, 410, 415
Beacon Press, 372
Blue Dolphin, 372
Broadman & Holman, 413

Canon Law Society of America, 363
Catholic Book, 369
The Catholic University of American Press, 372
Chalice Press, 412, 415
Cherry Lane Music, 375–76, 377
Christian Classics, 372
Confraternity of Christian Doctrine (CCD), 357, 358, 367, 386

Costello, 357, 363
Creative Communications, 407
Crossroad/Continuum, 369, 372–73, 406, 411

Daughters of St. Paul, 367
Dimension Books, 373
Distinctive Publishing, 375
Doubleday, 372

Eerdmans, 406, 415
Entourage Yearbooks, 404

Fordham University Press, 372
Forest of Peace, 389, 411, 419
Franciscan Media, 410, 415, 417

Georgetown University Press, 372

HarperSanFrancisco, 368, 389

Ignatius Press, 372, 414
Inner Traditions International/Bear & Co., 420
International Commission on English in the Liturgy (ICEL), 357, 358, 363, 364–65, 366, 385, 386
InterVarsity Press, 413

Johns Hopkins University, 412
Josey-Bass, 412, 420
J.S. Paluch, 386

Leavenhouse Publications, 377
Liguori, 354, 355, 356, 360, 366, 377, 378, 387, 400, 401, 407, 408, 409, 411, 415, 420
Lion Publishing, 372
Liturgy Training, 388, 420
(The) Liturgical Press, 364, 365, 366, 367, 368, 371, 374, 378, 383–86, 389–91, 393, 396–98, 400, 403, 405, 410, 413, 414, 415, 418, 419
Loyola Press, 406, 410, 415

Novalis, 388

Michael Glazier, 357
Macmillian, 357
Meriwether Publishing, 375
Morehouse Publishing, 406, 411

National Association of Pastoral Musicians (NAPM), 370
National Conference of Catholic Bishops (NCCB), 363
New City Press, 367, 405

531

Indices

New Leaf Press, 406
New World Library, 413, 418
Notre Dame Center for Pastoral Liturgy, 363

Orbis, 369, 371, 387, 402, 411, 415, 420
Oregon Catholic Press, 371, 404
Our Sunday Visitor, 367, 387, 396, 403, 410, 415, 420
Oxford University Press, 372, 389, 406

Paraclete Press, 406
Pastoral Press, 368, 369, 370–71, 387, 403
Pauline Books and Media, 396, 415, 419
Paulist, 361, 363, 367, 368, 371, 374, 402, 404, 405, 411, 414, 419, 420
Peter Li Education, 372
Pilgrim Press, 403, 406
Plough Publishing, 403
Prometheus Books, 405

Rowan & Littlefield, 393, 405
Religious Education Press, 372
Resurrection Press, 401, 413, 419, 420
Rose Printing, 376, 377

Saint Bede's Publications, 372
St. Anthony Messenger, 356, 358, 359, 360, 368, 373, 377, 383, 387, 402, 403, 405, 419, 420
St. Paul Books & Media, 373, 402
St. Martin's Press, 413
Servant Publications, 372, 388, 406, 411, 420
Sheed & Ward, 356, 360, 368, 371, 387, 401, 405, 411, 420
Simon & Schuster, 399
Standard Publishing, 413

Tabor Publishing, 420
Templegate, 403
The Thomas More Association, 368, 406, 412
Thomas Nelson, 368, 369
Trinity Communications, 372
Trinity Music, 371
Twenty-Third, 356, 387, 400, 401, 403, 404, 406, 407, 410, 411, 415

United States Catholic Bishops (USCB), 364, 365, 366, 369
United States Catholic Conference (USCC), 370
University of Notre Dame, 372
University Press of America, 392, 403

Vantage Press, 403

Viking Penguin, 403

Wm. C. Brown Co., 356
William H. Sadlier, 372
Wipf and Stock, 405, 406, 407, 410, 413, 414, 415, 419–22
World Library Publications, 404

Yearbook House, 354–55

Xavier Society for the Blind, 360

Zondervan, 406

Rivers/Creeks

Animas River Canyon, 199
Anthracite Creek, 231
Arkansas River, 227, 236, 240

Cimarron River, 194–95
Cochetopa Creek, 249
Colorado River, 193

Dunn's River, 279, 283, 307
Danube River, 339, 350
Dominguez River (Canyon), 226, 229, 235, 259, 265, 269–70

Gasconade River, 316
Gunnison River, 225–26, 237, 338

Little Dominguez River, 229, 235
Laroux Creek, 237

Matterhorn Creek, 200
Mississippi River, x–xi, 27, 44

Needle Creek, 199, 202, 252

Ohio River, 65

Platte River, 318

Rhine River, 318, 340

Slate River, 213, 225, 262
Stewart Creek, 249

West Elk Creek, 229

Yampa River, 229
Yukon River, 326

Indices

Roads

Alaskan Highway, 325

Black Bear, 190, 206

Colony Lakes, 249, 262
Cottonwood Creek, 221
Crystal Creek, 213

Dalton Highway, 326
Del Norte, 218

East Dallas Divide, 183, 188, 220
Eurotunnel (Chunnel), 329

Henson Creek, 223

Icefield Highway, 325

Kebler Pass, 208–9, 211, 213–14, 233–35, 260

Lake Como, 253, 256
Lone Cone, 219, 221, 226
Marine Highway, 217
Matterhorn Creek, 200

Nellie Creek, 223
North Smith Fork, 210

Oh-Be-Joyful, 222, 228, 232

Red Hassel, 281

Slate Creek/River, 222, 225, 228, 232
Snowmass Creek, 249
South Clear Creek, 247
South Colony Lakes, 249
South Fork of Silver Creek, 200
South Fork Lake Creek, 245
South National Avenue, 497–500

Top of the World Highway, 326–27

Owl Creed Pass, 194–95

Yule Pass, 213

Ships

Kloster Cruise Limited, 312–14
MS Seaward, 305–6, 308, 312–13
MS Skyward, 287, 294, 312
MS Starward 280, 282, 284, 294

MS Southward, 278–80, 282, 294
MS Sunward II, 294–97
Norwegian Caribbean Lines, 278, 280, 282, 284, 287–88, 294–95, 297, 299, 305, 310, 312
Royal Viking Line, 312
SS France, 288, 300
SS Norway, 288–91, 293–97, 297–301, 303–4, 306, 310–11, 313, 315
Viking Eir, 341
Viking Helgi, 347
Viking Mimir, 339

Trails

Anthracite Pass, 240

Bear Creek, 203
Beckwith Pass, 209, 211, 259, 276
Blank Gulch, 240
Blue Lakes, 183, 188–89, 220
Bright Angel, 193

Cascade Canyon, 233
Clear Creek, 244
Cliff Creek, 260, 276
County Line, 233, 238, 265
Coyote Ridge, 273
Crags Campground, 264
Crystal, 255
Cub Lake, 273

Dark Canyon, 231
Denny Creek, 239

East Spanish Peak, 261
Elliot Ridge, 264
Exclamation Point, 245, 262

Fire Mountain Ditch, 272
Four Mile Creek, 239

Glacier Gorge, 271
Grays Peak, 247
Gunnison Forks, 249

Hoodoo Creek, 212
Horsethief 200

Jenny Lake, 233

Kaibab, 193

Lawn Lake, 271
Lily Lake, 248

Indices

Lone Cone, 205, 219–20
Longs Peak, 192, 250

McClure Pass, 246, 265
Middle Fork of Cinnamon River, 195
Missouri Gulch, 245
Mount Harvard, 220
Mount Lamborn, 209–10

Navajo Lake, 206
Needle Creek, 199, 202, 252
Nellie Creek, 198
North Cottonwood Creek, 234

Pennsylvania Mountain, 276
Piburn, 274
Pole Creek, 234

San Luis Peak, 249
Sheridan Cross Cut, 196
Shoshone, 271
Skyline, 265
Smith Fork, 237
Smith Lake, 233
Snowmass Mountain, 249–51
SOB, 225–26, 257
South Fork of Clear Creek, 244
Spud Pass, 232
Sweeney Lakes, 234

Trail Rider Pass, 249–50

Ute, 271

Wahatoya, 261
Ward Lake, 265–66
Washington Gulch, 257
West Frisco, 218
West Spanish Peak, 261
Willow Creek, 258–59

Yankee Boy Basin, 183, 189, 198, 208
Yule Pass, 213

Universities/Colleges/Schools

Belmont Abbey College, 318
Cardinal Glennon College, 49–50, 52, 55–57, 60, 62–63, 181, 316, 318, 424–25
Catholic University of America, 318–19
Central Missouri State, 38, 241
Creighton, 274–76
Colorado Western, 236
Colorado State, 276
Forest Institute of Professional Psychology, 332, 411
Indiana University–Bloomington, 64, 186, 425
Kenrick Seminary, 52, 54, 316
LIMEX (Loyola's Institute for Ministry Extension Program), 127, 143, 411, 478
Loyola University, 127, 331
Maryknoll Seminary, 316
McAuley High School, 77–80, 83, 115, 170, 174, 195, 197, 199, 201, 204, 206–7, 282–83, 297, 299, 308–9, 321, 325, 392, 477, 483–84, 504
Missouri Southern, 80
(Southwest) Missouri State, x, 77, 83, 98, 105, 115, 129, 132, 174, 180, 330–32, 411, 427
Ozarks Technical Community College, 243
St. Joachim High School, 31–32, 35–36, 42, 45
St. Louis Preparatory Seminary South, 90–91, 316
St. Meinrad College, 59–61, 71, 185, 309, 425
St. Meinrad School of Theology, 57, 59, 63–64, 71, 74, 128–29, 181, 185, 187, 316–18, 351–52, 394, 425, 477, 482
School (College) of the Ozarks, 317
Seton Hall University, 336
Southeast Missouri State College, 46

U.S. States/Territories/Provinces

Alaska, 16–17, 217, 322, 325–28, 346, 373–75, 441, 808
Alberta, Canada, 325
Arizona, 188, 190, 193, 319, 324, 336, 423
Arkansas, 105, 172, 204, 331, 338, 394, 442

British Columbia, Canada, 325, 327

California, 188, 190–91, 319, 322, 324, 326–27, 331, 372, 386
Colorado, 85, 100–102, 172–73, 181–83, 187–90, 192–93, 195, 198–204, 206–10, 212, 214, 216–23, 226–29, 231–32, 234, 237–41, 244, 246–48, 251, 256–61, 263, 266, 268–74, 276–77, 297, 318, 320, 322, 325, 328–29, 332, 335–40, 375, 377, 404, 423, 427, 475, 477, 492–93, 495–97, 505

District of Columbia (DC), 57, 61, 318–19, 368–69, 474, 480

Idaho, 191, 319, 327
Illinois, x, 37, 66, 69, 316
Indiana, ix, 41, 57–59, 61, 63, 65–66, 69–70, 81, 185, 196, 208, 309, 316, 321, 330–31, 391, 394, 427, 429, 495

534

Indices

Iowa, 195
Kansas, 78, 206, 234, 257, 269, 273, 322, 504–5

Massachusetts, 323, 326, 425
Missouri, ix–xi, 1–2, 7, 10, 22, 28–29, 38–39, 44, 46–47, 49, 55–57, 62, 67–69, 73, 75–76, 80, 84, 88, 92, 95, 99, 115, 118–19, 135, 143, 157, 170, 172–73, 182, 185, 190, 211, 214, 216, 219, 221, 229, 232, 234, 240–41, 246, 248, 250, 252–53, 256–58, 260–61, 263, 265, 267, 269, 271–72, 277, 286, 289, 291, 293, 296, 300, 303, 305, 307, 309, 314, 316–17, 321, 323, 325, 329, 336–38, 340, 354, 356, 363–64, 366, 382, 407, 421, 423–26, 463, 475–77, 497–98, 504, 508–9
Montana, 325, 328, 505

Nebraska, 195, 274, 321, 333
New Jersey, 336, 404
New Mexico, 66, 181–82, 185, 188, 190, 193, 195, 272, 318–19

Ohio, 66, 330, 358, 378, 413, 426
Oregon, 190, 319, 406, 415

U.S. Virgin Islands, 289–90, 292, 298, 302, 304, 311
Utah, 208, 222, 224–25, 228, 232–33, 327, 468–69

Washington, 190, 319, 454
Wisconsin, 190, 195, 319
Wyoming, 232–33, 325, 327

Recent Books by Mark G. Boyer
Published by Wipf & Stock

Nature Spirituality: Praying with Wind, Water, Earth, Fire

A Spirituality of Ageing

Weekday Saints: Reflections on Their Scriptures

Human Wholeness: A Spirituality of Relationship

A Simple Systematic Mariology

Praying Your Way through Luke's Gospel and the Acts of the Apostles

An Abecedarian of Animal Spirit Guides: Spiritual Growth through Reflections on Creatures

*Overcome with Paschal Joy: Chanting through Lent and Easter—
Daily Reflections with Familiar Hymns*

Taking Leave of Your Home: Moving in the Peace of Christ

An Abecedarian of Sacred Trees: Spiritual Growth through Reflections on Woody Plants

Divine Presence: Elements of Biblical Theophanies

Fruit of the Vine: A Biblical Spirituality of Wine

Names for Jesus: Reflections for Advent and Christmas

Talk to God and Listen to the Casual Reply: Experiencing the Spirituality of John Denver

*Christ Our Passover Has Been Sacrificed: A Guide through Paschal Mystery Spirituality—
Mystical Theology in* The Roman Missal

Rosary Primer: The Prayers, The Mysteries, and the New Testament

*From Contemplation to Action: The Spiritual Process of Divine Discernment
Using Elijah and Elisha as Models*

Recent Books by Mark G. Boyer

Love Addict

All Things Mary: Honoring the Mother of God—An Anthology of Marian Reflections

Shhh! The Sound of Sheer Silence: A Biblical Spirituality that Transforms

What is Born of the Spirit is Spirit: A Biblical Spirituality of Spirit

Very Short Reflections—for Advent and Christmas, Lent and Easter, Ordinary Time, and Saints—through the Liturgical Year

Living Parables: Today's Versions

www.ingramcontent.com/pod-product-compliance
Lightning Source LLC
Chambersburg PA
CBHW081142290426
44108CB00018B/2419